MODERN HISTORY

The Rise of a Democratic, Scientific,
and Industrialized Civilization

BY

CARL L. BECKER

John Stambaugh Professor of History
Cornell University

SILVER, BURDETT AND COMPANY

NEW YORK   NEWARK   BOSTON   CHICAGO   SAN FRANCISCO

Copyright, 1931
By CARL L. BECKER

Printed in the United States of America

TO ALL TEACHERS
OF WHATEVER RACE OR COUNTRY
OF WHATEVER PERSUASION
WHO WITH SINGLENESS OF PURPOSE
HAVE ENDEAVORED TO INCREASE KNOWLEDGE
AND PROMOTE WISDOM IN THE WORLD
THIS BOOK IS DEDICATED

TO THOSE WHO READ THIS BOOK

Students often say to me: "I don't know any history; I think it would be a good thing to learn some." What they seem to mean is that they have never had a "course" in history, or have never read Gibbon's *Decline and Fall of the Roman Empire*, or Mr. Rhodes's *History of the United States from the Compromise of 1850*, or other books similar to these. But they are greatly mistaken if they think they "don't know any history." Every man, woman, and child knows some history, enough at least to stumble along in the world.

Suppose, for example, that you had awakened this morning totally unable to remember anything — all your other faculties working properly, but memory entirely gone. You would be in a bad way indeed! You wouldn't know who you were, or where; what you had done yesterday, or what you intended or other people expected you to do today. What could you do in that case? Wander about helplessly, seeing and hearing things, taking them in as altogether new, not at all knowing what they might mean in relation either to the past or the future You would have to discover your little world all over again, much as you discovered it in childhood; you would have to "re-orient" yourself and get a new running start. In short, you would be a lost soul because you had ceased to have any knowledge of history, the history of your personal doings and associations in the past.

For history is no more than things said and done in the past. It is as simple as that; and we might as well omit the word "past," since everything said and done is already in the past as soon as it is said or done. Done, but not done *with*. We have to remember many things said and done in order to live our lives intelligently; and so far as we remember things said and done we have a knowledge of history, for that is what historical knowledge is —

v

memory of things said and done. Thus everyone has some knowledge of history, and it is quite essential that everyone should have, since it is only by remembering something of the past that we can anticipate something of the future. Please note that I do not say *predict* the future. We cannot predict the future, but we can *anticipate* it — we can look forward to it and in some sense prepare for it. Now if memory of some things said and done is necessary, it seems that memory of more things ought to be better. The more we remember of things said and done (if they be the right things for our purpose), the better we can manage our affairs today, and the more intelligently we can prepare for what is coming to us tomorrow and next year and all our lives.

This is why it is worth while to take courses in history, or to read history books — even textbooks, even this book. The object should always be, not merely to learn enough to pass the examinations (although that is worth while too, and you will find in this book all that is necessary for that purpose), but to make an "artificial extension" of your personal memory. You cannot, of course, remember the events of the French Revolution as you remember the events that you took part in a year ago; but by reading books about the French Revolution you can create images or pictures of the men and events of that great upheaval; and by this artificial extension of memory you can observe these events "in the mind's eye," and hear these people speak with the mind's ear, in much the same way that you can still see, in imagination, events you took part in last year, or hear the friend who spoke to you then. The purpose of this book is to help you make this artificial extension of memory, help you stretch your memory over the last four hundred years, so that, by recalling the events that have occurred during that past time, you can more intelligently anticipate what is likely to occur during the years that are to come.

Of all the things said and done in the last four hundred years, only a very few of the most important could possibly be mentioned in a single volume like this one. If I had tried to say something about all the events, in all the countries, the book would have been no more than a bare list of names and dates. I thought it would be much better to omit a great many events, and even to say very little or nothing about some countries, so that there would be space enough to describe with some fullness of detail the events and people I did describe. By telling a good deal about a few events and a few people it would be possible, I thought, to make them seem real and perhaps even interesting. I have therefore selected those events and people, some having to do with one country and some having to do with another, which it seemed to me would best serve to explain how the European world of today came to be what it is. I have tried to relate these events in such a way that the essential facts of each, and their connection one with another, may be easily understood and permanently stored up in your memories. And to make this a bit easier I have placed with each chapter a kind of graphic representation of the course of events which I hope will enable you to take in at a glance the most essential things to be remembered.

The following persons were kind enough to read the manuscript, either in whole or in part; and by pointing out errors of fact, or suggesting changes in arrangement or in interpretation and emphasis, they have all been of very great service: Miss Jessie C. Evans, Head of the Department of Social Studies in the Simon Gratz High School, Philadelphia; Mr. Robert I. Adriance, Head of the Social Science Department in the High School, East Orange, New Jersey; Professor Sidney B. Fay of Harvard University; Professor Lewis R. Gottschalk of the University of Chicago. Miss Miriam A. Compton, a graduate student at the University of Minnesota, assisted in preparing the selected readings. And I desire to express my obligation to Miss Irene M. Gibson and to Mrs. Phyllis Cary, both of the editorial staff of Silver, Burdett and Company; to the former for her persistence and ingenuity in performing the difficult task of obtaining suitable illustrations; to the latter for her careful and intelligent preparation of the manuscript for the compositor. If the book has merits these friends have all contributed to them; its faults are all my own.

In securing the illustrations assistance was received from the staffs of a number of museums and libraries in this country and abroad. Acknowledgment is hereby made of all such assistance, and in particular of that received from the Archives Photographiques d'Art et d'Histoire; the New York Public Library; and Mr. William M. Ivins, Curator of the Department of Prints, Metropolitan Museum of Art.

CARL BECKER

ITHACA, NEW YORK

CONTENTS

LIST OF MAPS

A German Printing Shop in the Seventeenth Century

PART I

INTRODUCTION TO MODERN HISTORY

CHAPTER I. IN WHICH WE EXPLAIN WHAT MODERN HISTORY IS ABOUT

History is philosophy teaching by example. BOLINGBROKE.

Modern history is the history of our times and of our civilization. Any period of history is " modern " to the people who are living at the time. Caesar's wars in Gaul may have seemed far off and unreal to you when you read about them in your Latin class; but they were live events to Cicero, who was living in Rome at the time. They have become " ancient history " to us, just as the Great War will be ancient history to the people living in the year 2500 — if there are any people left then. For us, modern history is therefore the history of " our times." Modern history is our history.

Of course all history is our history in one sense. What men have thought and done in the past may still affect us, and it may have had some influence on what we do and think. Aristotle is called " the father of knowledge "; and the writings of Plato can still teach us much if we only take the trouble to read them. Whenever you see a fine building with white marble columns you are looking at a building that owes something to the Greek idea of beauty. In this sense all history is one, and is our history.

This is so because we are all human and have much the same desires, passions, hopes, and aspirations. Human nature, which makes history what it is, is much the same whatever period of history you may be studying. But although human nature remains the same, the manners and customs through which human nature expresses itself change greatly from age to age. For example, we can understand the Roman wars because the desires and passion which made the Romans fight are much the same as those which make men fight today. But the weapons which the Romans used

1

in fighting their wars were very different from those which we use. Differences in civilization are indicated by differences in the outward forms — the manners and customs — through which human nature expresses itself; and in this respect it is clear that our civilization differs very greatly from the civilization of the ancient world or of the Middle Ages.

Thus while all history is our history in the sense that all history is the work of human beings like ourselves, modern history is our history in a special sense. Modern history is the history of our civilization, and of those recent centuries during which our civilization has taken on the form with which we are familiar.

Five things to remember about modern civilization. Let us then ask what it is that makes modern civilization different from the civilization of earlier times. At first sight everything in modern life, from world wars to writing fluid, seems to be different from what it used to be; and since civilization is made up of everything men think and do, it would be possible to make an endless list of ways in which the civilization of our age differs from that of any previous age. Such a list would be too long, and we must be content to point out some of the most general and important differences. There are perhaps five things which make modern civilization different from the civilization of earlier times. To these five things we may give five names: (1) scientific knowledge; (2) economic interdependence; (3) humane feeling and democratic ideas; (4) nationalism; (5) internationalism. Having used these big words, let us see if we can find out what they mean.

1. *Scientific knowledge and how it has changed the conditions of life.* The principal thing which makes life in our day different from life in earlier times is that our trained scientists have learned how to make effective use of the forces of nature for the service of mankind. Because of the fact that these forces have been made to work for us, the conditions of life have changed more in the last hundred and fifty years than in the preceding two thousand years. If Socrates could have come to life in Paris in 1776, many things would have seemed strange to him; but he would not have had much trouble in making himself at home there. Once he had learned the French language, he could easily have taken up his former

occupation of going about and asking his fellow-citizens puzzling questions regarding the nature of truth and virtue. In two thousand years the outward conditions of life had not greatly changed.

But if Benjamin Franklin should enter Philadelphia today, with or without a loaf of bread under his arm, he would be less at home in his old home town after two hundred years than Socrates would have been in Paris after two thousand years. Franklin might recognize Independence Hall, if he should stumble upon it, but he would not, at first, know where to look for it. He would not know how to hail a street car or use a telephone, or what it was that made the automobiles go. He would not recognize the *Saturday Evening Post* which he had founded, and could not set type for it or run one of its presses. At every turn this greatly learned and much traveled citizen of the eighteenth century would be amazed — perhaps a little dismayed. It might be that he would prefer to return to the silent grave.

But if Franklin cared to remain in such a place as Philadelphia, he would soon understand all these things that at first seemed so strange. And the explanation would seem to him very simple after all. " I see," he would perhaps say, " that you have made great progress in *scientific knowledge.* You have gone much farther than we did in making practical use of this knowledge. This is what makes Philadelphia such a noisy, crowded, hustling city that I should never have known it. Yet this is just what we scientists were trying to do in my day; for even then we knew that by means of scientific experiment man would master the forces of nature and make them work for him."

This is the chief reason why modern civilization is different from the civilization of earlier times: Man has mastered the forces of nature and has made them work for him.

2. *Economic interdependence : How the countries of the world are becoming more dependent on each other.* Franklin would soon have noticed another thing. He would have seen that although man has mastered the forces of nature, the forces of nature have in a sense mastered man. In working for us, these new forces have changed the conditions of life, and we must submit to these new conditions whether we wish to or not. You can see for yourself

PART OF AN EIGHTEENTH CENTURY WALL-HANGING

Even in city streets, the mud was at times so deep that people who could afford it were carried about in sedan chairs borne by men or by horses.

many ways in which the railroad, the telegraph, and the automobile are changing the conditions of life. But the most general result of these changes is this: The people in every country are becoming more dependent upon each other, and upon the people of other countries, for the necessities and luxuries of life.

This is so because it is possible to travel and to send news and goods from one place to another much more easily and quickly than formerly. If the people living in any community had no means of communication with the outside world, they would have to raise all their food and make all their tools, clothes, and houses. In other words, the community would have to be *economically sufficient unto itself*. But if several communities within reasonable distances of each other had roads, horses, and wagons as means of transportation, one community might raise food, another make clothes, another tools and lumber; and each could exchange the surplus of what it raised or made with the others. These communities would then be, to the extent of these exchanges, dependent upon each other; they would be *economically interdependent*.

Before the nineteenth century practically the only means of travel and communication were horses and wagons, boats and sailing ships. Even with these limited facilities there was a good deal of travel and trade between the different countries of the world;

but each country was still largely dependent on what it could raise and make. Today, however, the railroad, the telegraph, the steamship, and the airplane are bringing all the countries of the world into much closer relation, and it is much less possible for any country to be economically self-sufficient.

You will understand this if you consider the food you eat, the materials that go to make up the house you live in, the clothes you wear, and the automobile you ride in, and then try to discover where all these things come from. You will understand it better, perhaps, if you consider some of the things that are necessary for every country to have. Coal is necessary. Italy has none, Great Britain a great deal. Cotton is necessary. Great Britain has none, the United States more than it can use. Rubber is necessary. No European country produces any, but a great deal is to be found in South America. Oil and iron are essential. There are rich deposits in some countries, none in others. International trade in these essentials binds the countries together, whether for good or ill.

Thus, on account of the use we make of the forces of nature, all countries are becoming more dependent on each other; and this *economic interdependence* is another thing that makes modern civilization different from that of earlier times.

3. *Humane feeling and democratic ideas.* Now that the peoples of the world know each other better and are more dependent on each other for many things, they are coming to have a more friendly feeling for each other.

It is a natural human instinct to be suspicious of what is unfamiliar. We are apt to think there must be something wrong or evil about people whom we do not know, especially if they live far away, speak a language we cannot understand, and follow quite different manners and customs. Our poor opinion of such people is strongly confirmed if their skins happen to be some other color than our own. But if by chance we come to know these curious beings, these " stranger-enemies," we usually find that underneath their odd clothes and queer-colored skins they are after all much like ourselves. We find that they have much the same desires and passions and aspirations, much the same virtues and vices. In short we find that they are, like ourselves, human.

UP-TO-DATE TRUCKING, 1773

An advertisement by James Sharp, maker of new-style "rolling carts and wagons." The broad wheels were designed to prevent heavy trucks from miring in the dirt roads. They also served the purpose of rolling the roads.

This is just what has happened during the last hundred years — the people of the world have become better acquainted with each other. They have become better acquainted because they travel more and meet each other more frequently, and because business relations bring them into more frequent contact. Besides, anyone who can read a Sunday newspaper or the subtitles on a moving picture travelogue may learn more about the manners and customs of such far-distant peoples as the Chinese or the South Sea Islanders than even an educated person knew a hundred years ago. The result is that people who belong to some other class, or country, or religion than our own seem less strange and " heathenish " to us. It is true that violent conflicts between classes and nations are still common enough, and these conflicts give rise to hatred and intolerance. We shall say something about those conflicts later. But in general it is true that during the last hundred years the thought and feeling of most people toward their fellow-men has become more friendly, more tolerant, and less divine.

One aspect of this humane feeling is sympathy with the misfortunes of others. More than ever before we sympathize with the misfortunes of others and feel that it is our duty to help the poor and relieve suffering. Never before has so much time and money been given for the relief of poverty, the care of the sick, and the prevention of disease. We no longer permit brutal treatment of the insane. Punishment for crime is not so harsh and cruel as it used to be. This means that we are better able than men were formerly to understand the misfortunes of others, and to realize that we ourselves might have been or may sometime be in the same unfortunate situation.

Along with the increase in humane feeling there has been an increase in *democratic ideas*. More and more people have come to believe in democracy. Most of us are now of the opinion that people should be allowed to govern themselves, instead of being governed by a king. But a democracy is more than a form of government. A true democracy is an expression of the idea that men are, or ought to be in some sense, equal. This idea is stated in our Declaration of Independence in these words: " We hold these truths to be self-evident: That all men are created equal; that they are endowed by their Creator with certain unalienable rights; that among these are life, liberty, and the pursuit of happiness." This does not mean that all men are created equal in height, color, intelligence, or virtue; it means only that one man's life and happiness is as important to him as the life and happiness of any other man is to that other man. Robert Burns gave fine poetic expression to this idea in the famous line, " A man's a man for a' that! " The religious expression of the idea is that " all men are equal in the eyes of God "; the legal expression is that " all men are equal in the eyes of the law." Perhaps the best expression of this idea is that " all men are equal in the possession of a common humanity."

Thus modern civilization is different from the civilization of earlier times bec᷒ humane feeling and democratic ideas are more common th᷒᷒᷒᷒ ᷒mer times.

4. *Nationalisn.* ᷒᷒ *the world is divided into independent nation-states.* Be᷒᷒᷒᷒ and 1918, wars have been going on in Europe more thn᷒᷒᷒᷒ of the time; and the last war was on a larger scale an᷒ fa᷒᷒᷒ ᷒structive than any previous one. If we think only ᷒ all th᷒᷒᷒ and of the hatred and cruelty they give rise to, we may w᷒᷒ hether the peoples of the world are not becoming less hum᷒᷒ ᷒riendly rather than more so. But when we said that peopl᷒ ᷒coming more friendly and humane, we were taking men at their best. Men are not always at their

Photo Hachette

COTTON WEAVING BY HAND LOOM

Compare this eighteenth century loom with that of a modern factory. Here the operator of the loom had to use both hands and feet. Reproduced from an engraving in *L'Encyclopédie* (see p. 207) published in the eighteenth century.

best, and there are times when whole nations fear and hate each other so much that they wage war with each other.

But if nations are becoming more dependent on each other for food and other necessary things, why should they ever fight? You might think that this dependence on each other would make them friendly. Sometimes it does. If one nation needs coal or oil or rubber which another country has, that may lead to friendly trade between them. But it may lead to violent disputes also; and if the two countries cannot settle their disputes by peaceable agreement, they often — since there is nothing in our modern system of government to prevent it — attempt to settle the disputes by war.

The reason for this is that although the countries of the world are becoming more interdependent in respect to trade and industry, they remain independent in respect to government. The theory of modern government is that each " state " or government is sovereign and independent. This means two things: (1) that the people within the territory over which the state or government rules are bound to obey the laws and government of that state; (2) that the state or government, in its relations with other states or governments, is the sole judge of the rights and interests of its own people; and that it is in duty bound to defend these rights and interests — peaceably if it can, by force if necessary. Since there is no international court or judge with power to settle disputes between nations, each state or government thinks that it is in duty bound to fight for its rights and interests if they cannot be defended in any other way.

But why is there not a " United States of Europe " as there is a United States of America? There might have been a United States of Europe if the people of Europe had been enough alike to form one nation. But Europe is divided into many nations. It is not easy to say what makes a nation. A common language does not by itself make a nation, because the people of England and the United States speak one language but form two nations, while the people of Switzerland speak three languages and form one nation. All we can say is that a nation is a group of people who feel that they are enough like each other and enough unlike other groups so that they wish to live under their own law and government. It is because Europe is made up of many such nations that it is divided into many sovereign independent states.

This group feeling, which we call *nationalism*, has become much stronger in the last two hundred years. The feeling of nationalism and the desire of each nation to govern itself are very important facts in modern civilization. The people of any nation — such as France or England or Poland or Germany — feel very strongly that they belong together, that they must be " patriotic " and loyal to their own government, and that it is the business of their government to look out for their interests even if other people have to suffer for it. They may feel friendly toward other peoples, and they know that all peoples will be better off if they get along peaceably. But still they feel that every country must look out for itself. Each country is easily led to think that some other country is

Photo Hachette

A CANNON FOUNDRY, EIGHTEENTH CENTURY

Taken from an engraving in *L'Encyclopédie*. The moulds are in the floor at the left. Workmen are preparing to let the moulten metal flow into them. The only mechanical device appears to be the lever which is used to lift the heavy slide in front of the furnace.

trying to do it an injury, and so fear and hostility are easily aroused and wars come.

Of course wars between countries have always been frequent enough. But in our modern civilization wars are likely to involve a great many countries, because all countries are becoming more closely related in respect to trade and industry. Wars are also becoming more destructive, partly because more countries are involved, but chiefly because our scientific knowledge enables us to use larger armies and more cruel and destructive weapons. Thus the last war, which began between Austria and Serbia, soon involved nearly all the countries of the world. It became a " world war "; and it was so frightfully destructive that we may well ask whether our civilization could survive another such world war.

5. *Internationalism : How the nations are trying to work together.* We often speak of the " progress of civilization," and we like to think of ourselves as more civilized than people were in former times. But if the " progress of civilization " brings a few more

world wars, does it not seem that civilization will end by destroying itself? This may happen; but it surely is not pleasant to look forward to, and perhaps the people of the world — or at least the people of Europe — will some day find a means of living together in friendly co-operation, without these frequent and destructive wars. This idea that the nations should and can work together in friendly co-operation we may call *internationalism*. The idea of internationalism has grown stronger during the last two centuries, and today it is more seriously talked about than ever before.

One of the chief objects of internationalism is, of course, to prevent war. You know that the Peace of Versailles, which ended the last war, established a League of Nations for the purpose of preventing war in the future. But you must not think that this idea of a league of nations is something new. As long ago as 1623, a French scholar, Emeric Crucé, published a little book called *The New Cyneas*, in which he proposed that the peoples of the world should abolish their armies and establish a world court for settling their disputes by peaceable means. Many similar schemes have been proposed by statesmen and philosophers during the last two hundred years. The present League of Nations is an attempt to put this old idea into practice.

Internationalism is not merely a movement to prevent war. It aims to promote the common good in other ways, and in times of peace. During the last hundred years, especially, there have been formed a great many international associations for all sorts of purposes — for the promotion of arts and letters, for the advancement of science and learning, for the relief of suffering and the prevention of disease, for promoting peace and conciliation, and the like. Such international associations tend to be more numerous and more world wide in their organization and in their objects. There are two reasons for this. First, the peoples of the world are becoming more closely related in their economic interests, and this makes such associations more necessary and desirable. Second, the railroad and the steamship and the telegraph make it very much easier to organize and carry on the business of such associations than it used to be.

Thus it is an important fact of modern civilization that the countries of the world are more and more working together for many purposes by means of international associations. The League of Nations is only one of many such associations. In this broad sense, internationalism is the result of those modern conditions which are bringing the people of the world closer together in their economic interests and in their thought and feeling. Mr. H. G. Wells, in his *Outline of History*, says that " a sense of history as the common adventure of mankind is as necessary for peace within as for peace between the nations." This phrase, " the common adventure of mankind," sums up very well what we mean by internationalism. Internationalism is just this growing sense that the millions of human beings crowded together on our little planet are after all in the same boat, embarked on the same voyage. In some slight measure we are beginning to realize that we shall wreck this voyage in the end unless we think of it as *the common adventure of mankind*.

QUESTIONS

1. What is meant by "scientific knowledge"? What important inventions have come into practical use during your lifetime? What things in a modern city like Philadelphia would most astonish Benjamin Franklin if he could come back to it?

2. What is meant by "economic interdependence"? What food would your community find it necessary to depend on if there were no means of transportation except horses and wagons, and no modern methods of preserving food?

3. What distant places have you visited? Why did you go to these places? How did you get there? What modern inventions help (1) to bring people of different communities into closer contact; (2) to make them more dependent on each other for the things they need?

4. What is meant by "humane feeling"? How many "humanitarian" organizations can you name?

5. Mention as many international organizations as you can. What are the chief international institutions designed to settle disputes between nations by peaceful means? What is meant by "nationalism"? by "internationalism"?

6. What do you understand by "patriotism"? Why do you feel more loyal to the United States than to other countries?

DETAIL OF THE CLOISTER AT ARLES
From a lithograph by Chapuy.

CHAPTER II. IN WHICH WE INTRODUCE THREE "THROW–
BACKS" TO SHOW WHAT LED UP TO MODERN HISTORY

History has for its object to fix the order of events throughout past time and in all places. SANTAYANA

A glimpse of three earlier stages in European history. We shall begin modern history with the seventeenth century — that is, about the year 1600. The chief reason for doing so is that the five characteristics of modern civilization described in the first part of Chapter I begin to be clearly discernible about that time. Nevertheless, there are no very sharply defined beginnings or endings in history. Wherever you begin, there are earlier events leading up to that beginning; wherever you end, there are, or will be, other events following after. Any chosen period of history is somewhat like a moving picture which represents the doings of certain people during a certain period of their lives. No doubt the picture has a unity and a significance of its own; but it is what it is — tragic or comic or a little of both — because something happened to the actors before the play began. Directors therefore often find it necessary to introduce a " throw-back," giving the spectators a glimpse of the early life of the hero or the villain. We may very well imitate this excellent practice by taking at least a glimpse at what happened in Europe before " modern history " began.

13

Let us imagine ourselves, then, ready to watch the drama of modern history from 1600 to the present time. That we may understand it better, the director kindly gives us a few throwbacks. A picture appears which gives us a glimpse of the period 1300–1600; the subtitle is " The Renaissance and the Reformation." Another picture, and we look still farther back, to the Middle Ages; the subtitle is " Medieval Civilization." Then a third picture appears, and we have before us " The Civilization of Ancient Greece and Rome." Let us see what these three throwbacks show us. We shall take them in reverse order: (1) The Civilization of Ancient Greece and Rome — a thousand years of history, from about 500 B.C. to 500 A.D.; (2) Medieval Civilization, 500–1300; (3) The Renaissance and the Reformation, 1300–1600. We wish to learn, as briefly as possible, what each of these three epochs in European history contributed to the civilization which we call modern.

I. The Civilization of Ancient Greece and Rome, 500 B.C.–500 A.D.

Greek civilization in the age of Pericles. When the people whom we call Greeks settled in Greece, they found in the eastern Mediterranean world (in Greece, in Crete, and in Asia Minor) a remarkable civilization, far more advanced than their own. This civilization they partly destroyed and partly appropriated, but in any case modified according to their peculiar genius, so that in the course of time there were established in Greece the political institutions and social customs, the art, and the philosophy of life, which we call the civilization of the ancient Greeks.

The most remarkable of the Greek peoples were the Athenians. When we speak of the " glory that was Greece," we commonly have in mind the brilliant civilization that flourished at Athens in the " Age of Pericles " (461–429 B.C.) and during the half-century following. At no time during this century did the total population of Athens exceed 300,000 — which is less than the present population of Buffalo, New York. Yet within a brief hundred years this handful of people produced masterpieces of art, literature, and philosophy which have rarely been equaled and perhaps never surpassed, and which have had a most profound and enduring influence upon the thought and culture of our own time.

It was during this hundred years that the Athenians perfected the Greek style of architecture, of which the most famous example was the Parthenon. At this time Phidias and Praxiteles executed, in gold and ivory and marble, those human figures (Athena, Hermes, Apollo, and Aphrodite) which for grace and beauty have rarely been equaled. At this time Thucydides wrote his *History of the Peloponnesian War*, which still ranks with the best examples of the art of writing history, and Xenophon wrote the *Retreat of the Ten Thousand*, which is still studied in college as a model of simple, lucid narrative. At this time appeared the masterpieces of Greek dramatic art — the plays of Sophocles, the somber tragedies of Euripides, the brilliant comedies of Aristophanes. At this time Socrates went about the streets of Athens asking his friends those puzzling questions about the nature of truth and virtue which wise men ever since have attempted in vain to answer. His pupil, Plato, preserved and

Photo Alinari

GREEK SCULPTURE, FIFTH CENTURY B.C.

Discovered in the Gardens of Sallust, Villa Ludovisi, Italy. It represents a Greek matron pouring incense into an incense burner.

dramatized and systematized the wisdom of Socrates in the famous *Dialogues* which furnished the starting-point of most later " idealistic " systems of thought. Following Socrates and Plato came the student and critic of both — Aristotle, who wrote so comprehensively and so profoundly on every subject that many philosophers still regard him as the greatest of thinkers. In producing these masterpieces, the Athenians also perfected the Greek language, " Attic Greek " — a language which those who know it tell us has never been surpassed as an instrument for presenting ideas with precision and subtlety, or for conveying sentiment and emotion in harmonious and beautiful form.

GREEK HORSEMEN, FROM THE PARTHENON FRIEZE

This frieze, which is forty inches high, ran around the four sides of the Parthenon. Many of the marbles from the frieze are now in the British Museum.

Greek civilization in the Hellenistic Age. This golden age of Athenian civilization was followed by what is called the " Hellenistic Age " — a period of about three centuries during which the Greek language and culture were spread throughout the entire eastern Mediterranean world. This diffusion of Greek culture was the result of the conquests of Philip of Macedon, and of his son, Alexander the Great. Within a brief period (334–323 B.C.) Alexander's armies swept over Asia Minor, Syria, Persia, and Egypt. After his death this great empire fell to Alexander's Greek generals and was divided into three independent governments — Macedon and Greece; the Seleucid Empire of Asia Minor, Syria, and Persia; and the Ptolemaic Empire of Egypt. The result was that in all these countries Greek became the official language, the language of polite society, of commerce, and of the schools. In short, Greek became the common language of the educated classes. The military conquests of Alexander were in themselves of slight importance. The important fact was the conquest

THE ERECHTHEUM, ATHENS

The Erechtheum, named after Erechtheus, the mythical king and founder of Athens, is justly famous for the beauty of its architecture. At the left is a porch, the roof of which is supported by lovely maidens, hence it is called the "Porch of the Maidens."

of the eastern Mediterranean world by the Greek language and the Greek culture.

It was in the Hellenistic Age that the Greeks made their chief contributions to science. In this age Euclid lived and worked out the system of geometry that is still taught in our high schools. Archimedes, who lived in Syracuse, developed higher mathematics, discovered the principle of specific gravity, and made practical inventions based on pulleys and levers. He said that with his levers he could " move the earth " — if he had a place to stand on. Eratosthenes computed the size of the earth, devised a system of latitude and longitude, and made a fairly correct map of the known world. Aristarchus demonstrated (although few people accepted his proof) that the earth and the planets move about the sun.

The chief center of scientific studies in the Hellenistic Age was Alexandria, in Egypt. But Athens retained its fame as a center of philosophical speculation, and at Athens there appeared two new philosophies which were to have a great influence in later times. One of these was founded by Zeno, who taught in the " Painted

Porch " in the market place. Since the Greek word for porch is
stoa, Zeno was called the *Stoic*, and his philosophy is known as
stoicism. Zeno taught that the great aim of life should be tranquillity of soul, and that this could be best attained by indifference
to both pleasure and pain. The other philosophy was founded by
Epicurus, who taught that the highest good could be attained, not
by avoiding pleasure and pain, but by seeking the highest satisfac-
tion of body and of mind. Zeno and Epicurus were less concerned
with the nature of the universe than Plato and Aristotle had been,
and more concerned with what men should do in order to be happy
in it. The Stoic said: " Steel your sensibilities so that life will
hurt you as little as possible." The Epicurean said: " Cultivate
your sensibilities so that you may enjoy life as much as possible."
From that day to our own, these two systems of practical morality
have had a profound influence on European thought. Today we
commonly think of a *stoic* as a man who bears pain or suffering
without flinching; whereas the word *epicure* we apply to one who
is too much given to the pleasure of eating.

The Roman Empire and why it was important. The Hellenistic
Age came to an end when the Romans (146–31 B.C.) conquered
the Eastern empires that Alexander had established. It was followed by the long period of the Roman world-empire. The
Greeks were an artistic and intellectual people. What they contributed to European civilization was, above all, *ideas*. These
ideas the Romans borrowed, without adding much to them, and
spread throughout the Western world. But the Romans contributed much of their own to European civilization. The Romans
were above all a practical people — doers rather than thinkers.
Their great achievement was to build up the most remarkable
political empire of ancient times — perhaps, all things concerned,
of any time. In doing this they mastered the practical arts of
military conquest, politics, and administration. The Greeks taught
the later Europeans what to think about the world; the Romans
taught them how to master it.

Rome was founded nearly a thousand years before Christ, by a
people called Latins. For a hundred years it was ruled by conquering Etruscan kings, but about 509 B.C. the Romans drove out the

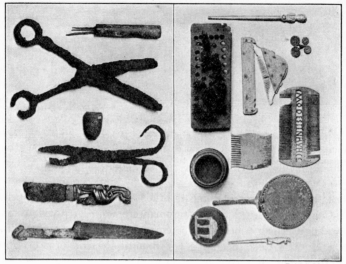

GREEK AND ROMAN TOILET ARTICLES AND DOMESTIC IMPLEMENTS

At the left are shown scissors, thimble, needles and case, and knives. At the right are combs, a brush, a round hand-mirror, pins, a rouge pot, and other articles.

kings and established the Roman Republic (509–31 B.C.). During the five hundred years of the republic the Romans were chiefly engaged in the slow but persistent conquest of the entire Mediterranean world. First they conquered Italy, then Carthage (their dangerous maritime and commercial rival in North Africa), then the Hellenistic empires of the East, and also Spain and Gaul in the West. For these conquests great armies were needed, and in the later republic powerful generals contended with each other for the mastery. The greatest of these was Julius Caesar, who overthrew the republic and established a " dictatorship." Augustus Caesar completed the work of Julius by organizing the government of the dictatorship and making it permanent. This is usually taken as the beginning of the Roman Empire (31 B.C.). Four centuries later the Emperor Constantine moved the government to Byzantium (Constantinople), and about the same time the empire was divided into two parts, the Western part being gov-

SILVER COINS OF THE ROMAN REPUBLIC

The first coin shows Roma, personified — a type head used on many early Roman coins. An elephant treading on a serpent was portrayed on a coin issued by Julius Caesar about 50 B.C. to commemorate one of his victories. The fourth coin shows Aeneas carrying Anchises.

erned by an emperor at Rome and the Eastern part by an emperor at Constantinople. The Western empire was destroyed by the invading German tribes, and the emperors ceased to rule at Rome in 476. The Eastern empire lasted until the conquest of Constantinople by the Ottoman Turks in 1453.

Roman civilization reached its highest development in the later republic and early empire (146 B.C.–180 A.D.). When the Romans conquered the East, they plundered it. Wealth poured into Rome, and wealthy Romans adopted the more luxurious and sophisticated life which they found in Athens and Alexandria. Many educated Greeks came to Rome, either on their own account or else as slaves. Greek books were translated into Latin, schools were established by Greek teachers, and the sons of Romans were taught in their homes by Greek slaves. Educated Romans wrote plays, histories, and essays, in which they imitated Greek models and copied Greek ideas. The great figures in Latin literature (Caesar, Cicero, Horace, Vergil, Lucretius, and Seneca), some of whose works are still taught in high school and college, were little more than imitators of the Greeks, adding little that was original. Nevertheless, they transmitted much of the Greek culture to the Western world, and they perfected the Latin language, from which were later derived the modern " romance languages " — Italian, French, Spanish, Portuguese, and Rumanian.

The Romans were original, not as thinkers but as doers. They were great builders. All over western Europe they built paved

Deutsches Museum, Munich

ROMAN WARSHIP, about 50 B.C.

This is one type of warship which helped the Romans to conquer most of the
Mediterranean world.

roads, so solidly constructed that they are still used. In the Forum
at Rome they constructed those splendid public buildings the
remains of which still stand. Tourists still visit the Colosseum,
a stadium, seating 45,000 people, which was used in part for the
gladiatorial exhibitions — the Roman equivalent of modern bull-
fights, prize fights, and football games. In architectural style
the Romans borrowed from the Greeks, but they invented the
round arch, which enabled them to erect more massive structures.
They also learned the secret of concrete, which has been redis-
covered in recent times. So effectively did they master the secret
that the immense dome of the Pantheon, a solid bowl of concrete
measuring 142 feet across, seems as secure today as it was when the
builders knocked the wooden supports from under it, eighteen
hundred years ago.

The greatest contribution of the Romans to modern civilization
was in the realm of government and law. At its greatest extent

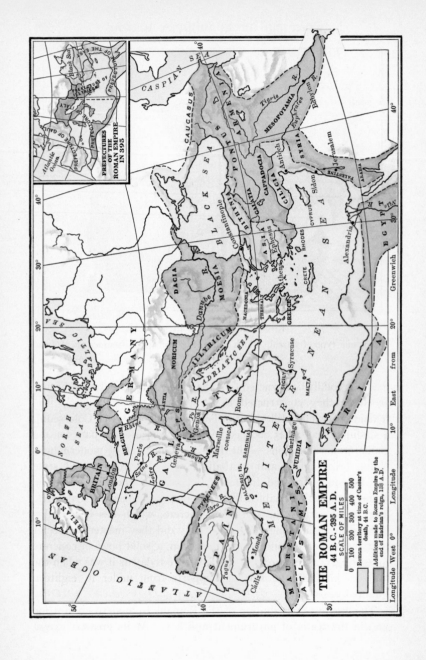

THE ROMAN EMPIRE
44 B.C. - 395 A.D.

SCALE OF MILES

0 100 200 300 400 500

Roman territory at time of Caesar's death, 44 B.C.

Additions made to Roman Empire by the end of Hadrian's reign, 138 A.D.

Longitude West 0° Longitude   East   from   Greenwich

PREFECTURES OF THE ROMAN EMPIRE IN 395

the empire included the entire Mediterranean world and more —
North Africa, Egypt, Syria, Asia Minor, all of Europe as far north
as the Danube and as far east as the Rhine, and the island of Britain to the frontier of Scotland. To govern this immense empire

in an age when there were neither
railroads nor telegraph lines required great political genius. As
finally organized by Constantine,
the empire was divided into four
divisions (*prefectures*), each having
its prefect subject to the emperor.
Each prefecture was divided into
dioceses, each having its vicar subject to the prefect. Each diocese
was divided into *provinces*, each
having its governor subject to the
vicar. The smallest unit of all was
the *city*, governed by a council and
magistrates under the supervision
of the governor. Thus there was
created a graded hierarchy of administrative officials from the emperor down to the local city officials.

Royal Ontario Museum of Archaeology

A CHILD'S TOY

This toy, made probably in the
second or third century A.D., belonged to a Roman child. It was
found at Fayum, in Egypt.

The administrative system of most countries today is modeled
more or less upon this ancient system which the Romans perfected.

During the five hundred years when the Romans governed the
Western civilized world they also perfected the civil law for the
administration of justice. The earliest Roman law was the Twelve
Tables, crude and harsh, suited only to a primitive society. But
when they made their conquests of Italy and beyond, they did not
apply this law to the subject peoples. For the administration of
justice in the provinces they built up a new code of law, based on
the practices that were common to the conquered peoples. This
was the *ius gentium* — "law common to all nations." During the
later period of the empire a number of famous judges, known as
iurisconsulti, modified and systematized the *ius gentium* by inter-
preting it in the light of "natural law" — that is, of law derived

from reason rather than from custom.   Finally, in the reign of the Emperor Justinian, the entire body of Roman civil law was reduced to a single systematic body of principles, known as the *Justinian Code*, or the *Digest* (534 A.D.).   The Justinian Code contains the essence of all that the Romans learned about the nature of political authority, of property rights, and of the rights of persons in their relations with each other.   During the last seven hundred years the Justinian Code has been studied in all the law schools of Europe; and even today it is, in modified form, the basis of the civil and administrative law of the European world.

Thus the modern world of Europe and America owes much to the ancient Greeks and Romans.   If we had to express in four words what we owe to these two peoples, the words would be *Greek ideas* and *Roman law*.

II. Medieval Civilization, 500–1300

Transition from Roman to medieval civilization.   In the third century, half-civilized peoples (mainly Germans) began to come into the Roman Empire across the Danube and the Rhine frontiers. Though often repulsed, they kept on coming.   During the fourth century they settled in various parts of the empire and were Romanized, very much as European emigrants to the United States are Americanized.   They learned the Latin language, lived as tenant farmers on the great estates, served in the armies, and not infrequently rose to high office in the army or the government. But in the fifth century they came in such conquering hordes that they could be neither Romanized nor repulsed.   The Saxons and the Jutes established themselves in Britain, the Franks in northern Gaul, the Visigoths in southern Gaul and Spain, the Vandals in Africa, the Heruli and the Lombards in Italy.   In the year 476 the barbarian chief Odoacer deposed Romulus Augustulus, the last of the Western emperors.   This date is therefore often taken as marking the end of the Western Roman Empire.

The conquering tribes, for the most part, did not *aim* to destroy Roman civilization.   On the contrary, the splendid roads and buildings, the ease and comfort of Roman life, seemed marvelous to them.   They wished to appropriate and to use these fine things.

But they were like rough children in a Sèvres china shop — they broke the Roman world to pieces, leaving only the fragments from which a new world might be constructed. They were too primitive to adopt the Roman way of life, too ignorant to maintain education or the useful arts, too incompetent to master the efficient Roman system of law and government. The result was that during five centuries (500–1000), civilization so far declined in the West that only a few chronicles, written in bad Latin, remain to inform us of the events of that time. The period of greatest ignorance was the latter part of the ninth century and the tenth century (850–1000), when men in western Europe knew nothing of the brilliant civilization that once flourished at Rome and Athens, and almost nothing of the civilization that still persisted at Constantinople and Baghdad.

Out of this age of confusion and ignorance there emerged a new type of civilization which reached its height during the twelfth and thirteenth centuries (1100–1300). We call it *medieval civilization* — the civilization that lies between ancient and modern times. What was it like? We may describe it briefly under three heads: (1) government and social classes; (2) economic life; (3) religion and philosophy.

Government and social classes. The first effect of the German conquests was that the Western Roman Empire was replaced by a multitude of unstable and warring powers. As a consequence, regular communication in western Europe came to an end. Roads and bridges fell into disrepair. Commerce declined, and cities decayed. Education and the useful arts all but disappeared. The German chieftains, unaccustomed to governing large countries, parceled out their possessions among their military followers. Communities became isolated and had to depend on themselves for economic support and military defense. The mass of the people looked to their military chieftain or great landowner for protection, and he in turn exacted from them obedience, services, and rents.

Thus in the course of centuries arose the " feudal system," which was well established in western Europe by the eleventh century. Feudalism was three things in one: (1) a form of land tenure; (2) a system of social classes; and (3) a method of government.

Everywhere in western Europe there was the great feudal " lord " (duke, earl, marquis, count, margrave, etc.). On his estate or " manor " lived the peasants, tilling the soil, subject to the lord's control, and owing him " feudal dues " (services and payments in money or in kind). He was the *overlord* of the land, they were servile *tenants* (feudalism as a form of land tenure). He was *noble* and privileged, they were *common* and unprivileged (feudalism as a system of social classes). He was *ruler*, they were *subject* (feudalism as a method of government).

As ruler, the noble lord was supported by other nobles, whose domains were held " in fief " from him in return for allegiance and military aid. They were his " vassals," armed and privileged like himself. For defense the noble had his strong castle, built perhaps on some high hill, or else surrounded by a moat filled with water and accessible only by a drawbridge. The castle was at once a home and a fortress. Here the lord lived and was supported and served by his peasants. (See Chapter VI for description of peasant life in the eighteenth century.) To his castle the lord and his vassals retired when hard pressed by some rival lord; from it they sallied forth to attack an enemy. The lord was himself the vassal of some powerful overlord, to whom he in turn owed allegiance and military aid. The overlord might perhaps be called a " king." But the king was usually a king in name only, since he often fought — and often in vain — to keep his powerful vassals in decent subjection. As a method of government, feudalism in the tenth century was little more than a regulated system of private war.

Out of feudalism, nevertheless, there at last emerged the " states " of modern times. By skill or good fortune some feudal lords managed to get the upper hand of their rivals. As their domains increased and their power grew, they enforced a stricter obedience on their own vassals and on all people within the region where their power was established. In this way, by the end of the Middle Ages, powerful kingdoms and principalities were established. The Duke of Normandy conquered England in 1066, and his successors created the English kingdom. Hugh Capet, whose ancestors were counts of Paris, became " king " in 987, and his successors created the Kingdom of France. It was one of his successors, Louis XVI,

AGRICULTURE IN THE FIFTEENTH CENTURY

Plowing, harrowing, sowing by hand, reaping with sickle, and binding. This illumination from a manuscript written in French is not very realistic, since all of these operations are represented as going on at the same time. In the background are the homes of the peasants, a walled town, and the castle of the owner.

who lost his crown and his head at the time of the French Revolution. The margraves of Brandenburg established the state which later became the Kingdom of Prussia; they were the ancestors of that William Hohenzollern who is now living in exile in Holland. In the thirteenth century Rudolph of Habsburg began to build up the state that was later known as Austria. In the Spanish peninsula appeared the kingdoms of Castile, Aragon, and Navarre, which were later united into the Kingdom of Spain.

As power was concentrated in the hands of kings and princes, the noble vassals lost the right of making private war, and became " subjects " of the king or the prince.   But they were still great landowners, managing their estates and exacting services and rents from their peasants.   They were still nobles, set apart from the common people.   They remained, in short, a privileged " aristocracy."   This is the origin of the aristocracies of European countries. Europe is still filled with people calling themselves dukes or counts or barons — the descendants of former privileged and powerful landowning aristocrats.

KNIGHTS IN ARMOR

These knights were drawn by one of their contemporaries to illustrate a twelfth century manuscript entitled "Hortus Deliciarum."   They may have taken part in one of the crusades.

Economic life. In the tenth and eleventh centuries, outside Italy, life was almost entirely rural.   In Spain, Gaul, and Britain, the fine towns of Roman times had all but disappeared. Money, banking, and forms of credit were virtually non-existent.   The only important form of wealth was land, and there were but two important economic classes — the noble proprietors and the servile peasant farmers. Even in the noble's castle, life was primitive and uncomfortable; food and clothes and other necessities were raised or made on the manor, and there were few if any luxuries.

But in the twelfth and thirteenth centuries a remarkable change occurred — industry and commerce began to flourish, towns sprang up, and the well-to-do adopted a more luxurious and sophisticated way of life.   This change was partly the result of the religious crusades, which were military expeditions to the Near East to conquer the Holy Land from the infidels.   During the twelfth and thirteenth centuries the crusaders, and the merchants and adventurers who followed in their train, brought back to western Europe many strange and desirable commodities — silks, tapestries, rugs, perfumes, dyes, spices, and precious stones. Gradually a thriving trade in these and other commodities was established between western Europe and the cities of Constantinople and Alexandria.

Commerce with the East stimulated industry in western Europe, and important cities developed on the river highways.

A FIFTEENTH CENTURY BAKESHOP

From a book printed in that century. This woodcut represents December and has the signs of the Zodiac inserted in the small circles.

As cities developed, their merchants and artisans wished to free themselves from the control of the feudal overlords. Sometimes they purchased their freedom; sometimes they obtained it by force. As a result, there were in western Europe in the thirteenth century many " free cities " — cities which had obtained from their former overlords — from king or noble — charters guaranteeing them the right of self-government and freedom from feudal dues and taxes. Within the town, artisans engaged in making a particular commodity or merchants engaged in a special line of trade were commonly united in a guild — the Guild of Tailors, the Hatters' Guild, the Guild of Goldsmiths, and the like. Each guild was a little closed corporation which enjoyed a monopoly of making and selling a particular commodity. Thus the cities freed themselves from the feudal system and from the control of the feudal nobles, and came to be governed by laws and customs suited to the needs of merchants and artisans. But after the cities were freed from the control of the nobles, they no longer enjoyed their protection. For defense or attack the towns maintained an armed militia and constructed high turreted walls, with massive gates guarding all the entrances.

Thus it happened that there were in all the countries of western Europe three classes — nobles, peasants, and townsmen (*bourgeoisie*). The peasants were subject to the nobles; the townsmen depended on the nobles to buy their wares. But otherwise the three classes had little in common. They had neither equality of rights nor any feeling of a common nationality. Much of modern history is concerned with the conflicting interests of these three classes. The peasants gradually won freedom from subjection to the nobles; the townsmen gradually won equality of rights and of political influence. But in the thirteenth century one thing, and one thing only, bound the people of western Europe together. This was a common religion — the Christian religion of the medieval church.

Religion and philosophy. Christianity was founded by Jesus of Nazareth, who lived in the reign of the Emperor Augustus Caesar. The teachings of Jesus were accepted by a few Jewish disciples and later carried to the " gentiles " (non-Jews) by the apostle Paul, who traveled throughout the Roman Empire preaching the new gospel. For two centuries the Christians were harshly persecuted. But in spite of persecution, or perhaps because of it, the followers of the new religion increased in numbers. In 313 Christianity was therefore granted toleration by decree of the emperor, and by the end of the century it was the accepted religion of the Roman Empire.

The German tribes that conquered the Western empire were easily converted to Christianity, and during the centuries of confusion that followed, while the power of the Roman Empire declined, the power of the Roman Christian Church increased. In the course of centuries its bishops and priests, looking to the Bishop of Rome as their leader, built up that most extraordinary and powerful institution — the Holy Catholic Church of medieval times. The medieval church reached the height of its power in the thirteenth century. What was it like and what did it teach?

The medieval church was something like a modern church, something like a modern state, and something like neither. It was a church-state which claimed the right to govern, not a country, but the " community of all true Christians," wherever they might be. Like a modern church, it taught a particular religious creed and provided a special form of worship. Like a modern state, it levied taxes, administered justice, and imposed penalties for the violation of its laws. The head of the church was the Bishop of Rome, the Pope, who claimed to be the Vicar of Christ and as such to exercise divine authority. His voice was the voice of God, his decrees were laws intended by God for the government of men. Subject to the Pope, in every country of western Europe, there were archbishops and bishops; and subject to the bishops there were the parish priests. Whatever language a man might speak, wherever he might live, to whatever king or prince he might be subject in temporal things, in spiritual things he was subject to the higher authority of the church. Even kings and princes were subject to the church, for kings and princes were Christians too, and could be deposed or excommunicated by the Pope. To withdraw from the church or to be excommunicated from it was to be placed beyond the protection of all law, human or divine.

PROCEEDINGS IN COURT

The judge with his law book, the clerk recording the proceedings. The man facing the judge seems to be arguing the case; the judge seems to be objecting. From a woodcut in a book printed in Lyon, France, in the fifteenth century.

Bishops and priests could exercise their authority freely, for they were not subject to the authority of the king or prince in whose country they resided. If they committed offenses, they were not tried in the civil courts of king or prince but in the church courts, and by the church law — the canon law. In the church courts, too, lay citizens were tried for certain offenses such as sacrilege, heresy, or theft of church property, and for offenses against religion. In respect to revenue, also, the church was independent of the state. Priests and bishops did not receive salaries from the state, nor were they supported by voluntary contributions. They administered an immense revenue, derived from the landed estates of the church and from the *tithe* or " tenth " — a tax which the church collected from all landowners. The church was a self-governing corporation not subject to the state, and a

en fuiant la mifere xiv .
courir. par victoire en ba

voibi feuner en toue temp
ne fuiffent nue greuce. Et

FRIAR PREACHING OUTSIDE A CHURCH

This scene is pictured in a French manuscript written about 1480. In the door-
way stands a monk. Outside pulpits were not uncommon in medieval times.

very wealthy corporation, disposing of a revenue far greater than
that of any king or prince or business corporation of that day.

Thus set apart from civil jurisdiction, the business of the bishops
and priests was to direct the people in all matters concerning their
spiritual and intellectual life. Priests and bishops and monks
were almost the only educated people. They controlled the schools
and the universities; they wrote most of the books; they decided
what was right for the people to read or have read to them. They
were the guardians of faith and knowledge, the agents of God, whose
duty it was to teach the people what they must do and what they
must think in order to be good citizens and good men.

In the thirteenth century, therefore, the chief contribution to
knowledge was made by the church theologians, or philosophers.
The most famous of these was Saint Thomas Aquinas. His great
work was the *Summa Theologica*, which was intended to be an
orderly statement of all knowledge. Saint Thomas said there
were two sources of knowledge. The highest source of knowledge

was the *revelation of Christian truth* which God had made through the Bible and the church. Christian truth could not be attained by reason, but must be accepted on faith. The other source of knowledge was *human reason*. The two kinds of knowledge — that which rested on faith and that which rested on reason — were different, but not inconsistent. With humble and uncritical faith Saint Thomas accepted the truth of God's revelation. With infinite patience he mastered all the learning of his day. With calm confidence he marshaled his learning to prove that experience and reason were in harmony with the mysterious truth of revealed religion. As an effort to reconcile Christian faith with human reason, the *Summa Theologica* has never been surpassed in comprehensiveness, in candor, or in the skill with which the author presents his arguments.

Besides the work of the theologians in systematizing knowledge, the Middle Ages made a great contribution to art, especially to architecture. The Gothic cathedrals of the thirteenth century were in their way a perfect expression of medieval civilization. Perhaps the most famous of the cathedrals is Notre Dame, in Paris. It is safe to say that it is still, after six hundred years, the most impressive building in that city of impressive buildings. After six centuries, there it still stands, secure and untroubled, as if built to ignore and to outlive the follies and errors of men. How perfectly it expresses both the humility and the confidence of the age of faith! With its somber hues, its flying buttresses, its lifted towers, how well it conveys a sense of the seriousness and the mystery of life! With its high altar, the intricate design of its springing arches, and the soft lights and shadowy vistas of its vast interior, how it disposes the mind to humility and to adoration! The influence of the Gothic style of architecture, as well as that of the Greek and Roman forms, has persisted to our own times, and may be noted in the buildings of any large city.

If we ask what modern civilization inherited from the Middle Ages, the answer is: (1) states ruled by kings and princes; (2) society divided into classes with distinct rights and privileges; (3) the Christian religion as organized in the Roman Catholic Church and interpreted by the medieval theologians.

The Cathedral of Notre Dame of Paris, Constructed in the Twelfth and Thirteenth Centuries

III. THE RENAISSANCE AND THE REFORMATION, 1300–1600

In the fourteenth and fifteenth centuries (1300–1500) many educated men turned from religious speculation to the study of the ancient Greek and Roman writers, or to the study of natural science. This movement in thought is called the Renaissance, and its chief effect was to discredit the religious and philosophical teachings of the medieval church. In the sixteenth century (1500–1600) many people broke away from the medieval church. This movement is known as the Reformation or the Protestant Revolt, and its chief result was to establish in western Europe many different and hostile religious faiths.

The Renaissance. The Renaissance was a " re-birth " or revival of interest in many things which the Middle Ages had cared little about. For one thing it was a revival of interest in the civilization and ideas of the ancient Greeks and Romans. In the early Middle Ages, although Latin was the language of the church and of scholarship, very little was known about the ancient Greek and Roman writers. But in the twelfth and thirteenth centuries, chiefly as a result of the crusades, the ancient writers began to be better known and more studied in the West, especially in Italy; and in the fifteenth century there were many men in Italy, in France, and even in England, who read Greek as well as Latin, and who felt that far more was to be learned from the ancient writers than from the theologians and philosophers of their own time.

These men were called *humanists*. The humanists of the fifteenth century were, above all, passionate admirers of the classical writers. They searched everywhere for lost manuscripts of Greek and Latin literature and discovered many, hitherto ignored and neglected, in the libraries and vaults of Western monasteries. They collected the writings of classical writers, housed them in libraries, studied and edited them, and in the latter part of the fifteenth century had them printed in those " original editions " which still bring high prices in the book market.

The greatest of the humanists was Erasmus. Erasmus was born, probably in 1469, in Rotterdam; but he studied in Paris, traveled in England, Germany, and Italy, and wrote, like all humanists, in

ERASMUS IN HIS STUDY (1469?–1536)

The inscription says: "Portrait of Erasmus of Rotterdam, made by Albrecht Dürer, from life . . . 1526." The initials A–D were Dürer's usual signature.

Latin. He corresponded with all the humanists of his time, and wrote many books. He was a great admirer and student of the ancient writers and edited many of their works. He remained a good Catholic, but he believed that the priests and theologians had falsified the simple moral teachings of Jesus; and he therefore published an edition of the New Testament — the first edition in the original Greek — in order to make clear the essential teachings of Christianity. But the most famous and the most influential of his books were the *Praise of Folly* and the *Colloquies*. These works, written in lively, colloquial, and witty Latin, expressed his ideas on the manners and customs of his time. The follies which he praised (ironically) were the folly of the monks, living useless lives devoted to ascetic practices; the folly of the theological professors, who discoursed endlessly on the hidden allegorical meaning of unimportant biblical passages; and the folly of popes and bishops, who thought that truth and virtue could be maintained by burning heretics and suppressing heretical books. Erasmus liked above all things clear and honest thinking; he disliked above all things intolerance and persecution. He was the greatest of the humanists because his books, more effectively than any others, propagated a *humane* philosophy of life, teaching that one's chief duties are to be intelligent, open-minded, charitable, and of good will to all men.

The Renaissance was also a rebirth of art. There was developed a new style of architecture, known as the Renaissance. It was a modification of the Greek and Roman forms of building. The most famous example of Renaissance architecture is the great church of St. Peter in Rome, begun in 1506 but not completed until the seventeenth century. The Renaissance style of architecture is still used, in modified form, in designing modern buildings. The Renaissance was even more famous for its achievements in painting and sculpture than for its architecture. In the history of painting no names rank higher than Leonardo da Vinci, Michelangelo, and Raphael (Italians, sixteenth century), or Rubens and Rembrandt (Dutchmen, sixteenth and seventeenth centuries).

A third aspect of the Renaissance was the revival of interest in geography, exploration, and natural science. In 1486 the Portu-

The Façade of St. Peter's, Rome

St. Peter's is the largest church ever built. Among the architects and artists who contributed to the design were Bramante, Raphael, Michelangelo, and Bernini. The huge cupola was designed by Michelangelo.

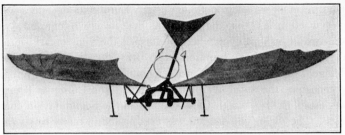

Courtesy Smithsonian Institution

AN EARLY MODEL OF A FLYING MACHINE

The great painter, Leonardo da Vinci, predicted that men would sometime learn to fly. His notebooks contain several designs for wings to be attached to the human body for that purpose. One of these designs, described about 1490 in a notebook now in the Library of Congress, was used by Paul E. Garber to make the above model, which is in the Smithsonian Institution in Washington.

guese navigator, Bartholomew Diaz, sailed around the southern point of Africa, and twelve years later Vasco da Gama sailed as far as India. In 1492 Columbus made the momentous discovery of America. These discoveries opened up a new and fascinating field of interest and endeavor. They were made possible by a new mechanical device, the mariner's compass, which began to be used in Europe in the fourteenth century. At this time gunpowder was improved and made practicable; and in the fifteenth century printing from movable type was invented and applied. Besides being an artist, Leonardo da Vinci was much interested in mechanics, invented various devices, and predicted that in time men would devise machines enabling them to fly in the air as the birds do. In the sixteenth century the Polish scientist, Copernicus, formulated the theory that the sun, not the earth, is the center of the solar system. Galileo, by observing a swinging lamp in a church, discovered the law of the pendulum, and by experimenting with falling bodies formulated one of the fundamental laws of mechanics. Thus in the time of the Renaissance many men turned from the study of religion and theology to the study of natural science, and they began to employ a new method of acquiring knowledge — the modern method of observation and experiment.

The Reformation or Protestant Revolt. In the year 1500 the medieval church was still, to all outward appearance, as secure as it had ever been. Throughout western Europe its doctrines were everywhere accepted; the Pope was everywhere recognized; the priests and bishops everywhere performed their customary duties. Yet during the next hundred years this situation was entirely changed. Half of western Europe renounced the faith and refused to recognize the authority of the church. The Lutheran Church was established in North Germany and in the Scandinavian countries. The Zwinglian religion was established in many Swiss cantons. The Calvinist religion was the recognized form in Holland and Scotland, in Geneva, and in some of the German states. The Anglican Episcopal Church was established in England. This transformation, known as the Reformation or Protestant Revolt, aroused intense bitterness and was accomplished only at the expense of widespread and ruthless persecution and devastating civil wars. What were the influences that brought about this profound upheaval? We may discuss them briefly under three heads: (1) religious reasons; (2) economic and social reasons; and (3) political reasons.

1. *Religious reasons.* The Reformation was started by Martin Luther, a teacher in the University of Wittenberg. In 1517 a man named Tetzel came to a nearby village selling " papal indulgences." It had long been the practice of the church to sell indulgences; and it was commonly believed that one who bought a papal indulgence would thereby be relieved of some of the penalties of sin. Tetzel was authorized to sell indulgences, and he went about it in a businesslike way, very much as an auctioneer might auction off his wares. Luther believed that Tetzel was deceiving the people by telling them that if they bought his indulgences they need no longer worry about their sins. In order to clear up the question of the true doctrine of indulgence he therefore posted on the church door at Wittenberg ninety-five " theses." These were ninety-five short statements relating to indulgences, and in posting them Luther was simply inviting learned professors to discuss the statements pro and con, in order to determine, if possible, what the true doctrine of indulgence really was.

The wording of the theses made it clear that Luther himself did not think it necessary for people to buy indulgences. " Buy indulgences if you like," Luther said in effect, " but the man who is really sorry for his sins does better than the man who pays money in order to escape the penalty of sin." Luther's theses raised a most fundamental question, which is quite as live a question today as it was then. The question is this: Should people be judged primarily by their outward acts or by their inward intentions? Luther said that the right inward feeling was more important than the correct outward act. He said: " Good works do not make the good man, but the good man does good works." In the sixteenth century this doctrine was called " justification by faith " as opposed to the doctrine of " justification by works."

Luther did not intend or expect to start a revolution. He hoped only to start a learned discussion in the University of Wittenberg. But much to his surprise the ninety-five theses were soon published, read, and discussed everywhere in Germany. He became suddenly

German Tourist Information Office

MARTIN LUTHER (1483–1546)

Reproduced from a painting by Lukas Cranach.

famous. The sale of indulgences declined. The Pope, Leo X, learning that an obscure monk was stirring up trouble, tried to suppress the discussion. But the discussion, once started, could not be suppressed. Learned men pointed out to Luther that his doctrine was similar to that of John Huss, who had been condemned and burned at the stake for heresy in the fifteenth century; that his doctrine was therefore contrary to the teaching of the church, and that he must recant it. Luther refused to recant, was excommunicated by the Pope, and saved his life only by retiring to a secluded castle (the Wartburg) under the protection of the Duke of Saxony. Throughout Germany thousands of people applauded Luther as a hero and a martyr, accepted his doctrines, and like him renounced the authority of the Pope. This was the beginning of the Protestant Lutheran Church, which in the sixteenth century was permanently established in many principalities of North Germany, and in Denmark, Norway, and Sweden.

Aside from Luther the two principal leaders of the Protestant Reformation were Ulrich Zwingli and John Calvin. In 1519 Zwingli began to teach Luther's doctrine of justification by faith, and under his leadership about half of the Swiss cantons broke away from the old church and established Zwinglian Protestant churches. John Calvin was a Frenchman who published in 1536 one of the most influential books ever written — *The Institutes of the Christian Religion*. It was a systematic treatise on religion and politics, based on the doctrine of justification by faith. Calvin had many followers in France (called *Huguenots*), but the king refused to support him and he went to Geneva, in Switzerland, where he established an independent church-state. From Geneva his teachings spread into Germany, Holland, England, and Scotland (Scotch Presbyterian Church), and in the seventeenth century to New England.

Why did the new doctrine of justification by faith spread so rapidly? As formulated by Luther and Calvin, this doctrine was too learned and philosophical for ordinary folk to understand. Luther himself was astonished, and we may well be astonished, to learn that this abstruse doctrine was welcomed so eagerly by thousands of common people everywhere. The reason is that the common people, who knew nothing and cared less about theological doctrines, knew very well why Luther objected to the sale of indulgences. They knew that popes and bishops were only too often more interested in worldly affairs than in religion. Pope Leo X, a collector of manuscripts and patron of literature and art, was the Vicar of Christ only in name. He scarcely believed the religion which he professed, and was reported to have said that since he had attained the papacy he proposed to enjoy it. Many bishops, following the example of the Pope, lived comfortable, worldly lives and seemed not to care whether people practiced Christianity or not, so long as they observed the ceremonials and ritual of the church. Frivolous and fashionable people were accounted good Christians enough if once or twice a year they confessed a few peccadillos to the priest and in public made a decent show of piety. In short, it seemed that to be a good Christian one needed only to observe the conventions of society, do as most people did, and not become involved in scandal or heresy.

Long before Luther's time thousands of common people felt that this was not enough. They were incensed at the cynical worldliness and indifference of the clergy. They regarded the sale of indulgences as a scandal — a shameless exploitation of religion for profit. They felt that Christianity was, or ought to be, something more than a conventional observance of rites and ceremonies. They felt that to be a good Christian one must " live the good life " — one must be right with God, not merely right with the bishop or the Pope.

These were the religious ideas which led many people to resist the authority of the church. But the people who opposed the church on religious grounds were likely to oppose it for economic and social reasons also. Let us see what these were.

2. *Economic and social reasons.* The teachings of Luther and Calvin were more popular in the towns than in the country. In the towns they were more popular among middle-class people than among the very poor or the very rich; in the country, more popular among the lesser nobles and country gentlemen than among the peasants and the great nobles. There were many exceptions to this rule, but in general the Protestant Reformation was the work of middle-class people in town and country. Why were the middle-class people more opposed to the old church than the upper classes were? The answer is that in the sixteenth century the church was largely controlled by the upper classes and administered largely for their benefit.

In each country the ruling aristocracy was composed chiefly of the ruling king or prince, the great nobles, the very wealthy financiers and business men, and the bishops of the church. Very wealthy men loaned money to needy kings and nobles and in return were provided with opportunities for making more money. The great nobles, being often at court, were in close touch with the ruling king or prince and in return for their support obtained from the king or prince many favors. One thing which the king could do for the nobles was to use his influence to get their sons appointed to high offices in the church; and in most countries in the sixteenth century a majority of the bishops, archbishops, and heads of monasteries were younger sons of the great nobles. This means that the wealth and power of the church were largely in the hands of men who by birth and social position belonged to the ruling aristocracy. This is why the bishops gave their chief attention to administering the church property, lived luxuriously in their episcopal palaces, lent dignity and color to the fashionable court society, and were mostly content with a formal and worldly religion that suited their aristocratic friends and relatives.

The middle-class people in town and country lived in a different world from that of the ruling aristocracy of nobles and bishops. The poor country nobles were rarely seen at court and received few favors from the king. Their sons might become parish priests, but the rich bishoprics were not for them. They looked with a jealous eye upon the wealthy court nobles who fawned upon the king and obtained from him smiles, pensions, and offices. The artisans and merchants and the lawyers and doctors living in the towns were looked down upon by the nobles and also by the bishops, who were likely to be of noble birth and who in any case did not associate on equal terms with shopkeepers and lawyers. The guilds were not so prosperous as they had once been. A few fortunate men were reaping the chief rewards of industry and commerce, and the town governments were falling more and more into the control of the very wealthy. Nobles were exempt from taxation, while the middle-class people paid taxes which the king as likely as not used to reward some favorite courtier. The bishop expected the middle-class people to contribute to the support of the church, although he regarded business as an ignoble occupation and taught that lending money for interest was a form of usury, contrary to religion and morality.

This is why middle-class people were more opposed to the church than the upper classes were. They felt that the church had fallen into the control of a wealthy aristocracy that looked down upon them and cared little for their interests. They felt that they had no control over the church that commanded their obedience, and

AUDIENCE GIVEN TO ENGLISH AMBASSADORS

From a painting by Carpaccio, late fifteenth century, now in the R. Accademia di Belle Arti, Venice. Note the Venetian costumes. In the early Middle Ages artists did not paint in proper proportions and perspective. The artists of the Renaissance, however, studied the human form and pictured it correctly. Compare this with the illustration on page 32. Although both of these were made about the same time, the figures painted by Carpaccio are much more correct in proportions. Carpaccio, an Italian, profited by the Renaissance, which came earlier in Italy than in France and Germany.

that the virtues which they prized — industry, frugality, sobriety — were no longer much practiced or preached by popes or bishops.

3. *Political reasons.* The middle-class followers of Luther and Calvin could not by themselves have broken away from the medieval church. The Reformation was successful because the reformers in many countries were supported by the ruling king or prince. Few kings or princes were interested in the doctrine of justification by faith or the doctrine of justification by works. They were for the most part interested in increasing their political power within their own countries. In the sixteenth century the church was still in many ways outside the king's authority. The immense property of the church was exempt from royal taxation. Bishops still administered justice in church courts in accord with the canon law. Every year large revenues were carried out of every country to the papal treasury, and the Pope was still able to interfere in many ways with the aims and ambitions of kings and princes.

The widespread popularity of the new teachings of Luther and Calvin offered an excellent opportunity for any king or prince to strengthen his political authority within his own country. If in any country the new teachings were accepted by a majority of the people, the king or prince could then safely support the heretics against the church. On the ground of defending the true religion, he could confiscate the property of the church in his country, suppress the taxes levied by the church, keep at home the revenues formerly paid to the Pope, and free himself entirely from papal interference. He could then authorize the establishment of the new Protestant religion. Moreover, the new church, its property and its ministers, would be subject to the political authority of the king or prince, since it depended on him for its existence. This is what happened in many of the countries where Protestant churches were established — in many German principalities, and in Holland, Denmark, Sweden, Norway, and England.

Thus the Reformation resulted in establishing in western Europe many religions and many churches. It broke the acknowledged authority of the medieval church, and strengthened the civil authority of kings and princes. All this was not accomplished without much strife and bloodshed. For a century and a half Europe was devastated by civil and international wars growing out of the religious conflict. Luther and Calvin were no more tolerant in matters of religion than the popes or the priests of the Catholic Church. At Geneva Calvin had Servetus burned at the stake for heresy. Luther said: " It is not for *Herr Omnes* (' Mr. Everyman ') to decide what should be rejected " in matters of religion; and he did all that he could to suppress other forms of belief than his own. Yet in the end the Reformation helped to spread abroad a spirit of toleration. After fighting over religion for more than a hundred years people became tired of such conflicts. When many religions were established, each claiming to be the true one, many people were sure to think: " They can't all be right. Perhaps none of them is wholly right."

We have now described briefly the three great epochs that led up to modern history: (1) the classical world of Greece and Rome; (2) the Middle Ages; and (3) the Renaissance and the Reformation. By the seventeenth century the civilization of western Europe was already taking on those modern characteristics that are familiar to us. Europe was already divided into many sovereign states contending with each other for independence or supremacy. Society was divided into three classes (nobles, peasants, and bourgeoisie) whose conflicting interests were to shape the domestic history of every country in modern times. Instead of one religion and one dominant church throughout western Europe, there were many religions and many churches. The chief European languages, more and more employed in place of Latin as a medium of literary expression, were beginning to take on their modern form; and learned men, ceasing to be exclusively interested in religion and theology, were already turning to those subjects which modern scholars have chiefly cultivated — classical studies, politics, economics, history, and natural science.

QUESTIONS

1. When did Greek civilization reach its height? Who were the chief Greek philosophers? dramatists? sculptors? Are there any buildings in your community in the " Greek style"? What famous monu-

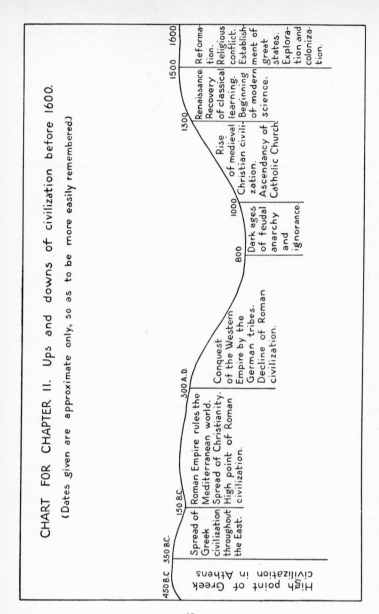

CHART FOR CHAPTER II. Ups and downs of civilization before 1600.

(Dates given are approximate only, so as to be more easily remembered)

450 B.C. 350 B.C. 150 B.C. 300 A.D. 800 1000 1300 1500 1600

High point of Greek civilization in Athens

Spread of Greek civilization throughout the East.

Roman Empire rules the Mediterranean world. Spread of Christianity. High point of Roman civilization.

Conquest of the Western Empire by the German tribes. Decline of Roman civilization.

Dark ages of feudal anarchy and ignorance.

Rise of medieval Christian civilization. Ascendancy of Catholic Church.

Renaissance. Recovery of classical learning. Beginning of modern science.

Reformation. Religious conflict. Establishment of great states. Exploration and colonization.

48

ment in Washington, D. C., is in the Greek style? How was Greek civilization spread over western Asia? What is the difference between *stoicism* and *epicureanism?* In general, what does modern civilization owe to the ancient Greeks?

2. When did the Romans conquer the East? How did this conquest influence Roman civilization? What countries were included in the Roman Empire? What material remains of Roman civilization still exist in Europe? What were the chief contributions of the Romans to European civilization?

3. Why did the Roman government break down in the West? How did feudalism become established? What did it contribute to European civilization? In what ways did the medieval church differ from modern churches? Who was Saint Thomas Aquinas? Tell all you can about his work, the *Summa Theologica.* What are the most noticeable architectural differences between a Gothic cathedral and a Greek temple? What did the Middle Ages contribute to European civilization?

4. What is meant by the "Renaissance"? Who were the "humanists"? Tell all you can about Erasmus and his writings. What important geographical discoveries were made in the fifteenth and sixteenth centuries? What new methods of acquiring knowledge were employed in the time of the Renaissance? What was the "Reformation"? What did Luther teach, and why were his doctrines so popular in the sixteenth century? Why were middle-class people more opposed to the church than upper-class people were? Why did many kings and princes support the Protestants? What did the Renaissance and the Reformation contribute to European civilization?

SELECTED READINGS

Brief accounts. C. J. H. Hayes and P. Moon, *Modern History,* chs. i–v. For excellent brief accounts of certain periods or aspects of ancient and medieval history, see J. H. Breasted, *Ancient Times,* chs. xv, xviii, xxi, xxvii–xxviii, and J. H. Robinson, *Introduction to the History of Western Europe,* chs. iii–iv, ix, xv–xix, xxii, xxv–xxviii. For art, literature, manners, and customs of France in medieval times, see P. van Dyke, *Story of France,* chs. xii–xv. The above books are well illustrated. For the history of dress and costume, see M. Evans, *Costume throughout the Ages.*

CHARLES I VISITS THE GUILDHALL

From a painting by S. J. Solomon in the Royal Exchange, London. On January 2, 1642, Charles I came with soldiers to the House of Commons for the purpose of seizing five members whom he accused of treason (see p. 63). No English king had ever before thus entered the House of Commons and no king has since done so. The king's plans had, however, been betrayed, and the Commons ordered the five members to take refuge elsewhere. When the king arrived, therefore, he could not discover them. He demanded of the Speaker where they were. The Speaker with great dignity replied, "May it please your Majesty, I have neither eyes to see nor tongue to speak in this place but as the House is pleased to direct me, whose servant I am here." This violation by the king of parliamentary liberties aroused great indignation.

PART II

THE AGE OF KINGS AND NOBLES

Why Part II is called the Age of Kings and Nobles. It is easier to remember and understand the course of events in history if we divide it into a few principal periods. You will see that in this book modern history is divided into four periods or parts. Part I was devoted to a general introduction to modern history, explaining in a brief way what the chief characteristics of modern history are and what the ancient world of Greece and Rome and the period of the Middle Ages contributed to modern history. Part II will deal with the seventeenth and eighteenth centuries, and this period in modern history we may remember as the Age of Kings and Nobles.

Of course there were kings and nobles in the Middle Ages; and there are still kings in some countries, such as England, today; and there are still nobles in most European countries. But in the Middle Ages the power of kings was often not very great, and since the eighteenth century — that is, since the French Revolution (1789) — kings and nobles have been going out of fashion. In the seventeenth and eighteenth centuries, however, the power of kings was well established in most countries; and in most countries the king ruled with the aid, and largely for the benefit, of a small class of nobles who were thought to be better than ordinary people and who enjoyed rights and privileges which ordinary people did not enjoy. In nearly every country there were also a small number of middle-class people who, on account of their wealth, exercised a good deal of influence and enjoyed advantages which were denied to the great mass of the people. In short, the nobles and the very wealthy middle class formed an aristocracy, and kings ruled with the support of this aristocracy and very largely for the advancement of its interests.

Abraham Lincoln, in his famous Gettysburg Address, said that in the United States we were engaged in a great experiment, the object of which was to see whether it was possible to establish

51

permanently a " government of the people, by the people, for the people." In the seventeenth and eighteenth centuries the theory and the practice were quite different from that. The prevailing idea then seemed to be that the best form of government was a government *of the people, by the king, for the nobles and the rich.* This is why the seventeenth and eighteenth centuries may well be called the Age of Kings and Nobles.

BRIDGE OVER THE RHINE, AT STRASBOURG
From an engraving by W. Hollar, made in 1630.

CHAPTER III. HOW THE ENGLISH MADE A REVOLU-TION, WERE NOT WELL PLEASED WITH IT, AND MADE ANOTHER MORE TO THEIR LIKING

Kings . . . have power of raising and casting down, of life and death, judges over all their subjects, . . . and yet accountable to none but God only. JAMES I

Give me the liberty to know, to utter, and to argue freely according to my conscience, above all other liberties. MILTON

The struggle for self-government in modern history. In the seventeenth century most countries were governed by kings who claimed to rule by the *will of God;* but in our day most countries are governed by elected parliaments or congresses claiming to rule by the *will of the people.* This change from government by kings to government by the people is the most important fact in the political history of modern times. The change came earlier in some countries than in others, and in no country was it brought about all at once. Government by the people has been won only slowly, and by hard struggle, usually only by revolution and bloodshed. One of the earliest and most important of these revolutionary movements occurred in England in the seventeenth century (1640-1689). We may speak of the events of this period as the " English Revolution."

The English Revolution was not democratic revolution. The English were better able than many countries to limit the power of their kings because they had what other peoples had not — a well-organized Parliament to carry on the struggle against them. In the seventeenth century the English Parliament was composed, as it is now, of two houses — the House of Lords and the House of Commons. Nobles and bishops sat in the House of Lords as they do now; but in the seventeenth century the members of the House of Commons were not elected by all the people, as they are now. They were elected by a few wealthy merchants and landowners. The men who sat in the House of Commons were mostly wealthy landowners called "country gentlemen," who were closely related to the nobles by birth and marriage. It was this closely related class of nobles and country gentlemen that really controlled the Parliament and carried on the struggle against the king.

The nobles and country gentlemen who sat in Parliament did not believe at all in democracy. They were unwilling to let the king govern as he pleased, because they wanted to have something to say about the government themselves; but they had no desire to allow the great mass of the people to have anything to say about the government. The English Revolution was thus not a democratic revolution but an aristocratic revolution. It was only the first stage on the road to government by the people.

Why the nobles and country gentlemen were not willing to let the king govern as he liked. As soon as James I became king (1603), the nobles and country gentlemen in Parliament began to quarrel with him, and attempted to limit his power. They did not quarrel with James because he was a cruel tyrant, or because they were poor and oppressed. They quarreled with James chiefly for two reasons: (1) because they were well able to take care of themselves without the king's aid; and (2) because they did not like James.

If the nobles had felt the need of a strong king to protect and aid them, they might not have attempted to limit his power. But since the English live on an island, they have never had to fear military invasion so much as other people — the French, for example. Moreover, they had recently defeated the most powerful king in Europe, Philip II, and since the destruction of his famous Armada they had felt more independent than ever. Thus the English people in the seventeenth century did not feel the need of a strong king and a large army to defend them. Besides, the

National Gallery, London

A SEVENTEENTH CENTURY POULTRY SHOP

Perhaps the lady will buy the hare also. Note the decoration under the counter and the live turkey in the basket. From a painting by G. Don.

English nobles and country gentlemen did not live at court as the French nobles did. They lived on their estates, and as most of them were very well off, they could take care of themselves and did not need to ask the king for money and favors. On this account, also, the English nobles were in a better position than the French to prevent the king from ruling as he pleased.

Not only did the nobles and country gentlemen feel independent of the new king — they did not like him. James I was a Scotchman, and therefore half a foreigner. He was clumsy and undignified and not used to English ways. He could not speak English well, although he spoke much and often, scolding the country gentlemen, and telling them that government was not their affair. They had been scolded by Elizabeth too, but they had been able to put up with that better because Elizabeth was an Englishwoman and very popular. The proud country gentlemen were in no mind to be scolded by this awkward Scotchman who spoke with a Scotch brogue and pretended to know more about the government of their country than they did.

So the country gentlemen quarreled with James from the very first, and with his son Charles, who succeeded James. The king was determined to govern as he pleased, while the nobles and country gentlemen were determined to prevent him from governing except with the consent of Parliament. But in the seventeenth century a king could not easily govern as he pleased unless he had two very important things. These two things were money and bishops. We must now see (1) how the king and Parliament quarreled about money, and (2) how they quarreled about bishops.

1. *The quarrel over money.* No king could govern as he pleased if he had to ask someone for money every time he needed a few thousand dollars. The French king, Louis XIV, had no trouble of this kind. But the English kings had to ask Parliament for money. It was customary, at the beginning of each reign, for Parliament to grant the king for life the income from certain taxes called tonnage and poundage duties. If the king could not get along with this revenue, he had to ask Parliament for more, and the Parliament, if it disliked the way he was governing, could refuse to give it to him unless he promised to do differently. This privilege was known as the " power of the purse." It was by keeping the purse in its own pocket, and by being very stingy in doling out money to the king, that the English Parliament was able to limit the king's power.

James I, although a Scotchman, was less economical than Elizabeth had been, and so he had always to be asking Parliament

National Gallery, London

A SEVENTEENTH CENTURY MUSICAL PARTY

From a painting by Velsen. The people of this century enjoyed music, as we do today. Two of them are singing, accompanied by a violinist.

for money. Since the nobles and country gentlemen did not like him or his way of governing, they never gave him enough. James then taxed the people without asking the consent of Parliament. James said that he was only doing what previous kings had done, and that he was therefore acting according to the law. This was true; but James made matters worse by claiming that he was not bound by the law anyway. He said he was responsible to no one, or to no one but God. " Kings," he said, " are rightly called gods, for that they exercise a manner or resemblance of divine power on earth. . . . God hath power to create or destroy. . . . And like power have kings : they make and unmake their subjects ; they have power of . . . life and death . . . and yet are accountable to none but God only."

This kind of talk about the " divine right of kings," as the theory is called, only made the country gentlemen more stingy than ever with their money ; and when Charles I became king (1625), they refused to give him any money for more than a year. Charles followed the practice of his father.   He collected taxes without asking Parliament.   He asked people for " loans," and many who refused were put in prison.   On account of his wars he could not raise enough money by these methods, and at last, in 1628, he had to ask Parliament to help him out.   Before giving him what he asked for, Parliament forced Charles to agree to the famous Petition of Right, which from that day has been regarded as one of the great safeguards of English liberty.

The Petition of Right stated that the king, by taxing people without the consent of Parliament, and by imprisoning people without fair trial in the courts, had violated certain ancient laws of England, such as those of the Magna Carta (1215).   It then petitioned the king that

no man hereafter be compelled to make any gift, loan, benevolence, tax, or such-like charge, without common consent by act of Parliament ; and that no freeman, in any such manner as is before mentioned, be imprisoned or detained.   All which they most humbly pray Your Most Excellent Majesty, as their rights and liberties according to the laws and statutes of this realm.

As soon as Charles got the money he needed, he dissolved the Parliament (1629).   For eleven years he did not call another, and in order to run the government he continued to levy taxes in the old way, just as if he had not agreed to the Petition of Right.   He even invented new methods of raising money, one of which was the collection of " ship money."   He commanded the counties to furnish ships for the navy, and since most of them had no ships, they were required to pay taxes in place of ships.   John Hampden, a rich country gentleman, refused to pay a ship-money tax of twenty shillings, claiming that the tax was illegal ; but when his case was brought to trial, the judge decided that the king had a legal right to collect ship money.

John Hampden was a very wealthy man, and he could well afford to pay a tax of twenty shillings.   The country gentlemen were not alarmed at the amount of the tax.   What alarmed them was the fact that the king seemed able to govern the country without any Parliament at all.   It was now nine years since there had been a Parliament in England, and if Charles could collect taxes and get the judges to decide that he had a legal right to do so, there might never be another one.

Meantime, this quarrel between the country gentlemen and the king over taxes had come to be mixed up with another quarrel. This other quarrel was the dispute between the Puritans and the bishops.

2. *The quarrel over religion: Puritans and bishops.* In the seventeenth century a king needed bishops almost as much as he needed money. One thing which greatly helped Louis XIV to rule in France was this: He appointed the bishops of the Catholic Church, and the bishops taught the people to be obedient to the king because God had given the king authority to rule them. The established church in England (the English or Anglican Church) was much like the Catholic Church, except that the Pope was not the head of it. The king was the head of the English Church. The king appointed the bishops, and the bishops ruled the clergy. Thus the English bishops could be as useful to the King of England as Catholic bishops could

THE DUTCH PREPARING TO INVADE ENGLAND

Probably in connection with the naval war between England and Holland, 1664–1665. Supplies and cannon are being hauled aboard. English warships were of the same type.

be to the King of France, so long as the people were satisfied with the English Church and were willing to obey the bishops.

The trouble was that in England there were many people who were not satisfied with the English Church. There were the *Separatists* who, like the Huguenots in France, wished to separate from the established church and worship as they pleased. The Separatists preached the modern idea of religious toleration, and being few in number, they were harshly persecuted as wild and dangerous people. Far more numerous were the *Puritans*. The Puritans were not satisfied with the English Church, since it reminded them of the Catholic Church. When the Puritans went to church, they could hardly have told that they were not in a Catholic Church if the priest had not read the service in English instead of in Latin. They were offended by all of those things which reminded them of the Catholic service — the priest's gown and the use of incense and crosses and saints' images. These things they called " popish practices," and they themselves were called Puritans because they wished to " purify " the Church of these popish practices.

The Puritans hoped that James I would agree with them, since he came from Scotland, where the ideas of the Puritans were very popular. But this was one reason why James would not agree with them. As King of Scotland he had had a hard time of it, because in Scotland the clergy, being chosen by the people, did not obey the king very well. James thought that the English Puritans, like the Scotch Presbyterians, wished to abolish the bishops and have the clergy chosen by the people. Therefore, in 1604, when some Puritan clergymen petitioned to have a few changes made in the church service, James became angry. " A Scotch Presbytery," he exclaimed, " agreeth as well with monarchy as God with the devil. Then Jack and Tom and Will and Dick shall meet, and at their pleasure censure me and my council. . . . Until you find that I grow lazy, let that alone. . . . No bishop, no king, as before I said."

" No bishop, no king " was Charles's motto as well as James's. During Charles's reign the number of Puritans greatly increased, and their opposition to bishops became more intense, especially on account of the conduct of William Laud, whom Charles appointed to be Archbishop of Canterbury in 1633. The new archbishop dismissed all of the clergy who refused to conduct religious services strictly according to the rules of the Prayer Book ; and Puritan writers who criticized the archbishop were fined and imprisoned, or had their ears cut off. These things made many people think that Charles and his new archbishop were Catholics at heart, and that they were secretly bent upon changing the church back into a Catholic Church. The future looked so black that thousands of Puritans fled to America, and founded the colony of Massachusetts, where they could establish a church that suited them.

Et genus, et inca inc, virtus ternus marig
Non into patitur nomen habere loco .

Ante feros Sigmanus ago promptum agmen ad arma.
Haudg parum debent parta trophosa mihi .

Archives photographiques d'art et d'histoire

MILITARY UNIFORMS AND EQUIPMENT, EARLY SEVENTEENTH CENTURY

The soldier at the left carries a musket (harquebus) so heavy that when firing he has to rest it in the forked staff which he carries in his right hand. In his left hand is the " match " — a wick or cord that burned slowly — used for firing it. The other soldier carries a species of battle-ax called a halberd.

Most of the Puritans remained in England, however. And in this period even the country gentlemen were becoming puritan in a sense, because it seemed to them that the church and the bishops were working hand in hand with the king to establish autocratic government by abolishing Parliament and restoring the Catholic religion. Puritans and country gentlemen therefore joined hands against the king and the bishops. It was this struggle of the Puritans and country gentlemen against the king and the bishops that started the first revolution.

How the Long Parliament started the first revolution, 1640. Strange as it may seem, the first English revolution (1640–1649) was precipitated by events occurring in Scotland. Although Charles was King of Scotland, the Scots really governed themselves through their Presbyterian Church, in which the clergy were elected by the people. Charles knew that he would never be able to govern Scotland as he did England, until there were bishops appointed by himself to govern the Scotch clergy. In 1637 he therefore tried to change the Scotch church into something like the English Church. The whole Scotch nation rose up in defense of its religion; and when Charles sent an army to conquer the country, the Scotch army defeated the king's army, occupied northern England, and refused to go home until it was paid (*Bishops' War, 1639*). Without money Charles could neither fight the Scots nor make peace with them. He was therefore forced to call the English Parliament and ask it to help him out. This was the famous " Long Parliament " (1640), which began the revolution.

The Puritans and the country gentlemen now had Charles in a tight place. Of course they refused to give him any money for the Scotch war until he promised to behave better in the future. They forced him to agree to certain new Constitutional Laws. One of these was the Triennial Act (1641), which provided that Parliament should be called at least once every three years. Other laws abolished ship money and made it illegal for the king to levy taxes without the consent of Parliament or to imprison people without a fair trial in the courts. These laws changed the form of government in England from an *absolute* monarchy to a *constitutional* monarchy. The king was still the head of the government, but according to these laws he could no longer rule except with the consent of Parliament. Charles had to agree to these laws, because he needed money and because the members of Parliament were all in favor of them.

After these Constitutional Laws were passed, the Parliament divided into two parties. The extreme Puritans wished to limit the king's power still more, and they wished especially to reform the church by abolishing the bishops and adopting a simple Puritan form of worship. But the nobles and most of the country gentlemen thought that enough had been done. Now that the king could no longer rule without the consent of Parliament, they no longer feared the bishops, and they never had liked the extreme Puritans who wished to make life sad and sober by doing away with sports and amusements and pictures and music. So, on the question of church reform, the country gentlemen parted company with the

TERRITORY CONTROLLED BY THE KING AND TERRITORY CONTROLLED BY
PARLIAMENT, 1642

extreme Puritans, and were ready to side with the king and the
bishops.

How the Civil War came and how it ended, 1642–1646. Charles
might have ended the revolution now if he had been willing to keep
quiet. But he was bound to get back all of his old power. He tried
to frighten Parliament by bringing some soldiers into the House of
Commons in order to arrest five of the chief leaders of the Puritan

party.   When this failed, he left London and began to gather troops in order to dissolve Parliament by force.   Parliament levied troops to resist the king, and so civil war began (1642).

Most of the nobles and country gentlemen preferred to be governed by the king rather than by a Puritan Parliament.   So they took their swords, mounted their horses, and went to fight as cavalry (" Cavaliers ") for King Charles.   Parliament had to take its soldiers chiefly from the Puritan townsmen and farmers of southern England.   Since they were not so used to guns and fighting as the country gentlemen were, the Parliament troops were at first defeated by the king's troops.   But after two years Oliver Cromwell, one of the country gentlemen who sided with Parliament, trained these Puritan " Roundheads " so that they could fight as well as the Cavaliers.   Besides its own army, Parliament had the aid of the Scotch army.   In 1643, the Scots, fearing that if Charles conquered England he might next conquer Scotland, agreed to fight for Parliament if Parliament would agree to establish the Presbyterian religion in England.

National Portrait Gallery, London

OLIVER CROMWELL, LORD PRO-
TECTOR OF THE COMMONWEALTH
(1599–1658)

Cromwell was not prepossessing in appearance. His pface was disfigured by a wart. His voice was harsh, and he was careless in his dress. Yet he was a man of great energy and action.

Thus the king had to fight two armies — the Scotch army and the Parliament army of Cromwell and Fairfax.   In 1644 Cromwell joined the Scotch army and badly defeated Charles at Marston Moor.   The result of this battle was that Charles lost control of northern England, and from now on he had to fight two armies — the Scotch in the north, and the Parliament army in the south.   In 1645 he was again badly defeated at Naseby.   The next year (1646) his army surrendered to General Fairfax, and Charles gave himself up to the Scotch army.   The Civil War was over.

How the king lost his head, 1649. When Charles surrendered, in 1646, no one dreamed of punishing him by cutting off his head. His enemies were willing to restore him to his throne if he would agree to certain terms. Since the king was helpless you might think this would have been a simple matter to arrange. The trouble was that the king had three enemies — the Scots, the English Parliament, and the army of Cromwell; and these three enemies were now almost as hostile to each other as they were to the king. They had been united in making war on the king; but they were hopelessly divided in making peace with him.

The Scots were willing to restore the king if he would agree to maintain the Presbyterian religion in Scotland and England. But Parliament was opposed to this. During the war the Puritans in Parliament had abolished the bishops and adopted a simple form of worship; but they were opposed to the Scotch system of having the clergy elected by the people. When the Scots found that the king had no serious intention of doing what they wished, they demanded their pay and went home, leaving the king in the hands of the English.

But now Parliament could not impose its terms on the king because Cromwell and the soldiers would not agree to them. Most of the soldiers were members of the various " dissenting " religions — Separatists or Independents, Baptists, or Fifth Monarchy Men. They had joined Cromwell's army because they had been persecuted for their religion, and they had thought they were fighting for religious liberty. They had fought well, they felt that they had won the war, and they were therefore unwilling to agree to any peace which did not give them the religious freedom for which they had fought. This was just what Parliament was unwilling to give them. Parliament had been willing to have these men fight its battles for it; but now that the war was over, it was ready to fine and imprison these old veterans and cut off their ears unless they joined the established Puritan Church. No wonder the soldiers refused to disband!

Cromwell, who was a member of Parliament, and the most trusted leader of the soldiers, proposed a plan which he thought all parties might agree to. " Let us restore the king to his throne," he said in

SOLDIERS IN CAMP, SEVENTEENTH CENTURY
In the background are the tents of the cavalry. Drawn by G. P. Rugendas.

effect, " and let the king in future agree to govern with the consent of Parliament. Let us restore the old church, with its bishops, since that is what most of the people want; but since the Puritans and Separatists and Baptists have served us well in the war, let us not persecute them any more but let them worship as they like, outside of the established church. And so let us have peace and liberty." This was a wise plan, but it was not what either king or Parliament or soldiers wanted.

Would it not, then, have been a good plan to dissolve Parliament, have a new election, and let the people decide what should be done? Perhaps it would have been. But neither the soldiers nor the Puritans in Parliament would do this, because they knew that the great majority of the people were now ready to support the king rather than the Parliament or the army. The people were tired of war and revolution; they were sorry for the king who had been so long a captive; they disliked the meddling of the soldiers in politics; they were not in favor of religious toleration or of a Puritan church. If the people had been allowed to decide, they would have

COSTUME ABOUT 1650

From an engraving by Hollar.   Left, a country woman of Strasbourg.   Right,
a woman of the upper classes in Antwerp dressed in a street costume.   Notice
that she is carrying a fan.

disbanded the army ; they would have restored the king and the old
church ; and they would have refused to grant religious toleration.

Cromwell and the soldiers were bound to have religious toleration
for themselves at all costs ; and since they had the power they got
their way.   Thinking that the king was the cause of all their difficulties, they decided to get rid of him.   In December, 1648, Colonel
Pride, with a troop of soldiers, came into the House of Commons
and drove out those members who would not agree to this (*Pride's
Purge, Dec. 6, 1648*).   The few remaining members, known as the
" Rump Parliament," then declared that they represented the
" people."   In the name of the people, they declared the king

guilty of treason and condemned him to death.   January 30, 1649, he was executed.   The Rump Parliament now declared the monarchy and the House of Lords abolished, resolved that " England shall henceforth be governed as a Commonwealth or free state," and devised a new seal bearing the words, " In the First Year of Liberty by God's blessing restored."   The first revolution was at an end.

How Cromwell governed England as a Commonwealth.   In spite of these solemn words, it was not really by God's blessing or by the will of the people that the king was executed or the Commonwealth established.   These things were done by Cromwell and the army, contrary to the will of the people, without any right at all except the right of might.

For nearly ten years Cromwell governed England by military force.   " I am as much for government by consent as any man," Cromwell once said, " but where shall we find that consent? "   It is not quite true that Cromwell was for government by consent. He wanted the people to consent to his government, which is not quite the same thing.   He tried several times to get the people to consent to his government, but they never did.   And so the Commonwealth was not a commonwealth at all, except in name.   Cromwell governed effectively; but his government was a military dictatorship, more autocratic and severe than that of Charles I had ever been.

Perhaps the best thing Cromwell did was this — for ten years he did away with religious persecution.   At least all Protestants who did not oppose his government were allowed to believe and worship as they liked ; and many people became so accustomed to this that it was never again quite possible to suppress all religious liberty in England, as it was in France.   But the chief result of Cromwell's government was that most people were sorry they had ever started a revolution.   During Cromwell's time the great majority of people came to dislike intensely two things — Puritans and soldiers.   The more Cromwell tried to force the people to adopt sober Puritan customs and habits, the more they disliked the Puritan customs and habits.   The more they were forced to obey a government of soldiers, the more they desired to get rid of a government by soldiers.   When Cromwell died in 1658, the great

THE GARDEN OF AN INN

From a painting by Jan Steen. So far as enjoyment in eating goes, men and dogs do not seem to have changed much since the seventeenth century. The same kind of outside tables and benches may be seen today in the gardens of European country inns.

majority of the people longed for a return of the good old times when they had had a king and a Parliament, when they had had a church with bishops in lawn sleeves and priests reading the Prayer Book, and when they had been permitted to follow old customs.

The restoration of 1660. Cromwell's son, Richard, could not control the army, and therefore he could not carry on Cromwell's system of government. The real power fell to General Monk, who thought it would be better to restore the king, since that was what most people wanted. He therefore assembled a Parliament which declared that " according to the ancient and fundamental laws of the kingdom, the government of England is and ought to be by king, lords, and commons." The son of Charles I, who had been living in exile in France, was invited to return, and in 1660 he was proclaimed King Charles II. This event is known as the Stuart Restoration of 1660.

Charles at once called a new Parliament. It was composed mainly of young country gentlemen who could not remember the oppressions of Charles I but who remembered very well the oppressions of Cromwell. They were therefore very hostile to everything that reminded them of the Puritan Commonwealth. So they re-established the old English Church with its bishops, and passed severe laws against the Puritans, the Separatists or Independents, the Baptists, and the Quakers. But although they were strong for king and church, they did not wish the king to govern autocratically, and so they did not repeal the Constitutional Laws of 1641. Thus the Restoration of 1660 was a restoration of king and Parliament, and of the old church without toleration for " Dissenters."

In 1660 the great majority of the English people were very happy to be rid of government by Puritans and soldiers, and to have back again the old government by king, Parliament, and the church. They thought that the great questions of government and religion were now settled. But after a time they discovered that this was not so ; and in 1688 they had to make a second revolution — a more quiet and careful revolution — in order to settle these questions. One reason why the Restoration of 1660 did not prove satisfactory in the end was that there were now a great many people who were not willing to belong to the old church. These Dissenters — Puritans, Independents, Baptists, and Quakers — kept on asking for religious toleration ; and as they had much political influence in the towns, it became more difficult, as time went on, to refuse their demands. But the chief reason why the second revolution occurred was this : The new king, Charles II, and his successor, James II, still thought, in spite of everything that had happened, that they could ignore Parliament and govern as they pleased. A second revolution was necessary to teach them better.

How Charles tried to govern as he liked, without setting out on his travels again. Charles II was very intelligent, but pleasure loving, cynical, and faithless. For years he had lived in exile and poverty. Now that he was restored to a life of ease and power, he was determined never to lose his throne or his head, as his father had done. " I will never set out on my travels again," he said. Yet he wanted to be a real king, like Louis XIV. Charles therefore had two main objects: (1) to keep his head on his shoulders and himself on his throne; (2) to outwit Parliament and rule as he pleased, if it could be done without being forced to "set out on his travels again." The clever rascal was shrewd enough to accomplish the first object, and at last, after many difficulties, to accomplish the second object also.

In order to do as he liked, Charles had of course to have money. His first Parliament had given him a large sum for life. But since this was not enough, he tried to make himself independent of Parliament by accepting money from Louis XIV. In 1670 Louis promised to give Charles a large sum of money if the latter would help him fight the Dutch and declare himself a Catholic (*Secret Treaty of Dover*). When this secret bargain became known, Charles found it less easy to manage his Parliament. People feared that he was trying to rule without the consent of Parliament, and that he was perhaps trying to establish the Catholic religion in England.

Victoria and Albert Museum, London

EARLIEST KNOWN ENGLISH SILVER COFFEE POT, 1681

The engraving reads: "The Guift of Richard Sterne Eq' to ye Honorable East India Comp."

The fear of Catholicism was greatly increased a few years later by the false rumor of a "Popish Plot." This was supposed to be a plot to establish the Catholic religion in England by murdering Charles and placing his brother James, who was known to be a Catholic, on the throne. The Popish Plot did not exist, but was invented by a liar named Titus Oates. Yet it was widely believed, and it created a great panic. A strong party known as the "Whigs" gained control of Parliament, and introduced the Exclusion Bill, to exclude James from the throne when Charles died. Charles finally persuaded Parliament not to pass the Exclusion Bill; but in order to do so he had to submit to the Whigs. Among other things, he had to agree to the Habeas Corpus Act (1679), which made it illegal for the king to imprison anyone without giving him a fair trial by jury. It is said that the Habeas Corpus Act would have been defeated in the House of Lords if the tellers who counted the votes had not in jest counted one fat lord as ten. If so, this was, as Trevelyan says, the " best joke ever made in England."

Although for a time Charles had to submit to the Whigs and govern as they wished, he soon recovered his popularity and was able to govern without them. The reason was this. As soon as the excitement over the Popish Plot died down, people began to think that the bitter struggle between the king and the Whigs had brought the country very near another civil war. People remembered the Civil War and the military government of Cromwell, and whatever happened, they did not want to go through that again. So the fear of Catholicism was replaced by a fear of civil war. It seemed safer to be governed by the king than by a Parliament whose party struggles threatened the peace of the land. Charles became popular. The clergy preached obedience to kings, and the bishops and country gentlemen sided with the king against the Whigs and the Dissenters. In 1681 Charles therefore dissolved Parliament, and during the rest of his reign, which ended in 1685, he governed as he liked, without calling any Parliament at all.

The second revolution, 1688. How James II was allowed to keep his head but not his throne. If James II could have kept the goodwill of the bishops and country gentlemen as Charles had done, he also might have governed as he liked. But James was a Catholic, and he was foolish enough to think that he could make England a Catholic country. He appointed Catholics to office in the army and in the church. He dismissed two of his loyal supporters because they refused to become Catholics. He issued a Declaration of Indulgence, granting freedom of worship to Catholics, and he ordered the bishops to read the declaration in the churches. These measures alarmed everyone and made enemies even of the bishops and the country gentlemen. Seven bishops, who asked to be excused from reading the declaration, were arrested and tried for sedition. The seven bishops became popular heroes, and even the king's soldiers cheered when they heard that the jury had declared the bishops " not guilty."

TOWER OF LONDON

From an engraving by Hollar, about 1649. The original Tower was built by William the Conqueror. Its walls were about fifteen feet thick. Although once a royal residence, it was a state prison in the seventeenth century. Prisoners were taken in or out by way of the entrance from the Thames shown in the foreground. The small boats are carrying passengers and the barges are carrying coal. At present the Tower is a national museum.

So the English decided to make another revolution rather than be governed by an autocratic king who was bent on establishing the Catholic religion. Now, James's sister, Mary, was a Protestant; and she was married to William of Orange, the ruler of the Netherlands, who was also a Protestant. Therefore, in June, 1688, seven prominent Englishmen wrote a letter to William asking him to come to England with an army. William accepted the invitation, and when he landed, James, deserted by everyone, even his soldiers, tried to escape to France. Some fishermen, thinking to please William, caught James and sent him back to London. But William was too shrewd to make a hero of James by cutting off his head, as Cromwell had made a hero of Charles I. So he set James free, and James obliged him by running off a second time.

The English did not want to call themselves revolutionists. Parliament therefore declared that James had "abdicated the government " by " withdrawing himself out of the kingdom." The throne was thus vacant, not because the people had driven him off from the throne, but because he had left it of his own accord. Parliament then offered the " vacant " throne to William and Mary, on condition that they would agree to a " Declaration of Rights." In 1689 the Parliament enacted the Declaration of Rights into law under the title of a Bill of Rights.

The Bill of Rights, like the Magna Carta (1215) and the Petition of Right (1628) and the Habeas Corpus Act (1679), is one of the great charters of English political freedom. The Bill of Rights declared it illegal for the king to do any of the following things: (1) to suspend the laws; (2) to deny jury trial to anyone accused of crime; (3) to inflict cruel or unusual punishments; (4) to deny the right of the people to petition the king; (5) to interfere with the freedom of elections to Parliament or with freedom of debate in Parliament; (6) to levy taxes or to keep a standing army without the consent of Parliament.

The Bill of Rights settled the *political* question of the relations of king and Parliament. After 1689 no English king ever seriously tried to rule without the consent of Parliament. This question the Revolution of 1688 settled very much as the Long Parliament had tried to settle it in 1641, and as Parliament had again tried to settle it in 1660. But the *religious* question was not settled in 1688 according to the agreement of 1660. In 1688 the people were ready to accept the ideas of Cromwell. So the Parliament of 1689 abolished the censorship of the press, thus establishing freedom of speech and the press. And it passed the Toleration Act which granted religious freedom to all Christians except Unitarians and Catholics. After 1688 even Unitarians and Catholics were not in practice interfered with much so long as they were loyal to the government.

What the English Revolution did and why it was important. For nearly a hundred years the English people had been engaged in discussion and conflict about religion and politics. Nearly everyone learned something from this experience. The kings learned that they could not rule as they liked, but must be content to rule as the Parliament liked — that is, as the nobles, country gentlemen, and wealthy merchants liked. The nobles and country gentlemen and merchants learned that it is easier to start a revolution than it is to stop one after it has begun. All the people learned that a government by soldiers is a bad government, even if the soldiers are good men. And nearly everyone learned that it is unreasonable to expect all people to think alike, and that to put a person in prison for holding a certain opinion about religion or politics does not prove that the opinion is wrong.

So, having learned these things, the English people ended their long revolutionary period by establishing an *aristocratic constitutional monarchy* — that is, a government in which the king should rule only with the consent of the nobles, country gentlemen, and wealthy merchants who were represented in Parliament. They kept the established English Church, governed by bishops appointed and paid by the government, but they no longer tried to compel anyone to belong to it. They also established certain individual liberties — that is, they gave to everyone a legal right to think as he liked and to speak and to print his opinions. Thus from the end of the seventeenth century the English people enjoyed a greater degree of self-government, of free speech, and of freedom of religion, than any other people in Europe, except perhaps the Dutch and the Swiss.

At the time, no one could see how important the English Revolution would prove to be. Most people in other countries thought that even this much liberty was unsafe, and they thought it unlikely that a people who refused to obey their king could ever be very prosperous or powerful. But in the eighteenth century they began to see that England, with its free government, its free religion, and its free thought was growing more prosperous and stronger than any other country. And so at the close of the eighteenth century, people in other countries, becoming tired of autocratic kings, looked with admiration on the English system of free institutions, and wished to have similar ones for themselves. This, then, is why the English Revolution is so important for modern history: It became a kind of example or model which the other peoples of Europe followed when they tried to get rid of autocratic government and establish free institutions.

CHART FOR CHAPTER III. Up-and-down struggle between king and Parliament in the seventeenth century:

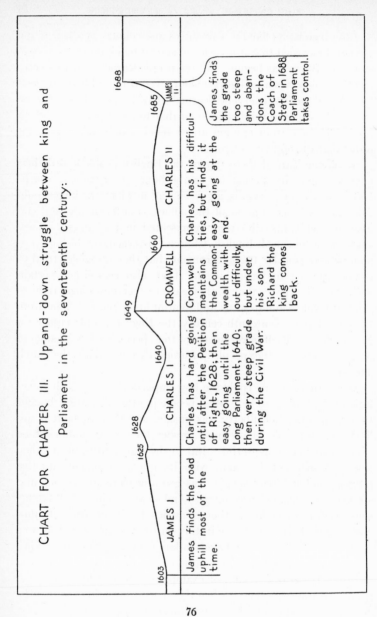

JAMES I	CHARLES I	CROMWELL	CHARLES II	JAMES II
1603	1625 1628 1640	1649	1660	1685 1688
James finds the road uphill most of the time.	Charles has hard going until after the Petition of Right, 1628; then easy going until the Long Parliament, 1640; then very steep grade during the Civil War.	Cromwell maintains the Commonwealth without difficulty, but under his son Richard the king comes back.	Charles has his difficulties, but finds it easy going at the end.	James finds the grade too steep and abandons the Coach of State in 1688. Parliament takes control.

QUESTIONS

1. Aristotle divided all government into three classes: (1) government of the one, (2) government of the few, and (3) government of the many. What other words may be used to describe these three forms of government? In which of these classes would you place England at the beginning of the seventeenth century? at the close? at the present time?

2. Why did the country gentlemen dislike James I? Why were they able to resist him? What is meant by the "divine right of kings"? What did James I mean by the phrase, "no bishop, no king"?

3. What was the Petition of Right? Why is it important in English history? Is there anything like it in the Constitution of the United States? in the state constitutions?

4. How did Charles I manage to get along without calling Parliament from 1629 to 1640? Why was he forced to call Parliament in 1640? Why did the country gentlemen unite with the Puritans to resist Charles I before 1640, and then quarrel with the Puritans after 1642?

5. Why did Cromwell decide to abolish the monarchy and establish the Commonwealth? How did he compel Parliament to abolish the monarchy? Why did the majority of people refuse to support Cromwell?

6. Why did Charles II succeed in keeping his throne, whereas James II failed to do so?

7. Compare the Petition of Right (1628), the declaration made by Parliament in 1660, and the Bill of Rights (1689).

8. If England had been a peninsula of Europe, as Denmark is, would England now be the great power it is? Why?

SELECTED READINGS

Brief accounts. E. P. Cheyney, *Short History of England*, chs. xiv–xvi. J. R. Green, *Short History of the English People*, chs. viii–ix. Robinson, *Western Europe*, ch. xxx. C. J. H. Hayes, *Political and Social History of Modern Europe*, I, ch. viii. F. Schevill, *History of Europe*, ch. xiii. Hayes and Moon, *Modern History*, ch. x. An excellent and much fuller account is G. M. Trevelyan's *England under the Stuarts*.

Biography. J. Morley, *Cromwell*. T. Roosevelt, *Cromwell*. Of Lord Macaulay's famous essays, those on Milton, Hampden, and Bacon fall in this period. Matthew Arnold's essay on Falkland describes a man who found it difficult to take sides in the Civil War, since he saw that there was right on both sides.

Historical novels. R. D. Blackmore, *Lorna Doone*. C. Doyle, *Micah Clarke*. Walter Scott, *The Pirate*, and *Old Mortality*, and *The Bride of Lammermoor*. A. Dumas, *The Black Tulip*. J. Drinkwater, *Mr. Charles, King of England* (a play). W. Besant, *For Faith and Freedom*.

Sources. Knowledge of history is derived from written records called *sources*. These are of many kinds — official documents, narratives written by people who took part in events, poetry and literature of the time, etc.

Extracts from the sources are to be found in the following manuals: Gardiner, *Constitutional Documents* (No. 10, the Petition of Right; No. 88, the Abolition of the Monarchy). Colby, *Selections from the Sources* (No. 70, Voyage of the *Mayflower* related by William Bradford; No. 78, Pepys's description of the London fire in 1666). Kendall, *Source Book* (No. 69, James I and the Puritans at the Hampton Court Conference; No. 72, a lively scene in the House of Commons in 1629; No. 73, Governor Winthrop's reasons for the Puritan migration to America in 1630; No. 81, Battle of Naseby; No. 90, Pepys's description of the return of Charles II to London; No. 90, Evelyn's description of the Trial of the Seven Bishops). Adams and Stephens, *Select Documents* (No. 239, the Bill of Rights). Cheyney, *Readings in English History.* Robinson, *Readings in European History.* J. G. Mudiman, *The Trial of Charles the First.* (Contains some new documents relating to this famous trial.)

Literature. The literature of a country throws light on its history. Among the great works appearing in the seventeenth century are the following: Shakespeare's *Hamlet;* Lord Bacon's *Advancement of Learning* and *The New Atlantis;* Milton's *Areopagitica* (a plea for freedom of the press), *Paradise Lost,* and *Authority of Elected Magistrates;* Bunyan's *Pilgrim's Progress.* There are two famous diaries kept by prominent men in the time of Charles II: Samuel Pepys's *Diary* and John Evelyn's *Diary.* The former describes in detail the daily doings of a busy man and gives an excellent picture of the manners and customs of the time. Among other things, it gives a vivid account of the great plague of 1665 and of the London fire of 1666.

FRENCH WROUGHT-IRON GATE OF THE SEVENTEENTH CENTURY

CHAPTER IV. HOW LOUIS XIV GOVERNED FRANCE AS HE PLEASED, WON MUCH GLORY WHILE HE LIVED, AND WAS LITTLE MOURNED WHEN HE DIED

The king, as king, is not regarded as a private personage; all the state is in him; the will of all the people is included in his will. BOSSUET

Why we give a chapter to the reign of Louis XIV. In the Middle Ages kings had little power. They were often weaker than the great feudal barons who were their vassals, and they often had to submit to the Pope. But gradually the kings gained the upper hand of the nobles, and were strong enough to defy the Pope. By the seventeenth century the kings in most countries were able to govern very much as they pleased. This is one reason why we may begin modern history with the seventeenth century. At that time Europe was divided into sovereign independent states, most of which were governed by absolute kings.

From 1562 to 1598 France had been racked by civil war. During the reign of Henry IV (1589–1610), peace was established. But under Richelieu, the famous minister of Louis XIII, revolts again broke out. In fact it was not until the time of Louis XIV (1643–1715) that the long struggle of the kings against the nobles and the Pope was completed. Louis was so successful in making everyone submit to him, and he made his power so much feared in Europe, that

LOUIS XIV (1638–1715)

From a portrait painted by Rigaud, in 1701. Louis appears in his robes of state, with high-heeled, buckled shoes, his scepter in his hand. This portrait shows especially well his " grand air."

all the kings and nobles of his time, and for a long time after, envied and admired him as the greatest king since Charlemagne. In this age of kings and nobles, Louis was thought to be the ideal king, France was the most powerful state in Europe, and everything French was taken as a kind of model to be imitated. This is why it is more important to know about Louis and France than about many other kings and countries.

Why the French people were willing to let Louis XIV rule very much as he liked. Louis became king in 1643, at the age of five. During the first eighteen years of his reign the government was really under the direction of his able minister, Cardinal Mazarin. But upon the death of Mazarin, in 1661, Louis took charge of affairs himself and determined to be master. At that time most people were ready to welcome a strong king. They thought it would be dangerous to limit the power of their ruler. Their English neighbors across the channel had tried to do that (see Chapter III) and, after fighting a civil war, had cut off the head of their king. This seemed to the French a kind of madness which they did not wish to imitate. Besides, the French had recently passed through a kind of civil war known as the *Fronde* (1648–1653). The Fronde, like the English Civil War, had started as an attempt to limit the power of the king, or of his minister, Mazarin; but it turned out to be only a useless struggle in which the people were at the mercy of the turbulent nobles. The French people remembered the unhappy days of the Fronde, and if anyone talked about limiting the power of the king, he was called a *frondeur*. The French people thought it was better to have a strong king than another civil war. One autocratic king was better than many petty tyrants.

The French were the more willing to submit to Louis because he pleased them and in many ways was fitted to be the kind of king they wanted. Louis was courteous, graceful, and dignified. It was said that even when playing billiards, he did so with the air of a man who ruled the world. He never doubted that he had the right to rule as he pleased, or the ability to rule wisely. This gave him the courage (and it takes a great deal) to decide every question, from the making of war to the style of dresses worn by the ladies of

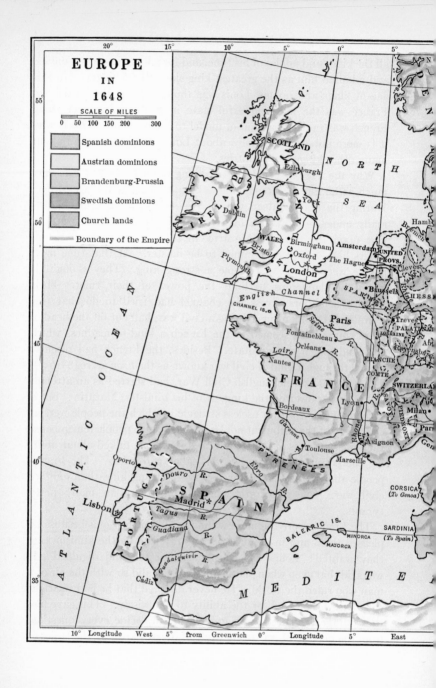

EUROPE
IN
1648

SCALE OF MILES
0 50 100 150 200   300

Spanish dominions
Austrian dominions
Brandenburg-Prussia
Swedish dominions
Church lands
Boundary of the Empire

SCOTLAND
Edinburgh
York
IRELAND
Dublin
WALES
Birmingham
Bristol
Plymouth
ENGLAND
Oxford
London
English Channel
CHANNEL IS.

NORTH SEA

Amsterdam
The Hague
UNITED PROVS.
Cleves
SPANISH
Brussels
HESS
Treves
PALATIN
LORRAINE
FRANCHE
COMTE
SWITZERLA
SAVOY
PIEDMONT
Milan
Par
Gen

Hamb
Brem
Flemish
Lu
Av
Regisbu
Ab

Paris
Fontainebleau
Seine R.
Orléans
Loire
Nantes
FRANCE
Bordeaux
Garonne R.
Lyon
Rhone
Avignon
Toulouse
Marseille

ATLANTIC OCEAN

Oporto
PORTUGAL
Douro R.
Lisbon
Tagus R.
Guadiana R.
Cádiz

SPAIN
Madrid
Ebro R.
PYRENEES

CORSICA
(To Genoa)

SARDINIA
(To Spain)

BALEARIC IS.
MINORCA
MAJORCA

MEDITE

Longitude   West   5°   from   Greenwich   0°   Longitude   5°   East

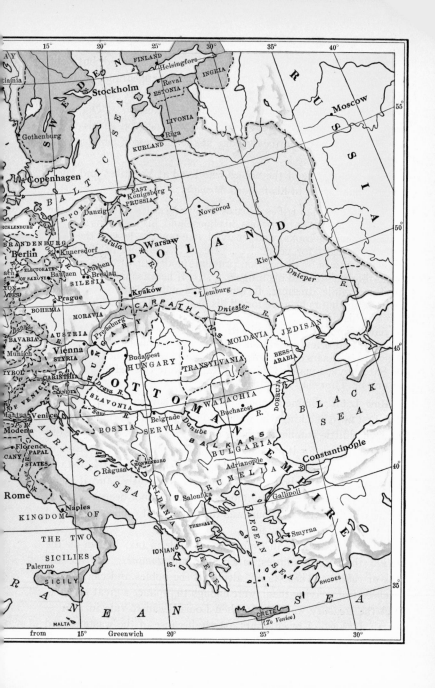

the court. Sure that he was right, Louis never hesitated, but went straight ahead, and this often gave him the appearance of being right even when he was wrong. Most important of all, Louis possessed the only substitute for genius — industry. "One must work hard to reign," he said; and he was as good as his word. Louis really worked hard every day at the business of being a great king.

Saint-Simon, one of the nobles who lived at Versailles and knew the king well, says in his famous *Memoirs:*

Naturally fond of trifles, he ceaselessly concerned himself with the most petty details of his troops, his household, his mansions: would even instruct his cooks, who received, like novices, lessons they had known by heart for years. . . . He . . . was fond of order and regularity; was by disposition prudent, moderate, discreet, master of his movements and his tongue. . . . If he was made to wait for anything while dressing, it was always with patience. He was exact in the hours he gave for all his day, with a precision clear and brief in his orders. . . . Thus, with a regularity which he never deviated from, he was served with the utmost exactitude. . . . On Sunday, and often on Monday, there was a Council of State; on Tuesday a Finance Council; on Wednesday a Council of State; on Saturday a Finance Council. Rarely were two held on one day or any on Thursday or Friday.

How Louis obtained money enough to govern as he pleased. The first need of a king who wished to rule as he pleased was money. Louis had little trouble in raising money, for the reason that he did not need to ask for it, as the English kings did. The institution in France which resembled the English Parliament was the Estates General. But this body had never met frequently, and it could scarcely be said to exist any more, since it had not been assembled for nearly fifty years. Louis was therefore free to collect taxes and use the money as he saw fit.

The principal taxes in France were the land tax, known as the *taille;* the customs duties, called *aides* and *douanes;* and the salt tax or *gabelle.* These taxes, although the nobles and clergy were excused from paying them, were enough to produce a great revenue. Yet the treasury was empty when Louis began to rule in 1661 — partly because of recent wars, partly because of the wasteful and corrupt methods of collecting the taxes. Louis soon remedied this

École Nationale des Beaux-Arts, Paris

A BALL IN THE TIME OF LOUIS XIII

From an engraving by A. Bosse. The men wear much lace, plumed hats, and pompons on their shoes. In the rear, at the left, are the musicians.

by appointing, as his minister of finance, an obscure official named Colbert. Colbert was a sour, disagreeable man, very ambitious, and jealous of all rivals. But he was an honest man, and a very able one. For eleven years Colbert served Louis faithfully, never trying to make the taxes less burdensome to the people but only more profitable to the king. By abolishing useless offices and improving the methods of collecting the taxes, he soon provided Louis with a very fine revenue. If Louis had not engaged in expensive wars, he would never have been hampered by lack of money as the English kings always were.

How Colbert tried to improve the commerce and industry of France. Besides increasing the king's revenue, Colbert wished to make France as wealthy and prosperous as possible. Louis was not much interested in questions of trade and industry, but he could see that a rich and thriving France would add to his glory as well as to his revenue. He therefore gave Colbert a pretty free hand in these matters.

Like most people then and now, Colbert thought of wealth chiefly in terms of money. In 1664 he said: " I suppose that anyone would readily agree . . . that it is simply and solely the abundance of money within a state that makes the difference in its grandeur and power." This being the case, Colbert's chief aim in all his measures was to have more money coming into the country every year than went out of it. In order to bring this about, he thought it necessary for France to sell more things to other countries than she bought of them. Colbert therefore tried to develop the manufactures of France so that she would have all the things she needed for her own people, and in addition a large surplus of things which she could export to other countries. Thus more money would always be coming into France than went out of it.

Colbert thought that this could not be done if everyone were allowed to make and sell things as he liked. He thought it was necessary for industry and trade to be supported and carefully regulated by the government. With the aid and regulation of the government he therefore introduced into France the manufacture of many things, such as linen, fine glassware, and tapestries, which France had been buying of other countries. He also got the king to issue more than a hundred and fifty edicts for regulating the " guilds " — that is, the little corporations of master workmen who had a monopoly of making and selling certain things. These edicts named the things which each guild could make, the quality of the product, the price at which it should be sold, and so on. One law provided that if a merchant made cloth not up to standard quality, a piece of the cloth should be fastened to a post in the market place, with the name of the maker attached. For a third offense the man himself was to be tied to the post, with the cloth attached to him.

By improving the industries of France in these ways, Colbert hoped to make it unnecessary for France to buy many things from foreign countries. But there were some things which could not be raised or made in France — or in any European country — such as cotton, sugar, pepper and other spices, dyewoods, coffee, and furs. These things were brought to Europe from the East or West Indies or from North America, chiefly by the Dutch and English East

BUILDING A SHIP IN A DUTCH SHIPYARD, ABOUT 1647

From a drawing by Wenzel Hollar. In such ships the Dutch carried on their immensely profitable trade with the East Indies. Their success annoyed Colbert and Louis XIV. Colbert tried to destroy Dutch trade by levying high tariffs on Dutch commodities. Louis tried to destroy Dutch independence by war (1672-1679). Neither attempt succeeded.

India Companies. As Colbert did not wish France to buy these things of the Dutch and the English, he tried to establish French colonies, and he organized a number of French trading companies. The most important of these companies was the French East India Company. The government furnished some of the money to start the company, and wealthy men were urged, and even required, to put money into it. The company was given a monopoly of all French trade with the countries between the Cape of Good Hope and the East India Islands, with the privilege of possessing all that it took from the natives, on condition that it should build churches and provide priests for converting them to Christianity.

How Colbert's measures strengthened the king. The plan which Colbert followed to make France rich and powerful was the same as that followed by other countries in the seventeenth and eighteenth centuries. This plan was known as the " mercantile system." It was a method of commercial warfare, and was based on the theory that one country could become wealthy and powerful only by making its rivals poor and weak. Colbert did not succeed in ruining the trade of his rivals, the Dutch and the English; but his measures did much to strengthen the power of the French king. They did this by placing the guilds and trading companies under the supervision of the government and by making the men who were engaged in business more dependent on the king for favors and opportunities.

All the guilds were now strictly controlled by the king's laws, and any guild that wanted new laws made or bad ones changed had to ask the king's consent. They even found that it was often impossible to keep the privileges which they already had without paying the king well for it. In the same way, men who wished to organize companies for undertaking new business ventures had to obtain a charter from the king. Of course the king did not ordinarily grant favors for nothing, and the wealthy business men had to pay him for the privileges he granted. Besides business opportunities, wealthy middle-class men often wanted important offices which would confer honor upon them and their families, or fine marriages for their sons or daughters, or titles of nobility for themselves. These things the king could give them, and for these things they were willing to pay also.

In this way, during the reign of Louis XIV a closer relation was established between the wealthy middle-class men and the king. As they became more dependent on the king for favors and offices, they became more loyal and obedient. The king was willing to reward them for their obedience, partly because they could pay him well, but chiefly because, by gaining the goodwill of these men and giving them high offices in the government, he became less dependent upon the nobles for political support. By granting favors to the wealthy middle class, Louis found it easier to reduce the turbulent nobility to submitting to his will.

How Louis kept the nobles in order. In the seventeenth century a king whose nobles did not obey him was not much of a king. Louis had very good reason to know this. He could remember, as a small boy, being hustled out of bed one cold winter's night in 1649 when the court was forced to flee from Paris to avoid being taken by the leaders of the Fronde. He never forgot or forgave this humiliating indignity which the rebellious nobles had inflicted on his sacred

THE CHATEAU AT VERSAILLES

From an engraving by Perelle, a contemporary of Louis XIV. Note the carriages, sedan chairs, and courtiers on horseback in the avenue. The château was the residence of the kings of France until the Revolution. It is now a national museum.

person.   Louis was therefore determined to do one thing at least, and that was, to keep the nobles in subjection.   This he did partly by depriving them of all important political offices but chiefly by making it amusing and profitable for them to obey him.

That it might be amusing for the nobles to obey the king, Louis built a splendid new royal residence at Versailles, near Paris, where he established the most brilliant court ever known in Europe.   The most influential nobles were encouraged, and even commanded, to leave their castles in the country, where life at best was dull, and to come and live with the king at Versailles.   Here the king provided amusements for them, and here he could keep his eye on them. The nobles could not well be discourteous or disobedient to the king while they lived in his house and ate at his table.   Almost without knowing it, Louis's noble guests fell into the habit of trying to please him.   The king's manners were imitated, his words repeated.   All smiled when the king smiled, all were sad when the king was sad, " all were devout when the king was devout, and all were sorry not to be ill when the king was ill."   If a noble at court displeased the king, he was sent back to the country to live in his own house, in which case everyone felt — and he did too — that he was in deep disgrace.

But the real reason why the nobles were willing to be humble servants of the king was that he was rich, while most of them were poor.   There were some rich nobles, and all of them together possessed a great deal of land.   But for a long time most of the nobles had been growing poorer.   The chief reason was this : Their income from the land, being fixed by custom, was about what it had been centuries before, while the cost of everything they had to buy was higher than formerly.   Besides, the nobles were extravagant, and life at the court was very expensive.   It was their need of money that made them humble servants of the king, who alone could pay their debts, provide them with pensions, arrange rich marriages for their daughters, or appoint their sons to offices in the army or the church.

Saint-Simon says, in his *Memoirs*, that when his father died, in 1693, a friend went the very next morning " to ask the king, as soon as his curtains were opened, to grant me the offices my father had

© *Ewing Galloway*

GALLERY OF MIRRORS IN THE CHÂTEAU AT VERSAILLES

Here Louis XIV received his courtiers in the morning. Here the German Empire was proclaimed after the Franco-Prussian war in 1871 (see Ch. XIV). Here, in 1919, the German delegates signed the Treaty of Versailles after the Great War (see Ch. XXII).

held. The king very graciously complied with this request, and in the afternoon said many obliging things to me. . . . The king exhorted me to behave well, and promised to take care of me." In these few words Saint-Simon tells us just how Louis mastered the nobles. He took care of them by giving them money and offices; but in return for this he required them to submit to him.

One of the principal ways in which Louis took care of the nobles was by giving them the higher offices in the church. These offices were much desired by the nobles because they were important and well-paid positions. By selecting his archbishops, bishops, and abbots from the old noble families, Louis placed the vast wealth and influence of the Catholic Church in their hands. But in return for this gift he expected his noble bishops to behave well. They could behave well only by teaching the people that they must obey the king because God had commanded them to do so.

We must now see how the noble bishops and abbots behaved well when Louis got into difficulty with the Pope.

How Louis quarreled with the Pope and what came of it. In the seventeenth century kings claimed to rule by the will of God, just as in our day presidents and ministers claim to rule by the will of the people. This theory of the "divine right of kings" was very popular in France. A famous bishop, Bossuet, wrote a book which he entitled *Politics Derived from the Holy Scriptures*, in which he proved from the Bible that to rebel against kings is the same as to rebel against God. Louis never doubted that God had given him authority to rule in France. But the Pope claimed to have authority from God also, and he thought the bishops of the church were bound to obey him as head of the church. Louis knew that he could not be an absolute king unless the bishops obeyed him instead of the Pope.

Louis and the Pope soon got into a quarrel over this question. In 1516 Pope Leo X had agreed that the French kings might appoint the bishops. But Louis was not satisfied with this, and in 1673 he issued an edict claiming that he had the right to appoint certain minor clergy as well as the bishops. Two bishops protested against this edict, and the Pope supported them. This raised a very important question, which was this: In case of a quarrel between the king and the Pope, must the bishops obey the king as head of the state, or must they obey the Pope as head of the church?

In 1681 Louis called an assembly of the French bishops in the hope that they would take his side in the quarrel with the Pope. The bishops were in a difficult situation. Since the king had appointed them, and since most of them were members of noble families, their worldly interests bound them to the king, but as officials in the church they were bound to the Pope. If they did not obey the Pope, it would be said they were not good Catholics; but if they did not obey the king, it would be said they were not good Frenchmen. The bishops would have preferred not to take sides at all. But Louis insisted, and so they finally prepared and signed a document known as the Declaration of 1682, or the Declaration of the Liberties of the Gallican Church.

This declaration stated that the Pope "has received authority from God only in things spiritual . . . and not at all in things temporal or civil. . . . In consequence of this we declare that kings are not subject to any ecclesiastical authority . . . and that they cannot be deposed . . . by the heads of the church." This meant that the Pope had the right to decide what the religious beliefs of the church were to be, but that in other matters the king had authority and the bishops were to obey him. This left the Pope very little authority over the church, and it gave the king a great deal. It almost made the king the head of the church.

The declaration was approved by the king, and so it became a part of French law. But the Pope refused to accept it, and for eleven years neither the Pope nor the king would yield. The quarrel over the " Gallican Liberties " became notorious in Europe — a kind of religious scandal which made many people wonder whether Louis intended to separate the French church from the Pope as Henry VIII had separated the English Church from the Pope. But Louis did not do this. In 1693 he made his peace with the Pope. The Pope agreed that Louis might have his way about appointing the minor clergy, and in return Louis agreed that the French bishops might sign a statement saying that they rejected the Declaration of 1682.

At the time this was thought to be a victory for the Pope. But the real victory was with the king. He got his way about appointing the clergy. Besides, although the bishops rejected the Declaration of 1682, the king did not annul the declaration, and it therefore remained a part of French law. Most important of all, the bishops did not reject the declaration because the Pope commanded them to do so, but because the king permitted them to do so. The Pope got something that he wanted, but he got it only with the permission of the king. From this time on, the power of the Pope over the French Church was very small, and the power of the king very great.

How Louis " converted " the Huguenots. Like many people then and now, Louis thought that anyone who did not agree with him must be a little stupid. Above all, Louis thought that people were stupid if they did not agree with him that the Catholic religion was the true one. It seemed to him that Frenchmen who did not accept the religion of their king must be even a little disloyal.

BEDCHAMBER OF LOUIS XIV IN THE CHÂTEAU AT VERSAILLES

The king's favorite courtiers were often received in this room, as Louis often
gave audiences before he arose.

The great majority of Frenchmen were Catholics, but there were
about 1,200,000 Frenchmen who were Huguenots. The Huguenots were Protestants, followers of John Calvin, and their religion
was therefore similar to that of the Scotch Presbyterians and the
English Puritans. In the sixteenth century the Huguenots had
been harshly persecuted; but in 1598 Henry IV had issued the
famous Edict of Nantes, which gave the Huguenots the same legal
privileges as other Frenchmen, and permitted them to practice
their own religion and educate their children in their own schools.

These privileges the Huguenots still enjoyed when Louis began
to rule in 1661. They were peaceable and industrious citizens who
lived in the towns and were, for the most part, engaged in industry
and commerce. Yet the Huguenots were much disliked and feared
by other Frenchmen. The chief reason for this was that they were
" heretics." The word *heretic* does not mean much to us, but in the
seventeenth century it was a terrible word. Then people feared
heretics in much the same way that we fear " Anarchists," and for
much the same reason — because they were thought to be dangerous

and disloyal people. Frenchmen were proud of their country, and to obey the king was a sign of patriotism, just as reverence for the flag is in our day. Why should the Huguenots not obey the king by accepting his religion? Why did they accept the religion of the Dutch and the English, who were enemies of the king? The Huguenots must be pro-Dutch or pro-English. So the people thought.

From the first, the Catholic clergy asked Louis to take away the privileges of these heretics. They told him that they were trying to convert the Huguenots to the true religion, but that it was difficult to do so as long as the king permitted them to practice a false one. For a long time Louis refused to take away the privileges of the Huguenots; he left the conversion of the Huguenots to the clergy. But about 1680 he changed his mind; he began to think it was *his* duty to convert the heretics.

At this time Louis was quarreling with the Pope, and he perhaps thought the bishops would be more willing to side with him if he did what the bishops wanted about the Huguenots. Besides, Louis began to think of converting the Huguenots because he began to think of converting himself. Being now about forty years old, he began to worry about his sins. " The king reads his Bible frequently," Madame de Maintenon wrote in 1679. " He confesses his faults. He thinks seriously of converting the heretics, and he will soon begin to work for that in earnest." Who could doubt that Louis was a good Catholic if he succeeded in converting the heretics? And perhaps God would forgive him his sins if he did God the service of forcing the Huguenots to give up their errors.

Louis began by excluding the Huguenots from public offices, forbidding them to become lawyers or doctors or to engage in the business of printing or selling books. Huguenots who refused to become Catholics were required to take soldiers into their houses and give them food and lodging. To escape such persecution, thousands turned Catholic. In 1685 Louis was told that nearly all the Huguenots were now converted. Thinking that this was so, Louis revoked the Edict of Nantes. As a result, the Huguenots were forbidden to worship in public. Their ministers were exiled. Their schools were closed. Thousands escaped to Holland, Ger-

Musée Carnavalet

A SHOP IN PARIS IN THE TIME OF LOUIS XIII

From an engraving by A. Bosse. Right: gloves, fans, laces, cuffs. Left: books, some of the titles being Seneca, Plutarch, Boccaccio, Machiavelli. The lettering below describes articles for sale at the shop.

many, England, and the English colonies in America, leaving their property behind but taking with them their knowledge and skill in the arts. Most of those who remained in France became Catholics at least in name. Those who resisted the new law were hunted down, killed or captured, imprisoned or sent to the galleys.

There was great rejoicing in France over the " conversion " of the Huguenots. Madame de Sévigné, a cultivated and gentle lady, probably expressed the common feeling when she said of the new law: " Everything that it contains is very fine, and no king ever has done or ever will do anything more memorable." But there were some intelligent persons who thought the measure a great mistake. Saint-Simon wrote in his *Memoirs*:

The revocation of the Edict of Nantes, without the slightest excuse, depopulated a quarter of the kingdom, ruined its commerce, weakened it in every direction. The king congratulated himself

on his power and his piety. The bishops applauded him; the
Jesuits made the pulpit resound with his praises. All France was
filled with horror and confusion; and yet there was never such
triumph and joy, such boundless laudation of the king.

**How Louis tried to make himself master of Europe as well as of
France.** Having made himself master of France, Louis wished to
make France the dominant power in Europe. When he took charge
of the government in 1661, the long Thirty Years' War, in which not
only France but most of the other nations of Europe had taken part,
was over, and the countries involved were willing to keep the peace.
Louis knew this, for he said: " Peace was established with all my
neighbors as long, in all probability, as I myself desired." Louis
was therefore free to keep the peace or to make war. He chose to
make war.

Louis chose to make war because he was ambitious for military
glory and because he knew that if he could wage successful wars it
would help him to rule as he pleased in France. Besides, France
was now the strongest power in Europe, and Louis thought this
would be a good time to make her still stronger. Like Henry IV
and Richelieu before him, Louis thought France would be much
stronger if she could extend her frontiers to the Rhine River. He
wished especially to annex to France the Netherlands and Franche
Comté, which belonged to Spain; and Lorraine, which was a part of
" the Empire " (see p. 107). If France could annex these three
provinces, she would be less easily invaded by her old enemies,
Spain and Austria.

To obtain these provinces Louis waged three wars: (1) the War
of Devolution (1667–1668), which was waged chiefly against the
Spanish; (2) the Dutch War (1672–1679), against Holland and
Spain; and (3) the War of the League of Augsburg (1688–1697),
against Holland, Austria, Spain, and Great Britain. These wars
were far more costly and less successful than Louis expected they
would be, but in the end he succeeded in adding to France the
province of Franche Comté, eleven towns in the Spanish Netherlands, and upper Alsace.

Besides these wars, Louis fought one more — (4) the War of the
Spanish Succession (1701–1713). In 1700 Charles II, the King of

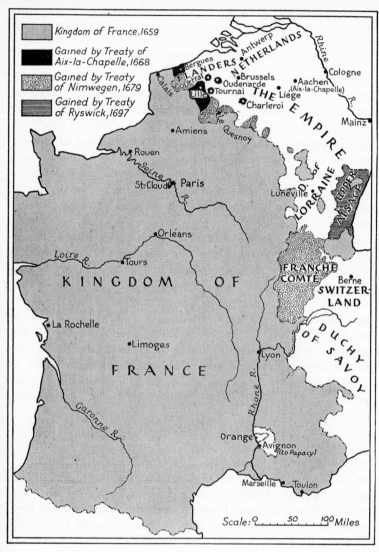

Legend:

Kingdom of France,1659

Gained by Treaty of
Aix-la-Chapelle,1668

Gained by Treaty
of Nimwegen, 1679

Gained by Treaty
of Ryswick,1697

FLANDERS
Antwerp
NETHERLANDS
Bergues
Courtral
Calais
Brussels
Oudenarde
Lille
Tournai
Charleroi
•Amiens
Quesnoy
Rouen
Seine
St-Cloud• Paris
Rhine
Cologne
•Aachen
(Aix-la-Chapelle)
Liège
THE EMPIRE
Mainz
D. of LORRAINE
Luneville
UPPER ALSACE
Orléans
Loire R.
Tours
KINGDOM OF
FRANCHE COMTE
Berne
SWITZER-LAND
La Rochelle
•Limoges
FRANCE
Garonne R.
Lyon
Rhone R.
DUCHY OF SAVOY
Orange
Avignon
(to Papacy)
Marseille• Toulon

Scale: 0   50   100 Miles

TERRITORIAL GAINS MADE BY LOUIS XIV

Spain, died without any direct heirs. By his will he left all of the Spanish Empire to Philip of Anjou, who was a grandson of Louis XIV. At that time the Spanish Empire included Spain, the southern Netherlands (Belgium), most of Italy, the greater part of South America, Central America, a part of what is now the United States, and the Philippine Islands. If this immense empire passed to a grandson of Louis XIV, it would be much the same as if it were given to Louis himself. So the other powers of Europe thought; and as France was already too strong, they united and fought for twelve years to prevent Louis from placing his grandson on the Spanish throne. The allies — of whom the most important were England, Holland, and Austria — won most of the battles. But in the end they permitted the Duke of Anjou to become King of Spain on condition that France and Spain should never be united under one ruler. In addition Spain was required to cede to the Duke of Savoy (who had joined the allies in 1704) the island of Sicily, and to cede to Austria the Spanish Netherlands, Naples, and Milan. England received from France Newfoundland, Nova Scotia, and the Hudson Bay territories, and from Spain Gibraltar and Minorca, besides certain rights of trading with the Spanish West Indian colonies. These agreements were provided for in the separate treaties of Utrecht, Rastatt, and Baden, which comprise what is commonly called the Peace of Utrecht (1713–1714). In 1720, to please Austria, the allies required the Duke of Savoy to cede to Austria the island of Sicily in exchange for the island of Sardinia, permitting him to take the title of King of Sardinia.

Thus Louis succeeded in making himself master of France, and in making France feared in Europe. But he failed to make France the dominant power in Europe. By waging war for thirty years he was able to add one province and a few towns to France, and to place his grandson on the throne of Spain. These wars conferred much " glory " on Louis, but they impoverished the people and nearly ruined the country, so that France was less prosperous and powerful at the end of Louis's reign than it had been at the beginning. When Louis died, in 1715, he was given a fine funeral. But the people all rejoiced. They were already growing tired of the " Grand Monarch " who won glory by making his people miserable.

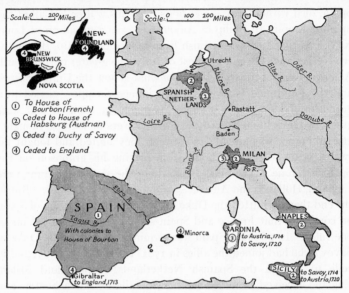

TERRITORIAL ADJUSTMENTS MADE BY THE TREATIES OF UTRECHT, RASTATT, AND BADEN, 1713–1714, AS MODIFIED BY THE EXCHANGE OF SICILY AND SARDINIA, 1720

Louis XIV is reported to have said: " I am the state " (*L'état, c'est moi*). Perhaps he never said it; but he might well have done so, for it was true enough. This is why his reign is important for the history of France and of Europe. Louis completed the work of the French kings in establishing the absolute power of the king. There was nothing further to be done along that line; and for nearly a hundred years — that is, until the French Revolution (1789) — there were no essential changes in the political or social institutions of France. So great was the fame of Louis, so great the prestige of French society, of French manners and customs, and of French art and letters, that during the eighteenth century the ruling classes in nearly every country in Europe looked upon France as the best governed and most civilized country in the world — the country whose institutions they would do well to imitate but could hardly hope to surpass.

CHART FOR CHAPTER IV. Louis XIV finds the road of despotic power easy to travel, except towards the end, when his expensive wars make the going a little harder.

| 1648 | 1661 | 1672 | 1678 | 1688 | 1697 | 1715 |

MAZARIN RULES FOR LOUIS XIV	LOUIS XIV RULES ON HIS OWN			
Civil war of the Fronde, 1648-1653, weakens royal power.	Louis reduces nobles to submission. Begins to build the royal palace at Versailles where he can keep his eye on the nobles.	Dutch War. Confers much glory on Louis. Franche Comté annexed to France.	Religious conflicts. Louis quarrels with the Pope. French bishops sign the Declaration of Gallican Liberties, 1682. Huguenots lose their privileges by revocation of Edict of Nantes, 1685.	War of League of Augsburg. With much effort and at great expense Louis gains Strasbourg.	France exhausted by the long and desperate War of the Spanish Succession, 1701-1713. The Duke of Anjou, grandson of Louis XIV, becomes King of Spain. Louis dies, 1715, not much mourned.

QUESTIONS

1. Why were the French people more willing to submit to the authority of Louis than the English people were to submit to the authority of James I?

2. How did Colbert increase the king's revenue? How did he try to improve the industry and commerce of France? Why was it to the interest of the business classes to be loyal to the king?

3. Why did Louis build the royal residence at Versailles? How did he manage to keep the nobles loyal and submissive?

4. Why did Louis quarrel with the Pope? What was the Declaration of the Liberties of the Gallican Church? Why did the French bishops have to serve two masters? Why was it to their interest to serve the king more faithfully than the Pope?

5. Who were the Huguenots, and what privileges had they under the Edict of Nantes? Why were they unpopular in France? Why did Louis think it necessary to "convert" them? When was the Edict of Nantes revoked, and what were the results of this action?

6. What were the four wars waged by Louis? What was his object in waging these wars? What did he gain by them? Were the French people better or worse off as a result of these wars? Why?

7. What is the importance of the reign of Louis XIV in the history of France? in the history of Europe?

SELECTED READINGS

Brief accounts. Hayes and Moon, *Modern History*, ch. vi. Robinson, *Western Europe*, ch. xxxi. J. H. Robinson and C. Beard, *Development of Modern Europe*, I, chs. i–ii. Hayes, *Modern Europe*, I, ch. vii. Schevill, *History of Europe*, ch. xiv. P. Van Dyke, *Story of France*, chs. xxxiii–xl. C. Seignobos, *Mediaeval and Modern Civilization*, chs. xxiii–xxiv, xxvi. C. Hugon, in *Social France in the Seventeenth Century*, gives an account of the manners and customs of the time. Voltaire's famous work, *The Age of Louis XIV*, contains chapters on literature and art in the time of Louis XIV.

Biography. C. J. Blennerhassett, *Louis XIV and Madame de Maintenon*. Madame Charles Vincens, *Louis XIV and la Grande Mademoiselle*. E. K. Sanders, *Bossuet*, and *Fénelon, His Friends and His Enemies*. B. Matthews, *Molière, His Life and His Times*. H. C. Puliga, *Madame de Sévigné*. L. Bertrand, *Louis XIV*. Madame Saint-René Taillandier, *Louis the Great and His Court*.

Historical Novels. The most famous of Alexandre Dumas's romances deal with the period of Richelieu, Mazarin, and Louis XIV: *The Three Musketeers; Twenty Years After; The Vicomte de Bragelonne*.

Sources. Robinson, *Readings in European History*, II, ch. xxxi, gives extracts from a variety of sources. See especially Bishop Bossuet's argument in favor of the divine right of kings, p. 273; Sir William Temple's account of France in 1671, p. 281; Madame de Sévigné's account of the king and his court at Chantilly, p. 283; Saint-Simon's portrait of the king, p. 285; the Revocation of the Edict of Nantes, p. 287. Some of these and other documents are in Robinson and Beard, *Readings in Modern European History*, I, chs. i, ii. Many people living at the time wrote letters and memoirs. Of these the most famous are Saint-Simon and Madame de Sévigné. See Saint-Simon, *Memoirs on the Reign of Louis XIV*, and G. Masson, *Selections from the Letters of Madame de Sévigné*. Warner's *Library of the World's Best Literature* gives extracts from Madame de Sévigné's letters, and from Bossuet's *Discourse on Universal History*.

Literature. Louis XIV encouraged literature and the arts. Some of the greatest of French writers lived at this time. Among the famous names are : Corneille, Racine, and Molière — writers of plays still given on the French stage; Fénelon, a bishop, who wrote on government, religion, and education; Pascal and Descartes, scientists and philosophers; La Bruyère, a satirist. See Molière's *Sganarelle*, in S. A. Eliot's *Little Theater Classics*, Vol. II; Fénelon, *The Adventures of Telemachus;* F. W. Warren, *Selections from Pascal.*

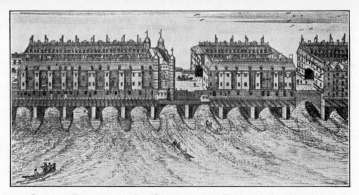

LONDON BRIDGE AND ITS SHOPS IN THE EIGHTEENTH CENTURY
From Stow's *Survey of the Cities of London and Westminster.*

CHAPTER V. HOW RUSSIA AND PRUSSIA APPEARED ON THE SCENE, AND HOW THE RIVALRIES OF THE GREAT POWERS INVOLVED THEM IN A THIRTY YEARS' WORLD WAR

A just cause of war is injury done us, and nothing else. GROTIUS

It is a permanent principle among princes to aggrandize themselves as much as they can. FREDERICK THE GREAT

What this chapter is about. In the preceding chapters we have been studying the internal history of France and England. We have seen how Louis XIV established an absolute monarchy in France, and how, as a result of the revolutions in England, a constitutional monarchy was established there. From the end of the English Revolution (1689) to the beginning of the French Revolution (1789) there were no further changes of great importance in the form of government of the European states. Since this is so, we may now turn to another aspect of modern civilization — that is, the external history of the European states, or the relations of European states to each other. This chapter will therefore have to do chiefly with the international rivalries and wars of the eighteenth century.

Some people say it is a waste of time to study about wars, because no good ever comes of war. But in studying history we have to

do with facts, whether good or bad ; and war has been a persistent
and stubborn fact in modern history.   It may well be that no
good, but only evil, has ever come of all these wars.   But if that
is so, then it is all the more necessary to learn something about
them in order to understand, if possible, why people keep on doing
something from which they get no good, but only evil.

One reason why wars have been so frequent in Europe is that
Europe is divided into independent sovereign states and it has
therefore seemed safer and more honorable for them to settle their
disputes by war than by arbitration.   Since each state has to look
out for its own interests, each state feels that it is necessary to be
as strong as possible in order to defend itself against aggression
or conquest by its rivals.   In the eighteenth century one way in
which it was thought a country could become more powerful was
by enlarging its territory and by forming alliances with other states.
Another way was by gaining control of colonies or trading privileges
in Asia or America, and thereby accumulating wealth.   The attempts of the European states to increase their power in either of
these ways naturally led to disputes which often resulted in war.
The wars of the eighteenth century were therefore chiefly of two
kinds : (1) territorial and dynastic — that is, wars fought in
Europe for the conquest of territory and for the establishment of the
ruling family of one country on the throne of another ; (2) maritime and commercial — that is, wars fought on the sea, or in Asia
or America, for the conquest of colonies, the control of trade, and
the increase of naval power.

In order to understand these wars and how they were related,
we must first learn something about the friendships and enmities
of the various European powers.

Why France and Spain were friends in the eighteenth century.
During most of the eighteenth century France and Spain were
friendly in time of peace and became allies in time of war.   Diplomats and statesmen must have found it odd to see these two countries hobnobbing together.   For two hundred years Spain had
been the ally of Austria, and France had regarded this powerful
Spanish-Austrian Habsburg combination as her natural and ever-
lasting enemy.   In the time of the Emperor Charles V (1519–

1556), in the Thirty Years' War (1618–1648), and in most of the wars of Louis XIV (1667–1697), France had fought against Spain and Austria. But in the eighteenth century Spain became a Bourbon power allied with France, instead of a Habsburg power allied with Austria.

This change came about as the result of the War of the Spanish Succession (1701–1713). The Peace of Utrecht (1713–1714) provided that Philip of Anjou, grandson of Louis XIV, should be king of Spain. Henceforth the Spanish kings, like the French kings, were descendants of Louis XIV, and the fact that both countries were ruled by the Bourbon family helped to bring them together. Besides, the Peace of Utrecht provided that the Spanish Netherlands and the Spanish provinces of Naples and Lombardy in Italy should be given to Austria. This also helped to bring France and Spain together, first because Spain no longer possessed territories on the frontier of France, and second because Spain wished to recover from Austria her lost provinces in Italy.

Thus France and Spain became friends in the eighteenth century because they were ruled by the same family, and because of a common hostility to Austria. But there was another thing which brought France and Spain together. They were both hostile to England.

Why France and Spain were hostile to England. The rivalry of Spain and England was no new thing. They had fought a long war in the time of Elizabeth and Philip II — a war which ended with the defeat of the famous Spanish Armada (1588). This war was partly due to differences in religion, but quite as much to commercial and colonial rivalry. In the eighteenth century the rivalry of Spain and England once more became important. Spain still possessed most of South America as well as valuable colonies in the West Indies. The trade with these Spanish possessions — especially the slave trade — was very profitable; but by the Treaty of Utrecht (1713) Spain had been forced to grant to the English South Sea Company the exclusive right to import slaves, as well as a certain amount of manufactured goods, into the Spanish colonies. By the same treaty Spain surrendered to England the famous rock of Gibraltar, and this requirement was a great humiliation to Spanish pride. Thus in the eighteenth century Spain was hostile to England because she hoped to recover Gibraltar and because she wished to deprive English merchants of their privilege of trading with her colonies.

The hostility of France and England was an old story also. In the fourteenth and fifteenth centuries they had fought the long Hundred Years' War. From 1688 to 1713 England was united with Austria and Holland in the desperate struggle to prevent Louis XIV from dominating Europe. In the eighteenth century England was still opposed to any extension of French territory in Europe, but the chief cause of hostility between the two countries was now colonial and commercial. Both countries had colonies in North America and in the West Indies. Both countries had established East India companies, and these two companies were now contending for the control of the East Indian trade.

France was therefore hostile to England for the same reason that Spain was. Both countries feared England as the leading colonial, commercial, and naval power of the world.

Thus it would have been clear to a careful observer of European politics about the year 1730 that, in case of a European war, France and Spain would be sure to unite against Austria on the Continent and against England in the colonies and on the sea. If these four states had been, as they were in the seventeenth century, the only great powers, you will easily see that the thing for Austria and England to do would be to unite against their common enemies, France and Spain. But the situation was now more complicated because, during the first half of the eighteenth century, two other countries began for the first time to play an important part in European affairs. These two countries were Prussia and Russia. We must now try to understand how Prussia and Russia came to meddle in the politics of the great powers, and who their friends and enemies were.

The rise of the Kingdom of Prussia, and the rivalry of Austria and Prussia for the leadership of Germany. In the eighteenth century the country which we think of as Germany and Austria was commonly known as " the Empire," or, to use the official title, " The Holy Roman Empire of the German States." The Empire

THE GREEN TREE INN, 1767, ON THE ISER RIVER, NEAR MUNICH

From a drawing by J. Stephan.   On the river are rafts transporting people and
merchandise.   In front of the inn a number of people are having refreshments.

was then divided up into a vast number of states or principalities,
the great majority of which were too small to be of any political
importance.   Besides Austria and Prussia, the most important
states were perhaps the following: Bavaria, Württemberg, Baden,
the Palatinate, Saxony, Hanover, Brandenburg; the city states
of Lübeck, Bremen, and Hamburg; and the bishoprics of Köln
(Cologne), Trier (Treves), and Mainz, which were called " ecclesiastical states " because the Catholic bishop was in each case also
the prince or ruler.   The rulers of nine of the most important
states were called " electors," because they elected the emperor.
Since the fifteenth century the electors had always chosen the
ruler of Austria to be emperor.

Thus all of the German states, including Austria, and with the
ruler of Austria as emperor, made up the Empire.   Now the actual
power of the emperor, outside Austria, was very slight indeed.   In
the sixteenth century the Emperor Charles V had tried to subjugate
the German princes but had failed to do so.   During the Thirty

Years' War the Emperor Ferdinand had tried it again, but he had failed even more completely. By the Treaty of Westphalia, which ended that war, the German princes were allowed to govern their little states very much as they liked. Henceforth they could coin money, make alliances with foreign powers, wage war (except against the emperor), and do most of the things which independent states could do. In fact the famous old Holy Roman Empire was now, as a political power, practically dead. It was already, as Voltaire in the eighteenth century wittily said of it, " neither Holy, nor Roman, nor an Empire."

Now that the German princes were virtually independent, the way was open for any one of them to build up another great state in Germany; and since the rulers of Austria had failed to keep the old Empire alive, perhaps some day this new German power might unite all Germany in a new empire. This was actually done by the rulers of Brandenburg, who first established the Kingdom of Prussia, then greatly enlarged it, and at last, in the time of Bismarck, founded the new German Empire which played so important a part in the Great War.

In 1648 the ruler of Brandenburg was Frederick William Hohenzollern, known as the Great Elector. At that time the Great Elector possessed territories in three different places: (1) the duchies of Brandenburg and Pomerania around Berlin; (2) the Duchy of East Prussia, separated from Brandenburg-Pomerania by the Polish territory of West Prussia; and (3) far to the west, near the Rhine river, the three little duchies of Cleves, Mark, and Ravensburg. These widely scattered possessions were the original territories of the Kingdom of Prussia; and the Great Elector Frederick William was the ancestor of that William II, King of Prussia and German kaiser, who is now living in exile in Holland.

Brandenburg was transformed into the Kingdom of Prussia during the period from 1648 to 1740. The Great Elector Frederick William (1640-1688) greatly strengthened the government by reducing the nobles to subjection and taking away the privileges of the local " estates " or assemblies. The Elector Frederick (1688-1713), in return for aiding the emperor in the War of the Spanish Succession, was permitted to take the title of King of

Prussia. From 1713, therefore, the rulers of Brandenburg-Prussia were electors of Brandenburg in the Empire and kings of Prussia.

But the real founder of Prussia was Frederick William I (1713–1740). He was a harsh old miser. When he became king he dismissed all the useless courtiers and flunkies of his court and forced his family to live in a simple and frugal way. He worked hard himself from morning till night and saw to it that everyone around him did the same. Sometimes, when the business of government did not require his attention, he wandered about the streets of Berlin, poking his royal nose into the kitchens of simple citizens in order to see whether the *hausfrau* was wasting food by giving her husband any needless luxuries. But this eccentric man was an able king, and he had one ambition. He wished his people to be thrifty and prosperous, so that he could raise money enough to equip a large army and make Prussia something more than a second-rate state. In this he largely succeeded. In the course of his reign he established a harsh but efficient government and built up an excellent army of about 80,000 men. He was too frugal, and perhaps too wise, ever to go to war. But he made Prussia respected, and in 1740 he was succeeded by his son, Frederick II, known as Frederick the Great, who fought two long wars, greatly increased the territory of his kingdom, and completed the task of making Prussia one of the great European powers (see pp. 116, 126).

The rise of Prussia entirely changed the situation in Germany. Hitherto there had been only one great power in Germany, and that was Austria. The ruler of Austria was, as we have seen, emperor in Germany, and as emperor he had very little political authority over the German princes. But the emperor still had much political *influence* in Germany, because the German princes, although they refused to be ruled by the emperor, commonly looked to him for protection against the intervention of any foreign power, such as France. But now there were two great powers in Germany — Austria and Prussia: two powers to which the small states could look for leadership and protection. Northern Germany was mainly Protestant in religion, and partly for this reason the states of northern Germany were inclined to look to Prussia as the leader. But southern Germany was mainly Catholic, and partly for this reason the states of southern Germany were inclined to look to Austria as the leader. This being the case, which of these two great powers would become the dominant power in Germany — Austria or Prussia? From 1740 to 1871 the great fact in the political history of Germany is this struggle between Austria and Prussia for the domination of Germany — a struggle which lasted till 1871, when the new German Empire, under the leadership of Prussia, was proclaimed at the close of the Franco-Prussian War (see p. 454).

Meantime, when Austria and Prussia began this struggle for leadership in Germany, they found themselves facing a new power in eastern Europe. This new power was Russia. Would Russia become the enemy of Austria? or of Prussia? or of both?

How Peter the Great made Russia a great power, so that it could meddle in the affairs of Europe. Before the eighteenth century no one thought of Russia as a European power. Her territory touched neither the Black Sea nor the Baltic, and her western frontier was four hundred miles farther east than it was in 1914. The Russian people were Christians, but they belonged to the Eastern Greek Church instead of to the Western Roman Catholic Church; and the Tartar conquest of the thirteenth century had left them half Oriental in their manners and customs. Besides, their kings or tsars had never been able to establish a strong government or an effective army; and so, being scarcely able to govern their own immense country, they were in no position to meddle in the affairs of any other.

Peter I (1672–1725) wished to change all this. He envied wealthy countries like Holland and England, and masterful kings like Louis XIV, who were able to make themselves obeyed at home and feared in Europe. He believed that Russia would never be the equal of these Western countries until she had the same institutions and customs which they had. In 1697–1698 Peter therefore visited Germany, Holland, and England in order to see with his own eyes how they managed things in these countries. He worked for a time as a laborer in the Dutch shipyards in order to learn shipbuilding; he stood in the gallery of the English House of Com-

PETER THE GREAT (1672–1725)

Peter was about thirty-five years old when this portrait was made, by J.
Kupetzky.   He was nearly six feet nine inches tall and of great strength.   At
times he worked sixteen hours a day in his shipyards.

mons, listening to the debates and trying to understand that curious
method of government; and everywhere he inquired into the progress of the arts and sciences, which he hoped to introduce into
Russia.

   Returning home, Peter gave the rest of his life to " Westernizing "
Russia.   He reorganized the government, modeling it upon that

of Louis XIV. He established the famous " Holy Synod " (council),
through which he hoped to control the powerful Russian church.
He brought German and Swedish military officers to Russia, and
with their help built up a large army trained to fight according to
Western methods. He reformed the government of the Russian
cities and tried to make them centers of industry like the Dutch
and German cities. He even ordered the men to shave their beards,
and the women to change the style of their dresses, so that the Russians would have the same customs as the people of the Western
countries. Wishing to have a port on the Baltic — a " window,"
as he said, through which Russia could look out upon the Western
world — Peter picked a quarrel with Sweden, and after a long war
with the famous and eccentric Charles XII he conquered the territory around the fine Gulf of Finland. There he established a new
city, called Peter's City or St. Petersburg (later Petrograd, and
now Leningrad), which he made the capital of his kingdom.

All these things Peter did so that Russia might be a prosperous,
well-governed country, capable of defending and promoting its
interests effectively by taking part in the affairs of western Europe.
Since Peter succeeded fairly well in doing this, he is called Peter
the Great.

From the time of Peter, Russia was, therefore, one of the six
" great powers " of Europe — that is, she was a country which
the other great powers had to reckon with in diplomacy and war.
What countries would Russia be likely to come into conflict with?
Naturally those that were nearest to her. Three countries touched
the European frontier of Russia: Turkey, Sweden, and Poland.
In the region of the Black Sea, Russia's chief enemy was therefore
Turkey; in the region of the Baltic, Sweden. In the region of
central Europe, the chief enemy of Russia would have been Poland,
if Poland had been strong enough to be an enemy. But Poland,
although an immense country, was so weak that it was merely a
prey for its powerful neighbors, Russia, Austria, and Prussia
(see p. 138). In central Europe the two chief rivals of Russia were
therefore Austria and Prussia.

**The rivalries of the great powers finally involve them in a new
" Thirty Years' War."** We have now discovered the principal

rivalries of the six great powers of Europe: (1) the rivalry of Austria and Spain in Italy; (2) the conflict of England with Spain and France in North America, in India, and on the sea; (3) the conflict of Austria and Prussia in Germany; and (4) the rivalry of Russia, Austria, and Prussia for the control of Poland.

These various conflicts of " interests," whether real or imaginary, at last involved the great powers in a series of three wars, following one upon the other in rapid succession; (1) the War of the Polish Succession, 1733–1739; (2) the War of the Austrian Succession, 1740–1748; (3) the Seven Years' War, 1756–1763. The first of these wars was fought only in Europe; but the last two were fought, not only in Europe, but in America and in India as well. In America the War of the Austrian Succession goes by the name of King George's War (1744–1748) and the Seven Years' War is called the French and Indian War (1754–1763).

Now it is important to keep in mind that all of these wars, although they have different names, were closely related. They were all parts of the same great struggle, which lasted, with brief intervals of peace, for exactly thirty years, from 1733 to 1763. In Europe, this was a struggle of France, Spain, Austria, Prussia, and Russia for the conquest of territory. In America, in India, and in the West Indies it was a struggle between England, France, and Spain for colonies, trade, and naval power. We may therefore rightly think of this great struggle as the " Thirty Years' World War " of the eighteenth century.[1]

The beginning of the Thirty Years' World War: The War of the Polish Succession, 1733–1739. In 1733 the King of Poland died, and all the kings and diplomats wondered whom the Polish diet (parliament) would elect as his successor. The diet might easily have chosen a king without any trouble if the other states had been content not to meddle. But Louis XV of France had married the daughter of a Polish prince, Stanislas; and he thought

---

[1] It should, however, be remembered that the struggle between France and England over colonial and commercial advantages in North America and India was not confined to this period. It began at least as early as the War of the Spanish Succession (1701–1713), and was continued as late as the Napoleonic wars which ended in 1815. This struggle between France and England in the eighteenth century is often called the " Second Hundred Years' War."

Metropolitan Museum

AN EIGHTEENTH CENTURY DYEING ESTABLISHMENT

An early advertisement, showing a press by means of which a pattern was stamped on the cloth. Signs like this were common in the American colonies also.

that if Stanislas became king, France would have Poland as an ally against her old enemy Austria. By distributing a good deal of money where it would do most good, Louis managed to get the diet to elect Stanislas, who was proclaimed King of Poland.

This did not suit the rulers of Russia and Austria, who wanted Augustus of Saxony to be King of Poland, so that Poland would be friendly to them instead of to France. They therefore sent an army into Poland, drove Stanislas out, and forced the diet to choose Augustus king (Augustus III). Since Louis could not easily send any army across Germany to fight for Stanislas in Poland, he decided to get revenge by invading and conquering Belgium, which belonged to Austria, and Lorraine, which was part of Germany. In this war France was joined by Spain, whose king thought the time had now come to recover the former Spanish provinces in Italy; and also by the Duke of Savoy, who hoped to annex to his duchy some of the Austrian territory in northern Italy.

The War of the Polish Succession was therefore fought, not in Poland, but in Belgium, in Lorraine, in Lombardy, and in Naples and Sicily. It began over the Polish succession, but ended in an attempt to partition Austria. Most of the fighting was over by 1735, but the preliminaries of peace were not signed till 1736 (*Treaty of Vienna*). By this treaty it was agreed: (1) that Augustus should be King of Poland; (2) that Austria should give up Naples and that the Spanish prince, Don Carlos, should be King of Naples and Sicily; and (3) that after a certain time Austria should have the Duchy of Tuscany in Italy in exchange for Lorraine, which should be annexed to France.

This war had given the European states a taste of Austria. In the next war they tried to devour her altogether.

The Thirty Years' World War continued: The War of the Austrian Succession, 1740–1748. The War of the Austrian Succession is usually said to have begun in 1740, when Frederick the Great invaded Silesia (see p. 120). But at that time two powers, England and Spain, were already at war. For a long time Spain had complained that English merchants were smuggling goods into the Spanish colonies contrary to the terms of the Peace of

Utrecht (1713–1714). This was true; but it was also true that Spanish privateers, pretending to be official coast guards, often illegally captured English ships and carried off their cargoes. In one of these conflicts an Englishman named Jenkins had one of his ears cut off. For eight years Englishmen were never allowed to forget that the Spaniards had cut off Jenkins' ear. On the other hand, the Spanish people were told that on one occasion an English captain had compelled a Spanish noble to cut off and devour his own nose. After many years of national grievances such as these, the honor of both countries was thought to be at stake, and in 1739 the English government declared war on Spain. This war is known as the War of Jenkins' Ear.

How the War of Jenkins' Ear might have ended we shall unfortunately never know, for it was soon submerged and lost in the War of the Austrian Succession. This was largely due to the appearance on the scene of one of the greatest kings and military leaders of the century — Frederick II, the Great (reigned 1740–1786).

Frederick was a thin, dried-up looking man, with cold eyes and a long sharp nose, as hard as iron both in body and mind. He seems to have been always old. Perhaps this was because he had a hard time of it, living under the harsh and cruel discipline of his father, old Frederick William. Frederick William thought the son of a king should be interested only in affairs of government, and especially in the army. But young Frederick cared nothing for these things — apparently. He occupied himself with music and literature. Like most of the other people of his time, he admired the French writers and thought them the only literary models. He therefore learned French — not very well, but well enough to write stilted verse in that language. He admired and imitated Voltaire, the famous French writer, and professed to think the Germans mere barbarians in things artistic and intellectual. All this infuriated Frederick William, who regarded his good Germans as the salt of the earth and cared for nothing but military and governmental affairs. Father and son quarreled furiously, and Frederick was so harshly treated that he once tried to escape. He was caught, and barely missed being shot for treason.

Old Frederick William would have been surprised and delighted

FREDERICK THE GREAT (1712-1786)

From a portrait by Menzel.   As a young man Frederick dressed in fine clothes,
as in the illustration on page 172; later he cared little about finery and to save
money kept his clothes until they wore out.   Frederick once said, "I am not the
man to sacrifice the interests of Prussia to those of the other powers."

to know that his frivolous and poetic son was to become a far abler
king than he himself, and one of the world's great generals.   As
soon as he became king, in 1740, Frederick gave his best energies
to the business of government.   He enlarged Prussia by the conquest of Silesia (1748) and by the annexation of West Prussia
(1772).   He strengthened the army and made it the best fighting

machine of Europe. He reclaimed waste lands, built canals, and improved the industries of his country, especially by developing the manufacture of woolens and linen. He proclaimed religious toleration, abolished torture as a means of punishment, and made reforms in the administration of justice. Before he died, in 1786, Frederick had made Prussia one of the great powers and had acquired for himself the reputation of being a great general, a great patriot, a great cynic, and a great humanitarian.

MAKING HATS, EIGHTEENTH CENTURY
An advertisement by H. Cutter, "Hat Maker."

Cynic and humanitarian — it seems a curious combination. But great characters do not easily lend themselves to the ordinary labels. Frederick was cynical because he had little faith in the capacity or virtues of mankind; and humane because, knowing the frailties of men, he did not expect too much of them. One day someone expounded to him the doctrine of Rousseau that " men are naturally good." Frederick replied, " Ah, my dear sir, you don't know the miserable human race as I do." Without vanity, and conscious of his strength, he could afford to ignore opposition and laugh at criticism. It is said that once, riding on horseback along the streets of Berlin, he saw a paper posted high up on a wall. Riding up to look at it, he read a scurrilous attack on himself. Calling an attendant, he said, " This is amusing, but it is too high up; put it lower down so that people on foot can read it." Then he rode on, chuckling no doubt. One of his first acts, upon becoming king, was the invasion and conquest of the Austrian province of Silesia. Learned men tried to prove from historical documents that Frederick had a legal claim to Silesia. But Frederick cared nothing for that. He said, " I take what I want; there will always be plenty of professors to justify what I do."

Such was the great Frederick — hard as iron, keen as a razor's edge, washed free of vanity and sentimentalism, indifferent, tolerant usually, brutal on occasion, scurrilous, witty, cynical. His long and successful reign began in 1740, and opened with the War of the Austrian Succession.

Frederick's father, old Frederick William, had built up an excellent army of about 80,000 men (see p. 110). The opportunity for the young Frederick to use this army came almost at once, in October, 1740, when Charles VI, ruler of Austria and of the Empire, died without leaving any son to succeed him. This raised the famous question of the Austrian succession. Charles VI, foreseeing this difficulty, had for many years been trying to get all of the European states to agree that when he died his daughter, Maria Theresa, should succeed him as ruler of Austria and as empress. All of the states of Europe had agreed to this, with one important exception. That exception was Bavaria; and when the Emperor Charles VI died, the Elector of Bavaria, who was very distantly related to the old emperor, claimed that he was the rightful heir of the Austrian government.

This was Frederick's opportunity. Since the Austrian succession was in dispute, it seemed possible that France and Spain might side with the Elector of Bavaria in the hope of getting some of the Austrian possessions for themselves. If there was to be a struggle for Austrian territory, Frederick wanted his share, and he decided to get his share first. Without any warning he therefore invaded the rich Austrian province of Silesia, which bordered on Brandenburg. He then notified Maria Theresa that if she would overlook this robbery and give him Silesia, without making any trouble about it, he would aid her in defending the rest of her possessions against the Elector of Bavaria. When Maria Theresa indignantly refused this offer, Frederick allied himself with Bavaria, and invited France and Spain to come into the war and take whatever other possessions of Austria they might wish or could get. After some

SOLDIERS IN CAMP, EIGHTEENTH CENTURY

From a drawing by G. P. Rugendas.   In the foreground is a cannon, and beside
it cannon balls and a barrel of powder.

hesitation both countries, together with the King of Sardinia, joined
Frederick and Bavaria in the war for the partition of Austria.
England, being already at war with Spain, naturally decided to join
Austria.

Thus the war was between England and Austria on the one side
and Prussia, France, Spain, Sardinia, and Bavaria on the other.   In
Europe it was fought in Belgium, Germany, and northern Italy for
the dismemberment of Austria; in America and India it was a
struggle for colonies, trade, and naval power.   The fighting dragged
on till 1745, but peace was not finally made till 1748 (*Peace of
Aix-la-Chapelle*).   This treaty provided: (1) that Maria Theresa
should be recognized as ruler of Austria, but that she should give
up Silesia to Frederick, Parma to Spain, and part of Lombardy to
Sardinia; (2) that all other conquests on both sides should be
restored.

The war and the peace really settled nothing.   Maria Theresa
was determined to recover Silesia at the first opportunity, and the
rivalry of Spain, France, and England in the colonies was just as

keen as ever. The Peace of Aix-la-Chapelle (Aachen) was really only a truce. Everyone believed that the war would soon be renewed. Therefore everyone began to prepare for this new war, and sure enough it came within a few years.

The Thirty Years' World War continued: The Seven Years' War, 1756–1763. 1. *How the war began in America, 1754.* The Seven Years' War really began in America two years before it began in Europe. In 1754 the French built a fort, which they called Fort Duquesne, on the upper Ohio River, where Pittsburgh now stands. No sooner was it built than the Governor of Virginia sent Colonel George Washington with a small force to capture the fort and drive the French out. This was the beginning of what is called the French and Indian War. Why was the possession of this fort of such vast importance as to involve France and England in a long and desperate war? To answer this question we must get a clear idea of where the French were located in America, and what they were doing there.

In the seventeenth and eighteenth centuries the French had established forts and trading posts along the St. Lawrence and the Great Lakes at Quebec, Montreal, Niagara, Detroit, and Sault Sainte Marie; on the Mississippi at New Orleans and near Saint Louis; and on the Maumee at Vincennes. These forts and trading posts were of value chiefly on account of the fur trade with the Indians. The soldiers overawed the Indians, the missionaries converted them, and the invaders gave them cheap colored cloth, bracelets, glass beads, and brandy. In exchange the Indians, especially when they were drunk, readily gave up their valuable furs, which the traders then sold in France for high prices. But before 1754 the French had had no trading posts on the Ohio River. This river they now determined to occupy, partly because it was the most direct route from their forts on the Mississippi to their forts on the St. Lawrence, and partly because they would thereby be able to control the Indian trade of all this middle-western country. This was why they built Fort Duquesne in 1754.

The English were determined not to allow the French to control the Ohio River because they also were interested in the middle-western country. English traders, with glass beads and rum, were

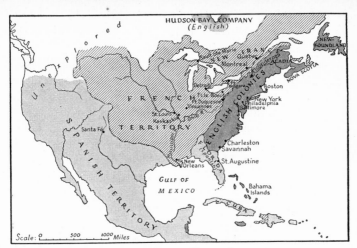

EUROPEAN POSSESSIONS IN NORTH AMERICA, 1750

already carrying on a profitable trade with the Indians along the
Ohio River. People from Virginia and Pennsylvania were crossing the mountains and taking up farms in what is now the state
of Ohio. Certain far-sighted men, like George Washington and
Benjamin Franklin, were interested in obtaining land in this region
in order to sell it at a profit; and for this purpose a number of
Englishmen and Virginians had organized the Ohio Company, which
had obtained from the English government a grant of 500,000 acres
of land near the present city of Cincinnati. If the French were
permitted to hold Fort Duquesne, they would soon establish other
forts farther down the river, overawe the Indians, and presently
all this rich country would be lost to the English.

Thus the French and Indian War began as a struggle for the
control of the Ohio Valley. We shall see presently how this struggle
ended; but first we must see how the war in America involved
all the European powers in the Seven Years' War in Europe.

2. *How England and France changed partners.* Now that they
were at war in America, France and England each sought allies
against the other, with the result that England obtained the assistance of her former enemy Prussia, while France obtained the assist-

ance of her former enemy Austria. This curious change of partners is called the Diplomatic Revolution, or the Reversal of
Alliance. Let us see how it came about.

When the war broke out in America the English king, George II,
was afraid France would attack his Duchy of Hanover in Germany. Since Austria had been the ally of England in the last war,
the English government now asked Maria Theresa to renew the
alliance, so that England could have her aid in defending Hanover
against France. But Maria Theresa cared very little whether
the English king kept Hanover or lost it. Her quarrel was not
with France, but with Frederick, who had taken Silesia in the last
war. Her one ambition was to recover Silesia; and since England,
as she thought, had given her very little help in the last war, she
was unwilling to renew the alliance for the coming war. Failing
to obtain the aid of Austria, England turned to Prussia and in
1756 signed the Treaty of Westminster with Frederick the Great,
by which the two powers agreed that, in case the war spread to
Germany, each would help defend the other's possessions.

The French king, Louis XV, was very indignant when he learned
that Frederick had made a treaty with England. Frederick had
been the ally of France in the last war, and Louis had expected
him to renew this alliance for the new war. Maria Theresa had
already asked Louis to make a treaty of alliance with her, but
Louis had refused to do so. It seemed contrary to all the rules of
the game that these ancient enemies should become friends overnight. But now that Frederick had apparently deserted France,
Louis felt that there was nothing left but to accept the offer of
Maria Theresa. Accordingly, in 1756–1757, these old and tried
enemies, France and Austria, signed a defensive and offensive
alliance (*First and Second Treaties of Versailles*).

Thus England and France changed partners for the new war
dance. It was now England and Prussia against France and
Austria. France and Austria were soon joined by Russia — whose
tsarina, Elizabeth, feared and hated Frederick — and also by
some of the small German states, notably Bavaria and Saxony.
This war was fought, as Voltaire said, " in the four quarters of the
globe " — in the East and West Indies, on the sea, in North

A BOOKSELLER'S ADVERTISEMENT, EIGHTEENTH CENTURY

The paper mill at the top is evidently run by water power. Among the books shown is one labeled "Spectators." At the left "Lloyd's Evening Post" is advertised.

America, and in Europe. In the last war the fighting in Europe had been carried on by a combination of powers who aimed to dispossess Maria Theresa and partition her empire. In the Seven Years' War the fighting was carried on by a combination of powers who aimed to dispossess Frederick the Great and partition his kingdom. Let us see how Frederick managed to survive this ordeal.

3. *How Prussia was saved from destruction by the genius of Frederick, the gold of England, and the death of Tsarina Elizabeth.* Frederick's position was a dangerous one. There he was in his little kingdom, with an army of no more than a hundred thousand men, surrounded on all sides by powerful enemies, each one with an army larger than his. On the east were the Russians, who could easily invade East Prussia at any time. On the south were the Austrians, ready to march directly into the province of Silesia. On the west were the French, who could strike at Brandenburg and Berlin from Saxony. Frederick was in a ring of fire; and more often than not during the long war his chances of escaping destruction seemed slight indeed.

One of the things that saved him was his own sheer genius and dogged persistence. Even these qualities would not have helped much if his enemies had been good fighters. Fortunately for Frederick, his enemies were slow to strike, they did not all strike at the same time, and when they won important victories they often foolishly failed to follow them up. In 1757 Frederick took effective advantage of these weaknesses. The Russians had gone home for the winter. One Austrian army held Silesia, while a combined French and Austrian army occupied Saxony. On November 5, Frederick suddenly attacked the latter army at Rossbach and won a crushing victory, dispersing the Austrian army and forcing the French army back to the Rhine. Then he turned to the east, and on the 5th of December defeated the second Austrian army at Leuthen and drove them out of Silesia.

These victories gave Frederick time to get his breath. But Prussia was neither a large nor a rich country, and without more money he could not go on fighting very long. Very fortunately for him, about this time the famous William Pitt, afterwards Earl of Chatham, became one of the King of England's most influential

National Portrait Gallery, London

WILLIAM PITT, EARL OF CHATHAM (1708–1778)

Pitt had a commission in the cavalry, but turned to politics in 1735. His eloquence won for him the name "The Great Commoner." When paymaster, his honesty became proverbial; he left the position with no more money than he had before. In 1756 he became prime minister.

ministers. Up to this time England had made little headway against the French in the colonies; and Pitt thought that if Frederick lost the war in Germany, the French would be free to devote all their energies to the war with England, and so England might lose the war in America. Pitt wished to give Frederick more effective aid, so that France would be kept busy in Europe. He therefore made a new treaty with Frederick, by which England agreed to maintain an army of 50,000 men in Germany, and to pay Fred-

BRITISH FAMILY GROUP

This painting by Hogarth shows a group of well-to-do people, typical of English society in the second half of the eighteenth century.   A butler is pouring tea.

erick about $3,250,000 each year.   With this aid Frederick was able to hold his own during the next four years.

But in 1761 the English aid was withdrawn.   The English king, George III, thinking that England had won the war against the French in America, desired to make peace.   He forced Pitt to resign and refused to make any further payments of money to Frederick, who was thus left to fight single-handed against France, Austria, and Russia.   His most dangerous enemy was Russia. Two years before, the Russian army had defeated Frederick decisively at Kunersdorf and might have ended the war by following up this victory.   What if the Russians should come again?   But once more fortune favored Frederick.   In 1762 the Tsarina Elizabeth died.   Her successor, Peter III, believing that the real enemy of Russia was Austria, had always opposed the war against Prussia. As soon as he became tsar he therefore abandoned Austria and sent an army to fight on the side of Frederick.   From this time on, Frederick had no difficulty in defending Prussia or even in keeping the disputed province of Silesia.

Thus the chief result of the war in Europe was that Prussia, instead of being destroyed, was permitted to become one of the great European powers. We must now turn to the war in America and India and see how England gained the upper hand there.

4. *How the English won an empire in America.* Colonel George Washington, coming up from Virginia in 1754 to drive the French out of Fort Duquesne, was defeated; and the next year (1755) the English general, Braddock, was defeated even more disastrously, largely because the British troops were not used to the Indian methods of fighting. The redcoats, moving in solid formation, were an easy mark for the redskins skulking in the woods. General Braddock was killed; his army was nearly wiped out; and the Indian tribes, judging from this easy victory that the English could not fight, nearly all sided with the French.

During the first four years the French and their Indian allies had the best of the fighting. But in 1758 the fortunes of war began to change. This was largely due to the great minister William Pitt, who inspired both the British and the colonists with the determination to win. Pitt was not content merely to win victories against the French; his aim was nothing less than to drive them out of America altogether. For this purpose a British fleet and a large British army were sent over to aid the colonial troops.

The great object was the capture of Quebec, the capital of French Canada. Standing high on the cliffs above the St. Lawrence River, it seemed almost impregnable. Yet it might be taken if two armies could attack it at once from two sides. Two expeditions were therefore planned. One army, under General Amherst, moved north by way of the Hudson and Lake Champlain; a second, under General Wolfe, was carried by the fleet up the St. Lawrence. If these two armies could strike at Quebec at the same time, it was thought there might be a chance of success.

But General Amherst was not able to reach Quebec as soon as he was expected to. He took Ticonderoga from the French, but it was no easy task to lead an army through the wooded country of northern New York, and General Wolfe had to do the best he could alone. He could really do nothing from the river, because the city and fort were so high above it on the bluffs. How could he get his army up the steep bank in face of a strong French army?

Photo Hachette

BALING AND SHIPPING RAW COTTON FROM THE COLONIES

From an engraving in *L'Encyclopédie*. Negroes are picking cotton (the artist
thought it grew on trees!), cleaning it, and packing it in bags to be carried by
ship to Europe. The colonies were not permitted to manufacture cloth.

It might seem impossible. But after long delays and many failures, Wolfe finally outwitted the French general, Montcalm, and
one fine morning the French were astounded to look out and see
the British army drawn up on the Plains of Abraham. On September 13 the French army was defeated, and the chief stronghold
of the French in America was occupied by the English.

The capture of Quebec was the decisive event of the war. Fort
Niagara had already been taken by General Forbes, and a year
later, with the capture of Montreal, the English were masters of
Canada. In 1761, when it was too late, Spain entered the war
on the side of France, in the hope that the combined navies of
France and Spain might drive the English out of the West Indies,
or at least defend their own colonies there. But they were hopelessly defeated. Within another year England had conquered, not
only many French colonies, but the Spanish island of Cuba as well.

5. *How the English became masters of India.* In the Seven
Years' War the English gained the upper hand in India as well as

in America. Since this was an important event in modern history, we must try to understand just what the French and English were doing in India.

For a long time before the war the French East India Company and the English East India Company had been competing for the profitable Indian trade. Both companies had settlements on the western and the eastern coasts of India. The principal French settlement was Pondicherry, not far from the English settlement at Madras; the principal English settlement was Calcutta, not far from the French settlement of Chandernagore. The inland country round these settlements was governed by native Indian princes (nabobs, rajahs, etc.) who were continually fighting each other, and who were sometimes friends and sometimes enemies of the French and English settlements. Now of course it made a great deal of difference to the trading companies whether the native princes were friendly or not. Unless they could establish friendly relations with the natives, they could not trade with them, and their settlements were in danger of being wiped out. Therefore each company was always trying to establish, with one or more native princes, alliances that would be advantageous to it and dangerous to its rival company. One way to win the friendship of a native prince was to aid him in his wars with other native princes. The native princes had large armies, but their methods of fighting were crude, while the English and French companies had small forces of Europeans and natives trained to fight in the European way. A native prince who could get one of these trained forces to fight for him could usually defeat his enemy, and for such aid the native prince was willing to pay well, by giving the trading company either privileges, or gold and jewels, or both. This meddling in native wars and politics was a dangerous business, but if successful it was a profitable business — at least for the officers of the trading companies. It was a Frenchman, Dupleix, who first learned to play this game effectively. But later an Englishman, Robert Clive, learned to play it even more successfully.

Let us see how Clive played this game in Bengal during the Seven Years' War. The Nabob of Bengal at that time was a certain Surajah Dowlah, who was hostile to the English at Calcutta, and

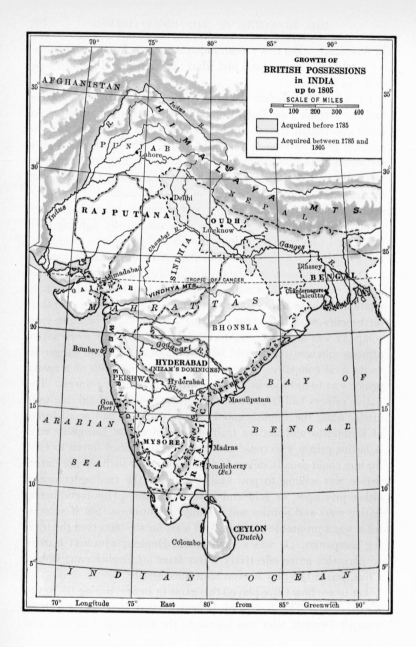

GROWTH OF
**BRITISH POSSESSIONS
in INDIA
up to 1805**
SCALE OF MILES

0   100   200   300   400

☐ Acquired before 1785

☐ Acquired between 1785 and
1805

AFGHANISTAN

HIMALAYA

PUNJAB
Lahore

Indus R.

RAJPUTANA

Delhi

OUDH
Lucknow

NEPAL

MTS.

SINDHIA

Chambal R.

Ganges

Ahmadabad

GAIKWAR

TROPIC OF CANCER

VINDHYA MTS.

BENGAL

Plassey

Chandernagore
Calcutta

MAHRATTAS

BHONSLA

Godavari R.

Bombay

WESTERN GHATS

PEISHWA

HYDERABAD
(NIZAM'S DOMINIONS)

Hyderabad

Kistna R.

NORTHERN CIRCARS

BAY   OF

Goa
(Port.)

ARABIAN

SEA

MYSORE

EASTERN GHATS

CARNATIC

Masulipatam

BENGAL

Madras

Pondicherry
(Fr.)

CEYLON
(Dutch)

Colombo

INDIAN   OCEAN

70° Longitude   75°   East   80°   from   85°   Greenwich   90°

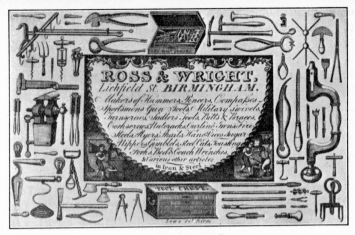

TOOL CHESTS AND THEIR CONTENTS

Can you think of any modern tools not shown among these Birmingham tools
used in the eighteenth century?

if he joined the French the English company would almost surely
be driven out of the province. Clive's little army was not strong
enough to defeat the army of the nabob, and so he entered into a
conspiracy to dethrone him.

One of the generals in Surajah Dowlah's army was a noble by the
name of Mir Jaffir who was quite willing to become nabob himself.
With Mir Jaffir, Clive therefore entered into a written agreement
to the effect that if Mir Jaffir and his troops would desert Surajah
Dowlah, Clive would help him to become Nabob of Bengal. In
return, Mir Jaffir promised that when he became nabob he would
grant certain lands to the company, and certain sums of money to
the officers. Clive's share was about $2,000,000. The treachery
of Mir Jaffir enabled Clive to defeat Surajah Dowlah at the Battle
of Plassey (1757). Surajah Dowlah was killed, Mir Jaffir became
nabob, and the English East India Company thus gained the upper
hand in all of this rich country of Bengal.

Thus you can see that the struggle in India was something more
than a mere struggle for trade. Each company wished not only
to control the trade of India, but to exploit the immense wealth

of the country by gaining a predominant political influence among the native princes. When the war ended, the French, having been defeated in America and Europe as well as in India, were forced to agree to the English terms. These terms were that the French East India Company, although allowed to retain five trading posts in India, should no longer make treaties with the native princes or meddle in any way with native wars or politics. This gave the English company the upper hand in trade and, what was far more important, left it free to become the master of India by extending its political influence among the native princes.

6. *The Seven Years' War ended by the Peace of Paris, 1763.* The war was ended by the Treaty of Hubertsburg and the Treaty of Paris (February, 1763), which together we may call the Peace of Paris. By the Treaty of Hubertsburg, between Frederick the Great and his enemies — Austria, Saxony, and France — it was agreed that Frederick should keep all of his possessions, including the province of Silesia. The war had lasted seven years, thousands of men had perished, a vast extent of country had been ravaged, and yet " not a hamlet had changed its ruler."

The result was far different in respect to the Treaty of Paris, between England, France, and Spain. By this treaty: (1) France surrendered to England all of her possessions in North America east of the Mississippi (except New Orleans) and also her West Indian islands of Grenada, Tobago, Dominica, and St. Vincent; (2) Spain surrendered Florida to England, in exchange for which England restored Cuba; (3) France gave to Spain, as compensation for the loss of Florida, New Orleans and all of the French possessions west of the Mississippi River; (4) in India the French East India Company retained five trading posts but was no longer permitted to take part in the politics and wars of the native princes.

Like all great events, the Thirty Years' World War of the eighteenth century had certain immediate results which everyone at the time could easily see. The immediate results of chief importance were two. In the first place, the war settled the fate of Prussia. Instead of being destroyed, as it might have been, Prussia became one of the six great powers of Europe. In the second place, by destroying the power of France in America and India, the war

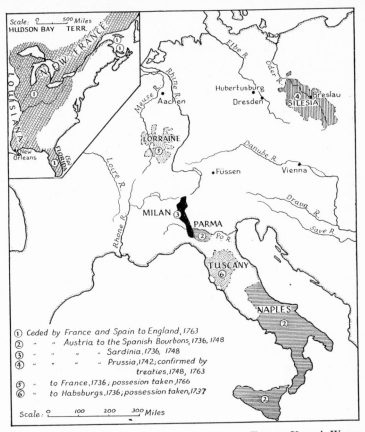

Scale: 0 ——— 500 Miles
HUDSON BAY   TERR.
NEW FRANCE
LOUISIANA
New Orleans
FLORIDA

Elbe R.
Oder R.
Hubertusburg
Dresden
SILESIA Breslau
Rhine R.
Meuse
Aachen
LORRAINE
⑤
Danube R.
•Füssen   Vienna
Loire R.
Rhone R.
MILAN ③
PARMA
② Po R.
Drava R.
Save R.
TUSCANY
⑥
NAPLES
②
②

① Ceded by France and Spain to England, 1763
② ,,   ,,   Austria to the Spanish Bourbons, 1736, 1748
③ ,,   ,,   ,,   ,, Sardinia, 1736, 1748
④ ,,   ,,   ,,   ,, Prussia, 1742; confirmed by
                       treaties, 1748, 1763
⑤ ,,   to France, 1736; possesion taken, 1766
⑥ ,,   to Habsburgs, 1736; possession taken, 1737

Scale: 0 ——— 100   200   300 Miles

TERRITORIAL ADJUSTMENTS RESULTING FROM THE THIRTY YEARS' WORLD
WAR OF THE EIGHTEENTH CENTURY, 1733–1763

made England the leading naval, colonial, and commercial power
of the world. But this war had certain remote results which no
one at the time could foresee. To understand the real importance
of the war it will therefore be well to keep these remote results in
mind also.

We must keep in mind, for one thing, that it was this same
Prussia, which England helped to preserve in the Seven Years'
War, that took the lead in founding the new German Empire of

1871 — the empire of Bismarck, and of Kaiser William II — which England helped to destroy in the war of 1914–1918. If the Seven Years' War had turned out differently — if Prussia had been destroyed then — it is possible that there would have been no modern German Empire. At least it would not have been created by Bismarck, or ruled by Kaiser William II. In this odd way the great war of the eighteenth century was a remote cause of the great war of the twentieth century.

Likewise the Seven Years' War was a remote cause of the two great events which soon followed it — the American Revolution and the French Revolution. The Seven Years' War nearly doubled the debt of England and, by giving her Canada and the Mississippi country, it increased the cost of defending her American possessions. It was to help meet these new expenses that the English government imposed the famous stamp tax on the colonies; and the Stamp Act, as everyone knows, was the beginning of a quarrel which led to the American Revolution and the independence of the thirteen colonies.

Meanwhile the French government had also contracted a heavy debt in the wars from 1733 to 1763. You may be sure that the French government, having been so badly defeated by England, was delighted to see the thirteen colonies rise up in rebellion against her old enemy, and in order to help disrupt the British Empire, the French government, in 1778, made an alliance with the thirteen colonies and furnished the money which enabled them to win their independence. This greatly increased the French debt, and it was to raise new revenue to meet the debt that the king was forced to call the famous Estates General of 1789 which began the French Revolution.

In these devious ways the wars of the eighteenth century influenced the course of modern history. By aiding Prussia in the eighteenth century, William Pitt helped to raise up a powerful enemy of England in 1914. By aiding England in the eighteenth century, Frederick the Great helped to create the British Empire which William II labored in vain to destroy in our own time. By depriving France of Canada, England prepared the way for the loss of her own colonies; and by aiding these colonies to win their

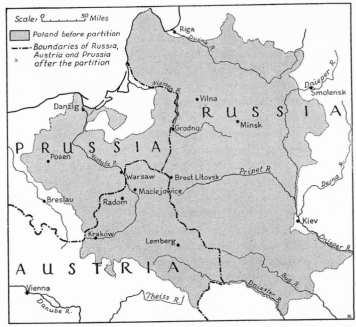

Scale: 0 _____ 50 Miles

☐ Poland before partition

—·—· Boundaries of Russia, Austria and Prussia after the partition

PARTITION OF POLAND, 1772, 1793, 1795

independence, the French king, Louis XVI, helped to bring on the revolution in which he lost both his crown and his head. Such is the tangled skein of historical events.

The results of the Thirty Years' World War of the eighteenth century may be summarized as follows: (1) France gained Lorraine but lost her colonial empire in America and India. (2) England made great gains in America and India. (3) Spain gained possessions in Italy. (4) Prussia gained Silesia.

How England lost her colonies and Poland was partitioned, 1772–1795. For thirty years after the Peace of Paris there were no general wars in Europe (1763–1793). But during this period important changes were made in the territorial possessions of the great powers. As a result of the American Revolution, in which France fought on the side of the colonies against England, England lost the most valuable part of her American colonial empire —

the thirteen colonies, and the territory lying between the Alleghany Mountains and the Mississippi River (1783). At the same time England ceded the province of Florida to Spain.

Meantime, the question which chiefly occupied the three eastern powers — Russia, Prussia, and Austria — was the partition of Poland. Poland was an immense country, but divided by religious and racial rivalries, and possessed of a government too weak to maintain its independence. For more than half a century its more powerful neighbors, especially Russia, had interfered in Polish affairs, and at last they resorted to the plan of each taking a convenient part of Polish territory. By the first partition (1772), Russia obtained that part of Poland lying east of the Dvina and Dnieper rivers; Prussia obtained that part of Poland known as East Prussia, including the important city of Danzig; Austria obtained the great province of Galicia. Realizing that unless they strengthened their government their country was doomed to destruction, the Poles endeavored to effect needed political reforms. This led to the second partition (1793), by which Russia obtained part of Lithuania, and Prussia obtained what was known as Great Poland and New East Prussia. The remainder of Poland was finally partitioned between Russia, Prussia, and Austria in 1795. The Poles remained subject to Russia, Austria, and Prussia until 1919, when their independence was restored.

QUESTIONS

1. Why were France and Spain friends after the Treaty of Utrecht? Why were France and England enemies in the eighteenth century? Why were Austria and Spain rivals?

2. What were the territories of the dukes of Brandenburg in 1648? How did the Duke of Brandenburg become King of Prussia? What did Frederick William I do to make Prussia a great state? Why were Prussia and Austria rivals in Germany?

3. What did Peter the Great do to "Westernize" Russia? Why did Russia become one of the European "great powers" in the eighteenth century? Why was Russia a rival of Austria? of Prussia? of Sweden?

4. What were the three European wars between 1733 and 1763? What were the main disputes in all these wars? Why may they be regarded as one war?

1713	1733	1739-1740	1748	1754	1763	1775	1783	1792 1795
Peace for the most part. New alliances formed. Spain and France unite against England and Austria. Rise of Prussia as rival of Austria in Germany. Rise of Russia as rival of Prussia and Austria.	War of the Polish Succession. France, Spain, and Sardinia vs. Austria. (Peace)	War of the Austrian Succession. France, Spain, and Prussia vs. Austria and Great Britain.	Peace.	French and Indian War in America, 1754, and Seven Years' War in Europe, 1756. France, Austria, Russia, and Spain vs. England and Prussia.	Peace. First Partition of Poland between Austria, Russia and Prussia, 1772. English colonies in America resist taxation.	American Revolution. War with England. Colonies win independence.	Peace.	Beginning of wars growing out of French Revolution. Second and Third Partitions of Poland.

Thirty Years' World War.
Frederick II enlarges and strengthens Prussia.
England takes French possessions in America and India.
Spain takes Austrian possessions in northern and southern Italy.
France acquires Lorraine.

139

5. How was the War of the Polish Succession settled? What caused the War of the Austrian Succession? State the terms of the Peace of Aix-la-Chapelle. Why did England and Austria "change partners" between 1748 and 1756? How did the Seven Years' War begin in America? Why did the French and English quarrel over the Ohio Valley? How did this war in America spread to Europe? How was Frederick the Great able to defend Prussia against the superior forces of Russia, France, and Austria? What were the French and English fighting about in India? What were the terms of the Peace of Paris, 1763?

6. What were the chief results of the Thirty Years' World War of the eighteenth century?

7. What possessions did England lose as a result of the American Revolution? Why was Poland, though a large country, unable to maintain its independence? What happened to the Kingdom of Poland in 1772, 1793, and 1795?

SELECTED READINGS

Brief accounts. Robinson, *Western Europe*, chs. xxxii–xxxiii. Robinson and Beard, *Development of Modern Europe*, I, chs. iv–vii. Robinson and Beard, *Outlines of European History*, II, chs. iii–iv. Hayes and Moon, *Modern History*, chs. vii–ix. R. L. Ashley, *Modern European Civilization*, chs. iii–iv. Schevill, *History of Europe*, chs. xv–xvii. Hayes, *Modern Europe*, I, chs. ix, xi–xii. Schevill, *Making of Modern Germany*, chs. i–ii. G. M. Priest, *Germany since 1740*, chs. i–iii. H. O. Wakeman, *European History*, pp. 289–310 (relations of Peter the Great and Charles XII of Sweden). E. F. Henderson, *Short History of Germany*, II, 148–218 (account of Frederick the Great in peace and war). Green, *Short History*, ch. x, sec. i (colonial struggle of England and France). F. Parkman, *Montcalm and Wolfe*, II, ch. xxvii (graphic account of the capture of Quebec). For English social history in this century see A. S. Turberville, *English Men and Manners in the Eighteenth Century;* S. G. Endore, *Casanova;* W. Hadley, *Selected Letters of Horace Walpole.*

Biography. S. Graham, *Peter the Great.* K. Waliszewski, *Peter the Great.* F. Schuyler, *Peter the Great.* E. A. B. Hodgetts, *Catharine the Great.* K. Anthony, *Catharine the Great.* M. L. Goldsmith, *Frederick the Great.* W. F. Longmans, *Frederick the Great.* W. F. Reddaway, *Frederick the Great.* N. Young, *Frederick the Great.* J. F. Bright, *Maria Theresa.* J. Morley, *Walpole.* F. Harrison, *Chatham* (William Pitt). Macaulay's essays on Chatham and Frederick the Great. Thomas Carlyle's monumental *History of Frederick the Great* is a classic in English literature. In the first three pages, Vol. I, ch. i, he gives a vivid portrait of the " interesting lean little old man." The famous friendship and quarrel of Frederick and Voltaire is recounted at length in Bk. XIV, ch. vi; Bk. XVI, chs. ii, vii, ix, xi, xii.

Historical novels. Thackeray's *Henry Esmond*, one of the best of all historical novels, deals with English history about the time of the Peace of Utrecht. Jane Porter's *Thaddeus of Warsaw* is a thrilling and once-popular romance of Polish history in the time of the partitions. L. Mulbach's *Old Fritz and the New Era; Frederick the Great and His Court;* and *Berlin and Sans-Souci.* D. Merejkowski, *Peter and Alexis, the Romance of Peter the Great.*

Sources. Robinson, *Readings in European History*, II, chs. xxxii–xxxiii. (How Peter founded St. Petersburg and tried to force the Russians to wear Western dress, pp. 309–310; relations of Frederick and Frederick William, pp. 319–323; Frederick's estimate of German literature, p. 326; Maria Theresa on the partition of Poland, p. 328, Clive's account of the Battle of Plassey, p. 342.) Robinson and Beard, *Readings in Modern History*, I, chs. iii–vii, x. (Arneth's description of Maria Theresa, p. 71; English trade in the West Indies, p. 74; Frederick on growing old, p. 81; Frederick on the duties of kings, p. 202; Joseph II on government, p. 213.) The *Memoirs of Catherine the Great* have been translated by Katherine Anthony. *Memoirs of Countess Golovine, a Lady at the Court of Catharine II.* The *Memoirs of Wilhelmina*, edited by Edith Cuthell, gives an account of German history and society in the time of Frederick the Great. Wilhelmina has been called the " Madame de Sévigné of Germany." An intimate account of Frederick the Great (perhaps not always strictly reliable) was written by his secretary or reader : *Frederick the Great, the Memoir of his Reader, Henri de Catt.*

A French Peasant's Cottage, 1749
From a drawing by J. G. Wille.

CHAPTER VI. THE FRENCH PEOPLE IN THE EIGHT-EENTH CENTURY: HOW THE FEW LIVED WELL WITHOUT WORKING, AND HOW THE MANY WORKED WITHOUT LIVING WELL

Certain savage-looking beings, male and female, are seen in the country, black, livid and sunburnt, . . . belonging to the soil which they dig. . . . They seem capable of articulation, and when they stand erect they display human countenances. They are, in fact, men. LA BRUYÈRE

No one who has not lived before 1789 knows how pleasant life can be. TALLEYRAND

Why we need a clearer picture of " the people." In writing history we often have to use words that refer, not to material things which everyone has seen and handled, but to ideas, which no one has seen or handled — splendid words, such as " government," " liberty," " revolution," and the like. Such words are likely to mean different things to different people. Humpty Dumpty, in *Through the Looking Glass*, said that he was the master of words and could make them mean anything he liked. We can't do that, but we ought to stop sometimes and see what some of these fine words do mean, or whether they mean anything.

In the last chapter we often used the words " England," " France," " Prussia." Perhaps we used such expressions as

" England made a treaty with Prussia," or " the English conquered North America," or " the English government declared war on Spain." Now of course the words " England," " Prussia," " government," when they are used in this way, stand for some person or persons; and since we are dealing with the wars of one country with another we are likely to form a picture of " the people " of each country acting as one person. Perhaps we have a vague image of the people of England joining hands with the people of Prussia, or rising up in anger to fight the French. And with that image in mind it is easy to suppose that if England won the war, all the English people were in some way better off than before, and all the French people worse off.

But this is not a correct picture of " the people " in England, or France, or any other country. If we say that " England declared war on Spain in 1739," what we mean is that the English government (the king and his ministers, with the assent of Parliament) declared war on the Spanish government. The only people who did any fighting were those in the navy, while the rest of the people went about their business much as before. Of course all Englishmen, being subjects of the English government, were supposed to act as if the Spaniards had greatly wronged them, and as if they would be greatly benefited by winning the war. But the great majority of the people of England were not really angry with the Spaniards. They knew nothing, and cared very little, about the rights and wrongs of Jenkins' famous ear, had nothing to do with the declaration of war, and were no better off on account of the glorious victories of the British navy. Likewise, in the Seven Years' War, the French peasant farmers had no grievance against the English farmers, and the only effect of the war on them, whichever side won it, was that their taxes were higher.

Thus when we think of the people of England, or France, or any other country in the eighteenth century, we must not think of them as one, but as many. We must think of the people as divided into more or less distinct classes, each with its own way of life, each with its own interests. Above all, we must not think of the people as all having an equal influence in deciding what their government should do, or as all equally benefited or injured by

AN EIGHTEENTH CENTURY FAIR IN ENGLAND

Ferris wheels before the time of Ferris. Note the mechanism by which the wheels are turned. From a drawing by Chodowiecki, 1774.

what it did. In this age of kings and nobles only the few, the nobles and the rich, had any influence in deciding what the government should do, and so what the government did — whether it levied a tax or waged a war — was done largely for the benefit of the few. It was taken for granted that what was good for king and nobles would be good for the common people.

Before we go on with the story of modern history we must therefore form a clearer picture of " the people " in this age of kings and nobles. And we shall try to form this picture by studying the system of society and government in France.

Why we ask the French people to sit for this picture. It may be impertinent to ask the French people to abandon business and pleasure and sit for a picture of " the people " in the Age of Kings and Nobles; but there are two reasons why we must do so. In the first place, the system of society and government in France was much the same as that in other countries. The people of France were perhaps more oppressed than those of England, Holland, or Switzerland; but they were less oppressed than those of Germany, Austria, or Russia. A picture of the French people will thus be representative — that is, much like a picture of the people in other countries, although not quite so bright as some would be or quite so dark as others.

But there is a second reason for choosing the French people as a model for our picture, and this reason is more important than the other. In the eighteenth century the French people were growing weary of government of the people, by the king, for the nobles; and in 1789-1795 they carried through a great revolution, the result of which was that the king lost his power and the nobles their privileges. This great French Revolution was one of the most important events in modern history, and therefore we shall presently (in Part III) have to study it with much care. But first we shall need to know a good deal about the system of government and society which the Revolution destroyed. That is why we ask the French people to sit for a picture of " the people " in the Age of Kings and Nobles, and why this chapter will be mainly devoted to a study of the system of government and society in France.

How the French people were legally divided into three classes or estates. In most countries today all the people, according to the law of the land, have the same rights and privileges. But in France in the eighteenth century, and in nearly every other country of Europe, the people were, according to the law of the land, divided into three classes or " estates." The clergy made the First Estate, the nobles made the Second Estate, and all the rest of the people made the Third Estate.

The First Estate was composed of about 130,000 clergy of the Catholic Church — bishops, abbots, monks, and parish priests. They possessed about one-fifth of the land; but, although they sometimes gave him a grant of money, they paid no taxes to the king. On the contrary, they levied and collected a tax, called the *tithe*, from all landholders. They had special courts of justice in which they were tried for offenses. They controlled education and to some extent could prohibit the publication of books which they did not like. The clergy thus formed a little company by themselves. They were supposed to perform certain services for society — they were responsible for the maintenance of religion, the education of the people, and the relief of poverty. It was in return for these services that they were favored with special privileges.

The Second Estate was made up of the nobles. There were about 110,000 nobles in France. They possessed about one-fifth of the land. They, also, could be tried and punished for offenses only in special courts. They paid very few taxes to the king, yet they collected rents from the peasants who lived on their manors. Many well-paid offices were reserved by the king for the nobles alone. In all the relations of life they were regarded as superior to ordinary people and could demand, as a right, to be so treated.

The Third Estate was composed of all the people who were neither nobles nor clergy — about 24,750,000. They had no special privileges as a class, but were called " Third Estate " merely to distinguish them from the two privileged orders. Thus nearly all the people of France were unprivileged. They were people of " base condition " — that is to say, in the eyes of the privileged nobles they were " the people."

The theory was that all three classes or estates were of equal importance and rendered equal services to society. But though the classes as a whole were considered to be of equal importance, the individuals composing them were not all given the same value. In the eyes of the law one clergyman, or one noble, was as important and as useful to society as 250 ordinary folk.

How the eyes of the law must have been poor, since they did not see things as they really were. The law does not always, or even usually, correspond exactly with the facts, and it was so in France in respect to the division of the people into classes. You must not suppose that all clergymen, or all nobles, were equally rich and powerful, or that all the common people were equally poor and helpless. On the contrary, many of the nobles and clergy were poor and without much influence, while some of the common people were very rich and powerful. In fact the real power and influence of people had come to depend more upon their wealth and manner of living than upon their rank ; and so the real division of the people was somewhat different from the legal division. We may represent the real division of the people by placing them on a kind of "social ladder" (see p. 147). You can easily see that the three estates, in scrambling up the social ladder, had become much mixed up, and the members of each of the estates had lost touch with each other. Many of the clergy and nobles were well toward the bottom, while some of the Third Estate had climbed so far up that they could grasp the skirts of the great

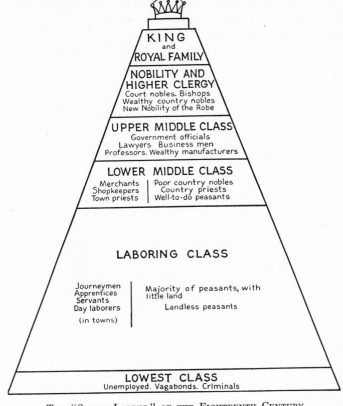

KING
and
ROYAL FAMILY

NOBILITY AND
HIGHER CLERGY
Court nobles. Bishops
Wealthy country nobles
New Nobility of the Robe

UPPER MIDDLE CLASS
Government officials
Lawyers   Business men
Professors. Wealthy manufacturers

LOWER MIDDLE CLASS

Merchants | Poor country nobles
Shopkeepers | Country priests
Town priests | Well-to-do peasants

LABORING CLASS

Journeymen | Majority of peasants, with
Apprentices | little land
Servants |
Day laborers | Landless peasants

(in towns) |

LOWEST CLASS
Unemployed. Vagabonds. Criminals

THE "SOCIAL LADDER" OF THE EIGHTEENTH CENTURY

nobles and bishops and even catch a glimpse of the king himself. The great majority of the people, however, remained very near the bottom of the ladder.

We have now a kind of bird's-eye or airplane view of "the people" as they were legally divided into estates or classes, and as they were arranged on the social ladder according to wealth and influence.

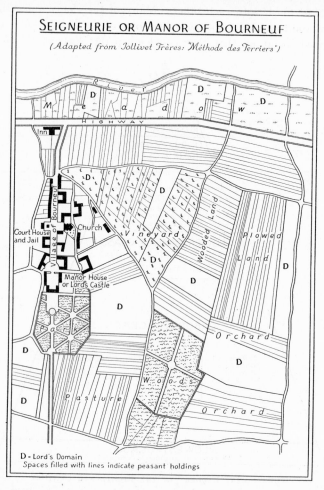

We will now come down to earth and get a " close-up " of some of these people as they went about their business or pleasure; and first let us visit a little community in the country.

The manor and the village: How the nobles, the priests, and the peasants were bound together through the land. Much of the land of France was still, as in medieval times, divided up into estates or *manors*. We shall visit the Manor of Bourneuf. The drawing on page 148 is not of an actual manor, but it is typical — that is, it represents fairly well what any manor was like. You will notice the castle or manor house, the woods and parks, and the land called *domain*. All this belongs to the lord of the manor, and what is raised on the domain belongs to him. Then you will notice the village where the peasants live, and the many strips of plowed land, pasture, and wooded land held by the peasants. Although each peasant works his land and cannot be dispossessed of it, he does not own it. The lord of the manor, whom we will call the Count of Bourneuf, is the overlord of all the peasants and the proprietor of all the farms; therefore each peasant has to pay him certain rents and perform for him certain services.

In this way the lord of the manor with his domain land and the peasants with their little farms form a compact community. But there is another person who belongs to this community. In the village will be a parish church, and there will be a parish priest to conduct the religious services and look after the religious welfare of the peasants. He is called a *curé* because he has the cure or the care of souls. But this priest, whom we will call Father Joseph, is not chosen by the people of the village. He is appointed — very likely by the lord of the manor, the Count of Bourneuf. The reason for this is that one of the remote ancestors of the count gave the land for the church and provided the money to build it; and in return for this gift he required that the lord of the manor should always have the right of appointing the parish priest.

Thus we have on the manor of Bourneuf a little community of about one hundred people. All three of the estates are represented here — there is a noble, a priest, and peasants; and all are bound together by the land.

How the peasant, Jacques Bonhomme, works hard for a poor living. Let us follow one of the peasants, whom we will call Jacques Bonhomme (" James Simplefellow "), into his cottage in the village. It is a small stone house, with a thatched roof. The main room is living-room, dining-room, and kitchen combined, with a large fireplace for cooking, a solid table and chairs, and a cupboard or two. On the mantel is a crucifix, in the corner a spinning-wheel. The room is lighted by a single window, perhaps a large one. There

A WELL-SUPPLIED FARM KITCHEN IN ENGLAND, EIGHTEENTH CENTURY

English farmers in general lived much more comfortably than French peasants.
The farmer who lived here had a cheese press, a churn, and an abundant supply
of bacon.

may be another room, or perhaps an attic, for sleeping — cold in
winter and hot in summer.

Here Jacques Bonhomme lives with his wife and children. He
will be unfortunate if he has no children to help him — unfortunate, also, if he has too many to provide with farms when he dies.
But whether the children are few or many, all rise early and
work hard. Perhaps Jacques Bonhomme has a rough wooden
plow, and perhaps an ox to draw it. Otherwise he must use a
spade, or draw the plow himself, unless he can get his sons or his
wife to draw it for him. He sows his grain by hand, reaps it with
a sickle, and threshes it with a wooden flail or tramps it out with
his heavy shoes. Jacques Bonhomme and his family live on vegetables and rye bread, with sometimes a rare feast of eggs or meat.
In the evenings they gossip with the neighbors, and then it is " early
to bed and early to rise " for another laborious day.

On Sundays and fast days Jacques Bonhomme, or at least his
wife, goes to church, and now and then to a wedding or a funeral
or a village church festival on the green. But they have few amusements. They never take a vacation or make a journey, for they
cannot afford it. They do not write letters, for they cannot write ;
or read books, for they cannot read. Besides, they have no time.
They must toil ceaselessly in order to live and perhaps, by desperate
economy, save a little money with which to buy an acre or so more
of land from the lord's domain. For the farm is theirs to possess

as long as they live, and when Jacques Bonhomme dies his sons will inherit it. If there are several sons, one may choose to become a priest, while another may go off to town and be apprenticed to a shopkeeper.

Many peasants are worse off than Jacques Bonhomme; some are better off. Jacques Bonhomme would himself be better off than he is if he could keep all that he raises from his farm. But that is what Jacques is beginning to complain of bitterly — he cannot keep all that he makes by his hard labor. He cannot keep it all because he has three masters, and to each of these he must give something each year. These three masters are (1) the lord of the manor; (2) the church; (3) the king.

How Jacques Bonhomme helps to support one of his masters — the lord of the manor. The lord of the manor, the Count of Bourneuf, lives in his castle or manor house, a large stone house with many rooms. Some nobles are wretchedly poor and have little to live on in their bare, cold houses. But the Count of Bourneuf happens to be a rich noble, and his castle is filled with fine furniture, has pictures and tapestries on the walls, and has rugs on the floors. It is perhaps not very warm in winter. But everyone is used to that, and the count does the best he can with plenty of wood for the huge fireplaces, plenty of good food and wine for the table, and plenty of servants to work for him and make everything as comfortable as possible. The count and his family and friends amuse themselves as best they can, with conversation, music and dancing, card-playing, and perhaps a little reading. The count does not labor with his hands — he is not permitted to; but he may, if he wishes, manage his domain lands, and look after the peasants on the manor who owe him rents and services.

Jacques Bonhomme can see the castle from the village. He looks up to the count, and to his wife and sons and daughters, with awe and reverence — or perhaps with hatred — as superior beings. He knows that they belong to another world than his and that when he meets them by chance in the streets or the fields he must doff his cap, and be pleased if they deign to give him a good-day or submissive if they ask him to do them a favor. What he knows best of all is that every year the count or his agent will come to demand the rent in money (*cens*), or in grain (*champart*). It may be that in addition Jacques will have to work one day in the week on the lord's domain, while the count's sons, in pursuit of game, are perhaps riding over the fields of Jacques and tramping down the grain. For this too is the right of the lord. And when Jacques dies, his sons, before they can inherit the farm, must pay a fee to the count.

Perhaps all this seems right enough to Jacques Bonhomme so long as the count lives in his castle and takes a fatherly interest in his people. For in that case Jacques will know his lord by sight and will sometimes have a bit of conversation with him about the farm; if he is ill he may send up to the castle for food or medicine; if the wind blows off his thatch the count will perhaps put on another; or he may give him another cow in place of the spotted one that died, or not press for the rent if the harvest has been bad. So long as the count, his master, is also a kind of father, it seems right to Jacques to be obedient and pay the rent.

But the count is likely to find life dull in the country, especially in the winter. So he may get out the coach and take his family to the neighboring city of X——, where he has a town house, and where it is more amusing; or, if he can afford it, he will go to Versailles and live at the king's court, where it is most amusing of all. In that case he will leave a lawyer to collect the rents. The lawyer will be sure to collect the rents, but he will not be a father to Jacques or look after him when he is in trouble. In that case Jacques will begin to ask himself, " Why should I pay rent to someone who does not live in the castle? "

How Jacques Bonhomme helps to support a second master — the church. It may be that Jacques Bonhomme will go to the village priest, Father Joseph, and grumble about his troubles. " Why does the count not live at home? " he will ask. " Why do I pay rent to a stranger who does nothing for me? It is not right." Father Joseph will sympathize with Jacques, for he, too, thinks the count ought to live in the castle and take care of his people; but he will tell Jacques not to complain, because the world is like that and there is nothing to be done about it.

Father Joseph will sympathize with Jacques, even though he

does belong to the privileged First Estate, for he may have been born of peasant parents himself. At all events he is poor, too, and lives no better than the peasants. Besides, he lives with them day by day and shares all their joys and sorrows. When their children are born he baptizes them; when they are grown up he marries them; when they die he buries them. He is their friend and teacher, who tells them what it is right to think and to do. Jacques may not always do what Father Joseph tells him to, but he looks up to him because he represents the church, and the church is one of his masters also.

To this second master, the church, Jacques has to pay every year the tax called the *tithe*. The tax is supposed to be a tenth of what is raised on the farm. In reality it is not so much as that — perhaps no more than a twentieth. But every year it has to be paid. It should rightly be paid to Father Joseph for the support of the village church, for education, and for the relief of poverty among the peasants. This would not be so bad. But Father Joseph complains — and Jacques Bonhomme might well complain — that very little of the tithe is kept in the parish for these purposes. Most of it has to be carried away to some monastery, or more likely to the bishop of the diocese, a grand personage whom Jacques Bonhomme never sees because, when the bishop is not living at the king's court at Versailles, he lives in the city of X——.

Two masters ought to be enough, but Jacques Bonhomme has one more, and that is the king.

How Jacques Bonhomme helps to support a third master — the king. Jacques Bonhomme never sees the king, but he knows that he lives far away, in Paris or Versailles, in a wonderful palace, and that everyone must obey him without question. A poor peasant may complain of the count, but Heaven would surely punish the man who might be so rash as to question the right of the king to do what he thought wise. The power and majesty of the king is represented to Jacques Bonhomme in the person of the king's agent, the *intendant*, who lives in the city of X——. Perhaps Jacques does not see even the intendant, but only his representative, the *sub-delegate*. It is this sub-delegate, the servant of the servant of the king, who comes every year to collect the king's taxes.

To him, also, Jacques Bonhomme has to pay a part of his small earnings. He has to pay (1) the *taille*, or land tax; (2) the *vingtième* or twentieth, which is a kind of income tax; and (3) the *capitation*, or poll tax. Besides, Jacques has to buy from the king a certain amount of salt for his table and a certain amount for curing meat and for other purposes. It may be that he does not need so much salt. He has to buy it just the same. The sub-delegate is not much interested in Jacques Bonhomme or his troubles, although the king allows the intendant a certain sum for the relief of poverty in the village. The sub-delegate wants the money so that he can pay it over to the intendant. The intendant must have the money so that he can send it on to the king's ministers, who spend it in keeping up the splendid palace at Versailles, in feeding the nobles who live there with the king, or in paying for the wars which the king has to wage with Austria, or Prussia, or England.

Thus Jacques Bonhomme has to help support three masters: (1) the lord of the manor, to whom he pays rent; (2) the church, to which he pays tithes; and (3) the king, to whom he pays taxes. When he has paid all these, how much does he have left of his small earnings? Something less than half. And so it is with the other peasant farmers — the great majority of the French people. At least one-half of what they raise goes to support the nobles, the clergy, and the king.

The nobles, the clergy, and the king ought to live very well with all this money. The king lives very well, but not all of the nobles or the clergy do. Only a few of the nobles are rich enough to live luxuriously, and the great majority of the clergy — the 60,000 parish priests — are as poor as the peasants. The 138 bishops and the heads of the numerous monasteries, these are the clergy who take the tithes and the revenues of the church lands and live well on them.

The tax and the tithe which the king and the church took from poor Jacques Bonhomme were carried off to the city of X——, where the bishop and the intendant live. Very likely the Count of Bourneuf, when he got into his coach and went off to the city of X——, took with him some of the rent which Jacques had paid

PARIS STREET SCENES, EIGHTEENTH CENTURY
"Brooms for sale, brooms." On the right are shown workmen unloading coal.
Sketches by Boucher.

over to him. Let us go then to the city of X——, and see what
the count and the bishop and many other people — shopkeepers,
lawyers, and officials — are doing there.

The city of X——, and the little and big people in it. Only a
small part of the French people lived in cities in the eighteenth
century. The largest city was Paris, with a population of about
600,000, and the next largest was Lyon, with a population of 130,-
000. Altogether there were about 78 cities, with a population of
not more than 10,000 each. In these cities there were perhaps
2,000,000 people — less than there are today in the single city of
Paris. We will suppose that the city of X——, which we are now
to visit, has a population of 10,000. It is not a real city, but a
typical city, as the manor of Bourneuf was a typical manor.

In the city of X——, there are vagabonds, criminals, and men
without employment. These people form the lowest class. There
are also many day laborers and domestic servants, whom we may
speak of as belonging to the laboring class. Above them are

people engaged in business — butchers, bakers, and candlestick-makers — the shopkeepers and merchants who make and sell the things which the people in the city need to have. These, and the town priests, belong to the lower middle class. Above them, in the upper middle class, are officials and people engaged in some profession. There will be the city officials — a mayor and councilmen; and there will be the king's intendant, who collects the taxes; lawyers and judges connected with the high court of justice known as the *parlement;* and the professors in the university, if there happens to be a university in the city of X——. Above these is still another class, composed of the nobles who have town houses here, the abbot who governs the monastery, and the bishop who governs the diocese.

We must stop to say a word about the bishop, because he is a very important personage. France is divided into 138 dioceses, and a bishop presides over each one. The Bishop of X—— will have charge of the cathedral church in the city of X——, he will administer the church lands, and supervise the parish priests in the villages of the diocese, including Father Joseph whom we already know. The king appoints the bishops; and you might suppose that he would appoint, as Bishop of X——, some parish priest who had served long and faithfully. But he will not do this. Father Joseph can never hope to be promoted to be Bishop of X——, for the king chooses his bishops from the noble families. The Bishop of X—— may therefore very well be the brother or the uncle or the cousin of the Count of Bourneuf. Let us suppose that the Bishop of X—— is the brother of the count. As bishop, he will live in the episcopal palace and have the title of Monseigneur.

What the people in the city of X—— live on, and how some of them are ambitious to better their condition in life. The Count of Bourneuf and his brother the bishop are the most important people in X——, and they have money enough to live well. The count has his rents and the produce from his domain. The bishop has the rents from the church lands, and most of the tithe collected from Jacques Bonhomme and the other peasants in the diocese. If Monseigneur is a serious and high-minded bishop he may use most of his money for churches, schools, and charity, and spend

ENGLISH APPRENTICES WORKING AT LOOMS

The industrious apprentice (right) and the idle apprentice (left).   From a series of engravings by Hogarth illustrating "Industry and Idleness."

very little on himself.   But if he lives too simply, people will complain, because a bishop is expected to live well and maintain the dignity of his position.

The lawyers, judges, officials, and professors live on their fees, or on salaries.   Most of them cannot live so well as the count and the bishop, but they hope to have better houses and make a better show than the merchants and shopkeepers.

The two lower classes live on what they can sell.   The laborers sell their services, and the shopkeepers sell their wares.   Of course they hope the count and the bishop and the lawyers and judges and professors and officials will all live luxuriously and spend as much money as possible, so that business will be lively and the town prosperous.

The merchant or the shopkeeper will not try to make a show. He will live economically, and by working hard try to save money. He knows that he is not important by reason of his birth, like the noble, or by reason of his position, like the judge.   He knows that if he is ever to become anybody, it will be through the power of money. His ambition is therefore to save money, so that he can make his son a physician, perhaps, or buy him a small office connected with the parlement. Then his son may some day hope to marry the daughter of a lawyer, or a judge, and so rise from the third class into the second. While the shopkeeper dreams of making his son a lawyer or a judge, the judge dreams of marrying his son to the daughter of some noble, so that he may rise from the second class to the first. Meantime, what can the count and the bishop hope for, since they already belong to the first class? The count and the bishop may be perfectly satisfied; but it is quite possible that they also want something more than they have. In that case, they will find it necessary, in order to get what they want, to run off to Paris and Versailles.

What the count and the bishop want, and why they go to Paris and Versailles to get it. The Bishop of X—— will be a very unusual bishop if he does not desire to be promoted to a larger and more important diocese. Perhaps he aspires to become an archbishop. If he is very ambitious he may even hope to become a cardinal. His brother, the Count of Bourneuf, wishes nothing for himself, perhaps; but if he has sons and daughters he will wish to do as well as possible for them. To his eldest son he will leave the manor of Bourneuf. He will expect his second son to enter the church and become a bishop; and he will expect his third son to obtain some distinguished and well-paid office in the king's household or in the king's army. For his daughter he must try to make as brilliant a marriage as possible. He will think himself unfortunate if he has more than one daughter or more than three sons. Children are a blessing to be sure, but the count cannot easily arrange for more than four.

These are perhaps the ambitions of the Count of Bourneuf and of his brother, Monseigneur the Bishop. Neither of them can get what he wants by remaining in the little provincial city of X——. It is the king who can give Monseigneur his promotion, and help the count to settle his troublesome children in life. But the best offices and the most brilliant marriages will be for those nobles and bishops who are on the spot, and the king is likely to forget those who do not come to pay their respects to him. The count and Monseigneur will therefore think it necessary to run up to Paris and Versailles, at least for part of the year. Let us follow them and see what is going on among the rich and powerful who live near the king and seek to obtain from His Majesty, or from His Majesty's ministers, smiles, pensions, and offices.

Why Paris is more important than other cities. The count and Monseigneur will not run up to Paris in their motor cars or on a fast express train. They will have to manage with a heavy closed coach drawn by four horses; and if the city of X—— is two hundred miles from Paris it will take them two or three days to make the journey, unless they travel night and day, with relays. But sooner or later they will rumble over the cobbles through one of the many guarded gates into the narrow streets of the famous city.

The count and the bishop will know, but will take it as a matter of course, that Paris is a famous city. It is famous because it is the largest city in Europe — with its population of over 600,000, larger even than London. It is famous because it is the center of wealth, of commerce and industry, of science, literature, and art. It is famous because it is the capital of France, the chief state in Europe; and it is celebrated the world over for its public buildings and private palaces where so many distinguished people have lived and so many historic events have occurred.

The count and Monseigneur might have seen, as they crossed the river, the splendid palace of the Louvre (today one of the great art galleries of the world), which had once been the residence of the king. They might have seen adjoining the Louvre another royal residence, the Tuileries, which the king still used when he came from Versailles to Paris. They might have visited the Duke of Orléans at the Palais Royal near by, or the Prince of Condé at the Palais Bourbon across the river, or the king's brother, the Count of Provence, at his palace in the Luxembourg Gardens. Perhaps, as they crossed the Pont Neuf ("New Bridge"), Monseigneur may have bestowed a careless glance on the cathedral of Notre Dame, which had been standing there on the island since the thirteenth century, gray and serene, lifting its towers above the city.

STREET VENDORS IN PARIS, EIGHTEENTH CENTURY
Left: "Buy my larding needles, my pots and spoons."   Right: A girl selling
fish.   Drawn by E. Bouchardon.

The count and Monseigneur will not stop in Paris, for they have
seen it before. They will pass rapidly through, driving twelve
miles to Versailles, where the king is. But we may be excused
for remaining in Paris long enough to see some important people
whom we did not see in the little city of X——.

The great majority of the people of Paris in the eighteenth century were much the same as the people of X——. In Paris, as in
other cities, there were a great number of laborers, of small shopkeepers and merchants, of lawyers, judges, officials, and a few
nobles and bishops. But Paris, being the capital of France and
the largest city, naturally attracted adventurous and ambitious
men from all over the country. In Paris, therefore, we shall find
a class of very rich people — merchants, speculators, and bankers
— which we did not find in the smaller city. These people made
a new kind of aristocracy, an aristocracy of money instead of
an aristocracy of birth.

In Paris shrewd men found many opportunities for making great
fortunes. Some of the industries were very profitable. The
Guild of Goldsmiths, for example, was a wealthy corporation, and

Photo Hachette

THE ESTABLISHMENT IN WHICH THE FAMOUS GOBELIN TAPESTRIES WERE MADE

A gentleman is showing two ladies the tapestry on the loom. Weaving was one of the best-paid industries of the time. The Gobelin tapestry factory was established in the sixteenth century and is still in operation. From *L'Encyclopédie.*

this industry was largely controlled by a few men who in the course of time had enriched themselves. Other men acquired fortune through their connection with the great foreign trading companies. Still others enriched themselves by speculating in the grain trade. In years when the harvest was bad they would buy up all the wheat in some province or other, and then sell it at exorbitant prices to the starving people. One of the most profitable businesses was controlled by a corporation known as the *farmers-general.* This corporation was composed of about sixty men who paid the king a certain sum every year in return for the right to collect the indirect taxes — the customs and tariffs. As they collected far more than they paid the king, the business was a good one. In 1763 a man named Jacques Delhante took what little money he had, borrowed enough more to make 1,200,000 francs, and by paying this large sum became a member of the corporation. As an officer of the corporation he received a salary of 41,000 francs for many years. With this salary, together with his profits as a member of the corporation, he paid back what he owed, and left an estate when he died in 1792 of 2,500,000 francs.

But Jacques Delhante acquired something more than great wealth. After he became a member of the corporation of the farmers-general he purchased from the king an office — " Secretary to the King in the King's Household " — and the possession of this office, after twenty years, conferred on him a title of nobility which was inherited by his sons. There were in France many offices which conferred on their holders such titles. The principal offices in the king's household, in the parlement of Paris, in the Chamber of Accounts, and in the Privy Council — all these, and many others, conferred upon the holders a title of nobility. Of course the king did not give these offices for nothing; they had to be paid for, and only the wealthy could pay for them. If a man had money enough, he did not need to purchase an office. He could buy a title of nobility outright — for a million francs or so.

Thus we find at Paris a new aristocracy rising out of the common people, an aristocracy of money. The people of great wealth, however acquired, looked down on the ordinary merchants and officials, and began to tread on the heels of the privileged nobles. They built fine houses in Paris. They bought land of the poorer nobles, built themselves splendid country houses, and collected rents from the peasants like any lord of the manor. In time they hoped, by purchasing an office or a title, to become nobles themselves and intermarry with the old families. Then they, or at least their children, might also go to Versailles, and be received at court, and ask the king for favors and pensions.

Now we may go on to Versailles, where we shall find some of these new nobles, and the Court of Bourneuf and his brother, Monseigneur the Bishop of X——, and many other nobles and bishops, all ready to serve the king and to be served by him.

How the king lived in a very large house, because he had a large family and many guests. The palace at Versailles, with its beautiful gardens, was built by Louis XIV as a royal residence (see p. 90). As a residence it has long since been abandoned, and now weary tourists wander every day through its stately galleries and innumerable small chambers, pausing to look with hushed and dispirited admiration at the pictures and tapestries. The place is lifeless and a little tawdry in its empty grandeur. But in the eighteenth century it was the center of life and power, for it was still the dwelling place of the king and of the king's household.

In this immense dwelling lived the king, with his wife and children, and with his brothers and their wives and children, and with such royal princes as he could endure and their wives and children. To minister to the needs of all these exalted personages there were many "gentlemen-in-attendance" and "ladies-in-waiting," together with innumerable guards and servants of high and low degree. And always, coming and going, were many guests — nobles and bishops and cardinals, high officials of state, and ambassadors of foreign courts. In so large a family a few more or less made little difference; and the arrival of the Count of Bourneuf and his brother, the Bishop of X——, would scarcely be noticed. Yet some small and not too sweet-smelling rooms would be found for them; and in the morning, when the king received his guests in the grand Hall of Mirrors, they would come forward and pay their respects to him by bowing very low. Then they would mingle with the throng again, much flattered if His Majesty had welcomed them with a smile and a gracious word or, as a signal favor, had given them the royal hand to kiss.

Why so many exalted personages bowed very low before the king. The nobles and peers of France might be charmed with the king's conversation, or despise him as a dull and stupid man. But every day they stood in attendance and bowed low for all that, because the king of France was more than a man. He was more than a ruler. He was a symbol, just as our flag is a symbol. When we take off our hats to the flag we mean to express our loyalty to the country. The flag is, therefore, sacred. For the same reason the person of the king was sacred, and when the nobles and bishops bowed low before him they were doing homage to the power and majesty of France.

But there is a great difference between doing homage to a king and doing homage to a flag. When we take off our hats to the flag we do not expect to get anything from it. The flag cannot give us an office or a contract. For such favors we must write to the President or to the secretary of the interior. But when the Count of Bourneuf and his brother, the Bishop of X——, bowed very low to Louis XVI, they knew well that he was something more than a symbol of France. They knew that he was a king who ruled by divine right, whose word was law, and who could grant them a favor or put them in prison according to his humor.

But the king, however much legal authority he might have, could not govern France all by himself. No one man can govern a country unless a great many influential people are willing to support his government. So it was in France. The king governed France by means of a long-established system of administration, and this government was supported by the great and the powerful — the nobles, the bishops, and the wealthy people of the middle class.

How the king governed France by means of a system of administration. The king had a great many officials of government who did what he told them to do. The most important officials were the six ministers, who made up the Council of State. The king frequently called the council together, to get the advice of his ministers and to give them orders. These ministers were especially important because each one had charge of certain great affairs. They were (1) the chancellor of France; (2) the controller of finance; (3) the secretary of war; (4) the secretary of foreign affairs; (5) the secretary of the navy; and (6) the secretary of the king's household. These high officials were all appointed by the king, and if they did not do as he wished he could dismiss them and appoint others who would.

When the king had given orders to the ministers, they in turn passed these instructions on to the intendants. France was divided into thirty-two divisions, called *intendancies*, and over each intendancy the king appointed an intendant. We have already seen how the intendant of X—— collected the taxes from the peasants. But the intendants not only collected the king's taxes, they carried out the king's orders in all matters; and if they did not obey the king, or the king's ministers, they too would be dismissed.

Besides the ministers and the intendants, the king had his courts of justice. The highest of the king's courts were the parlements — thirteen in all — of which the most important was the parlement of Paris. There were also several hundred minor courts of justice in the different parts of the country. All of these courts tried and punished people for crimes and offenses according to the law and custom of the land. But the king was not bound by the law. He could at any time, by signing his name to a slip of paper called a *lettre de cachet* ("sealed letter"), direct his police officers to arrest and imprison any person and keep him in prison until further notice. The king did not need to give any reason for keeping the person in prison, except that it was his will.

To pay all of these officials, and hundreds of less important ones, the king used the huge revenue which he obtained from the taxes. Some of these taxes we have seen the intendant and the sub-delegate collecting from Jacques Bonhomme. They were the direct taxes — the *taille*, the *vingtième*, and the *capitation*. Besides these, there were the indirect taxes — the salt tax (*gabelle*) and the customs and tariffs collected by the farmers-general. If anyone refused to pay the taxes, he was arrested and had his property taken. To compel obedience to the king and his officials there were the police and, if necessary, the entire military force of the army.

Of course the king would have been helpless if the people had all refused to obey the intendant, if the intendant had refused to obey the ministers, if the ministers had refused to obey the king, and if the army had refused to suppress all this disobedience. But the king had in fact little difficulty, for his officials obeyed him, and the people obeyed the ministers, as a matter of course. Why was this so?

The great mass of the people were poor peasants, and they obeyed the king's officers without question, because they were ignorant and helpless and could not have acted all together even if they had thought of doing so. But it never even occurred to them to do so. If you had asked a peasant, Jacques Bonhomme for example, why he obeyed the king, he would have been dumbfounded. "What!" he would have exclaimed, "not obey the king? But that is unheard of! Does not the count obey the king? And does not the bishop obey the king? Do they not bow very low before him? How should a poor peasant not obey the king when the great ones of the earth are humble before him?"

The peasant would have been right. The king's power was safe as long as the rich and powerful were submissive. The king was able to govern France as he pleased because he was supported by the nobles, the bishops, and the wealthy people; and these people supported him because he governed France for their advantage. It was a government of the people, by the king, for the nobles and the rich.

Why the nobles, the bishops, and the rich supported the king's government. It is easy to see why the nobles supported the king. The nobles were a privileged class. They had one-fifth of the land, collected rents from the peasants, and yet paid no taxes to the king. If all this did not satisfy them, the king could give them something more. At this very moment the Count of Bourneuf is at Versailles asking the king for favors. He is asking the king, or the king's minister, to make one of his sons a bishop and to appoint another to an office in the army. Of course the count will not get what he wants if he goes about stirring up trouble for the king. If the count does anything so foolish as that, the king will delicately hint that his presence at Versailles is not desired. Some morning the king will take occasion to say to the count, in the presence of all the court and in a very loud voice: " Count, I fear that the exciting life we lead here at Versailles is bad for the health of such of my subjects as are discontented; for them the quiet of the country is far better." The count will understand that he is expected to start at once for his castle on the manor of Bourneuf; and he will go home knowing that all the courtiers are laughing at him and that neither of his sons will be provided with an office. But if he is properly submissive the king will give him the offices he desires — at least, if he has not already filled all the vacancies by appointing the sons of other nobles.

It is also easy to see why the bishops support the king. The bishops are the governing officials of the church, which is a powerful and privileged corporation. It is the king who has, by giving them their offices, turned over to them a large part of the immense revenues of the church. Besides, nearly all of the bishops are of noble birth, and thus what is good for the nobles is generally good for the bishops. The Bishop of X—— is the brother of the Count

MAN OF FASHION GETTING DRESSED
It's evidently a very serious business.   From a drawing by Moreau.

of Bourneuf.   Therefore the bishop will probably do what he can
to help the count get offices for his son, and the count will do what
he can to help the bishop get his promotion.   It is a family affair.
The bishops and the nobles are really one class, one group of powerful families, with many privileges.   Since the king does not deprive
them of their privileges, why indeed should they wish to deprive
him of his power?

It is true there are many poor nobles, and many poor priests,
who neither ask nor obtain favors from the king.   But they do
not count; for if they are too poor to get anything out of the
king, they have for that very reason little influence to make trouble
for him.

But the nobles and the bishops are not the only people who find
it to their advantage to support the king.   Rich men and men who

hope to become rich, men who hold high office and men who hope to hold such offices — these also support the king. The sub-delegate hopes to become an intendant, the intendant hopes to become a minister, the minister hopes at least that he will not be dismissed in disgrace. The business man who has acquired a little wealth, the banker who has acquired more, the speculator who has made a good strike — such men think of buying good offices or dream of being admitted to the corporation of the farmers-general. All these people of the Third Estate are pushing up from office to office, from wealth to greater wealth. They are pushing up toward the top, and at the top they see a shining goal, a great reward. This shining goal, this great reward, is a title of nobility, which they hope to obtain, if not for themselves, at least for their children. They know that it is the king who can help them; but they know that he will not help them unless they help him with their money, their influence, and their loyalty. Those who are successful will not think the king has too much power.

How society and government in other countries differed from that in France. The system of government and society in other countries did not differ much from that in France. Most countries were governed by absolute kings. (In the smaller German countries the rulers were called dukes, counts, margraves, etc.). The exceptions were: (1) England and the Dutch Republic, in which the power of the government was controlled largely by parliaments elected by the wealthy classes; and (2) the Swiss Confederation, in which the power was in the hands of assemblies elected by the mass of the people. In most countries, as in France, the power of the king rested on the support of a privileged nobility, and usually on that of an established church. This was true even in England and the Dutch Republic, only in these countries the influence of the privileged classes was exercised through a parliament. In most countries, as in France, there was a wealthy middle class. In England this class was larger and more influential than in France; in Germany, Austria, and Russia it was smaller and less influential. In most countries, as in France, the mass of the people were peasant farmers living on the great estates of the nobles. In England more of the peasants owned their land and they were freer from the

Germanisches Museum, Nürnberg

SERVANT WOMEN IN GERMANY

With a good stiff neck, or a yoke, fairly heavy loads could be carried quite easily.

control of the nobles; in central and eastern Europe they were less free than in France, being for the most part serfs, bound to the soil.

In this chapter we have had a new picture of the people of France — the people divided into the privileged and the unprivileged, the rich and the poor, the influential and the helpless; and a new picture of the government of France — *government of the people, by the king, for the nobles and the rich.* And, if we except the little Swiss democracies, this picture may be taken as typical of the society and government of Europe as a whole during the seventeenth and eighteenth centuries — the Age of Kings and Nobles.

QUESTIONS

1. When we say "the people of France" did so and so, we are making a generalization. What is a generalization? Why is it necessary to make general statements in writing history? Why are general statements about "the people" of any country never quite true? In what sense are they true?

2. What classes of people made up the three "estates" in France in the eighteenth century? In what respects were the nobles and clergy "privileged classes"? Are the classes which exist in America today, such as the capitalist class, the laboring class, etc., privileged classes in the same sense?

3. How did the *legal* class distinctions differ from the *actual* class distinctions in eighteenth-century France? On the "Social Ladder" (p. 147), why are the government officials, wealthy business men, etc., placed higher than the poor country nobles? Why are the parish priests placed lower than the bishops?

4. How were the three classes of nobles, clergy, and Third Estate represented in the life of the Manor of Bourneuf? How were they bound together through the land? Explain how Jacques Bonhomme was subject to three masters. What was his attitude toward the Count of Bourneuf? toward Father Joseph? Why was Father Joseph more intimate with Jacques Bonhomme than he was with the Bishop of X——?

5. What classes of people lived in the city of X——? Why were the interests of the Count of Bourneuf and the Bishop of X—— much the same? Why did the merchants and laborers of the city of X—— wish the bishop to live luxuriously? In what ways did Paris differ from other cities in France? Why was there a larger class of rich people in Paris?

6. Why did the Count of Bourneuf and the Bishop of X—— find it desirable to run up to Paris and Versailles for a part of the year? What people did they find living at Versailles? Why were they polite and submissive to the king? How could the king help them to get what they wanted? How could they help the king?

7. How did people manage to climb up the social ladder? How did they manage to fall down?

8. Why is it true to say that the government of France was a government of the people, by the king, for the nobles and the rich?

9. How did the system of government and society in England, Switzerland, and the Dutch Republic differ from that in France? In what respects were the mass of the people in these countries better off than those of France? In what respects were the mass of the people in central and eastern Europe worse off?

10. Why is it appropriate to describe the seventeenth and eighteenth centuries as the "Age of Kings and Nobles"?

SELECTED READINGS

Brief accounts. Robinson, *Western Europe*, ch. xxxiv. Robinson and Beard, *Modern Europe*, I, chs. viii–x. Robinson and Beard, *Outlines* II, chs. v–vii. H. E. Bourne, *Revolutionary Period in Europe*, chs. i–ii. Hayes, *Modern History*, I, chs. xiii–xiv. Ashley, *Modern Civilization*, ch. v. E. R. Turner, *Europe since 1789*, pp. 1–42. D. M. Kettelby, *Modern*

Times, chs. i–ii. Seignobos, *Contemporary Civilization*, pp. 92–106. For detailed description of France in the eighteenth century, see E. J. Lowell, *Eve of the French Revolution*, especially ch. iii (on the clergy), ch. vi (on the nobles), ch. xi (Paris), ch. xii (on provincial towns), ch. xiii (on the peasants); and a similar work by a famous French writer, H. A. Taine, *Ancient Régime*, especially Bk. I, chs. ii–iii (on the nobles), Bk. II, ch. i (court life), Bk. V, ch. i (peasants). For life in country and town in England, see W. E. H. Lecky, *History of England in the Eighteenth Century*, II, 97–115, 203–228, 241–265; H. See's *Economic and Social Conditions in France* is the best account in English of the subject.

Historical novels. A. Dumas, *The Queen's Necklace* and *Joseph Balsamo*.

Sources. Robinson and Beard, *Readings in Modern European History*, I, chs. viii, xi. See especially pp. 138–145, 161–172, 225–235. Some of the same selections are in Robinson, *Readings in European History*, II, ch. xxxiv. Arthur Young, an Englishman interested in farming, traveled in all parts of France in 1788–1789. He wrote a detailed account of what he saw, and his book, *Travels in France*, is one of the chief sources for conditions in France on the eve of the Revolution. Some selections from the *Travels* are given in Robinson and Beard, *Readings*. Thomas Jefferson was in France for several years preceding 1789. His correspondence contains his impressions of society and government in France. Madame de Staël's *Germany* is a description of Germany by one of the ablest Frenchwomen of the time.

LARGE FACTS TO REMEMBER ABOUT PART II

1. *In the seventeenth century:* (*a*) English Revolution results in establishment of authority of Parliament over king; (*b*) Louis XIV completes work of establishing absolute monarchy in France.

2. *In the eighteenth century:* (*a*) Peter the Great makes Russia a European great power; Frederick William and Frederick the Great make Prussia a European great power; (*b*) Thirty Years' World War, 1733–1763: conflict for territory in Europe and for commerce and colonies in America and India; resulting extension of Prussia, Russia, and Austria in Europe and ascendancy of England in America and India.

3. *System of government and society in the seventeenth and eighteenth centuries.* Government of the people, by the king, for the nobles and the rich.

VOLTAIRE AT THE TABLE OF FREDERICK THE GREAT

From a painting by Menzel. Frederick is at the far end of the table, turned toward Voltaire, who is addressing him.

PART III

THE AGE OF POLITICAL REVOLUTION

Why Part III is called the Age of Political Revolution. In the eighteenth century many people were beginning to think that government of the people, by the king, for the nobles and the rich was oppressive and unjust. They began to ask why nobles and priests should be thought better than other people. They began to ask why the majority of the people, who worked hard for a poor living, should be taxed to support the few, who already had enough to live in idleness. They began to ask whether it was true that God had intended kings to rule as they pleased, or whether he had not rather intended them to rule as the people pleased.

As a result of this discontent and these questionings there occurred, between 1775 and 1815, three great events which brought the Age of Kings and Nobles to an end — or nearly so. The first of these events was the American Revolution (1775–1783), by which the English colonies in America won their independence and established the Republic of the United States. The second of these events was the great French Revolution (1789–1795), which abolished the old system of society and established the French Republic. The third of these events was not so much an event as a man — Napoleon, who, by toppling over many thrones (1799–1815), prepared the way for the spread of new ideas and institutions throughout Europe.

In 1815, after twenty-five years of revolution and war, most people wanted peace and quiet. Rulers and wealthy people, especially, were afraid of the new ideas of " Liberty, Equality, Fraternity " which the French and American revolutions had let loose in the world; and for many years they tried to keep the world " safe for monarchy and aristocracy " by repressing all popular movements. But the new ideas were too strong to be repressed permanently. The middle and lower classes kept on demanding political liberty, equality of rights, and national independence; and

173

gradually the old form of government by kings and nobles was replaced in nearly every country of Europe by some form of government by the people.

In Part III we shall therefore study the history of a hundred years — roughly, from 1789 to 1889. During this period the chief public question that occupied the hopes and fears of people, the question on which political parties divided, was that of the form of government. Should governments be controlled by kings and nobles as formerly? Or should the wealthy middle classes be permitted to share with them in the control of the government? Or should all the people be permitted an equal share in the control of the government? The chief result of this hundred years of controversy was a widespread political revolution. In 1789 the form of government in nearly every European country was absolute monarchy. In 1889 the form of government in nearly every European country was some form of government by the people. This is why we shall call Part III the Age of Political Revolution.

People do not engage in widespread and long-continued revolution until they have acquired new and important ideas about government and society. First of all, therefore, we must learn something about the new ideas which were making their way in Europe in the eighteenth century — ideas which furnished the ideals and the inspiration for the French Revolution of 1789 and for the political changes of the hundred years from 1789 to 1889.

A SESSION OF THE ACADEMY OF SCIENCES

CHAPTER VII. HOW THE REVOLUTION WAS ACCOMPLISHED IN MEN'S MINDS BEFORE THEY MADE IT THE WORK OF THEIR HANDS

Since no one has a natural authority over his kind, and since might does not make right, there remains only agreement as the basis of all authority among men.
ROUSSEAU

In the eighteenth century people began to have many new ideas. The title of this chapter is a modification of the famous statement by the French writer, Chateaubriand: " The French Revolution was accomplished before it began." What he meant was that the French people had ceased to believe in the divine right of kings and in many other ideas on which the old system of government rested. They had already condemned the old system before they began to destroy it. Thus the Revolution was accomplished in their minds before they made it the work of their hands.

This revolution in men's minds — in their way of thinking — came about very slowly, and perhaps we should call it an evolution rather than a revolution. But at least we may say that by the eighteenth century most educated people had come to have new ideas about the material world and about the world of human society. These new ideas are closely connected; but we may best consider them under four main heads: (1) new ideas about things and their relations; (2) new ideas about man and the power of his mind; (3) new ideas about the rights of man and the nature of government; (4) new ideas about the rights of states and their relations.

I. New Ideas about Things and Their Relations

For a long time people were afraid of the forces hidden away in material things. Of course everyone has ideas about things, because everyone has to do with things all the time. Yet most people have only practical ideas about things. They think of wood as something with which to build houses or a fire; they think of fire as something which will cook their dinners or warm their houses. But there are always some unusual persons who like to know for the mere sake of knowing.

Great men in all ages have had this desire to learn for the sake of learning, but it is only in recent times that it has been much directed to the study of material things. The ancient Greeks had plenty of curiosity, but they were more interested in man than in things. The Romans were a practical people, who took things as they found them, being too busy conquering and governing the world to spend much time asking that explosive and fruitful little question, "Why?" Then for a long time, during the Middle Ages, most people were afraid of the secret forces hidden away in material things; and anyone who had a laboratory filled with bottles, retorts, and strange-looking instruments, was looked upon as an evil person — a sorcerer in league with the devil.

When did people cease to fear the secret forces of nature? When did they cease to think of them as evil forces to be shunned, and come to think of them as beneficent forces to be mastered and made use of? The silent change which took place in people's ideas about nature and her laws is one of the most important events in modern history — far more important than the wars and battles that made much more noise at the time; for without this change modern science, and the mastery of material forces which depends on science, would have been impossible.

As early as the thirteenth century a few individuals (such as Roger Bacon) were aware that the study of nature would be useful instead of harmful; and in the fifteenth and sixteenth centuries such men as Leonardo da Vinci, Copernicus, and Kepler were

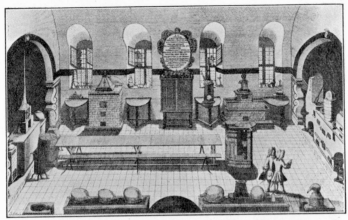

CHEMICAL LABORATORY OF THE UNIVERSITY OF ALTDORF, ABOUT 1720

From a drawing by Puschner. This laboratory is equipped with retorts and ovens. The university's income from its endowment was only $4000 yearly.

making important discoveries. But even as late as the seventeenth century the church and the universities were still hostile to natural science, and scientists who boldly announced their discoveries were more likely to be persecuted than honored.

The greatest scientist of the early seventeenth century was Galileo. Let us see how he discovered some of nature's laws and how he got into trouble by announcing these discoveries too boldly.

How Galileo discovered some laws of nature, and was persecuted for his pains. Galileo was born in Italy, in the town of Pisa, in 1564. He first studied medicine, but he gave that up because he did not want to become a doctor. He was one of those rare persons who refuse to engage in the " practical " affairs of life, but must spend all their time asking " How? " and " Why? " He therefore became a professor — first a professor of mathematics in the University of Pisa, and afterwards a professor of natural science in the University of Padua.

One day, when he was only nineteen years old, Galileo was sitting in the church at Pisa. A lamp hanging from a long chain was swinging back and forth. Thousands of people, including Galileo, had seen the swinging lamp before. But this time Galileo's curiosity

GALILEO (1564–1642)
From a painting in the Bodleian Library, Oxford University.

was aroused. He watched the swinging vessel, and as he watched
it he noticed that with each oscillation from side to side it moved a
shorter distance and also more slowly. An interesting question
arose in Galileo's mind — namely, how did the time of the movement compare with the distance? Having no wrist watch, Galileo
felt his pulse. He found that the number of pulse beats was the
same for each swing of the vessel, no matter what the length of the

swing might be. Galileo had discovered something about the way material things behave. He had discovered the law of the pendulum, and realized that by means of a pendulum time could be accurately measured. To sit in church and discover a law of nature was perhaps a new way of worshiping God.

In Galileo's time everyone supposed that a heavy body would fall to the ground more rapidly than a light one. It seems reasonable to suppose so; and at that time no one doubted it, because the Greek philosopher, Aristotle, had taught that the rate of falling bodies was in proportion to their weight. But Galileo was so curious about such things, and he had so little respect for Aristotle, that he made the scientific experiment of dropping heavy and light bodies at the same time from the same height in order to see with his own eyes how they behaved. Again he made a discovery. He found that all bodies, light or heavy, fall from a given height with equal rapidity (making allowance for the friction of the air). Galileo had discovered another law of nature — the law of falling bodies.

When Galileo announced this discovery, the professors in the University of Pisa refused to believe him. They supposed Aristotle must know better than a young fellow like Galileo. Galileo then proposed to prove that Aristotle was wrong. Leading a crowd of professors and students to the famous Leaning Tower of Pisa, he climbed far up and released at the same instant a very large and a very small cannon ball. They reached the ground at the same instant. The learned professors were astounded. They saw with their own eyes that the two weights reached the ground at the same time; but they were unwilling to believe that Aristotle could be mistaken, and it was very humiliating for them to admit that this young professor knew more than they did. Therefore they said that he had undoubtedly used magic. Instead of being praised for discovering a law of nature, Galileo was regarded with suspicion. Too much curiosity about the forces of nature was still a dangerous thing, and shortly afterwards Galileo found it convenient to leave Pisa.

How Galileo discovered a law of human nature, which was that people in authority do not like to be made fun of. Galileo was interested in astronomy as well as in mechanics. By means of an improved telescope he discovered many things hitherto unknown about the sun and the moon, the milky way, and the planets of Venus and Jupiter. The chief importance of these discoveries was to confirm the theory of Copernicus that the earth and the other planets moved around the sun instead of the sun around the earth.

Since the new theory was contrary to the teachings of the church, and seemed to be contrary to the teachings of the Bible, the theologians and the bishops and the Pope began to take note of the famous professor. Like many other people, Galileo was fond of popular applause; and as he had a sharp tongue, he could not resist making fun of the theologians who did not accept his theories. In 1632 he published a book entitled, *Dialogue on the Two Principal Systems of the World*. It was not a dry, scientific treatise, but a kind of story, in the form of a lively dialogue or argument between three characters named Salviati, Sagredo, and Simplicio. Salviati presents the theory of Galileo clearly and effectively; Sagredo is a modest pupil willing to learn; but Simplicio ("Simpleton") is a stupid person who with foolish reasons tries to defend the old system. Simplicio was intended, of course, to represent the theologians and professors who did not accept the Copernican system; and by making him ridiculous Galileo seemed to be making fun of the theologians and the Pope. In fact that is what he was doing.

Unwilling to be made ridiculous, the Pope summoned Galileo before the Holy Inquisition at Rome. His teaching was condemned as contrary to the teachings of the Bible. He was declared to be " vehemently suspected of heresy," and in order to avoid the consequences of heresy he was ordered to renounce his doctrine that the earth moves around the sun. Galileo knew what the consequence of heresy was likely to be, for he could remember very well the year 1600, when Giordano Bruno was burned at the stake for that crime. He had no desire to suffer such a fate; and perhaps he reasoned that the truth of his theory would neither be disproved by his denying it nor confirmed by his being burned to death for refusing to deny it. At all events, Galileo recanted. He

SIR ISAAC NEWTON (1642–1727)

said that he had no desire to oppose the teachings of the Bible, and he said that he no longer believed that the earth moved around the sun.

Galileo was now seventy years old. He had done his work in the world. In spite of his denial, he continued to believe that the earth moved around the sun, for belief cannot be compelled by force. Since Truth cannot be burned for heresy, it does not need to bow before Authority; and we may suppose that the earth continued on its way after the trial as if nothing at all had happened.

Why the persecution of scientists went out of fashion towards the end of the seventeenth century. Galileo died in 1642. That very year the great English scientist, Isaac Newton, was born. For his discoveries Newton was honored in his lifetime, and when he died in 1727 his funeral was a public event, celebrated with pomp and circumstance in the presence of nobles, bishops, and high government officials. Between the death of Galileo and the death of Newton a great change had occurred — the practice of persecuting scientists had largely gone out of fashion.

The work of Galileo himself did much to bring about this change; and while Galileo was still living, the study of nature found a powerful champion in Francis Bacon, lord chancellor of England in the time of James I. Bacon did not make scientific discoveries himself, but he wrote two books which had a wide influence. These were *The Advancement of Learning* and the *Novum Organum*. In these works Bacon maintained with great eloquence that the learning of the philosophers and theologians was of little value. For, he said, they are too much inclined to spin their theories out of their own heads, " as the spider worketh his web "; and so they " bring forth indeed cobwebs of learning, admirable for the fineness of the thread and work, but of no substance or profit." Bacon therefore urged men to study nature and thus acquire new knowledge which might be of practical benefit to mankind. His writings had a great influence on account of their merits, but also because the author was a man of rank and a high official.

Besides the writings of Bacon and the discoveries of Galileo and other scientists, there was another influence which helped to make the study of nature popular. This was the growing indifference to religious controversy. The Thirty Years' War in Germany (1618–1648) and the English Civil War (1642–1646) were in large part wars of religion. After every war people begin to ask, " What is the use of war?" It was especially so in the middle of the seventeenth century. Many people began to ask, " What is the use of these religious wars which settle nothing? Is it not better to study nature, which leads to knowledge, than to dispute about religion, which leads to hatred and bloodshed?" Thus many intelligent people turned away in disgust from religious controversy and began to think that the hope of mankind lay in the discoveries of science. One evidence of this new interest was the founding of scientific societies. The most important of such societies were: the Royal Society of London (1662); the Royal Academy of Science at Paris (1666); and the Royal Academy of Science at Berlin (1700).

One of the members of the Royal Society of London was Isaac

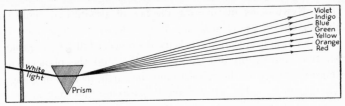

LIGHT PASSING THROUGH A PRISM

Newton.   Few men have had a greater influence on modern history than Newton.   He did not lead conquering armies or rule a great kingdom; but in the eighteenth century he ruled the thoughts of men.   Let us see how he did it.

How Newton discovered that objects have no right to their colors, having borrowed them from the light.   Newton's first great discovery was made in a simple way.   Holding an ordinary glass prism in his window, he saw that the light passing through it was thrown on the opposite wall in seven different colors.   From this he concluded that white light is a blend of seven different kinds of rays; and that each of these different kinds of rays, in passing through the prism, is *refracted* (bent out of a straight line) to a different degree, so that each ray, separated from all the others and falling on the wall in a different place, shows there its proper color.   (See the figure above.)

If this was so, why, Newton wondered, are some objects one color and some another?   This he thought must be because objects do something to light when it falls on them.   Objects receive light differently.   Some objects are very hospitable; they open the door wide, take light in with all its different rays, and shut the door again.   Such objects, having absorbed all the rays, appear black. Other objects are less hospitable; they take in all of the rays except one kind — let us say the red rays; and the red rays, finding the door shut in their faces, fly back to the eye of the observer.   Such objects appear red.   Some objects will have nothing to do with light or any of its rays.   Such objects appear white.   Thus Newton discovered that color is not a property of objects.   A red book is a book which has stolen and concealed all the rays of light except red, leaving the red rays outside to conceal the theft.

How Newton, by discovering the law of gravitation, made one universe out of many worlds. Before Newton's time men had asked the simple questions, " Why do objects fall to the ground, instead of falling up into the sky? Why do the planets circle around the sun, and the moon round the earth, instead of going off at a tangent?" The first of these questions they had answered by saying that the earth pulls objects to itself by a force, which they called " gravitation." The second question they answered by saying that the sun pulls the planets, and the earth pulls the moon, by a force just sufficient to balance the force which, by itself, would drive them off at a tangent. Was this force which pulls the moon to the earth and the planets toward the sun the same as the force which makes objects fall to the ground? Before Newton's time some men had guessed that it was; but no man had been able to prove it. What Newton did was to prove it.

How Newton proved this we can easily understand by help of the figure on page 185. Suppose that, when the moon arrived at point A in its orbit, the earth should suddenly let go of it. In that case the moon would move in a straight line, and B is the point it would reach in one minute. But the earth does not let go. It keeps pulling the moon, and so at the end of one minute the moon finds itself at C instead of B. This means of course that in one minute the earth has pulled the moon down from B to C. This distance could be calculated, and Newton found that it was about 15 feet. Thus we may say that the earth attracts the moon by a force which makes the moon " fall " 15 feet in one minute.

Now what Newton wanted to know was this: Is this force which makes the moon fall 15 feet in a minute the same as the force which makes all bodies fall to the ground? How could he determine this? We know that near the earth bodies fall very rapidly. Galileo's cannon ball, if it weighed ten pounds, must, falling from the top of the Tower of Pisa, have fallen about 180 feet in less than a second. But suppose the Tower of Pisa were as high as the moon, and suppose Galileo could have taken his ten-pound weight to the top and dropped it from point A in the moon's orbit. He knew that from such a height it would move, in the first minute of its fall, very slowly. Therefore what Newton had to find out was this: If any body, such as a ten-pound weight, could be dropped from point *A* in the moon's orbit, how far would it fall in the first minute? Would it fall from *A* to *D* — that is, 15 feet? Well, Newton did not need a tower as high as the moon to answer this, for he had something better — he had Galileo's law of falling bodies. By means of this law he figured out mathematically that any body, if it could be carried up to the moon's orbit and dropped from point *A*, would fall in the first minute just the distance from *A* to *D* — that is, just as far as the moon "falls" in one minute.

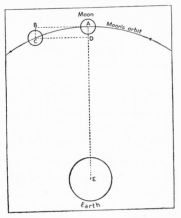

Thus Newton, with the help of Galileo, proved that the force by which the earth holds the moon in its orbit is the same as the force which makes bodies fall to the ground. By similar methods, he proved that this

EFFECT OF THE FORCE OF GRAVITY

force is also the same as that by which the sun holds the planets in their orbits. In the end Newton made it possible for scientists to accept the idea that ordinary gravitation is a force that operates uniformly throughout the universe. Other men had discovered certain special laws of nature. Newton discovered one universal law of nature — that all bodies, great or small, whether planets or grains of sand, attract each other by a uniform force, in proportion to the mass of the bodies and inversely in proportion to the square of the distance between them. Newton tied all matter together with one law, and so we may say that he made one universe out of many worlds.

The work of Newton turned the attention of learned men to the study of nature. In the eighteenth century many inventions were made. Something was learned about chemistry; much about electricity; and most of all about mathematics, physics, and mechanics. The older studies of theology and metaphysics fell out of favor, and natural science, or "natural philosophy" as it was then called, was regarded as the most important branch of learning.

This was in itself a great revolution in thought; but we should not have needed to learn so much about Galileo and Newton if they had influenced the thinking of none but learned men. What is important for us is that the new ideas of nature and natural law influenced the thinking of ordinary people about human life — about the nature of man, about his rights, and about the organization of government and society.

We must now see how the scientific idea of nature and natural laws entered the heads of ordinary people and changed their thinking about man and the power of his mind.

II. NEW IDEAS ABOUT MAN AND THE POWER OF HIS MIND

Why ordinary people became interested in the Newtonian philosophy. Newton's great book, the *Principia*, was first published in 1686. At that time not twenty men in Europe knew enough mathematics to understand it; yet by the middle of the eighteenth century ordinary people everywhere were eager to learn something about what was called the "Newtonian philosophy." Men went about giving popular illustrated lectures on the subject, and many books were published in English, French, and Italian (including some written especially for " the ladies ") which explained in simple language the meaning of Newton's discoveries. " Few people read Newton," said Voltaire, " because one must be learned to understand him; but everybody talks about him." Why should everyone talk about the work of a man whose books no ordinary person could understand?

Ordinary people talked about Newton for the same reason that in our time ordinary people talk about Darwin. The name of Darwin stands for a new idea of the world and of man's place in it; and most people, even though they may never have opened the *Origin of Species*, know something of Darwin and the Darwinian philosophy of evolution. In the eighteenth century the name of Newton stood for a new idea of the world and of man's place in it; and that is why ordinary people, who never opened the *Principia*, were eager to learn about the Newtonian philosophy. What was this new idea of the world and of man's place in it? We can best understand what it was by contrasting it with the older idea which had survived from the Middle Ages.

In the Middle Ages the world was regarded as a mystery and man as a poor creature who could never solve this mystery. It was thought that men were naturally disposed to evil, so that if they were allowed to think and to act for themselves they would be sure to do evil deeds and to think wrong thoughts. Therefore it was supposed that God had given kings and princes authority to govern men's acts, and the church authority to govern their thoughts. The duty of men was to obey this divinely established authority of state and church without question; and no one supposed that men could ever, here on earth, be made much wiser or better, or the conditions of life under which they lived be much improved.

This was surely a depressing view of man and his earthly fortunes. But since the time of the Renaissance many men had ventured to think better of mankind. After all, it seemed that the scientists — men like Copernicus and Galileo — were able, by using their own reason, to learn something about God's universe that the church did not know. If this was so, was the world after all an unsolvable mystery? Had God actually given truth into the keeping of the church? Might not the mind of man be capable of discovering the truth about that world? These were some of the questions people began to ask themselves.

The popular books about Newton gave clear answers to these questions. According to the Newtonian philosophy, as these books explained it, it seemed as if God had said to mankind: " I have created an interesting world for you to learn about and to use. I have designed the world according to a rational plan; and I have given you a rational mind, capable of understanding that plan. That is all I can do, and you must make the best of it. By following reason and experience you may in time learn all about the universe and its laws and so in the end solve all your difficulties." This is why ordinary people were eager to learn about the Newtonian philosophy: It provided them with a democratic idea of the universe, and made man the master of his own fate. It enabled them to believe that men were capable, by means of reason, of indefinitely increasing knowledge; and through knowledge, of becoming always wiser and better. It enabled them to believe that mankind, through its own effort, was capable of making progress towards perfection.

How " the philosophers " applied Newton's idea of a democratic universe to government and society. This new idea that God had given men reason and intended them to use it was a terrible explosive. If it got into the heads of ordinary people it was sure to upset kings and destroy the power of bishops and popes. You can easily see how this was so. If God had intended men to be guided by reason, it is clear that he could not have intended them to give blind obedience to kings and churches. Thus, for those who accepted the Newtonian philosophy, the democratic idea of the universe led directly to the democratic idea of government and society.

All the leading thinkers and writers of the eighteenth century accepted the Newtonian philosophy. For that reason perhaps they were often called " the philosophers." They were not professors of philosophy in colleges, or writers of books about metaphysics. They were mostly writers of plays, novels, histories, and popular books about science, religion and morality, education, economics, and politics. Through these books they spread among ordinary people the new idea of the world and of man's powers; and on the basis of this idea they preached the modern democratic faith — freedom of thought, freedom of religion, and political freedom.

The philosophers were not in agreement on all of these points, but on one point they were agreed. They agreed that truth was something to be discovered by thinking; and therefore they all believed that men must be free to think. One of the most influential of the philosophers was the Frenchman, Voltaire (1694–1778). His dramas, novels, histories, tracts, and letters fill ninety ordinary volumes. For fifty years, with all the resources of a brilliant mind, he preached freedom of thought and denounced cruelty and oppression in all its forms. Above all others, Voltaire stands as the champion of reason and tolerance.

Why Voltaire went to England, and why he could not live in Paris when he returned. As a young man, Voltaire won a reputation in Paris for his plays and the brilliance and wit of his conversation. But his biting wit often got him into trouble; and on one occasion he offended the powerful Chevalier de Rohan. This eminent per-

son, too proud to fight a duel with a commoner, had his lackeys give Voltaire a beating in the street, and then used his influence to have him sent to the Bastille. By promising to leave France, Voltaire obtained his freedom; and in 1726, at the age of thirty-two, he went to England, where he lived three years.

In England Voltaire was free to say what he pleased, and no one gave him a beating for it, or sent him to prison. On the contrary he was treated with great consideration, and he was delighted with a country where no one was oppressed for his religion, and where literary men and scientists were highly respected. In 1727 he at-

VOLTAIRE (1694–1778)

François Marie Arouet, son of a French notary, took the name Voltaire soon after he came of age. He was about forty when this engraving was made.

tended the funeral of Newton and was amazed to see " a professor of mathematics buried like a king." While in England, Voltaire wrote a book called *Letters on the English* which was published there in 1733. In it he criticized the intolerance of the French government and church by praising the free institutions and customs of England. " The English, as a free people," he said, "choose their own road to heaven." There the nobles are " great without insolence, and the people share in the government without disorder."

In 1734, after he had returned to France, Voltaire's *Letters on the English* was published again, in his own country, and people read it with eagerness and delight. But such a book displeased the government and the church, and it was ordered to be burned by the public hangman as "scandalous, contrary to religion, to morals, and to respect for authority." This was of course the best advertisement any book could have, and more people read the work after it was condemned than before. But in order to avoid the Bastille, Voltaire went to live with friends at the château of Cirey, in Lorraine, where he remained for fifteen years. Afterwards, since it was still unsafe to live in Paris, he built a fine house at Ferney, near Geneva.

These experiences of Voltaire's made a deep impression on him. It was humiliating to think that only in foreign countries — in England, Holland, Prussia, or Switzerland — could a Frenchman say what he thought about religion and politics. Thus Voltaire came to have a passionate hatred of oppression, and all his life he made war on intolerance and persecution for opinion's sake. He did this both by his writings and by his acts.

How Voltaire made war on intolerance by his writings. Besides his *Letters on the English*, Voltaire wrote plays which thousands of people saw at the theaters. He wrote amusing tales, such as *Candide;* books on science, such as *The Philosophy of Newton;* and all the time he wrote letters — thousands of letters — to all sorts of persons throughout Europe. Among his correspondents was Frederick the Great, whom he admired, visited, and quarreled with. In all of these works, sometimes with wit and humor, sometimes with burning indignation, Voltaire carried on an uncompromising crusade against intolerance.

Voltaire was also a historian. One of his friends, Madame du Châtelet, said she could not read histories because they related a "mass of petty events without connection and without consequence — a thousand battles which decided nothing." But Voltaire thought there was something worth learning from history. For Madame du Châtelet, and for other people like her, he therefore wrote a general history of the world from the earliest times. This work he called *An Essay on the Manners and Spirit of Nations* (1756). This was the greatest of Voltaire's writings, and it had perhaps a greater influence than any other in spreading his ideas.

But how could Voltaire, merely by relating the history of past

times, convince people that persecution and intolerance were unjust
and useless? He did this chiefly by making it appear that the
greatest advancement in knowledge and civilization occurred when
there was greatest freedom of thought — that is, in the time of the
Greeks and Romans, during the Renaissance, and in the seventeenth
and eighteenth centuries — whereas in the Middle Ages, when the
church had most power and thought was most restricted, there was
the greatest ignorance and wretchedness; these were the " Dark
Ages." Voltaire painted the ancient world in brighter colors and
the Middle Ages in darker colors than either deserved; but for
that very reason his history had a great influence in convincing
people that the intolerance of the church was the great obstacle to
enlightenment and progress.

As Voltaire grew older his hatred of persecution in the name of
religion increased. He was not an atheist, nor an enemy of religion; but he was an enemy of any and all religions that were opposed to freedom of thought. Therefore he was a bitter enemy of
the Catholic Church in France, which at that time used its great
power to suppress other forms of religious belief. When Voltaire
was about sixty-five years old he began to make frequent use of the
word *infâme* ("infamous thing"). Letter after letter to his
friends he closed with the phrase, *Écraser l'infâme!* (" Crush the
infamous thing!") The phrase became famous. To crush the
"infamous thing" became the chief mission of Voltaire in life.
The "infamous thing" was not the Catholic Church but the spirit
of intolerance, the spirit of persecution in all its forms.

How Voltaire made war on intolerance by his acts. In 1762
Voltaire was sixty-eight years old, rich and famous, living in comfort, and associating with the distinguished persons who came from
all parts of Europe and America to do him honor. He might well
have thought that his work was done. But instead of taking his
ease, the famous old man now came voluntarily to the aid of certain
obscure persons who had suffered unjust and cruel treatment. The
most famous case of this sort was that of Jean Calas.

Jean Calas was a Huguenot shopkeeper who had lived an honest
and respectable life at Toulouse for forty years. One evening in
October, 1761, his eldest son, Mark Anthony, committed suicide

by hanging himself in his father's shop. Someone started the rumor that Mark Anthony had been murdered by his father and brother in order to prevent him from turning Catholic. The rumor spread like wildfire, and Jean Calas and his son were tried for murder by the parlement of Toulouse. There was no evidence of murder. But the people and the magistrates were blinded by religious hatred of the Huguenots. The property of Calas was confiscated; his two daughters and one son were forced to embrace the monastic life; and Jean Calas himself was first tortured and then broken on the wheel — the most cruel punishment known to the law.

Voltaire studied this case long and carefully. He became convinced that Calas was innocent. The cruel punishment of an innocent man, due solely to religious hatred, aroused him to a white heat of indignation, and he set himself to get the decision reversed. He printed a clear statement of the facts, had Madame Calas brought to Paris and cared for, and got all his friends to use their influence with the officials of the government. At last, after three years of hard work, the case of Calas was retried at Paris and the verdict was reversed. The children of Calas were given their freedom, and Voltaire gave money and obtained money from friends for their necessities. The " case of the Calas " became famous throughout Europe, and nothing Voltaire ever did brought him more honor or admiration as the champion of human rights.

By the close of his life Voltaire had conquered a realm more powerful than that of the king — the realm of public opinion. Neither church nor state dared interfere with him. In 1778, fifty-two years after taking refuge in England, he returned in triumph to Paris. At the frontier of France the customs officers stopped his carriage to ask if it contained any contraband goods. " Nothing but myself," Voltaire replied. He was allowed to pass. In Paris he was crowned and applauded at the theater and followed by admiring crowds in the street. It is said that one day a stranger asked an old woman, " Who is that man who is much followed by the people? " The woman replied, " That is the saviour of Calas."

Voltaire's great influence was due partly to his unselfish service in behalf of oppressed persons and partly to the fact that he lived long and wrote much. But it was due chiefly to the fact that everybody read his works eagerly because they were so well written. No one ever wrote more simply, more clearly, or with greater liveliness and charm. His ninety volumes of argument, wit, ridicule, and irony did their work. When Voltaire died, in 1778, the people of France no longer believed in the divine right of kings or priests to govern the thoughts of men.

III. New Ideas about the Rights of Man and the Nature of Government

Why the French people admired the English form of government. People who believe in freedom of thought usually believe also in freedom of government. By the end of the eighteenth century few people believed in the divine right of kings to govern as they pleased. This does not mean that many people believed that kings ought to be abolished or that all the people could be given an equal share in government. It means only that people had come to have a new idea about the nature of political authority. This new idea was that kings and rulers, instead of deriving their authority from the will of God, derived their authority from the will of the people — or at least of some of the people.

One thing which made this new idea popular in France was the success of England under a constitutional government. In 1689 most people in France thought the English were trying a dangerous experiment in giving so much power to Parliament and so many liberties to the people. (See Chapter III, p. 74.) But in the eighteenth century the English people got on very well with this form of government. They defeated the French in three wars, took away their colonies, and became the leading colonial and commercial power in the world. After 1763 many Frenchmen therefore asked themselves this question: " Why does England always defeat France in war? Would France not be more successful and better off if she had a government like that of England? "

The writings of the philosophers did much to make them think so. Voltaire's *Letters on the English* praised the free institutions of England, where " the people share in the government without disorder." Rapin, a Huguenot in exile in England, wrote a *History of England*, which was widely read in France; and most educated

Frenchmen had read Delolme's *English Constitution*. Above all, Montesquieu, in his famous book *The Spirit of the Laws*, praised the English government as a kind of ideal system. Through these books and a host of others, Frenchmen learned to think well of the English form of government and to desire the political liberties enjoyed by Englishmen.

How John Locke devised a theory of government which the Americans and the French made use of. Few people like to be called " rebels." Therefore, when they engage in revolution they look around for a theory of government which will make their action seem right and meritorious. This is what the English did, in the seventeenth century, when they cut off the head of Charles I (1649) and later dethroned James II (1688). Of course if kings ruled by divine right, then the English were rebels against God as well as against the king. So English writers tried to find a theory of government which would make it right for them to resist an autocratic king. Theories are not difficult to find, and the English found several. But the one which became popular in the eighteenth century was the theory of " natural rights."

The theory of natural rights was well stated by John Locke, who published in 1690 a work entitled *Two Treatises of Government*. His object was to show that the English people had a right to dethrone James II in 1688. His theory of government may be stated briefly thus: (1) All men have certain natural rights — a right to life, to liberty, and to the possessions which they acquire by their own labor. (2) God gave men reason in order that they may know what their natural rights are and in order that they may devise a government to protect them in these rights. (3) Men therefore owe obedience to the government they have established, as long as the government protects them in their rights. (4) When any government ceases to do this, the men who made it may destroy it. Thus Locke tried to prove that the English were not rebels against James, but that James was a rebel against them.

You can easily see that this is both a democratic theory and a revolutionary theory. It affirms that governments are made by men, for the protection of their natural rights, and may be overturned when they cease to protect those rights. Any people wishing to change their form of government would be glad to borrow so convenient a theory. In the eighteenth century Locke's theory was borrowed by the Americans and the French.

Locke's essay on civil government was read by all the leaders in the American Revolution, and it furnished them with the theory by which they justified the revolt against England. Thomas Jefferson was especially familiar with Locke's work, and he was simply repeating Locke's ideas when he wrote in the Declaration of Independence:

We hold these truths to be self-evident: that all men are created equal; that they are endowed by their creator with certain unalienable rights; that among these are life, liberty, and the pursuit of happiness; that to secure these rights, governments are instituted among men, deriving their just powers from the consent of the governed; that whenever any form of government becomes destructive of these ends, it is the right of the people to alter or to abolish it.

Locke's book had a great influence in France also. The philosophers, who accepted the Newtonian idea of natural law in the material world, found it easy to accept the idea of natural rights in the world of human society and government. "Natural law," said Voltaire, "is that which Nature teaches all men. . . . Human rights should be founded, in all cases, on the law of nature." When the French people became dissatisfied with the autocratic government of the king, they found it easy to deny the theory of the divine right of kings and to replace it with the theory of the natural rights of man.

The philosopher who had the greatest influence in making the natural rights theory popular in France was Jean Jacques Rousseau. Rousseau was a queer, unhappy person, at times on the verge of insanity. But insanity and genius are sometimes closely allied. Whether insane or inspired, the life and writings of Rousseau have had a profound influence on modern history; and therefore we need to know more about this mad genius than about many other far more normal and respectable people.

How Rousseau lived as a vagabond for thirty-seven years and then suddenly discovered that he was a genius. Jean Jacques

Rousseau was born in Geneva, June 28, 1712.   A few days later
his mother died, and he was left to grow up without training or
education.   He learned a little Latin, something about engraving,
something about music, much about trees and flowers, and more
than was at all necessary about meanness and vice.   He tried many
occupations but was too restless and infirm of purpose to succeed
in any.   He drifted about from one place to another, without definite object, living in idleness and poverty.   What he liked best
was to do as he pleased from day to day, to wander in the woods,
or to lie and dream of the fine things he would do if the world would
only give him a chance.

At the age of thirty-seven Rousseau was living in a dirty little
hotel in Paris, so far a complete failure in life.   During thirty-seven
years of aimless and varied experience he had acquired certain
fixed likes and dislikes.   He liked to be alone a good deal, because
he was not accustomed to society or at ease with strangers.   He
liked the country better than the city.   He understood and sympathized with the poor and the ignorant and the unhappy but
disliked the rich, the well-born, the cultivated and pretentious
people of fine society.   Never having submitted to restraint or
discipline, he had a passionate dislike of any form of compulsion.
He had, too, a settled feeling that something was wrong with the
world because it did not give him the success or the happiness that
he deserved.   These likes and dislikes help to explain the ideas
Rousseau set forth in his books.

One day in 1749 Rousseau was walking to the prison of Vincennes
to visit his friend Diderot, who was shut up there for writing *Letters
on the Blind for the Use of Those Who See.*   In his hand he carried
a copy of the *Mercury of France;* and as he walked along he read in
that journal that a prize had been offered for the best essay on the
subject, *Has the Progress of Science and the Arts Contributed to the
Corruption or the Purification of Morals?*   Rousseau tells us that
this announcement suddenly filled his mind with the most brilliant
ideas.   The result was that he wrote an essay on the subject,
which won the prize.   In this essay he argued that when men lived
a simple, primitive life, without cities, they were virtuous and
happy; but that with the increase of knowledge, the accumulation

Bibliothèque Nationale

JEAN JACQUES ROUSSEAU AT MONTMORENCY

A drawing from life made by the painter Houel after dining with Rousseau.

of wealth, the growth of cities and the luxurious life of cities, people became corrupt and unhappy.

The publication of this essay made Rousseau suddenly famous. Eminent philosophers sought his acquaintance. Idle, fashionable ladies, wanting a new excitement, came to his dirty little hotel to visit him. To be rid of them he was rude and outspoken; but that only convinced them that here was a new kind of philosopher — an "original," a genius. Thus Rousseau discovered his one great talent — that of a writer of books containing original ideas. He found that if he merely set down the ideas that came into his head, instead of trying to think as other people did, other people would find his ideas original and interesting. Therefore Rousseau, having first gained fame by teaching that the progress of art corrupted morals, devoted himself to the art of writing great books. His great books, which were all written within a short time, were: *The New Héloïse* (1761); *Émile* (1762); *The Social Contract* (1762); and *The Confessions* (1782).

How Rousseau taught that men would cease to do evil if no one tried to compel them to be good. In all of these works Rousseau taught that men are naturally good and that if they do evil, it is chiefly because the conditions in which they live make it impossible to do otherwise. This was Rousseau's own experience. He felt that he himself was naturally good because he had good and kindly intentions toward everyone; yet he knew, and confessed with the greatest frankness, that he often did evil. This he said was because his good intentions were thwarted by circumstances. Instead of blaming himself for his bad acts, he blamed " society " — the bad conditions under which he was forced to live. So Rousseau reasoned that all men had good intentions, like himself; and he concluded that if the conditions in which men lived were what they should be, and might be, all men would do good deeds instead of evil deeds.

What then was wrong with society? What were the bad conditions which made men do evil deeds? These bad conditions were chiefly: (1) the unequal distribution of wealth, which enabled the few to live in idleness and luxury and compelled the many to toil constantly and live in poverty and wretchedness; (2) the inequality of rank and privilege which gave to a few an unfair advantage; (3) a false system of education, which taught people to value rank, wealth, or social position more than talent, virtue, or service to others. These conditions Rousseau denounced in all his works. He taught that society was so organized that the few corrupt people had all the privileges and power, whereas the mass of the people, who were mostly simple, honest, kindly, and virtuous, lived in subjection and slavery.

How were these bad conditions, this subjection of the virtuous many to the corrupt few, to be remedied? First of all by establishing a just government. Rousseau's ideas on government were presented in *The Social Contract*. That famous little book opens with the words, " Men are born free, and are everywhere in chains. . . . How was this change made? I do not know. What can make it legitimate? I think I can answer that question." In *The Social Contract* Rousseau tried to answer the question, " What is it that gives any government the right to make laws and compel people to obey them? " Rousseau did not urge men to change their governments by force; he urged them to change their ideas about the right of governments to use force.

Rousseau followed Locke in thinking that all men have certain natural rights and liberties. This being so, he argued that no man could justly be deprived of his natural rights and liberties without his own consent. In society as it existed men had been deprived of their rights and liberties without their consent. In a justly organized society every man would give up his right to act for himself and agree to act only for the good of all. Thus each man would agree to be bound by the will of all; and therefore no government, whether monarchy or republic, would have a rightful authority over men unless it had been established by the consent of all the people.

In this way Rousseau made out that governments derive their legitimate authority from the consent of the governed instead of from the will of God. Rousseau did not say that kings ought to be abolished. But he did say that all men had the same natural rights; that all the people had the right to establish whatever form of government they thought wise; and that when they did establish such a government it would be possible to abolish those bad customs and institutions which made men wretched and to replace them by good customs and institutions which would make men happy.

In 1762, after the publication of *The Social Contract* and *Émile*, Rousseau was forced to leave France. He lived for eight years in exile. He became half mad from thinking that the world, including all his friends, had turned against him. Until the end of his life he fancied himself a hunted man and wandered about, living and dying in wretchedness. His *Émile* was condemned by the parlement of Paris in June, 1762; but during the next twenty-five years his works were read by everyone. Mallet du Pan says that in 1788 he saw Marat reading *The Social Contract* and expounding its doctrines to an applauding crowd in the streets of Paris. No man did so much as this unhappy Jean Jacques Rousseau to convince people that they might all become happy by changing their political and social institutions.

With all these new ideas about the rights of man and the nature of government, it would be strange if we could not find some new ideas about the rights of states and their relations. There were such ideas, and we must now see what they were.

IV. New Ideas about the Rights of States and Their Relations

How the idea of Holy Church and Holy Empire gave way to the idea of international law and a league of nations. In the Middle Ages most of the people of Europe, except the Russians and the Turks, had the same religion and were united in the same church — the Holy Catholic Church. For this reason they thought that they ought all to live at peace under the guidance of one empire — the Holy Roman Empire. It is true that they fought among themselves a good deal of the time, and that the Holy Roman Empire had little actual power outside of Germany, except sometimes in Italy. But nearly everyone thought that this was not as it should be. Since Europe made one Christian community, it was thought that all the peoples of Europe should live at peace under one Holy Empire and one Holy Church. This notion we may call the medieval idea of European unity.

By the seventeenth century most people had come to see that this ideal was no longer a possibility. The Reformation had divided Europe into Catholic and Protestant countries; and at the same time there had arisen powerful states, such as England, France, Spain, and Sweden, whose rulers claimed that they were subject neither to pope nor to emperor, but to God alone. Besides, in the sixteenth and seventeenth centuries these states were constantly engaged in long and destructive wars with each other — wars far more destructive than those of the Middle Ages. The kings, having more power and more money, raised larger armies; and these armies now fought with muskets and cannon instead of with swords, pikes, and bows and arrows. So people began to ask themselves, "What is the good of all these destructive wars? Must the disputes of states always be decided by force and violence? Since the peoples of Europe no longer have one church, and since the states of Europe cannot be united into one empire, is there not some other method of uniting them so that they may live in peace and friendship?"

By the seventeenth century men began to propose new answers to these questions. Since it seemed no longer possible to unite the peoples of Europe under a common religion, some men began to seek for a common law which might unite them. This was the beginning of modern international law. And since it seemed impossible to unite the states of Europe under one empire, other men began to ask whether it would not be possible to unite them in a league or federation for certain purposes. This was the beginning of the modern idea of a league of nations. The medieval ideal of church and empire thus gave way to the modern ideal of law and federation.

How Hugo Grotius tried to find the rights of war and peace in the law of nature. Hugo Grotius (1583–1645) was a learned Dutchman, who published in 1625 one of the most famous books ever written, which he called *The Rights of War and Peace* (*De jure belli et pacis*). In the introduction to this book he tells us why he wrote it. "I saw prevailing throughout the Christian world a license in making war which even barbarous nations would have been ashamed of, recourse being had to arms for slight reasons or for no reason; and when arms were once taken up, all reverence for divine or human law was thrown away." Besides, said Grotius, there are learned men who say that "for a king, who has an empire to maintain, nothing is unjust which is useful," and that in affairs of state he who has the might has the right. Grotius wrote his

BOOKSHOP OF LACKINGTON, ALLEN, & CO., LONDON

In this eighteenth century shop, according to the advertisement, "above half a million volumes are constantly on sale." From an engraving by Walker.

book to prove that states, like individuals, were bound by rules of right and justice. He tried to prove that there was such a thing as international law, and that states were bound by this law.

But where is this " international law " to be found? Grotius found it in the law of nature. All men, he said, belong by nature to one society — the society of the human race; and as members of this society, all men are bound to act justly towards each other. Kings are independent of any human law, but like other men they are bound by nature to act justly towards each other. But how can we know what this natural law of just action is? This, said Grotius, we can discover by reason and experience. What action is just according to reason; and what action have the wise and learned in all ages agreed to regard as just?

Well, for example, reason tells us that it is right for a person to defend himself against attack; and all people in all ages have so well agreed on this point that it has become a proverb: " Self-preservation is the first law of nature." Kings then must have the right to defend their kingdoms against attack, because this right is according to reason and the judgment of mankind. In the same way Grotius argued that a king or a state has a natural right to punish another king or state for an injury which has been done, because this right is also according to reason and the judgment of mankind. These were the two rights of war which Grotius found — the right to wage war in self-defense, and the right to wage war to punish a state for an injury it had done.

Grotius went on to establish in the same way the rules that states were bound to follow in carrying on a war once begun. He does not deny that states have a right to make war, but he says that states have a right to make only just wars and to carry them on only in a just and humane way, in so far as war can be so carried on. Other writers, notably Pufendorf and Vattel, wrote books on international law. The aim of these writers was much the same as that of Grotius — to find an international law which ought to be followed by states in their relations to each other. All these books, and especially the book of Grotius, were widely read and greatly praised; but the states of Europe continued to act very much as they had done before. They continued to wage unjust wars. They paid little attention to this international law which ought to restrain them.

What could be done about that? Was there any way of compelling them to act justly? Grotius has little to say about any practical methods of preventing unjust wars, but he does make one interesting suggestion. " It would be useful," he says, " and indeed it is almost necessary, that certain congresses of Christian powers should be held, in which disputes among some of them may be decided by others who are not interested, and in which measures may be taken to compel the parties to accept peace on just terms." Grotius had tried to find an international law; and in this statement he hints at an international government to enforce the law.

Other men made much of this idea of an international government or federation of states. These schemes may be regarded as the ancestors of our own League of Nations. Let us see what some of them were.

How Emeric Cruce invited all the rulers of the world to form a league of princes. In 1623 there was published at Paris a little book by Emeric Cruce, called *The New Cyneas* (*Nouveau Cynée*). If you wish to know why the book was called by this title, read the conversation between Cyneas and Pyrrhus in Plutarch's *Life of Pyrrhus*. Cruce does not discuss the " right " of war; he points out that war is destructive and inhumane and useless because it injures those who win as well as those who fail. He says:

Human society is one body, of which all the members are in sympathy in such manner that it is impossible for the sickness [injury] of one not to be communicated to the others. Now this little book contains a universal policy, useful to all nations, and agreeable to those who have some light of reason and the sentiment of humanity.

Cruce first discusses the cause of wars, showing that they arise from greed, jealousy, and ambition; and the effects of wars, showing that they are all harmful and none useful. Since this is so, and since everyone would be better off if there were no more wars, he proposes that all of the rulers of the world should be invited to send ambassadors to meet in a common assembly, perhaps in Venice. The Pope, he thinks, might invite all the Christian rulers, and the King of France might invite all the non-Christian rulers. This assembly might then act as a court to settle all disputes arising between states; and it might be given authority by the rulers to compel states to accept its decisions. Thus war could easily be abolished if the rulers were willing to see it abolished.

Many advantages, Cruce thought, would follow from the abolition of war. If princes were no longer in danger of being attacked, their armies could be reduced, the soldiers could engage in useful occupations, taxes would be less, wealth would increase, and governments could devote themselves to the arts of peace instead of the art of war. If all nations lived at peace, they could all have the same money and the same weights and measures, and commercial tariffs could be abolished. Thus the intercourse of the peoples of the world with each other would be increased, mutual fear and religious hatred would disappear, and all would learn that friendship and charity are better roads to happiness than jealousy and conflict.

Cruсé was an obscure scholar, and his humane little book was almost unknown in his day. Being a wise man, he scarcely expected that many people would heed what he said. His book, he said,

perhaps will be useless. I have wished, nevertheless, to leave this testimony to posterity. If it serves nothing, patience. It is a small matter to lose paper and words. I have said and done what was possible for the public good, and some few who read this little book will be grateful to me for it, and will honor me, as I hope, with their remembrance.

He had to wait nearly three hundred years for this grateful remembrance.

How a duke, a Quaker, and a priest each devised a plan for a league of states. In the seventeenth century the most famous plan for a federation of Europe was known as the Grand Design of Henry IV. It was not written by Henry IV, but by Henry's minister, the Duke of Sully. Sully proposed to reduce all the states of

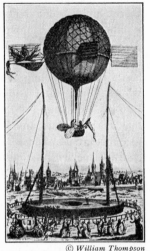

© *William Thompson*

EXPERIMENT IN BALLOON
TRAVEL IN 1784

M. l'Abbé Berteau and M. Marvaux left Dijon at 5 P.M. April 25 and arrived safely at Magni-les-Auxone at 6:25.

Europe to fifteen —six hereditary monarchies, six elective monarchies, and three federated republics. The territorial limits of these states were then to be fixed in such a way as to satisfy everyone as much as possible. This having been done, he thought they might all agree to recognize the right of each country to its territory, its religion, and its form of government. Then he proposed that they should unite to establish a common assembly, with six minor councils, for settling such disputes as might arise among them. For enforcing these arrangements there was to be a common European army for which each state would contribute men and money in proportion to its population and wealth.

Another scheme was devised by William Penn, the founder of Pennsylvania, who in 1693 published a short *Essay towards the*

Present and Future Peace of Europe. Penn's essay was not read by many people; but towards the close of the long and disastrous War of the Spanish Succession a French priest, the Abbé Saint-Pierre, published a scheme for abolishing war which was often reprinted and much talked about in the eighteenth century. The Abbé Saint-Pierre was a busy, absent-minded man, " whom every-one laughs at, but who is himself serious and never laughs." He had a passion for improving everything and everybody, and so he wrote project after project — " Project for Making the Roads Passable in Winter," " Project for Reforming Beggars," " Project for Making Dukes and Peers Useful," etc. One day it occurred to him that it would be well to abolish war. The idea, he says, " struck me with astonishment by its great beauty. It has oc-cupied all my attention for fifteen days. . . . I betook myself with ardor and joy to the greatest enterprise that could come from the human mind." The result was his *Project for Making Peace Perpetual.*

Saint-Pierre's idea was that the twenty-four states of Europe, great and small, including Russia but not Turkey, should form a perpetual union, in order to preserve peace in Europe. To remove the chief causes of war, Saint-Pierre proposed to fix once for all the form of government and the territorial boundaries of all the states. It would be the duty of the federal government to protect each ruler against insurrections from within and against conquest from without. To prevent commercial and colonial wars, the limits of the colonies of the different states were to be likewise fixed, and there was to be a commercial code in which the tariffs and trade laws " may be equal and reciprocal towards all nations." Such disputes as might still arise would be referred to the federal govern-ment for arbitration and settlement. If, in spite of all these pre-cautions, any ruler attempted to make any war not authorized by the federal government, he should be declared " an enemy of European society," and all the other powers would then make war on him to compel him to keep the peace.

How the philosophers of the eighteenth century ridiculed Saint-Pierre, denounced war, and hoped for peace. The good Abbé's *Project for Making Peace Perpetual* was first published in 1713, and several times thereafter.   It was familiar to the philosophers, and Rousseau wrote a brief summary of it, together with his own comments.   The philosophers desired peace, but none of them thought that the Abbé Saint-Pierre's scheme would work.   They thought that wars were made by rulers to gratify their ambitions. How then, they said, can you expect kings to stop making war, when they are the very persons who benefit by it?   " Is there a single sovereign in the world," Rousseau asked, who will agree to a project which " forces him to be just, not only with foreigners, but even with his own subjects? "   The Abbé's *Project*, Voltaire said, was an " excellent scheme, incapable of execution."

Nevertheless, throughout the eighteenth century, the philosophers passionately denounced war as inhuman and worse than useless. " It is absurd," said Voltaire, " that nations should perish because . . . princes have reasoned badly.   Let them [the rulers] fight out their quarrels in a closed field if they please; but that an entire people should be sacrificed to their interests, that is the horrible part."   The philosophers hoped to abolish war too; but they did not think it could be done by a league of states or of rulers.   They thought that war would disappear only when people became en- lightened.   They thought that gradually, with the progress of knowledge, people would become intelligent enough to establish just governments, and that just governments would be wise enough to see that war is a foolish way to settle disputes.

We have now reached the end of a long chapter.   In this chapter we have seen how people were coming to have new ideas about many things.   The philosophers had taught them to believe that the mind of man, if left free to think, could increase knowledge indefinitely, and that, with the increase of knowledge, government and social institutions could be made more just and humane. These new ideas, which are to be found in the writings of the phi- losophers, were all systematized and presented in the famous Ency- clopaedia (*L'Encyclopédie*) edited and carried through with much difficulty by Denis Diderot, and published between 1751 and 1772. This great work, to which most of the philosophers contributed, contains many illustrations, some of which are reproduced in this book.   Thus the minds of the people were prepared for social and political changes.   Neither the people nor the philosophers expected such changes to come, nor did they wish them to come through revolution and war, accompanied with hatred and cruelty and the shedding of blood.   Yet that is how they did in fact come.   We must now study the great French Revolution which brought about many of the changes which the philosophers desired, but in other ways than the philosophers had intended.

QUESTIONS

1. Mention some ways in which modern life has been affected by recent scientific discoveries.   What was the new idea of nature which became popular in the seventeenth and eighteenth centuries?   In what way was this new idea the basis of modern science and invention?

2. What is the "Copernican theory" of the solar system?   When did Galileo live?   How did he discover the law of the pendulum?   the law of falling bodies?   How did he get into trouble with the church authorities?

3. How did Newton discover the nature of light?   What is meant by the "universal law of gravitation"?   How did Newton discover this law?   Why were people in the eighteenth century so much interested in the "Newtonian philosophy"?

4. Who were "the philosophers"?   Why did Voltaire's writings have such an influence upon the people of his time?   What were some of his writings?   What does he stand for in the history of thought?

5. What new ideas about government became popular in the eighteenth century?   How did John Locke justify the English Revolution of 1688?   What is meant by saying that government rests on "natural rights"?   How did this theory differ from that held by James I and Louis XIV?   How did the ideas of Locke influence the history of the United States?   of France?

6. How did Rousseau's early life influence his ideas?   What did he mean by saying that "men are born free, and are everywhere in chains"?   by saying that "man is naturally good; it is society that corrupts him"?   What are the principal ideas of his *Social Contract?*   How did *The Social Contract* support the doctrine of "sovereignty of the people"?

7. What was the medieval idea of European unity?   Why did this ideal cease to be practicable in the sixteenth and seventeenth centuries?   What idea of European unity has prevailed since the seventeenth century?   What did Grotius mean by saying that states, although sovereign and independent, were subject to the law of nature and reason?   How did Emeric Crucé propose to abolish war?   How did his scheme for abolishing war differ from the scheme of Sully and of Abbé Saint-

CHART FOR CHAPTER VII.   Showing how new ideas about man and nature slipped in, in the midst of more spectacular events.

Struggle between king and Parliament in England

Thirty Years' War in Germany, 1618-1648

Thirty Years' World War of the Eighteenth Century

1600 10 20 30 40 50 60 70 80 90 1700 10 20 30 40 50 60 70

BACON:
Advancement of Learning | Novum Organum | GALILEO: Dialogue on the Two Principal Systems of the World

NEWTON: Principia | LOCKE: Two Treatises on Government

VOLTAIRE:
Letters on the English | Essay on Manners

ROUSSEAU:
Discourse on the Progress of Science and the Arts | Émile, and The Social Contract 1762 | The New Héloïse 1761

209

Pierre? How did these schemes of the seventeenth and eighteenth centuries differ from the present League of Nations?

8. What is meant by saying that "the Revolution was accomplished in men's minds before they made it the work of their hands"?

SELECTED READINGS

Brief accounts. Robinson, *Western Europe*, ch. xxxiv. Robinson and Beard, *Modern Europe*, I, ch. ix. Robinson and Beard, *Outlines*, II, ch. vii. Hayes and Moon, *Modern History*, ch. iii. Seignobos, *Contemporary Civilization*, ch. iii. Schevill, *History of Europe*, ch. xviii. Bourne, *Revolutionary Period*, ch. iii. Hayes, *Modern Europe*, I, 196–201, 414–426. Lowell, *Eve of the French Revolution*, chs. x, xviii–xix (on Montesquieu and Rousseau). H. S. Williams, *History of Science*, II, chs. iv–v, xi–xii (Copernicus, Galileo, and Newton). Libby, *History of Science*, ch. v (Bacon). Marvin, *The Living Past*, ch. viii. On "the philosophers" see also S. Mathews, *French Revolution*, pp. 52–72; *Cambridge Modern History*, VIII, 1–35; J. B. Bury, *History of the Idea of Progress*, chs. vi–ix.

Biography. H. Vrieland, *Hugo Grotius*. A. D. White, *Seven Great Statesmen*. (Includes an essay on Grotius.) J. J. Fahie, *Galileo*. J. Morley, *Voltaire*, and *Rousseau*, and *Diderot and the Encyclopaedists*. Sorel, *Montesquieu*. Leon Say, *Turgot*.

Sources. Robinson and Beard's *Readings in Modern History*, I, ch. ix, gives extracts from the writings of Bacon, Voltaire, Diderot, Rousseau, and Montesquieu. Some of these are in Robinson, *Readings in European History*, II, 380–386. For a sample of Galileo's *Dialogue on the Two Principal Systems of the World* see Williams, *History of Science*, II, 84 ff. One of Voltaire's most popular and amusing tales is *Candide*, published in translation by the Modern Library Company. Locke's *Essay on Civil Government* and Rousseau's *Social Contract* and *Émile* are all published in Everyman's Library. Emeric Crucé's *New Cyneas* has been edited and translated by T. W. Balch (1909).

Musée Carnavalet

FESTIVAL TO THE SUPREME BEING. (See p. 252.)

CHAPTER VIII. HOW THE FRENCH PEOPLE STARTED OUT TO MAKE A SMALL REVOLUTION AND ENDED BY MAKING A GREAT ONE

Liberty consists in the power to do anything that does not injure others.
Declaration of the Rights of Man

What everyone knows about the French Revolution. The English historian, Lord Macaulay, said that he found it useful, before reading a book on any subject, to recall what he already knew about that subject. We may well follow his example. What do we know about the French Revolution? What does " everybody know " about the French Revolution?

Well, everyone knows that Louis XVI and Marie Antoinette were the ill-fated sovereigns of those troubled times. Louis was a shy, well-meaning man, who liked to hunt better than to occupy himself with affairs of state. When asked whether the Estates General should meet at Paris or Versailles he is reported to have said, " At Versailles, on account of the hunting." Marie Antoinette was an Austrian princess who came to France as a young girl. Beautiful and gracious, she was at first admired by the people, but the gaiety and extravagance of her life at court soon made her unpopular. She became involved in the famous " Diamond Necklace Affair," a sordid intrigue which reads like a modern

detective story.   On account of her extravagance she became popularly known as Madame Deficit; and everyone has heard how, on
being told that the people lacked bread, she said, " Why don't they
eat cake? "   So at the outbreak of the Revolution the people of
Paris had lost their admiration for the fat king who liked to hunt and
for the beautiful queen who amused herself in the splendid palace at
Versailles.

Perhaps everyone has heard also of the other great personalities
of the Revolution.   There was Mirabeau, a noble who espoused the
people's cause — Mirabeau, the great orator who defied the king
and swayed the National Assembly by his passionate eloquence.
There was the Abbé Sieyès, a member of the privileged clerical
order, who wrote the famous pamphlet entitled, *What is the Third
Estate?* and answered the question by saying, " Hitherto it has
been nothing; henceforth it will be everything."   Afterwards asked
what he did during the Revolution he is reported to have said, " I
lived through it."   There was Danton, a rough-faced man with
tousled hair, who needed only a sash and dirk, and a red kerchief
round his head, to be taken for a pirate — the " Tribune of the
People," who boasted that he had " made the insurrection of
August 10 " which ended the monarchy, and at his trial regretted
that he had organized the Revolutionary Tribunal which condemned him to the guillotine.   And there was Robespierre —
" Robespierre the Incorruptible," — a precise, humorless man
with a thin face and sharp nose, with a mind like " pale ale," who
preached the new gospel of the " Reign of Virtue and the Reign of
Terror."

Above all, everyone knows that the Bastille was taken on July
14 — a day which the French people now celebrate as the anniversary of their liberty, just as we celebrate the 4th of July as the
anniversary of our independence.   Everyone knows that the nobles
and the clergy lost their privileges; that Louis XVI lost his throne
and his life; that during the Reign of Terror hundreds of people,
including Marie Antoinette, had their heads cut off by the guillotine.
These things everybody surely knows already.   What everyone
needs to know is why these events occurred and how they were
connected; and in learning why they occurred and how they were

MARIE ANTOINETTE (1755–1793)

From a portrait by Madame Vigée-Lebrun.

213

connected, we shall perhaps learn some other things even better worth knowing.

How the Estates General was called together in 1789 in order to help the king pay his debts. Revolutions are not likely to occur unless a great many people are discontented with the existing system of government and society and have some ideas about how things can be improved. This was particularly true of the French Revolution. The great majority of the people had good reason to be dissatisfied (see Chapter VI), and the philosophers had filled the heads of people with new ideas about the rights of man and the duties of governments (see Chapter VII). This discontent and these new ideas may therefore be called the fundamental causes of the Revolution; they were the influences that made it what it was.

LOUIS XVI (1754–1793)

The king was about twenty-one when this engraving was made.

But great revolutions are commonly started by some particular circumstance or event which acts like a spark of fire falling into a barrel of powder. The particular circumstance which started the French Revolution was the king's need of money. Poor King Louis XVI, when he came to the throne in 1774, inherited a large debt, some of which had been contracted by Louis XIV to pay for his disastrous wars, and some by Louis XV to pay for *his* disastrous wars. It was difficult to pay off this debt because every year the expenses of the government were greater than the annual revenue from the taxes. People are often glad to see a new king on the throne, because they hope he will do better than the old one. The French people therefore rejoiced when Louis XVI ascended the throne. They thought him a good young man; and when he appointed the famous philosopher Turgot as his minister, many people thought that the financial difficulties of the government would be ended.

Turgot showed the young king how he could easily solve his money difficulties. Your tax collectors, he said, are corrupt, and put much money into their own pockets. Your court at Versailles is too expensive; there are too many useless officials there and too many idle nobles. Besides, the nobles and the clergy, who possess two-fifths of the land of France, ought to pay taxes like other people. Then, too, the country would be more prosperous and better able to pay taxes if industry were open to all men instead of being a monopoly of the guilds, and if commerce, instead of being hampered by tariffs, were entirely free. Within two years Turgot abolished the guilds, the grain tariff, and the *corvée*, which was a tax in labor obliging the peasants to work on the king's highways. He cut down the expenses of the court, increased the revenue, and began to pay the debt. If the king had stood by Turgot there might have been a reformation of France without a revolution. But of course the nobles, the clergy, the useless officials of the court, and the queen who liked to have money to spend, all combined against Turgot. The king, who was a good man but a weak one, could not withstand all this pressure. So in 1776 Turgot was dismissed and his reforms came to nothing.

Two years later (1778), the king made an alliance with the Americans, and in support of the war against England he had to borrow more money. After the American war he kept on borrowing, so that in 1787 the poor king was at the end of his tether. The treasury was empty, and no one would lend the bankrupt government anything more. So the king asked the nobles and clergy to pay taxes like other people. The nobles and clergy refused and complained of the extravagance of the ministers. Not knowing what else to do, the king issued a decree levying new taxes, including a land tax and a stamp tax.

Such decrees had to be " registered " by the parlements. The parlement of Paris refused to register the new decrees. The judges said they had no authority to grant new taxes. Perhaps the judges had been reading Rousseau's *Social Contract*, which proclaimed the new theory that the authority of government is derived from the consent of the governed. At all events, the judges declared that the new taxes could be authorized only by the French people ; and they therefore asked the king to call together the old Estates General. The Estates General was somewhat like the English Parliament. It had been established about the beginning of the fourteenth century, and was composed of representatives from the three estates — the nobles, the clergy, and the Third Estate. During the next three centuries the kings had sometimes summoned this body to assist them. But the Estates General had never met regularly or secured any right of legislation, as the English Parliament had done. Since 1614 it had indeed never been assembled for any purpose. The judges in the parlement now asked the king to revive this old institution. The Estates General, they said, since it represented the nation, would have authority to grant new taxes.

The king tried to force the parlement to register his decrees. But people everywhere sided with the parlement and demanded the calling of the Estates General. The king was forced to yield; and in August, 1788, he therefore summoned the Estates General to meet in May, 1789, in order to say what should be done about the debt and the taxes.

Why the people forgot about the taxes and began to talk about a constitution. There was much excitement and rejoicing when it was learned that the king had invited the people to elect representatives to the Estates General. Everywhere people were asking, " What shall we instruct our representatives to do when the Estates General assembles ? " Hundreds of pamphlets were written, and when the people voted for representatives they also drew up written documents, called *cahiers*, for the latter's guidance. From the pamphlets and the cahiers we know why the people of France were dissatisfied with the existing government and what they expected the Estates General to do when it assembled in May, 1789.

The peasants were dissatisfied because they had to pay rents for the farms which they felt belonged to them, and perform various services for the nobles. The nobles were dissatisfied because they had less influence than formerly, and because the king sold titles of nobility to so many rich capitalists and merchants who were now more powerful than the old noble families. The bishops were dissatisfied because for a long time the king had been depriving the church of its privileges and confiscating its property. But the most dissatisfied people of all were the educated and well-to-do middle-class people. They had been reading Voltaire, and Montesquieu, and Rousseau, and many other " philosophers." They no longer believed in the divine right of kings, or in the sacred character of bishops, or in the superior merit of nobles. " Are we not as intelligent and as worthy as the nobles and bishops who look down upon us as inferiors? Why should not we, who work hard and live virtuously, have the same rights as frivolous nobles and idle priests? " The middle class had long asked and answered these questions.

POPULAR CARTOON, 1789

The peasant is carrying the nobility and the clergy on his back. The rabbits are eating his crops, but he is not allowed to kill game.

Thus each class had some grievance of its own. But there was one grievance which all classes had in common. All classes — at least all educated people — felt that France was badly governed. France was no longer, as in the great days of Louis XIV, feared and envied by all Europe. In all the wars of the last fifty years, with the exception of the American war, France had been losing power and prestige. Prussia and Russia had risen to be great powers; and above all, England had conquered India and America at the expense of France. Why was this? People began to think it must be because France was badly governed. Since England always defeated France, it must be because a constitutional government, such as England had, was more efficient than an autocratic government such as France had. So nobles, clergy, and middle class alike were beginning to think that France would be better governed if the people had some share in making the laws.

This belief was strengthened by the American Revolution. The French people sympathized with the Americans and helped them to win their independence. Lafayette and many other Frenchmen went to America to fight under General Washington, and they returned to France with many good things to say about Americans and about the liberty and equality which prevailed in the New World. When Lafayette returned to France, he brought with him a copy of the Declaration of Independence, which he had framed and hung up in his house in Paris. Beside it he left a vacant space; and when his friends asked him what the vacant space was for, he said that he was waiting for the time when France should have a declaration of rights, which he would then place beside the American Declaration of Independence.

Thus it happened that when the Estates General met on May 5, 1789, the French people had almost forgotten about the debt and the taxes. They were all talking about the constitution which France ought to have; and they looked forward to the Estates General with enthusiasm, because they expected the Estates General to adopt a constitution. They all agreed that the laws ought to be made, not by the king alone, but by the king with the consent of a legislative assembly elected by the people.

On this point the clergy, nobles, and Third Estate were all agreed; but on one important point they were not agreed. The nobles and clergy wished this legislative assembly to be so elected and organized that the nobles and clergy would be able to make the laws; the middle-class deputies wished it to be so elected and organized that the middle-class people would be able to make the laws. As soon as the Estates General met, the members began to quarrel over this question.

Why the members of the Estates General took a long time deciding whether they should sit in three rooms or in one. There were 1214 members of the Estates General — 308 chosen by the clergy, 285 chosen by the nobles, and 621 chosen by the common people or Third Estate. In previous meetings of the Estates General it had been the custom for each of the three estates to sit and to vote in a room by itself. The nobles and clergy wished to follow this old practice. But the deputies of the Third Estate

Bibliothèque Nationale

COSTUMES PRESCRIBED FOR THE DEPUTIES TO THE ESTATES GENERAL

Clergy (left), nobility (center), Third Estate (right).

wished to adopt a new practice — they wished the 1214 deputies all to sit in one room and vote as one assembly.

This dispute, which lasted for eight weeks, was more important than you might think. If the Estates General sat as three separate assemblies, then no measure could be adopted unless it were approved by a majority of the deputies of each of the three estates; and so the clergy alone, or the nobles alone, could prevent the adoption of any reform which deprived them of any of their privileges. But if the Estates General sat as a single assembly, measures would be decided by a simple majority of the whole body, and in that case the deputies of the common people, being more numerous than the deputies of the nobles and clergy combined, would have a better chance to adopt such reforms as they desired, even if the nobles and clergy were opposed to them.

So the quarrel went on week after week, and nothing was done about making a constitution. The deputies of the common people began to suspect that the king and the nobles and clergy were not much interested in a constitution. They suspected that the king would side with the nobles and clergy, and that the nobles and clergy would be willing to have the king dissolve the Estates General rather than allow it to be controlled by the deputies of the Third Estate. On June 17 the Third Estate therefore passed a momentous resolution. They declared that, since they represented 96 per cent of the French people, they alone were competent to make a constitution. They declared themselves alone to be a National Assembly of the French Nation. They declared that they had been elected by the French people to make a constitution, and that they would proceed to make one, whether the nobles and clergy joined them in that business or not.

Collection of M. Henry Marcel

MIRABEAU (1749–1791)

From a painting by Boze. Mirabeau was a noble, but was chosen to represent the Third Estate in 1789. He was a very effective extemporaneous orator, and the most notable popular leader during the first two years of the Revolution.

This was a new idea, and the whole Revolution is contained in it. It was as much as to say that there was only one class of citizens in France, and that a noble or a bishop was of no greater importance than any other person. Such a high-handed resolution could not be allowed to pass unnoticed; and so, on June 23, the king assembled all the deputies in royal session in order to hear his decision. He declared that the resolution of the Third Estate was null and void, and he ordered the three estates to sit separately for the decision of all important matters. But the king had delayed too long. On June 24 more than half of the clerical deputies (parish priests, who sympathized with the common people) deserted their fellows and joined the Third Estate. On June 25 forty-seven nobles followed their example. Encouraged by this support, and inspired by the eloquence of their leader, Mirabeau, the Third Estate paid no attention to the king's decision. Again the king yielded. " Oh, well, confound it, let them stick where they are ! " he is reported to have said, and so he ordered the deputies all to sit as a single body. Thus the Estates General came to an end, and was replaced by the National Assembly.

Most people supposed that it would take the National Assembly no more than three or four months to make the constitution, and that then it would dissolve and the " revolution " would be ended. But the National Assembly sat for more than two years, and it did much more than make a political constitution; it made a pretty complete overturning of all the old institutions of France. We must now see why it was that the National Assembly, which began with the intention of making a small revolution, ended by making a great one.

Why the people of Paris got excited and destroyed the Bastille. One reason why the National Assembly made a great revolution in the end was because the king tried to suppress the little one which it had begun. The poor king, left to himself, would probably have done nothing. But he was not left to himself. The king's brothers, and the queen, and many nobles and bishops were now much alarmed for fear that the National Assembly, being controlled by the deputies of the common people, would deprive the king of his powers and the nobles and clergy of their privileges. They therefore urged the king to make use of the army to overawe the city of Paris, dissolve the National Assembly, and so end the Revolution before it went any farther. The king yielded to this bad advice. He gradually gathered about 30,000 soldiers in and around Paris; and on July 11 he dismissed his minister Necker and certain other ministers who opposed his plan.

As soon as the people of Paris heard that Necker was dismissed, they rose in insurrection. Food was scarce in the city, and the idle, ragged crowds in the streets were easily stirred by Camille Desmoulins, a young orator who made a fiery speech in the gardens of the Palais Royal urging the people to resist the soldiers. The hungry people needed little urging. Joined by many of the king's soldiers who were friendly to them, they pillaged the bakeries and the wine shops. They broke into the City Hall, where they found guns and powder. Joined by many respectable middle-class people, they turned to the Bastille, an ancient royal prison which in

THE FALL OF THE BASTILLE

From a drawing by Prieur. Note the various sorts of weapons carried by the people. The entrance by way of the drawbridge has been forced and cannon are being brought up.

their eyes was the very symbol of tyranny and oppression, and which was supposed to contain arms and ammunition. So on the famous 14th of July (1789), the people attacked the Bastille. After a feeble resistance the governor surrendered, seven astonished prisoners were liberated, and the people began the joyous task of demolishing the thick walls of the hateful dungeon.

The king made no serious effort to suppress the insurrection, perhaps because neither the officers nor the soldiers were willing to fire on the people. But the well-to-do citizens of Paris were as much alarmed at the lawlessness of the mob as they were at the presence of the king's soldiers. They did not enjoy having their shops pillaged or the windows of their houses broken. So they quickly organized a government of their own for the city of Paris, supported by a citizen militia called the National Guard. Lafayette was made commander of the National Guard, and the astronomer Bailly was made Mayor of Paris. Thus through the establishment of the *Commune*, as the new municipal government was called, the middle-class people of Paris were in a position to preserve order against the mob and also to defend the city against the king's troops.

Once more the weak king yielded. On July 15 he promised the National Assembly to remove the troops ; and two days later he came from Versailles to Paris, rode down between the silent ranks of the National Guard, and gave his approval to the new city government. Someone handed him a little knot of ribbon, such as all the people were wearing.   It was the famous tricolor — red, white, and blue — which had been adopted during the insurrection as a revolutionary emblem. With this symbol of defeat stuck in his hat, Louis XVI returned to Versailles amidst the cries of the people, " Long live the king ! "   However long he might live, the days when a king of France could rule by " divine right " were over.

How the peasants became impatient and made a revolution of their own. Paris was not the only place of insurrection. All through central and northern France the peasants were making a revolution of their own. When the peasants voted for representatives to the Estates General they asked for one thing — to be freed from the feudal dues, the rents and taxes which they paid to the nobles for their land. The peasants cared nothing for political reform. They were not interested in a constitution. But the deputies of the Third Estate were mostly lawyers and business men, who were interested only in political reform, and cared little about the feudal dues. They had almost forgotten the peasants and their grievances.

The peasants did not wish to be forgotten; and as the National Assembly sat week after week without doing anything for them, they began to take matters into their own hands. In July occurred what is known as the " Great Fear." A curious rumor spread rapidly through the country. In village after village the cry would be raised, " The brigands are coming ! " Then the peasants would arm themselves with whatever came handy — pikes, scythes, pitch-forks, axes. If no brigands appeared, the peasants, being armed, made war on something far more hateful than brigands. They went to the castle of their lord or *seigneur* and asked him to give up the deeds and contracts which bound them to pay the rents and

services for their land.   If the seigneur gave up the deeds and contracts, the peasants destroyed them.   If he resisted, they tried to
break into the castle, and often, in order to destroy the hated
documents, demolished it, just as the people of Paris had demolished
the Bastille.   From this time on, whether the deeds and contracts
were destroyed or not, the peasants refused to pay the feudal dues
and resisted all attempts to compel them to do so.

**How the National Assembly spent the night of August 4 making
good resolutions which it took them two years to carry into effect.**
While the peasant insurrections were going on, the National
Assembly was sitting at Versailles discussing the new constitution.
But at last the reports of the peasant disorders became so alarm-
ing that something had to be done.   So the National Assembly
appointed a committee to gather information and report.   The
committee reported on August 3.   It told the Assembly that the
peasants were everywhere burning and destroying property; that
the king's officers were helpless; and that the National Assembly
ought to do something to suppress the peasants and restore order.
The Assembly therefore decided that it would for the moment stop
discussing the constitution and discuss the peasant insurrection.
It decided to take up the report of the committee the very next
day — August 4.

The nobles in the National Assembly were more interested in
the doings of the peasants than anyone else was, for if the peasants
did not pay the feudal dues the nobles would lose most of their
incomes.   Some of the nobles, talking the matter over among
themselves, thought that if they volunteered to give up some of the
feudal dues, perhaps the peasants might be persuaded to go on
paying the others.   Therefore, when the Assembly met on the
evening of August 4, the Duke of Aiguillon, one of the largest
landowners in France, got up and made a short speech.   He said
that the peasants had a real grievance, and that something should
be done for them.   He therefore proposed: (1) that the nobles
and clergy should pay their share of taxes to the king; (2) that
the peasants should no longer be required to perform the personal
services for their seigneurs; (3) that the peasants should go on
paying the rents for a term of years, when these also should cease.

This proposal was received with no great enthusiasm. A deputy of the Third Estate, Dupont de Nemours, said that the peasant uprisings ought to be put down before any concessions were made to them. Finally, an obscure deputy, Guen de Kerengal, made a rousing speech on behalf of the peasants, picturing their misery, and calling on the privileged classes to make sacrifices for the welfare of all. When he sat down, so we are told, "enthusiasm seized all hearts." Carried away by this enthusiasm, deputy after deputy arose, and on the spur of the moment moved to abolish some privilege or abuse. At last, in the small hours of the morning, the secretary passed to the president of the Assembly a slip of paper on which he had written: "Adjourn the session; everyone has lost his head." And so, after proclaiming Louis XVI "Restorer of French Liberty," the famous session of the night of August 4, 1789, came to an end.

Archives photographiques

POPULAR CARTOON, 1789

Represents the triumph of the peasant after the abolition of the feudal dues. The peasant is riding the noble. On his sword is written: "Full of courage." It supports a rabbit which he has killed. The tag hanging from his pocket says: "Peace and concord." The clergyman carries a scales, one pan of which is weighted by "Equality and liberty," the other by "Relief for the people."

During this one famous night the National Assembly had voted to abolish the feudal dues, the hunting rights, the sale of public offices, the church tithes, the privileges of the nobles and clergy in respect to taxation — in fact most of the privileges of the upper classes. "Just like our Frenchmen," said Mirabeau. "They spend an entire month wrangling over syllables, and in a night overturn the whole of the ancient order of the kingdom!" But this overturning was as yet only decreed on paper. The decrees of August 4 constituted only a kind of program of reform which it took the National Assembly two years to carry into effect.

Thus it happened that the National Assembly, starting out to make only a political revolution, ended by making also an economic and social revolution, and a religious revolution. We shall now take up each of these revolutions in turn; and first the political revolution.

The political revolution: The Declaration of Rights and the Constitution of 1791. After the 4th of August the National Assembly took up again the business of making a constitution. The main features of the constitution were soon determined, but it was not completed or proclaimed until September, 1791 (see p. 235). For this reason the first French constitution is called the Constitution of 1791.

Prefixed to this constitution is a short document known as the Declaration of the Rights of Man. This document has the same importance for French history that our Declaration of Independence has for our history. Both documents proclaimed those principles of natural rights which Locke and Rousseau had defined; and for half a century or more these principles provided a kind of gospel for many people in many lands who were trying to win political freedom by revolution. It is worth while to learn the essential parts of these two documents, since they have had so great an influence in modern history.

In the Declaration of Independence the theory of natural rights is expressed thus:

We hold these truths to be self-evident; that all men are created equal; that they are endowed by their Creator with certain unalienable rights; that among these are life, liberty, and the pursuit of happiness; that to secure these rights, governments are instituted among men, deriving their just powers from the consent of the governed; that whenever any form of government becomes destructive of these ends, it is the right of the people to alter or to abolish it, and to institute new government, laying its foundations on such principles and organizing its powers in such form as to them shall seem most likely to effect their safety and happiness.

In the French Declaration of the Rights of Man the same ideas are expressed, although in a slightly different form:

Men are born and remain equal in rights. . . . The aim of every political association is the protection of the natural and imprescriptible rights of man. These rights are liberty, property, security, and resistance to oppression. The source of all sovereignty is essentially in the nation; no body, no individual, can exercise authority that does not proceed from it [that is, the nation] in plain terms. Law is the expression of the general will. All citizens have the right to share personally, or by their representatives, in its formation [that is, the formation of the law].

On the basis of these principles the National Assembly made the Constitution of 1791. All citizens were guaranteed freedom of religion, freedom of speech, and freedom from arbitrary arrest and imprisonment. The special privileges of the nobles and clergy were abolished. New courts were established in which justice was administered and offenses punished, on equal terms for all persons. Public offices were open to all alike. The king no longer ruled by divine right; his powers, like those of any other official, were defined by law. The laws were made by a legislative assembly of one chamber, composed of representatives elected by those citizens who possessed a certain amount of property. The king might veto such laws temporarily but his main business was to administer and execute the laws; and to assist him in administering the laws, the country was divided up into eighty-three divisions, called "departments," in each of which a local government was established, composed of officials elected by the citizens of that department.

This was the political revolution. The Constitution of 1791 did not last very long, and France has had many constitutions since. But the two fundamental principles upon which the Constitution of 1791 was based were never afterwards really abandoned by the French people. These two principles were: (1) that the government derives its authority from the will of the people; and (2) that all citizens have equal rights before the law.

Such a political revolution could not be made without making a social and economic revolution also. We must now see how the National Assembly changed the social and economic institutions of France.

The social and economic revolution: How class divisions were abolished, and wealth redistributed. On the night of August 4, 1789, the National Assembly had decreed that " the feudal system is forever abolished in France." It was easy to declare this, but difficult to carry it into effect. The National Assembly tried to make a distinction between those rents and services of the peasants which had originated in *personal servitude* and those which had originated in *property rights*. The former they declared abolished at once; the latter were to be abolished as soon as the peasants had paid the rents for a certain number of years. The peasants, learning that the feudal dues had been abolished, could not understand why they should pay anything more. And when anyone tried to compel them to pay, they began to riot again. So the National Assembly never really settled the question of the feudal dues; but before the Revolution was over, in 1793 during the Reign of Terror, another assembly, the National Convention (see p. 239), settled this question once for all by abolishing the feudal dues without requiring the peasants to pay anything at all. Thus in the end the nobles lost their rents and the peasants obtained their land free of all obligation.

Since the nobles had lost their authority over the peasants and no longer had any special legal privileges, it seemed useless to have any nobles at all. So the National Assembly, on June 19, 1790, passed the following decree: " Hereditary nobility is forever abolished; in consequence, the titles of prince, duke, count, marquis, viscount, vidame, baron, knight, messire, écuyer, noble, and all other similar titles shall neither be taken by anyone whomsoever nor given to anyone." By various laws (see p. 230) the clergy were also deprived of their special privileges, and so these two classes or estates — nobles and clergy — lost the special privileges which they had formerly enjoyed. But there were still certain privileged corporations in France, such as the financial corporation known as the *farmers-general of the taxes*, the legal corporations known as *parlements*, and the industrial corporations known as the *guilds*. These also the National Assembly abolished. The most important of these were the guilds. Each guild had a legal monopoly of making and selling certain things. On March 2, 1791, the National Assembly abolished these legal monopolies, and laid down the principle that " every person shall be free to engage in such business or to practice such profession, art, or craft as he shall find profitable."

These measures constituted a social revolution. The French people were no longer a collection of classes and corporations, each having its own special rights and privileges.   Henceforth the French people made one class in which all individuals were, according to the law, equal in rights.

Of course this does not mean that all people were made equal in wealth, in intelligence, or in social position and influence.   Nothing can make people equal in intelligence or in power and influence. But something can be done to make the distribution of wealth more equal; and one of the most important results of the French Revolution was this: A great deal of the land of France changed hands. Before the Revolution was over, the National Assembly confiscated the lands of the church and much of the land of the nobles.   During the Revolution a good deal of this land was offered for sale.   Some of it was bought by the peasants and a larger part by the middle class. Thus much of the land of France passed from the hands of the nobles and clergy into the hands of the common people.   In 1793, in order to keep the land divided up among the people, the National Convention passed a new law of inheritance, which provided that when a man died his landed property must be divided up more or less equally among his children or near relatives.

This was the social and economic revolution.   It aimed: (1) to abolish all legal classes and corporations; (2) to make all citizens equal before the law; (3) to effect a more equal division of wealth among the people.   We must now turn to the religious revolution.

The religious revolution: How the National Assembly deprived the Catholic Church of its property and its former privileges.   The National Assembly abolished all the old laws that deprived people of religious freedom.   Protestants and Jews were granted their civil rights.   Henceforth all people were free to be of any religion or of no religion, just as they liked.   The Catholic clergy were no longer a separate class or estate but citizens, and, like all citizens, subject to the civil laws and the civil courts; and they lost their former power of preventing the publication of books which they did not like.   To diminish the power of the Catholic Church still more, the National Assembly deprived it of most of its property. On August 4, 1789, the church tithes were abolished, and later all of the land of the church was confiscated and taken over by the government.

Musée Carnavalet

PARIS IN 1759

From a painting by Raguenet. At the time of the Revolution Paris had changed very little. The bridge is the Pont-Neuf. This section was the center of the city and of the revolutionary activities. Notre Dame, the Hôtel de Ville, the Tuileries, the Conciergerie, the Palais de Justice, the Palais Royal — these were all within a short distance of the Pont-Neuf. (See the map of Paris, p. 248.)

If the National Assembly had stopped at this point, the Catholic Church would have been in the same position as other religious bodies. It would have been a religious association, like the Huguenots, free to believe and worship as it liked, but without any financial support from the government. There would then have been a complete separation of church and state, and the Catholics would have had the same freedom and the same privileges as other people. But the Catholic Church was too powerful to be treated in this way. The church had so long enjoyed special privileges that it was not willing to be placed on an equality with other churches. On account of its great influence, the National Assembly did not think it quite safe to give it so much freedom without governmental control. So the National Assembly, in order to keep the powerful Catholic Church under the thumb of the government, tried to transform it into a national church, which would be subject to the government because its clergy would be government officials paid by the state.

This object the National Assembly tried to accomplish by passing a law called the Civil Constitution of the Clergy (July, 1790). By this act each of the civil divisions called departments was to be also a religious diocese or bishopric. Bishops and parish priests were no longer to be appointed. They were to be elected; and they were to be elected, not solely by the people who were Catholics but by all citizens (including Huguenots, Jews, and free-thinkers) who had the right to vote for civil officials. The bishops and priests, thus elected by the citizens, were to be paid a salary by the government, just as other officers of the state were paid by the government. The Pope was no longer to have any authority over the church in France, although he was still permitted to define its doctrines and beliefs.

Thus the National Assembly tried to transform the Catholic Church into a state institution of religion, supported and controlled by the government, just as our public schools are state institutions of education, supported and controlled by the government. It may seem odd to us that Protestants and Jews, and even those who did not believe in Christianity at all, should be permitted to vote for Catholic bishops and priests. But this seemed right enough to many members of the National Assembly — and that for two reasons. First, the bishops and priests were to be paid by the government out of the state revenues; and since all citizens contributed by taxes to the state revenues, why should not all citizens have a voice in choosing the bishops and priests? Second, many members of the National Assembly thought that the chief business of bishops and priests paid by the government was to teach those practical moral virtues which would make good citizens. For this reason also it seemed right that all citizens, whatever their religious beliefs might be, should share in choosing the bishops and priests that were to teach them.

But the Catholic clergy and people thought this a very unreasonable and unjust measure. They said that since the National Assembly had taken away the church lands, the government was under obligation to pay the bishops and priests out of this property. They said that the business of Catholic bishops and priests was to teach the Catholic religion, and not merely the moral virtues; and so it was absurd and unjust to allow Protestants, Jews, and atheists to choose the clergy of a religion in which they did not believe and of which they were bitter enemies. Most of the bishops and priests therefore refused to accept the Civil Constitution of the Clergy, especially after the Pope commanded them not to. The National Assembly ignored the Pope and required the bishops and priests to take an oath of allegiance to the Civil Constitution; and later penalties were imposed on those who refused to take the oath.

This measure of the National Assembly had a very important influence upon the course of the Revolution. Two-thirds of the parish priests and all but seven of the bishops refused to take the oath of allegiance; and they were so much opposed to the religious measures of the National Assembly that the majority of them became opposed to the Revolution altogether. Thus by 1791 most of the nobles and clergy, and a great many of the people, had become "counter-revolutionary." That is, they had come to regard the Revolution as a dangerous movement which, if allowed to go on, would overturn everything in France and create a condition of anarchy. They wished, therefore, to suppress the Revolution altogether and to give back to the king his former powers and to the nobles and clergy their former privileges.

The king himself was now one of the counter-revolutionists. He too wished to suppress the Revolution. He was ready to use any means to suppress the Revolution; and in order to suppress it he tried first of all to run away from it.

Why the king ran away to Varennes and how he was brought back to Paris. Louis XVI was a shy man of few words, and like many weak, shy persons he had the bad habit of saying "Yes" even when he meant "No," merely to get rid of the people who pestered him. The result was that no one could be quite sure whether the king was for the Revolution or against it. When hard-pressed by the National Assembly, he promised publicly to accept the reforms that were made; but when the queen and the nobles at court scolded him for yielding, he privately promised them to see what could be done to get rid of the National Assembly and abolish all its reforms.

But how could the king get rid of the National Assembly? In July, 1789, when he tried to use the army to dissolve the National Assembly, Paris had risen in insurrection and raised a National Guard, and many of the king's troops had joined the people. Later, on the 6th of October, the king and the court had been partly persuaded and partly forced by Lafayette and the National Guard to come from Versailles and reside in Paris. What could the king do in Paris, where he was carefully watched, and where he had no troops that could be relied on? The poor king did not know what to do. But the queen and the nobles at court had a plan. They were always urging the king to escape from Paris, gather the troops in other parts of France, and return at the head of an army. Then, they told the king, all his loyal subjects, seeing that he meant business, would rally around him, with the result that the National Assembly and the disloyal city of Paris would have to submit.

Bibliothèque Nationale

WOMEN STARTING FOR VERSAILLES

From a contemporary print. A crowd of women marched from Paris to Versailles October 5, to ask for bread for their children. The crops had been scanty, and the poor in the cities were suffering. Although Lafayette protected the royal family, the mob broke into the château and frightened the queen.

Louis hesitated to do this, because it would mean civil war. But at last he decided to try the plan. The thing that decided him was the Civil Constitution of the Clergy. Louis was a devout Catholic. He might have accepted the other reforms of the National Assembly, and he did reluctantly assent to this one; but when the Pope rejected the Civil Constitution, Louis felt that he must do something desperate to suppress the Revolution and recover his former powers. So secret plans were made to escape from Paris and join the army of General Bouillé near the eastern frontier of France. Accordingly, on the night of June 20, 1791, the king and the queen and their children got quietly into a coach, slipped unnoticed out of Paris, and drove rapidly away on the road to Metz.

It is likely that the scheme would have failed in any case, because even the soldiers of General Bouillé's army sympathized with the

National Assembly. But the king never reached the army. He might have done so, perhaps, if he had been content to travel uncomfortably in an ordinary carriage. But majesties do not like to travel uncomfortably. The coach was an enormous affair, built expressly for the journey, in order that the royal family might ride at their ease. People in the little towns through which they passed, seeing this grand coach, naturally wondered who it could be that traveled with so much magnificence. Suspicion was aroused; at one of the towns someone recognized the king; and finally, at Varennes, the royal party was detained. Meantime the National Assembly, as soon as it was learned that the king had escaped, sent some officers on his trail to arrest him. The officers arrived at Varennes on June 21; and when they presented the decree of arrest to the king, Louis exclaimed, " There is no longer a king of France ! "

King or not, Louis was brought back under guard to the city of Paris. As the splendid coach rolled through the streets, the king was hooted by the people; and the royal family, hot and dusty from the long ride, re-entered the Tuileries, where they were kept under close watch until the National Assembly could decide what ought to be done with a king who ran away.

The flight of the king made a great sensation in Paris and through-out all France. It emboldened some people and frightened others. Some people, of whom Danton was one and Madame Roland another, said, " Well, since the king has shown that he is determined at all hazards to crush the Revolution, he is no longer to be trusted. The thing to do is to depose him and establish a republic." But most people, including a majority of the National Assembly, were frightened at the idea of a republic. They said, " We cannot do without a king; and so we must find some way to make the king accept the Revolution, and hold him to his promise." So the National Assembly decided to revise the political constitution, on which they had been working for two years, in the hope that the king would find it more to his liking; but they also decided that while they were revising the constitution, the king should be deprived of his duties and kept under guard.

For two months the National Assembly was engaged in revising the constitution and putting it into final shape so that it could be presented to the king. At last this work was finished; and on September 14 the king came before the National Assembly and read a letter, written the day before, in which he formally accepted the constitution. There was general rejoicing. " We are free at last," one of the deputies wrote. " The harness is off our backs! " On September 30, 1791, the National Assembly was dissolved. On the following day the new Legislative Assembly provided for in the Constitution of 1791 convened, and the Revolution seemed to be over. The king himself had said so. " The end of the Revolution has arrived," he wrote. " Let the nation return to its own cheerful nature."

If the king really thought that the Revolution was over he was sadly mistaken. On the contrary, during the next three years the Revolution passed into a second stage, far more radical and violent than the first. In 1792 France became involved in war with Austria. The war led directly to the fall of the monarchy, the establishment of a republic, the execution of the king and queen, and the famous Reign of Terror. We must now learn something about this second phase of the Revolution.

The insurrection of August 10, 1792 : How the king was deposed. The leading party in the Legislative Assembly which assembled on October 1, 1791, was known as the *Girondist* party (because some of its leaders came from the district of the Gironde). The Girondists were mostly young men, representing the most radical sentiment of the time, and anxious to prove their ability and their loyalty to the Revolution. The principal leader was Brissot, an able journalist. He was supported by a number of brilliant if wordy orators, among them Vergniaud and Gensonné. These and other Girondist leaders were inspired and kept up to the mark by Madame Roland, an eager and passionate patriot, in whose apartment they often met to discuss their plans.

The Girondists felt that the Revolution was not yet complete. They did not as yet demand the abolition of the monarchy, but they were extremely hostile to the king and wished to restrict his power even more than had already been done. They suspected, with good reason as it turned out, that the king and the queen were secretly asking aid from the Emperor Leopold, brother of the queen and ruler of Austria, and from the King of Prussia. They knew that most of the former nobles and clergy in France were hostile to the Revolution and would gladly see the armies of Austria and Prussia invade France for the purpose of suppressing it. Besides, there were the *émigrés* — nobles and clergy who had left France and were now living in foreign capitals — in Vienna, Berlin, London, and St. Petersburg. It was notorious that the emigrant nobles were trying to get the foreign powers to come to the assistance of the French king. All these powerful people were counter-revolutionists. They were working for a revolution against the Revolution; and to attain their object they were willing to accept the aid of foreign powers. This was what the Girondists feared — a counter-revolution aided by foreign powers. They felt that unless the Revolution destroyed the counter-revolution, the counter-revolution would destroy the Revolution.

As it happened, in the winter of 1792 both the Girondists and the counter-revolutionists were inclined to think that a war would not be a bad thing. The queen and the court party believed that if a war broke out, the people would rally to the support of the king. The Girondists believed that a war would arouse patriotic sentiment against the emigrant nobles and the king. " The Revolution needs a war to insure its success," one Girondist leader said. Occasions for dispute between France and Austria were not lacking, and on April 20, 1792, the Legislative Assembly declared war against the emperor on the ground that he was conspiring with the emigrant nobles to restore the king to his former powers. When the queen heard that war was declared she exclaimed, " So much the better ! " But it was not so much the better for the poor queen. On the contrary, the war led directly to the insurrection of August 10 and the fall of the monarchy.

The war began in Belgium, a province of Austria, where an Austrian army was stationed near the French frontier. But the French troops fought badly, partly because they feared that some of their officers, who were ex-nobles, were in sympathy with the counter-revolution. In the first battle, no sooner did the Austrians appear than the French troops ran away and even killed their leader, General Dillon, who tried to stop them. To make matters worse,

Prussia soon joined Austria, and the Prussian army, under the Duke of Brunswick, moved toward the French frontier in Lorraine.

When it was learned that the French troops, instead of beating the Austrians, were running away from them, there was the greatest excitement throughout France, and especially in Paris. Petitions were presented to the Legislative Assembly, demanding that the king be deposed. But the Legislative Assembly refused to depose the king; and the people of Paris, not knowing what to expect, became more and more excited and irritable. This excitement and irritation reached the boiling point when, one day late in July, there was handed about the city a printed document known as the " Brunswick Manifesto." People read this curious document with amazement and anger. It was dated July 25, and was signed by the Prussian general, the Duke of Brunswick. The manifesto declared that the emperor and the King of Prussia were invading France for the purpose of suppressing the rebellion against the French king. It commanded all Frenchmen to submit to the invading armies, and it threatened to treat as rebels all who resisted. But especially, the manifesto threatened the city of Paris; for it declared that if the people of Paris " dared to defend themselves," they would be shot down without mercy and their rebellious city would be destroyed.

Neither the emperor nor the King of Prussia was responsible for this absurd manifesto. It was prepared by the emigrant nobles, who had badgered the weak Duke of Brunswick into signing it. But the people of Paris did not know that. They took it for what it purported to be, an official declaration of the purposes of the emperor and King of Prussia; and in their eyes it proved conclusively what they had long suspected — namely, that Louis XVI and Marie Antoinette were conspiring with the enemies of France for the purpose of suppressing the Revolution.

The effect of the Brunswick Manifesto was just the opposite of what the emigrant nobles had hoped. They had supposed that it would terrify the inhabitants of Paris into submission. But instead of submitting, the people of Paris organized another insurrection — the famous insurrection of August 10, 1792. The city was at this time divided into sixty " sections." Directed by

Danton, Santerre, and other popular leaders, the people in many of the sections were organized and armed. At midnight on August 9 the church bells were tolled as a signal that the insurrection was about to begin. The rioters first set aside the city government or Commune of 1789 and established one of their own, known as the

Archives photographiques

DANTON (1759–1794)

From a contemporary portrait in the Musée Carnavalet. He was a leader in the insurrection of August 10, 1792, by which the king was deposed, and also in organizing national defense in 1792–1793.

Commune of August 10. They also got control of the National Guard. But the great event was the attack on the king's palace, the Tuileries. Many of the king's guards refused to fire on the people, and themselves joined the insurrectionists; but one company of Swiss guards heroically defended the palace until the king ordered them to cease firing, which they did, only to be surrounded and massacred.

When the people swarmed into the Tuileries they did not find the king there. The king and the queen had taken refuge with the Legislative Assembly. But this did not help them much, for the people forced their way into the assembly hall and demanded that the king

be deposed. Many of the members of the Assembly were absent, and those present were either in sympathy with the people or else easily intimidated. So the Legislative Assembly, submitting to force very much as the English Parliament had submitted to Cromwell's army (see Chapter III), voted to suspend the king until a new assembly could be elected by the people to decide his fate. Louis and Marie Antoinette were imprisoned in the Temple (a fortified building once used by the Knights Templars), and the duties of the king were taken over by a Provisory Executive Council of which Danton was the leading member.

The new assembly, which was to decide the fate of the king, was soon elected. It met on September 21, 1792, and remained in session until October 26, 1795. This assembly was the famous National Convention. It was the National Convention that abolished the monarchy, established the republic, executed Louis XVI, organized the "Terror," and successfully defended the Revolution against the united powers of Europe.

How the National Convention established the republic, repulsed the foreign armies, and executed the king, September, 1792– January, 1793. The National Convention was elected to decide what should be done with the king. Very few of the deputies thought it would be safe to restore the king to his old position, because they knew he did not sympathize with the Revolution. Yet most of the deputies hesitated to abolish the monarchy, because if they abolished the monarchy there seemed nothing for it but to establish a republic, and a republic was something new, which they were a little afraid of. When the deputies thought of a republic, they thought of the little city republics of ancient Greece and Rome, or of the Swiss Confederation or the Dutch Republic, or else of the thirteen republics of America. It seemed that all the existing republics were loose federations of small states; and people feared that if France became a republic it would break up into a number of small states bound together in a federation. How could such a weak government defend itself against the powerful military monarchies of Prussia and Austria? This was why the deputies hesitated.

When the deputies assembled on September 21, no one supposed that they would take the great decisive step on that day. All day they talked about other things, and they were about to adjourn for dinner when one of the Paris deputies, Collot d'Herbois, got up and said: "There is a question which you cannot postpone until tomorrow; which you cannot postpone until this evening; which you cannot postpone a single instant, without being unfaithful to your vows to the nation: that question is the abolition of royalty." Thus the question was raised. Still the deputies hesitated. But within a few moments all hesitation vanished. Perhaps the deputies were tired of being uncertain. At all events, with almost no discussion at all, the famous act was passed: "The National

Convention unanimously decrees that monarchy is forever abolished in France." Then the deputies relieved the tension by cheering, stamping on the floor, and throwing their hats into the air.

Having abolished the monarchy forever, the deputies went out to dinner. People in the streets were crying, "Long live the republic!" In the evening people came into the assembly hall to congratulate the Convention, assuring the deputies that they would shed their blood for the safety of the "republic." The Convention had not yet established a republic, but people were taking it for granted that one must exist, since the monarchy was abolished. On September 22 the Convention passed a decree that "henceforth public documents shall be dated from the first year of the French Republic." On September 25 it decreed that "the French Republic shall be one and indivisible." Thus the first French Republic was established by tacit consent. "The republic," said Robespierre, "glided in furtively between the factions."

The most pressing question that now confronted the Convention was the defense of the country against the Austrian and Prussian armies. On the second of September, three weeks before the Convention assembled, the Prussians had taken Verdun. What was to prevent them from taking Paris? Fear of the Prussians led to the famous "September massacres." On September 2-6, bands of people terrorized the city, broke into prisons, and brutally murdered about a thousand counter-revolutionary priests and members of the nobility (both men and women) who were confined there. The government of Paris did nothing to prevent the massacres. These crimes in the name of liberty were the work of a few, but they were encouraged or condoned by many, on the ground that it was necessary to terrorize the counter-revolutionists in order to prevent them from aiding the oncoming Prussians.

But on September 20, the day before the National Convention assembled, the Prussians were checked at Valmy; and before the year was out the French armies were everywhere victorious. In October the Prussians retreated into Germany. General Custine took Mainz, and soon the "left bank" (West bank) of the Rhine was in the possession of the French. More important still, General Dumouriez won a decisive victory against the Austrians at Jemappes on November 6; and before the end of the year 1792 the French had conquered all Belgium. Dumouriez was the hero of the hour. The Convention, not content with the conquest of Belgium, authorized him to cross the Rhine and conquer Holland.

These victories made the republic popular and inspired the people with new enthusiasm for the Revolution. The most enthusiastic began to ask, " Why not carry the Revolution into other countries? Other people live under the tyranny of kings, and they too must wish to be free. Why should not the French people come to the aid of the oppressed of all countries? " So on November 19, 1792, the National Convention passed a famous decree, known as the Propagandist Decree. This decree, addressed to all the people of Europe and translated into all languages, announced that the French armies would gladly come to the aid of any people who wished to free themselves from the tyranny of kings and nobles. Thus the National Convention threw down the gage of battle to all European governments. It declared the universal revolution of all peoples against all kings.

Meantime, the Convention had to decide what was to be done with the king, who was still imprisoned in the Temple. At first the majority of the deputies were not in favor of executing the king. But opinion began to change after November 20, when there was discovered in the Tuileries an iron chest containing the king's secret papers, among which were letters proving that the king had often written to foreign kings asking them for military aid against the revolutionary parties in France. On January 15, 1793, the Convention voted unanimously that the king was guilty of treason against the nation. Many of the deputies demanded that the people be given a chance, by ballot, to approve or disapprove this decision, but the proposal was rejected by a vote of 424 to 283. Finally the vote was taken on the question of whether the king should be put to death. The roll was called and each deputy was given a chance to say why he voted for or against the execution of the king. For twenty-four hours, amidst intense excitement, the roll-call went on. At eight o'clock in the evening of January 17 the decision was announced: for death, 387; against death, 334.

On January 21, 1793, Louis, the descendant of kings who had

Archives photographiques

EXECUTION OF LOUIS XVI, JANUARY 21, 1793
From an engraving in the Musée Carnavalet.

ruled in France since 987, was carried in a tumbril through crowded streets to the guillotine. Weak and petulant and always a little ridiculous in life, he met death with dignity and high courage. The executioner, Samson, wrote an account of the king's behavior on the scaffold:

He himself helped us to take off his coat. He made some difficulties when it came to binding his hands, which he nevertheless held out when his confessor told him this would be the last sacrifice. . . . He then allowed himself to be led to the spot where he was fastened down, and then called out very loudly, " People, I die innocent ! " Then, turning to us, he said, " Sirs, I am innocent of that of which I am accused ! I hope my blood will consolidate the happiness of all Frenchmen." Then the knife descended, and there were a few shouts of " Long live the nation ! "

How the Convention was threatened by foreign armies and internal insurrection, 1793. The execution of Louis XVI convinced the kings of Europe that they too were in danger. As early as 1790 a famous Englishman, Edmund Burke, had predicted in his *Reflec-*

tions on the French Revolution that the Revolution in France would prove a menace to all established governments. At that time few people agreed with him. In England, and in most Continental countries, many people sympathized with the French in their effort to win political liberty. Rulers and statesmen felt that the uprising in France was perhaps an advantage to them, since it had weakened the French government and demoralized the French armies. But by the beginning of 1793 the prophecies of Edmund Burke seemed to be coming true. The National Convention had conquered Belgium and the left bank of the Rhine. It had executed the French king and proclaimed a war of all peoples against all kings. At last the governments of Europe were convinced that something must be done to suppress this dangerous revolution. The result was the formation of what is known as the First Coalition.

The first of the great powers to join Austria and Prussia in the war was England. The imprisonment of Louis XVI had greatly alarmed the English. The conquest of Belgium alarmed them still more. The execution of the king horrified as well as alarmed them. This event, said the English minister, William Pitt, is the most "atrocious crime known in history." Perhaps he had forgotten the execution of Charles I in London in 1649. However that may be, on January 22 the English government broke off all relations with France, and on February 1 the National Convention declared war on England. France was then at war with four states — Austria, Prussia, England, and Holland. These four were soon joined by Spain, Portugal, Sweden, Naples, and Sardinia.

The object of the First Coalition, thus formed, was to dissolve the National Convention, restore the monarchy in France, and place on the throne the young son of Marie Antoinette. In compensation for these services the European powers expected from France some cession of territory. In the spring and summer of 1793 the coalition armies carried everything before them. March 20 the Austrians won the decisive battle of Neerwinden against General Dumouriez, and followed up this victory by the conquest of Belgium. In July the Prussians recovered Mainz and the left bank of the Rhine. In August the English fleet took the French seaport of Toulon, and meantime the Spanish armies crossed the Pyrenees into southern

France.   Thus in the summer of 1793 the National Convention had to meet invasion by the coalition armies on all fronts.

At the same time the Convention was threatened by serious internal insurrections.   In Normandy, Brittany, and the south of France the counter-revolutionary priests and nobles had organized the people against the revolutionary government.   They were now supported by many people who had formerly supported the Revolution.   The most important of these were the Girondists.   To understand how the Girondists came to join the counter-revolutionists we must learn something about the party conflicts in the Convention.

When the Convention first assembled, in September, 1792, there were three main parties in it.   First the Girondists, who had been the leading party in the Legislative Assembly.   They numbered about 160 deputies, and were led by Brissot, Condorcet, and Roland in the Convention, and by Madame Roland outside of it.   The Girondists sat on the right,[1] which meant that whereas in the Legislative Assembly they had been the most radical party, they were now, in the Convention, regarded as the most conservative party.   Sitting on the left, high up in the back, were about fifty deputies (twenty-five of whom came from Paris) who were known as " the Mountain," or the Jacobin, party.   The chief leaders of the Jacobins were Robespierre, Marat, and Danton.   A third party, the largest of all, sat in the center.   It was called " the Plain " or " the Marsh."   It was strong in numbers but uncertain in policy, and was led by Barère — an able man, devoted to the Revolution, but a clever politician, prepared to support whatever policy seemed most expedient.

For nearly nine months the Convention was distracted by a bitter and irreconcilable conflict between the Girondists and the Jacobins.   The Jacobins were at first weak in numbers, but they knew what they wanted, and they had the powerful support of the people of Paris who, in the cafés, in the streets, and in the gallery of the Convention applauded their own deputies and intimidated the Girondists.   It was the Jacobins, backed by the people of Paris,

[1] The custom was, and still is, for conservative parties to sit on the right, radical parties on the left, and moderate parties in the center of the assembly hall.

that forced the execution of the king. Afterwards they charged the Girondists with "royalism," because many of the Girondists voted against the execution of the king. When General Dumouriez, who was a Girondist, lost the Battle of Neerwinden, the Jacobins charged the Girondists with the military failures. The bitter conflict reached a crisis on May 31, when an insurrection was organized in Paris against the Girondists. The following day the Tuileries, where the Convention was sitting, was surrounded by the municipal troops under General Hanriot. The deputies wandered about the Tuileries gardens seeking an exit, but every gate was guarded. The Convention was itself imprisoned, and likely to remain so until it took action against the Girondists. Yielding to force, the Convention, on June 2, voted to expel twenty-two of the leading Girondist deputies. From this time on the Convention was dominated by the Jacobins.

The forcible intervention in the deliberations of the Convention by the city of Paris was deeply resented throughout France, but especially so in the south, where many of the Girondist deputies came from. More than half of the local governments protested against the expulsion of the Girondists, and some of the Girondist deputies escaped to their homes in the south of France and organized an armed resistance to the Convention and the Jacobins who now controlled it. By the middle of July the cities of Marseille, Bordeaux, and Lyon had joined the counter-revolutionists. Thus in the summer of 1793 the Convention was confronted by the double danger of invasion from without and widespread insurrection from within. It was this double danger that resulted in what is called the Reign of Terror.

How the Jacobins saved the Revolution by means of the Terror, 1793–1794. In June, 1793, the Convention adopted a republican constitution. It was approved by popular vote, and formally proclaimed on August 10, 1793. It is known as the "Constitution of the first French Republic," but it was never in fact put into force. In October, 1793, the Convention declared that "the provisional government of France is revolutionary until the peace."

This revolutionary government, known as the government of the Terror, was directed by a Committee of Safety appointed by the

Convention and responsible to it. Its decrees were approved by the Convention and carried out by appointed officials in the provinces, known as "deputies on mission" or "national agents." In each district there was a revolutionary committee of local patriots whose business it was to keep a list of all inhabitants who were suspected of being unfriendly to the Jacobin government. To suppress all opposition, the famous Law of Suspects was passed (September, 1793). Suspects were defined as all those who "by their conduct, their relations, their remarks or their writings show themselves as partisans of tyranny . . . or enemies of liberty." To deal with suspects the Revolutionary Tribunal was created. Between March, 1793, and July, 1794, the Tribunal tried and condemned to death about 2600 persons. Many of these were enemies of the Revolution in all its forms. Such was Marie Antoinette. Some had been good revolutionists, but had turned against the Jacobins. Such was Madame Roland. Some had been good Jacobins but had incurred the enmity of the Committee of Safety. Such was Danton. Some there were who never meddled in politics, but were unfortunate enough to be denounced by a malicious neighbor. Innocent or guilty, they were herded into the prisons, from the prisons brought before the Tribunal, and from the Tribunal carried in tumbrils through the crowded streets to the scaffold. Daily the people watched the spectacle of the guillotine, until the dropping of heads in the basket became too commonplace to be thrilling. During the Terror the guillotine stood on the square formerly known as the *Place Louis XV*, then known as the *Place de la Révolution*. Here hundreds of people were sacrificed in the name of liberty. The square is now called the *Place de la Concorde*.

The chief task of the Terror government was to build up an army adequate to suppress the internal insurrections and to repel the armies of the Coalition. For this purpose the law known as the *Levée en Masse* was enacted. It declared that "until the foreign armies shall have been driven from the soil of the republic, all Frenchmen are in permanent requisition for the service of the armies." This act provided soldiers enough; but it was easier to obtain soldiers than to equip them, and easier to equip them than to plan victorious campaigns. Fortunately for the Jacobins the

Bibliothèque Nationale

SKETCH OF MARIE ANTOINETTE RIDING TO HER EXECUTION

The painter David drew this rough sketch as the cart bearing the queen passed along the rue Saint-Honoré.   The queen's hair had been cut off, and her hands bound behind her.

man for the task was found — Lazare Carnot. Carnot was an honest man, a tireless worker, and an able administrator.   Under his direction the armies were equipped and disciplined, able officers were appointed, and for the first time the operations of the various armies were directed as parts of one great campaign of national defense.

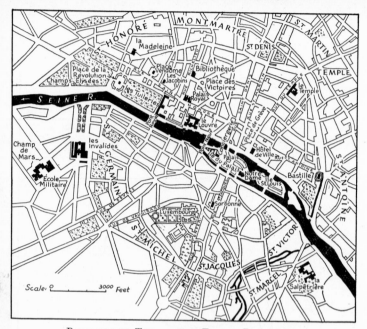

PARIS IN THE TIME OF THE FRENCH REVOLUTION

Note the location of places mentioned in the text. The Conciergerie was the chief prison during the Terror. Next door was the Palais de Justice, where the Revolutionary Tribunal sat.

The internal insurrections were ruthlessly suppressed. In October the city of Lyon surrendered, and about four thousand of its inhabitants were either shot or drowned in the river. Other rebellious cities hastened to make their peace and were more leniently treated. Before the year was out the insurrections were for the most part at an end. Meantime the foreign armies were gradually pushed out of French territory, and during the next year the French again made conquests beyond the frontier. In June, 1794, General Jourdan won the Battle of Fleurus, which forced the Austrians out of Belgium. General Pichegru followed up this decisive victory by crossing the Rhine, and by February, 1795, the French were masters of Holland as well as of Belgium. In this year also the left bank of the Rhine was again conquered, and the Spanish were driven across the Pyrenees. In April, 1795, the Prussians made peace with France, recognizing the Rhine as the French frontier. In July peace was made with Spain. The First Coalition was thus broken, and the National Convention had achieved the dream of every French government since the time of Richelieu. It had conquered for France her " natural frontiers " — the Rhine, the Alps, the Pyrenees.

How the Jacobins, after having saved the revolution, destroyed themselves, 1794. The danger from the coalition was not yet over before violent factional conflicts arose within the Convention. In these conflicts three men stand out as leaders — Hébert, Danton, and Robespierre. Hébert was a scurrilous writer who every day filled his newspaper, the *Père Duchesne*, with bloodthirsty denunciations of the " enemies of the Revolution " — that is, those whom Hébert disliked. He was popular in Paris, where his paper was eagerly read, and for this reason he was influential with the city government. In March, 1794, Hébert tried to stir up an insurrection in Paris in order to intimidate the Convention and gain control of the Committee of Safety. Paris refused to support him, the insurrection fizzled out, and on March 24 Hébert and some of his followers were condemned to death.

With Hébert disposed of, the Committee turned on Danton. Danton was one of the outstanding figures of the Revolution. He was a coarse, passionate man, a powerful orator, and a leader of great practical sense and effectiveness in time of crisis. In defending himself at his trial, he boasted: " I made the insurrection of August 10 " (1792). It was more or less true, and from that day until July, 1793, he was the most influential man in the Convention and on the Committee of Safety. He deplored the futile conflict between the Jacobins and the Girondists, disliked Robespierre (" The man has not sense enough to cook an egg," he said), and had little sympathy with the frenzied state of mind that brought to the guillotine so many men whose only crime was that they had incurred the suspicion of the super-patriots. In July, 1793, he was dropped from the Committee of Safety, and from that time his influence waned, while that of Robespierre increased.

One day in January, 1794, a delegation of weeping women came to the Convention begging the release of their relatives from prison. At that time the danger from the Coalition armies was largely over, and many people felt, therefore, that the time had come to relax the severity of the Terror. Danton was one of them. " I had rather be guillotined," he said on one occasion, " than guillotine others." When Danton lifted his powerful voice in favor of mercy the Committee became alarmed, as well it might. If public opinion turned against the Terror, those who were chiefly responsible for it would be the first victims. None knew this better than Robespierre and his friends. To save themselves they charged Danton with being concerned in a Royalist plot to restore the monarchy. Danton made no serious effort to save himself. Advised by a friend to escape from France, he made the famous reply : " Does a man carry his country away with him on the soles of his shoes? " Early in April, 1794, he was brought to trial and condemned to death. He was proud and contemptuous to the last. Passing Robespierre's house on the way to the guillotine, he stood in the tumbril and shouted : " Vile Robespierre! The scaffold claims you too. You will follow me."

The prophecy proved a true one; but for three months Robespierre was the outstanding figure in the Convention and on the Committee of Safety. Robespierre was an austere and fastidious man, secretive and self-contained. Few people liked him, but many admired him, and the mass of the people had confidence in his integrity and patriotism. He lived a simple, laborious, and blameless life. Many revolutionary leaders, including Danton, were charged, and rightly charged, with using their influence to make money. Robespierre never was. He was known as " the Virtuous," " the Incorruptible." Besides, he was a master of platitudes. His long-winded speeches were filled with phrases about liberty, humanity, virtue — phrases which people liked to hear. These phrases he voiced with a fervor and solemnity which made people think of the Revolution as something sacred — something for which life itself was a small sacrifice.

Robespierre is something of an enigma, and a furious battle of the books has been fought over him. Some writers maintain that he was a sincere patriot and humanitarian who suffered martyrdom in the vain effort to bring about a social revolution in behalf of the mass of the people.   Others maintain that he was no more than a sinister intriguer who crushed his enemies in order to gratify his love of power.   Perhaps he was a little of both, since good and evil are strangely blended in the human heart.   We may think of him as a sincere fanatic who believed that the Revolution was destined to regenerate France, and all mankind, by making all men virtuous. But perhaps he was also, without knowing it, a vain and ambitious man who convinced himself that he and his devoted followers were the only virtuous ones.   The Revolution would therefore, in his opinion, be a failure unless these virtuous ones gained control and used their power to destroy the immoral and the corrupt.   It was apparently Robespierre's idea that the Terror, which had been organized to defend the Revolution against foreign enemies, should be continued in order to establish in France a " Reign of Virtue." " Without Terror," he said, " Virtue is helpless."   Again he said : " A man is guilty against the republic if he takes pity on prisoners ; he is guilty if he does not believe in virtue ; he is guilty if he is opposed to the Terror."

Chief among the virtues was hatred of the enemies of the Revolution, and chief among the enemies of the Revolution was the Catholic Church.   During the Terror fervent revolutionists therefore conceived the idea that the Catholic Church must be abolished and Christianity itself destroyed.   In Paris and many other places the churches were closed and the Christian religion denounced as a degrading and unpatriotic superstition.   That people might the more easily forget the Christian religion a new calendar was adopted (November, 1793).   The Year I was to begin with the establishment of the republic, September 22, 1792.   New names were given to the months, *Vendémiaire* (Sept. 22–Oct. 21) being the first month ; and each month was divided into three periods of ten days each, thus abolishing the Christian Sunday.   Using this calendar every day, the people would be constantly reminded of the Revolution and of the new era of human happiness which it had ushered in.

But the Jacobins were not content with abolishing the old religion. They wished to replace it with a new one — a religion of patriotism.

The new religion, like the old, would have its dogmas, its saints, its form of worship. Its dogmas would be the principles of the Revolution — "Liberty, Equality, Fraternity." Its saints would be the great men who had formulated the creed of the Revolution and those who had suffered martyrdom in its defense. Its worship would take the form of public festivals celebrating the great events of the Revolution or the ideas on which it was based.

Of all the Jacobins, none was more interested in establishing the new religion than Robespierre; and his ideas on the matter were embodied in a decree of the Convention establishing the Worship of the Supreme Being (May 7, 1794). This decree declared that the French people recognized the existence of the Supreme Being and the immortality of the soul. It declared that the chief duties of man were " to detest bad faith and tyranny, to punish tyrants and traitors, to relieve the unfortunate, . . . to defend the oppressed." That the people might associate this new faith with the Revolution, it was decreed that every year there should be held four great festivals to celebrate the four great events of the Revolution. These great events were the taking of the Bastille, July 14, 1789; the deposition of the king, August 10, 1792; the execution of the king, January 21, 1793; and the insurrection, May 31, 1793, that led to the fall of the Girondists.

The new religion was solemnly inaugurated on June 8, 1794. The members of the Convention, together with a great crowd of people, assembled in front of the Tuileries. Presently Robespierre appeared, dressed in a violet coat and carrying a bouquet of flowers. Mounting a platform, he delivered a long oration on religion as the necessary foundation of good government. Then he led the people in procession to the Tuileries gardens, where a group of wooden statues had been erected. The statues represented Atheism surrounded by Vice and Folly, and Wisdom threatening them with destruction. To complete the allegory Robespierre set a torch to the statues of Atheism, Vice, and Folly. Unfortunately the wood was not very dry, and instead of burning cleanly it made a great smoke, so that in the end Wisdom herself, although emerging triumphant, was seen to be all smudged and blackened. It was a bad omen. Worse than that, it was ridiculous, and made the

ARREST OF ROBESPIERRE, JULY 27, 1794
From a drawing by Barbier, engraved and published in 1796.

people laugh at the moment when they were expected to be most impressed.

After the establishment of the new religion of liberty and humanity the Terror reached its height. The Revolutionary Tribunal was reorganized and the judges were given a freer hand in the trial and condemnation of suspects. The prisons were filled to overflowing. People were tried, condemned, and guillotined in batches. During the forty-nine days following June 10, 1794, there were about 1376 executions — more than during the thirteen months preceding.

Such methods of introducing the Reign of Virtue which Robespierre had dreamed of did not succeed. People were easily bored by the new religion and revolted by the bloodshed apparently required to establish it. Since no one was any longer safe, the Convention became restive under the increasing domination of the Committee of Safety; and since Robespierre was the outstanding figure on the Committee, various groups in the Convention united to destroy him. The crisis came on July 27. Robespierre was slated to make a speech; but the Convention for the first time would not listen to him. When he tried to make himself heard, someone shouted, "The blood of Danton chokes him!" In a terrific uproar, amidst cries of "Down with the tyrant!" the Convention decreed the arrest of Robespierre and four of his most loyal followers. They were tried and guillotined the next day, July 28, 1794 (10 Thermidor, Year II). This was the end of the Terror.

How the Revolution came to an end, October 26, 1795. The men who destroyed Robespierre had no intention of ending the Terror, but much to their surprise they found that in destroying Robespierre they had undermined their own power. Public opinion turned strongly against the Committee of Safety, the Revolutionary Tribunal, and the man who had been chiefly responsible for their activities. The Convention gradually yielded to this change of opinion. The Committee of Safety was deprived of its former powers, the Tribunal was transformed into an ordinary court, the Girondists who had been expelled were recalled. The chief members of the old Committee of Safety — Barère, Collot-d'Herbois, Billaud-Varenne — became every day more unpopular, and at last were tried and banished.

Public opinion not only turned against the Terror, it turned against the democratic republic also, since the democratic republic was associated with the Terror. The Convention therefore drafted a new constitution, more moderate and conservative than that of 1793. This was the Constitution of 1795, known as the Constitution of the Directory, under which France was governed until Napoleon assumed power in 1799. The new constitution provided for an executive board of five "directors," and two legislative chambers called the Council of Ancients and the Council of Five Hundred. France was still a republic, but not a democratic republic, since the right to vote was limited to people with a certain amount of property.

When the Constitution of the Directory was adopted in 1795, Royalist sentiment was so strong that the Convention feared the people might elect a majority of Royalists to the legislative bodies and so prepare the way for a restoration of the Bourbon monarchy. To prevent this the Convention passed what is called the Decree of Two-Thirds — a decree providing that in the first elections two-

Bibliothèque Nationale

A Session of the Convention Interrupted by an Invasion of the People

From a drawing by Monnet.   On May 20, 1795, workmen killed a deputy,
Féraud, and bore his head into the meeting of the Convention.

thirds of the members of the Convention must be chosen for the
Council of Ancients and the Council of Five Hundred.

The Decree of Two-Thirds was so unpopular in Paris that the
people organized an insurrection against the Convention.   Supported by 30,000 of the National Guards, the insurgents prepared
to attack the Convention at the Tuileries.   For its defense the
Convention had only some 4000 soldiers.   But Barras, who was in
charge of the defense, managed to procure a few cannons.   Acting
on the advice of a young artillery officer by the name of Napoleon
Bonaparte, he disposed his cannons so as to command the narrow
streets that led to the Tuileries gardens.   Coming up the narrow
streets, the insurgents were met by a raking fire of grape-shot, which
soon dispersed them.   Thus ended the famous insurrection of 13
Vendémiaire (October, 1795).

Having prepared the way for a new government, the work of the
National Convention was done.   For three years it had governed
France.   It had maintained the Revolution against its enemies —
enemies from without and enemies from within.   But in order to
accomplish this it had resorted to such ruthless methods of terror

and bloodshed that the people were exhausted, disillusioned, and still divided by furious hatreds. October 26, 1795, the great revolutionary assembly met for the last time. At two o'clock it passed its last decree: "The National Convention declares its mission fulfilled and its sessions closed." A deputy asked: "What time is it?" From across the benches a solemn voice replied: "The hour of Justice."

Justice has had many hours. Perhaps this was one of them.

QUESTIONS

1. What was the Estates General? How did it differ from the English Parliament? Why was it assembled in 1789? What did the people expect it to do? How do we know what they expected it to do? Why did the three estates quarrel over the method of casting their votes? Why was this quarrel important? How was the Estates General changed into the National Assembly?

2. Describe the uprising which resulted in the taking of the Bastille, July 14. Why was this event important?

3. What events led up to the famous "night of August 4"? What did the National Assembly do on that night? How did the events of that night change the character of the Revolution?

4. What were the chief provisions of the Constitution of 1791? How did it change the government of France? Compare the Declaration of Rights with the American Declaration of Independence.

5. To what extent did the National Assembly abolish social and economic privileges? How did the peasants benefit by the economic laws?

6. What laws were passed affecting the property and organization of the Catholic Church? Why did these laws make many people "counter-revolutionists"?

7. Write one sentence (not too long) stating in general terms the changes in French government and society made by the National Assembly between 1789 and 1791.

8. How did the Revolution change in character after 1791? What were the aims of the counter-revolutionists? Who were the Girondists, and why did they favor a war with Austria in 1792? What was the first result of this war? Tell what took place during the insurrection of August 10, 1792.

9. Why was the National Convention elected? When did it meet? When and how was monarchy abolished? What was the situation that led to the September massacres? What charges were brought against the king? What was the "Propagandist Decree"? What effect did

CHART FOR CHAPTER VIII. Rise and decline of the revolutionary spirit in France, 1789-1795.

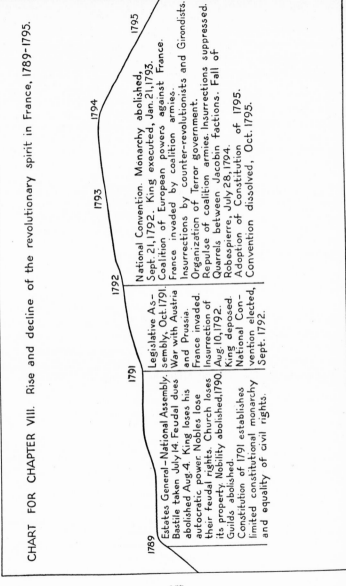

1789	1791	1792	1793	1794	1795

1789

Estates General—National Assembly. Bastile taken July 14. Feudal dues abolished Aug.4. King loses his autocratic power. Nobles lose their feudal rights. Church loses its property. Nobility abolished.1790. Guilds abolished. Constitution of 1791 establishes limited constitutional monarchy and equality of civil rights.

1791

Legislative Assembly, Oct.1791. War with Austria and Prussia. France invaded. Insurrection of Aug.10,1792. King deposed. National Convention elected, Sept.1792.

1792

National Convention. Monarchy abolished, Sept. 21,1792. King executed, Jan.21,1793. Coalition of European powers against France. France invaded by coalition armies. Insurrections by counter-revolutionists and Girondists. Organization of Terror government. Repulse of coalition armies. Insurrections suppressed. Quarrels between Jacobin factions. Fall of Robespierre, July 28,1794. Adoption of Constitution of 1795. Convention dissolved, Oct.1795.

these actions of the Convention have on the attitude of foreign governments towards the Revolution? What was the First Coalition, and what were its aims? What success did its armies achieve in the spring and summer of 1793?

10. Why was the situation of the Convention very desperate in the summer of 1793? How did it organize the government of the Terror? How did it deal with persons suspected of being enemies of the Revolution? Who were the Jacobins, and how did they triumph over the Girondists? How were the armies raised and organized in 1793? What were the decisive victories against the First Coalition?

11. Tell all you can about Hébert, Danton, and Robespierre. How did the Jacobins try to destroy the Catholic Church and the Christian religion? What new religion was established in France in 1794? Why did Robespierre think it necessary to continue the Terror after the foreign armies had been driven out of France? How did the Terror come to an end?

SELECTED READINGS

Brief accounts. Robinson, *Western Europe*, chs. xxxv–xxxvi. Robinson and Beard, *Modern Europe*, I, chs. xi–xiii. Robinson and Beard, *Outlines*, II, chs. vii–ix. Hayes and Moon, *Modern History*, pp. 295–334. Hayes, *Modern Europe*, I, ch. xv. Ashley, *Modern Civilization*, ch. vi. Schevill, *History of Europe*, pp. 405–438. Seignobos, *Contemporary Civilization*, pp. 106–149. Van Dyke, *Story of France*, chs. xiii–xiv. Brief histories of the Revolution: C. D. Hazen, *The Revolution and Napoleon;* L. Madelin, *The French Revolution;* S. Mathews, *The French Revolution.* Carlyle's *French Revolution* is a classic in English literature, famous for its brilliant portrayals of personalities and descriptions of events. The chapter entitled "The Spires at Midnight" describes the preparations for the insurrection of August 10, 1792.

Biographies. H. D. Sedgwick, *Lafayette.* H. Belloc, *Marie Antoinette.* J. G. Palache, *Marie Antoinette.* P. E. L. Dumont, *Recollections of Mirabeau.* H. Belloc, *Danton* and *Robespierre.* H. Beraud, *My Friend Robespierre.* Ida M. Tarbell, *Madame Roland.* C. Young, *A Lady Who Loved Herself* (Mme Roland). L. Madelin, *Figures of the Revolution.* H. Beraud, *Twelve Portraits of the Revolution.*

Historical Novels. A. Dumas, *The Taking of the Bastille* and *The Chevalier de la Maison Rouge.* R. Sabatini, *Scaramouche.* Dickens, *Tale of Two Cities.* Victor Hugo, *Ninety-Three.* Anatole France, *The Gods Athirst.* W. S. Davis, *The Whirlwind.*

Sources. Robinson and Beard, *Readings in Modern Europe*, I, chs. xi–xiii. The same selections in Robinson, *Readings in European History*, II, chs. xxxv–xxxvi. F. M. Anderson's *Constitutions and Other Select Documents* contains most of the official documents. The *Memoirs* of Madame de Campan, a lady-in-waiting to the queen, give an interesting account of court life. Arthur Young's *Travels in France* gives the impressions of an Englishman as to the conditions in France in 1788 and 1789.

NAPOLEON DISCUSSING THE PRELIMINARIES OF CAMPO-FORMIO
From a drawing by Le Thière.

CHAPTER IX. HOW NAPOLEON SET FRANCE RIGHT SIDE UP AND TURNED EUROPE UPSIDE DOWN; AND HOW EUROPE RETALIATED BY SENDING NAPOLEON OFF TO ST. HELENA

Power is never ridiculous. NAPOLEON

Was Napoleon a great man? Most writers, even if they do not admire him, concede that Napoleon was one of the few supremely great men of history; but some writers admire him so little that they deny him greatness altogether. Mr. H. G. Wells, in his famous book, *An Outline of History*,[1] says that Napoleon failed to do anything great because he lacked a " noble imagination." Lacking that,

Napoleon could do nothing more than strut upon the crest of his great opportunity like a cockerel upon a dunghill. The figure he makes in history is one of almost incredible self-conceit, of vanity, of greed and cunning, of callous contempt of all who trusted him, and of a grandiose aping of Caesar, Alexander, and Charlemagne which would be purely comic if it were not caked over with human blood.[1]

That is a vigorous and definite estimate of Napoleon, to say the least. And there is much truth in it. Napoleon was not a lovable

[1] H. G. Wells, *An Outline of History*. The Macmillan Company.

259

man — perhaps not strictly an admirable one. His selfishness, his egotism, were unbounded. He seems never to have doubted that what he wanted was the thing that ought to be done. " Power is never ridiculous," he said. In his eyes *might* and *right* were much the same thing. To obtain power for himself he scrupled at nothing — no pretense was too shameful, no conduct too cruel or ruthless, no sacrifice of men's lives too great, if thereby he could gain his ends. Humane feeling, friendship, gratitude — these were but words. " When a king is said to have been kind, the reign is a failure," is one of his epigrams. He also said that " men are like figures, which only acquire value in virtue of their position." Napoleon had an unsurpassed genius for action, for management, for arranging things to the best advantage for a desired end. That was perhaps why he thought of men as " figures," as things to be arranged, to be given positions, to be played with like chessmen. This was indeed his great weakness. He could never understand that people are not things, and cannot to any good purpose or lasting advantage be treated as objects to be played with.

Perhaps this is why he lost the game in the end. But while the game lasted he was, if not a great man, at least a great player. Like him or not, we cannot ignore him, because the people of his time could not ignore him. From 1799 to 1815 he was the central figure, the observed of all observers, admired, feared, and wondered at by all the kings, statesmen, and peoples of Europe. Great or not, Napoleon was the most striking and influential personality of modern times.

We must therefore know what he did and what was done to him. We must know (1) what Napoleon did in France ; (2) what he did and what he tried to do in Europe ; and (3) why Europe objected to him and at last sent him off to St. Helena.

I. What Napoleon Did in France

How Bonaparte made a name for himself, 1796–1799. October 4, 1795, the day after the insurrection of 13 Vendémiaire was " snuffed out with a whiff of grapeshot," word went round that this was the work of young Bonaparte. " Yes, but who is this fellow Bonaparte ? " people asked. No one seemed to know.

The fellow Bonaparte was then twenty-six years old.   Born in Corsica, of obscure parents, he had had little education or experience, although he had read much in military science and military history and in 1792 had watched with a discerning eye the insurrectionists at work on the famous 10th of August.   Tremendously ambitious, and with unlimited confidence in himself, he was waiting for an opportunity to make himself known.   He looked at this time both younger and older than he was — a very slight, slender, wiry youth, with a large head, long straight black hair, deep-set somber cold gray eyes, thin and sharp but finely molded features.   A striking face it was, not easily forgotten, as clear cut as if made to be stamped on coins and medallions.

In 1796 France was still at war with Austria, and Bonaparte was appointed by the Directory government to take charge of the armies in Italy.   Imagine, then, this young stripling, five feet two inches tall, inexperienced and unknown to fame, coming to Italy to take over the command from Masséna, Berthier, and Augereau — all older, experienced, and famous.   They did not like the idea.   They decided they would ignore the young upstart.   Augereau especially, a large blustering man, said that he would show this " General Vendémiaire " his proper place.   On April 11, near Genoa, the old generals had their first interview with young Bonaparte.   The new general kept them waiting.   Then he came quietly into the room, in his general's uniform, hat on head.   " He began to speak at once.   In a hard voice, in brief, precise, trenchant phrases, he gave his orders, explained what he proposed to do, and with a gesture dismissed his subordinates."   The generals said not a word, but saluted and went out.   It was not till he was outside that Augereau recovered his voice.   With a loud oath, he said to Masséna : " This little runt of a general frightened me.   It is impossible to understand how he made me feel that he was the master from the moment he looked at me."

Many men were afterwards to have the same experience.   There was something about Bonaparte, some hypnotic power in the cold gray eyes, that enabled him to impose his will on others.   " His eyes," said Cambacérès, " seem to penetrate your head."   The old generals, Augereau and Masséna, could not meet those eyes.

They obeyed and were silent. They not only obeyed Bonaparte, they admired him and remained ever after his devoted servants.

It was the same with the soldiers. This cold selfish egotist somehow managed to inspire them with confidence, and not only with confidence but also with undying devotion — even with affection. His brief proclamations to the soldiers are famous, and none more so than the first one addressed to the army in Italy (March 27, 1796):

Soldiers! You are naked and hungry. The government owes you much, but can give you nothing. Your patience and your courage are admirable; but they can win you neither glory nor prestige. I will lead you to the most fertile plains in the world. Rich provinces and great cities will be in your power; there you will find honor, glory, riches! Soldiers of Italy! Will you lack courage or constancy?

Bonaparte won the soldiers as quickly as he won his generals. They called him " Little Corporal," " Bony," " The Little One," and other affectionate names. At last the soldiers had a master whom they would follow to the ends of the earth. They followed him because they loved him, because they had confidence in him, and last but not least, because they knew he would lead them to " honor, glory, riches."

Bonaparte's promises to the soldiers were soon made good. In a number of brilliant campaigns he defeated the Austrians and drove them out of northern Italy. Then he crossed the Alps into southern Germany, where a French army under General Hoche was ready to unite with him. Confronted by two armies, the Austrians were induced to sign the Treaty of Campo-Formio (1797). By this treaty the Austrians recognized the Rhine as the French frontier, thus ceding Belgium, and sanctioned the political changes which Bonaparte had already effected in northern Italy. The Italians had welcomed the French as liberators, and under the direction of Bonaparte they abolished many of the old inequalities and established two small republics, both modeled upon that of France. One of these, comprising the territory around Genoa, was called the Ligurian Republic. The other and more important one, with Milan as its capital, included the greater part of northern Italy and was called the Cisalpine Republic. In return for freeing the Italians from Austria and giving them institutions similar to those of France, Bonaparte exacted heavy indemnities and sent off to Paris many of their famous works of art, some of which may still be seen in the Louvre. Although nominally independent, the Italians soon found that they had only exchanged one master for another.

These victories made Bonaparte famous. Back home in France people read of his exploits. They learned that he had ended the war with Austria. They learned that he had acquired the Austrian province of Belgium and made northern Italy virtually a French dependency. Meantime the glorious war was costing nothing. On the contrary it brought indemnities into the treasury, and the soldiers were sending to their relatives in France gold and silver, which were much better than the worthless paper money. People were amazed, but also delighted. They were watching Bonaparte. What would he do next?

How Bonaparte became master of France, 1799. At the request of the Directory government Bonaparte returned to Paris, where he received an ovation. But he did not wish to remain in Paris, for in Paris, where there was nothing for him to do, he felt that his sword would " grow rusty." He therefore proposed to make a conquest of Egypt, as an effective way of interfering with British interests in the Mediterranean. The Directory government had little faith in the venture ; but it was so alarmed at the popularity of Bonaparte that it was glad to get rid of him on any terms. With an army and a fleet Bonaparte arrived in Alexandria in July, 1798. Egypt was soon conquered. But in August the British Admiral Nelson destroyed the French fleet at the Battle of the Nile, leaving Bonaparte and his army virtually imprisoned in the country they had conquered.

Meantime the European powers, alarmed by the French control of northern Italy and the conquest of Egypt, organized a new coalition, known as the Second Coalition. In 1799 the coalition armies recovered northern Italy, and from Holland and Switzerland threatened to invade France once more, as they had formerly done in 1793. Here was an opportunity for Bonaparte to win new laurels — if he could get back to France. Luck seemed often to favor him, and never more so than in this instance. Leaving his army in Egypt, he managed by happy chances to avoid capture by the British and arrived in France in October, 1799. When they learned of his safe arrival, people were wild with joy. " In the theaters the performances were interrupted by cheers and patriotic songs; elsewhere crowds gathered, and people embraced each other, weeping with joy and enthusiasm."

Unfortunately for Bonaparte, France was half saved before he returned, by the French victory at the Battle of Zürich. But in spite of that victory the Directory was easily overthrown. It was so corrupt and so inefficient that it now had few friends and many enemies. We are not to suppose that Bonaparte was the only one who was conspiring to overthrow the old government. The Jacobins were plotting to establish a democratic republic like that of 1793. The Royalists were plotting to restore the Bourbon monarchy. Even within the government itself there was a party, led by the Abbé Sieyès, laying schemes for a " revision of the constitution." What Sieyès needed to carry through his scheme was the support of a popular military leader. When Bonaparte returned to France, General Moreau said to Sieyès, " There is the man you need."

Sieyès and Bonaparte were brought together and a conspiracy was soon hatched. Sieyès was at that time one of the five directors who constituted the executive branch of the government. Two other directors, Ducos and Barras, were induced to join the conspiracy, and some of the members of the two legislative bodies (Council of Ancients and Council of Five Hundred) also supported it — among them Bonaparte's brother, Lucien, who was president of the Council of Five Hundred. November 9 the three directors resigned, the troops were put under the command of Bonaparte, and on the pretext of a Jacobin plot, the councils were directed to meet next day at Saint-Cloud, just outside of Paris. It was hoped that in the quiet village of Saint-Cloud the two councils could be persuaded to dissolve after appointing three provisional " consuls " to revise the constitution. The three consuls were to be Bonaparte, Sieyès, and Ducos.

The affair did not go so smoothly at Saint-Cloud as was hoped. The Council of Ancients played its part well enough, but violent opposition came from the Council of Five Hundred. Thinking to overawe the Five Hundred, Bonaparte entered the hall. Crying " Down with the Dictator," the members surrounded him, shoving him about. For once in his life Bonaparte was frightened. He lost his head, and in the end had to be carried half-fainting from the hall by some officers. The day was saved by his brother Lucien, who ran out to the soldiers, told them that Bonaparte had been threatened " with daggers," and begged them to save him. After some hesitation the soldiers entered the hall with fixed bayonets, and the members of the Five Hundred fled in terror, escaping through the windows into the gardens — into oblivion.

© *Braun et Cie*

NAPOLEON AS CONSUL, ABOUT 1801
From a painting by Appiani.

The same night some members of the two councils returned and passed the necessary decrees. Each council appointed from its own members a committee of twenty-five. They also appointed Bonaparte, Sieyès, and Ducos provisional consuls, and then declared the councils permanently dissolved. Thus ended the famous *coup d'état* of 18 Brumaire, Year VIII, which ended the Directory and began the rule of Napoleon. When people learned what had been done, they only shrugged their shoulders and went on with their business. No one knew what Bonaparte would do, but most people felt that he would do better than the Directory. This feeling was reflected on the stock market. Within a week the shares of the Consolidated Third (government debt) rose in value from eleven points to twenty.

How Bonaparte established a new government which pretended to be a republic but was really a dictatorship, 1799–1804. Before the 18 Brumaire, Bonaparte allowed all of the various parties to think that he would serve their plans. At least so he afterwards told Madame de Rémusat, in these words:

> I saw the Abbé Sieyès and promised to execute his wordy constitution; I received the leaders of the Jacobins, the agents of the Bourbons; I accepted advice from everyone, but gave none except such as would serve my plans. . . .
> Everyone fished in my lake, and when I became the head of the state, there was not even a single party in France which did not hope to gain something from my success.

Bonaparte had no faith in popular government, but he did not feel strong enough to abolish the republic at once. The government which he first established was in form a republic, but in reality a kind of dictatorship. It was called the Decennial Consulate (1799–1802). The constitution, drafted by Bonaparte himself, named three consuls to serve for ten years. All executive power was conferred on the First Consul, Bonaparte. To advise him, he appointed a Council of State. There was also a Senate composed of distinguished men, a majority of whom were appointed by friends of Bonaparte. To give the government the appearance of a republic, there were two legislative assemblies — the Tribunate and the Legislative Assembly; but they had little power, and the members were not elected by the people but appointed by the Senate. To strengthen the power of the First Consul a separate law provided that there should be in each of the eighty-three departments into which the country was divided a " prefect " appointed by the First Consul and responsible to him. Thus effective power was in the hands of the First Consul, supported by a Council of State, a Senate, and the prefects in the departments.

When the constitution was officially proclaimed and read in Paris, two old women were standing in the crowd listening. One of them was deaf. " I cannot hear," she said. " What do you see in this new constitution? " The other replied, " I see Bonaparte in it." No more incisive judgment could have been pronounced on the new constitution. Not only was Bonaparte in it — there was little else in it. In form the new government was a republic; in reality it was a dictatorship. People understood this well

Bibliothèque Nationale

CROSSING THE ALPS THROUGH THE ST. BERNARD PASS

In 1801 Napoleon crossed the Alps into Italy, took the Austrians somewhat by surprise, and won the Battle of Marengo. From a lithograph by Victor Adam.

enough, but they were willing to have it so; and when the constitution was presented to the people for approval or disapproval, it was approved by a vote of 3,011,007 to 1526.

The First Consul exhibited at once his marvelous talent for efficient administration. As prefects in the departments he appointed able men who soon established orderly government where confusion had existed under the Directory. A new and stable currency replaced the depreciated paper money which had formerly circulated. New taxes, heavy but reasonably just and honestly collected, restored the credit of the government by providing an adequate revenue. Meantime, the War of the Second Coalition was ended. Making a spectacular crossing of the Alps, Bonaparte descended into the plains of Lombardy, where he defeated the Austrians at the famous Battle of Marengo and recovered for France the control of northern Italy (*Peace of Lunéville, 1801*). The next year he managed to make peace with England also (*Peace of Amiens, 1802*). For the first time since 1793 France was at peace with all the world. It seemed that the long wars growing out of the Revolution were at an end, and people looked forward to a period of peace and prosperity. What more could be asked of Bonaparte than this — that within three years he had established orderly government in France and peace in Europe?

In 1802 Bonaparte's popularity was such that he thought it safe to take another step towards absolute power. He asked the people to vote on the question, " Shall Napoleon Bonaparte be made consul for life? " Again the people approved by an overwhelming majority, thus establishing the government known as the Life Consulate (1802–1804). For the first time the name " Napoleon Bonaparte " was officially used in place of " Citizen Bonaparte." Napoleon gave up the pretense of being a Republican. He openly ridiculed the Republicans as " ideologues." He abandoned the simple Republican manner of living at the Tuileries, and introduced the pomp and ceremony of a royal court, gathering about him the nobles and ladies of the old aristocracy. " Only this kind of people know how to serve," he said. Yet he made it plain to the Royalists that he had no intention of restoring the Bourbon monarchy. His intentions were indeed perfectly plain; and two years later, after the suppression of a Bourbon plot to assassinate the consul, he once more asked the people to vote, this time on the question whether he should be permitted to take the title of Emperor. This the people also approved, by a vote of 2,959,891[1] to 2567. Thus was established the hereditary empire (1804).

Yet Napoleon claimed that he ruled by consent of the people. It was substantially true. They had voluntarily conferred upon him his autocratic power, and in these early years, at least, the great majority of the French people gladly submitted to his authority. What is the explanation of this? For six years they had carried on the great Revolution to free themselves from the Bourbon autocracy. Why should they now so eagerly welcome the autocracy of Napoleon?

Why the people of France gladly submitted to the authority of Napoleon. Of course people submitted to Napoleon for many reasons — because he was a fascinating personality who knew how to win allegiance and exact obedience; because he was a military

---

[1] Since this was a smaller vote than that for the Life Consulate, Napoleon falsified the returns and gave out to the papers 3,574,898 as the vote in favor of taking the title.

CORONATION OF NAPOLEON IN NOTRE DAME, 1804.

From a painting by David. It was supposed that Napoleon would kneel before the Pope and be crowned by him. Instead, he took the crown, turned his back on the Pope and the altar, crowned himself, and then crowned Josephine kneeling before him.

genius who won brilliant victories; because he was a skillful politician and an efficient administrator; because he was a great actor,
always in the spot-light, stirring the emotions of men and gratify-
ing their instinct for the dramatic and the grandiose. But people
submitted to Napoleon for two more important reasons: (1) because they had lost faith in the republic, and (2) because Napoleon
had saved for them the advantages they had gained from the Revolution.

In 1793 people had gone through blood and fire for the republic.
They had thought of the republic as something sacred, a form of
government that would bring happiness to mankind. This emotional faith had died hard, and in 1799 there were still many good
Jacobin Republicans, especially in the army. But the mass of the
people had grown cynical about the republic. The republic was
associated in their minds with the Terror, to which they looked
back with aversion, or with the Directory government, which had
proved to be one of the most feeble and corrupt ever seen in France.
Thus in 1799 most people in France preferred an autocrat who
would govern well to a republic that governed badly.

But if people had lost faith in the republic why were they not
willing to restore the old Bourbon monarchy? There was the
brother of Louis XVI, the Count of Provence, who now claimed to
be the rightful king of France. There was a strong Royalist party,
composed of priests and ex-nobles, who were working for the restoration of the Bourbon " pretender " as Louis XVIII. Why did the
majority of the people prefer Napoleon to Louis XVIII?

The reason is that the Bourbon pretender was determined, if ever
he became king, to undo the work of the Revolution and punish
those who had taken a leading part in it. He would restore to the
nobles their ancient privileges and subject the peasants to the old
feudal obligations. He would re-establish the Catholic Church
and restore to it the lands which had been taken from it and sold
to peasants and middle-class people. Above all, he would punish
by imprisonment, exile, or death, those men who had taken a leading part in the Revolution, and especially the " regicides " — those
members of the National Convention who had voted for the execution of his brother, Louis XVI. Priests and ex-nobles favored the

STREET COSTUMES

Photo Hachette

The two on the left represent styles about 1804; those on the right, a few years later. Long trousers, top hat, and something resembling the modern dress coat are in evidence (right). The frock coat — later called the Prince Albert — is recognizable (left).

program because they would benefit by it. But the mass of the people — peasants, middle-class people, officers in the army, and revolutionary politicians — were opposed to it because they would lose the benefits the Revolution had conferred upon them.

In 1794 Mallet du Pan, a shrewd observer, expressed the feeling of the majority of the people in these words:

The mass of the people cares as little for the republic as for royalty, and simply clings to the advantages . . . which the Revolution has conferred upon them. They will accept the law from any master who knows how to bind them by their hopes and fears.

Napoleon was that master. He knew how to bind the people by their hopes and fears. They submitted to him gladly, because he saved them from a restoration of the Bourbon monarchy and preserved for them the benefits of the Revolution.

Napoleon made it clear from the first that he did not wish to undo the work of the Revolution. After the *coup d'état* of the

18 Brumaire he said: "The romance of the Revolution is ended; we must begin its history." He wanted people to forget the furious party struggles, the bloodshed, the dream of an ideal republic or a Reign of Virtue. All that was " romance." He wanted them, as loyal Frenchmen, to accept the Revolution as an accomplished fact, and to unite with him in building a stable régime on the basis of the changes in rights and privileges which the Revolution had effected. We must now see what Napoleon did to maintain the revolutionary changes. His work may be considered under three heads: (1) the church and religion; (2) the five codes; (3) education.

1. *The church and religion.* One question which the Revolution had left unsettled was that of the Catholic Church. In 1793–1794 the National Convention had tried to destroy the Catholic Church. The effort was a failure. In 1799 more than half the people in France were Catholics. A majority of the old bishops and priests, led by the Pope, still refused to recognize the republic as the legitimate government, and they still claimed the church lands which the revolutionary governments had confiscated and sold to the people.

Napoleon cared little about religion in itself, but he realized that it might be a powerful influence either for or against any government. He once said: " If I had to govern a nation of Jews I would rebuild Solomon's Temple." Having to govern a nation largely Catholic, he felt that it was highly necessary to gain the goodwill of Catholics. The Revolution could never be regarded as settled, or his own power be firmly established, until the Pope and the French bishops recognized the republic and renounced their former rights and possessions. Napoleon therefore at once entered into negotiations with the Pope, Pius VII, and after many months of controversy induced him to sign with the French government a formal agreement which is known as the Concordat of 1801.

The Concordat was a brief but very important document. It defined the relations between the Catholic Church and the French government. It provided that Napoleon should appoint the bishops, that the bishops should appoint the priests, and that both bishops and priests should be paid salaries by the government.

Thus Napoleon restored the church to a privileged position in the state.   In return he obtained from the Pope important concessions. The Pope wished the Catholic religion to be the only one recognized by the government.   This Napoleon refused, thus preserving the religious freedom which the Revolution had established.   The Pope wished to have the confiscated lands of the church returned to it.   This also Napoleon refused, and in the end the Pope agreed that neither he nor his successors would ever " disturb in any manner the possessors of the confiscated church lands." Thus the Concordat restored the Catholic Church to a privileged position; but in signing the Concordat the Pope recognized the republic which the Revolution had created and the validity of the revolutionary laws by which the church property had been confiscated and sold.

The proclamation of the Concordat was celebrated with great pomp and ceremony in the Cathedral of Notre Dame.   After the ceremony Napoleon asked General Delmas: " Well, what did you think of it? "

" It was a fine hocus-pocus," the general replied.   " One thing only was wanting — the presence of the million men who gave up their lives to destroy what you are building up."

Many people agreed with General Delmas.   Ardent supporters of the Revolution felt that the reconciliation with the Pope and the restoration of the church to a privileged position was a backward step — that it was undoing the work of the Revolution.   But this was not really so.   By signing the Concordat Napoleon conceded little and gained much.   What did he gain?   He won the approval of the majority of the Catholics in France.   He maintained the religious freedom which the Revolution had established. Above all, the Pope, in signing the Concordat, formally recognized the republic as the legitimate government of France.   It was as much as to say that the Catholic Church and all good Catholics at last recognized the Revolution as an accomplished fact.

2. *The five codes.*   The revolutionary assemblies had passed many laws affecting the rights of persons and property — laws abolishing the nobility, the guilds, the parlements; laws abolishing feudal obligations on the land; laws concerning marriage and

divorce, the authority of fathers, the rights of children; laws defining crimes and regulating the procedure in courts of justice. In these laws there was much that was not clear, much that was incomplete, much that was inconsistent. In 1799 French law was therefore a confused mass of ancient customs and revolutionary legislation, so that even lawyers often found it difficult to say just what the law was.

This means that French law needed to be codified — that is, the confused mass of custom and revolutionary legislation needed to be reduced to a brief, clear, and systematic statement. The National Convention began this task of codification but never finished it. It is one of Napoleon's chief titles to fame that he completed the work of codification. Of course the actual work was done by the lawyers, but without Napoleon to urge them on, the lawyers would never have finished. Napoleon got the lawyers together and kept them at work. He insisted that it was better to have an imperfect code than not to have any code at all. The reports of the lawyers were discussed at length in the Council of State, with Napoleon presiding and taking part in the debates. The sessions sometimes lasted from seven o'clock in the evening until three or four in the morning. Eminent councilors and lawyers would sometimes fall asleep in the small hours; but Napoleon kept them at their task. "Wake up, gentlemen!" he would exclaim. "We must earn our salaries." After several years of labor five codes were completed, having to do with civil and criminal law and procedure and with commercial law.

The most important of the codes was the Civil Code (1804). It defined the rights of persons and the law of property. In the main it accepted the changes brought about by the Revolution. It was based on the principle that all persons are free and equal before the law. In defining the law of property the Civil Code accepted the work of the Revolution in abolishing feudal obligations on the land. In respect to the law of inheritance, it provided that when a man died a considerable part of his property must be equally divided among his heirs, thus making it more difficult to build up great landed estates such as had existed before the Revolution.

The Criminal Code (1810) also accepted, in the main, the work of the Revolution. Penalties for crimes were made the same for all people. Penalties were still harsh and included the death penalty and imprisonment for life, but torture and the more cruel punishments were abandoned. Arbitrary arrest and imprisonment were no longer legal, and the procedure (that is, the form of trial) gave to accused persons rights not enjoyed before the Revolution. The trial was public; the accused was given the aid of a lawyer and was permitted to bring witnesses to testify in his defense; and the verdict in cases of crime was rendered by a jury of citizens. Thus the Criminal Code also perpetuated important changes brought about by the Revolution.

The codes established by Napoleon not only perpetuated the work of the Revolution — they also made it easy for the average citizen to know what the law was, what he might do and what he might not do, and what would be the consequences of his acts. It was partly for this reason that the Civil Code, especially, has had a great influence on the law of many countries besides France. At the present time the French Civil Code, with some modifications, is the law of Italy, Belgium, Holland, Bavaria, Baden, and our own state of Louisiana (this last being due to the fact that Louisiana was once a French colony). The Civil Code was, in fact, perhaps the chief way in which the French Revolution influenced the institutions of other European countries.

The Civil Code has been well described as " the summary and the correction of the French Revolution." Later, at St. Helena, Napoleon himself said, " My glory chiefly consists, not in having won forty battles, but in having established the Civil Code."

3. *Education.* Before the Revolution the schools were mainly controlled by the church. The most famous colleges were those of the Jesuit and Benedictine monks. The special purpose of such colleges was to train men for the church or the law; their general purpose was to maintain the Catholic faith, the supremacy of the church, and the authority of the king. The revolutionary leaders were of course opposed to this system of education. Their idea was that the government should control education, and that it should provide free public schools for all citizens. In their view the object of the schools should be to make good and loyal citizens.

The National Convention discussed the subject of free public schools at great length, but it was too busy ever to carry out its projects. Napoleon continued and completed the work of the National Convention. If the government did not control education, he said, the monks would come back and manage the schools as they did formerly. " The recall of the Jesuits I will not permit! " he exclaimed. " Let no one mention that idea to me again." After years of discussion and experimentation, Napoleon therefore established what he called the Imperial University (1808). It was not a university as we understand the term. The Imperial University included the entire system of education — primary schools, high schools (*lycées*), and schools of higher learning. The organization of all these schools, the subjects to be taught, the appointment of teachers, the payment of salaries — all this was controlled by the government; that is, by Napoleon. This was necessary, according to Napoleon, in order that " good principles " might be taught by " good methods." " Good methods," he said, " make good minds; good principles make good citizens."

The fact is that Napoleon wished to control the schools for the same reason that he wished to control the church. He cared little about education or religion except as they could be used for political ends. He hoped that the bishops and the teachers, since they were appointed and paid by the government, would teach the people to be " good citizens " — that is, loyal to him. He had prepared for use in the schools a " Catechism " which the children were expected to learn. Part of it ran as follows:

LESSON VII. CONTINUATION OF THE FOURTH COMMANDMENT

Question. What are the duties of Christians toward the princes who govern them, and what in particular are our duties toward Napoleon?

Answer. Christians owe to the princes who govern them, and we owe in particular toward Napoleon, our emperor, love, respect, obedience, fidelity, military service, and the taxes laid for the defense and preservation of the empire. . . .

Q. Why are we bound to all these duties toward our emperor?

A. Because God . . . established him as our sovereign and has made him the minister of His power and His image upon the earth.

Q. What ought to be thought of those who may be lacking in their duty toward our emperor?

A. According to the Apostle Saint Paul, they would be resisting the order established by God himself and would render themselves worthy of eternal damnation.

Napoleon's schools were not very good ones. Catholics would not send their children to his schools. It was difficult to get good teachers, partly because the pay was small, partly because the government interfered too much with the teachers' activities, both within the schools and outside of them. Nevertheless, Napoleon's establishment of a system of public schools controlled by the state was of great importance in two ways: (1) It prevented the church from recovering the control of education which it had formerly enjoyed. (2) It helped to perpetuate the revolutionary idea that the government should establish schools freely open to all citizens. In fact France has today what Napoleon aimed to establish — a uniform system of public schools (primary schools, high schools, and universities) supported and controlled by the government, providing instruction for all citizens on equal terms.

A brief statement of what Napoleon did for France. Napoleon preserved the equality of rights which the Revolution established. He established an hereditary empire, and in organizing the imperial government he simplified and systematized the system of centralized administration which had existed under the kings before the Revolution. His hereditary empire did not endure. After 1815 the Bourbon monarchy was restored. In 1848 a republic was established. In 1852 the hereditary empire was restored (Napoleon III). In 1871 there was established the third French Republic, which still exists. Thus in the end France came back to the revolutionary ideal of a republic. But under all these forms of government the equality of rights established by the Revolution, and the centralized administration fashioned by Napoleon persisted with slight changes.

II. What Napoleon Did in Europe

Why Napoleon was not satisfied with one country to govern. An ordinary man would have been satisfied with one country to govern. But Napoleon was not an ordinary man. Governing France was not enough for him; he wished to govern the greater part of Europe as well — and in truth he nearly succeeded. One war followed another, and every victory increased his power, until by 1811 all of Continental Europe west of Russia and Austria was more or less subject to his authority. What was Napoleon's object? Was he inspired solely by selfish ambition, by the love of glory? Or did he have some great plan in his head for the better government of Europe?

It is difficult to answer this question, since human motives are never simple. Napoleon was a man of such boundless energy that he could not resist the temptation to meddle in the affairs of other European countries. Besides, he was ambitious — one of the most ambitious men that ever lived. Like all men of genius he wished to be remembered and acclaimed for having done great things. But still he was intelligent enough to know that he would not be long remembered for waging war aimlessly, merely for the sake of winning battles. He knew that his name would be soon forgotten unless he created something of lasting value. And so Napoleon was always the statesman, who made his wars and battles serve a political purpose.

What was this purpose? We need not suppose that from the very first Napoleon had a clear idea, a well-matured plan for the reorganization of Europe. But as his conquests were extended, first in Italy, then in Germany, he gradually worked out a scheme for a European empire. By 1811 this scheme was fairly clear. Speaking to Fouché, one of his intimates, he said:

How can I help it if a great power [destiny] drives me on to become Dictator of the world? . . . I have not yet fulfilled my mission, and I mean to end what I have begun. We need a European code of law, a European court of appeal, a uniform coinage, a common system of weights and measures. The same law must run throughout Europe. I shall fuse all the nations into one. . . This, my lord duke, is the only solution that pleases me.

Napoleon never succeeded in fusing the nations of Europe into one nation. But by 1811 he had created a kind of federation of European states under one imperial authority, and in many of the dependent states he had already established the system of equal rights which France had won by the Revolution. We must now see how he accomplished all this.

The first extension of French power beyond the Rhine: The " sister republics," 1797-1799. The famous French diplomat Talleyrand, once said: " The conquest of the natural frontiers [the Rhine, the Alps, the Pyrenees] was the work of the Revolution; all the rest was the work of Napoleon." We have already seen how the French frontier was extended to the Rhine in the time of the Revolution (p. 249). The first extension of French power beyond the Rhine was made by the young Bonaparte in 1797, when he drove the Austrians out of northern Italy. The two little republics, the Cisalpine and the Ligurian republics, which were then established in North Italy, were modeled upon the French Republic, and although they were nominally independent, they soon found that they were little more than dependent states, protégés of the French government. People referred to them as little sisters of France — " sister republics."

When Bonaparte went off to Egypt in 1798-1799 the Directory government created some more sister republics. In Holland there were many people who wished to imitate the French Revolution — to sweep away the old inequalities and establish a more democratic republic. The French government took up the cause of the republican party in Holland, and by means of diplomatic pressure and military force the Dutch Republic was reorganized and took

TALLEYRAND (1754-1838)

One of the ablest diplomats of the nineteenth century. Although he was Bishop of Autun before the Revolution, he espoused the popular cause until the Terror, when he left France. He served Napoleon as minister of foreign affairs, but deserted him in 1814 and helped to establish the Bourbons, whom he supported till 1830. Then he helped to establish Louis Philippe on the throne. One of the many witticisms attributed to him is: "Language was given to man in order to conceal thought." Very appropriate for a diplomat.

the name of the Batavian Republic. In much the same way the Swiss Confederation was transformed into the Helvetian Republic, and the Kingdom of Naples in southern Italy was transformed into the Parthenopean Republic. Thus when Napoleon made peace with Austria (1801) and England (1802), French political influence was already predominant in the little sister republics beyond the Rhine — in Holland, Switzerland, and northern and southern Italy. Napoleon's next extension of French influence was in Germany.

How Napoleon began to undermine the influence of Austria in southern Germany: The Act of Secularization, 1803. Between 1803 and 1806 the political organization of Germany was greatly changed. These changes are important, not only because they help us to understand Napoleon's empire, but because they made the political geography of Germany much what it is today. For these reasons we must try to understand these changes.

First of all we must try to get a clear idea of Germany as it was before 1803. It was a most curious hodge-podge of states, big and little, all united in what was called " the Empire," or more exactly " the Holy Roman Empire of the German States." The most important states were Austria and Prussia, each one strong enough to rank with the great powers of Europe. Then there were a number of secondary states, smaller than Austria and Prussia, but still of considerable size. The chief of these were Oldenburg, Saxony, Hanover, Nassau, and Hesse-Cassel in central and northern Germany; and Bavaria, Württemberg, Baden, and Hesse-Darmstadt in southern Germany. Finally, there were some hundreds of very small states — many more than can be shown on an ordinary map. Some of these were city states, some were ecclesiastical states (cities or territories ruled by bishops of the Catholic church), others were insignificant possessions of innumerable counts, barons, and knights of the Empire.

All of these hundreds of states were united in the Empire. The emperor was chosen by nine of the more important rulers, known as " electors "; and for centuries the electors had always chosen as emperor the Habsburg ruler of Austria. There was also an imperial diet, in which the various states were represented, either directly or by proxy. But the diet had almost no power at all, and the emperor, outside of Austria, had very little. German politics turned very largely on the rivalry of the two great states, Austria and Prussia. The small states sided with one or the other as their interests seemed to demand. The principal states of South Germany — Bavaria, Württemberg, Baden, and Hesse-Darmstadt — were inclined to side with Austria against Prussia. But in one important matter the interest of Austria was opposed to that of the South German states. Within the boundaries of Bavaria, Württemberg, Baden, and Hesse-Darmstadt were located hundreds of the tiny states — city states, ecclesiastical states, imperial counts, knights, etc. Naturally the rulers of Bavaria, Württemberg, and Baden were more than willing to take over the government of the tiny states within their boundaries, and they would long since have done so except for the opposition of Austria. Here was a situation which Napoleon could make use of. By helping the larger states take over the tiny states within their boundaries, he could bind them to France and so weaken the influence of Austria in South Germany.

The beginning of this agreeable business of wiping out the small German states goes back to the Treaty of Basel between France and Prussia in 1795. By that treaty Prussia ceded to France her territory west of the Rhine, on condition that Prussia should later be compensated for her loss of territory by taking over certain small German states east of the Rhine. By the treaties of Campo-Formio (1797) and of Lunéville (1801) Austria also agreed that those German states which ceded territory to France should be compensated in the same way. Thus there was lodged in the heads of the rulers of the secondary German states a most attractive idea. This idea was that with the aid of Napoleon they could enlarge their own territories and increase their wealth and power by annexing the territory and taking over the government of the small states lying within their boundaries. The result was that in 1803 there was enacted by the German diet a decree which for convenience we may call the Act of Secularization. By this act all the city states except six, and all the ecclesiastical states except one, lost their independence and were incorporated with the larger states within whose boundaries they were located. The states that profited most by this act were Prussia and the four South

German states of Bavaria, Württemberg, Baden, and Hesse-Darmstadt.

The South German states found this business so agreeable that they at once began to take over the innumerable tiny principalities ruled by counts, barons, and knights. Napoleon urged them on. The tiny states were of no use to him, but the four chief states of southern Germany could help him against Austria, and the more he helped them the more they were likely to help him. To a subordinate he once expressed his purpose with brutal frankness:

The small rulers in Germany want to be protected against the big; the big rulers want to rule according to their fancy. Now I want [from the rulers of Germany] men and money, and as it is the big rulers and not the small rulers who can give me both men and money, I leave the former in peace, and the latter must get on as best they can.

The knights, threatened with destruction, appealed to Austria for protection. The Emperor Francis threatened to make war on the Duke of Bavaria unless he left the knights undisturbed. Thereupon Napoleon made treaties with Bavaria and the other South German states, promising them, in case of victory against Austria, to " round out their territories conveniently." This was the beginning of the war between France and Austria in 1805. Meantime, France had been at war with England since 1803, and early in 1805 Russia had joined with England. In 1805, therefore, France was at war with the three powers, England, Russia, and Austria. This is known as the War of the Third Coalition.

War of the Third Coalition, 1805: How Napoleon formed the Rhine Confederation and ended the Holy Roman Empire, 1806. When the Austrian General Mack invaded Bavaria, Napoleon's army was still in northern France and Belgium, where it had been gathered for an attempt to invade England. With more than usual rapidity he moved his army in five divisions south to the upper Rhine, where it confronted General Mack at Ulm. Then, feigning a direct attack upon the Austrian general, Napoleon executed one of his most spectacular victories by rapid flank movements of his armies to the north and east, thus cutting off the retreat of the Austrian general. With scarcely any fighting at all General Mack

© *Braun et Cie*

NAPOLEON IN CAMP AT AUSTERLITZ, 1805
From a painting by Lecomte du Noüy.

surrendered his entire army (*Capitulation at Ulm, October, 1805*).
As this victory was won chiefly by marching, the French soldiers
said that they won the battle by " their legs instead of their arms."

Napoleon then pushed eastward along the Danube and on
December 2, 1805, won a complete victory over the combined
Austrian and Russian armies at Austerlitz. The Russians, complaining that the Austrians were responsible for the defeat, went
home in disgust; and the Austrian Emperor Francis was compelled
to make the humiliating Peace of Pressburg.

The Peace of Pressburg (December 26, 1805) provided that
Austria should cede all of her scattered possessions in South Germany to Bavaria, Württemberg, and Baden. In addition Austria
agreed that Bavaria and Württemberg should become kingdoms,
and that these states, together with Baden and Hesse-Darmstadt,
should no longer be included in the Holy Roman Empire, or be in
any way dependent on Austria. Thus Napoleon took another step
in destroying the old German political system. With South Germany in his power, and his victorious armies encamped from the
Rhine to the frontiers of Austria, he was prepared for the next step.
This was the formation of the Rhine Confederation.

All the states in South Germany, big and little, now knew that their fate depended on Napoleon. In 1806 they all had their representatives in Paris bidding one against another for favors. On July 17, 1806, the representatives of Bavaria, Württemberg, Baden, Hesse-Darmstadt, and twelve other states in South Germany were each in turn presented with a document known as the Constitution of the Rhine Confederation. Each of the sixteen representatives was given twenty-four hours to sign this document, and each was told that if he refused to sign it, the state which he represented would forthwith cease to exist. Each of the representatives signed.

The Constitution of the Rhine Confederation was in the form of a treaty between France and each of the sixteen states included in the confederation. The confederation was to be entirely independent of Austria and the old Empire. Napoleon was declared to be the " Protector " of the confederation, and each of the states in it was bound to support Napoleon in any war he might become engaged in. Finally all of the states in South Germany not named in the confederation (all of the innumerable tiny states ruled by counts, barons, knights, etc.) were abolished as states and incorporated in the states that composed the confederation.

The formation of the Confederation of the Rhine prepared the way for the end of the old Holy Roman Empire. In August, 1806, the diet of the Empire was abolished, and the Emperor Francis issued a pathetic document in which he formally renounced the title of Emperor which his family had held for more than three centuries. He was permitted to take the title of Emperor of Austria, but this title had no more meaning than the title King of Austria would have had. The only empire in the real sense was now the Napoleonic empire, and of this empire South Germany was a part, in the form of a protected confederation.

How Napoleon changed the sister republics into kingdoms, for the benefit of his family, 1805-1806. While building up his power in South Germany, Napoleon was also engaged in binding the little sister republics more closely to his empire. As long as France was a republic it was right that the little dependent states should also be republics. But after Napoleon assumed the title of Emperor, it was more in keeping that they should be kingdoms. They could then be bound more closely to the empire by turning them over to members of Napoleon's family. Fortunately for this scheme Napoleon had several brothers (Joseph, Louis, Jerome, and Lucien) besides a stepson (Eugène de Beauharnais).

The first of these republics to be transformed into a kingdom was the Cisalpine Republic in northern Italy. March 15, 1805, Napoleon issued a decree to the effect that, in view of the " request " of the Cisalpine Republic, the " Emperor of the French is King of Italy." A constitution was drawn up for the new kingdom, and Napoleon traveled down to Milan, where with great pomp and ceremony he was crowned with the famous old iron crown of the Lombard kings. Napoleon did not intend to remain king himself; but the crown was declared to be hereditary in his family, and the next year Eugène de Beauharnais became King of Italy in his place. Northern Italy thus became, not a part of France, but a part of Napoleon's empire. Since the old Kingdom of Sardinia and the Ligurian Republic had already been annexed to France, the imperial authority now included all of Italy as far south as the frontier of the Pope's dominions.

The next year Napoleon took another step in subjecting Italy to his empire by transforming the old Parthenopean Republic into the Kingdom of Naples and Sicily. By a decree of March 30, 1806, he declared that " by right of conquest " Naples and Sicily " make up part of the Grand Empire," and that " we recognize as King of Naples and Sicily our well-beloved brother Joseph Napoleon. . . . The King of Naples shall be forever a grand dignitary of the empire, under the title of Grand Elector." Since England controlled the sea, the island of Sicily was never really a part of this new kingdom, but Naples (that is, all of southern Italy) was until 1808 governed by Joseph Bonaparte under the direct supervision of the Emperor Napoleon.

In the same year Holland, then called the Batavian Republic, was also made over into a kingdom. The chief official of the Batavian Republic was at that time a very old man, nearly blind, by the name of Schimmelpenninck. One day this old man received a polite letter from Talleyrand, Napoleon's minister for foreign affairs. In this letter Talleyrand said that Napoleon was much concerned about the health of his friend Schimmelpenninck and wondered if the time had not come to relieve him of the burdens of government by " consolidating " the political institutions of Holland. Schimmelpenninck replied that his health was excellent, and that Holland was very well satisfied with its present government. Another letter from Talleyrand soon followed, in which Schimmelpenninck was informed that Napoleon had made up his mind that the government of Holland must be changed, and that the Dutch must at once send a commission to Paris to discuss the matter. Since the Dutch had no powerful friends to protect them, they sent the commission. Without any beating about the bush, Napoleon told the commissioners that Holland must have a king. Otherwise the Dutch could have any institutions they liked, but a king they must have, and he would give them one — his brother, Louis Napoleon Bonaparte. He gave the commissioners eight days to decide. If they refused to accept Louis as their king, he, Napoleon, would be forced, " in the interests of peace," to annex Holland to France.

Of course the Dutch submitted, and on May 24, 1806, there was signed at Paris a treaty which announced to the world that, since their High Mightinesses representing the Batavian Republic had *requested* that Louis Napoleon be made King of Holland, " his Majesty [Napoleon] *defers* to this opinion and authorizes Prince Louis Napoleon to accept the crown of Holland." Thus the Kingdom of Holland, like the Kingdom of Italy and the Kingdom of Naples, became part of Napoleon's empire.

Napoleon had two brothers still unprovided with kingdoms to rule. Lucien he quarreled with. But there was Jerome. Was there no kingdom for Jerome? The very next year, sure enough, a kingdom was provided for him too. But a war with Prussia was necessary before that could be done.

How Napoleon conquered Prussia and made three small states out of it, 1806–1807. During the ten years from 1795 to 1805 Prussia had stood aside while Austria was three times defeated and weakened by the loss of territory. This was a fatal mistake. Napoleon was of course glad to remain friendly with Prussia while he was fighting Austria. But now, having firmly established his power in Holland, in Italy, and in South Germany, he was ready to deal with Prussia. He made it plain to the King of Prussia that he must either bind himself to France by a defensive and offensive alliance or prepare for war. The Prussians were not willing to bind themselves to France. They remembered the glorious days of Frederick the Great and believed that their army was still the best in Europe. Disputes arose over many questions — particularly over Hanover, which Napoleon had half promised to turn over to Prussia but now threatened to restore to England. Napoleon became more and more arrogant, the Prussians more and more exasperated, and so in September, 1806, war broke out between France and Prussia.

Napoleon's army was then in South Germany, along the Main River. The Prussians moved their armies to the west towards the lower Rhine, expecting Napoleon to meet them there in order to defend France from invasion. Instead of doing that, Napoleon marched his army to the east, and then north down the valley of the Elbe River, thus coming in behind the Prussians and cutting off their retreat, very much as he had cut off the retreat of General Mack at Ulm. The Prussians then turned back, and the two armies, each in two divisions, met at Jena and Auerstadt, October 14, 1806. The Prussian armies, which were not nearly so good as the Prussians thought them, were entirely defeated and virtually destroyed. Eleven days later Napoleon entered Berlin in triumph. Within six weeks from the beginning of the war, Prussia was a conquered country, its chief cities occupied by French troops.

In this war Prussia had been joined by Sweden, England, and Russia, thus forming what is known as the Fourth Coalition. Neither Sweden nor England could be of much help, but the Russian armies had still to be met. In February, 1807, Napoleon, aided by the Poles, met the Russians at Eylau, where a bloody and indecisive battle was fought. Although the Russians retreated, they were scarcely defeated. Russia then tried to get Austria to join the coalition; but Austria now played the same part that Prussia had formerly played — she remained neutral. With Austria neutral and Prussia helpless, Napoleon finally inflicted a crush-

© *William Thompson*

CARRIAGE USED BY NAPOLEON DURING THE RUSSIAN CAMPAIGN, 1812

Compare this with the high-powered motor cars at the disposal of Marshal Foch during the Great War. Yet Napoleon had to travel much farther than Foch.

ing defeat upon the Russians at the Battle of Friedland, June 14, 1807.

After this defeat the tsar, Alexander I, was ready to make peace. In July the three sovereigns — Napoleon, Alexander, and Frederick William of Prussia — met at Tilsit, on the Nieman River, to arrange the treaties. Since Frederick William was virtually a conquered king, he had little influence. His fate depended on the other two. In all the comings and goings of the three sovereigns he was, therefore, as the French historian Thiers says, " a little in the rear — isolated, like misfortune." He had nothing to do except listen to the others and accept whatever terms Napoleon and the tsar could agree upon; and the terms agreed were essentially those Napoleon desired. Several treaties were finally arranged — treaties between France and Prussia, and treaties between France and Russia. These treaties constitute what is known as the Peace of Tilsit, July 7, 1807.

By the Peace of Tilsit, Prussia was deprived of all her territory west of the Elbe River and of all of her Polish provinces, thus being left with her original provinces of Brandenburg, Pomerania, and Silesia. Besides, French troops remained in Prussia, and in the following year Napoleon required the Prussian army to be reduced to 42,000 soldiers, so that after 1807 Prussia remained a secondary state about the size of Bavaria, virtually under the domination of France.

Out of the territory taken from Prussia Napoleon created two new states. The Polish territory formerly belonging to Prussia was erected into the Duchy of Warsaw, nominally independent, but really governed by the French ambassador at Warsaw and the French general who commanded the Polish army. At the same time the territory west of the Elbe River formerly belonging to Prussia was united with certain other German states to make the new Kingdom of Westphalia, to be governed by Napoleon's brother Jerome as king. Meantime the three Hanse cities (Hamburg, Lübeck, and Bremen) and the city of Danzig were occupied by French troops and virtually governed by Napoleon's generals. Thus Napoleon destroyed Prussia as a great power and brought North Germany under the sway of his empire.

One other thing Napoleon accomplished by the Peace of Tilsit. He made peace with Russia, and the tsar and Napoleon agreed for the future to be friends and allies. Alexander agreed to help Napoleon against England, if England refused to make peace, and Napoleon agreed to help the tsar against the Turks, if the Turks refused to make peace. Napoleon, by his blandishments, led the tsar to think that from now on the two great powers, France and Russia, would share Europe between them and in due time proceed to the conquest of the world. This was almost certainly not Napoleon's real purpose, but he made the tsar think it was.

Napoleon's empire in 1810 and his plans for extending it. By 1807 Napoleon's imperial authority extended far beyond the frontiers of France. It included virtually all of Continental Europe west of Russia and Austria. We may represent that imperial authority by a diagram (see page 291).

By comparing this diagram with the map on page 290, you can easily see both the extent and the character of the Napoleonic

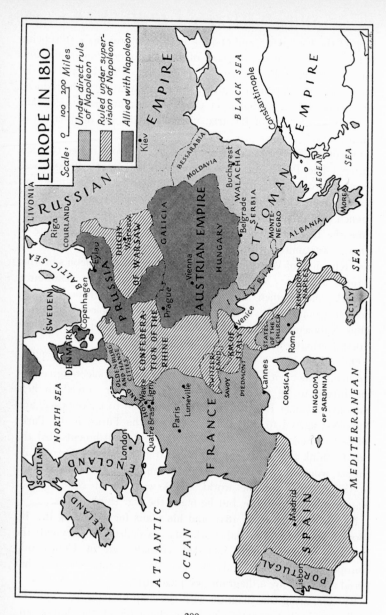

EUROPE IN 1810

Scale: 0   100   200 Miles

Under direct rule
of Napoleon

Ruled under super-
vision of Napoleon

Allied with Napoleon

SCOTLAND

IRELAND

ENGLAND

London

NORTH SEA

ATLANTIC

OCEAN

DENMARK

SWEDEN

Copenhagen

BALTIC SEA

Riga

LIVONIA

COURLAND

Eylau

PRUSSIA

DUCHY
OF WARSAW

Warsaw

Kiev

RUSSIAN   EMPIRE

GALICIA

BESSARABIA

MOLDAVIA

Bucharest

WALACHIA

Belgrade

SERBIA

MONTE-
NEGRO

ALBANIA

BLACK SEA

Constantinople

OTTOMAN   EMPIRE

AEGEAN

SEA

MOREA

OLDENBURG
AND HANSE
CITIES

CONFEDERA-
TION OF THE
RHINE

Vienna

Prague

AUSTRIAN EMPIRE

HUNGARY

Venice

ILLYRIA

Rome

STATES
OF THE
CHURCH

KINGDOM OF
NAPLES

SICILY

Rotterdam

Waterloo

Quatre Bras

Ligny

Paris

Lunéville

FRANCE

SWITZER-
LAND

Savoy

KM. OF
ITALY

Piedmont

Cannes

CORSICA

KINGDOM
OF SARDINIA

MEDITERRANEAN

SEA

Madrid

SPAIN

PORTUGAL

Lisbon

empire. What Napoleon was doing was this: He was gradually breaking up the great states like Prussia and Austria; he was gradually creating a number of secondary states; he was subjecting these secondary states, in one way or another, to the directing authority of a single European empire.

EMPEROR NAPOLEON

—France—	Military—	—Kingdoms ruled—	—Protectorates—	States—
governed under the emperor through the Senate, the prefects, and the administrative services	districts governed under the emperor by French generals	by members of the Bonaparte dynasty	Swiss Federation Confederation of the Rhine	virtually subject
	Hanse Cities Danzig	Km. of Italy Km. of Naples (after 1808 governed by Murat) Km. of Holland Km. of Spain (p. 295) Km. of Westphalia (in 1810 a part of Rhine Confed.)		Prussia Duchy of Warsaw

Yet Napoleon was not content merely to unite the states of Europe into one federated empire. He wished also to establish throughout Europe a certain uniformity of rights and institutions. Therefore, as fast as he extended his imperial authority beyond the frontiers of France, he introduced, or tried to introduce, into the subject countries, the *equality of rights* and the *administrative system* which had been established in France. Napoleon wished to confer upon Europe what he regarded as the beneficial results of the French Revolution.

These changes were never fully made in the subject countries of the empire. But generally speaking, by 1810 the French system of administration and the French Civil Code had replaced the institutions of the Old Régime in Holland, Switzerland, in the German countries along the Rhine, in parts of South Germany, and in all of Italy. Napoleon never completed his empire. He had scarcely made more than a beginning when he was overthrown. But from this beginning it is clear what he had in mind to do. If he had succeeded there would have been in Europe, not many sovereign states, but perhaps a federation of states under the control of the Napoleonic empire.

The Romans maintained peace in the Western world for two

hundred years. They established a high level of prosperity and civilization. Do you think Napoleon's empire, if he had succeeded, would have done as much? Would it have been better for Europe in the long run if he had succeeded? Would the Great War of 1914 have been avoided? It is possible. But the historian can at best tell only what happened, not what might have happened. What happened was that after 1807 Napoleon found it increasingly difficult to manage the vast and complicated empire which he had built up, and after 1810 it came crashing down on his head, burying him, as it were, in the ruins.

III. Why Europe Became Tired of Napoleon and Sent Him Off to St. Helena

Why Napoleon failed to maintain his European power. Many reasons could be found for Napoleon's failure; but there is one reason which includes all the rest. Napoleon failed because, as is the case with most of us, his mind had a " blind side " — a side with no windows in it. He could clearly see that people are often influenced by fear, force, cupidity, vanity, love of comfort — in a word, by material self-interest; and no one was ever more skillful in getting people to do what he wanted by playing upon these motives. But one thing Napoleon never quite understood. He never understood that people are sometimes influenced by emotions, sentiments, or ideals which may be more or less directly opposed to their material self-interests; nor did he ever quite understand that these motives may sometimes be far more powerful than the other kind.

Now there were three very powerful general sentiments or ideals which were directly opposed to Napoleon's imperial schemes. One of these was the loyalty of the ruling aristocracies in Europe to the governments and institutions which Napoleon was trying to destroy. Kings and nobles in every country were opposed to Napoleon's schemes because he threatened the independence of their respective states. Besides, kings and nobles regarded Napoleon as the very personification of that dreaded enemy, the French Revolution, because he was actually doing in Europe what the Revolution had done in France — he was depriving the kings of their power and the nobles of their privileges.   Thus the ruling classes in Europe were opposed to Napoleon, not only because he threatened their material interests but because he aroused in them a powerful emotional sentiment — loyalty to their own kings.

But how about the common people?   We might suppose that they would support Napoleon, since he freed them from the yoke of kings and gave them equal rights with the privileged classes. Napoleon apparently thought so.   When his brother Jerome became King of Westphalia, Napoleon assured him that his German subjects, once having experienced the advantages of French institutions, would never wish to be restored to Prussian government.   It is true that at first many Germans and Italians welcomed Napoleon as a deliverer.   They imagined that their dream of political liberty and equality of rights might now be realized. But they found that Napoleon's government was little less burdensome than that of their former kings.   So as time passed the people in Germany, in Italy, and even in France, became restive.   However beneficial Napoleon's government might be in a material way, they still cherished the ideal of political liberty.   They wanted to govern themselves instead of being governed, however well, by him.

Finally, the Napoleonic conquests intensified the powerful sentiment of nationality.   After all, it was not pleasant for Italians and Germans to see the French armies overrunning their countries. They resented being dominated by foreigners, even though they might benefit by it in a material way.   On the whole they were more prosperous and better governed than formerly ; but they felt that these benefits were purchased at a heavy price.   French officials and army officers and soldiers were everywhere about — on the streets, in the cafés, in the theaters ; and they were likely to be arrogant and supercilious.   Italians and Germans found this humiliating.   In the end they felt that it would be better to be governed by their own people, even by their kings and nobles, than by the conceited Frenchmen who lorded it over them.

Napoleon's empire might have been a good thing for Europe if the people of Europe had cared for nothing but their material comfort and well-being.   But the larger his empire grew, and the more effectively his imperial authority was established, the more he encountered the opposition of these three intangible but powerful sentiments: (1) the loyalty of the upper classes to their kings; (2) the aspiration of the middle classes for political liberty; and (3) the angry resentment of all classes against the meddling of Frenchmen in their affairs. Victor Hugo said that " God finally became bored by Napoleon." Perhaps this is another way of saying that the people of Europe finally became bored by him. We must now see how, after 1807, Napoleon's difficulties increased, and how his great empire finally collapsed.

How Napoleon tried to destroy English commerce by the Continental system, and found it a bigger job than he thought it would be, 1806-1812. Napoleon had always disliked the English. He called them a nation of " shopkeepers," thinking that they cared only for money and that their political power depended solely on their extensive commerce. In 1806–1807 Napoleon therefore devised a grand scheme, known as the " Continental system," for the destruction of English commerce. The object of Napoleon's scheme was to close the European ports to the importation of English manufactured and colonial commodities. He was quite willing, even anxious, to have England buy goods of the European countries. But he wanted England to pay for these goods in money. In this way Napoleon hoped to drain England of her gold, with the idea of lowering prices in England, and ruining English merchants and traders. England of course wished to prevent Napoleon from carrying out his purpose; so she used all her power to keep the European ports open and force her goods into Europe.

Napoleon soon found that he could not keep English goods out of Europe. There were three points on the European coast where English goods were entering, in spite of all he could do. These were: (1) the great German ports of Hamburg, Lübeck, and Bremen, near the mouths of the Elbe and Weser rivers; (2) the Dutch ports round the mouth of the Rhine; (3) the port of Lisbon, in Portugal, which for more than a hundred years had been friendly with England. Napoleon therefore determined to get these three regions more directly under his control.

LONDON CUSTOM HOUSE

From a drawing by Rowlandson, in *The Microcosm of London*, published in 1808.
At this time Napoleon was trying to destroy English commerce.

In 1807 he made an alliance with the King of Spain for the conquest and partition of Portugal. But before this was carried out, a quarrel between the Spanish king and his son so weakened the Spanish government that Napoleon thought it would be simpler to conquer Spain itself, and then take possession of Portugal. He thought the conquest of Spain would be a simple matter. He would march a small army to Madrid, take possession of the government, and that would end the business. It would, he said, take a month or two and require about 25,000 men. Well, he sent his army to Madrid and transferred his own brother Joseph from the throne of Naples to the throne of Spain (1808). That much was easily done.

But much to Napoleon's surprise, this did not end the affair. Far from it. The Spaniards were a very proud people, with an intense feeling of national independence. They were infuriated by Napoleon's action; and so, although their army had been defeated and their government overthrown, they did not submit. They organized a popular national resistance, a kind of guerilla warfare, and Napoleon found that in order to maintain his power in Spain he required, not merely 25,000 men but 300,000. Besides, the English sent an army under Wellesley (afterwards the famous Duke of

Wellington who led the English at the Battle of Waterloo) to help the Portuguese; and so Napoleon was unable even to carry out his original purpose, which was to get control of the port of Lisbon.

Meantime, the heroic resistance of the Spanish people encouraged the people of Germany and Austria. If the Spanish people could resist Napoleon, why couldn't they do so? So the people of South Germany began to organize secretly; and the Austrian government thought that the time had now come to free Germany from Napoleon's power. In 1809 Austria therefore made war on Napoleon once more. For the first time Napoleon was forced to accept a war which he would have preferred to postpone. He tried to get his ally, Alexander of Russia, to keep Austria quiet. But the tsar's friendship for Napoleon was now cooling, and he did nothing.

Napoleon had therefore to wage war with Austria in 1809, when he was deep in Spanish difficulties and wished to busy himself with the commercial war with England. It was a more difficult war than the previous one against Austria. In crossing the Danube at Aspern and Essling, he got himself into a trap; but he managed by a clever trick to get out, and finally defeated the Austrians at the Battle of Wagram (1809). Then the Austrians, as usual, made peace. They made peace by ceding the province of Galicia to the Duchy of Warsaw, and the provinces round the Adriatic to Napoleon, who erected them into the " Illyrian provinces " (*Peace of Vienna, October 10, 1809*). Thus Napoleon won the war. But he barely won it. Wagram was not so brilliant a victory as Austerlitz, and one has a feeling that Napoleon's power in Europe had begun to slip. For the first time he was forced to do certain important things before he was ready to do them. He was no longer controlling circumstances as he seemed to do formerly; on the contrary, circumstances were beginning to control him. The great imperial machine which he had constructed was beginning to run away with him.

All this time Napoleon had kept up the commercial war against England, and after the Austrian war he endeavored to prosecute it more vigorously. In order to control more effectively the ports on the north coast, he abolished the Kingdom of Holland and annexed to France both Holland and the north coast of Germany as far east as Lübeck (1810).   Partly for the same reason he annexed the Papal States also (1809), thus gaining control of Rome and the mouth of the Tiber.   At the same time he issued several decrees imposing drastic penalties for the importation of English or colonial goods into Europe.   These measures greatly restricted English imports, and if Napoleon could have continued them for several years the result might have been disastrous for British commerce. But unfortunately for Napoleon he soon quarreled with the Tsar Alexander, and this quarrel marks the beginning of the end, not only of the Continental system, but of Napoleon's empire.

How Napoleon quarreled with the tsar, and how the Russians defeated Napoleon by not knowing when they were beaten, 1812. In 1807 Napoleon had convinced the Tsar Alexander by his cajoleries that the alliance with France would mean great things for Russia — the occupation of Constantinople, for example.   But as time passed the tsar began to see that Napoleon was only making use of him for his own ends.   His friendship for Napoleon therefore became every year a little cooler, and in 1811 the two great men quarreled in good earnest.   Alexander complained that the closing of Russian ports by the Continental system was injuring Russia more than it injured England, and all for the benefit of France. He was offended by the annexation of North Germany to France. He was alarmed because Napoleon, having divorced his first wife, Josephine, had married Marie Louise of Austria, thus forming an alliance that boded no good to Russia.   But what disturbed the tsar most of all was the fear that Napoleon intended sooner or later to deprive Russia of the province of Lithuania, in order to restore the ancient Kingdom of Poland.   Allied with Austria, and with Poland under his control, he could dispense with Russia and bring southeastern Europe, including Constantinople, within the sphere of his empire.

So convinced was the tsar that Napoleon intended to restore the Kingdom of Poland that he decided to do it first.   In 1812 the tsar accordingly proclaimed the restoration of Poland, of course under Russian suzerainty, and sent a Russian army to the Polish frontier to carry out the project.   Napoleon could not permit this, so he gathered a great army in Saxony in order to resist the tsar.   In

June he crossed the Niemen River into Lithuania with an army of about 450,000 men. He doubtless expected the Russians to defend Lithuania; and he hoped that after he had defeated the tsar in a decisive battle or two, the tsar would make peace with him on his own terms. That is what the Austrians had always done, and why should the Russians not do the same?

But the Russians refused to play the game in that way. Instead of defending Lithuania, the Russians retreated. First they retreated to Smolensk, the gateway to Old Russia; defeated there they again retreated on the road to Moscow. At Borodino they made another stand; barely defeated there, with great losses on both sides, the Russian army again retreated, to Moscow and beyond, leaving the ancient and beloved capital open to Napoleon, whose army entered the city on September 14. Surely, Napoleon thought, the tsar would make peace now that Moscow was in his hands. He was astonished to find that the government officials, together with most of the wealthy and important people, had abandoned Moscow. In Moscow he found neither an army to fight nor a government to negotiate with. Russia was a large country. There was plenty of room in it for all concerned — for the French as well as for the Russians. The tsar and his officials were far away in St. Petersburg, and there the tsar remained, making no sign.

Napoleon remained in Moscow until October 19, waiting for the tsar to make peace. Moscow soon caught fire and burned for several days. Some historians say that the Russians deliberately set fire to Moscow. In any case a deserted city, without police protection, filled with foreign soldiers camping in empty houses, was almost certain to catch fire. But of course the Russians believed the French had deliberately set fire to the city; and the destruction of their ancient and half-sacred capital infuriated them, so that they were now more than ever determined on no account to submit to Napoleon. Their armies might not defeat him, but their immense country would. They would let him stay as long as he liked, and go when he got ready, and see what good it did him. Once more Napoleon had blundered. Once more he had encountered the incomprehensible force of a nation's resentment and

Musée de Versailles

MARSHAL NEY AND THE REAR-GUARD IN THE RETREAT FROM MOSCOW, 1812

Marshal Ney is in the center, with a gun in his left hand.   To the left is a wagon with wounded.   Note that after every shot the muskets had to be loaded from the muzzle with powder and the bullet pressed down by a ramrod.   How many shots could one soldier fire in an hour?   How many can be fired from a modern repeater, or from a machine gun?

resistance.   He could not meet it.   Five weeks he remained in Moscow, and then, with an army diminished by desertion and illness, he retreated through rain and sleet and snow, over the same road he had come.   It was a rout.   The soldiers died by thousands from exposure or want of food.   Thousands deserted.   Thousands were mercifully taken or killed by the Russian troops that hung on the rear and flanks of the retreating army.

Between June 24 and September 15, Napoleon had taken into Russia about 530,000 soldiers.   When he recrossed the Niemen River in December, 100,000 soldiers crossed with him.   What had become of the others?   Of that immense army, 50,000 had deserted; 130,000 were prisoners; 250,000 had perished.   It was an unparalleled disaster — an entire army of half a million destroyed, and nothing accomplished.

How Napoleon was defeated by his enemies, deserted by his subjects, and sent off to Elba, 1813-1814. The retreat from Moscow was more than a military disaster. It destroyed the myth that Napoleon was unbeatable. He had won so many victories that people had come to think that fate was somehow on his side. Now his enemies took courage, thinking that fortune had at last deserted him.

Napoleon hurried back to Paris to raise a new army in order to hold his power in Germany, against a new coalition of European powers. In March, 1813, Russia and Prussia formed an alliance, but for some months Austria refused to join, because she was almost as much afraid of Russia as of Napoleon. At first, therefore, Napoleon had to meet only the Russian and Prussian armies. These he defeated in May, 1813, but instead of pushing his advantage he agreed to a truce, hoping to win the tsar to his side again by promising to give up Poland. But the tsar stuck to the alliance with Prussia, and in the summer Austria joined the coalition. The war was then renewed, and on October 16–19, 1813, at the great Battle of Leipzig (sometimes called the Battle of the Nations) the coalition completely defeated Napoleon and drove his broken army back across the Rhine into France.

Instead of invading France at once, the allies entered into negotiations with Napoleon. They did this for two reasons. First, they found it difficult to agree among themselves as to what they should do with Napoleon and France in case they were victorious. Second, they were not sure how the French people would take an invasion of France. The French people, who cared little about helping Napoleon keep his power in Germany, might resent an invasion of their country. The allies remembered the national resistance to invasion in 1793, and they wondered if that would happen again. For these reasons the allies offered to make peace with Napoleon if he would be content with France alone — France with her natural frontiers, the Rhine, the Alps, and the Pyrenees. They gave Napoleon until December 2 to accept these terms. Napoleon accepted these terms at the last moment, but his acceptance did not reach the allies on December 2, and so they crossed the Rhine into France and began the march towards Paris.

The allies were probably glad that Napoleon's reply did not reach them in time; for they had now learned that the French people would probably not support Napoleon very vigorously. They therefore no longer wished to make peace with Napoleon, but to get rid of him altogether and restore the Bourbon monarchy in France. To reassure the French people, they accordingly issued what is known as the Declaration of Frankfurt (December 1, 1813), in which they explained that in invading France they were not making war on the French people, but upon Napoleon only. They said that they had offered Napoleon generous terms of peace, which he had rejected. Therefore, they said, it was Napoleon's fault that they were invading France, and they hoped the French people would side with them against Napoleon, who had so long disturbed the peace of the world. The allies asked the French people to desert Napoleon, just as President Wilson, in his famous notes of 1918, asked the German people to desert Kaiser William.

Well, the French people did virtually desert Napoleon. They had become weary of his exploits, especially now that he was fighting a losing battle. His continual wars meant that every year the taxes were higher, every year more young men were conscripted for the armies — and all for a European empire which did them little good. Besides, every year Napoleon's government of France became more despotic and he himself less approachable and more irritable. So it was almost with indifference that the French people watched Napoleon make his last desperate resistance. Fighting brilliantly against overwhelming odds, he was driven slowly back along the Marne River towards Paris. Learning, too late, that Paris was being attacked in his rear, he retired to Fontainebleau.

The allied armies entered Paris on March 31, 1814. But the government of Napoleon had already collapsed. The French Senate, under the lead of Talleyrand, had already arranged with the allies for the restoration of the Bourbon monarchy; on April 2 it voted to depose Napoleon, and four days later it proclaimed Louis XVIII King of France. Beaten by his enemies and deserted by his friends, Napoleon would still have fought on; but when even his generals refused to obey him he gave up. On April 11 he signed his abdication, resigning for himself and his heirs the thrones of

Musée de Versailles

NAPOLEON SAYING FAREWELL TO HIS GENERALS AFTER THE ABDICATION AT
FONTAINEBLEAU, 1814

From a painting by Vernet. Napoleon's secretary described this incident:
"Napoleon took General Petit in his arms and kissed the flag, and the silence
. . . was broken only by the sobs of the soldiers."

France and Italy. In return, the allied governments agreed that he
might retain the title of Emperor; and, in order that he might have
something to govern with this magnificent title, they gave him the
tiny island of Elba, on condition that he would never leave it.

**How Napoleon came back from Elba, was joyously received,
again defeated, and at last carried off to St. Helena, 1815.** Having
now, as they thought, got rid of Napoleon forever, the allies signed
with Louis XVIII the first Treaty of Paris (May 30, 1814). By
this treaty, peace was declared between France and the allied
powers. The boundaries of France were declared to be the same as
they had been on January 1, 1792, so that France was given, not
the Rhine frontier, but very nearly the same frontier that she had
had before the Revolution. No indemnity was exacted by this
treaty. The allies assumed that all the trouble had been caused by

Napoleon and that France, being as glad to get rid of Napoleon as they were, would now behave herself in a becoming manner.

But Napoleon was not quite done for yet. On February 26, 1815, he slipped out of Elba and landed on the south coast of France. Two things led him to suppose he might recover his power. The first was that the allied powers, who were now assembled at Vienna trying to arrange a settlement of the Europe which Napoleon had turned upside down, had recently got into a serious quarrel over the disposal of Poland and Saxony. At one time Austria, England, and France were on the point of making war on Russia and Prussia, and partly for that reason Napoleon thought the time was ripe to return. He also knew that the Bourbon government in France was now very unpopular. After nine months the peasants and middle classes were thoroughly dissatisfied with the new king, Louis XVIII, and especially with the returning emigrant nobles and priests who gathered about him, thinking to get back their former privileges and property.

So Napoleon returned to France, landing at Cannes on March 1, 1815. His journey to Paris was a triumphal march. Everywhere the people greeted him with joyous enthusiasm. Meeting some old soldiers sent to arrest him, the " Little Corporal " threw open his coat with a dramatic gesture and invited them to fire on their former leader. They threw down their arms and embraced him, weeping. Everywhere it was the same; and when Napoleon reached Paris, poor old Louis XVIII had already bundled his family into carriages which were trundling off toward the Belgian frontier.

For a " Hundred Days " Napoleon again ruled in France. Once more he raised an army — the last one he ever commanded — and moved north into Belgium, where the English and Prussians were located. On June 15–16 he succeeded in dividing the English forces of Wellington and the Prussian forces of Blücher at Ligny and Quatre Bras. As his object was to take Brussels, the capital of Belgium, Napoleon moved northward on that road until he was stopped by Wellington at Waterloo. Meantime, Napoleon had sent Grouchy to follow the Prussian general, Blücher, who had retreated from Charleroi along the road to Wavre, and keep him from joining Wellington. On the 18th of June Napoleon launched his army against Wellington at Waterloo for five hours in vain; and of course, while he was expecting Grouchy to look after Blücher, Wellington was hoping that Blücher would give Grouchy the slip and come to the aid of the English. As it happened, Blücher's army was sighted about four o'clock in the afternoon, coming from the direction of Wavre. Blücher's arrival turned the virtual defeat of Napoleon into a rout. He had lost 30,000 soldiers and all of his guns; and when he reached Paris on June 21, still determined to resist the approaching allies, he found that his power had collapsed in France as well as in Europe. The emperor had played his last card and lost the game.

On July 7, 1815, the allies again entered Paris. Once more Louis XVIII was restored to the throne, and once more he signed a treaty with the European powers — the second Treaty of Paris (November 20, 1815). By this treaty an indemnity of 700,000,000 francs was exacted from France, and as a guarantee of good behavior and the payment of the indemnity, foreign troops were to be stationed in France for a period of years (actually until 1818).

This time the allies were determined to take no chances with Napoleon. Stripped of his titles, and publicly proclaimed an "enemy and disturber of the tranquillity of the world," he was carried off to the distant isle of St. Helena, where he was carefully guarded by a British garrison. Napoleon was forty-eight years old when he landed on the island of St. Helena. For six years, in that silent and lonely retreat, far from the world's affairs, the little man in the cocked hat, who for fifteen years had shaped the destinies of Europe, fretted away his life in idleness and despair. He died on May 5, 1821, at the age of fifty-four.

QUESTIONS

1. How would you define a "great man"? Was Napoleon a greater man than Lincoln? than Shakespeare? What were the qualities that enabled Napoleon to accomplish more than ordinary men?

2. How did Napoleon first become famous? What was the Treaty of Campo-Formio? the Cisalpine Republic? What is a *coup d'état*? How was the Directory overturned?

3. What were the chief features of the Constitution of the Decennial Consulate? How was Napoleon's government modified in 1802? in

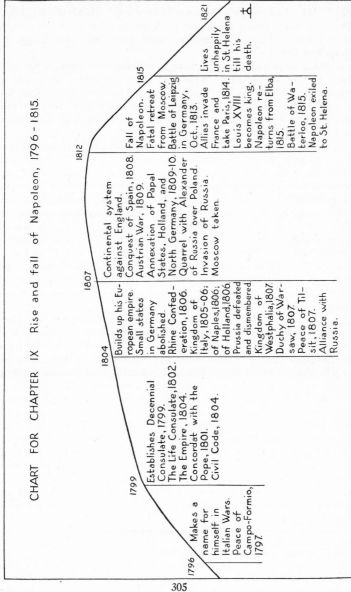

CHART FOR CHAPTER IX Rise and fall of Napoleon, 1796 - 1815.

1796
Makes a name for himself in Italian Wars. Peace of Campo-Formio, 1797.

1799
Establishes Decennial Consulate, 1799. The Life Consulate, 1802. The Empire, 1804. Concordat with the Pope, 1801. Civil Code, 1804.

1804
Builds up his European empire. Small states in Germany abolished. Rhine Confederation, 1806. Kingdom of Italy, 1805-06; of Naples, 1806; of Holland, 1806. Prussia defeated and dismembered Kingdom of Westphalia, 1807. Duchy of Warsaw, 1807. Peace of Tilsit, 1807. Alliance with Russia.

1807
Continental system against England. Conquest of Spain, 1808. Austrian War, 1809. Annexation of Papal States, Holland, and North Germany, 1809-10. Quarrel with Alexander of Russia over Poland. Invasion of Russia. Moscow taken.

1812 1815
Fall of Napoleon. Fatal retreat from Moscow. Battle of Leipzig in Germany, Oct., 1813. Allies invade France and take Paris, 1814. Louis XVIII becomes king. Napoleon returns from Elba, 1815. Battle of Waterloo, 1815. Napoleon exiled to St. Helena.

1821
Lives unhappily in St. Helena till his death.

1804? Why had the people ceased to care much about the republic? Why were they willing to submit to Napoleon? Why did Napoleon use the name "Citizen Bonaparte" until 1802, and then change to "Napoleon Bonaparte"?

4. What steps did Napoleon take to maintain the changes brought about by the Revolution? What was the Concordat? Why was it important? What was the Civil Code? What ground is there for saying that the Civil Code was Napoleon's greatest title to fame? How did Napoleon organize the public schools? What part of Napoleon's work in reorganizing France was permanent?

5. Do you think Napoleon worked out his plan for the reconstruction of Europe beforehand, or worked it out as he went along? What were the causes of the war with Austria in 1805? What changes were made in the political organization of Germany between 1803 and 1806? in the political organization of Italy? What were the results of the war with Prussia in 1807? What was the extent of Napoleon's empire in 1807? What were the various dependent states? How did Napoleon aim to change the social and economic institutions of Germany and Italy?

6. What was Napoleon's aim in establishing the "Continental system"? How did he become involved in the conquest of Spain? In what way did he miscalculate the difficulties? How did the Spanish affair lead to the Austrian war of 1809? How did Napoleon try to strengthen the Continental system in 1810?

7. What were the causes of the breach between Russia and Napoleon in 1812? Why was the "Polish question" important for Alexander? for Napoleon? What did Napoleon expect to accomplish by the Russian campaign in 1812? Why did he go on to Moscow? Why did he remain in Moscow five weeks? Why did he retreat from Moscow without having made peace? Why was the retreat a disaster?

8. Why did Austria not join Russia and Prussia in the spring campaign in 1813? What terms were offered Napoleon in the summer of 1813? What was the importance of the Battle of Leipzig? Was this a more decisive battle than Waterloo? Give the reason for your answer.

9. What terms did the allies offer Napoleon at Frankfurt in November, 1813? Why did they hesitate to invade France? Why did the French people not support Napoleon with much enthusiasm in 1814? What were the terms of the first Treaty of Paris? Why did Napoleon return to France in 1815? What were the terms of the second Treaty of Paris?

SELECTED READINGS

Brief accounts. Robinson and Beard, *Modern Europe*, I, chs. xiv–xv. Robinson and Beard, *Outlines*, II, chs. x–xi. Robinson, *Western Europe*, chs. xxxvii–xxxviii. Hayes and Moon, *Modern History*, ch. xiii. Hayes, *Modern Europe*, I, ch. xvi. Seignobos, *Contemporary Civilization*, chs. vii–

viii.   Schevill, *History of Europe*, pp. 438–466.   Ashley, *Modern Civiliza-
tion*, ch. vii.   For more detailed accounts, see Bourne, *Revolutionary
Period*, chs. xii–xxvi; Van Dyke, *Story of France*, chs. xlvi–xlviii; Hazen,
Revolution and Napoleon. For the changes in Germany, see Schevill,
Making of Modern Germany, ch. iii; G. M. Priest, *Germany since 1740*,
chs. iv–vii; E. F. Henderson, *Short History of Germany*, II, chs. vi–vii.

Biography.   H. A. L. Fisher, *Napoleon.*   (A brilliant brief life, in the
" Home University Library.")   R. M. Johnson, *Napoleon.*   E. Ludwig,
Napoleon.   (An interesting and detailed account of Napoleon the man.)
J. C. Ropes, *The First Napoleon.*   (Much attention to military campaigns
and battles.)   J. H. Rose, *The Personality of Napoleon.*   D. Merezh-
kovsky, *Napoleon the Man.*   J. H. Rose, *The Life of Napoleon.*   A. Four-
nier, *Napoleon the First.*   (The last two are virtual histories of the time.)
Lord Rosebery, *Napoleon, the Last Phase.*   (An account of Napoleon at
St. Helena.)   J. R. Seeley, *A Short History of Napoleon I.*   (A brilliant
work, on the thesis that Napoleon's main aim was to destroy England, and
that he built up his European empire for that purpose.)   F. M. Kircheisen,
Napoleon.   (A recent life by one of the leading authorities on Napoleon.)
W. C. Russell, *Horatio Nelson* (the famous English admiral).   W. O.
Morris, *Wellington.*   Joseph McCabe, *Talleyrand.*   N. Forssell. *Fouché,
the Man Napoleon Feared.*

Historical novels.   Tolstoy, *War and Peace.*   (One of the greatest of
historical novels.)   Thackeray, *Vanity Fair.*   (A picture of life in England
about 1815. Contains a famous description of the Battle of Waterloo.)
Dumas, *The Whites and the Blues.*   Conan Doyle, *The Exploits of Brigadier
Gerard.*   Balzac, *An Historical Mystery.*   H. S. Merriman, *Barlasch of the
Guard.*

Sources.   Robinson and Beard, *Readings in Modern History*, I, chs. xiv–
xv.   (Napoleon's proclamation explaining the *18 Brumaire*, p. 322.
Madame de Rémusat relates anecdotes about Napoleon, pp. 324–326.
Bourrienne's description of the Marengo campaign, p. 326.   Treaty of
Lunéville, p. 329.   Madame de Rémusat tells why the French submitted
to Napoleon, p. 333.   Napoleon describes conditions in France after five
years of his government, p. 334.   Berlin and Milan decrees, pp. 346–349.
Decrees of Napoleon abolishing feudalism, the Inquisition, and monasticism
in Spain, p. 354.   Constant's description of the crossing of the Beresina
on the retreat from Moscow, p. 357.   Las Casas' description of the voyage
to St. Helena, p. 368.)   The same selections in Robinson, *Readings in
European History*, II, chs. xxxvii–xxxviii.   Anderson, *Select Documents.*
(Contains constitutions, treaties, the Concordat, and many other official
documents.)   Of the many memoirs written by contemporaries, some have
been translated: Bourrienne, *Memoirs of Napoleon;* Meneval, *Memoirs of
Napoleon.*   (Bourrienne and Meneval served as Napoleon's secretaries.)
Madame de Rémusat, *Memoirs.*   (The work of a cultivated and witty lady
who was not very friendly to Napoleon.)   The *Memoirs* of Talleyrand
(Napoleon's minister of foreign affairs, one of the ablest diplomats of
Europe).   *Memoirs of the History of France during the Reign of Napoleon,
dictated by him at St. Helena.*   (An account of Napoleon's career, placing
all his acts in the most favorable light.)

THE ARRIVAL OF THE MAIL
From an old English print, engraved by G. Hunt..

CHAPTER X. HOW THE GREAT POWERS TRIED TO SAFE-GUARD EUROPE AGAINST REVOLUTIONS, AND HOW THE PEOPLE KEPT ON MAKING REVOLUTIONS IN SPITE OF THEM, 1815–1848

The golden age of the human race is not behind us, but ahead of us; our fathers will never see it, our children will see it some day; it is for us to prepare the way.
SAINT–SIMON

Why this chapter is divided into three parts. When Napoleon was sent off to St. Helena, not many people were altogether sorry. Even the French people, who had admired Napoleon and were proud of the glory he had conferred on France, were tired of constant war, and so they were inclined to say, " Well, he was a great man, but he turned the world upside down too much."

The kings, statesmen, and nobles of Europe of course felt much more strongly about it. They were very glad indeed to get rid of Napoleon. They regarded the Revolution as a kind of wild outburst of anarchy and atheism, and Napoleon's exploits as the natural result of the Revolution. They commonly referred to the Revolution as " Jacobinism," and to Napoleon's activities as " Bonapartism," and to them these words had much the same frightful sound that the word " bolshevism " has for many people today. For nearly twenty-five years the rulers and statesmen had been fighting Jacobinism and Bonapartism, and in 1815 they felt that at last they had the upper hand. For the first time they felt secure. They were firmly convinced that through their efforts European civilization had been saved from destruction. Naturally, therefore, they wished as far as possible to restore the political system of Europe as it had been before the Revolution and Napoleon came to disturb it. They felt that if they could dress Europe up again in its old clothes it would behave as it had formerly done.

But the kings and nobles who felt that the political system of Europe could be set back twenty-five years were mistaken. Their fear and hatred of Napoleon blinded them to the reality of things. Europe would never again behave as it had done before 1789. For the Revolution had occurred, and Napoleon had lived and performed his extraordinary exploits, and these were facts which could not be undone by looking the other way. People might be tired of Napoleon and his wars, but the revolutionary ideal of " Liberty, Equality, Fraternity " was too attractive to be abandoned. Sooner or later the mass of the people would demand a share in the control of their own governments.

For some years after 1815 the upper classes had things much their own way. They made what was called the " Settlement of 1815 " at the Congress of Vienna. Afterwards they organized the " Concert of Europe " and by diplomacy and force tried to suppress radical ideas and revolutionary movements. For ten years they were fairly successful; but then a more liberal spirit spread abroad, which culminated first in the revolutions of 1830–1832, and later in the widespread upheaval known as the " revolutions of 1848." We may therefore conveniently divide this chapter into three parts: (1) the Settlement of 1815 and the Concert of Europe; (2) the revolutions of 1830–1832; and (3) the revolutions of 1848.

I. THE SETTLEMENT OF 1815 AND THE CONCERT OF EUROPE

How the great powers made the Settlement of 1815 at the Congress of Vienna, 1814–1815. The fall of Napoleon's empire left innumerable questions to be settled — the boundaries of Austria, Russia, and Prussia; the fate of Poland; the political organization of Italy and Germany. To settle all these questions a congress of the European powers was assembled, which is known as the Congress of Vienna, 1814–1815.

It was a brilliant company that assembled in the ancient capital of Austria. There was Tsar Alexander of Russia, Emperor Francis of Austria, and King Frederick William of Prussia. There were the most famous statesmen of Europe, among them Castlereagh and the Duke of Wellington from England, Nesselrode from Russia, Hardenberg from Prussia, the famous Metternich from Austria, and the still more famous Talleyrand from France. Besides the official representatives, innumerable ladies and gentlemen of Europe's social aristocracy came to dance and gossip and intrigue. The mass of the people had no representatives at the Congress of Vienna and no way of making their wishes known there. It was an assembly of kings, nobles, and other high-placed favorites of fortune who knew not what the people were thinking. They themselves were thinking that the days of war and revolution were over, that all the nonsense about liberty and equality was a thing of the past.

Although many small states were represented, the principal decisions of the Congress of Vienna were made by the five great powers — Russia, Austria, Prussia, England, and France. After much discussion and some bitter quarrels a great many treaties were drafted and signed. These treaties, together with the second Treaty of Paris which restored the Bourbon monarchy in France, constituted what the statesmen of that time called the Settlement of 1815. In making that settlement the great powers were guided by three main aims, which they called the principles of *compensation*, *restoration*, and *guarantees*.

Compensation. Each great power, and each little power too, wished to get as much as possible for itself in the way of territory and political advantage. France obtained less than the other great powers, but by the second Treaty of Paris she acquired a little more territory than she had had before 1789. Prussia wanted all of her former territory back again, but since Russia demanded the greater part of Poland, Prussia was " compensated " by taking Swedish Pomerania, one-third of Saxony, and a large block of territory on both sides of the Rhine, which included such important cities as Cologne and Koblenz. Austria received back her former

ADJUSTING THE BALANCE OF POWER AFTER NAPOLEON'S ABDICATION

From a contemporary cartoon. The great powers at the Congress of Vienna
are quarreling over the spoils. Great Britain is taking all the money out of
the chest. Russia and Prussia are squabbling over Saxony and Poland. Austria is sitting on Poland and has Italy near by. The small powers in the background are patiently waiting to see what, if anything, is left for them.

province of Galicia; and for the loss of Belgium, which she did not
want, she received Salzburg, the Tyrol, and the Italian provinces of
Venetia and Lombardy. England received nothing on the continent of Europe, but she added to her colonial possessions the islands
of Malta and Ceylon, and the Cape of Good Hope, besides some
territories of less importance in Africa and the West Indies.

Restoration. Besides adding to their own possessions, the great
powers wished to safeguard Europe from the radical ideas which
might lead to revolution. This they sought to do by restoring, as
far as possible, the old ruling dynasties which had been overturned
by the Revolution or by Napoleon. The Bourbon kings were
restored in France, Spain, and Naples. The old rulers were
restored in the Papal States, Tuscany, Sardinia, and some of the
German states. The hundreds of tiny German states that had
disappeared between 1803 and 1806 were not restored; but Germany was still divided into a great number of states (thirty-eight in

EUROPE in 1815

German Confederation ·········

SCALE OF MILES

0   100   200   300   400

ATLANTIC OCEAN

SWEDEN

NORWAY

Bergen

Christiania

NORTH SEA

DENMARK

Copenhagen

Schleswig

HOLSTEIN

MECKLEN-
BURG

Berlin

Bremen

Hanover

Magdeburg

Göttingen

Lützen

Auerstadt

Gotha

WEIMAR

SAXON

Frankfurt

Koblenz

Cologne

NETHERLANDS

WESTPHALIA

Amsterdam

The Hague

Düsseldorf

Hamburg

Elbe

P·R·U

UNITED

KINGDOM

Glasgow

Edinburgh

Newcastle

Belfast

Dublin

Liverpool

Limerick

IRELAND

WALES

Manchester

Birmingham

London

The Severn

Le Havre

Brest

Rouen

Paris

Seine R.

Orléans

Loire R.

Tours

Dijon

Lyon

Rhone R.

Waterloo

Ligny

Lille

Fleurus

Jemappes

Ham

Metz

Valmy

Strasbourg

Basel

Berne

Zürich

Geneva

Forney

SWITZERLAND

Innsbruck

TYROL

AU

Munich

Stuttgart

Heidelberg

BADEN

WÜRTTEMBERG

Bayreuth

BAVARIA

Danube

Salz

BAY OF BISCAY

Bordeaux

FRANCE

Toulouse

PYRENEES

Ebro R.

Burgos

Douro R.

Corunna

Oporto

SPAIN

Madrid

Salamanca

PORTUGAL

Lisbon

Tagus R.

Guadiana R.

Valencia

Sevilla

Guadalquivir R.

Granada

Cádiz

C. Trafalgar

Tangier

Gibraltar
(Br.)

Marseille

Toulon

Nice

Marengo

Turin

Novara

KINGDOM OF SARDINIA

LOMBARDY

Milan

Parma

Modena

Verona

VENETIA

Venice

Lucca

Florence

Siena

PAPAL STATES

CORSICA
(Fr.)

ELBA

Civitavecchia

Rome

Naples

MEDITERRANEAN

MOROCCO

ALGERIA

Algiers

TUNIS

Palermo

MALTA
(Br.)

Longitude 5° West 0° 5° Longitude 10° East

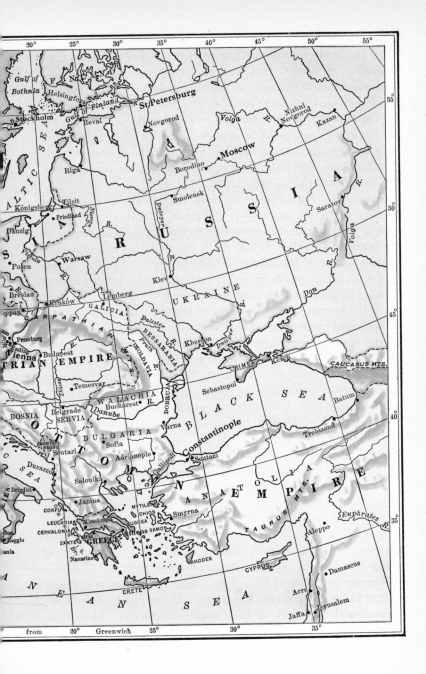

all) ; and in place of the old Empire there was now a German Confederation, so devised that Austrian and Prussian influence was
again dominant in Germany, as it had been before 1789. Italy was
likewise divided into many small states whose autocratic rulers were
for the most part bound hand and foot to Austria. Thus with the
old autocracies restored in most states, and with Austrian influence
once more predominant in Italy and Germany, the great powers felt
that they had done much to safeguard Europe from the danger of
revolutions and radical ideas.

Guarantees. For twenty-five years Europe had suffered from
military aggression on the part of France. Above all, the statesmen at Vienna wished to guarantee Europe against this danger in
the future. This they tried to do by creating what was called the
" Rhine barrier." The country which could be most easily overrun
by French armies was Belgium. To strengthen this frontier against
France, Belgium and Holland were united to form one kingdom
under the famous old Dutch House of Orange. It was hoped that
this enlarged kingdom, supported by England, would be an adequate
barrier against French aggression on the lower Rhine. Just south
of Holland-Belgium was the territory given to Prussia. It was
hoped that the possession of this territory would give Prussia a
special interest in guarding the Rhine against France. Still further
south was the Swiss Confederation, which was now " neutralized "
— that is, each of the great powers signed a treaty agreeing not to
violate the neutrality of Switzerland. This arrangement was also
directed primarily against France.

Thus the statesmen at Vienna tried to establish a lasting peace by
turning away from new ideas and holding fast to old ideas. For
establishing peace within the countries they could think of nothing
better than to restore, so far as possible, the old ruling dynasties.
For establishing peace between the countries they could think of
nothing better than to redistribute territories and peoples in such
a way as to make a better " balance of power."

**How the great powers formed the Concert of Europe to suppress
radical ideas and preserve the peace.** Many people were disappointed with the work of the Congress of Vienna. Most educated people at that time were familiar with the *Grand Design of*

Henry IV and with the Abbé Saint Pierre's *Project for Making Peace Perpetual* (see pp. 205 and 206), and many people were optimistic enough to suppose that the congress might try to establish some sort of a league of states for preventing war. The congress did not even discuss such a plan, but there was one prominent statesman who took the idea seriously. This was the Tsar Alexander. Alexander was something of a religious mystic, and the burning of Moscow and the subsequent overthrow of Napoleon convinced him that God had intended him to do something striking for the welfare of mankind and the brotherhood of nations. Acting on this conviction, Alexander drafted and signed, and induced the King of Prussia and the Emperor of Austria to sign, an extraordinary document known as the Holy Alliance. In this document the three sovereigns agreed that they would take the gospel of Christ as their sole political guide, and that henceforth they would treat each other as brothers should, and govern their subjects as fathers should govern their children.

Out of courtesy to Alexander most of the rulers of Europe signed the Holy Alliance, but they did not take it seriously. Statesmen were amazed that anyone in his senses should expect them to take the gospel of Christ as a guide to politics. They agreed with Castlereagh that the " Holy Alliance is a piece of sublime mysticism and nonsense." Ignoring Alexander's fantastic scheme, the great powers accordingly adopted a different method of preserving peace. November 20, 1815, the four great powers (England, Russia, Austria, and Prussia) signed the secret Treaty of Alliance against France. By this treaty they agreed to act in concert to maintain Louis XVIII on the throne of France and to suppress any dangerous revolution which might in the future " convulse France." In addition they agreed to " renew their meetings at fixed periods " for the purpose of maintaining the peace of Europe. In 1818 France herself was admitted to this alliance for certain purposes. This alliance of the great powers is known as the Concert of Europe, and its chief purpose was to suppress revolutionary movements that might lead to war or overturn the Settlement of 1815.

The revolutions so much feared by the rulers and statesmen of the great powers were not long in coming, and they were brought about by the very measures taken by terrified governments to prevent them. In Austria, for example, nothing could be printed until it passed the government censor. Officials examined all the foreign books at the customs houses in order to see that no liberal ideas crossed the frontier. In the universities government spies slipped into the lecture rooms to see that the professors taught no dangerous notions, and a list of all books taken out of the library by professors was turned in to the government. Students were required to attend church and go to confession, and they were forbidden to hold public meetings for the discussion of political or religious questions. Thus the government tried to encourage the right ideas by laws prohibiting the discussion of any ideas.

In Germany similar methods were adopted. During the Napoleonic wars the students of the University of Jena had formed a patriotic society known as the *Burschenschaft*. Chapters were later established in sixteen German universities. In October, 1817, representatives from these societies met at the Wartburg Castle, where Luther had once taken refuge, to celebrate the three-hundredth anniversary of the German Reformation. At the meeting speeches were made in commemoration of the liberation of Germany from papal authority and from the Napoleonic despotism. Harmless episodes of this sort were regarded by the governments of Austria and Prussia as manifestations of a dangerous revolutionary movement, and a few years later they got the German diet to pass a series of laws known as the Carlsbad Decrees. These decrees provided for the abolition of all unauthorized student societies, for the establishment of a strict censorship of the press in every German state, and for the establishment at every German university of a government agent to supervise the lectures of professors and the activities of students.

Even in England, where freedom of speech and the press had prevailed for more than a century, a repressive policy was adopted by the Conservative government. After the Napoleonic wars, business was less thriving and many people were out of work. There were some labor riots. Meetings were held at which laborers demanded political reform. At Manchester a great meeting was addressed by " Orator " Hunt, a labor leader, who proposed that the government should be petitioned to grant the laborers the right to vote. The meeting was regarded as dangerous. Troops were sent in to disperse it, and some people were shot down. The frightened government professed to see in these activities the sinister beginnings of an English Reign of Terror. Accordingly, in 1817 it suspended the Habeas Corpus Act which for a hundred years had guaranteed the English people against arbitrary arrest and imprisonment; and in 1819 it passed the Six Acts, popularly known as the " Gag Laws," which greatly restricted freedom of speech, of the press, and of public discussion.

All these repressive measures encouraged the very ideas and activities they were designed to prevent. Prevented from meeting and speaking in the open, people organized secret societies, met under cover of the night, and aired their grievances by candlelight. The most famous of these secret societies was the *Carbonari* (" Charcoal Burners "). Organized in Italy, it spread to other countries. By 1820 the political pot began to bubble in every country. But what really startled the kings and statesmen of Europe was an actual revolution in Spain. In January the Spanish soldiers revolted and forced Ferdinand VII to proclaim the old Spanish constitution adopted in 1812, in the time of Napoleon. Following this example, the soldiers of Naples revolted and forced the King of the Two Sicilies (Naples and Sicily) to proclaim the same constitution. These revolutions, by overturning the Settlement of 1815, created the very situation which the Concert of Europe was organized to deal with.

The result was that in 1820 the great powers met in a conference at Troppau to consider what they should do about the revolution in Naples, and two years later another conference was assembled at Verona to deal with the revolution in Spain. The powers found, however, that it was easier to talk about acting in concert for the purpose of suppressing revolutions than it was to act in concert when confronted by a particular revolution. France was keen to suppress the revolution in Spain; Austria was keen to suppress the revolution in Naples. England was unwilling to take any part in intervening in Naples and strongly opposed to any intervention at all in Spain. The outcome was that the Naples revolution was

READING THE NEWSPAPERS IN A CAFÉ IN PARIS

From an engraving by Boilly. As the cost of a subscription was rather high, frequently several people would subscribe for one paper and pass it from one to another.

suppressed by Austria, with the consent of Russia and Prussia; and the Spanish revolution was suppressed by France, with the consent of Russia, Prussia, and Austria, but in face of a strong protest by England. Meantime, in 1821, the Greeks had revolted against Turkish rule, and a third conference of the great powers was called to meet at St. Petersburg in 1825. But the conference never met, because the powers were so divided on the question that it seemed useless to try to settle it by concerted action, and in the end the Greeks won their independence (1829).

For the first time since 1815 the great powers had failed to suppress a popular revolution. This failure may be taken as the end of the so-called Concert of Europe. The English minister Canning announced the end of the Concert in a famous saying: " The time for Areopagus and the like of that is past. Europe is once more back to the situation in which every nation is for itself, and God for all."

Meantime the old fear of revolution and war had greatly abated. In 1830 only very old people could remember the French Revolution, and only the old or the middle-aged could remember very vividly the stirring events of Napoleon's day. But the " younger generation," the men and women under thirty, could not remember the Revolution at all, and even the Napoleonic wars were things they had heard of rather than experienced. The great Napoleon himself, who had died in 1821, was already becoming something dim, a figure half forgotten, half mythical. Thus it happened that as the years passed people remembered less vividly, or not at all, the dangers of war and revolution which had seemed so real in 1815, and were less averse to new ideas and a modification of political and social institutions.

The failure of the Concert of Europe and the rise of a more liberal spirit prepared the way for the revolutionary movements of 1830. In many countries — in Italy, Germany, Poland — these movements, like the similar movements of 1820, were suppressed. But in three countries — France, Belgium, and England — they succeeded. We must now learn something about these three successful revolutions.

II. THE REVOLUTIONS OF 1830–1832

The July Revolution in France, 1830: How Charles X tried to undo the work of the great French Revolution of 1789. In France the Restoration of 1814–1815 had restored the Bourbon monarchy by placing Louis XVIII on the throne, but it had not restored the ancient privileges of the nobles and clergy. In 1814 Louis XVIII granted to the French people a constitution known as the Charter of 1814. The charter promised to keep the Civil Code which Napoleon had established; that is to say, it promised to keep the equality of rights which had been won by the great Revolution. The charter also provided for a measure of political freedom. According to the charter, the king could rule only with the consent of a legislature consisting of two chambers — a Chamber of Peers appointed by the king and a Chamber of Deputies elected by those people who paid rather high taxes. Only about 80,000 people out of a population of 30,000,000 had the right to vote for members of the Chamber of Deputies. Thus the Bourbon monarchy was restored; but it was now a *constitutional* instead of an *autocratic* monarchy.

The majority of the people were pretty well satisfied with this arrangement, and no serious difficulties arose as long as Louis XVIII

FRENCH CHAMBER OF DEPUTIES, 1845
From a drawing by Daubigny.

reigned, since he was content to govern according to the charter.
But many of the former nobles and clergy — especially those who
had emigrated during the Revolution and had lived abroad during
the Napoleonic empire, were not content with the charter or with
any form of constitutional government. They had come trooping
back to France in 1815, expecting to recover all the property and
privileges they had lost. Since they were more conservative than
the king they were called " Ultra-Royalists."

Among the leaders of this party were famous writers, such as
Chateaubriand and Joseph de Maistre. But the chief leader was
the king's brother, the Count of Artois. Of all the enemies of the
Revolution he was the most bitter. In 1824 he became King
Charles X and he at once set about to restore, so far as possible, the
privileges of the nobles and clergy. A law was passed appropriating
about 30,000,000 francs a year to pay the nobles for the property
they had lost during the Revolution. The king also tried to get
the legislature to pass other laws favorable to the nobles and clergy.
He made no secret of his purpose. " I would rather saw wood,"
he said, " than be a king of the English type." His minister,
Polignac, said that the object of the king was " to reorganize society,
to restore the clergy to its former preponderance in the state, to

create a powerful aristocracy and surround it with privileges."
His object was, in fact, to undo the work of the great Revolution
and to restore the autocratic monarchy and the privileged classes
of nobles and clergy.

As soon as this became clear, the Chamber of Deputies refused to
support the king's measures, and when he dissolved the Chamber
the people elected deputies who opposed him more strongly than before.   Since the Chamber of Deputies refused to support him, the
king decided to ignore it.   In July, 1830, he therefore issued three
famous ordinances, known as the " July Ordinances."   One of these
dissolved the Chamber that had just been elected ; another abolished
the freedom of the press ; a third changed the law of voting so that
only those classes of people who supported the king's measures
would have the right to vote.   By these ordinances the king virtually set aside the Charter of 1814, and restored the autocratic
monarchy.   The immediate result of these actions was the July
Revolution of 1830.

**How the lower-class Republicans drove Charles X off the throne,
and how the middle-class Moderates placed Louis Philippe on it.**
The July Revolution was confined to Paris, and it lasted only a few
days.   The fighting was done by the lower-class people who,
under the lead of Cavaignac and Lafayette, demanded the establishment of a republic.   They began by tearing up the cobblestones and
building barricades across the narrow winding streets.   Behind
these barricades they fought the king's soldiers.   As soon as the
soldiers took one barricade and passed on, it was reconstructed
again.   The king's soldiers were not very keen to fire on the people
anyway ; and so after three days of fighting they retired out of
Paris, and the king retired with them as gracefully as he could.
Seeing that he was beaten, Charles X promised to withdraw the
hated ordinances and to rule according to the charter.   But the
insurgents said that it was too late for that.   They had won the
revolution, and now they demanded a republic — the Republic of
1793.

The Republican party of Lafayette and Cavaignac established its
headquarters at the Hôtel de Ville (City Hall).   Meantime, a more
moderate revolutionary party had established its headquarters at

BREAKING UP THE PRESSES OF THE NEWSPAPER *LE TEMPS*, JULY 27, 1830

An episode in the Revolution of 1830 in Paris. From a lithograph by
Delaporte.

the Palais Bourbon across the river. This party, which included
the famous historians Guizot and Thiers, represented the middle-
class people who were strongly opposed to Charles X but were by
no means in favor of a republic. They had taken no part in fighting the king's soldiers. Their part in the revolution consisted in
assembling at the Palais Bourbon and talking about it. They were
willing to have the workmen erect barricades and fight Charles X
until he was brought to his senses. But when Charles promised to
withdraw the ordinances and rule according to the charter, they
would willingly have recognized him as king again. Yet what could
they do? The Republicans had a military force, led by the great
Lafayette, while they had no force at all except their tongues. So
the parties — the talkers and the fighters — faced each other across
the river, the middle-class Moderates at the Palais Bourbon, the
lower-class Republicans at the Hôtel de Ville.

This was the situation when, on July 30, the young historian
Thiers and the shrewd old diplomat Talleyrand proposed that Louis

Philippe, the Duke of Orleans, should be recognized as king in place of Charles X. They felt that Louis Philippe might satisfy both parties. He was a prince of royal blood, and so the Moderates and even the Ultra-Royalists might be satisfied to have him for their king. On the other hand, he had supported the Revolution of 1789 in its early years. He had fought with the revolutionary armies in Belgium at the Battle of Jemappes. Since 1815 he had not been on friendly terms with his relations, Louis XVIII and Charles X. But he was a well-known figure in Paris. He was often seen walking through the streets carrying an umbrella, and he had been known to stop and talk with ordinary people. For these reasons it was hoped that the Republicans might accept Louis Philippe as king in spite of the fact that he was of royal blood.

The Moderate party at the Palais Bourbon therefore invited Louis Philippe to take the title of " Lieutenant-General of the Kingdom." Louis accepted the title and on July 31, dressed in a general's uniform and wearing the tricolor, he rode across the river from the Palais Bourbon to the Hôtel de Ville. Crowds of people watched this famous ride, for the point of it was to see what the Republicans would do. Would they accept Louis Philippe or not? It really depended on Lafayette, who commanded the armed forces of the Republicans. Neither party could succeed without the support of Lafayette's great name and fame. In this crisis Lafayette preferred to make a king rather than to fight for the uncertain cause of the republic. He therefore appeared on the balcony of the Hôtel de Ville and embraced Louis Philippe before all the people. This was one of those dramatic events which the French people enjoy so much. It meant that the Republicans accepted Louis Philippe as king.

The July Revolution of 1830 was a slight affair compared to the great Revolution of 1789. It was not a great social upheaval, nor did it even change the form of government very much. The charter was modified so as to diminish the king's powers slightly and to extend the suffrage a little. But in general the government of France under Louis Philippe, who ruled till 1848, was much the same as it had been under Louis XVIII and Charles X. It was still a government for and by the wealthy people. For this reason the

BIVOUAC OF THE FRENCH NATIONAL GUARD IN THE COURTYARD OF THE
LOUVRE, DECEMBER 22, 1830

From a painting by Gassies. There was street fighting during the month of
December and the National Guard was called into action.

reign of Louis Philippe is often called the period of the " bourgeois
monarchy." Balzac, in his powerful novels, has described French
society during the bourgeois monarchy, when money was the golden
key to social influence and political power.

The wealthy and well-to-do middle-class people were well satisfied with the results of the July Revolution, but the working-class
Republicans were very much disgruntled. They had done the real
work of the revolution, and when they had accepted Louis Philippe
they had expected to have something done for them. But they
were not even given the right to vote. The Republican leader, Cavaignac, said : " We have yielded because we are not yet strong
enough. Later it will be different." Later it was different. In
1848, as we shall presently see, there was another revolution, which
overturned the government of Louis Philippe and established the
second French Republic.

**How the Belgians revolted in 1830 and won their independence
from the Dutch.** In 1814–1815 the great powers had united Holland and Belgium in order to create a strong state to guard the
lower Rhine against France. It was an unwise arrangement be-

cause the Dutch and the Belgians were really two different nations. Although they elected representatives to the legislature, the Belgians felt that the Dutch really controlled the government and that they, the Belgians, were ruled by a foreign people. They complained that the taxes bore more heavily on them than on the Dutch, and that the Dutch king, William I, tried to compel all public officials to use the Dutch language. But their chief grievance was that the Dutch, who were Protestants, were hostile to their own religion, which was Catholic.

These grievances were of long standing, and therefore as soon as the Belgians heard that the French had started a revolution in Paris, they started one of their own in Brussels. All classes of Belgians wanted to be independent of Holland; but the Belgians, like the French, were divided into two parties over the question of the kind of government to be established. The lower-class Radicals wanted a republic, but the upper-class Moderates wanted a constitutional monarchy. As in France, the Moderates proved stronger than the Radicals. A constitution was adopted which provided for a king, and for a legislature to be elected by the wealthy and well-to-do people. Prince Leopold of Coburg was invited to be the king of the new Belgian state. Thus there was established in Belgium, as a result of the revolution, a moderate constitutional monarchy very similar to the July monarchy in France.

But the Belgians found it was easier to establish a government than it was to win their independence. The Dutch king, William, was determined to suppress the rebellion in Belgium; and since he had a good army, while the Belgians had none, he would probably have succeeded if the great powers had not interfered. Prussia, Russia, and Austria were disposed to help the Dutch king suppress the Belgian revolution, but their attention was soon diverted from Belgium to Poland, where a revolution broke out in November, 1830. Besides, the new French king, Louis Philippe, threatened to help the Belgians if Russia and Prussia came to the assistance of Holland. The English government felt that it would be unwise to subject the Belgians to a government they disliked, and it was especially anxious to prevent the French from sending an army to help the Belgians, for fear that France might thereby gain some Belgian territory. In the end, therefore, largely through the influence of France and England, King William was forced to recognize the independence of Belgium. The great powers, at a conference held in London, agreed to the separation of Belgium and Holland, and they all signed a treaty agreeing to respect the independence of Belgium. This " neutralization " of Belgium was really accomplished in 1833, but due to the stubbornness of King William the definitive treaty was not signed until 1839.

One other successful revolution occurred at this time — the enactment of the Reform Bill in England. Perhaps, strictly speaking, this shouldn't be called a " revolution." No barricades were erected, and no fighting occurred — only a little rioting. But still, the conflict in England over the Reform Bill was much like the conflict in France over the Charter of 1814, and the outcome of the conflict was much the same in England as in France. For these reasons we may call the enactment of the Reform Bill a " revolution," like the others.

Parliamentary reform in England: How the Industrial Revolution put the old system of representation out of joint. Since the seventeenth century England had been a constitutional monarchy in which the king ruled with the consent of Parliament. Parliament was supposed to represent and give effect to the wishes of the people. It consisted of a House of Lords and a House of Commons. The House of Lords was composed of those nobles who possessed a hereditary right to sit in it, and of certain bishops of the English Church. This body therefore represented the landowning aristocracy — still the most powerful class in England.

The House of Commons was composed of members elected by certain people. Each county sent two members, who were chosen by all those men who owned land in the county worth forty shillings a year. Certain towns, or boroughs, sent two members each, chosen by those people (usually a small number) who had the right of voting. The House of Commons was thus supposed to represent the farmers in the counties and the middle-class people in the towns or boroughs.

This system of representative government was not so bad in the seventeenth and early eighteenth centuries because then the county members represented the farming classes pretty well, and the members from the boroughs represented the people engaged in industry and trade. But in the early nineteenth century this was no longer true. The explanation is to be found in that very important movement of the nineteenth century which is known as the Industrial Revolution. The Industrial Revolution was the result of the invention of machines, and of the discovery that natural forces, such as water power, steam, and electricity, could be used to run the machines. The most profound and widespread transformation of modern life brought about by the use of the power-driven machines with which we are all familiar did not occur until the late nineteenth and early twentieth centuries, as we shall see later (Chapters XVI–XVII). But in the late eighteenth and early nineteenth centuries the use of power-driven machines had already begun to transform the indus-

ENGLISH INN AND POSTHOUSE, ABOUT 1829

From a sketch by Eugène Lami in *Voyage en Angleterre*.

trial life of England. Between 1733 and 1792 six important inventions were introduced into the manufacture of cloth. Eli Whitney's cotton gin was a machine for picking the seeds out of raw cotton. Arkwright's water frame was a machine run by a water wheel. The other inventions — the fly-shuttle, the power loom, the jenny, and the mule — were machines for spinning and weaving more rapidly. For running the new machines water power was first used, but was gradually replaced by steam power. As early as 1690 a Frenchman, Denis Papin, made a steam engine. Thomas Newcomen made a better one in 1705. But it was James Watt who made the steam engine of practical use. In 1769 he patented a "condenser" which saved two-thirds of the coal required by the earlier engines, and later he devised a method by which the pistons of the engine could be used to run the wheels of other machines.

The use of such machines transformed the cloth industry. Formerly a farmer's wife could set up a hand loom in her kitchen and weave cloth in her spare time. But the new machines were cumbersome and expensive. Only a man of means, a " capitalist," could afford them or the large buildings, " factories," in which they were installed. Thus the cloth industry came to be centered in large factories, with many machines, and many workers to tend them, all under one management. Besides, the factories had to be located where there was water power or a supply of coal. In England this meant that the great cloth and iron industries moved from the towns and boroughs of southern England to north-central England, where there was coal and water power. And the result of this was that the towns and boroughs of southern England declined in population or disappeared altogether, while in northern England there grew up new and populous cities, such as Manchester, Birmingham, Leeds, and Sheffield.

The new type of industry also changed the conditions of life in the country. Formerly many farmers had made their living partly by spinning and weaving cloth which they sold to the dealers who came around periodically in their wagons and collected it. But the farmer's wife could not make cloth on her hand loom so cheaply or so well as the machines made it in the factories. Hence the farmers, for the most part, lost this source of income, and many of them got into debt and were forced to sell their farms and move into the industrial cities where they, or more likely their wives and children, worked in the factories tending the machines.

The boroughs which had the right of sending members to the Commons were, with few exceptions, those which had been given that right in the seventeenth century, when the towns of southern England were the centers of industry. But in the early nineteenth century many of these boroughs had ceased to be towns at all, except in name. Many of them were no more than small hamlets where a few families lived, or mere names of places where no one lived. Boroughs of the former type were called " rotten boroughs," because it was easy for some noble or rich man to buy the votes of the few electors who still lived in the borough. Boroughs of the latter type were called " pocket boroughs," because the

DINING-HALL OF AN ENGLISH ORPHAN ASYLUM

From an aquatint by Pugin and Rowlandson in *The Microcosm of London*, published in 1808. The room was heated by a fireplace at the far end.

right to choose the members of the Commons from those boroughs passed to the noble or the rich man who had acquired the land on which the borough had formerly stood.

Thus most of the borough members were chosen, not by the people engaged in industry and trade, but by the rich nobles or landowners who controlled the borough elections. Meantime, the great centers of industry in England — the cities of Manchester, Sheffield, Birmingham, and Leeds which had developed as a result of the Industrial Revolution — had no representation at all in Parliament. The rich manufacturers who controlled the cotton and iron industries and the mass of the laborers who worked in their factories complained, like the mass of the farmers in the country, because there was no one in Parliament whose business it was to speak for them.

So it happened that in the early nineteenth century the old system of parliamentary representation was out of joint. England was still a constitutional monarchy in which the king ruled with the consent of Parliament. But Parliament no longer represented either the farmers or the industrial classes. The nobles who sat in the House of Lords by hereditary right had the greatest influence in deciding who should be elected to the House of Commons from the counties and from the pocket and rotten boroughs. We might almost say that the House of Commons represented, not the people in town and country, but the great noble families.

Sooner or later the middle and lower classes were sure to object to a government which was so largely controlled by a few noble families. There had in fact been much talk of "parliamentary reform" in the late eighteenth century, before the French Revolution. Associations had been formed for promoting the cause of reform, and in 1793 measures were proposed in Parliament for changing the method of electing members of the House of Commons. Then the French Revolution and the Napoleonic wars had intervened, and these exciting events had driven all thoughts of reform out of most people's heads. But gradually the fear of revolution and of radical ideas had diminished in England as elsewhere, and after 1820 the demand for parliamentary reform was once more the great question of the day.

The Reform Bill of 1832: How the English people took a cautious step towards democratic government. On the question of parliamentary reform the English people were represented by the three political parties. The Tory (Conservative) party was supported chiefly by noble families, the country gentry, and the clergy of the Anglican Church. These people opposed parliamentary reform. We may suppose them to have argued somewhat as follows: "Why change anything? Able men are sent to Parliament now. If you begin to extend the right of voting there will be no stopping until everyone has the right to vote, and then you will have government by the people, which will mean by the poor and ignorant people. We are opposed to democratic government because that is a kind of despotism — a 'despotism of the majority' — which would be as bad as the despotism of a king."

The Whig (Liberal) party had as its leaders some of the most famous noble families of England; but since the Revolution of 1688 this party had been supported by the wealthy industrial class in the cities. The Whig nobles therefore supported parliamentary reform because their wealthy middle-class supporters favored it. The Whigs were as much opposed to democracy as the Tories. But they said that the educated and well-to-do people in the towns ought to have a voice in government. " The question is," said the famous historian Macaulay, " whether a hundred drunken potwallopers in one place, or the owner of a ruined hovel in another, shall be invested with powers which are withheld from cities renowned to the ends of the earth for the marvels of their wealth and industry." The Whigs therefore demanded only " partial reform." They asked that the system of election should be so changed that the wealthy and well-to-do middle classes in the towns and cities would have a proper representation in Parliament.

The Radical party, like the Republican party in France and the Radicals in Belgium, was composed mainly of working people in country and town, although it had as leaders and spokesmen certain distinguished writers and scholars, such as Jeremy Bentham, James Mill, and the historian George Grote. The philosopher Jeremy Bentham had formulated two principles of government. He said: (1) that the object of government was " the greatest good to the greatest number "; and (2) that in the control of government " every man ought to count for one and none for more than one." The Radicals accepted these democratic principles. They therefore demanded a thoroughgoing " democratic " reform of Parliament.

In 1830 the popular demand for parliamentary reform in England was greatly strengthened by the success of the July Revolution in France. Earl Grey, the leader of the Whigs, asked the Tory prime minister, the Duke of Wellington, to introduce a reform bill into Parliament. The " spirit of the times " was such, he said, that Parliament must be reformed peaceably, or else the people would make a revolution in England as they had in France. But the Duke of Wellington refused. He is reported to have said that " if he had the task of creating a new Constitution he could not hope to create such perfection [as the existing English Parliament] at once,

but his great endeavor would be to form some description of legislature which would produce the same results."

This famous declaration of the duke's only increased the demand
for reform. In 1831 the Whigs came into power, and Earl Grey
introduced into Parliament a reform bill. But the House of Commons was about evenly divided on the question, and so the prime
minister dissolved Parliament, in the hope that a new election
would return a greater number of members favorable to the reforms.
The election was held in the midst of great excitement, and the
result was that many of the old members who had voted against
reform were defeated. The Whigs then introduced another reform
bill, which was passed in the House of Commons by a large majority.
The House of Lords promptly rejected it by a large majority.
Here, then, was a deadlock. What was to be done?

At last the people began to take a hand in the business. They
began to call for the abolition of the House of Lords. Nottingham
Castle was burned down. In Birmingham 150,000 people assembled and declared they would pay no more taxes until the reform
bill was passed. In Bristol shops were plundered and buildings
destroyed; for three days the city was in the hands of the mob.
Once more the Whigs brought in a reform bill — the Reform Bill of
1832. The House of Lords rejected it. Earl Grey then resigned,
whereupon the king asked the Duke of Wellington to form a Tory
ministry, hoping that he would draft a bill which the Tory House of
Lords would pass. When this became known the National Political
Union, an association favorable to reform, prepared for armed
rebellion. Birmingham blacksmiths worked all night making
arms. Plans were made to prevent the king's troops from leaving
London. The country was on the verge of revolution and civil
war. The Tories began to waver, and the Duke of Wellington
found that he could not form a ministry. His followers told him
that it was useless, since the excitement was such that the House of
Commons would never pass any Tory measure. So the duke gave
it up. He told the king that there was only one thing to do, which
was, to ask Earl Grey to form another Whig ministry.

This the king did. But Earl Grey told him it was useless to form
any ministry unless he would force the House of Lords to pass the

THE BIRMINGHAM TALLYHO

Coaches passing the Crown Inn at Holloway, 1828. From an aquatint by
Bently.

reform bill. There was one way the king could do this. He could
appoint a sufficient number of new peers to pass the bill. In order
to avoid a civil war the king promised to do this. But the mere
promise was enough, for the House of Lords preferred to pass the
reform bill rather than have a lot of new peers appointed. Thus
the reform bill was passed by both the Commons and the Lords and
became a law in 1832.

**What the Reform Bill of 1832 accomplished, and why some
people were satisfied and some not.** The Reform Bill of 1832 was
not a very drastic reform. It deprived fifty-seven rotten and
pocket boroughs of their two representatives each, and thirty other
boroughs of one representative each. It increased the representation from the counties by sixty-two members and gave to cities not
before represented a total of sixty-three members. It also changed
the suffrage. Borough members were now to be chosen by all
" householders " who lived in houses worth ten pounds a year;
county members, by farmers owning farms worth forty shillings a
year and farmers leasing land worth fifty pounds a year. The
Reform Bill did not make the government of England democratic. It conferred no political power on the mass of the people.

What it did was to deprive the landowning aristocracy of its exclusive power of government by conferring political power upon the wealthy and well-to-do middle class in the cities and counties.

What did the people think of this partial reform? Some liked it very much, some only a little, and some not at all. The Whigs — especially the middle-class people in the towns — were of course well pleased, because it benefited them chiefly. The Tories did not like it much; but still, after it was over they accepted the accomplished fact, although they grumbled about it a good deal. The people who were really dissatisfied with the results of the Reform Bill were the Radicals — the mass of working people in the towns. They felt, like the Republicans in France, that they had done much to carry through the reform by their insurrections and then had got nothing out of it. They therefore kept on demanding further reform. Their demands were formulated in a document known as the " People's Charter," which contained six points: (1) annual Parliaments, (2) manhood suffrage, (3) vote by ballot, (4) equal electoral districts — that is, each electoral district to be composed of the same number of people; (5) abolition of property qualification for members of Parliament, and (6) payment of members of Parliament. This movement on the part of the working classes and those who sympathized with them was known as the Chartist movement — a movement for democratic government which continued for twenty years and more.

III. The Revolutions of 1848

Why the revolutions of 1830 made people more hopeful about the future prospects of mankind. Most people are subject to varying moods, being at one time despondent and at other times full of hope. Society at large seems to be affected in the same way, so that in the history of thought we find alternating periods of hope and despair. The time after 1815 was not a period of hopefulness. In those years people lived under the shadow of oppression — the oppression of political opinions and activities by frightened conservative and autocratic governments. The mass of the people, glad to have peace again, busied themselves with making a living. Those who had aspired to political liberty had little hope of ever obtaining it. The thought of the time was therefore somewhat gloomy and depressed. Poets and writers were inclined to turn away in disgust from the questions of the day, and to find consolation in writing about themselves or about events and people in the remote past. Popular authors like Byron and Chateaubriand wrote a good deal about the sad state of their own souls. Historians like Thierry described in brilliant colors the life of France in Merovingian times. Novelists like Walter Scott wrote romances of the age of chivalry, such as *Ivanhoe*. Such writers represent what is called the " Romantic movement " in the history of thought. After 1830 the thought of the time did not cease to be romantic, but it became less gloomy and depressed. The Revolutions of 1830 had a great deal to do with this change. Young men, especially, were encouraged by these successful revolutions to think that political liberty and social reform were after all not impossible to obtain. Poets and writers in nearly every country wrote more about the political and social problems of the present and less about the state of their own souls and the departed glories of the Middle Ages. Thus the mood of depression following the Napoleonic wars gradually gave way to a mood of hope. Once more, as in the years before 1789, people looked forward with enthusiasm to better times coming for the battered old world.

This faith in better times coming reached its height in the years just preceding the revolutions of 1848. It took different forms with different people, and in different countries. For convenience we may say that it took three main forms: (1) the form of *humanitarianism* — the belief in the possibility of abolishing poverty and social injustice; (2) the form of *political idealism* — the belief in popular government; (3) the form of *international pacifism* — the belief that war would shortly disappear among civilized nations. It will be worth while to study these ideas a little, even if we have to omit some of the political and military events of the revolutions of 1848.

Optimistic faith in human progress: Humanitarianism. Of course there have always been humane people in the world. Ancient philosophers, such as Socrates and the Stoics, and many religious sects, such as the Anabaptists and the Quakers, preached the

New York Public Library

A Cartoon of 1848

The crowned heads of Europe are frightened by the sudden appearance of the
great sea-serpent "Liberty."

brotherhood of man and denounced all forms of cruelty as crimes
against humanity.   But humanitarianism is especially characteristic of the last hundred and fifty years, and never perhaps was it
stronger than in the period between about 1830 and 1848.   It finds
best expression in the literature of the time.   Fifty years ago young
people read, with more delight than they do now, such books as
Harriet Beecher Stowe's *Uncle Tom's Cabin*, Victor Hugo's *Les
Misérables*, and Charles Dickens' *Oliver Twist* and *David Copper-
field*.   These stories are a little too sentimental for our taste, but
the point is that they were designed to arouse strong sympathy
with the poor and oppressed.   They are sentimental and they were
intended to be.   They are saturated to the weeping-point with the
humanitarian sentiment of their time.

Humanitarianism is also reflected in the social legislation of the
first half of the nineteenth century.   In France many inhumane
practices, including slavery in the colonies, were abolished during
the Revolution.   Slavery in the colonies, restored by Napoleon,
was again abolished in 1848.   Slavery in the British colonies was
abolished in 1833; and in England itself, during the thirty years

from 1820 to 1850, a host of inhumane laws and practices were swept away.   The death penalty for petty crimes was abolished, and laws were passed for the protection of workers — especially women and children — employed in certain industries.   These early measures mark the beginning of that great body of humanitarian legislation which now exists in nearly every country — laws for the prevention of cruelty and oppression, for the protection and assistance of the weak, and for the care of the helpless.

Faith in a better time coming inspired many men to write books showing how it could be brought about by changing the conditions of economic and social life.   These writers are often called Socialists, or Utopian Socialists (see page 332).   The best known of these are Robert Owen, Saint-Simon, and Fourier.   Robert Owen was an English manufacturer who believed that the misery of the working classes was due to the struggle between the employers and the wage-earners.   To show how this could be remedied, he established a little

Bibliothèque Nationale

SAINT-SIMON (1760–1825)

From a lithograph by Perrot. Saint-Simon fought in the American Revolution, was imprisoned in Paris during the Terror, and later acquired a fortune in land speculation.   This he later lost in scientific experiments.

community at New Lanark where the managers and workers all had a share in the ownership and the profits of industry.   The enterprise succeeded so well that Owen tried to establish a similar community in Indiana at a place called New Harmony. Fourier and Saint-Simon were French writers who proposed that the production of wealth should be managed by the government and the wealth thus produced be distributed among all people according to some just principle.   Many attempts were made, both in France and the United States, to establish little communities on the basis of Fourier's idea.   The most famous of these was the experiment at Brook Farm in New England. You could learn something about this famous social experiment by reading a life of Margaret Fuller, or one of Nathaniel Hawthorne, both of whom took part in it.

Most of these attempts to establish an ideal society failed after a few years. But they illustrate the faith in the approaching regeneration of society which was so common at the time. This faith, as it was held by many people in the period before 1848, is well expressed by Saint-Simon. " The imagination of poets," he said, "has placed the Golden Age of humanity at the cradle of the human race. . . . The Golden Age of humanity is not behind us; it is yet to come, and will be found in the perfection of the social order. Our fathers have not seen it; our children will one day behold it. It is our duty to prepare the way for them."

Bibliothèque Nationale

FOURIER (1772–1837)

From a lithograph by Gigoux. Fourier led an uneventful existence as a broker, and spent all his leisure time writing and studying.

Optimistic faith in human progress: Political idealism. The period from 1830 to 1848 was a period of political idealism as well as one of humanitarian sentiment. The news of the July Revolution in Paris gave courage to thousands of men who were beginning to despair of ever attaining the political liberty which they so much desired. This was perhaps especially true in Germany. For example, the German writer, Ludwig Börne, tells us that in the summer of 1830, at the age of forty-four, he was ill and despondent and ceased to interest himself in politics. But the news of the Paris revolution came like an electric shock, giving him new life and hope. Too impatient to remain in Frankfurt, he went to France in order to see this glorious revolution with his own eyes. At Strasbourg the first " cockade " he saw, on a peasant's cap, was " like a little rainbow, after the flood of our time. . . . But when the bright tricolored flag greeted my eyes, . . . my heart beat so violently that I was on the point of fainting. . . . This is the one color of the French liberty that will be ours."

Of all the political idealists of this time the greatest was the Italian, Joseph Mazzini. Mazzini was born in Genoa in 1805. He had a very frail body, but a very active mind, and a conscience that never left him in peace. He was a great reader of the Bible, of the Roman historian Tacitus, and of the English poet Byron; and he was thoroughly familiar with the history of the French Revolution and with the democratic theories of Rousseau upon which the French Republic of 1793 was based. Mazzini's principal trait was passionate sympathy with the poor and helpless and a desire to aid them. The wretched condition of his brother Italians, living under tyrannical governments, preyed on his mind, and so one day he abandoned all thought of getting on in the world and gave himself heart and soul to the cause of human freedom.

Mazzini had a very simple faith, which nothing could shake. He believed that men were naturally good, and that they would behave as they ought to do if they were once freed from tyranny and injustice. In 1831 he organized a secret political society called " Young Italy," the object of which was to teach the Italian people what their rights were and how to obtain them. Like Rousseau, Mazzini believed that all men had certain natural rights and that these rights were the same for all men. These rights were expressed in the famous motto of the French Revolution — " Liberty, Equality, Fraternity " — which Mazzini changed to " Liberty, Equality, Humanity." To obtain these rights, Mazzini advised the people to rise up in revolution, abolish the existing governments and laws, and establish over all Italy a single government of free citizens —" One, Independent, Sovereign, Republican."

Mazzini wrote a great many articles and pamphlets in which he set forth his ideas with so much clarity, force, and passionate sympathy that many people, especially young men, accepted him as an inspired prophet. In Italy they took him at his word and started a number of revolutions; but these were easily suppressed by the Italian rulers, and from 1831 to 1848 Mazzini lived in exile, first in Marseille, afterwards in London. In London he made a bare living writing literary articles and teaching Italian, and he had to be content with a smelly little room in a dingy lodging house. Banishing Mazzini from Italy really increased his influence, for it made him a great European figure. Societies on the model of Young Italy were everywhere organized — Young Germany, Young Switzerland, Young Hungary, Young Ireland, Young Europe — and all these societies kept in touch with each other and with Mazzini. For Mazzini was more than a patriot, more than a lover of Italy. He was a lover of mankind; and it was his idea, and the idea of his disciples, that the coming revolution would be an international affair. A revolution in Italy would be a signal for revolutions in every country. These revolutions would overwhelm the old governments; each country would become a nation of free citizens governing themselves under a democratic republic; and all these free republics would then live together in peace and harmony.

By 1845 Mazzini was the best beloved and the worst hated man in Europe. Thousands of poor people looked upon him as an inspired prophet, while rulers and statesmen and nobles and bishops looked upon him as a madman. Royal heads stirred uneasily on their pillows at night wondering what this violent and bloodthirsty " Anarchist " was up to. As like as not the bloodthirsty Anarchist would be teaching London organ-grinders to read and write; or carrying a coal scuttle up three flights of stairs in order to help his overworked landlady; or perhaps writing another revolutionary pamphlet by candlelight in his dingy room.

Optimistic faith in human progress: International pacifism. The idea that war can be abolished is an old one. We have already seen that in the seventeenth and eighteenth centuries able men had written books to show that the governments might abolish war by establishing a European federation of states (see p. 204). Ordinary people had read these books about peace and war, but they had done nothing about the matter themselves. They had waited for kings and governments to act. But in the nineteenth century they began to do something on their own account. They began to organize popular societies, with the object of influencing public opinion in opposition to war.

The first of these, the New York Peace Society, was organized in August, 1815, with about thirty members. In December of the same year Noah Worcester and William E. Channing founded the Massachusetts Peace Society. In 1816 William Allen, an English Quaker, organized the London Peace Society. Within the next forty years many similar societies were formed — first in England and the United States, afterward in other countries. These societies published peace pamphlets, and periodicals such as the *Advocate of Peace* (American) and the *Herald of Peace* (English). They also offered prizes for the best essay on the means of abolishing war. Most of the essays advocated the formation of a " congress of nations " (another name for " league of nations "), and some of them were published and widely read. The object of the peace societies was to convince people and governments that " war is inconsistent with the principles of Christianity, and the true interests of mankind; and to point out the means best calculated to maintain permanent and universal peace."[1]

The founders of the peace societies were mainly church people and noted philanthropists. But in the period after 1830 many noted political leaders became interested in the peace movement. One of these was Charles Sumner, Senator from Massachusetts. He delivered a number of notable and widely read addresses, such as " The True Grandeur of Nations " (July 4, 1845), in which he tried to show, not only that war was contrary to religion and humanity but that it was likely to disappear under the conditions of modern civilization. Richard Cobden, a prominent member of the English Parliament, was also a powerful advocate of peace. His great remedy for war was " free trade." He said that war was most likely to be caused by trade disputes; that trade disputes were due to protective tariffs and the conflict over colonies; and that when all nations adopted free trade (as England did in 1846), they would no longer have any use for colonies, disputes over trade would cease, and the causes of war would largely disappear.

So the peace movement grew stronger every year. In 1843 the peace societies held a peace congress in London, which was attended by 300 delegates, thirteen of whom came from the United States.

[1] *Constitution of the London Peace Society.*

But the first great international peace congress was held in Brussels in 1848. Delegates attended from the United States, England, and most of the countries of Europe. Many enthusiastic speeches were made prophesying the end of war. In order to hasten that desired end the congress passed resolutions urging the governments of the various countries to do three things: (1) to form a congress of nations; (2) to agree to decide their disputes by arbitration; (3) to agree to reduce their armies and navies.

Thus in the year 1848 there was a very hopeful feeling abroad in the world. People were much inclined to think that the world was rapidly growing better and that the time was soon coming when poverty and suffering would disappear, when just governments controlled by the people would be everywhere established, and when all the nations would live together in peace and harmony. This widespread feeling prepared the way for the great upheaval known as the revolutions of 1848.

The Revolution of 1848 in France: How the second republic was established and why it was short-lived. For ten years there had been increasing dissatisfaction with the government of Louis Philippe. Many middle-class Moderates demanded an extension of the suffrage, and laws doing away with the corrupt practices by which the government controlled elections. The lower-class Republicans, led by Cavaignac and Lamartine, still hoped to see a democratic republic established in France. Meantime a workingman's Socialist party had been established by Louis Blanc, who had worked out a scheme for the reorganization of industry which he called the system of " national workshops." By this scheme the great industries would be owned and operated by the managers and workers together, and all would share in the profits. Thus the Moderates were demanding electoral reform, and the Republicans were hoping to establish a democratic republic, while the Socialists wanted not only a democratic republic but a socialistic reorganization of industry as well.

The government of Louis Philippe refused to consider any of these reforms. It even tried to prevent the discussion of reform by making it illegal to hold political meetings without a permit. So the people held banquets, and after dinner talked politics. In

ATTACK ON THE CHÂTEAU-D'EAU IN 1848

From a lithograph by Jules David. The Republicans tried to reach the
Tuileries, where Louis Philippe was, but were held at this barricade.

February, 1848, arrangements were made for a great banquet in
Paris. When the government refused to permit a banquet to be
held, the people determined to hold it anyway. They raised barricades, resisted the police, and cried, " Down with Louis Philippe ! "
As in 1830, the king's troops made little effort to suppress the uprising. Louis Philippe became frightened and fled from Paris, as
Charles X had done in 1830. The revolutionists then proclaimed
a republic, and formed a provisional government.

The provisional government consisted of five Republicans and
four Socialists. The socialists demanded that steps be taken to
carry out Louis Blanc's scheme for national workshops. This the
Republicans did not wish to do, and it could not be done very well
anyway in the midst of a revolution; and so all that the provisional government did was to offer a small weekly wage to all
men who had no employment. The result was that crowds of men
came flocking to Paris, and soon there were about 110,000 men in
the city receiving a weekly wage from the government. As the

government had little or nothing for them to do, they spent their time pleasantly in the cafés talking politics. They cared little about Louis Blanc's scheme of national workshops, and they soon found new leaders who talked wildly and enthusiastically about the " social revolution " which would do away with private property and get rid of the bankers and all rich people. The provisional government was helpless before the hundred thousand armed men who marched up and down the streets threatening everyone who opposed them. For months these so-called Socialists had everything their own way, terrorizing the city and the government.

Making the best terms they could with the Socialists, the provisional government meantime called for the election of a National Assembly to draft a new constitution for France. The National Assembly, elected by all men over twenty-one years of age, assembled in Paris in May, 1848. The first thing it did was to restore order in Paris. All people of property were now thoroughly frightened by " socialism," and a middle-class army was organized to support the National Assembly. The Republican leader, Cavaignac, was appointed general and " Dictator," and after four days of bloody fighting in the streets of Paris the working-class Socialists were dispersed and driven out of the city. Ten thousand people were killed or wounded. This episode was known as the " bloody June days " of 1848.

The National Assembly then drafted a new constitution for France. The new constitution provided for a president and a single legislative body, both elected by the people. The new form of government was thus a " democratic republic," much like the Republic of 1793. It is known in French history as the " second republic." The first elections under this new republican government were held in December, 1848, and May, 1849. For president the people elected Louis Napoleon, nephew of Napoleon I, by an overwhelming majority, while about two-thirds of the members chosen for the Assembly were men who were not in favor of a republic.

This curious result needs a little explaining. There are two explanations. First, during the years since 1815 the people of France had come to regard the first Napoleon as a great hero and patriot who had made France admired and feared in Europe. The peasants, especially, thought of him as a kind of superman who had given them their lands and freed them from the control of the nobles. They therefore thought that his nephew, Louis Napoleon, must be a great man because he bore a great name. In voting for Louis Napoleon, they voted for a name instead of a man. Secondly, the bloody June days had greatly alarmed people all over France. The peasants were told that the Socialists desired to take away their lands and to destroy morality and religion. They were told that the Republicans were not much better than the Socialists. The peasants therefore thought of Republicans and Socialists as very radical and dangerous men. Hence they said, " We will be on the safe side and elect conservative men to the new Assembly — men who will not try to take away our lands and destroy our religion."

Thus the Republic of 1848 had a bad start. The bloody June days had made people distrust Republicans as well as Socialists. The republic was scarcely established before people lost faith in it. No wonder it did not last long. It lasted until 1852, when Louis Napoleon abolished it and established the second empire. We shall see later how easily he did that. But first we must see how the revolutionary movement spread over Europe, what it did in other countries, and how it failed there also.

The Revolution of 1848 in Italy, Germany, and Austria: Why it succeeded for a time and then utterly failed. The revolution in Paris was like a spark falling into a powder barrel — it produced a great explosion. The news of the downfall of Louis Philippe spread rapidly throughout Europe, and within a few weeks the people in Italy, Germany, and Austria were in open rebellion against the autocratic governments under which they lived. In one way these revolutions were all alike. They were all inspired by the desire of the people for political liberty. In each of the states into which Italy and Germany were divided, the revolutionists demanded the establishment of a constitution, by means of which the people should be given a share in government. In Austria the chief racial groups — Bohemians, Hungarians, Poles, and Serbo-Croats — demanded local self government within the empire.

VIEW OF ZÜRICH, SWITZERLAND, EARLY NINETEENTH CENTURY
In the foreground at the right is an open· air café.

The revolutions came so suddenly, and were so widespread, that at first the various rulers could not resist them. They made concessions by granting, or promising to grant, what the people demanded. Even the most powerful rulers, the King of Prussia and the Emperor of Austria, had to give way at first. In Berlin the people erected barricades, and for many days the city was in a state of turmoil. On March 18, Frederick William, hoping to prevent bloodshed, came out on the balcony of his palace to speak to the people. They refused to listen, until he took off his hat as a sign of respect. So the king took off his hat and then promised to call an assembly to aid in forming a constitution for Prussia.

The Austrian Emperor Ferdinand and his famous minister, Metternich, hardly knew what to do first, since they saw revolutions in full swing everywhere they looked — in Bohemia, Hungary, Poland, Venetia-Lombardy, and even in the streets of Vienna. Metternich was so unpopular that, in fear of his life, he fled in disguise to England. The emperor made promises. He promised to permit the Bohemians to govern Bohemia as they liked. He promised the same to the Hungarians. To pacify the Germans he called an assembly to meet in Vienna to form a constitution for the empire. Vienna nevertheless remained in a state of turmoil. In May, 1848, the poor emperor removed his toppling government to Innsbruck and shortly after abdicated in favor of his young nephew, Francis Joseph.

Thus at first the revolutionary movement seemed to be successful. The people were everywhere jubilant. But these bright hopes were soon dashed. After the first few months everything went from bad to worse, and within little more than a year the entire revolutionary movement had hopelessly collapsed.

There were many reasons for the collapse of the revolutionary movements of 1848, and the reasons were somewhat different in different countries. But perhaps the chief reason in every country was that the revolutionists could not agree as to what should be done. Some were satisfied with their old hereditary rulers but wanted political privileges given to the well-to-do middle classes. Others wanted to abolish hereditary rulers altogether and have a democratic republic. Besides, the revolutionists were divided by religious differences and by racial and national hatreds. And finally, as in all revolutions, a great many people took part who did not know what they wanted — except, perhaps, to make a disturbance. The confusion and rioting and bloodshed which everywhere resulted from these divisions and hatreds made it easier for the rulers to suppress the revolutions and recover their old power in the end.

In Italy the revolution was at first directed by the Moderate middle classes, who forced the rulers to grant constitutions giving the middle classes political privileges. This did not at all satisfy the Republican followers of Mazzini, who very soon organized more violent revolutions in some places. Republics were established in Florence and Rome. Mazzini himself, after long years of exile, returned to Italy, took charge of the revolution at Rome, and for some months was the virtual ruler of the ancient city of the popes and the Caesars. This, Mazzini thought, was the beginning of the great revolution to which he had looked forward so long. He expected that the Roman republican revolution would spread to all Italy, and from Italy to all Europe.

But the result was not as Mazzini hoped. The Republican revolutions at Rome and Florence were not to the liking of the Moderate middle-class people. They were frightened by the bloodshed and turmoil that accompanied the revolutions at Rome and Florence. "This is going too far," they said. "After all, the old system was better than this." Thus many well-to-do people who had supported the movement in its early stages turned away from it and were ready to support the rulers in restoring the old forms of government.

The revolution in the Austrian Empire failed even more completely, and for similar reasons. In Bohemia, a bitter quarrel developed between the Germans and the Czechs. The German inhabitants of Bohemia wanted to be united to Germany; the Czechs wanted to keep Bohemia separate from Germany. In Hungary the Magyars were divided into the Moderates, led by Francis Deák, and the Republicans, led by Kossuth. Besides, there were many Slavic peoples in Hungary, such as the Croats and the Rumanians, who hated the Magyars as much as the Magyars hated the Austrians. In Vienna the lower-class workmen got control of the revolutionary movement, and this frightened the middle-class Moderates, who were glad enough to see the emperor recover his power in Vienna. Thus the emperor gradually recovered all his old authority, first in Bohemia, then in Italy and Austria proper, and at last in Hungary (August, 1849).

In Germany the revolutionists wanted something more than constitutional government in each of the several states. They wanted in addition *national unity* — that is, a more effective federal government for the whole of Germany. To accomplish this object the people elected a national assembly which sat at Frankfurt, and is known as the Frankfurt National Assembly (May, 1848 – May, 1849). It included many of the ablest scholars and the most distinguished political leaders of Germany. All members of the assembly were in favor of establishing a strong federal government for Germany, but they differed as to the best method of organizing such a government. There were about two hundred Republicans who wished to establish a federal republic, similar to that in the United States; but the majority was in favor of making the federation an hereditary empire. Then there was the question of whether Austria should be included in the German federation. It seemed wrong to exclude the German people of Austria; but how could the Austrian Germans be included without also including the entire Austrian Empire, with its large population of Czechs, Poles, Magyars, Croats, and other non-German peoples? This was the chief question which the Frankfurt National Assembly had to decide.

The assembly finally voted to exclude the Austrian Empire from the new German federation. A constitution was drafted which provided for a legislature consisting of an upper chamber representing the states (excluding Austria), and a lower chamber representing the people (including the Germans of Austria).

Deutsches Museum, Munich

MAIL COACH USED ON THE ROYAL BAVARIAN STATE MAIL LINE, ABOUT 1830

On March 28, 1849, it was voted that Frederick William of Prussia should be the executive head of the federal government, and a committee was appointed to invite him to approve of the constitution and take the title of German Emperor. But Frederick William refused to take the title of Emperor. The Austrian Emperor, having suppressed the revolution in Austria, made it plain that he would not permit Austria to be excluded from the new German federation if he could help it. Frederick William was unwilling to risk a war with Austria. He wanted to be Emperor of Germany but he was not willing to fight for it.

Thus the work of the Frankfurt National Assembly all went for nothing. The members gradually dispersed, and in a short time the old Confederation of 1815 was restored. Nearly all the German rulers withdrew the constitutions they had granted. But Frederick William, although he refused to approve of the constitution for the German federation, did keep his promise to grant a constitution to Prussia. The Constitution of Prussia (January, 1850) gave a great deal of power to the king, but it established a legislative parliament consisting of an upper chamber composed of peers, and a lower chamber (*Landtag*) elected by the people in such a way that the very wealthy people chose most of the members. This was not a very liberal constitution, but at least it was a constitution. It remained in force in Prussia until 1919.

How the revolutions of 1848 had important results in spite of the fact that they failed. People often learn more by failure than by success. What they usually learn by failure is to try again, or to try some other method of achieving the desired end. Perhaps the most important result of the failure of the revolutions of 1848 was that it helped to change the trend of political thought in Europe. It made people lose faith in violent revolution as a means of obtaining political liberty. Most of the things that people had tried to obtain by the revolutions of 1848 were actually obtained a few years later — between 1860 and 1875. During these years, as we shall see presently (Chapters XII–XIV), Italy won her national independence, Germany was unified under Prussian leadership, the Austrian Empire was reorganized, France became a republic, and in all these countries the people gained a share in the control of their governments. But these results were not obtained by uprisings of the people against their governments. They were obtained for the most part by the governments themselves, mainly through diplomacy and war. In the following chapters we shall learn how the people won political liberty by other means than those used in the revolutions of 1848.

QUESTIONS

1. Why is this chapter divided into three main parts? What is meant by the "Settlement of 1815"? What was the Holy Alliance? the Concert of Europe? Why did the people keep on making revolutions? How were the revolutions of 1820 suppressed?

2. What kind of government was established in France by the Charter of 1814? Who was Charles X, and how did he bring on the July Revolution of 1830? What two parties carried through the revolution? How did their ideas differ? Why was Louis Philippe chosen as king? What was accomplished by the Revolution of 1830 in France?

3. Why did the Belgians desire to be independent of Holland, and how did they win their independence? What was the "neutralization" of Belgium?

CHART FOR CHAPTER X. Showing the revival of liberal and revolutionary spirit.

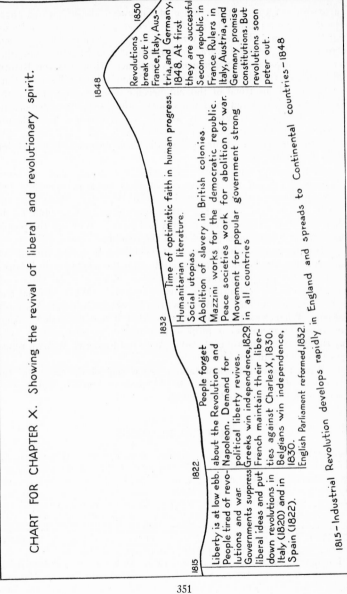

1815

Liberty is at low ebb. People tired of revolutions and war. Governments suppress liberal ideas and put down revolutions in Italy (1820) and in Spain (1822).

1822

People forget about the Revolution and Napoleon. Demand for political liberty revives. Greeks win independence,1829 French maintain their liberties against Charles X, 1830. Belgians win independence, 1830.
English Parliament reformed,1832.

1832

Time of optimistic faith in human progress. Humanitarian literature. Social utopias. Abolition of slavery in British colonies. Mazzini works for the democratic republic. Peace societies work for abolition of war. Movement for popular government strong in all countries

1848

1850

Revolutions break out in France,Italy, Austria,and Germany, 1848. At first they are successful Second republic in France. Rulers in Italy, Austria, and Germany promise constitutions. But revolutions soon peter out.

Revolutions soon peter out—1848

1815—Industrial Revolution develops rapidly in England and spreads to Continental countries—1848

4. How was the English House of Commons elected before 1832? Why did it not represent the people? Tell all you can about the Industrial Revolution in England. Why did it make a reform of Parliament more necessary? What were the three parties in England, and what were their ideas about parliamentary reform? How was the Reform Bill of 1832 carried through Parliament? What did this bill accomplish?

5. Why did the trend of thought become more hopeful after 1830? What was the humanitarian movement; the liberal and democratic political movement? Who was Mazzini, and how was his influence exerted? Describe the peace movement which took place in the first half of the nineteenth century. How did these new ideas help to bring about the revolutions of 1848?

6. Why were people dissatisfied with the government of Louis Philippe? How did the Revolution of 1848 begin in France? Tell something about Louis Blanc and his socialistic ideas. What were the "bloody June days" of 1848? How was the second republic established in France, and why did it get a bad start? Why did the people choose Louis Napoleon as president of the republic?

7. How do you explain the fact that revolutions broke out throughout Italy, Austria, and Germany immediately after the revolution in France? What was the object of all these revolutions? What political differences existed among the revolutionists in each country? What national and racial differences existed? Why was the Frankfurt National Assembly elected? What was the chief question that it had to settle? What kind of government did it propose to establish for Germany? Why was the Austrian Empire excluded? Why did Frederick William refuse the title of German Emperor?

8. Write a brief statement (about 200 words) of the causes of the revolutions of 1848 and the reasons why these revolutions were at first successful but soon completely failed.

SELECTED READINGS

Brief accounts. Robinson and Beard, *Modern Europe*, II, ch. xvii–xx. Robinson and Beard, *Outlines*, II, chs. xii–xvi. Robinson, *Western Europe*, chs. xxxix. Hazen, *Modern Europe*, chs. xvi–xviii. Hayes, *Modern Europe*, II, ch. xix. Seignobos, *Contemporary Civilization*, chs. ix–x. Ashley, *Modern Civilization*, chs. ix–xi. Schevill, *History of Europe*, chs. xx–xxiii. For more detailed treatment, see Hazen, *Europe since 1815*, chs. i–viii; G. M. Trevelyan, *British History in the Nineteenth Century*, chs. ix, xiv–xv; G. Slater, *Making of Modern England*, chs. v, vi, ix; C. K. Webster, *Congress of Vienna;* W. A. Phillips, *Confederation of Europe*.
Biography. McCabe, *Talleyrand.* G. B. Malleson, *Prince Metternich.* B. King, *Mazzini.* H. E. King, *Letters and Recollections of Mazzini.* G. M. Trevelyan, *Lord Grey of the Reform Bill.* G. M. Trevelyan, *John*

Bright. J. A. Hobson, *Cobden the International Man.* G. D. H. Cole, *Robert Owen.*

Historical novels. George Eliot, *Felix Holt.* Charles Kingsley, *Alton Locke.* Victor Hugo, *Les Misérables.* Charles Dickens, *Oliver Twist.* Nathaniel Hawthorne, *Blithedale Romance.*

Sources. Selections illustrating the revolutions of 1830 and 1848 are in the following: Anderson, *Select Documents;* Robinson and Beard, *Readings in Modern History,* I, ch. xvi, and II, chs. xix, xx; Robinson, *Readings in European History,* II, chs. xxxix–xl. For autobiographies of prominent men, see the *Memoirs* of Talleyrand and of Metternich, *The Life of Robert Owen Written by Himself,* and *The Autobiography of John Stuart Mill.* Mazzini's ideas are best given in his *Duties of Man* (Everyman's Library). The best formulation of the contemporary ideas of political liberty and popular government is in J. S. Mill's *Liberty* and his *Representative Government* (Everyman's Library). Many extracts from sources and secondary writings are given in J. F. Scott and A. Baltzly, *Readings in European History since 1814,* chs. i–iii, v.

THE ARRIVAL OF A FRENCH FAMILY AT A HOTEL
From a page of silhouettes in *L'Illustration*, 1855.

CHAPTER XI. THE SECOND EMPIRE IN FRANCE: HOW LOUIS NAPOLEON BECAME A GREAT MAN BY VIRTUE OF BEING THE NEPHEW OF HIS UNCLE

From time to time there are created men . . . in whose hands the destinies of their country are placed. I believe myself to be one of those men. NAPOLEON III

Why revolutions went out of fashion after 1850. For sixty years before 1850 there were many popular revolutions in Europe, and some of the important changes in government and society were the outcome of these revolutions. During the sixty years following 1850 there were many important changes in government and society also, but they were for the most part not brought about by popular revolutions. We may say that after 1850 popular revolutions, as a means of effecting political changes, went out of fashion.

One reason was that people were discouraged by the failure of the revolutionary upheaval of 1848. Before 1848 men had looked forward with hope and confidence to better times coming, when war and poverty would cease and people would be justly governed because they would govern themselves. Then revolutions had broken out all over Europe and for a few months the better times coming seemed to be coming with a rush, through the effort of the people to take things into their own hands. But then, quite as suddenly, the revolutions were all suppressed, and in spite of all the confusion and bloodshed, governments were even more repressive than before. Consequently people were discouraged.

354

They were inclined to say: " If freedom could ever be won by violent methods, it could have been won this time. It must be that violent revolution is not the best way to win freedom."

Besides losing faith in popular revolution as a means of bringing about better conditions, many people lost faith in the possibility of bringing about better conditions in any way. " After all," many people were inclined to say, " the world will always be what it has been — a place where the few are powerful and happy, while the many are poor and helpless." After 1850 the trend of thought was less *optimistic* and *humanitarian,* more *pessimistic* and *realistic.* This change in the trend of thought is well illustrated by the sudden popularity of the great German philosopher, Schopenhauer. In 1850 Schopenhauer was sixty-two years of age. Many years before, he had published a book called *The World as Will and Idea,* in which he maintained that life is evil and that the best anyone can do is to avoid the evil of life as much as possible by ceasing to struggle. But no one paid much attention to Schopenhauer and his pessimistic philosophy of life until after 1850, when he suddenly became popular. His books were republished, studied in the universities, and widely read, for people were now in a frame of mind to accept his pessimism. It is likely that life never seemed so good to Schopenhauer as in these later years when everyone was praising his books, which taught that life is an evil.

Thus for many years after 1850 people were more inclined to accept the world as they found it. If they did not abandon the hope of political freedom and social reform, at least they were more disposed to follow the lead of rulers and statesmen. As it happened, during the twenty-five years after 1850 three men in three countries rose to prominence and became the central figures of that time. These three were Louis Napoleon, Camillo Cavour, and Prince Bismarck. They were not opposed to political changes. They were, indeed, very much in favor of them; but they did not believe that these changes could be brought about by popular revolutions. They believed that whatever changes were made could best be made by the established governments, by means of diplomacy, war, or legislation. Since the people were in a mood to follow these great men, many of the great changes of the period from 1850 to 1875 were the outcome of the ambitions and rivalries of these three men.

In this chapter and the next two we shall study the doings of these leaders. First of all we must learn about Louis Napoleon and the second empire, which he established in France.

Why the people chose Louis Napoleon to be president of the second republic. We have already seen that the chief result of the Revolution of 1848 in France was the establishment of the second republic, and that the people of France, by an overwhelming majority, chose Louis Napoleon to be president of the republic. This meant that for some reason the people of France had great faith in Louis Napoleon. We must first of all try to understand why that was so.

Until 1848, Louis Napoleon had had a somewhat romantic career. He was the son of Louis Bonaparte, King of Holland (1806–1810), and the nephew of the great Napoleon Bonaparte. When Napoleon Bonaparte's son died in 1832, Louis Napoleon became the head of the Bonaparte family and heir to whatever claims and expectations of a political sort the family had. The claims were slight enough, since the great Napoleon had renounced the imperial title for himself and his heirs. But Louis Napoleon never quite lost the hope of some day playing a great part in the history of France. " I believe," he said on one occasion, " that from time to time there are created men whom I will call *providential*, in whose hands the destinies of their country are placed. I believe myself to be one of these men."

Louis Napoleon scarcely looked the part of a great man. Like his famous uncle, he was a short little man, with a body too long for his legs; and his large head, deep-set somber eyes, and black mustachios gave him somewhat the appearance of the villain in a melodrama who pursues but never obtains the fair lady. Indeed, until 1848 the man was something of a joke, more laughed at than feared. He started two insurrections against the Citizen King, Louis Philippe — one in 1836, one in 1840. Both were complete failures. In 1840 the French government condemned him to perpetual imprisonment at Ham, but feared him so little that he was allowed to escape to England, where he lived in exile for several years. Yet all these comic opera adventures surrounded the little man with an air of romance which made people at least take note of him.

People took note of him less for himself and his achievements than for his name. The name *Napoleon* was not one to be forgotten. Frenchmen remembered the splendid achievements of the first Napoleon and took pride in the " glory " he had conferred on France. In the dull years after 1830 they recalled the lonely figure in the white waistcoat and cocked hat on the desert isle of St. Helena, and it seemed to them that his punishment had been severe — too severe. The English had kept him prisoner there, and it was said that they had treated him badly. Many books were published about the great Napoleon. Among these was one supposed to have been written by Napoleon himself, called *Memoirs Dictated by Napoleon at St. Helena.*

Musée de Versailles

NAPOLEON III (1808–1873)
From a portrait by Flandrin, 1863.

Another was the *History of the Consulate and the Empire* by the well-known politician Adolphe Thiers. A third was a little volume by Louis Napoleon, called *Napoleonic Ideas.* The gist of these books was that Napoleon had accomplished great things for France and would have accomplished greater things still if his enemies, especially the English, had not interfered with his plans and carried him off to die on St. Helena. So there grew up in France what is called the " Napoleonic legend " — a great admiration for Napoleon Bonaparte and all that the name stood for, a kind of hero-worship which forgot most of the evil he had done and remembered chiefly the good. In 1840 his body was brought back from St. Helena and with much pomp and ceremony was interred in Paris. Visitors to Paris came daily in crowds to visit the hero's tomb, and throughout France the peasants, regarding him as a kind of demigod who had liberated them from feudal serfdom, gave his portrait the place of honor in their homes.

It was Louis Napoleon who profited by all this worship of the Napoleonic name. People contrasted the achievements of the present king, Louis Philippe, with those of Napoleon Bonaparte, to the great disadvantage of the former. They began to ask themselves: " Was not France happier and more powerful under the Bonaparte empire than it is now under the stodgy and timid Citizen King? Perhaps Louis Napoleon, whom we have laughed at, is a great man too. Perhaps it is his ' destiny,' as he says, to complete the work begun by his famous uncle. Perhaps! Who knows? " Thus it was that people came to have faith in Louis Napoleon because he bore a great name.

This was why, in 1848, seven million Frenchmen voted for Louis Napoleon to be president of the republic.

How Louis Napoleon established the second empire, 1852. From the moment he became president, Louis Napoleon set about to overthrow the republic and make himself emperor. Already popular, he became month by month more so. He often presided at public occasions and went about making speeches — very clever speeches they were, too, for Louis Napoleon knew how, by saying undisputed things in a very solemn way, to convince every class of people that he was its friend and would do what it wanted done. In this way he convinced the Catholics that he was a good friend of religion, and the business men that he was a defender of property, and the laboring men that he would protect them against the rich. And so for two years the people of France became more and more convinced that their president was a great man, whose destiny it was to accomplish some great thing for France.

But the more people admired Louis Napoleon, the less they thought of the republic of which he was president. The new republic had had a bad start. It had been born in the midst of confusion and bloodshed, and the rioting and lawlessness of the so-called Socialists in 1848 (see p. 344) had made people think that the republic was a weak form of government which would not be able to protect property or preserve order. And so it happened that in 1849, when the elections were held for members of the Chamber of Deputies, only about one-fourth of the members were Republicans. With a president who was determined to restore the Bonapartist empire, and a legislature of which the majority were monarchists, the new republic had indeed little chance of enduring.

For two years (1849–1851) the president and the Legislative Assembly quarreled over every conceivable question. The object of each was to put the other in the wrong and obtain the support of the people for its own projects. But in this quarrel the Legislative Assembly was under a great handicap because it was itself divided into hostile groups: (1) Republicans, who wanted to preserve the republic; (2) "Orleanists," who wanted to restore the Orleans monarchy; and (3) "Legitimists," who wanted to place the successor of Charles X on the throne. Louis Napoleon cleverly fostered all these quarrels and divisions in order to frustrate the efforts of the Legislative Assembly and convince the people that the republic was a failure. He urged the Legislative Assembly to pass a law greatly restricting the right to vote, and then, when the legislature did this, he made himself popular by complaining that they had tried to usurp authority by taking away the rights of the people. At last, in 1851, when his term of office was about to expire, he asked the Legislative Assembly to revise the constitution, so that he might be re-elected to the office of president. The Legislative Assembly refused to revise the constitution. Thus the final issue was this: Should Louis Napoleon retire to private life, or should he be continued in power? On this question the great majority of the people were on the side of Louis Napoleon; they did not want him to retire, any more than he wanted to himself. Knowing this very well, Louis Napoleon proceeded to carry out a *coup d'état* — a little revolution of his own.

This famous event occurred on December 2, 1851, the anniversary of the coronation of Napoleon in 1804. As president, Louis Napoleon appointed the minister of war and the minister of police, and so he had the military force in his hands. During the early morning hours the chief political leaders were arrested and imprisoned. Soldiers were stationed in the legislative chamber, and in other important points in Paris. The telegraph and the post office were taken over by the president. Meantime placards were put up in the streets stating that the president had assumed the authority of restoring universal suffrage, of dissolving the Legislative Assembly, and of calling the people to vote on a proposed revision of the constitution. The people, he said, were the " only sovereign " authority in France, and to them he would submit the quarrel between himself and the Legislative Assembly. There was some opposition in Paris to these high-handed proceedings. Three barricades were erected and 150 people killed. But the opposition was easily put down, for the mass of the people were ready to see Louis Napoleon assume authority. On December 20 the people of France, by a vote of 7,439,216 to 640,737, sanctioned the acts of the president and authorized him to revise the constitution.

The new constitution was soon prepared and published. It was carefully modeled on the first constitution, proclaimed by Napoleon in 1799 — the Constitution of the Decennial Consulate. It provided that Louis Napoleon should be president for ten years, and conferred on him the authority to govern France with the aid of a Council of State, a Senate, and a Chamber of Deputies. The Council of State was to be appointed by the president, the Senate partly so. The Chamber of Deputies was to be elected by universal suffrage, but its powers were chiefly confined to voting for or against measures presented to it by the president. In reality the new constitution made the president, Louis Napoleon, virtually the ruler of France. So little opposition was there to this form of government that Louis Napoleon soon asked the people to vote again — this time on the question of whether he should take the title of Emperor. On November 21, 1852, the people voted, 7,824,189 to 253,145, in favor of transforming the republic into an hereditary empire. On December 2, 1852, Louis Napoleon was accordingly proclaimed Napoleon III, Emperor of the French. Thus was the second empire established in France.

Why the people of France forgot about political liberty for ten years. The second empire lasted nearly twenty years — until the Franco-Prussian War of 1870. French historians commonly divide the history of this empire into two periods. The first period (1852–1860) they call the period of the " Autocratic Empire," because during these years Napoleon kept all power strictly in his own hands. The second period they call the period of the " Liberal

Empire," because during those years Napoleon gradually conceded certain powers to the Chamber of Deputies. We shall learn something about the Liberal Empire later, in connection with the Franco-Prussian War (Chapter XIV). Now we must see what Napoleon succeeded in accomplishing during the period of the Autocratic Empire.

The truth is that during the first decade of the empire Napoleon succeeded so well that the world was much astonished, and he must have been somewhat astonished himself. For ten years he was the central figure, not only of France, but of Europe as well.

The great majority of the French people eagerly welcomed the empire. After the bloody days of the Revolution of 1848, and the uncertainties and weaknesses of the republic, they were more than willing to exchange the semblance of political liberty for a government that seemed to be efficient and was certainly brilliant. No one paid much attention to the Chamber of Deputies, which deliberated in secret session and rarely ventured to oppose the projects which the emperor laid before it. It was much more interesting to watch the soldiers, in bright new red-and-blue uniforms, who were everywhere in evidence, or to read about the doings of the imperial court, which imitated as well as it could the brilliant court of the first Napoleon. Most interesting of all was the romantic figure of the emperor, who could often be seen riding with the empress in the Bois de Boulogne, or with a flourish of trumpets galloping down the avenue at the head of the Imperial Guard. The silent and self-contained little man with the somber eyes became the " Man of Destiny," the source of power and the molder of fashions. Politicians turned to him for favors, and all the smart young men noted the cut of his clothes, grew " imperials," and endeavored to cultivate mustachios as neatly waxed and pointed as might be.

Napoleon was acclaimed because he made the empire a good show, well worth watching; but that was not the only, or even the chief, reason for his power. His great success during the first ten years was due partly to his own shrewd policy, partly to fortunate circumstances. Let us see first what the fortunate circumstances were, and then what good use Napoleon made of them.

How the discovery of gold in California helped to make Napoleon a great man. Shakespeare said that " some are born great, some achieve greatness, and some have greatness thrust upon them." Many things contributed to thrust greatness upon Napoleon III. We have already mentioned some of them. He had a glamorous name. People were disgusted with the government of Louis Philippe, tired of revolution, and afraid of socialism and radical republican experiments. All these circumstances contributed to Napoleon's greatness. But the thing that probably did most to make people satisfied with Napoleon's government was the fact that the period from 1850 to 1860 was one of great business prosperity. Prices were steadily rising, and most people, having a little more free money in their pockets than usual, were quite content with things as they were. Moreover, since this new prosperity came in with Napoleon's empire, most people were likely to think that he had brought it about.

Perhaps he did. But economists are inclined to say that the business prosperity of that time was largely due to the discovery of gold in California in the year 1848. As a result of that event the amount of gold in the world was steadily increased, and as the amount of gold increased, the value of any definite amount of it — for example a dollar or a franc — declined. This meant that money, the dollar or the franc, would buy less than formerly, which is only another way of saying that prices were higher. Whatever the cause may have been, the fact remains that between 1850 and 1860 the general level of prices in France, and in other countries too, became every year a little higher. This was good for all those who had something to sell — farmers and manufacturers and shopkeepers — and for those who wished to launch new enterprises, and for the bankers who wished to lend them money for the new enterprises. The decade was a kind of " boom period," and even the laboring class profited because jobs were plentiful and wages not so bad. During this time, therefore, the majority of the people were generally able to live pretty well and pay their debts and have a little to put in the bank. So they were, for the most part, well content, and the republic seemed well lost for a government that brought prosperity in its train. Napoleon's

PARISIANS DISCUSSING THE HIGH PRICE OF BREAD, 1853

From a sketch in the *Illustrated London News*. Rising prices, which please merchants, are not pleasing to housewives with small budgets. Note the costumes of the common people and the long loaves of bread under one girl's arm. The French still make such loaves.

empire seemed to provide the people not only with a brilliant show but with the money to enjoy it.

Napoleon did not discover gold in California, nor did he create the business prosperity which followed that event; but he was shrewd enough to take advantage of favorable circumstances. He said that previous governments in France had failed because they favored one class or party at the expense of others. The government of Charles X had favored the nobles and the clergy; the government of Louis Philippe had favored the business men and bankers. Napoleon said that it would be his policy to promote the interests of all classes equally. Perhaps he did not quite do that; but at least he aimed to do something to please every class or party that might prove troublesome if he neglected it. The classes that Napoleon aimed to please, by favoring their ideas or promoting their material interests, were chiefly four: (1) the Catholic clergy; (2) the great landowners; (3) the business men; and (4) the laborers.

How Napoleon tried to please the Catholic clergy. As we have seen, one very powerful party in France was the Bourbon or Legitimist party — that is, the party that still thought Charles X had been wrongfully deposed in 1830 and still professed allegiance to the Count of Chambord, as the " legitimate " king. This party was composed chiefly of the Catholic clergy and the great landowners, especially the great landowners who were descended from the old noble families. These two groups still possessed much influence, and Napoleon knew that he must do something to disarm their opposition, at least, even if he could not win their wholehearted loyalty. He never won the support of the old nobles, but by winning the support of the clergy he split the Legitimist party in two and so undermined its influence.

Napoleon did two things especially to please the clergy and the Catholics. First of all he made himself the champion of Pope Pius IX. In 1849 Pius had been deprived of his temporal political power and exiled from Rome by Mazzini and his followers, who thereupon established the short-lived Roman Republic. In that same year, while he was still only president of the French Republic, Napoleon sent troops to Italy and helped to overthrow Mazzini's republic. It was thus partly through Napoleon's support that the papal government was restored in Rome ; and for twenty years it was largely through Napoleon's support that the Pope was able to maintain his political power. The pro-papal policy of Napoleon was naturally very pleasing to the French Catholics and especially so to the clergy.

In the second place, Napoleon did much to increase the influence of the Catholic Church in the schools. The great Revolution of 1789 had deprived the Catholic clergy of many privileges. Among these privileges none was more valued than the control of education. Ever since 1789 the public schools had been controlled by the government, and many restrictions had been placed on the establishment of private schools by the Catholics. The government of Louis Philippe had been especially " anti-clerical " in matters of education — that is, opposed to the employment of Catholic priests in the public schools and unfriendly to the private schools established by Catholics. The Catholics therefore complained bitterly that the schools of France were anti-religious, that they taught the children to be " free-thinkers," and that this was the chief reason for the growth of immorality and of dangerous political doctrines such as socialism. Napoleon pleased the clergy and the Catholics by favoring the Catholics in the schools. Certain courses in the University of Paris which they complained of (history and philosophy) were discontinued. The establishment of Catholic primary schools was made easier, so that the number of such schools rapidly increased and far more children were educated by Catholic priests.

These measures won over the majority of the Catholic clergy, who commonly acclaimed Napoleon as the champion of religion and morality.

Once he had won the clergy to his side, Napoleon had little to fear from the Legitimist party; but he did what he could to please the great landowners, especially those who belonged to the old noble families. He welcomed them at the court when they deigned to present themselves. He willingly appointed them to high office. But the chief thing Napoleon did to disarm the opposition of the old nobles was to aid them in enlarging their landed estates.

The ancient nobility of France was of course much less wealthy and powerful than it had been before 1789. During the Revolution many nobles had been deprived of their estates, and these were only partly restored in 1815. Besides, the law of inheritance established by the Civil Code (see p. 274), which required that estates should be divided upon the death of the owner, made it difficult to maintain their estates from generation to generation. The noble families felt that they could never recover their former influence in government and society unless they could become again, as they had been before 1789, a great landowning class. To increase their landed possessions was therefore one of the chief ambitions of the old noble families. Napoleon helped them to do this by making it easy for them to purchase land. A " Land Bank " (*Crédit Foncier*) was established (afterward absorbed into the Bank of France), which, at low rates of interest, made long term loans secured by mortgages on land. Many nobles made use of the

Metropolitan Museum of Art
CARICATURE OF CRINOLINE DRESSES, 1855
From a cartoon by Daumier. The first lady is finding it difficult to enter the cab.

bank to enlarge their estates, and this friendly policy diminished
the opposition of the old aristocracy to the empire.

How Napoleon tried to please the business men and the laborers.
Napoleon was not a man to harbor grievances or to punish enemies
for the fun of it. A vindictive man, in his place, would have found
many enemies to punish. He had suffered great humiliations
under the government of Louis Philippe, and Louis Philippe had
notoriously governed in the interest of the business men and the
bankers. Napoleon exiled the Orleanist princes and confiscated
their estates, but he showed no hostility toward the business men
and bankers who had supported the Orleanist government. On
the contrary, he made a special effort to promote the interests of
this powerful class.

For example, although convinced that free trade would prove
beneficial to France in the long run, Napoleon maintained for some
years the tariffs and other restrictions on imports, because he knew
that the manufacturing class was favorable to such restrictions.

He revised the patent and bankruptcy laws so that the owners of industries would profit more if their enterprises proved successful and suffer less if they failed.   Above all, Napoleon was interested in the success of great public enterprises, such as the building of railroads, steamships, and telegraph lines.   It is difficult to realize that in Napoleon's day locomotives and steamships were novelties, much as the airplane is in our day.   Many people could not see that they would ever replace sailing ships and wagons as the chief means of travel and transportation.   Someone said that the railroads were after all " only rich men's toys," which the people as a whole could hardly be expected to pay for.   But Napoleon was convinced that steam and electricity were the forces of the future — that they would revolutionize industry and the conditions of life — and he was eager to use the power of the government to help this revolution along.

One of the difficulties was that the new enterprises (railroads, steamships, telegraph lines) required for their development a great deal of money — more than the ordinary capitalist or corporation possessed or was willing to risk.   To meet this difficulty Napoleon assisted in promoting an institution known as the " Commercial Bank " (*Crédit Mobilier*).   It was not quite like an ordinary bank, but rather a joint-stock company which made loans and issued notes.   People invested their money in it by buying shares which paid annual dividends ; but it was especially designed to loan large sums of money, at low rates of interest, for the promotion of great industrial enterprises and public works.   Among other things, it supplied much of the capital for extending the French railroads and its telegraph service, for establishing transatlantic steamship lines, for rebuilding Paris, and for consolidating the gas companies that lighted the capital.

For six or eight years the Commercial Bank was a tremendous success — a kind of Aladdin's lamp which turned everything into gold.   People who bought shares in 1852, at 500 francs a share, were able to sell them in 1855 at 1982 francs per share ; or if they kept their shares, they received that year a dividend of 178 francs per share, which was much the same as lending money at 35% interest.   No doubt the institution was a somewhat speculative affair, which could not go on forever making a great deal out of a little. But for many years it created at least the illusion of unprecedented business activity and prosperity. The many people who doubled their money in it were well content with the empire and still more content with the little emperor who seemingly had only to wave his wand, like a wonderful magician in a fairy tale, in order to bring shining coins and crisp notes into everybody's pocket.

Napoleon did not forget the laboring classes either — the peasant farmers and the industrial workers. He always professed a great interest in the " social question " — the question of the poor and what to do with them. In 1844, when he was imprisoned in the fortress at Ham and time was heavy on his hands, he wrote a little book called the *Abolition of Poverty*. He said that just as the great achievement of Christianity had been to abolish slavery and the great mission of the Revolution of 1789 had been to abolish serfdom, so the great mission of the democratic revolution of the nineteenth century was to abolish poverty. For the first time in history this could be done, he said, because modern science and mechanical inventions made it possible to increase the production of wealth to the point where everyone could have enough. But the poor could never get their share through socialism. They could get their share only through a government strong enough and intelligent enough to make proper laws for increasing the production and regulating the distribution of wealth.

The empire was such a government — so Napoleon said. He called his empire a " democratic empire." He possessed autocratic power, to be sure, but he said that this power had been freely conferred upon him by the vote of the people. Thus his empire was democratic because his great power was derived from the popular will. For this reason it was above all the mission of his empire to solve the social question, which it would do by ruthlessly suppressing foolish movements like socialism and making whatever laws were necessary in order that the mass of the working people might get their fair share of the good things of life.

Napoleon did not really do much for the peasants. But then he didn't need to. The steadily rising prices made good times for them. They thought him a great man anyway, because his name was Napoleon, and they were all the more inclined to support him because the village priests told them that he was a friend of religion and the church.

The laborers in the towns called for more attention than the peasants. Wages were going up, but not so rapidly as the cost of living. Besides, it was chiefly among the town laborers that the dangerous doctrine of socialism made its converts, and they were the people who were most likely to support revolutions against the government. So Napoleon did what he could to help the laboring class. With the money obtained from the confiscated Orleanist estates he built some model workingmen's cottages. He permitted the laborers to form labor unions for certain purposes. He made a law providing for the settlement of wage disputes by arbitration. But the most important thing Napoleon did to help the laboring class was to undertake a great number of public improvements, thus creating a greater demand for labor of all sorts. It was during Napoleon's time that much of the old city of Paris was virtually rebuilt. Scores of houses were torn down, streets were widened, and parks were laid out, all according to the splendid design of a French magistrate by the name of Baron Haussmann. The most striking part of Paris as we see it today, from the Louvre to the Arc de Triomphe, owes much of its surpassing beauty to the reconstruction designed and partly carried out during the reign of Napoleon III. All this building greatly increased the demand for labor, tended to increase wages, and thereby helped to keep the workingmen of Paris contented. Incidentally, of course, widening the streets made it less easy to build barricades, in case the laboring class felt disposed to begin another revolution.

Thus, by a combination of favorable circumstances and shrewd measures, Napoleon established his empire on a firm foundation between 1852 and 1860. During the same period he managed also to become the most influential person in international affairs, the central figure of European diplomacy. We must see now how this came about.

How Napoleon talked about peace but soon made war: The Crimean War, 1853–1856. Many people are opposed to war when

FRENCH REGIMENT EMBARKING ON THE ST. VINCENT AT CALAIS
From the *Illustrated London News*, 1854. The St. Vincent was an English ship
used as a troop ship during the Crimean War.

there isn't any. They think rightly that war is a useless waste
of life and property. Yet when circumstances are favorable to
war, most people rush eagerly into it, forgetting that it is a useless waste of life and property. Napoleon was like other people
in that — he talked peace but made war.

Napoleon talked peace partly because he wished to reassure the
great powers of Europe. In 1852 the great powers were not much
in favor of Napoleon's empire. They remembered that the first
Napoleon had spent much of his time in making wars of conquest.
They remembered that in 1815 they had signed a treaty never to
permit the Bonaparte dynasty to be restored in France. But
now the Napoleonic empire was re-established, and the great
powers were asking themselves, " Will Napoleon begin at once to
make wars of conquest, following the example of his great uncle? "
Napoleon knew well that if he showed any intention of trying to
conquer Belgium or the left bank of the Rhine, the great powers
would combine against him. He knew that inside and outside

France people were saying, "The empire means war!" In the years 1851–1852 Napoleon therefore made a great point of denying this. "A spirit of distrust leads certain persons to say that the empire means war; but I say that the empire means peace." He repeated this many times. The only conquests the empire would make, he said, were the conquests of peace.

Peace or no peace, Napoleon wished to play a part in European affairs. One of the chief objections to the former government of Louis Philippe was that the Citizen King had been too timid in dealing with other countries, so that France had lost its former influence and prestige. Besides, Napoleon was trying to follow in the footsteps of the great Napoleon, and he felt that the second empire would be a little ridiculous if it did not do something to carry on the traditions of the first empire. He felt that the successor of Napoleon Bonaparte must be a big man in Europe as well as in France. Louis Napoleon was therefore bound to take a hand in the affairs of Europe somehow, and he was not averse, even, to a little war, if one could be staged in such a way as not to unite all the great powers against him.

The opportunity for his little war came in connection with the "Eastern question" — the perennial question of the Ottoman (Turkish) Empire in Europe. It had long been the ambition of Russia to weaken the Ottoman Empire by extending her influence in the Balkan countries, with the ultimate object of getting possession of Constantinople. In 1853 a quarrel arose between Napoleon and the Turkish government over the "Holy Places" in Palestine. Partly in order to please the Catholics in France Napoleon claimed, on the basis of an old treaty of 1740, the right of maintaining certain places connected with the birth of Christ in behalf of the Roman Catholics who made pilgrimages there. The sultan made some concessions to Napoleon in this matter, whereupon the Tsar Nicholas claimed, on the basis of an old treaty of 1774, the right of protecting the Greek Catholics throughout the Ottoman Empire. The sultan, on the advice of France and Great Britain, refused to grant this right. The tsar then sent Russian troops into the Turkish provinces of Moldavia and Walachia (modern Rumania), and when he refused to withdraw the troops, the Turkish govern-

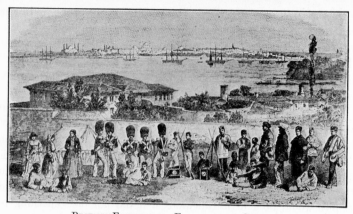

BRITISH FOOTGUARDS ENCAMPED AT SCUTARI
From an early daguerreotype. The heavy shakos must have been hot, besides
being excellent targets for the enemy.

ment declared war on Russia (1853). Great Britain and France
then sent their fleets into the Black Sea and shortly after also
declared war on Russia (1854). Thus began the Crimean War, in
which the Tsar Nicholas found himself fighting with three powers
— Turkey, France, and Great Britain.

The tsar had not counted on so many enemies. He despised
Napoleon and had not supposed, in any case, that France would
go to war over the Turkish question, in which it had no real interest. He knew well that Great Britain was opposed to his projects
against Turkey, but he had thought it would be possible to make a
bargain with that country which would keep her out of the war.
In 1853 he had said to the British ambassador that Turkey was
the " sick man " of Europe, that the sick man was bound to die
soon, and that Russia and Great Britain might well divide the
remains between them. He had proposed, therefore, that Great
Britain should take Egypt and Crete, whereas the tsar, for his part,
would occupy Constantinople temporarily and organize the Balkan
countries as independent states under Russian protection. Great
Britain had refused to make this deal, but the tsar apparently
thought that she would now stand aside until Russia had defeated
Turkey and then go in for her share.

The tsar was therefore much surprised when he found himself at war with France and Great Britain as well as with Turkey. To make matters worse, Austria threatened to join the allies unless the Russian troops were withdrawn from the Turkish provinces. After a confused and indecisive campaign the tsar accordingly withdrew his troops from Moldavia and Walachia. The cause of the war was thus removed, and the war itself seemingly at an end.

But Great Britain and France were not yet satisfied. Although the British ministry was divided on the question, the war spirit was strong among the people, who demanded that the ambitious tsar should be taught a lesson. Napoleon, especially, was not satisfied. He had a personal grudge against the Tsar Nicholas because Nicholas had not yet fully recognized the imperial government in France. Nicholas, in his official correspondence, would not address Napoleon as " My Brother," which was the proper way, but only as " My dear Friend," which was quite improper. Besides, Napoleon had not as yet won any glory for himself or gained any prestige for France out of the war. He was therefore all for continuing the war until some humiliating defeat was inflicted upon Russia, such as might compensate for the humiliation of the Russian invasion of France in 1814–1815. Great Britain and France accordingly decided to make a conquest of Sevastopol. Sevastopol was the great Russian naval base on the north shore of the Black Sea, in the region of Crimea. By taking Sevastopol, France and Great Britain would deprive Russia of its chief foothold on the Black Sea, and of the naval base which was essential for any future attack upon Constantinople.

Thus the war which started as a quarrel between Russia and Turkey over Moldavia and Walachia, ended as a French and British expedition for the conquest of Sevastopol. The undertaking proved far more difficult than either power expected. The British and French fleets were unable to enter the port of Sevastopol because the Russians had sunk battleships in the harbor, so that it was necessary to send armies inland to take the city from behind. For eleven months the city was besieged; but at last, in September, 1855, after a murderous assault, it was taken. To take Sevastopol and win this little war required the sacrifice of more than

TURKISH FORT OF FIDIEH-TABIASSI

From the *Illustrated London News*, 1854. View of the town and plain of
Schmula. Note the crescent on the flag.

half a million men, a great number of whom died from sickness
occasioned by infected food and inadequate sanitary and hospital
facilities. At the close of the war an international congress was
assembled at Paris in order to arrange the terms of peace.

**The Congress of Paris of 1856, and how it conferred glory on
Napoleon.** The Congress of Paris was composed of representatives from all the countries which had taken part in the war, and
of some, such as Austria, which had taken no part. It required
nearly a month for the distinguished representatives of all these
countries to give final and formal sanction to the treaties, the terms
of which had for the most part already been determined before
the congress assembled. The principal provisions of the treaties
of the Congress of Paris of 1856 were the following:

1. The Black Sea was declared to be " neutralized " — that
is, no country was to be permitted in future to send war vessels
into it, or maintain forts or arsenals on its shores, but every country was to be free to send its merchant vessels into it.

2. The Danube River was declared to be freely open to navigation by the ships of all countries.

3. The provinces of Moldavia and Walachia were declared to be autonomous — that is, free to govern themselves, but bound to recognize the " suzerainty " of the Sultan of Turkey.

4. The Ottoman Empire was admitted to the " European Concert " — that is, for the first time the Turkish government was recognized by the international law of Europe as possessing equal rights and obligations with the other European powers. The great powers agreed further to recognize and guarantee the independence and territorial integrity of the Ottoman Empire, in return for which the sultan expressed his intention to deal justly in the future with " the Christian population of his empire."

The Crimean War and the Congress of Paris conferred great " glory " on Napoleon. For a month many distinguished statesmen and diplomats were gathered at Paris and were welcomed and entertained by Napoleon, who was the host of the occasion, and who presided at the sessions of the congress. No sovereign could longer refuse to " recognize " the emperor after accepting his hospitality, or neglect to address Napoleon as " My Brother." In all this business Napoleon played so conspicuous and distinguished a part that he felt he was now the big man of Europe who could, like the first Napoleon, safely meddle in European affairs for the benefit of all peoples and the greater glory of France.

It is not very clear what part Napoleon hoped to play in European affairs; but he had apparently a real conviction that it would be a good thing if the oppressed peoples could realize their aspirations for national unity and independence. He was shrewd enough to see, what was true, that the sentiment of nationalism was one of the strongest forces of the time. This sentiment was especially strong in Italy, in Germany, in Poland, and in the countries that made up the Austrian Empire. Napoleon therefore dreamed much, and talked quite a little, about helping oppressed nations to win their freedom. At least he often expressed his sympathy for the national aspirations of the Italians, the Germans, and the Poles.

But all this sympathy with oppressed peoples was united with a strong desire to increase the power of France. Napoleon thought, as most statesmen do, that the more powerful his own country was, the better it would be for mankind. It seemed to Napoleon that the country in whose affairs he could take a hand with the best chance of increasing the power of France, and, at the same time, of doing something for oppressed peoples, was Italy. He therefore often expressed his particular sympathy with the Italians in their desire for national independence. " Something must be done for the Italians," he said; and he said it so often without doing anything that at last, in 1858, an Italian patriot, Orsini, attempted to assassinate Napoleon as a kind of reminder that he had as yet done nothing for Italian freedom. Far from exhibiting any vindictiveness against Orsini, Napoleon professed to see something providential in his act. He took it as a sign that now was the accepted time to do something for the Italians, and immediately afterward he set about in earnest to help the Italians win their independence from Austria.

This brings us to the next great event in European history — the freeing of Italy from Austrian domination and the establishment of the Kingdom of Italy (1861). It also brings us to the second of the three great personalities who played an important part in the history of this time — Count Camillo Cavour. In the next chapter we shall learn something about Cavour, and how he managed to achieve the political unification of Italy, and what part Napoleon played in that great event.

QUESTIONS

1. Why was Louis Napoleon popular in France? What was the "Napoleonic legend"? Why was the second republic unpopular? What was the *coup d'état* of 1851? What were the essential features of the constitution of the second empire?

2. How did the discovery of gold in California in 1848 make it easier for Louis Napoleon to establish his power and popularity? What measures did he adopt to please the Catholics? to please the business men? to please the working classes? What was the *Crédit Foncier?* the *Crédit Mobilier?* Why did Louis Napoleon wish to rebuild Paris?

3. What was the cause of the Crimean War? Why did Louis Napoleon become involved in it? Why is it called the "Crimean" War? What were the provisions of the Peace of Paris in 1856?

4. Why did Louis Napoleon wish to play an important part in European politics? Why was he especially interested in Italian affairs?

CHART FOR CHAPTER XI. Rise of Louis Napoleon to power, 1840-1860.

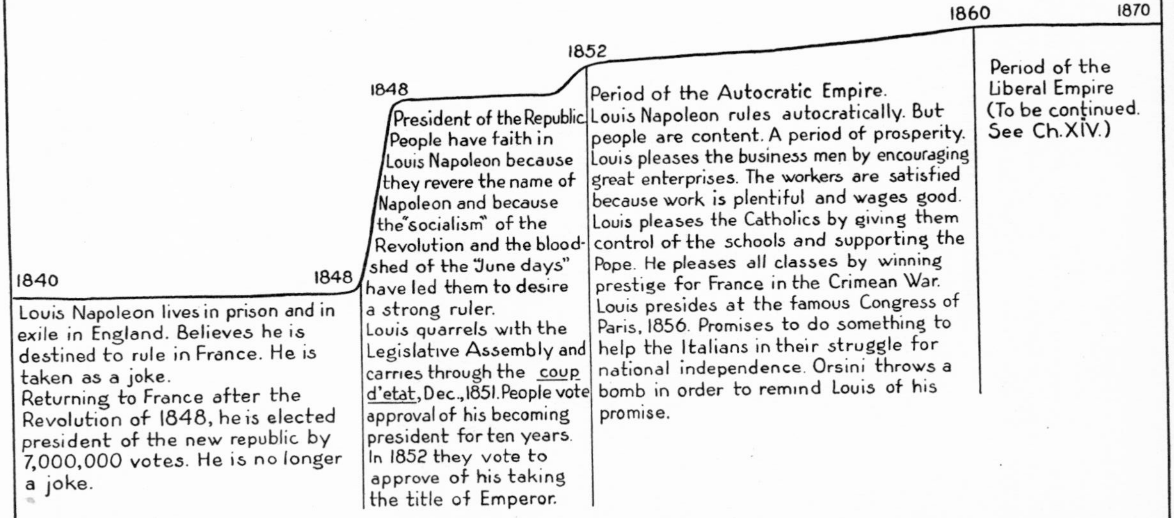

1840

Louis Napoleon lives in prison and in exile in England. Believes he is destined to rule in France. He is taken as a joke.
Returning to France after the Revolution of 1848, he is elected president of the new republic by 7,000,000 votes. He is no longer a joke.

1848

President of the Republic. People have faith in Louis Napoleon because they revere the name of Napoleon and because the "socialism" of the Revolution and the bloodshed of the "June days" have led them to desire a strong ruler.
Louis quarrels with the Legislative Assembly and carries through the coup d'etat, Dec., 1851. People vote approval of his becoming president for ten years. In 1852 they vote to approve of his taking the title of Emperor.

1852

Period of the Autocratic Empire. Louis Napoleon rules autocratically. But people are content. A period of prosperity. Louis pleases the business men by encouraging great enterprises. The workers are satisfied because work is plentiful and wages good. Louis pleases the Catholics by giving them control of the schools and supporting the Pope. He pleases all classes by winning prestige for France in the Crimean War. Louis presides at the famous Congress of Paris, 1856. Promises to do something to help the Italians in their struggle for national independence. Orsini throws a bomb in order to remind Louis of his promise.

1860

Period of the Liberal Empire (To be continued. See Ch. XIV.)

1870

377

Was Orsini's attempt to assassinate Louis Napoleon an important event? If so, why? If not, why not?

5. How long did the second empire last? Why do we turn aside from the story of the second empire in 1859 to take up the story of Cavour and Italian independence?

SELECTED READINGS

Brief accounts. Robinson and Beard, *Modern Europe*, II, 57-72. Robinson and Beard, *Outlines*, II, 381-392. Hazen, *Modern Europe*, ch. xix. Hayes, *Modern Europe*, II, 149-163. Seignobos, *Contemporary Civilization*, ch. xi. Hazen, *Europe since 1815*, ch. ix. Schapiro, *European History* (revised ed.) ch. xiii. Seignobos, *Europe since 1814*, ch. vi. An interesting book on the growing popularity of Louis Napoleon is A. L. Guerard, *Reflections on the Napoleonic Legend.*

Biography. P. Guedalla, *The Second Empire.* (More of a biography than a history.) F. A. Simpson, *The Rise of Louis Napoleon.* F. H. Cheetham, *Louis Napoleon.* (An account of his life until 1848.) A. Forbes, *Napoleon the Third.*

Sources. Robinson and Beard, *Readings in Modern History*, II, ch. xix, sec. 59. Anderson, *Select Documents.* (Contains the official decrees of the *coup d'état* of 1851 and the constitution of the empire.) Napoleon was described by some contemporaries who admired him and by others who despised him. Among the former were his American dentist, T. W. Evans (see the *Memoirs of Dr. Thomas W. Evans*), and the English economist, N. W. Senior (see *Conversations with Distinguished Persons During the Second Empire*). Among the latter was Victor Hugo, who wrote *The History of a Crime* (the *coup d'état* of 1851) and *Napoleon the Little.* Many of Napoleon's writings are in *The Life and Writings of Louis Napoleon*, 2 vols. Illustrative extracts from the sources: Scott and Baltzly, *Readings in European History*, ch. vii, sec. 1.

The French Army Arriving at Maglianella, Siege of Rome, 1849
From a drawing by Raffet.

CHAPTER XII. THE UNIFICATION OF ITALY, 1859–1870: HOW CAVOUR DID WHAT MAZZINI WISHED TO DO, IN A WAY THAT MAZZINI NEVER WOULD HAVE DONE IT

Anyone can govern by martial law. CAVOUR

I am free; free because I am a man, made in God's image, inherently possessing in myself the powers and aspirations and destinies of all humanity. MAZZINI

How the way was prepared for the work of Cavour. The great event in Italian history during the nineteenth century was the unification of Italy — that is, the union of all the small states (except the tiny Republic of San Marino with a total population of about eleven thousand, which still exists) into one Kingdom of Italy. This great event was accomplished between 1859 and 1870; and the man who stands out as the principal figure in its accomplishment is Cavour. Mazzini dreamed of a united democratic Italian Republic. More than any other man, he inspired the Italians with the desire for Italian unity. But it was Cavour who really did most to unite Italy, although his united Italy was neither a republic nor strictly democratic.

As we already know, Italy had long been politically divided into many states. Since 1815 the chief divisions had been: Lombardy-Venetia, which was a province of the Austrian Empire;

the Kingdom of Sardinia; the duchies of Modena and Parma; the Grand Duchy of Tuscany; the Papal States; and the Kingdom of Naples and Sicily. In none of these, except Sardinia after 1849, did the people have any share in the government; and in all of them, except in Sardinia, the tyrannical governments were maintained against the wishes of the people, largely through the influence of Austria.

Ever since 1815, and even before that time, the Italians had been greatly dissatisfied with this state of affairs. They had long asked themselves these questions: " Why is it that the French people and the English people have been for centuries united under one government, and have therefore been great powers, while the Italians are divided into many governments, none of which has any importance in the world? Why is it that the French and the English have won political freedom, while the Italians are subject to tyrants? Are not we a capable and an intelligent people too — as capable and intelligent as the French or the English? " They remembered that in ancient times the Romans governed the world; that in medieval times Italy was the home of free republics; and that in the sixteenth century Italians were the intellectual leaders of Europe. " How is it," they asked themselves, " that in these advanced days of scientific progress and political liberty we count for nothing? "

To these questions the Italians found one sufficient answer. The chief reason for their present weakness, they said, was that for three centuries Italy had been the prey of foreigners; for three hundred years Spain, or Austria, or France, or all of them together, had invaded and plundered and made use of the country for their own ends. In the nineteenth century it was Austria that was keeping them in subjection. Therefore, in order to win that political importance in Europe to which they were entitled, they must first of all free themselves from Austrian domination and then establish a single strong government for all of Italy. Once Italy was free and politically united they would play a great part in Europe, as the English and the French had done.

No one had done so much as Mazzini to inspire the Italians with the desire for national independence and unity. But Mazzini's plans had all failed, and after the collapse of the revolutions of 1848 Italian patriots had less faith in Mazzini and were inclined to think that their objects could be attained only by following the lead of some one of the Italian governments. There was only one government in Italy which could or would take the lead in the movement for Italian freedom. That government was the government of Victor Emmanuel II, King of Sardinia (the Piedmont); and after 1848 Italian patriots more and more rallied round the Kingdom of Sardinia as their proper leader.

For this there were two principal reasons: (1) The Kingdom of Sardinia was governed by a native Italian dynasty which alone of all the ruling houses in Italy was not subject to Austrian influence. Charles Albert, the father of Victor Emmanuel II, had led the war against Austria in 1848–1849, and in 1849 had granted a constitution which Victor Emmanuel had kept, so that Sardinia was the only

Photo Alinari

VICTOR EMMANUEL II (1820–1878)

In twenty-one years Victor Emmanuel rose from King of Sardinia to the head of a united Italy. He is here shown in the uniform of a general.

Italian state that possessed a liberal government. Thus Italian patriots naturally turned to the only government that was hostile to Austria and that was liberal in form. (2) In 1852 Count Camillo Cavour became the prime minister of Victor Emmanuel; and Cavour not only passionately desired to win national independence and unity for Italy, but he had a definite practical program for doing so. It was Cavour, above all, who won over the Italian patriots to follow the lead of Sardinia.

Who was this remarkable man, Cavour?

Count Camillo Cavour (1810–1861): What manner of man he was, and especially how he differed from Mazzini. Cavour was born in Turin in 1810, of noble parents. Educated at a military school, he became at the age of sixteen an officer of engineers.

Afterwards imprisoned for his liberal political views, he resigned from the army in 1831 and for the next seventeen years devoted himself to managing the family estates near Turin. Cavour was a born manager. He had what is called a practical mind — a mind interested in things and affairs and easily capable of master-

CAVOUR (1810–1861)

Considered by some historians the greatest statesman of the nineteenth century.

ing the details of any business. During these years Cavour therefore learned all about soils and crops and how to reduce the cost and increase the profits of a large agricultural enterprise. This experience was important for Cavour's later political career. It made him a rich man, and because he was a rich man the wealthy and powerful people of Italy had more confidence in him as a political leader. They thought that he could not be a " visionary idealist," like Mazzini, since he had been so successful in managing a large farm. Being a rich man, Cavour was himself less likely to harbor any dangerous political ideas. He was more likely to have the ideas which rich men are likely to have, and to think that the well-to-do are more to be trusted with political power than the poor and improvident. Besides, all this experience in managing his estates made it easier for Cavour, when he became the first minister of Victor Emmanuel, to manage the affairs of the government.

During this long time when he was managing his estates, Cavour never lost interest in politics. He often visited France and England. For England especially Cavour had a great admiration. He knew English history and was familiar with the political and social customs of England. He sat for days in the gallery of the House of Commons watching the performance and endeavoring, like Peter the Great at an earlier time, to master the practical working of the British system of parliamentary government. This system of government, in which the wealthy and educated people shared with the king in making the laws, was the kind Cavour wanted for his own country. " If I were an Englishman," he said at this time, " my name would not now be wholly unknown." Like most great men, Cavour wished to be known for having done some great thing. He felt that with his wealth and talents he could win renown for himself and do something worth while for his country in a political way, if only his country possessed a form of government which would give him an opportunity.

At the first opportunity Cavour therefore took an active part in political life. That opportunity came in 1847, when the censorship of the press was abolished in his country. He began by establishing a newspaper, *Il Risorgimento*, in which he advocated a constitutional government for the Kingdom of Sardinia and afterwards favored the war in 1848–1849 for the liberation of Italy from Austrian domination. In this way he made a name for himself as a liberal patriot, an ardent nationalist, and a man of great knowledge and astuteness in political affairs. And so, in 1850, soon after a constitutional government had been established, Victor Emmanuel made Cavour minister of commerce and agriculture. It was the least important office in the king's ministry. But Victor Emmanuel, who was a shrewd judge of men, said to his prime minister, D'Azeglio, " I warn you that this man who enters the cabinet by the little back door will soon turn you all out." The warning proved true. Cavour knew so much more than the other ministers and exhibited so much more energy, capacity for work, and practical ability, that two years later the king made him prime minister.

From that moment Cavour was virtually the director of Victor Emmanuel's government, and Victor Emmanuel's government was the center of the movement for Italian independence and unity. What then was Cavour's plan for the liberation of Italy, and how did it differ from that of Mazzini?

No two men of the same nation could well differ more than Cavour and Mazzini. Mazzini was a slender man with a thin face and large, somber, serious eyes. He looked what he was — the orator, the poet, the philosopher. Mazzini wrote poetry; his political papers dealt with general ideas and the philosophy of government and human rights; his speeches were moving appeals addressed to the emotions of men. He believed that few, if any, existing governments would do any good thing for human liberty, and that Italian freedom could be won only by the people themselves, by means of popular revolutions which would destroy the existing governments and establish in their places a democratic

MAZZINI (1805-1872)

republic. Cavour was the opposite of Mazzini in all this. Cavour was a short, stocky man, with a big round head, shrewd eyes that seemed to be keeping secrets behind half-closed lids, and a firm but good-natured mouth which seemed to say, " Now let's get down to business." Cavour's big round head was full of facts and figures. He wrote no poetry; Italian though he was, he cared nothing for music; and if he read philosophy, it was rather as a relaxation than as a guide to practical life. His speeches

and his writings were concerned with economics, with business and agriculture, the details of legislative measures, and the practical aspects of political or diplomatic action. Cavour was essentially a man of affairs rather than of ideas. A friend said of Cavour that his mind was " always at the level of events." This describes Cavour. He was a strong swimmer in the sea of actual circumstances, never submerged by them, always breasting them easily, but rarely raising his eyes to the heavens seeking the unattainable. Cavour counseled men to make the most of the actual world. Mazzini endeavored to lift them to the level of a better one.

Cavour's plan for the unification of Italy was therefore far more practical, far less idealistic, than that of Mazzini. Cavour had but little faith in undirected revolution initiated by the people.

He believed that Italian unity must be achieved, if at all, under the direction of the Kingdom of Sardinia, supported by the rest of Italy and aided by some foreign power such as France. Briefly, therefore, Cavour's plan was: first, to make war on Austria and drive her out of Italy; and second, to unite all of Italy under a constitutional monarchy, with Victor Emmanuel as king of Italy.

But careful preparations had to be made before Sardinia could wage war against Austria with any hope of success. From 1852 to 1859, Cavour was chiefly engaged in these preparations. He had to do four things: (1) strengthen Sardinia and give it a liberal government which the moderate party throughout Italy would approve; (2) win the support of the Republican followers of Mazzini to his project for unification; (3) make a treaty of alliance with Napoleon III; (4) bring about a war with Austria without any intervention on the part of the European powers. Let us consider these points in order.

Cavour's preparations: (1) How he strengthened Sardinia and gave it a good name among the moderate Liberals throughout Italy. Cavour had first of all to give Sardinia a government of which the middle-class Liberals throughout Italy would approve. This was congenial work for him, because he was himself a genuine Liberal. He sympathized neither with the nobles who distrusted all liberal government however conservative it might be, nor with the Republicans who distrusted all monarchical government however liberal it might be. Cavour, like the middle-class Liberals throughout Italy, wanted some such government as England had, in which the king and his ministers were responsible to Parliament, and in which the Parliament was controlled by the people of property.

When Cavour became prime minister he therefore carried on the government according to the English practice. He assumed that he could not remain prime minister unless his measures were supported by a majority in the parliament. He relied for support upon the moderate parties of the Center; and in order to obtain their support he passed laws that were favorable to the middle-class people whom these parties represented. He therefore formulated measures for restricting the privileges of the Catholic

Church, for improving agriculture, for extending the railways, for making Genoa one of the finest ports on the Mediterranean, and for promoting business prosperity by protective tariffs and favorable commercial treaties. He strictly maintained the constitutional rights of freedom of speech and of the press and of religion.

ITALIAN MONEY-CHANGER

From a sketch by Dura. This woman makes change for people in the street. The little booth hold her bags of money.

During the years 1852–1859 he built up a well-equipped and well-trained army of about 50,000 men.

In this way Cavour soon succeeded in giving the little Kingdom of Sardinia a good name abroad as well as at home. Throughout Europe, but especially in Italy, people of liberal views were watching Cavour and his work. "Here at last," they said, " is one Italian state that is decently governed and is strong enough to take care of itself without the aid of a foreign power. This little country is becoming prosperous. It has good roads, and business is thriving. Above all, this is the one Italian state where a man is free to say what he likes without fear of arrest. All this is because it has a constitutional government in which the people have a voice in making the laws." This is what the moderate Liberals throughout Italy were saying. " This," they said, " is what we have always wanted for all Italy, and if Cavour is aiming to give Italy this kind of government we are for him."

Cavour's preparations: (2) How he won the support of the Republican followers of Mazzini. The Republican followers of Mazzini were less easily won over. Mazzini himself and some of his followers were never won over. Mazzini was too much opposed to monarchical government in any form. He thought that Italy united under a monarchy would still be unfree. He could not be convinced that Cavour was a sincere patriot who was working for the welfare of the people. He thought him only a clever politician who was serving the ambitions of the ruling dynasty of Sardinia.

But there were many Republicans whose desire for the union of Italy was stronger than their desire for a republican government. The leader of these was Daniele Manin. Manin was a Venetian, one of the wisest and most disinterested of the Italian patriots. He had taken a leading part in the Revolution of 1848 in Venice, and in establishing the short-lived Republic of Venice. After the failure of that venture he lived in exile, still a Republican and still working devotedly for Italian freedom. He was an admirer of Mazzini and had formerly been his loyal disciple; but by 1855 Manin was beginning to think that Italian unity could never be achieved under Mazzini's leadership or by Mazzini's methods. He was therefore ready to abandon the ideal of a republic for Cavour's ideal of a constitutional monarchy, if he could be sure that Cavour aimed to establish a united Kingdom of Italy and not merely an enlarged Kingdom of Sardinia. Many Republicans throughout Italy thought as Manin did, and in 1855 he issued on their behalf a famous manifesto, which read in part as follows:

The Republican party again . . . performs an act of abnegation and sacrifice on behalf of the national cause. Convinced that before everything *Italy must be made*, it says to the House of Savoy [the government of Victor Emmanuel]: "Make Italy and we are with you! If not, not." It says to the constitutionalists [to Cavour]: "Plan to make Italy and not to aggrandize Piedmont; be Italian patriots, and not exclusively Piedmontese, and we are with you! If not, not."

This manifesto made a great impression, and the phrase " if not, not " became a kind of motto of those Republicans who were ready to abandon Mazzini for Cavour.

Cavour did all he could to encourage this movement among the Republicans. He had conferences with Manin and assured him that what he wished to do was to establish a united Kingdom of Italy, and that when this was done the Kingdom of Sardinia would cease to exist. In 1857 Manin took the lead in forming a "National Society " of Italian patriots for helping on the cause. Cavour was delighted with this project. As prime minister of King Victor

Emmanuel, Cavour could not, of course, have open dealings with professed Republicans who were conspiring to overthrow their own governments. But early in the morning, before daybreak, Joseph La Farina, one of Manin's friends, used to come to Cavour's study by a private stairway to talk over the plans of the National Society. " Go ahead and prosper," Cavour is reported to have said to La Farina. " But if you fail, or if I am molested on your account by the Chamber or by Diplomacy, I shall be forced to deny you like Peter."

The National Society went ahead, and it prospered. It kept secretly in touch with Cavour, and it became the organization which won over a great body of Republican patriots to support the projects of Cavour.

Cavour's preparations: (3) How he made a bargain with Napoleon to fight Austria, and how his ideas and those of Napoleon differed as to what would come of it. Cavour had long foreseen that he would some day need Napoleon's aid. That was why, in 1855, he sent 15,000 Sardinian troops to help Napoleon fight in the Crimean War. Many of his countrymen thought this a foolish thing to do, since Sardinia had no interest in the Crimea. But Cavour wished to win the gratitude of Napoleon, and he wished to have little Sardinia represented in the peace congress at Paris. There he managed to raise the " Italian question " and to lay before the assembled diplomats the wretched condition of the Italians, which he made them understand was due to Austrian interference. Old Prince Metternich, the famous Austrian statesman, watching these events, said, " There is only one diplomat in Europe, but unfortunately he is against us. He is M. de Cavour."

Thus the stout little man laid his schemes to win the support of Napoleon. He succeeded. Napoleon was grateful for Cavour's support in the Crimea, and we have already seen that in 1858, after the attempt of Orsini to assassinate him, he determined to " do something for the Italians " (see p. 376). That very year Cavour was fairly well prepared for the war with Austria, if he could get the aid of Napoleon. In 1858 the two men therefore had a famous interview, which they attempted to keep secret. Napoleon was at Plombières, a small village near the Sardinian

frontier where it was understood he had gone for a few days' rest
and quiet. One day a stumpy little man in spectacles turned up,
and was at first looked at suspiciously by the police, who thought
him another Italian conspirator come to take Napoleon's life. It
was Cavour. He was a conspirator, sure enough, but he had only
come by appointment to talk with Napoleon. Just what the two
men said to each other we don't know; but we know what they
agreed to do, and we can be fairly sure that in certain important
matters they tried to deceive each other.

Cavour wanted Napoleon to help Sardinia defeat Austria. Austria defeated, he hoped that certain things would happen. He
hoped that while the war was going on, or afterwards, the people
in the other Italian states would overthrow their governments
and then agree with the people of Sardinia to unite in one Italian
state, with its capital at Rome and with Victor Emmanuel as its
king. He hoped that the National Society would take the lead
in these popular revolutions. He hoped that the affair would
move swiftly, and that within a short time there would be formed
a united Italy strong enough to take care of itself without the aid
or the interference of any foreign power. It is safe to say that
Cavour did not reveal these hopes to Napoleon. He said that he
wished to free Italy from Austrian domination, and asked Napoleon to help him.

Napoleon was willing to help free Italy from Austrian domination. He also hoped that, when that was accomplished, certain
things would happen. But his hopes were different from those of
Cavour. Napoleon hoped that Sardinia would be satisfied by
adding to its territory the two Austrian provinces of Venetia and
Lombardy. He hoped that Italy would then be united, not into
a single state, but into a loose federation of states — the enlarged
Kingdom of Sardinia, Tuscany, the Papal States, and the Kingdom of Naples and Sicily. Napoleon suggested that the nominal
head of this federation should be the Pope. He probably hinted
that the real head would be the enlarged Kingdom of Sardinia.
He doubtless thought, but did not say, that the situation thus
created would enable France to have the controlling influence in
Italian affairs. In short, Napoleon hoped to free Italy from Aus-

trian domination in order to subject it to French influence. Need-less to say, he did not reveal these hopes to Cavour.

With these different views as to the outcome, and leaving each other in the dark as much as possible, the two statesmen made their bargain. The bargain was explicit enough. Napoleon promised that if within a certain time Austria made war on Sardinia, France would come to the aid of Sardinia with an army of about 200,000 men in order to " free Italy to the Adriatic." If they were successful, Austria should be forced to cede Lombardy and Venetia to Sardinia. In return for Napoleon's aid in taking Venetia and Lombardy from Austria, Cavour promised to cede to France the Sardinian province of Savoy and the city of Nice — places inhabited largely by French-speaking people. To cement this alliance it was agreed that the fifteen-year-old daughter of Victor Emmanuel should marry Napoleon's " fine young cousin," Prince Napoleon Bonaparte. The prince was in fact not so very young, nor so very fine either.

Thus the two men agreed to drive Austria out of Italy, each one hoping something would come of it that did not appear on the surface. We shall presently see how this agreement at cross-purposes prospered. But first there was one other thing Cavour had to do before the scheme could be carried out in any fashion. He had to badger Austria into declaring war on Sardinia before a given date.

Cavour's preparations: (4) How he managed to bring about war with Austria, and how, with the aid of the Austrian emperor, he finally succeeded. Napoleon promised to aid Cavour only if Austria " attacked " Sardinia. It would not do at all for Sardinia to attack Austria, for that would be a war of aggression which could not be justified. What Cavour had to do, therefore, was to badger Austria into being the aggressor. He did all he could, and since he was the ablest diplomat in Europe that was a good deal. He used every opportunity to irritate the Austrian government. Napoleon did his share too. On New Year's Day, 1859, speaking openly to the Austrian ambassador at a diplomatic reception, he said: " I regret that our relations with your government are not so good as they were." This simple statement was understood to be a threat — almost equivalent to a threat of war. A little later Victor Emmanuel made matters worse — that is, better — by making a threat of his own. In a speech before the Sardinian parliament he said that Sardinia could not " disregard the cries of grief that arise to us from so many parts of Italy." This was nothing less than an announcement that Sardinia was prepared to become the champion of Italian freedom against Austria.

All Europe could now see that Cavour and Napoleon were determined to badger Austria into war. Cavour made no secret of his intentions. " I shall force Austria to declare war against us," he said to some English visitors. Yet there were two principal difficulties which threatened to drive Cavour to despair. One was that the great powers might succeed in preventing the war. The other was that Napoleon might yield to the wishes of the great powers and withdraw his promise.

The English were friendly to Cavour and to the cause of Italian independence. But they wondered what Napoleon was up to. The prospect of a great French army marching into Italy reminded them too much of the first Napoleon's conquest of Italy to be agreeable. The Tsar of Russia, Alexander II, had no love for Napoleon, and feared his Italian schemes as much as the English did. Both Russia and England wished Italy to be free, but if it was to be subject to any foreign power, they preferred that it should be subject to Austria rather than to France. These powers therefore proposed to assemble a European congress to " settle the Italian question." Cavour knew that a congress would spoil all his plans, but he could not afford to reject the proposal and so lose the sympathy of England. The most he could do was to insist that Sardinia should be a member of the congress, hoping that Austria would not consent to this. Meantime he mobilized his army on the Austrian frontier.

Now that the great powers were becoming excited, Napoleon began to lose interest in " doing something for the Italians." His remarks to the Austrian ambassador aroused so much comment that he hastened to assure Austria that he did not mean anything by them. After all, he said on one occasion, there can be " no question of war with Austria for the next five years." Cavour

PUBLIC LETTER-WRITERS IN ITALY

From a sketch by Dura. The old lady is apparently telling the man that her
daughter wants a letter written — a love letter no doubt.

was in despair. It is said that he gave up hope, talked of burning
his papers, resigning his office, and even of committing suicide.
Indeed everything would have been lost if the Austrian government had been wise enough not to play Cavour's game. If it had
simply done nothing, or taken the advice of the English government, all of Cavour's carefully laid plans would have gone up in
smoke. But the emperor, Francis Joseph II, and the military
party at Vienna were not to be restrained. They insisted that the
little upstart Kingdom of Sardinia should be taught a lesson. The
Austrian government committed the blunder of doing just what
Cavour hoped it would do. It sent an " ultimatum " to Cavour,
demanding in peremptory terms that the Sardinian army on the
frontier should be demobilized within three days, failing which
Austria would make war on Sardinia.

April 23, 1859, Cavour was sitting in the parliament chamber,
when news was brought that a special Austrian ambassador, Count
von Kellersperg, had arrived. This news raised Cavour from the
depths of despair. He received the count politely, read the ultimatum, and said that within three days precisely Austria should
have its answer. On April 26 the Austrian demands were rejected.
Knowing well that Austria would now " attack " Sardinia, and
that Napoleon could scarcely fail to carry out his promise, Cavour

turned with a happy smile to his companions and said: " The die is cast ! We have made history — now let us go and dine." On April 29 the Austrian troops invaded Sardinia, and the war was on.

The war for the liberation of Italy: Battles of Magenta and Solferino, June, 1859. It seems as if the Austrian commander, Count Gyulai, might have defeated the Sardinian army before the French arrived. But for three weeks he did nothing but march and countermarch and dig trenches, as if considerately waiting for Napoleon to arrive on the scene. As soon as he arrived in Italy, Napoleon announced : " We are going to second the struggle of a people reclaiming its independence, and to rescue it from foreign oppression." On June 4, 1859, the united French (100,000) and Sardinian (30,000) forces met the Austrians and defeated them in the first important battle of the war — the Battle of Magenta. This victory enabled the allies to take possession of the city of Milan, the capital of Lombardy. Napoleon and Victor Emmanuel, riding at the head of their armies through the streets of Milan, were welcomed as liberators by the people ; but more observed than the two sovereigns was Cavour, the little man riding behind them with the generals, easily recognizable in his civilian clothes and famous round spectacles. To him were accorded the loudest cheers of all.

Driven from Milan, the Austrians made their stand at Solferino, near the frontier of Venetia. Here the allies came up with them on June 24. The Battle of Solferino was one of the most extensive and deadly conflicts known up to that time. On a battle front of twelve miles, some 260,000 men were engaged. Artillery played a great part in the battle, the allies alone having over 300 heavy pieces. With a keen eye for the dramatic, Napoleon had with him a balloon detachment under M. Houdan, a famous aëronaut of that time. All through the muggy June day masses of men struggled and fought, deafened by the roar of cannon, choked by the sulphurous sultry air, falling by the thousands from wounds or exhaustion. When night came on 10,000 men were missing, 23,000 were wounded, 4500 were dead. The immediate object of the French and Sardinians was to dislodge the Austrians from the heights of Solferino. This they succeeded in doing, so that the battle was a victory for the allies. But it was not a decisive victory. The Austrians retired in good order, withdrawing into the four powerful fortresses of the famous " Quadrilateral " — Mantua, Peschiera, Verona, and Legnano — which guarded the entrance to Venetia.

" Great battle — great victory! " So Napoleon telegraphed to the empress, Eugénie. But as he surveyed the situation after the battle he found the victory so little to his liking that he refused to fight any more. Instead of continuing the war, Napoleon made peace with the Austrians and took his army back to France.

The war for the liberation of Italy: Why Napoleon deserted Cavour in the middle of the war. There were many reasons why Napoleon refused to continue the war after the Battle of Solferino. It was fine to ride down the streets of Milan, with flags waving and bands playing, and receive the plaudits of a grateful people. It was less fine to ride over the battlefield of Solferino, looking at the piled-up bodies of the dead and listening to the moans of the dying. Napoleon was a humane man, and the ghastly slaughter of that day sickened him. He could not but ask: " Is the liberation of Italy worth such a price? If so, can I ask Frenchmen to pay it? "

Besides, the war was not yet over. Far from it! Venetia could not be taken until the Austrians were dislodged from the four fortresses of the Quadrilateral, and it would take months to do that, even if it could be done at all. Meantime the Germans were becoming alarmed at Napoleon's march through Italy. They were mobilizing. They were negotiating with Austria. Even if Napoleon went on with the war, could he win it? It was extremely doubtful. Napoleon decided that he would better make peace now, after a great victory, than later, after a possible defeat.

More important still, things were not going as Napoleon wished in Italy itself. After the Battle of Magenta Napoleon had issued a proclamation saying: " Italy shall henceforth be master of her own destinies! " Napoleon III liked to imitate the first Napoleon in all things, and in none more than in the making of fine phrases. But he did not really wish the Italians to be master of their own destinies, and when they took him at his word he was annoyed. After the Battle of Magenta the people of Modena, Parma, and Tuscany, instigated by the National Society and encouraged by Cavour, rose up in rebellion and sent their rulers into exile. In Romagna the people renounced the papal government and sent the Pope's legate back to Rome. The people of all northern Italy were ready to carry out Cavour's plan — ready to unite with Sardinia for the formation of a united Italy.

Napoleon did not like all this. He did not approve of revolutions. He did not want Italy to be united in a single strong state, but in a weak confederation of little states. Above all, he did not want the Pope to lose his political power. Napoleon had won the support of the Catholics in France by supporting the Pope, and French troops were at that moment in Rome bolstering up the feeble government of the Pope. But the war with Austria had started popular revolutions which threatened to destroy the political power of the Pope. Thus with one hand Napoleon was holding the Pope up, while with the other he was knocking him down. This was serious. It was more than serious — it was ridiculous.

The French Catholics did not hesitate to point out to Napoleon how serious and ridiculous it was. They had always been opposed to the war for aiding Cavour, whom they regarded as the arch-enemy of the church. Now they loudly demanded that Napoleon give it up. " We told you so," they said in effect. " The war is turning out just as we said it would. It is bound to destroy the Pope and to create a powerful state which will be a dangerous rival of France. End the war, and come home where you belong."

For all of these reasons Napoleon decided to get out of the war while he could do so with some credit. On July 11 he therefore met the Emperor Francis Joseph at Villafranca, and there the two sovereigns arranged the preliminaries of a treaty of peace. They agreed that Venetia should remain with Austria; that Lombardy should be annexed to Sardinia; that the rulers of Modena, Parma, and Tuscany should be restored, although " without force "; that Romagna should again be subjected to the Pope. They agreed further that the Italian states, including the Austrian province of Venetia, should be united in a loose federation under the honorary presidency of the Pope, and that the Holy Father should be requested to make certain reforms in the government of his dominions. Having arranged these preliminaries, Napoleon took his army back to France. In November the agreements at Villafranca were embodied in the Treaty of Zürich.

Thus Napoleon abandoned Cavour when the struggle for Italian freedom was only half won. He tried to console the Italians by saying, " Now we shall see what the Italians can do by themselves."

How the Italians, in spite of Napoleon's desertion, took the first step in the creation of a united Italy. Cavour was a hard-headed, practical man, but under great strain he sometimes lost his head and acted like a madman. When he learned that Napoleon was bound to make peace, he tried to prevent it; and when that failed he tried to convince Victor Emmanuel that Sardinia should go on with the war alone. According to one story, in a long and heated interview Cavour argued with the king, pleaded with him, and at last grew insolent and bullied him.

" Calm yourself," Victor Emmanuel said. " Remember that I am king."

" I am the *real* king ! " Cavour shouted. " The Italians recognize me first of all ! "

" What do you say? You the king? *You are a rogue !* "

Victor Emmanuel was so angry that he turned his back on his prime minister; and Cavour was so angry that he rushed out of the room — probably slamming the door, if there was one. The king immediately summoned his chief of staff, Della Rocco, and said to him : " Do you know what Cavour wants? He wants me to continue the war alone. I am as furious as he is over this peace, but I don't lose my compass — I don't lose my reason."

The king was right. It was useless for Sardinia to continue the war alone. Victor Emmanuel therefore signed the peace which Napoleon had negotiated. But he signed it only " in so far as it concerned him " — that is, only in respect to Lombardy and Venetia. Cavour gave up his office as prime minister rather than sign the treaty. For days his rage continued, subsiding gradually like a volcano intermittently throwing out hot lava.

" This peace will never be made! " he said. " This treaty will never be executed! If necessary I will take Margherita [1] by one hand, and Mazzini by the other. I will turn conspirator [striking his breast]. I will become a revolutionist! But this treaty shall not be carried out! We will do what the emperor did not dare to accomplish. By God! *We* will not stop halfway! "

Wild words! Yet Cavour was right too. The treaty was never carried out except in part — except as it concerned Lombardy and Venetia. The rulers of Modena, Parma, and Tuscany were never restored, nor was the federation under the honorary presidency of the Pope ever formed. On the contrary, within two years the Kingdom of Italy, which Cavour desired and which Napoleon did not desire, was a reality.

All this did not come about by Cavour's turning revolutionist and joining hands with Mazzini. It came about chiefly because of two things: (1) because the people of Modena, Parma, and Tuscany insisted on being united with Sardinia; and (2) because Napoleon could not prevent them from doing this without losing Savoy and Nice.

Napoleon had agreed to help Sardinia drive Austria out of Italy if Victor Emmanuel would cede Savoy and Nice to France. But now, since Napoleon had failed to carry out his part of the bargain fully, Victor Emmanuel refused to carry out his part. Napoleon felt that he must have Savoy and Nice at all costs. The French people, never very keen for the war, were now asking whether they were not to get anything for all the lives sacrificed in the cause of Italian freedom. So in order to satisfy the French people, Napoleon made another bargain with Victor Emmanuel. He agreed that if Victor Emmanuel would cede Savoy and Nice to France, he, Napoleon, would make no objection to the annexation of Parma, Modena, Tuscany, and Romagna to Sardinia.

Seeing that all was not lost, Cavour became prime minister again, and continued with his plans for Italian unity. It was arranged that the people of Nice and Savoy should hold a " plebiscite " (that is, should go to the polls and vote) to decide whether they wished to be annexed to France; and that similar plebiscites should

[1] Margherita was a conservative leader, and a bitter enemy of Cavour's policies.

be held in central and northern Italy to decide whether the people there wished to be annexed to Sardinia. The plebiscites were held in April, 1860, and in each case the decision was almost unanimously in favor of annexation. The first parliament of the enlarged Sardinia met April 2, 1860. In it was represented all of Italy except Venetia, the Papal States, and the Kingdom of Naples. Victor Emmanuel was now king over 11,000,000 people instead of 5,000,000.

This was the first great step in the union of Italy. The next step was the union of Naples and Sicily to the enlarged Kingdom of Sardinia.

The Neapolitan revolution: How two enemies, Cavour and Garibaldi, worked together for the union of Italy. Italians honor three men above all others as the founders of modern Italy: Mazzini, Cavour, and Garibaldi. Mazzini was the prophet, preaching the gospel of freedom. Cavour was the statesman, devising the practical political program. Garibaldi was the picturesque military adventurer, recklessly leading his followers to victory. These three men never liked or trusted each other. Mazzini denounced Cavour as an intriguer betraying the sacred cause of liberty by asking the aid of Napoleon, the man who had set his heel on liberty in France. Cavour distrusted Mazzini as a dangerous idealist likely to upset the best-laid plans, and Garibaldi as a child likely to burn down the house with his firecrackers; while Garibaldi, for his part, was incapable of understanding Cavour's statesmanship and never forgave him for ceding to France the city of Nice, where he was born. Yet these three men, each in his own way, contributed to the same end — the union of Italy.

Garibaldi was born in Nice, in 1807. He joined the society of Young Italy, took part in Mazzini's insurrection in Savoy in 1834, was condemned to death, and afterwards escaped to South America, where he organized an Italian Legion which took part in the many South American wars of the time. Returning to Italy in 1848, he organized a band of free-lances to fight in the war against Austria. In 1849 he helped to defend Mazzini's Roman Republic. Barely escaping from that ill-fated venture with his life, he lived for some years in exile, sailing the sea in a Peruvian bark, or making candles on Staten Island. In 1854 he once more returned to Italy and settled down on a farm on the island of Caprera. His adventures had made him a picturesque figure, known to all Italians, worshiped by many for the dangers he had passed through, feared by a few for the indiscretions he might commit. As Mazzini looked the poet and Cavour the business man, Garibaldi looked the pirate and desperado in his slouch hat, heavy beard, and famous red shirt. Yet through all his rough adventures he remained as simple as a child, as tender-hearted as a woman. He knew nothing of strategy or statecraft, of intrigue or compromise. He knew only courage and honesty, he knew only that tyrants were hateful, that all honest men should abhor tyrants and all courageous men go and fight them. Garibaldi was the humanitarian Knight Errant of Liberty, rigged out in the garb of a modern freebooter.

When there was fighting in Italy, Garibaldi always emerged from retirement or exile; and so in 1859 we find him leading, with dash and courage, a company of volunteers in the war against Austria. When that war was ended, he turned his eyes to Naples and Sicily, where the people were in revolt against their king, Francis II. To aid the Neapolitans, Garibaldi collected some eleven hundred adventurers, provided them with arms and red shirts, and on May 5, 1860, this famous company of the " One Thousand " set sail from Genoa in two small steamers to overthrow the government of Francis II, which was supported by an army of 124,000 men. The enterprise seemed foolhardy. But Garibaldi never asked whether an enterprise was foolhardy. His vocabulary did not contain the word. And as it happened he succeeded in this foolhardy enterprise. He succeeded because neither the people nor the soldiers of Francis II were loyal to their king. After a few weeks of desperate fighting, Garibaldi was master of Sicily. Then he crossed to the mainland of southern Italy. With scarcely a struggle the king and a remnant of his army retreated, and on September 7 Garibaldi entered Naples, where he was hailed as the liberator of eleven millions of people.

In Sicily Garibaldi had assumed the title of Dictator in the name of Victor Emmanuel; and now that Naples and Sicily were won, he began to talk of marching on Rome, overthrowing the Pope,

LANDING OF GARIBALDI IN SOUTHAMPTON

From an old print. Garibaldi visited England in 1864, where he was given an enthusiastic reception. Note his cape and neck scarf. He did not dress in conformity with the fashions of the time.

and proclaiming the union of Italy from the steps of Saint Peter's Cathedral — all in the name of Victor Emmanuel.

Meantime, up in Turin, Cavour was watching with anxious eyes the exploits of Garibaldi. Cavour had secretly encouraged the expedition of Garibaldi. He was glad that Garibaldi had succeeded in overturning the government of Francis II. Above all things he wanted Naples and Sicily to be united to the Kingdom of Sardinia. But he was alarmed at the prospect of an expedition against the Pope. Napoleon had consented to the enlargement of Sardinia. He might, by careful management, be induced to consent to the annexation of Naples and Sicily. But Cavour knew that Napoleon would never consent to the destruction of the political power of the Pope. Yet Garibaldi was a child when it came to political and diplomatic questions of that sort, and besides, since he disliked Cavour, he could not be trusted to listen to any advice that Cavour might offer.

What Cavour had to do, therefore, was to get Victor Emmanuel and his army as quickly as possible into southern Italy in order to take the direction of affairs out of the hands of Garibaldi. This was not so easy as it might seem. The Sardinian army would have to march across the papal territory, and the Pope would never give his consent to that. What then would Napoleon do if Victor Emmanuel marched through the papal territory without the Pope's consent? Fortunately for Cavour, the people of the two eastern provinces of the Pope's dominions, Umbria and the Marches, wished to be annexed to Sardinia, and were prevented only by a papal army of foreign adventurers led by a French Catholic by the name of Lamoricière. Cavour therefore complained to Napoleon that French subjects were conspiring against Sardinia on papal territory. He said that he would not go near the city of Rome or interfere with the papal power in any way. He would march through Umbria and the Marches, deal with the mercenary army of Lamoricière, and then leave the people of Umbria and the Marches to decide whether they wished to remain loyal to the Pope or be annexed to Sardinia. It is said that Napoleon gave Cavour a verbal message: " Act if you must, but act quickly."

Cavour acted quickly. In September, 1860, Victor Emmanuel led his army into Umbria and the Marches, defeated the army of Lamoricière, and then went on to Naples. In November the remnant of the army of Francis II was defeated at Capua, and a few months later the unfortunate king fled, an exile, to Rome. Garibaldi welcomed Victor Emmanuel and was quite willing to surrender the direction of affairs to him. But at first he made one condition, which was that Victor Emmanuel should dismiss Cavour, whom Garibaldi regarded as a traitor to Italy because he had ceded Savoy and Nice to France. Victor Emmanuel refused to dismiss Cavour, and in the end Garibaldi acquiesced. To show that there was no enmity, the two men, Garibaldi and Victor Emmanuel, rode together through the streets of Naples. The king offered Garibaldi titles and wealth, honors and rewards; but Garibaldi refused to take any of these things. With only a little money in his pocket, and a bag of seeds for his farm, he sailed away to his home in Caprera.

How the work of Cavour was completed by the establishment of the Kingdom of Italy, March 17, 1861. When Garibaldi sailed away to Caprera, Cavour must have given a sigh of relief, for the happy end of all his labors was now in sight. The Sardinian parliament had already, in October, 1860, declared in favor of the annexation to the Kingdom of Sardinia of all the people of central and southern Italy who should by popular vote express their approval of that measure. Plebiscites were immediately held in Umbria, the Marches, and in the Kingdom of Naples and Sicily; and in each case the majority in favor of annexation was overwhelming — the total vote being 1,962,00 for and only 12,180 against it.

With these annexations completed, the population of the Kingdom of Sardinia had been increased, within less than two years, from 5,000,000 to about 22,000,000 people, and the territory over which Victor Emmanuel ruled included all of Italy except Venetia and the " Patrimony of Saint Peter " — that is, the city of Rome and the immediately surrounding country. The first parliament of this greater Sardinia met in Turin, February 18, 1861. On March 17 the name " Kingdom of Sardinia " was changed to " Kingdom of Italy," and Victor Emmanuel was solemnly proclaimed " by the grace of God and the will of the nation, King of Italy."

One great problem still confronted Cavour. This was the " Roman question." Pope Pius IX was exceedingly angry at the turn events had taken — as well he might be, since the creation of the new Kingdom of Italy had deprived him of more than two-thirds of his ancient dominions. He refused to recognize the new kingdom, and denounced Victor Emmanuel as a king " despising every right, trampling upon every law." What attitude, then, should the government of Victor Emmanuel take toward the Pope? There were many who wished to make an end of the Pope's political power at once by taking possession of Rome and making that city the capital of the kingdom. There were others, such as D'Azeglio, who were willing to leave the Pope alone, renounce all intention

SWITZERLAND

L. Geneva

Geneva

Rhone R.

L. Maggiore

L. Como

L. Garda

TYROL

Drava R.

AUSTRIA-HUNGARY

Save R.

1866

VENETIA

Trieste

LOMBARDY **1859**

Magenta

Milan Solferino

Villafranca

Padua

Venice

PIEDMONT

Turin

Po R.

PARMA **1860**

Genoa

MODENA **1860**

ROMAGNA **1860**

STATES OF THE MARCHES

SAN MARINO

ADRIATIC SEA

Gulf of Genoa

Arno R.

Florence

ELBA

TUSCANY **1860**

1860

1860

UMBRIA **1860**

CHURCH

CORSICA

Ajaccio

1870

Tiber R.

Rome

SARDINIA

SARDINIA

Cagliari

T Y R R H E N I A N

S E A

Naples

Mt. Vesuvius

CAPRI

1860

KINGDOM OF THE

Gulf of Tarentum

M E D I T E R R A N E A N   S E A

Palermo

Messina

TWO SICILIES

1860

Mt. Etna

Tunis

MALTA

THE UNIFICATION OF ITALY, 1859-1870

SCALE OF MILES

0   25   50   75   100   150

Kingdom of Sardinia, 1859.   Nice and
Savoy ceded to France, 1860

United to Kingdom of Sardinia, 1859-60,
to form Kingdom of Italy

United to Kingdom of Italy, 1866

United to Kingdom of Italy, 1870

8°   Longitude   10°   East   12°   from   14°   Greenwich   16°

of taking possession of Rome, and be satisfied with Turin as the capital.

Cavour agreed with neither of these parties. He felt that the great dream of a united Italy would never be realized until the papal territory was included within the Kingdom of Italy, and he was determined that Rome, the great historic city, should be the capital. He felt that Rome must be the capital of united Italy, not only because it was the center of all the traditions of Italy's greatness, but also because keeping Turin as the capital would perpetuate the old jealous rivalry between the peoples of central Italy and the Piedmont. But Cavour was utterly opposed to all projects for the forcible annexation of the papal dominions. For one thing Napoleon, whose troops were still in Rome, would object to it, and a conquest of the Papal States without his consent might end in a war between Italy and France. Besides, the Pope was not an ordinary petty ruler. He was the head of the great Catholic Church; and Cavour knew that he would still be a power in the world even if he were dispossessed of his political power. Cavour therefore wanted to get the Pope to surrender his political power voluntarily, and thus avoid future hostilities between the church and the Kingdom of Italy. Cavour's ideas prevailed. The parliament formally declared in favor of the principle that Rome should be the future capital of the Kingdom of Italy, provided the consent of Napoleon and the Pope could be obtained.

Cavour's work was done. In the prime of life, at the age of fifty-one, he took to his bed, worn out with eleven years of ceaseless labor and nervous strain. He died on June 6, 1861. His last intelligible words were: " Italy is made — all is safe."

Italy was indeed made, but not yet quite finished, since neither Venetia nor the Papal States were yet parts of the Kingdom of Italy. Within ten years two great European events made it possible to complete the unification of Italy, although not in the manner desired by Cavour. In the Austro-Prussian War of 1866 Italy joined Prussia and forced Austria to cede Venetia; and in 1870, when Napoleon's empire was overthrown as the result of the Franco-Prussian War, the government of Victor Emmanuel at last, although without the Pope's consent, took possession of the city of Rome.

This brings us to the next great event in European history —
the unification of Germany.

QUESTIONS

1. What were the chief states in Italy in 1852? How were they
governed? How did Austria exercise a dominant influence?

2. Why did most Italians object to this situation? What did they
want? Why did they have less faith in Mazzini's methods of freeing
Italy after 1848? Why did they look to Sardinia as a leader with greater
confidence after 1852?

3. Who was Cavour, and what had he done before 1850? How did
he differ from Mazzini in character and temperament? in political
ideas? in plans for freeing Italy?

4. How did Cavour aim to win the confidence of middle-class Liberals throughout Italy? How did he work with Daniele Manin and the
National Society to win the support of the Republicans?

5. Why did Cavour think Italy could not win her freedom without
the aid of France? Why did Mazzini object to receiving aid from
France? What was the agreement entered into by Cavour and Napoleon at Plombières?

6. What was the importance of the Battle of Magenta? of Solferino? Why did Napoleon withdraw from the war after Solferino?
What were the provisions of the Treaty of Zürich?

7. How was the union of Sardinia with the duchies of Modena,
Parma, and Tuscany brought about? Why did Napoleon object to
this, and why did he not prevent it?

8. Who was Garibaldi, and what did he do for the unification of
Italy? Why did Cavour think it necessary to send the Sardinian army
through the Papal States to Naples? How was Sardinia enlarged as
a result of the revolution in Naples and Sicily?

9. When was the Kingdom of Italy proclaimed? Why was it
desirable to declare Rome the future capital?

10. Write a brief statement (not more than fifty words) of the essential
differences between Mazzini's ideas and methods of freeing Italy and
those of Cavour.

SELECTED READINGS

Brief accounts. Robinson and Beard, *Modern Europe*, II, ch. xxi.
Robinson and Beard, *Outlines*, II, ch. xvii. Hayes and Moon, *Modern
History*, ch. xvii. Hazen, *Modern Europe*, ch. xx. Hayes, *Modern
Europe*, II, 163–175. Schapiro, *European History* (revised ed.), ch. xiv.
Turner, *Europe since 1789*, ch. xi. Schevill, *History of Europe*, ch. xxvi.
A more detailed account is in Hazen, *Europe since 1815*, ch. x.

CHART FOR CHAPTER XII. Unification of Italy, 1852-1871:

Principal stages in the risorgimento (resurrection) of Italy.

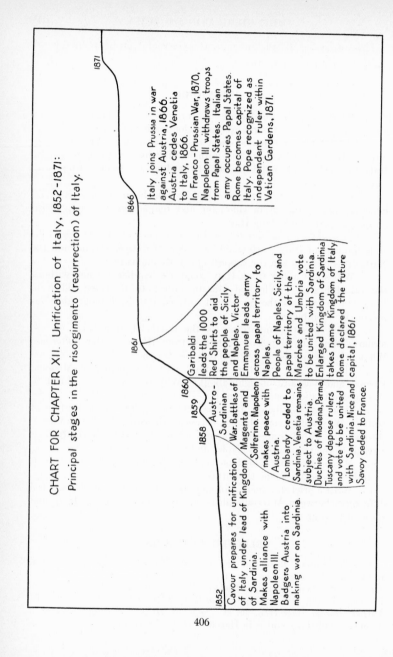

1852
Cavour prepares for unification of Italy under lead of Kingdom of Sardinia.
Makes alliance with Napoleon III.
Badgers Austria into making war on Sardinia.

1858

1859
Austro-Sardinian War. Battles of Magenta and Solferino. Napoleon makes peace with Austria.
Lombardy ceded to Sardinia. Venetia remains subject to Austria.
Duchies of Modena, Parma, Tuscany depose rulers and vote to be united with Sardinia. Nice and Savoy ceded to France.

1860

1861
Garibaldi leads the 1000 Red Shirts to aid the people of Sicily and Naples. Victor Emmanuel leads army across papal territory to Naples.
People of Naples, Sicily, and papal territory of the Marches and Umbria vote to be united with Sardinia. Enlarged Kingdom of Sardinia takes name Kingdom of Italy. Rome declared the future capital, 1861.

1866
Italy joins Prussia in war against Austria, 1866.
Austria cedes Venetia to Italy, 1866.
In Franco-Prussian War, 1870, Napoleon III withdraws troops from Papal States. Italian army occupies Papal States. Rome becomes capital of Italy. Pope recognized as independent ruler within Vatican Gardens, 1871.

1871

Biography. Evelyn Martinengo-Cesaresco, *Cavour*. M. Paléologue, *Cavour*. A. D. White, *Seven Great Statesmen*. (Contains an essay on Cavour.) P. Orsini, *Cavour and the Making of Modern Italy*. W. R. Thayer, *Life and Times of Cavour*. B. King, *Mazzini*. J. W. Mario, *The Birth of Modern Italy*. (Very favorable to Mazzini and Garibaldi, but hostile to Cavour.) J. A. R. Marriott, *Makers of Modern Italy, Mazzini — Cavour — Garibaldi*. G. M. Trevelyan, *Garibaldi and the Thousand* and *Garibaldi and the Making of Italy*. G. S. Godkin, *Life of Victor Emmanuel II*. R. Flenley, *Makers of Nineteenth Century Europe*.

Historical novels. Marion Crawford, *Saracinesca* and *Don Orsino*. (Pictures Roman society after the unification.)

Sources. Robinson and Beard, *Readings in Modern History*, II, ch. xxi. (Extracts from the writings of Mazzini, Cavour, Napoleon, Garibaldi, and Pope Pius IX.) Anderson, *Select Documents*. A. Werner, *Autobiography of Giuseppe Garibaldi*. Scott and Baltzly, *Readings in European History*, ch. vii, sec. 3.

THE NEW BRIDGE OVER THE RHINE AT COLOGNE
From a sketch in *L'Illustration*, 1855.

CHAPTER XIII. THE UNIFICATION OF GERMANY: HOW BISMARCK BEGAN THE UNIFICATION OF GERMANY BY DIVIDING IT INTO THREE PARTS.

Germany has its eyes not on Prussia's liberalism, but on its power. . . . The great events of our day will not be decided by speeches and resolutions of majorities . . . but by blood and iron. BISMARCK

Introducing a great man, Otto von Bismarck. The unification of Germany was the great event in German history in the nineteenth century, just as the unification of Italy was the great event in Italian history. In many ways the two events present striking similarities. Germany, like Italy, had long been divided into many states. The Germans, like the Italians, had long desired political liberty and national unity. In both countries the people had tried, and failed, to attain these desired ends in the revolutions of 1848. A few years later (1859–1861) Italian unification was accomplished under the leadership of Cavour, the prime minister of the King of Sardinia; and at about the same time (1862–1870) the unification of Germany was accomplished under the leadership of Bismarck, the prime minister of the King of Prussia. First of all, therefore, let us see how Bismarck became the prime minister of the King of Prussia, and then what manner of man he was.

After the Revolution of 1848 the King of Prussia had granted a constitution to his people. The Prussian constitution was not a very liberal one. It provided for a legislature of two chambers, a

408

Chamber of Peers and a Chamber of Deputies (*Landtag*), elected in such a way that the majority of the deputies represented the very wealthy people. Besides, the parliament had little control over the administration and execution of the laws, since the king could appoint and dismiss his ministers without asking the consent of the parliament. The real power of government was thus still largely in the hands of the king and his ministers; and during the ten years from 1851 to 1861, the king and his ministers had often violated the constitution, especially in respect to the guarantees of freedom of speech and the press and freedom from arbitrary arrest and imprisonment.

As a result of this situation there had developed a conflict between the two principal parties in the Prussian parliament: (1) the Conservatives, who represented mainly the nobles and the Prussian landed aristocracy, and (2) the Progressive Liberals, who represented the middle-class people. The latter resented the king's violation of the constitution and wished to make him and his ministers responsible to the parliament; the former generally supported the king and his ministers and did not wish to see the parliament obtain control of the government. The Conservatives controlled the Chamber of Peers, but the Progressive Liberals were the strongest party in the Chamber of Deputies.

This was the situation when, in 1860, the king and his minister of war, Albrecht von Roon, presented to the parliament certain bills for the enlargement of the army. The reforms, which called for thirty-nine new regiments, would require a great deal of money. The Chamber of Peers was willing to grant the money. But the Landtag hesitated and finally, in 1862, refused outright to give its consent. King William had either to abandon his measures or to carry them through without paying any attention to the parliament. At first neither course seemed possible. The king was not willing to abandon his military reforms, since he felt that the future of Germany depended on a strong Prussian army; but his prime minister, Von Hohenlohe, was unwilling to assume the responsibility of carrying the reforms through without the consent of the Landtag. The king was therefore about to resign, and had written out and signed an abdication of the throne, when Von Roon advised him to appoint as prime minister a man named Otto von Bismarck. This man, Von Roon said, was devoted to the king and would assume any amount of responsibility. King William tore up his abdication, had an interview with Bismarck, and after some delay appointed him to be his prime minister (1862). From that day until his resignation in 1890 Bismarck was the central figure in German history.

German Tourist Information Office
BISMARCK (1815–1898)

This extraordinary man, Bismarck, whose name will ever stand out as the creator of the German Empire, was born of noble parents, in Brandenburg, in 1815. After graduating from the university, he lived for some years the life of a country squire, managing the family estates. Like Cavour, he emerged from private life to enter politics just before the Revolution of 1848. But unlike Cavour, he was opposed to the revolution. He was opposed to the granting of the Prussian constitution in 1851. This was indeed the chief difference between Cavour and Bismarck — a difference in political ideas. Cavour was a genuine Liberal, who believed that the people could govern themselves better than any king could do it for them. Bismarck was a genuine Conservative, who believed that any government controlled by the people was already on the "toboggan slide" towards socialism, and that socialism must lead in the end to anarchy and ruin.

Bismarck's political philosophy was the result of a good-humored but cynical attitude toward mankind. He knew the weaknesses and vices of men rather better than he knew their virtues. This knowledge never embittered him. He was genial and friendly, liking his fellow-men well enough — perhaps because he did not expect too much of them. But not expecting too much of them, he distrusted their capacity to govern themselves. He believed, therefore, that good government rested in the long run on force and fear, and that the best form of government was the monarchical — a government in which the people would be governed for their own good by the king and his ministers.

Side by side with this genial cynicism there was in Bismarck's mind a curious strain of mysticism. Bismarck said that he often found in the Bible a " confirmation of his faith in a Divine Providence and a God who ordered the universe and chose the instruments of His inscrutable will." Thus to the cynicism of a Frederick the Great, Bismarck united the reverence of a Cromwell. He believed that God had destined Prussia and her Hohenzollern kings to accomplish a great work in the world. He had chosen the Hohenzollerns to create the great state of Prussia and through Prussia to create a greater Germany. This work they must carry through, with or without the consent of the people. From the moment that King William chose him to be prime minister, Bismarck therefore regarded himself as a chosen instrument of God, whose chief work was to bring about " the unification of Germany under Prussian leadership."

Bismarck's plan for the unification of Germany and why it was difficult to carry out. Bismarck quite agreed with King William that the first step was to strengthen the Prussian army. When he was appointed prime minister, in 1862, he therefore advised the king to go on with his military reforms without paying any attention to the parliament. This was done. The taxes were collected, and the thirty-nine new regiments organized, just as if the parliament had not rejected those measures. In addition, under the direction of Albrecht von Roon and another very able military man, Helmuth von Moltke, the entire Prussian army was made more efficient in organization, training, and equipment. For example, the army was equipped with a new type of gun, the " needle gun " — that is, a gun which could be loaded at the breech instead of at the muzzle. Since it could be loaded more quickly than the old type, the needle gun was far more effective. Within a few years the Prussian army was the most efficient army in Europe; and not the least of its advantages was that the other countries did not yet know that it was the most efficient.

Ignoring the parliament, supported by the king, and backed by a powerful army, Bismarck was now in a position to work out his plans for the unification of Germany. The plan which he adopted and carried through was: (1) to make war on Austria and exclude her from the German Confederation; (2) to enlarge Prussia by annexing a good part of northern Germany; (3) to unite all the German states, except Austria, in a federal union so constructed that Prussia would be the dominating state and the King of Prussia the real ruler.

The plan was simple enough in itself, but difficult to carry out because there was at this time no united or enthusiastic approval either of Bismarck or his plan. Bismarck was not yet the great national hero that he later became. Prussian middle-class Liberals hated the man for ignoring the parliament in carrying through his army reforms, and they were suspicious of any plan he might devise for German unification, because they knew he was opposed to popular government. Prussian Conservatives — the aristocratic ruling class to which Bismarck himself belonged — disliked Bismarck personally. Prussian Junker though he was, Bismarck often expressed, in caustic witticisms, his contempt for the stupidity of his own class, and with few exceptions the most influential Conservatives regarded him as a braggart upstart who was likely to stir up trouble and lead the king into dangerous courses.

But Bismarck's chief difficulty at first was the war with Austria. Bismarck was not much interested in the unification of Germany unless Prussia became the dominant power in the new federation. To accomplish this, Austria had to be excluded; and since Austria would never voluntarily withdraw, it was necessary to force her out by means of a victorious war. The difficulty was to find a good pretext for such a war. Cavour had been able to rely upon the united support of the Italians, because they regarded Austria as a foreign country. But the Germans did not regard Austria as a foreign country. The Austrians were as much German as the Prussians. Even in Prussia there was no strong anti-Austrian feeling that could be aroused in support of a war. In bringing about a war with Austria, Bismarck had therefore to play a lone hand in order to keep his plans well covered, sometimes even from

the eyes of the king.   King William was an honest, even if a somewhat dull man, and Bismarck knew that he would never approve
of a war of aggression against Austria.   What Bismarck had to
do was to make use of circumstances in such a way as to provoke
.a war with Austria, and at the same time make it appear that
Prussia was the injured party.

**How Bismarck used his diplomatic skill to bring about a war
with Austria.**   In the art of diplomacy, Bismarck was a past master,
ranking with Talleyrand, Metternich, Cavour, and Disraeli. He
possessed an amazing knowledge of the governments of Europe,
of the statesmen and diplomats with whom he had to deal, of the
personal relationships and party intrigues and political interests
that were likely to be of use or hindrance to him.   He knew the
value of newspapers and used them systematically for conveying
such information as might suit his purposes.   Not the least of his
qualities was an unusual power of fascinating men, of impressing
them with a sense of his rugged strength and simple honesty.   A
giant of a man he was, calm and deliberate, always master of himself even when pretending to be angry.   Genial and good-natured,
he liked nothing better than to sit and chat and tell stories, smoking his long pipe, with beer and sandwiches conveniently at hand.
Few men there were who could resist his charm and none who could
outwit him for long, or be sure they had detected the real purpose
behind the casual remarks made with such pursuasive, childlike
simplicity.

With all his genius for diplomacy, Bismarck could not of course
create events that would be useful to him.   But he could use those
that occurred with extraordinary skill.   His primary purpose was
to quarrel with Austria while remaining on good terms with all the
other great powers.   Fortunately for him, an international question arose in 1863 which fitted in admirably with this primary
purpose.   This was the famous Schleswig-Holstein affair.

Schleswig and Holstein were two provinces comprising the southern part of the Danish peninsula.   The people of Holstein were
German, the people of Schleswig partly German and partly Danish.   Both provinces were ruled by the King of Denmark, who was
Duke of Schleswig and of Holstein.   This situation had long created

difficulties, since the king wished to incorporate the two duchies into the Kingdom of Denmark; and while the Danes of Schleswig were favorable to this, the Germans in both provinces were opposed to it, desiring rather to be entirely separated from Danish rule. In this perennial quarrel the great powers had intervened in 1852 when they signed a treaty with the Danish king, known as the London Protocol, to the effect that the King of Denmark should continue to be Duke of Schleswig and of Holstein, on condition that the two provinces should never be made an integral part of the Danish kingdom. Nevertheless, in 1863 King Christian of Denmark violated this agreement by signing a constitution which incorporated Schleswig and Holstein into the kingdom.

This act raised the " Schleswig-Holstein question." It was an extremely complicated question because so many conflicting interests were involved. The German people were interested because the people of Schleswig-Holstein were mainly Germans. The German diet was interested because the province of Holstein was a member of the German Confederation. A German prince, the Duke of Augustenburg, was interested because he had certain hereditary claims to the duchies which had been renounced in 1852 — claims which he presently revived on the ground that the Danish king had violated the London Protocol of 1852. The great powers were interested because they had signed the London Protocol, which the King of Denmark had now violated. How could Bismarck make use of such a complicated question to bring on a war with Austria?

Besides his main aim of making war on Austria, Bismarck wished in the end to annex Schleswig and Holstein to Prussia, thus giving Prussia excellent ports on both the North Sea and the Baltic. In attempting to use the Schleswig-Holstein question for his purposes, he was confronted with a double danger. One danger was that the great powers (Russia, France, and England) might interfere and re-establish the old agreement of 1852. Another danger was that the German diet might, with the aid of Austria, interfere and establish the two duchies as a separate German state under the Duke of Augustenburg. Bismarck had, if possible, to prevent intervention on the part of either the great powers or of the German diet. In dealing with the powers he maintained that it was not necessary for them to intervene, on the ground that the fate of Schleswig and Holstein was essentially a German question. In dealing with the German diet he maintained that the status of Schleswig and Holstein was essentially an international question, since it had been settled by the London Protocol of 1852, to which the German diet was not a party.

This way of arguing was a bit inconsistent, but in the end Bismarck had his way. Great Britain and Russia were both friendly to Prussia and kept their hands off. The German diet could do nothing without the approval of Austria; and Austria at last fell in with Bismarck's plan, which was that Austria and Prussia should act together in dealing with the matter. Therefore in 1864 Austria and Prussia made joint war on Denmark in order to force the Danish king to observe the Protocol of 1852; and then, having defeated Denmark, they forced the king to cede Schleswig and Holstein to them on the ground that the war had annulled the treaty of 1852. With Schleswig and Holstein in the joint possession of Austria and Prussia, it was easy for Bismarck to quarrel with Austria over the disposal of the two provinces. Austria presently brought this quarrel before the German diet, whereupon Bismarck sent Prussian troops into Holstein and dispossessed the Austrians. Austria was now at a disadvantage — she had either to abandon Schleswig and Holstein or make war on Prussia. If she did the former, Bismarck would have obtained one of his objects — the annexation of Schleswig and Holstein to Prussia; if she did the latter, Bismarck would have obtained what he most wanted — a war with Austria in which Austria could be made to appear the aggressor.

Austria, supported by the German Confederation, prepared for war with Prussia. Bismarck was able to convince King William that Austria was the aggressor. And so came the Austro-Prussian War of 1866.

The Austro-Prussian War of 1866: Why the German states sided with Austria, Italy with Prussia, and France with neither. In this war Austria was supported by all of the important German states — Bavaria, Württemberg, Baden, Hesse-Darmstadt, Hesse-

Cassel, Nassau, Hanover, and Saxony. The rulers of these states sided with Austria because they felt that if Austria were excluded from the German Confederation they would be at the mercy of Prussia. The people of these states favored Austria partly because many of them were, like the Austrians, Catholics in religion; and partly because many of them were Liberals in politics who knew that Bismarck, if he established a united Germany, would be opposed to a Liberal government for united Germany. The Austro-Prussian War was therefore a German civil war. Its object was to decide, not whether Germany should be united, but whether Austria should be excluded from the united Germany.

Bismarck did not expect the southern German states to support Prussia, and it suited his plans that Nassau, Hesse-Cassel, and Hanover should support Austria. If these latter states supported Austria in a war in which Prussia was successful, that would furnish him with a pretext for annexing them to Prussia — which was what he did when the war was over. Bismarck was more concerned with the attitude of foreign countries — Russia, Italy, and above all, France. The goodwill of Russia Bismarck had obtained in 1863, when he had given some diplomatic support to the tsar in suppressing a Polish insurrection. Italy was not likely to aid her ancient enemy, Austria; and in fact Italy agreed to aid Prussia, by invading the Austrian province of Venetia, provided Prussia made no objections to the annexation of Venetia to the Kingdom of Italy.

But the chief question was: What would Napoleon III do? Surely it would not be to the interest of France to have a powerful German state, dominated by the military Prussia, established directly across the Rhine. All the great kings and statesmen of France — Henry IV, Richelieu, Louis XIV, and Napoleon — had tried to keep Germany weak by keeping her divided. Would Napoleon III abandon this policy? In order to sound Napoleon on this question, Bismarck had an interview with him in October, 1865, at Biarritz. What the two men said to each other is not known, but it seems that Napoleon agreed to remain neutral in case of a war between Austria and Prussia. This does not mean that Napoleon abandoned the traditional French policy towards

A SQUARE IN ROTHENBURG

This square has changed but little in the course of centuries.

Germany. It means only that he misjudged the situation. He probably thought, as most people did, that Austria, not Prussia, would be successful in the war, or else that neither party would be wholly successful. In either case, a civil war would weaken Germany and enable France, at the right moment, to step in on one side or the other and exact from both parties some territorial concessions on the Rhine. Contrary to his expectation, the fighting lasted only six weeks and ended in a complete victory for Prussia.

The Austro-Prussian War of 1866: Battle of Königgrätz, July 3; Peace of Prague, August 23. The war began in June, 1866. While the Austrians were slowly mobilizing, the Prussian armies disposed of their enemies in western Germany. Within two weeks they defeated the Hanoverian army, occupied the capitals of Hanover, Saxony, and Cassel, and captured the Elector of Hesse-Cassel and the King of Hanover. Meantime, Von Moltke sent three armies by different routes into Bohemia to meet the Austrians. On July 3 the two armies met near the villages of Sadowa and Königgrätz. Until two o'clock it seemed as if the Austrians might win, but the arrival of the crown prince with re-enforcements turned the hard-fought battle into a complete victory for the Prussians. The Prussians lost 10,000 men; the Austrians 40,000.

The Austrian armies retreated, followed slowly and cautiously by the Prussians until the spires of Vienna were in sight; and meantime the armies of the South German states — Bavaria, Württemberg, Baden, and Hesse-Darmstadt — were defeated, and the governments of these states asked for peace. Within six weeks from the beginning of a war which most people thought Austria would win, all Germany appeared to be at the mercy of Prussia. What is the explanation of this astounding victory?

" The needle gun is king," said the London *Times*. That was only part of the explanation. The victory was due chiefly to one of the world's great strategists and generals — Helmuth von Moltke. It was said of Von Moltke that " he could be silent in seven languages." A calm, austere man, Von Moltke was, who said little but thought much. He had but one loyalty — to Prussia and her king; but one interest — the Prussian army; but one desire —

to make that army the most perfect military machine in the world. For years he had given his days and nights to training and equipping the Prussian army in the most up-to-date and efficient manner, and long before the war with Austria he had worked out the strategy of the war to the last detail. Every movement of the armies was calculated, every emergency foreseen and provided for. The Hanoverians of a certain city, in order to delay the Prussians, had destroyed a bridge across the river; but the Prussians, foreseeing that the bridge would be destroyed, had long since measured it, and had brought along with them a temporary bridge to fit, which they set up in a few hours. Above all, two novelties adopted by Von Moltke gave the Prussians a great advantage. One was the needle gun, which could be fired four times while the Austrian muzzle-loader was fired once. The other was the open formation, which enabled each man to move more freely and take advantage of the terrain, concealing himself somewhat behind bushes, fences, or mounds of earth. These advantages were fully revealed at

Von Moltke (1800–1891)

He might be called the first to use scientific methods of warfare.

the Battle of Königgrätz, where the Austrians lost four times as many men as the Prussians.

The European world, unaware of these advantages, was astounded at the swift completeness of the Prussian victory. " The world is coming to an end! " exclaimed Cardinal Antonelli. Lord Malmesbury said that the war " alarmed all nations." For centuries the statesmen of Europe had counted on Germany to be weak by virtue of her division into many small states, weak by virtue of the ancient rivalry of two equally strong powers — Prussia and Austria. Now, overnight, Prussia had suddenly emerged as the master. What would this ruthless Prussia, directed by the ruthless diplomacy of Bismarck, do with her victory? Dismember Austria? Threaten France? Aim at universal empire, as Napoleon had done?

The alarmed statesmen were as much astounded by Bismarck's moderation in victory as they had been by his ruthlessness in bringing on the war. Having won the war, he wished to let Austria off as easily as possible. In his *Reminiscences*, written thirty years after the war, Bismarck says that King William was bitterly opposed to his policy of moderation, wishing rather to " punish " Austria by exacting heavy indemnities and large cessions of territory. Whether or not this was so is uncertain. What is certain is that Bismarck wished to make peace with Austria as quickly as possible, and to be as lenient with her as possible.

The treaties negotiated between Prussia, Austria, and Italy together make up what is called the Peace of Prague (August 23, 1866). The terms of the Peace of Prague were: (1) that Austria should cede Venetia to the Kingdom of Italy; (2) that Austria should pay a small indemnity to Prussia; (3) that the old German Confederation should be dissolved, and that Prussia should have a free hand to organize a new confederation in North Germany; (4) that neither Austria nor the South German states should be included in the North German Confederation; (5) that the South German states — Bavaria, Württemberg, Baden, and Hesse-Darmstadt — should be free to form a confederation of their own, with Austria excluded, if they chose.

Thus the century-long rivalry of Austria and Prussia for the control of Germany was ended. Austria was no longer a German power. The fate of Germany was henceforth virtually in the hands of Prussia. Bismarck at last had his opportunity to " unify Germany under Prussian leadership." How would he do it?

How Bismarck enlarged Prussia and organized the North German Confederation, 1866–1867. Bismarck's first step in consolidating Germany was to enlarge Prussia. This was done by annexing Schleswig and Holstein, Hanover, Hesse-Cassel, Nassau, and the city of Frankfurt. The people of these countries did not wish to be annexed to Prussia, but they were not consulted. Since they were conquered countries, Bismarck said, they must submit to the terms imposed by the victor. Yet it was not from motives of revenge that Bismarck acted. He annexed Schleswig and Holstein in order to give Prussia their excellent ports on the North Sea and the Baltic. (Later it was through this territory that Prussia built the famous Kiel Canal.) The countries of Hanover, Hesse-Cassel, and Nassau were annexed because they lay between the Prussian territory on the Rhine and the Prussian territory east of the Elbe River. Annexing them filled in the gap and gave Prussia a continuous territory from the frontier of France to the frontier of Russia. With these annexations Prussia became, not only the largest state in Germany (excluding Austria), but larger than all the others combined. After 1866 Prussia possessed two-thirds of the population and two-thirds of the territory of Germany.

With Prussia thus enlarged, Bismarck proceeded to form the North German Confederation. Unlike the federations of Switzerland and the United States, the North German Confederation was the union of one enormous state with twenty-one small states. In such a union the great state would be likely to dominate the others. As a matter of fact the Constitution of the North German Confederation was cleverly designed to subject the small states to Prussian control without actually annexing them. The constitution was first approved by the rulers of the twenty-two states, then adopted by a convention of deputies elected by the people, and finally proclaimed in July, 1867. With some slight modifications after the Franco-Prussian War (when the King of Prussia took the title of Emperor, and the South German states were included) this constitution remained in force until 1918. Since it was Bismarck's device for achieving the " unification of Germany under Prussian leadership " we must try to understand how it worked.

Bismarck said that the constitution was intended to recognize three main forces in the actual life of Germany. These were: (1) the predominant position of Prussia; (2) the tradition of political independence in the different states; and (3) the growing force of liberal ideas throughout Germany. The constitution recognized the predominant position of Prussia by making the King of Prussia president (after 1871 emperor) of the confederation; it recognized the tradition of independence in the various

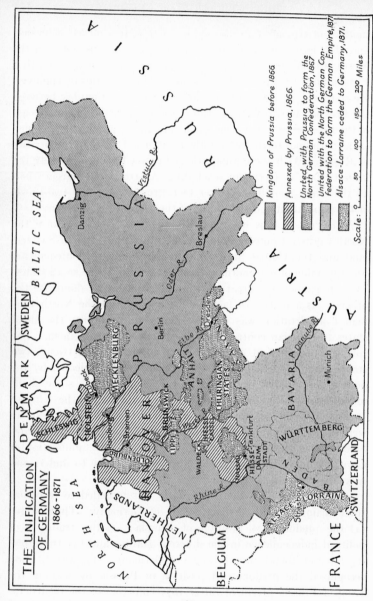

THE UNIFICATION
OF GERMANY
1866-1871

Kingdom of Prussia before 1866

Annexed by Prussia,1866.

*United with Prussia to form the
North German Confederation,1867*

*United with the North German Con-
federation to form the German Empire,1871*

Alsace-Lorraine ceded to Germany,1871.

Scale: 0   50   100   150   200 Miles

R U S S I A

BALTIC SEA

SWEDEN

DENMARK

P R U S S I A

Danzig

Vistula R.

Breslau

Oder R.

MECKLENBURG

Berlin

Elbe R.

Dresden

S A X O N Y

ANHALT

THURINGIAN
STATES

AUSTRIA

BAVARIA

Danube R.

Munich

LÜBECK

HOLSTEIN

SCHLESWIG

H A N O V E R

Bremen

BRUNSWICK

Weser R.

LIPPE

HESSE

WALDECK

OLDENBURG

WÜRTTEMBERG

HESSE
DARM-
STADT

Frankfurt

B A D E N

Rhine R.

Strasbourg

ALSACE

LORRAINE

SWITZERLAND

NORTH SEA

NETHERLANDS

BELGIUM

F R A N C E

states by creating an upper legislative chamber (*Bundesrat*) composed of forty-three deputies (after 1871, sixty-one) appointed
by the rulers of the various states; it recognized the force of liberalism by creating a lower chamber (*Reichstag*) composed of deputies elected by a democratic suffrage. Thus in *form* the North
German Confederation was a federation of independent and equal
states for certain common objects; and in form it created a government in which the laws were made by the representatives of
the people. But in practice this was not so. In practice the confederation was a device which placed the real control of affairs
in the hands of the Prussian king and his ministers. To understand this we must see how the new federal government worked.

First of all we must remember that Prussia had its own government, entirely apart from the government of the confederation;
and since Prussia was two-thirds of Germany, two-thirds of Germany was thus for most matters subject to the government of
Prussia. In Prussia the king was the real director of the government. Besides this, the King of Prussia was president of the
confederation and, as such, exercised extensive power throughout
Germany. He commanded the armies of the confederation. He
controlled foreign affairs and made treaties. He practically controlled the Bundesrat. The members of the Bundesrat voted
by instruction from the rulers who appointed them. The King
of Prussia thus controlled the votes of the seventeen members
whom he appointed for Prussia, and his personal influence with
the rulers of the small states was such that he rarely had any difficulty in obtaining the five additional votes which were necessary
to make a majority. The Bundesrat was thus a council of the
ruling princes in which the King of Prussia was the dominant influence, and since no laws could be passed without the consent of the
Bundesrat, no laws could really be passed without the consent of
the King of Prussia.

The only part of the government of the confederation not controlled by the King of Prussia was the Reichstag. The Reichstag
was elected by the people of Germany. But the Reichstag had
no control over the president or his ministers. It could not ini-
tiate laws, but only discuss those presented to it by the president

and his ministers. Its one check on the president (King of Prussia) and his ministers was that it could reject such proposed laws. This was something, but not much, for the number of parties in the Reichstag was such that the president and his ministers could almost always get a majority for the laws which they wanted passed. Many years afterward a German writer said of the Reichstag that it was not so much a law-making body as a " debating society."

Many people were surprised that Bismarck, who was known to be entirely opposed to government by the people, had been willing to concede even this much to the people in the way of government. One reason probably was that he felt that the lower working classes would be as much opposed to the wealthy middle-class Liberals as he was, and would therefore be inclined to support the Conservatives against the Liberal parties. This was the idea of the Socialist leader, Lassalle, who is supposed to have had some influence on Bismarck at this time. Another reason was that he knew that the people who were most in favor of a unification of Germany were the very people who were most attached to the idea of popular government. It was in order to get their support for the unification of Germany that he favored a popularly elected Reichstag. He said afterwards that it was a species of " political blackmail " that he paid the people to keep them quiet. He felt that the Reichstag could always be managed by the king and his ministers. For twenty-seven years he managed it, but not always as easily as he had hoped.

Thus the first stage in the unification of Germany was accomplished. The old Germany, like ancient Gaul, was now divided into three parts: (1) Austria; (2) the North German Confederation; (3) the four independent South German states — Bavaria, Württemberg, Baden, and Hesse-Darmstadt. As a result, the relation of these three parts to each other was entirely changed. The relation of the South German states to the North German Confederation has to do with the final stage in the unification of Germany. We shall consider that presently. But first we must see what effect these events had on the situation of Austria and the organization of the government of the Austrian Empire.

How the autocratic Austrian Empire was transformed into the constitutional Austro-Hungarian Monarchy, 1867. The Austrian Empire had always been a curious state, unlike any other. In some ways it was not so much a state as a network of political influence centering in a dynasty and an army. The Emperor Francis Joseph, head of the Habsburg dynasty, in his capital at Vienna ruled many peoples and exercised political influence over many others. He ruled directly the Germans of Austria, the Italians of Venetia and Lombardy, the Czechs of Bohemia, the Magyars of Hungary, the Poles of Galicia, and the Serbo-Croats of Croatia, besides many other Slavic groups. In addition the emperor exercised a dominating influence throughout Italy and Germany. Sitting at Vienna, in the center of this network of political connections, the Austrian emperor acted as a kind of guardian for the powers of Europe — a guardian whose business it was to safeguard Italy, Germany, and southeastern Europe from the dangerous ideas of nationalism and political liberalism.

The events of 1859 to 1867 rudely tore this web of political connections in two, much as a broom might tear down half of a spider's web. First, the Italian war and the founding of the Kingdom of Italy (1861) destroyed Francis Joseph's influence in Italy; then the Prussian war and the founding of the North German Confederation (1867) destroyed his power in Germany. Excluded from both Italy and Germany, the emperor found his power within his own dominions beginning to crumble also. He had to make what terms he could with his own dissatisfied subjects. The result was the reorganization of the old Austrian Empire into the dual monarchy of Austria-Hungary (1867).

The Emperor Francis Joseph found himself in trouble immediately after the Italian war of 1859. The war had cost much money, so that the emperor had to borrow some to pay for it. But the German financiers of Austria refused to lend the money until the emperor made some concessions to the people in the way of self-government. To meet this demand Francis Joseph called together a " Council of the Empire " composed of representatives of all the different national groups. The members of the council asked the emperor to grant a constitutional government for the empire;

but they differed as to the form of government to be adopted. The representatives of Bohemia, Hungary, Galicia, and other non-German nations, demanded that each nation should be allowed to establish a government of its own, all of these to be then loosely federated under the emperor. This plan would have made of the empire a loose federation of practically independent states. The representatives of the Austrian Germans were opposed to this plan. They wanted a single united government under the emperor, but they demanded a parliament, for the empire as a whole, which would share with the emperor in the business of governing.

The majority of the council were in favor of the first plan. Accordingly in 1860 the emperor granted a constitution, known as the *Diploma*, which allowed the national groups to establish each its own government. But the Germans were so dissatisfied with this that the following year the emperor modified the Diploma by issuing what was called the *Patent*, which restricted the powers of the several local governments and established a central parliament for the whole empire. The Germans liked this scheme better, but the Magyars and the Czechs were so incensed that they refused to send representatives to the new parliament. The result was that the first constitutional reforms of Francis Joseph worked badly in part of his empire and did not work at all in the rest of it.

Then came the Austro-Prussian War of 1866. During the war the emperor withdrew his grant of constitutional government altogether. But the hopeless defeat in 1866 forced him to take up the question of constitutional reform once more. The difficulty was that if he satisfied his German subjects he would offend his non-German subjects, while if he satisfied his non-German subjects he would offend his German subjects. Since he could not satisfy them both, he decided to satisfy as well as possible the two most powerful national groups and let the others get on as best they could. The two most powerful groups were the Germans of Austria and the Magyars of Hungary. They were the largest groups within the empire and, besides, they occupied the strongest position geographically, being in the center of the empire along the Danube River. Francis Joseph therefore allowed the Germans and the Magyars to devise a form of government for the empire that would satisfy them.

The two men who took a leading part in the negotiations were Count Beust of Austria and Francis Deák of Hungary. The result was the drafting of a constitution known as the " Compromise," which transformed the Austrian Empire into the dual monarchy of Austria-Hungary — a constitution which lasted until 1918. By this constitution the empire was divided into two practically independent states — Austria and Hungary. Under the Hungarian government was all that part of the empire east of the Leith River, except Galicia. The government of Hungary was placed in the hands of a cabinet of ministers responsible to a parliament elected by the people, but elected in such a way that the Magyars had virtually complete control of it. Thus the eastern part of the empire was turned over to the Magyars, who governed not only themselves but also the various Slavic groups within the Kingdom of Hungary. The capital of the Kingdom of Hungary and the seat of the parliament was Budapest. Under the Austrian government was all of the empire west of the Leith River, together with the Polish province of Galicia. Its capital was at Vienna, and its parliament was elected in such a way that the landowning and wealthy classes had a dominant influence. It was in the government of Austria that the emperor, Francis Joseph, retained his influence. Possessing executive power and the right to appoint the ministers, he was able, by playing off the rivalry of the various national groups against each other, to direct the affairs of Austria largely in the interests of the Germans. He had very little influence in Hungary. He was King of Hungary, but he had virtually no control over the ministers or the parliament.

Thus the old Empire was divided into two independent states. In the state of Hungary the Magyars had control; in the state of Austria the emperor and the Germans were the dominating influence. In both states the Slavic groups were more or less still in the position of subject nationalities without self-government. The arrangement was well characterized by Count Beust, who said to Francis Deák, " You manage your barbarians and we will manage ours." By " barbarians " he meant the Slavs.

Practically independent for all matters of internal government, the two states of Austria and Hungary were nevertheless united in their relations to other states. Francis Joseph was Emperor of Austria and King of Hungary, so that the two states were united by having the same ruling dynasty. Besides the two parliaments already mentioned, one for Austria and one for Hungary, there was also a dual parliament representing both states. This dual parliament was composed of sixty members elected by the parliament of Hungary and sixty members elected by the parliament of Austria. The dual parliament sat alternately in Vienna and in Budapest, and it passed measures having to do with the common defense of the two states. There were three ministers of the dual government appointed by the emperor — a minister of foreign affairs, a minister of war, and a minister of finance.

You may ask why, since these two states of Austria and Hungary were independent in all matters of internal government, they united for common defense against foreign powers. The Magyars and the Germans were separate nations, and neither had any love for the other. Why did they not separate entirely? The reason was that neither was strong enough to make a great power, capable of defending itself. The Magyars feared that if they did not unite with the Germans for defense they would be unable to maintain their independence against the Slavic people — particularly the Russians — who surrounded them on all sides. The Germans felt that if they did not tie themselves up with the Magyars they would be absorbed into the new Germany and become subject to Prussian domination. So the two groups joined in this curious dual monarchy for defense, because the Magyars feared the Russians and the Austrian Germans feared the Prussians.

Thus with the creation of the Austro-Hungarian Monarchy the Austrian Germans, numbering about eight millions, were definitely excluded from the new Germany that Bismarck was engaged in creating. Meantime, what of the four independent South German states of Bavaria, Württemberg, Baden, and Hesse-Darmstadt? In the old Germany they had always depended upon Austria to defend them from Prussian aggression on the one hand and from French aggression on the other. Unable now to look

GROUP OF MIDDLE-CLASS GERMANS, ABOUT 1870

The balcony of Professor Schroedter's house in Karlsruhe. The man leaning against the railing is the professor. The man smoking a cigar is Anton von Werner, the artist who drew this sketch.

to Austria for protection, could they maintain their independence? Or would the fear of France force them to join with the North German Confederation? The latter was what Bismarck hoped. We must now see how Bismarck labored to bring about a situation which would force the South German states to join the North German Confederation and thus complete the unification of Germany.

Why the South German states preferred to remain independent of the North German Confederation. The people of South Germany for the most part were sorry to see Austria excluded from the new Germany, and for the present they had no desire to join with the North German Confederation. To join the North German Confederation would be to subject themselves to Prussian domination, and they feared and disliked the Prussians for three reasons especially.

First, the South Germans were, and still are, a different people from the Prussians. The Prussians were a practical, hard-headed people. They were excellent administrators, rulers, and warriors, and though somewhat hard and unimaginative, were quite capable of managing everything, including other people. The South

Germans were far more easy-going, more intellectual and artistic, more humane and tolerant, less aggressive. They disliked the hard, unimaginative Prussians and some sure instinct told them to beware of giving Prussia any chance to meddle with their affairs.

Second, besides this difference of temperament, there was a difference in religion. The South Germans were mostly Catholics; the North Germans mostly Protestants. In all Germany, exclusive of Austria, the Catholics were only about one-third, the Protestants two-thirds. The South Germans therefore hesitated to join the North German Confederation because they feared that the Protestant majority might try to impose restrictions on their religion.

Finally, the South Germans were more liberal in political ideas than the Prussians. It was in South and West Germany that the influence of the French Revolution had been most effective. In South Germany, especially, the ideals of " Liberty, Equality, Fraternity " had never lost their hold since the time of Napoleon. Even the aristocratic classes in the south, particularly in Bavaria, had little sympathy with the autocratic traditions of the Hohenzollern dynasty of Prussia — traditions of which Bismarck was well known to be an ardent supporter.

For all of these reasons the South German states preferred to remain independent as long as they could. This does not mean that they were opposed to the unification of Germany. It means only that they did not like Bismarck's method of bringing it about. The South Germans had desired a united Germany that would include the Austrian Germans; and if Austria were excluded, they desired a united Germany that would be more liberal in government, and less dominated by Prussia, than the one which Bismarck was engaged in constructing.

Bismarck knew very well how the South Germans felt about Prussia, and why they did not desire to join the North German Confederation. Yet unless they were included in the new Germany, the work of unification would be only half done. Bismarck was determined if possible to bring the South German states into the confederation. In order to bring this about he did what he could (1) to make the South Germans fear Prussia less and France more; and (2) to badger France into making war on Germany, so that the South German states would be forced, in self-defense, to join the northern confederation.

How Bismarck tried to win the goodwill of the South Germans, 1867–1870. Bismarck's success in the Austrian war and in establishing the North German Confederation had made him popular in Prussia. The famous historian, Von Treitschke, who had formerly been a Liberal and as such had distrusted Bismarck, now became one of his ardent admirers. " A man who has accomplished so much at a single stroke must be right against every one," he exclaimed. After 1867 there were therefore many Prussians who urged Bismarck to complete the unification of Germany by force — to compel the South German states to join the confederation whether they wanted to do so or not.

Bismarck resisted all such advice. He made no effort to coerce the South German states into a political union with the northern confederation, but he did much to unite them by voluntary agreements, especially in economic and military matters. In 1867–1868 military conventions were entered into which provided for joint action by the South German states and the North German Confederation in case of a defensive war against France. More important was the revision of the old *Zollverein* (Customs Union). In 1818 free trade had been established between all the provinces of the state of Prussia; and between 1818 and 1842 free trade had been established between Prussia and all the other German states except the three Hanse towns of Hamburg, Lübeck, and Bremen. These agreements, which united practically all Germany into one customs district, were known as the *Zollverein*. In 1867–1868 the arrangement was renewed between the South German states and the northern confederation. But the new agreements went farther than the old. They provided that there should be a *Zollparliament*, composed of deputies elected by the people in North and South Germany. The purpose of the *Zollparliament* was to discuss the economic and commercial interests of Germany as a whole, and to devise uniform laws in the interest of all the states, south as well as north.

Besides endeavoring to win the goodwill of the South Germans,

German Tourist Information Office

CUTLERY PLANT IN THE RUHR DISTRICT

This factory, built in the early nineteenth century, was run by water power.

Bismarck did what he could to increase their fear of France. This was not difficult to do, since Napoleon was now asking for those compensations which he had expected to get as a reward for remaining neutral in the Austro-Prussian War of 1866. In 1866 Napoleon asked Prussia to consent to the annexation to France of that part of Bavaria which was called the Rhenish Palatinate. Bismarck told Napoleon that it was not a matter that concerned Prussia, and then he showed Napoleon's letter to the King of Bavaria, in order to prove to him that France had designs on Bavaria. Next Napoleon asked for Belgium. Bismarck discussed the matter, but made no promises. Finally, Napoleon proposed to buy Luxembourg, a small duchy on the Rhine ruled by the King of Belgium and defended by a Prussian garrison. The King of Belgium was willing to sell Luxembourg, but Bismarck got the matter referred to a conference of the great powers at London which decided against the sale but provided that the Prussian garrison be removed and the duchy " neutralized."

In all of these affairs Bismarck played a very shrewd game. He fooled Napoleon to the top of his bent, accomplishing two purposes.

He made it plain to the South German states that they were menaced by the aggressive policy of Napoleon and that if all of Napoleon's projects had been blocked they had Bismarck and Prussia to thank for it. Yet Bismarck was not satisfied with making the Germans fear that Napoleon might make war on Germany. It was necessary to bring Napoleon to the point of actually making such a war.

How Bismarck tried to bring about the Franco-Prussian War of 1870. Some historians think that Bismarck was solely responsible for the Franco-Prussian War of 1870. But if many people in France had not desired the war as much as Bismarck desired it, all of Bismarck's carefully laid plans would probably have come to nothing. The responsibility of France for the war we shall consider in the next chapter. Here we are concerned only with Bismarck's part in it. That Bismarck did all he could to bring about a war with France is certain. In his *Reminiscences* he says: " I assumed that a united Germany was only a question of time, and that the North German Confederation was only the first step in its solution . . . but I did not doubt that a war with France must take place before a united Germany could be realized." Such a war was necessary in order to strengthen the sentiment of German nationalism and to convince the South Germans that their only safety lay in a union with the powerful Prussia. But much as Bismarck wanted war with France, he could not attack France. He must manage to get France to attack Germany. His opportunity came in 1870, in connection with the " Spanish throne question." Just as he had made use of the Schleswig-Holstein question to bring on a war with Austria in 1866, so now he seized upon the Spanish throne question to bring on a war with France.

In 1868, as a result of a revolution in Spain, Queen Isabella was deposed. Possessing a throne with no one on it, the revolutionists began to look for a king. They offered the throne in turn to the Duke of Aosta, to Prince Ferdinand of Saxe-Coburg, and to the Duke of Genoa. Each one declined the offer. Then the revolutionists offered the throne to Prince Leopold of Hohenzollern, a cousin of the King of Prussia. Prince Leopold also declined the

offer (1869).   But Bismarck, foreseeing that the French government would dislike much to see a Prussian prince on the throne
of Spain, sent a secret agent to Madrid to request the Spanish
revolutionists to renew the offer to Prince Leopold.   The result
was that in 1870 the Spanish throne was once more offered to
Prince Leopold, and this time he accepted it (July 2, 1870).   This
was the Spanish throne question which Bismarck hoped would
embroil France and Prussia.

The acceptance of the Spanish throne by Prince Leopold had
precisely the effect in France that Bismarck hoped for.   The French
government protested vigorously, on the ground that the dynastic
union of Spain and Germany would be an intolerable menace to
France; and it even went so far as to say that it would " not permit " a Hohenzollern prince to be King of Spain.   The French
ambassador, Benedetti, was sent to Ems, where the King of Prussia happened to be, to demand of King William that he, as head
of the Hohenzollern family, should order Prince Leopold to withdraw his acceptance of the Spanish throne.   King William refused.
Bismarck was now quite happy.   It seemed almost certain that
France would make war on Prussia in order to prevent Prince
Leopold from becoming King of Spain.

But then, on July 12, it was announced that Prince Leopold,
on the advice of his father, had voluntarily withdrawn his acceptance and would not after all become king of Spain.   Bismarck
took it for granted that the French government would be entirely
satisfied with the withdrawal of Prince Leopold, and that no war
would result.   He was so disappointed that he determined to
resign his office as Chancellor of the North German Confederation.   He was then in the country, and on July 13 he went to Berlin to consult with his friends Von Roon and Von Moltke about
his resignation.   He invited the two men to dine with him, but
the certain prospect of peace made them all so despondent that
they could neither eat nor drink with any pleasure.   While they
were sitting at dinner Bismarck received from King William a
telegram which stated that the French government had made
some new demands.   It was not satisfied with the simple withdrawal of Prince Leopold, but asked in addition that King Wil-

liam should promise never in the future to permit a Hohenzollern to sit on the Spanish throne.

This was the famous Ems telegram. When he had read it, Bismarck felt more cheerful, for he saw at once that he could use this telegram in such a way as to infuriate France and bring on the war after all. If the French government wanted peace, it had made a stupid blunder. If it wanted war, it had done just the right thing to bring it on. Leaving Bismarck and his friends sitting in Berlin with the Ems telegram before them, we must now turn to Paris in order to see whether the French government wanted peace or war, and why it made this extraordinary demand after all cause of quarrel seemed to have disappeared.

QUESTIONS

1. What was the Confederation of 1815? How many states were included in it? Why were the German people dissatisfied with this form of government? What was Bismarck's plan of unification? How did it differ from that favored by most Germans? Compare Bismarck and Cavour.

2. How did Bismarck become the prime minister of King William of Prussia? How did he carry through the military reforms? Why were the Progressive Liberals opposed to Bismarck's policies? Why were the Conservatives not very favorable to him?

3. What was the "Schleswig-Holstein question"? How did it lead to the Austro-Prussian War of 1866? What states sided with Austria in this war, and why? What part did Italy take in the war? Why did Napoleon remain neutral? What was the importance of the Austro-Prussian War? What were the provisions of the Peace of Prague, 1866?

4. What states were annexed to Prussia after the Austro-Prussian War? What were the reasons for annexation? Describe the North German Confederation of 1867. How did Prussia exercise a dominating influence in this confederation? How long did this constitution remain the basis of the government of Germany? How was it modified in 1871?

5. How was Austria's position in Europe changed by the events of 1859–1867? How was the government of the Austrian Empire changed in 1867?

6. Why did the South German states fear Prussia? What did Bismarck do to lessen this fear? How did he try to make the South German states fear France? Why did he do this?

7. What was the "Spanish throne question"? How did Bismarck make use of it to bring on a war with France?

CHART FOR CHAPTER XIII. Unification of Germany, 1862-1871:

Principal stages in the rise of the German Empire.

1862	1863-1865	1866	1867	1868-1871
Bismarck becomes minister of King William of Prussia. Carries through army reforms without consent of the parliament.	Bismarck uses Schleswig-Holstein question to bring on a war with Austria.	Austro-Prussian War. Prussia defeats Austria and her allies-Saxony, Hanover, Bavaria, Württemberg, Baden, and Hesse-Darmstadt. Peace of Prague. Old confederation dissolved. Prussia is free to form a new confederation in North Germany without interference from Austria.	North German Confederation established. Includes all German states except Austria, Bavaria, Württemberg, Baden, and Hesse-Darmstadt. King of Prussia is president of the confederation. Bundesrat represents the states. Reichstag, elected by universal manhood suffrage, represents the people.	Austrian Empire transformed into the Austro-Hungarian (Dual) Monarchy by the constitution adopted in 1867. The four South German states join in the Franco-Prussian War, 1870. They enter the confederation, 1871, which then becomes the German Empire. (Ch. XIV.)

SELECTED READINGS

Brief accounts. Robinson and Beard, *Modern Europe*, II, ch. xxii. Robinson and Beard, *Outlines*, II, ch. xviii. Hayes and Moon, *Modern History*, ch. xviii. Hazen, *Modern Europe*, ch. xxi. Schevill, *History of Europe*, ch. xxvii. Hayes, *Modern Europe*, II, 180–211. Schapiro, *European History* (revised ed.), ch. xv. More detailed accounts: Schevill, *Making of Modern Germany*, chs. iv–v; Priest, *Germany since 1740*, chs. viii–x; Hazen, *Europe since 1815*, ch. xi; R. M. McBride, *Towns and People of Modern Germany*.

Biography. C. G. Robertson, *Bismarck*. E. Ludwig, *Bismarck*. C. Lowe, *Prince Bismarck*. Munroe Smith, *Bismarck and German Unity*. A. D. White, *Seven Great Statesmen*. R. Flenley, *Makers of Nineteenth Century Europe*.

Sources. Robinson and Beard, *Readings in Modern History*, II, 142–158. *The Reflections and Reminiscences of Prince Bismarck*, 2 vols. (Not always to be relied upon, since they were written years after the events described.) *Prince Bismarck's Letters to his Wife*, translated by F. Maxse. The provisions of the Prussian constitution defining the right to vote for members of the *Landtag* are given in Schevill, *Making of Modern Germany*, p. 217; Scott and Baltzly, *Readings in European History*, ch. vii, sec. 2.

THE PONT SULLY, PARIS
From an etching by Lepère.

CHAPTER XIV. THE FRANCO–PRUSSIAN WAR, 1870–1871: HOW LOUIS NAPOLEON LOST AN EMPIRE, AND HOW VICTOR EMMANUEL WON A CAPITAL, KING WILLIAM A CROWN, AND THE FRENCH PEOPLE A REPUBLIC

We are still fighting Louis XIV. LEOPOLD VON RANKE

How Louis Napoleon's most loyal friends badgered him into a war with Germany. Of course the mass of the French people did not want war with Germany. They had no influence, and no great interest in the matter, being fully occupied with the difficult business of making a living. Napoleon himself was not very keen for the war, and if he had been left quite free to do as he liked there would perhaps have been no war. But Napoleon was surrounded by many loyal and influential friends who assured him, with great confidence, that a war with Germany was the best thing that could happen. Who were these loyal but misguided friends, and why did they think that a war with Germany was a good thing for France?

The loyal friends who badgered Napoleon into the war were called " Ultra-Imperialists " — that is, they were more Imperialist than the emperor. The party included many influential officials in the government and the army, many members of the Chamber of Peers and the Chamber of Deputies, and most of the fashionable people who gathered daily at the imperial court to do homage to the emperor, and to the empress Eugénie, who was herself a most ardent Imperialist. These were the people who had always supported the empire as the ideal form of government for France, the people who had always been proud of Napoleon's power at home and of his prestige abroad. But during the ten years following 1860 (the period of the Liberal Empire, see p. 360) Napoleon's power had declined, and in 1870 the empire seemed less firmly established than it had been in 1860. The Ultra-Imperialists blamed Napoleon for it, and they insisted that he should do something striking to revive his waning popularity.

First of all, after 1860 Napoleon had gradually "liberalized" the government. He relaxed his control of the press, and in 1870 he sanctioned a new constitution which lessened his own power and increased that of the ministers and the Chamber of Deputies. Far from being satisfied with these concessions, the people demanded further concessions. Moderate Liberals urged that the emperor transfer all authority to the ministers and the Chamber. The old Republican spirit revived, and under the lead of the brilliant young Gambetta many people were looking forward to the time when the empire would be replaced by a republic. These changes greatly alarmed the Ultra-Imperialists. They felt that Napoleon should have kept the power in his own hands. They felt that in liberalizing the empire he had endangered its existence.

Napoleon's friends were even more alarmed by his blunders in foreign affairs. In 1859 he had helped Cavour against Austria, but had withdrawn when the war was half finished, and afterwards he had prevented the new Kingdom of Italy from taking possession of Rome. The French people criticized him for doing so much for the Italians; the Italians criticized him for not doing more. In 1862–1867 he intervened in Mexico and at great cost established an empire there under the Austrian prince, Maximilian, only to abandon the enterprise when the United States protested. Most serious of all, in 1866 he had remained neutral in the Austro-Prussian War, thus allowing Bismarck to build up a powerful German federation across the Rhine without gaining any territorial compensations for France. What a stupid thing to do, Napoleon's critics were saying, to stand aside and see Prussia enlarged and Germany united without doing anything to prevent it until it was too late!

Thus in 1870 the Ultra-Imperialist friends of Napoleon felt that he had made serious blunders. They were infuriated to think that the Man of Destiny was being laughed at by his enemies. Something must be done to restore the prestige of the emperor in France and in Europe. And what indeed could restore the prestige of the emperor more effectively than a successful war with Germany and the cession of some German territory to France?

Such was the situation when, on July 2, 1870, it was announced that Leopold of Hohenzollern had accepted the throne of Spain. Most Frenchmen thought that a Hohenzollern prince on the throne of Spain would be a menace to France. The prospect reminded them of the sixteenth century, when Germany and Spain were united under the Emperor Charles V. The French government protested vigorously, going so far as to say in effect that it would not permit a Hohenzollern prince to become King of Spain. Benedetti was sent to interview King William of Prussia, who happened to be at Ems. Benedetti was instructed to ask King William to use his authority, as head of the Hohenzollern family, to compel Prince Leopold to withdraw his acceptance. The king declined to compel Leopold to withdraw, but said that if he should withdraw voluntarily he, the king, would approve of it. Thus it seemed that war between France and Germany was inevitable.

But then, on July 12, it was announced that Prince Leopold, acting on the instructions of his father, Prince Anthony, had withdrawn his acceptance and would after all not become King of Spain. Most people took it for granted that this ended the quarrel. Since this was precisely what the French government had asked for, it seemed impossible to suppose that it would ask for anything more. The famous French politician and historian, Guizot, said that it was the greatest diplomatic triumph which France had won in his time. King William said that a millstone had been lifted from his heart. Napoleon said that there was no longer any quarrel. It was as if an island, over which two countries disputed, had suddenly disappeared. What was there left to dispute about?

Ollivier, the prime minister of France, rejoiced to think that the danger of war was over.   Bismarck, as we have seen, thinking that peace was assured, was so discouraged that he decided to resign. The general opinion throughout Europe was that the quarrel had ended in a great diplomatic victory for France.   French honor seemed more than safe ; it appeared triumphant.

Nevertheless, within a week France declared war on Prussia. How did this come about?   It came about because Napoleon was persuaded by the Ultra-Imperialists to make a further demand on King William — the demand for " future guarantees " — and this demand Bismarck made use of to create a war frenzy which could not be resisted.

Napoleon himself did not want war.   Upon hearing of the withdrawal of Prince Leopold, he said : " It is a great relief to me ; war is always a great adventure."   Yet Napoleon knew that some people would not be satisfied.   To the prime minister, Ollivier, he wrote : " The country will not be satisfied, but what can be done about it ? "   The " country " would have been quite well satisfied. Napoleon was not thinking of the country.   He was thinking of the Ultra-Imperialists.   The opinions of the Ultra-Imperialists meant more to Napoleon than the opinions of others, because he had to live with them.   The people in his drawing-rooms and at his dinner table were Ultra-Imperialists of the most violent sort. When he went to his palace at Saint-Cloud on the afternoon of July 12 the empress, the Duc de Gramont, General Bourbaki, and many others were there.   They gathered round him.   " Peace is assured," he told them.   They were dismayed.   " The empire will fall like a house of cards ! " the empress is said to have exclaimed. General Bourbaki said something about breaking his sword for very shame.   Napoleon was an old man, suffering from illness. He had not the decision of character which he had had formerly. He could not stand nagging.   He wanted to satisfy everyone, especially those with whom he was daily associated.   He allowed himself to be persuaded ; and so about seven o'clock, on July 12, he authorized the Duc de Gramont to send an official dispatch to Benedetti at Ems.   Benedetti was instructed to demand of King William that he should not only approve of the withdrawal of Prince Leopold, but also " give assurance that he would not again authorize his candidature."

This was the famous demand for future guarantees. Neither Ollivier, the prime minister, nor any other minister in the government knew anything of it until the next day. Napoleon, yielding to the clamor of the Ultra-Imperialists, was solely responsible.

The next day, July 13, Benedetti met King William on the promenade at Ems and presented the demand according to his instructions. The king replied courteously that he had not yet received official notification of Prince Leopold's withdrawal, but that when he did he would approve of it. As for the future guarantees, he could not bind himself. If Benedetti had been content with this reply, the war might have been avoided. The French government would perhaps have been satisfied with the king's approval of the withdrawal of Prince Leopold. But Benedetti pressed the king a second time to give his promise. He became " almost impertinent." It is very easy to be impertinent to a king. King William, who had a fine sense of his own dignity, was much irritated, and at last he said: " It seems to me, Mr. Ambassador, that I have so clearly expressed myself to the effect that I can never make such a declaration, that I have nothing more to add." Lifting his hat, he moved away.

The Ems telegram: How King William and Bismarck helped to make the war inevitable. Even so, the matter might have been settled peaceably. But now King William did an unusual thing. Contrary to all diplomatic precedent, he authorized Bismarck to make public the negotiations between himself and Benedetti. It is difficult to say why the king did this — certainly not because he wished to bring on a war with France. Benedetti had made him angry, it is true, and Bismarck had been scolding him a little for not being firm enough with Benedetti. Perhaps the king wished to show Bismarck and everyone else how firm he could be. Whatever the reason, he now authorized his secretary, Abeken, to telegraph to Bismarck a statement of what had occurred, giving Bismarck permission to publish the statement in the newspapers. Abeken thereupon sent to Bismarck the famous Ems telegram, which was in substance as follows:

His Majesty writes me: "Count Benedetti spoke to me on the promenade, in order to demand from me, finally in a very importunate manner, that I should bind myself for all future time never to give my consent if the Hohenzollerns should renew their candidature [to the Spanish throne]. I refused, at last somewhat sternly, as it is neither right nor possible to undertake engagements of this kind *à tout jamais* ['forever']." His Majesty has since received a letter from the prince. His Majesty . . . has decided . . . not to receive Count Benedetti again, but only to have him informed through an aide-de-camp that His Majesty had received from the prince confirmation of the news which Benedetti had already received from Paris [news of the withdrawal], and had nothing further to say to the ambassador. His Majesty leaves to Your Excellency [Bismarck] whether Benedetti's fresh demand and its rejection should not at once be communicated both to our ambassadors and to the press.

We must now return to Bismarck at Berlin, where we left him at the close of the last chapter, sitting at dinner with Von Roon and Von Moltke, very much depressed because there seemed no longer any prospect of war. It was while they were sitting there that Bismarck received the Ems telegram from King William. What happened then, Bismarck tells us in his *Reminiscences*. Although written many years after, the account (given below) is probably true enough.

I read the telegram out to my guests, whose depression was so great that they turned away from food and drink. . . . I put a few questions to Moltke as to our military preparations. . . . He answered that if there was to be war he expected no advantage to us in deferring the outbreak. . . . In view of the attitude of France our national sense of honor compelled us, in my opinion, to go to war. . . . Under this conviction, I made use of the king's authorization, which included a command [this is not true], to publish the contents of the telegram; and in the presence of my two guests I reduced the telegram by striking out words, but without adding or altering, to the following form:

After the news of the renunciation of the Prince of Hohenzollern had been officially communicated to the imperial government of France by the royal government of Spain, the French ambassador at Ems made the further demand to His Majesty the king [William] that he would bind himself for all future time never again to give his consent if the Hohenzollerns should renew their candidature. His Majesty thereupon decided not to receive the French ambassador again, and sent to tell him through an aide-de-camp that His Majesty had nothing further to communicate to the French ambassador.

After I had read out the condensed edition to my two guests, Moltke remarked: "Now it has a different ring." . . . I went on to explain: "If in execution of His Majesty's order I at once communicate this text . . . not only to the newspapers, but also by telegraph to all our embassies, it will be known in Paris before midnight, and not only on account of its contents, but also on account of the manner of its distribution, will have the effect of a red rag on the Gallic bull. Fight we must, if we do not want to act the part of vanquished without a battle." . . . This explanation brought about in the two generals a revulsion to a more joyous mood. . . . They had suddenly recovered their pleasure in eating and drinking and spoke in a more cheerful vein.[1]

Did Bismarck "falsify" the Ems telegram? Much has been written on this question. At least this much is certain, that Bismarck's wording of the telegram was intended to make the Germans think that the French ambassador had insulted the Prussian king and to make the French people think that the Prussian king had insulted the French ambassador. The effect of publishing his version of the telegram was precisely what Bismarck hoped. On July 14 the streets of Berlin were filled with excited people clamoring for war with France; the streets of Paris were filled with excited people clamoring for war with Prussia. Perhaps Napoleon and his ministers might still have avoided war. But even the prime minister, Ollivier, who had sincerely desired to prevent war, now felt that it was necessary to vindicate the "honor" of France. Mobilization of the French armies began on July 15; on July 19 France declared war on Prussia.

The Franco-Prussian War, 1870–1871: How the French armies proved incompetent and suffered defeat. Thanks to Bismarck's propaganda, all Germans felt that Napoleon was making an unprovoked war of aggression on Germany. Accordingly the four South German states immediately joined Prussia and the North German Confederation. From the first, France was thus con-

---

[1] *Bismarck the Man and the Statesman.* Translated from the German. Harper and Brothers.

fronted with a united Germany. The Germans had 385,000 soldiers immediately available for the invasion of France. Yet the French were confident of winning. Marshal Leboeuf boasted that the army was ready " down to the last button on the last gaiter." The French cry was " on to Berlin." The confident expectation was that the French armies would quickly cross the Rhine, and that the smaller German states would welcome the French as liberators, much as the Italians had formerly, in 1859, welcomed them as liberators.

But in fact the French had completely misjudged the situation. Their armies were inferior to the German armies in organization, equipment, and leadership. From the first day of French mobilization, confusion reigned everywhere, partly on account of official corruption, partly on account of bad management. Commanders arriving at the front found cannon without ammunition, horses without harnesses, and guns provided with cartridges too large or too small for the bores. General Michel telegraphed from Belfort : " Can't find my brigade. Can't find the general of the division. What shall I do ? Don't know where my regiments are." When Napoleon arrived at Metz on July 28, thirteen days after the beginning of mobilization, he discovered that there was still not a single army corps ready to take the field.

The only things the French generals were adequately provided with were military maps of Germany — which they never needed to use. The German armies, perfectly equipped and intelligently led, moved with swift precision to the frontier and crossed into Alsace and Lorraine. Thus thrown on the defensive, the French attempted to hold Metz and Strasbourg. August 6, General MacMahon was defeated at Wörth and retired to Châlons. The Germans pushed on, outwitted and defeated General Bazaine (Aug. 18) and bottled him and his entire army up in the fortress of Metz (Sept. 1). Napoleon had meantime joined General MacMahon at Châlons. General MacMahon desired to retire in defense of Paris, while gathering re-enforcements. From a military point of view this was probably the proper thing to do ; but officials at Paris telegraphed the general that a retreat would be followed by revolution in Paris and the collapse of the empire. Napoleon

BISMARCK ESCORTING NAPOLEON III TO KING WILLIAM

From an engraving by Camphausen. At the Battle of Sedan, September 1, 1870, Napoleon and his army were taken prisoners by the Germans. Napoleon is in the right rear seat.

446

and General MacMahon therefore moved eastward, but slowly and inexpertly, and when it was too late decided after all to retreat. The Germans caught them at Sedan, where, on September 1, the French army was surrounded and captured. September 2, Napoleon telegraphed to Paris: " The army has been defeated and captured. I myself am a prisoner." Within a month the Germans had shut up one French army in Metz, and captured another. They then moved on to Paris.

Napoleon's pathetic telegram: " I myself am a prisoner," reached Paris September 3. The next day the Legislative Assembly met. A crowd of people invaded the Chamber crying: " Down with the empire! Long live the republic! " Gambetta, Jules Ferry, and others went to the Hôtel de Ville and there, before a shouting mob, proclaimed the republic. A provisional Government of National Defense was hastily formed to take charge of affairs and prepare Paris for the oncoming Germans. Among the members of the new government were Gambetta and Jules Favre. Gambetta was for fighting to the last ditch, but the majority of the members were willing to make peace if no French territory was ceded. The Germans demanded the cession of Alsace and Lorraine. " Not an inch of our territory! " Jules Favre replied; and so the Government of National Defense prepared to hold Paris, hoping that General Bazaine would break through the Germans at Metz and come to their assistance. General Bazaine made no serious attempt to escape from Metz. He wasted a month in fruitless and treasonable negotiations with Bismarck, and then, before his supplies were entirely exhausted, surrendered his entire army of about 175,000 men (October 27). The premature surrender of Bazaine was a godsend to the Germans, since it released their armies for the siege of Paris. Paris made a heroic defense. In January, 1871, the people, in order to keep warm, cut down the fine trees in the *Champs Élysées* and the Bois de Boulogne, and for food were reduced to anything they could get — cats and dogs for preference, rats at two francs each for those who could afford nothing better. Gambetta, escaping in October from Paris in a balloon, established a branch of the Government of National Defense at Tours (later moved to Bordeaux) and tried to rouse the

GAMBETTA ESCAPING FROM PARIS IN A BALLOON

From *L'Illustration*, Oct. 15, 1870. Gambetta was minister of the interior in the provisional government created in Paris after the capture of Napoleon III. He escaped during the siege of Paris in order to rouse the country and organize an army for the relief of Paris.

country for the defense of Paris. But the raw levies which he enlisted were no match for the seasoned soldiers of Von Moltke; and on January 28 the city of Paris, reduced to actual starvation, surrendered.

The Franco-Prussian War, 1870–1871 : The Peace of Frankfurt, May 10, 1871. Since the Government of National Defense had no proper authority to cede French territory, a National Assembly was elected by the people of France for the purpose of making peace with Germany. Republicans like Gambetta wished to continue the war, rather than cede Alsace and Lorraine, but the people generally were in favor of peace at any price. The National Assembly was therefore composed mainly of representatives of the old monarchist parties — Legitimists and Orleanists, with a sprinkling of Bonapartists, and some Republicans elected from Paris and

Musée Carnavalet

LIFE IN PARIS DURING THE SIEGE, 1870–71

From a painting by Pille. People are in line before a municipal canteen waiting to receive food.

the other large towns. The Assembly met at Bordeaux, February 12, 1871. Five days later it elected Adolphe Thiers " Head of the Executive Power." Thiers was now the most popular man in France. He had first become prominent in connection with the Revolution of 1830. He had served as a minister under Louis Philippe. He was the author of a famous and popular history, *The Consulate and the Empire*. He had tried to prevent the Franco-Prussian War, but after it broke out made a tour of Europe in the vain effort to obtain the assistance of the great powers on behalf of France. So the Assembly, having chosen Thiers " Head of the Executive Power," empowered him to negotiate the peace with Germany.

The French and German negotiators met at Versailles, in the famous old palace of Louis XIV. Bismarck stated his demands — a huge indemnity and the cession of Alsace, most of Lorraine (including Metz), and the city of Belfort. The Germans demanded Alsace and Lorraine for two reasons. The first was a sentimental reason. The two provinces had formerly been parts of the Holy Roman Empire. The French had obtained the three chief cities of Lorraine — Metz, Toul, and Verdun — in 1559, and the province of Alsace in 1648. The people of Lorraine were French-speaking, those of Alsace mostly German. The people of both provinces had long since become satisfied with French rule, and a popular vote in 1871 would have been overwhelmingly in favor of remaining part of France. But German national sentiment demanded the recovery of these old " imperial lands." The second reason was military and strategical. The possession of Strasbourg and Metz would give Germany a great advantage in time of war. Moltke said that Metz in German hands was worth 100,000 soldiers. Bismarck was not very keen for demanding so much. "I do not like so many Frenchmen in our house against their will," he said. But Moltke and King William were determined to have Alsace and Lorraine.

Thiers and the French negotiators made a desperate effort to get better terms. At one time in the discussion Thiers burst out in furious anger: "These negotiations are nothing but a sham. Make war then! Ravage our provinces, burn, slaughter! . . . We will fight you to our last breath. We may be defeated, but at least we will not be dishonored." Bismarck was not sure whether Thiers was in earnest. He knew that Europe was becoming alarmed at the extraordinary success of Prussia, and he feared that if peace were not speedily made the great powers might intervene. He therefore got Moltke and King William to make some slight concessions. He said that the French might keep Belfort, provided the German army were allowed a triumphal march through Paris. On these terms the peace was made. The preliminaries were agreed to at Versailles, and the final treaty was signed at Frankfurt, May 10, 1871.

The Treaty of Frankfurt provided (1) that France should cede all of Alsace and part of Lorraine, including Metz; (2) that France should pay an indemnity of 5,000,000,000 francs ($1,000,000,000); (3) that certain French fortresses should be occupied by German troops until the indemnity was paid.

Thus ended the Franco-Prussian War of 1870–1871 — the most important European war between 1815 and 1914. The immediate results of this famous war were three: (1) the completion of Italian unification; (2) the completion of German unification; (3) the establishment of the third French Republic. We must now learn something about each of these.

Results of the Franco-Prussian War: (1) Completion of the unification of Italy. The first immediate result of the Franco-Prussian War was the completion of Cavour's plans for the unification of Italy. When Cavour died in 1861 the Kingdom of Italy had been established, but it did not yet include either the province of Venetia or the city of Rome and the territory round about (see p. 404). The province of Venetia was obtained from Austria during the Austro-Prussian War of 1866 (see p. 420), but so long as Napoleon supported the Pope the Italian government did not venture to take possession of Rome. The Franco-Prussian War, forcing Napoleon to abandon the Pope, provided the Italian government with the opportunity it had been waiting for. As soon as the war started, the king,

CARICATURE BY GILL

Germany is pictured painting the former French provinces of Alsace and Lorraine a Prussian blue.

Victor Emmanuel, with Bismarck's approval, marched 60,000 troops into the Papal States, and on September 20, 1870 — less than three weeks after the Battle of Sedan — they occupied the ancient capital of Italy. The Pope's subjects were allowed to decide whether they preferred to be united to the Kingdom of Italy or remain under papal rule. They voted 130,000 to 1500 in favor of becoming subjects of Victor Emmanuel.

In spite of conquest, in spite of the wishes of his subjects, Pope Pius IX refused to yield. He did not indeed make any forcible resistance — or very little. His army was far too small to contend against the army of Victor Emmanuel, and at the first bloodshed the Pope ordered his troops to cease firing.   Having made it clear to the world that he did not yield voluntarily, the Pope retired to his palace in the Vatican Gardens and there he remained, refusing to recognize Victor Emmanuel as king, refusing to give up his former rights, and refusing to make any treaty with the Italian government.

What could the king do with this Pope who refused to recognize him?   To be sure Pius IX was an Italian, and Victor Emmanuel might have put him in prison or sent him into exile, as he would have imprisoned or exiled any other Italian who refused to recognize the government.   But it was not easy to treat the Pope in this way. As head of the Catholic Church, the Pope was an international figure, and far too powerful to be treated as an ordinary person. The Italian government therefore allowed the Pope to remain in his palace without interference.   In 1871 it passed the Law of Papal Guarantees, which established the relations of the papacy to the Italian government.   The law declared the person of the Pope to be sacred and inviolable.   Certain places in Rome — the Vatican, the Lateran, Castel Gondolfo, and their gardens — were declared to be without the jurisdiction of the Italian government, subject entirely to the Pope.   Within these places the Pope was recognized as a foreign power.   Here he could rule with his court as he had formerly ruled, receiving and sending ambassadors as he had formerly done.   In addition, the Italian government granted to the Pope an annual revenue of about $650,000 as an indemnity for the territory which he had lost.   From that day to this the Pope has ruled his tiny realm within the city of Rome.   But the Pope did not recognize this settlement.   Pius IX and his successors refused to accept the annual revenue granted by the Italian government.   Until the year 1929 (see p. 790), they acted on the theory that the Italian government was a usurping government and that they themselves were prisoners within the Vatican Gardens.

The Italian government acted on a different theory.   It assumed that the vote of the Pope's subjects made Rome a legitimate part of the Italian kingdom.   The capital of the kingdom, formerly removed from Turin to Florence, was moved from Florence to

Rome. Thus in 1871 Cavour's dream of a united Italy with its capital at Rome was at last realized. (See map, p. 403.)

Results of the Franco-Prussian War: (2) The completion of the unification of Germany. The occupation of Rome by the Italian government was only a by-product of the Franco-Prussian War, but the establishment of the German Empire was a direct and intended result of it. Bismarck had desired the war for one reason only — because he believed that it would make it possible to complete the unification of Germany by uniting the South German states with the North German Confederation. In this his judgment proved correct. The people of South Germany, convinced that the war was one of pure aggression on the part of France, felt that they must in the future secure the powerful support of Prussia. A famous Bavarian, Prince Von Hohenlohe, tells us in his *Memoirs* that Bavaria was induced from necessity, rather than from inclination, to enter the confederation in order to preserve her independence against French aggression. It was for this reason that Bavaria, and to a less extent the other South German states, at last agreed to join with the North German Confederation. (See map, p. 424.)

In general the southern states accepted the constitution of the North German Confederation as it was formulated in 1867, but in some respects they reserved to themselves privileges of self-government which the other states did not possess. At the same time it was agreed that the confederation should take a new name — the German Empire (*Deutsches Reich*) — and that the King of Prussia, as head of the federation, should no longer be called " President " but " German Emperor." This was Bismarck's idea. King William at first refused to take the new title. " What have I to do with the fancy-ball major? " he asked. King William was very proud of the title " King of Prussia," and he feared that if he took a new title people would think he did not sufficiently prize his old one. But Bismarck insisted that the new title was necessary, partly because it would revive the glorious traditions of the ancient medieval Empire, partly because the kings of Bavaria and Württemberg would perhaps find it less humiliating to be second in rank to the German Emperor than to the King of Prussia.

Bismarck had his way in the end; and on January 18, 1871, King William was formally proclaimed German Emperor. This ceremony occurred in the famous Hall of Mirrors, in the royal palace at Versailles where the kings of France had formerly lived. In this very Hall of Mirrors, where French courtiers had so often congratulated Louis XIV on his victories in Germany, the new German Empire was now proclaimed, while the German armies were besieging the city of Paris. The event marks a turning-point in European history. For two hundred years France had been the "first state of Europe." After 1871 the new German Empire of Bismarck's creation held that desired position until June 28, 1919, when deputies of the Reich entered the Hall of Mirrors to sign the Peace of Versailles that ended the Great War.

Referring to the Franco-Prussian War, the German historian Von Ranke said to the Frenchman Thiers: "We are still fighting Louis XIV." In 1919 the French premier, Clemenceau, might equally well have said to the German deputies: "We are still fighting Bismarck." It was another Frenchman, Auguste Comte, who said: "The living are ruled by the dead."

Results of the Franco-Prussian War: (3) Establishment of the third French Republic, 1870–1875. When Napoleon was captured at the Battle of Sedan, the second empire collapsed. The hastily formed provisional Government of National Defense directed affairs during the war, only to be replaced by the National Assembly which was elected to make the peace. The National Assembly, sitting first at Bordeaux, moved afterwards to Versailles, where it negotiated the Treaty of Frankfurt which ended the war.

The first thing the National Assembly had to do after ending the war with Germany was to fight a little civil war with the city of Paris. In Paris, after the siege was over, an insurrectionary government was established — a kind of "dictatorship of the proletariat," known as the Commune of Paris. The leaders of the Commune refused to recognize the National Assembly because they feared (with good reason) that the National Assembly intended to restore one of the old monarchical governments in France. Since the Commune had its own army, the army of the National Assembly had to lay siege to Paris, and at last to fight its way desperately

LIFE IN PARIS DURING THE SIEGE, 1870–71

From *L'Illustration*, January 7, 1871. Killing an elephant at the Jardin des
Plantes (zoological and botanical gardens) for food.

through the streets of the city. The "Communards" were treated
as traitors. Some who surrendered were shot down in their tracks.
Thirteen thousand were afterwards condemned to death. Seven
thousand or more were exiled to New Caledonia. Throughout
France the people sympathized with the National Assembly. The
Communards were generally regarded as dangerous Anarchists, as
"Reds," whose aim was to destroy morality and the social order,
and who therefore deserved the harsh treatment which they
received.

After the suppression of the Commune of Paris the chief questions
in everybody's mind were: "What form of government shall be
adopted for France — monarchy or republic? Who has authority
to decide this question?" The National Assembly had been
elected to govern France temporarily while making peace with
Germany. It had not been elected to make a constitution for
France or to govern it indefinitely. Nevertheless, the National
Assembly assumed the right to make a constitution, and then went
on governing France for four years before making one. What is
the explanation of this?

The explanation is that the National Assembly was divided into three parties, each of which had its own plan for a permanent government of France. There was first the Republican party, led by Gambetta, which wished to establish a republic; second, the Orleanist party, which wished to restore the Orleanist monarchy, with the Count of Paris as king; third, the Legitimist party, which wished to restore the Bourbon monarchy with the Count of Chambord as king. There was one government to be established, three different plans for it, and no majority in the Assembly for any plan. Until some compromise could be arranged between these conflicting aims, no constitution could be adopted.

For two years (1871–1873) the National Assembly governed France without even attempting to frame a constitution. The government was directed by Adolphe Thiers as president, with a ministry composed of Republicans and Orleanists. Under the presidency of Thiers, the government paid to Germany the five billion indemnity exacted by the Treaty of Frankfurt, and made certain necessary reforms in the local government and in the organization of the army. President Thiers then felt that the National Assembly could not with decency longer delay the making of a constitution. Thiers had formerly been a supporter of the Orleanist party, but he was now convinced that a majority of Frenchmen desired a republic. After all, he said, a republic is " the system which divides us least." Besides, as he again said, there are two candidates for the throne, but " unfortunately only one throne." In 1873 Thiers therefore brought forward certain proposals for a moderate republican form of government — a Chamber of Deputies and a Senate to be elected by the people, and a president to be elected by the Chamber of Deputies, the Senate, and certain other persons appointed by the local governments. Thiers hoped that these proposals would be radical enough to satisfy many Republicans and conservative enough to satisfy many Orleanists.

But the Orleanists were not yet ready to abandon hope of restoring the monarchy. They therefore joined with the Legitimists to reject Thiers's proposals, whereupon Thiers resigned as president. The two monarchist parties then elected Marshal MacMahon (an Orleanist) to succeed Thiers as president. Thus

PAYING THE INDEMNITY to GERMANY

From *L'Illustration*, July 22, 1871. Arrival of a load of coin at the Bank of
France at Strasbourg.

in control of the Assembly, the Orleanists and Legitimists endeavored to arrange a compromise plan for restoring the monarchy.
On three essential points of this plan the two parties were agreed.
These were: (1) that the Count of Chambord, the Legitimist pretender, should be king first, and that upon his death (since he
had no heirs) he should be succeeded by the Count of Paris, the
Orleanist pretender; (2) that the National Assembly should not
elect the Count of Chambord king by right of popular sovereignty,
but should simply *declare* him king by right of inheritance; (3) that
the Count of Chambord, once declared king, should then grant to
his subjects a moderately liberal constitution.

On these three points the two parties agreed; but on a fourth
essential point they could not agree. They could not agree on the
symbol or flag to be adopted. The Orleanists wished to adopt the
tricolor, the emblem of the Revolution; but the Count of Chambord insisted that the white flag of the old Bourbon monarchy
should be adopted. This dispute might seem a trivial matter, but
in reality it was not so. In refusing to give up the white flag, the

Count of Chambord was really refusing to recognize the validity
of those foundation principles of the Revolution — the principle of
popular sovereignty and of equality of rights.   The Orleanists
were wise enough to know that the French people, although they
might accept a king, would not accept one who refused to recognize
the Revolution as an accomplished fact.   As Marshal MacMahon
said, " If we proclaim the white flag, the muskets will go off of their
own accord."   He meant that to proclaim the white flag would be
the signal for revolution and civil war.

As soon as this plan broke down, the Orleanists hastened to unite
with the moderate Republicans to form a constitution which would
satisfy them both.   " Not being able to make the monarchy," said
the Count of Paris, " it is necessary to organize a constitutional
government with the executive placed above party struggles. . . .
I do not see why we should be alarmed at the idea of calling this
government a republic."   The Orleanists and the moderate Republicans (Republicans like Thiers as distinguished from Republicans
like Gambetta) were especially afraid that if they delayed too long
one of two things might happen — either (1) there might be another
revolution, resulting in the establishment of a radical democratic
republic like that of 1793 or that of 1848; or (2) public sentiment
would once more become favorable to the restoration of the Bonapartist empire.   These fears, and the influences which established
the Constitution of 1875, were exactly expressed by the Duke of
Broglie, who said:

In one word, a republic which resembles a constitutional monarchy, a constitutional monarchy which resembles a republic and
which differs from it only in the constitution and the permanence of
the executive — that is the sole alternative which remains to the
friends of liberty.   Every other republic would be the Convention
[of 1792–1795], every other monarchy would be the [Bonapartist]
empire.

**How the third French Republic was designed to resemble a
monarchy with the king left out.**   The Constitution of 1875 provided for a president, a Senate, and a Chamber of Deputies.   The
Chamber of Deputies was the *democratic* element in the constitution;
the Senate was the *aristocratic* element; the president was the *royal*
element.

The Chamber of Deputies was to be elected by the people, by universal manhood suffrage. No law could be passed without the consent of this chamber, and all tax bills had to be initiated in it. Its chief function was to enable the mass of the people to safeguard their interests, to prevent the wealthy upper classes from running the government in their interest alone.

But it was felt that if the popular Chamber of Deputies had complete control of the government it might disregard the interests of the wealthy and the educated. The Senate was designed to prevent this by acting as a check on the Chamber of Deputies. The Senate was therefore not elected by the people directly. One-third of the members were chosen for life by the National Assembly. (This has since been changed so that there are now no life-senators). Two-thirds were to be chosen by electoral assemblies in each department, composed of the senators and deputies for the department, together with certain local officials. The expectation was that the Senate would be composed of elderly men, wealthy for the most part, and accordingly cautious and conservative in their views. The chief function of the Senate was to exercise a conservative check upon hasty or radical measures favored by the mass of the people, thus safeguarding the rights and interests of the upper classes.

The president was elected for a term of seven years by the members of the Senate and of the Chamber of Deputies all sitting together as one body. The president was expected to represent no party or class, but to represent impartially the state or the nation as a whole. He appointed the cabinet of ministers; but all of his official acts had to be " countersigned by a minister," and the ministers were " jointly responsible to the two chambers." This meant that the cabinet of ministers could not carry through any important measures without the consent of the Chamber of Deputies and the Senate. Consequently the president could not appoint any ministers he pleased, to carry through any policy he liked, but only such ministers as the majority of the Chamber and the Senate desired, to carry out the policy they liked. Whenever any cabinet of ministers ceased to have the support of a majority of the Chamber and the Senate, it had to resign office and the president had then to appoint a new cabinet of ministers agreeable to the chambers.   Thus the executive power was not in the hands of the president, as it is in the United States, but in the hands of the ministers who, in turn, were responsible to the chambers.   To this extent the French system of government resembled the English system, and to this extent the powers and duties of the French president were similar to those of the English king.

Thus, after changing her mind many times since 1789, France at last decided that a republican government suited her best. The third French Republic is not a " democratic republic " like those of 1793 or of 1848.   It is a conservative republic.   But it is at least based on universal manhood suffrage, and after weathering all the storms of half a century seems as firmly established today as any government in Europe.

QUESTIONS

1. How did Napoleon "liberalize" the empire after 1860?   What successes or failures did he have in foreign affairs?

2. Why did the French government object to Leopold of Hohenzollern as king of Spain?   What measures were taken to prevent his becoming king?   Why did Prince Leopold withdraw his consent to become King of Spain?   What effect did most people think this act would have on the question of war?   What did Bismarck think about it?   What did the Ultra-Imperialists think?   What did Napoleon and King William think?

3. How was Napoleon induced to make the demand for "future guarantees" and what was this demand?   Why did King William send Bismarck the Ems telegram?   What did the telegram say?   What changes did Bismarck make in the telegram, and what was his purpose in doing so?   Did he "falsify" the telegram?

4. Why were the French so easily defeated in the Franco-Prussian War?   Describe the German plan of campaign.   What were the results of the Battle of Sedan?   Why was it necessary to elect a National Assembly in France in 1871?   What were the terms of the Treaty of Frankfurt?

5. What were the three chief results of the Franco-Prussian War? How did the German Empire of 1871 differ from the North German Confederation of 1867?   After the Kingdom of Italy took Rome in 1871, what privileges were accorded to the Pope?

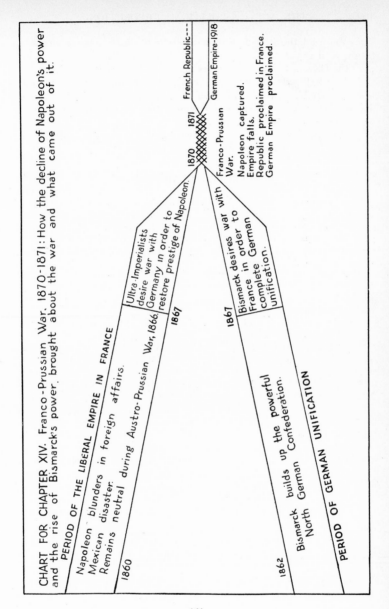

CHART FOR CHAPTER XIV. Franco-Prussian War, 1870-1871: How the decline of Napoleon's power and the rise of Bismarck's power brought about the war and what came out of it.

PERIOD OF THE LIBERAL EMPIRE IN FRANCE

Napoleon - blunders in foreign affairs.
Mexican disaster.
Remains neutral during Austro-Prussian affairs.

1860

Ultra-Imperialists desire war with Germany in order to restore prestige of Napoleon.

Austro-Prussian War, 1866.

1867

French Republic - - - -

German Empire - 1918

1871

1870

Franco-Prussian War.
Napoleon captured.
Empire falls.
Republic proclaimed in France.
German Empire proclaimed.

1867

Bismarck desires war with France in order to complete German unification.

Bismarck builds up the powerful North German Confederation.

1862

PERIOD OF GERMAN UNIFICATION

461

6. Why did the French National Assembly delay making a constitution until 1875? Why did Thiers resign as president in 1873? Why were the Orleanists and Legitimists unable to restore the monarchy?

7. In what respects did the Constitution of 1875 differ from the Radical Republican constitutions of 1793 and 1848? In what respects does the government of France resemble that of the United States? in what respects that of England?

8. Write a brief account of the chief political changes brought about in Europe during the period from 1859 to 1875.

SELECTED READINGS

Brief accounts. Hazen, *Modern Europe*, ch. xxii. Hayes, *Modern Europe*, II, 175–180, 196–206, 331–345. Schapiro, *European History* (revised ed.), pp. 242–250, 321–328. Hazen, *Europe since 1815*, chs. xii–xiii. Seignobos, *Contemporary Civilization*, ch. xi. Summary of events in Italy, Germany, and France from 1849 to 1871: Ashley, *Modern Civilization*, ch. xii.

Biography. Lives of Bismarck and Napoleon already cited. F. T. Marzials, *Life of Gambetta*. P. B. Gheusi, *Gambetta*. F. Le Goff, *Life of Thiers*.

Historical novels. Émile Zola, *The Downfall*.

Sources. Robinson and Beard, *Readings in European History*, II, 158–165, 208–216. Anderson, *Select Documents. Memoirs of M. Thiers, 1870–1873*, translated by F. M. Atkinson. Accounts of the war and the siege of Paris by people who were in France at the time: E. B. Washburne, *Recollections of a Minister to France;* A. Forbes, *My Experience of the War between France and Germany;* Edwin Arnold, *Inside Paris during the Siege;* E. A. Vizetelly, *My Days of Adventure.*

A RUSSIAN PEASANT AND HIS WIFE
From a sketch made in 1871.

CHAPTER XV. SHOWING HOW POLITICAL LIBERTY PROSPERED IN TWO EMPIRES, RUSSIA AND GREAT BRITAIN, 1830–1885

No man is good enough to govern another man without that other's consent.
ABRAHAM LINCOLN

The importance of dates in general and of 1871 in particular. People often say that it is difficult to remember dates. No doubt it is, if one tries to remember them for no good reason. Historical dates are like hooks in a closet — the one you need to remember is the one your hat is hanging on. Therefore don't try to remember all dates, but those only on which important events may be hung — such, for example, as 1789, on which you may hang the French Revolution; or 1914, on which you may hang the Great War.

Another such date to remember is 1871. This date is important because it marks the end of those dramatic and decisive events which we have been studying in the last three chapters. And why are these events so important? They are important because they were in a sense the culmination of political struggles which had been going on for more than half a century. Ever since 1815 the great political question in nearly every country of Europe had been the old one raised by the French Revolution: Shall the people be ruled

by kings and nobles, or shall they rule themselves through representative assemblies of their own choosing? In 1830 some gains
were made by the middle classes in France, Belgium, and England.
In 1848 more was attempted (but nothing gained) in France, Italy,
Austria, and Germany. Then came the dramatic events of 1859–
1871, the result of which was the establishment of at least some
measure of popular government in four of the great European
countries — France, Italy, Germany, and Austria-Hungary. Remember that all the closely related events described in the last
three chapters occurred within twelve years. For convenience,
hang them all on the date 1871.

If you had been living in 1871 you would naturally have associated
certain other great events with those that had recently occurred
in France, Italy, Germany, and Austria — three events, especially,
which might have confirmed you in the belief that you were living
in a time of rapid progress toward political liberty and human freedom. These three events were: (1) the American Civil War
(1861–1865); (2) the emancipation of the serfs in Russia (1861);
(3) the Reform Bill of 1867 in England.

The first of these events we shall not describe. It is necessary
only to remember that it ended in the preservation of national unity
and the abolition of slavery in the United States. People living
at the time naturally associated the American Civil War with the
Italian wars of independence and the German wars of unification.
In their minds all these wars were victories for human liberty and
the principle of nationalism. The other two events which you
should associate with this date are concerned with the progress of
liberal government in Russia and the British Empire. The present
chapter will deal more fully with these.

I. LIBERAL REFORM IN RUSSIA, 1855–1881

How the tsar, Alexander II, freed the serfs, 1861. In 1855, when
Alexander II became tsar, the Russian people still lived under
institutions much like those of France in the time of Louis XIV.
The tsar ruled as an autocrat, by " divine right," supported by
privileged nobles and a state church — the Orthodox Greek Church.
Anyone who criticized the government or the church was likely to

Photo Hachette

RUSSIAN PEASANT LIFE

This shows a typical peasant cottage of the nineteenth century, built of logs and covered with thatch. The barn and cowshed are attached to the house.

be sent to prison or exiled to Siberia. The great mass of the people, some fifty million peasant farmers, were serfs bound to the soil and subject to the nobles on whose estates they lived.

But since 1815 many Russians, inspired by ideas of " Liberty, Equality, Fraternity," had become dissatisfied with this state of affairs. They began to talk of " reform," and even of " revolution." Secret societies were formed, literary magazines founded, and books from abroad smuggled in and circulated. The leaders of the movement included nobles, lawyers, teachers, and officers in the army. During the reign of Alexander's father, Nicholas I (1825–1855), it was still dangerous to talk of " reform." In 1834 a brilliant young man, Alexander Hertzen, was arrested for being present where songs uncomplimentary to the tsar were sung. Later he was banished to Novgorod for criticizing a policeman. In 1847 he left Russia and the next year went to Paris to take part in the Revolution of 1848. For many years he lived in London, where he wrote works in denunciation of the Russian system of government and society. After the death of Nicholas in 1855 his works were smuggled into Russia and had a great influence in promoting the reform movement. Hertzen's *Memoirs* give an excellent account of the conditions in Russia. But Hertzen was only one of many who worked for the liberation of Russia.

One object of the reformers was the abolition of serfdom. Hertzen himself wrote against serfdom, which he denounced as a kind of " baptized property." The great Russian writer, Turgenev, who also lived abroad, wrote *Recollections of a Sportsman*, in which the misery of the peasants and the brutality of their masters are graphically portrayed. In those years opposition to serfdom spread in Russia, as opposition to slavery spread in the United States. *Uncle Tom's Cabin*, which made so many people pity the negro slaves, circulated in Russia and made people pity the peasant serf. Sympathy for the serf was part of the " humanitarian " movement of the time.

When Alexander became tsar in 1855 he felt that something must be done about serfdom. The peasants themselves, returning from the disastrous Crimean War, started insurrections in many parts of the country. So the tsar said : " We live in such an age that in time emancipation must come about. . . . It is better for it to come from above than from below." Accordingly, after much discussion, Alexander issued the Edict of Emancipation (1861). The peasants ceased to be bound to the soil and were freed from the personal control of the nobles. The most difficult question was what to do with the land. The nobles wanted it all. But the peasants wanted their farms freed from all rents and services to the nobles. A compromise was therefore arranged. The nobles kept some of the land, and the peasants were given some. But the nobles, in return for giving up the rents and services formerly paid by the peasants, were paid certain sums of money by the government ; and then the government got its money back, principal and interest, by requiring the peasants to pay annual taxes for forty-nine years. At the end of that time the peasants would not only be personally free men but would own their farms, free from rents and services to the nobles.

The arrangement did not wholly satisfy either party. The nobles complained because they were not paid enough ; the peasants, because they had to pay too much. Many nobles, not used to handling large sums of money, squandered what they received and were worse off than before. As one noble said, " Formerly we kept no accounts and drank champagne; now we keep accounts and drink beer." Thrifty peasants prospered and bought more land. Lazy or unfortunate ones got into debt, lost their farms, and drifted to the cities to join the poverty-stricken classes there. In spite of all, the peasants gained what most men desire more than anything else — personal freedom.

How Alexander nearly granted a constitution, and why he was prevented, 1881. Another object of many of the reformers was political liberty. They admired the political systems of England, Belgium, and France. " Russia," they said, " will never play her part in advancing European civilization until she adopts the liberal institutions that have made England and France the leading states of Europe." They urged the tsar to permit freedom of speech and of religion, to establish local governments controlled by the people, and to grant a national legislature composed of elected representatives. These reformers were called " Westerners " or Liberals. Opposed to them were the " Slavophiles " or Nationalists. " Russia," the Slavophiles said, " will never become great by imitating other people. Russia is Russia, a peculiar nation which will do her part in civilization only by developing her own peculiar institutions." The program of the Slavophiles was a little vague. In fact they had no program. To the Slavophile party belonged such men as Dostoievski and Tolstoy, passionate lovers of mankind, who had little faith in the power of laws to make men good; while to the Western or Liberal party belonged such men as Hertzen, Turgenev, and Kropotkin — lovers of mankind too, but convinced that political liberty was the first essential step to the regeneration of Russia.

The tsar refused to grant a national constitution; but the emancipation of the serfs, which freed the peasants from the discipline of the nobles, made some change in local government necessary. So after 1861 two sorts of local institutions were established. (1) For the administration of justice, local courts were created, modeled somewhat on the English system and providing for jury trial in criminal cases. (2) For other matters — such as the man-

© *Press Cliché*

RUSSIAN PEASANT HOUSE AND BARNS IN THE PROVINCE OF MOSCOW

agement of poor relief, schools, prisons, and hospitals — local
assemblies were established: (*a*) district assemblies, elected by
the nobles, city people, and peasants, and (*b*) provincial assemblies,
composed of representatives elected by the district assemblies.

To the Liberals, Russia seemed now about to enter a new era of
political freedom. But their hopes were soon dashed. The new
local institutions worked badly. Officials proved ignorant and
corrupt, and there were bitter quarrels between the nobles and the
city people and between the nobles and the peasants. To make
matters worse, in 1863 the people of Russian Poland rose in insurrection demanding "national independence." The Slavophiles
were able to say: "We told you so! This is what comes of
borrowing the institutions of other countries — confusion and
anarchy and the dismemberment of Russia!" So the timid tsar
changed his mind about reform, and after the Polish Revolution
was suppressed the local reforms and liberties were to a great
extent withdrawn.

The result was that after 1870 the reform movement in Russia
changed its character. Old-fashioned Liberals became discouraged.
Many young men became indifferent. "Our fathers," they said,
"had a childish faith in 'Liberty, Equality, Fraternity'; but as
for us, we have faith in nothing." This difference between the old

and the new generation is the theme of Turgenev's novel, *Fathers and Sons*, and it was he who coined the word *Nihilists*. The younger people were Nihilists because they scoffed at everything and had faith in nothing (*nihil*). But not all young men were Nihilists. Many of them said that the reforms had failed because of the ignorance of the peasants. They said, " We must go among the peasants as missionaries, teaching them." So a great many of these devoted young men and women, disguising themselves by wearing old clothes and tarring their hands, went to work with the peasants, hoping to spread among them the revolutionary doctrines of Proudhon and Bakunin (see p. 536). But they found the peasants stolid and immovable, and soon gave up. Most of them joined a third group of reformers who called themselves " Terrorists." The Terrorists said, in effect: " Everything has been tried in vain — argument, persuasion, education of the peasants. Since mild measures fail, we must strike terror into the hearts of the oppressors. We will throw bombs until every official, from the tsar down, realizes that his life is in constant danger. When they give us the liberty we demand we will no longer resort to violence. "

Between 1879 and 1881 many officials were assassinated, and three attempts were made to kill the tsar. Once more the tsar changed his mind. Upon the advice of his minister, Loris-Melikoff, he had prepared a document which promised certain reforms in the government. March 13, 1881, Alexander signed the order for the publication of his promise ; but on the afternoon of the same day, as the tsar was returning from a drive, he was killed by a bomb thrown under his carriage.

The result of this act was different from what the Terrorists hoped. Russia was terrorized indeed. The new tsar, Alexander III, withdrew the promise of liberal reforms, and for the next twenty-five years a policy of " tsarist repression " prevailed, such as Russia had not known since the time of Nicholas I. Consequently, in the eyes of the world the failure of liberal political reform in Russia was charged to the Terrorists. The martyred Alexander was known as the " Tsar Liberator," and his reign was counted as a step forward in the progress of human freedom.

II. Democratic Political Reform in England, 1867-1885

How the " spirit of the times " induced the English people to take another cautious step towards democracy. In 1832, as we have already seen (p. 333), a kind of revolution occurred in England, the result of which was to extend political power to the wealthy middle classes. Besides the Reform Bill, the English Parliament passed many other laws, before and after 1832, abolishing abuses or modifying old customs. The barbarous criminal code was reformed (1821). Certain restrictions on the rights of Catholics were removed (*Catholic Emancipation Act, 1829*). Slavery was abolished in the colonies (1833). The first of the Factory Acts, designed to protect workers in industries, and better laws for the relief of the poor, were enacted (1833). The outworn and corrupt government of the cities was reformed (1835).

Meantime, the working classes were not at all satisfied with the Reform Bill of 1832, which they had helped to force through Parliament but which conferred no political privileges on them. From 1838 to 1848 they therefore kept up a continuous agitation for further reform of Parliament. In what was known as the " People's Charter " (see p. 334), they demanded the following reforms: (1) annual parliaments; (2) manhood suffrage; (3) vote by ballot; (4) equal electoral districts; (5) removal of property qualification for members of Parliament; (6) payment of members of Parliament.

These famous six points of the charter were all designed to give the poor man equal political rights with the rich. The " Chartist movement " reached a kind of climax in 1848, at the time of the revolution in Paris. A petition to Parliament was prepared, supposed to have been signed by five million people, and April 10 was set as the day for a great parade and the presentation of the petition. To prevent riots, the government gathered troops in London under the lead of the aged Duke of Wellington. On the appointed day a heavy rain dampened the enthusiasm of the Chartists, the parade fizzled out, and the monster petition — loaded into five cabs to be carried to Parliament — was found to contain no more than two million signatures, many of them fictitious.

For ten years after the fiasco of 1848 the Chartist movement declined; but in the decade from 1860 to 1870, though the name " Chartism " was not used, the question of parliamentary reform again became a live one.   Hitherto neither of the two dominant parties had been willing to grant any extension of the suffrage to the mass of the people.   Both parties — Whig (now calling themselves Liberal) and Tory (now calling themselves Conservative) — were supported by the upper classes, who were well satisfied with the privileges which they possessed and wished not to share them with the working classes in country and town.   But about 1865 certain leaders in the Liberal and Conservative parties felt that the demand for further parliamentary reform could no longer be entirely ignored.

One reason for this was the vague but sometimes very powerful influence called the " spirit of the times."   All the great events of the ten years from 1860 to 1870 seemed to show that Europe was " going democratic."   In Italy, Germany, and Austria, hitherto the centers of reaction, the people were winning at least some degree of political liberty.   Even in the France of the Emperor Napoleon III the mass of the people could vote for representatives in the Assembly.   The people of England could ask, and did ask: " Shall England, always regarded as the home of political liberty, lag behind in the general advance towards democratic government? "

One very important evidence of the spirit of the times was the outcome of the American Civil War.   English laborers were directly affected by the Civil War.   When the southern ports were blockaded, the supply of cotton was cut off and thousands of laborers in English cotton mills were thrown out of work.   The suffering which they endured with much patience and self-restraint won them widespread sympathy and contributed to the feeling that their demands for political rights should be granted.

In addition to that, the outcome of the Civil War helped to convince the English people that democracy was the coming form of government and that they might as well make the best of it.   Generally speaking, the conservative ruling classes, whether Whig or Tory, hoped that the South would win the war; the laborers hoped the North would win. John Bright, a popular leader and a powerful orator, told the laborers why the privileged classes wanted the South to win:

Privilege thinks it has a great interest in the American contest, and every morning, with blatant voice, it comes into our streets and curses the American Republic. Privilege has beheld an afflicting spectacle for many years past. It has beheld thirty millions of men happy and prosperous, without emperors, without kings, without nobles — except such as are made by eminence in intellect and virtue, without state bishops and state priests — those vendors of the love that works salvation, without great armies and great navies, without a great debt and great taxes; and Privilege has shuddered at what might happen to old Europe if this great experiment should succeed.

No doubt this was oratorical exaggeration, but there was much truth in it for all that. Conservative journals, such as the *Morning Post* and the *Edinburgh Review*, said very frankly that if the North won the Civil War, " Democracy will have won its greatest victory since the world began." They admitted frankly that they hoped the North would not win, because if it did it would be very difficult, if not impossible, to resist the demand for democracy in England.

Thus the spirit of the times was working for a more democratic government in the world. Moreover as it happened, during these years there came to the front in English politics two able men who were aware of the spirit of the times and decided to make use of it for the advantage of their respective parties. These men were Benjamin Disraeli, leader of the Tory party, and William E. Gladstone, leader of the Whig party.

Disraeli and Gladstone: Two great men who had little in common except their devotion to England and their dislike of each other. Benjamin Disraeli was one of the most striking personalities of the nineteenth century. His father, Isaac, was a Jew who turned Christian, and the author of *Curiosities of Literature* — a book widely read in its day. The young Benjamin educated himself by associating with the scholars and men of letters who frequented his father's house and by reading whatever he found interesting in his father's well-stocked library. For many years he was known chiefly as a writer of books and as a picturesque society character.

He began his career at the age of twenty-one by publishing a novel
— *Vivian Grey* (1826). He attracted attention by appearing at
dinners wearing green-velvet trousers, low shoes adorned with silver
buckles, sleeves fringed with fine lace, and hair ostentatiously and
foppishly done in long ringlets. His conversation, unless he per-
versely chose to be conspicuously
silent, was as brilliant as his costume.
People were alternately puzzled, delighted, and infuriated by the aptness
of his caustic wit, the cryptic and
double-edged quality of his paradoxes.

In 1837 this social dandy and man
of letters entered Parliament. It was
supposed to be but another of his
eccentricities. His first speech, elabo-
rately rhetorical and delivered with
the mannerism of an actor, was received with jeers and laughter. He
ended by saying, " I sit down now,
but the time will come when you will
hear me." The prophecy seemed as
preposterous as it was conceited. A
Jew, a man of letters, a wit, a notorious dandy given to green-velvet
trousers and delighting in Oriental
rhetoric — who indeed could picture
such a fellow commanding the serious

DISRAELI AS A YOUNG MAN

From a sketch in *Fraser's Magazine*. Note the sandals, lace
cuffs, curls, rings, and watch
chain of the complete dandy.
The letters on the mantel are
from his admirers.

attention of the prosaic and easily bored men who sat on the
benches of the House of Commons with hats pulled down over their
eyes? Nevertheless that miracle happened. By 1867 Disraeli was
recognized as the outstanding leader of the Conservative party.

About the same time another able man, William Ewart Gladstone, had come to be recognized as the leader of the Liberal party.
Gladstone was as unlike Disraeli as one great statesman could well
be unlike another. He was the son of a Scotch merchant-prince
of Liverpool. He was educated in schools designed for the sons of
gentlemen — Eton and Oxford. He early attracted attention,

not by doing or saying unaccustomed things, but by doing and
saying what people expected him to do and say, better than they
expected he would. In his dress, his manners, and his ideas, he
followed the conventional modes. He was serious, devoutly religious, systematically industrious, and gifted with a solid and
powerful mind which rarely condescended to wit, persiflage, or

National Gallery, London

WILLIAM EWART GLADSTONE
(1809–1898)

From a painting by Millais.

paradox. He wrote much, but always on serious subjects seriously
treated — on religion, on Homer,
on finance. Finance was a subject
which his Scotch mind delighted in
and easily mastered. It was said
of him that he was the only man
who could make the dull details of
a financial budget interesting to the
House of Commons.

Gladstone at first joined the Tory
(Conservative) party, and at the
age of twenty-three entered Parliament (1832). He was at that
time opposed to the Reform Bill,
thinking that " along with partial
good " it would bring " a melan-
choly preponderance of mischief."

He believed that the Bible justified the institution of slavery,
but he advocated the education and the gradual emancipation
of slaves in the British colonies. In 1846 he followed his party
leader, Robert Peel, in abolishing the old system of protective
tariffs; and during the years that followed adopted, with much
travail of spirit, so many liberal views that he could no longer
remain in the Conservative party. He therefore joined the Liberals, and rapidly rose to be their outstanding leader. Gladstone's
power over his contemporaries came less from his intellect than
from his character — less from his ideas than from the emotional
fervor with which he held them and the marvelous felicity with
which he expounded them. He was a heaven-born orator. His
voice was as commanding as his presence. It is said that fifteen

thousand people in the Waverley market at Edinburgh could hear him without difficulty. Whether they understood him or not, people listened entranced to the easy flow of his long and complicated sentences, to the rhythmical rise and fall of his singularly flexible and melodious voice.

Thus these two men, Disraeli and Gladstone, confronted each other as the leaders of their respective parties. From 1865 to the death of Disraeli in 1881, English politics was a dramatic duel between these different and hostile personalities. Different as they were, neither had much faith in the capacity of the people to govern themselves. Yet one of the first notable results of their bitter rivalry was that through their joint efforts the government of England was made more democratic.

The Reform Bill of 1867: How Disraeli took "a leap in the dark," and how Gladstone profited by it. According to the Reform Bill of 1832, the right to vote in the cities was limited to "ten-pound householders" — persons owning or occupying houses worth ten pounds a year ($50). In 1866 Gladstone proposed to extend this right to "seven-pound householders." Even so moderate a reform was opposed by many Liberals on principle. Gladstone's bill was therefore defeated by a combination of Conservatives and Liberals. The Liberal ministry resigned, and a new Conservative ministry was formed under Lord Derby as prime minister, with Disraeli as leader in the House of Commons.

National Portrait Gallery, London

DISRAELI, EARL OF BEACONS-
FIELD, IN LATER LIFE

This portrait was painted at the time when he was leader of the Conservative party. Compare it with the one reproduced on page 473.

The defeat of Gladstone's bill, much to the surprise of everyone, aroused great popular excitement. In his last speech Gladstone coined the phrase which became a party slogan: "You cannot fight against the future; time is on our side." The agitation was greatest in the cities. John Bright, the idol of the workers, employed his eloquence to stir the people to action. He reminded them that in 1832 their fathers had used force to get the great Reform Bill passed, and he hinted that they might do as much now:

You know what your fathers did thirty-four years ago, and you know the result. The men who, in every speech they utter, insult the workingmen, describing them as a multitude given up to ignorance and vice, will be the first to yield when the popular will is loudly and resolutely expressed. If Parliament Street, from Charing Cross to the venerable Abbey, were filled with men seeking a reform bill, these slanderers of their country would learn to be civil, if they did not learn to love freedom.

A National Reform League was formed, and arrangements were made for a great public meeting to be held in Hyde Park. To prevent the meeting, the government had the park gates locked — an act which defeated its own purpose, since it only confirmed the popular belief that reform was necessary. The enraged people broke down the heavy iron railings, swarmed into the park, and held their meeting in spite of locked gates and government orders.

Parliamentary reform thus became once more the order of the day. Disraeli and many Conservatives realized that they could not hold office long unless concessions were made. Lord Derby, the prime minister, therefore decided to bring in another reform bill. Lord Derby himself did not like the idea very much. He described the proposal to extend the suffrage to the people as taking a " leap in the dark." The famous historian and man of letters, Thomas Carlyle, called it " shooting Niagara." Many Conservatives reconciled themselves to it by saying that by granting reform themselves they would at least have the advantage of " dishing the Whigs " — stealing the thunder of the Liberals. The new bill, a moderate one, was introduced into the House of Commons by Disraeli. Moderate as it was, it soon appeared that no majority could easily be obtained for it. The Liberals opposed it because it was a Conservative measure, and many Conservatives opposed it in spite of that fact. Rather than suffer defeat, Disraeli therefore accepted many amendments offered by Gladstone. In 1867 the bill was finally carried by the Conservative ministry, but as amended it was as much Gladstone's bill as it was Disraeli's.

The Reform Bill of 1867 was therefore the joint work of the two enemies, Disraeli and Gladstone. Its provisions were as follows: (1) Some small boroughs lost their representation in Parliament, and some large cities were given added representation. (2) The right to vote was given to many tenant farmers in the country. (3) In the cities the right to vote was given (a) to all householders, no matter what the value of their houses, and (b) to men living in lodgings worth ten pounds a year.

The new law extended the right to vote to a million men, chiefly in the cities, thus doubling the electorate. It did not establish the universal manhood suffrage demanded by the People's Charter, but it was a most important step in that direction. Both of the old parties now recognized that political privileges could no longer be confined to the wealthy few, but must inevitably be extended, for good or for evil, to the many poor.

Disraeli no doubt hoped that the workers who were thus granted the right to vote would, in common decency, vote for the party which conferred that right upon them. If so, he was disappointed. The first election (1868) under the new law resulted in a sweeping victory for the Liberals, and Gladstone became prime minister with a larger majority in the House of Commons than any prime minister had had since 1832.

The reform bills of 1884–1885: How the English people took another step in the direction of democratic government. During the first Gladstone ministry (1868–1874) many reforms were enacted, but chiefly in connection with Ireland (see p. 487). In respect to parliamentary reform one measure only was enacted. This was the adoption of the " secret ballot " in 1872. But in his second ministry (1880–1885) Gladstone carried through Parliament the reform bills of 1884 and 1885.

The first of these had to do with the suffrage. The Reform Bill of 1867 had extended the suffrage to the poor people, chiefly those in the cities. The Reform Bill of 1884 provided that the same " household " suffrage should be established in the counties as already existed in the cities — that is, every person who owned or occupied a house, or part of a house used as a separate lodging, was given the right to vote. Thus the laborers in the country were given the same right of voting as that already enjoyed by the poor people in the cities.

The Reform Bill of 1885 had to do with representation. People may have equality in respect to the right of voting for representatives but still lack equality in respect to the number of representatives they may elect. Before 1885 this had been notably so in England. Most boroughs had two representatives in Parliament, no matter whether they had few or many inhabitants. One of the six points of the People's Charter had demanded " equal election districts." The idea was that if Manchester, for example, had five times as many inhabitants as some other borough, it ought to have five times as many representatives in Parliament. The Reform Bill of 1885 was based on this democratic principle. It divided the country into new election districts, so that each district would have about fifty thousand inhabitants and would choose one member of Parliament. The effect of the law was to give populous cities and counties a greater number of representatives than they had formerly had. The county of Lancaster, for example, had formerly chosen only eight members of the House of Commons. Under the new law of 1885 it chose twenty-three members.

Thus in this second period of Parliamentary reform (1867–1885) political privileges were extended to the mass of the people. Some men — and all women — were still excluded from the right of voting. But by 1885 England was at least committed to the principle that the people as a whole, and not merely the upper classes of wealth and education, were to share in the privileges of government.

Meantime, during the last three-quarters of the nineteenth century, while the government of England itself was becoming more democratic, the right of national self-government was being conceded to some of the English colonies — to Canada, Australia, New Zealand, and South Africa. We must now learn something of that process by which the British Empire has become in part a voluntary association of free peoples.

III. The Establishment of Self-Government in Some of the British Colonies

How England lost part of her empire by trying to govern it too much: The American Revolution, 1775-1783. In the seventeenth and eighteenth centuries England built up a great empire — in North America, in India, in the West Indies. At that time statesmen and economists thought that colonies were valuable possessions, especially if they could supply the mother country with things which the mother country could not herself produce. For example, South Carolina and Jamaica were valuable to England because they could supply England with cotton and sugar, neither of which was raised in England. Without sugar or cotton colonies, England would have had to buy these commodities from foreign countries — the Dutch or the French perhaps — and to pay for them by sending money to the French or the Dutch.

In order that the colonies might benefit the mother country, the English government supervised their activities in various ways. With few exceptions there was in each of the American colonies a royal governor, appointed by the British government to assist the colonial assembly in governing the colony and especially to see that no improper laws were passed by the assembly. The trade and industry of the colonies were strictly regulated by many acts of Parliament, known as the Trade and Navigation Acts. In general the Trade and Navigation Acts prohibited the colonies from buying or selling many things in foreign countries. For the most part the commodities they exported had to be exported to England or to an English colony, while the things they imported had to be imported from England or an English colony.

In 1765 the British government levied a stamp tax in the colonies. Then came the famous quarrel that led to the American Revolution. The dispute concerned the rights of the colonies. The British government claimed that the colonies had only such rights as Parliament might be willing to give them. The colonies claimed that they possessed certain rights, derived either from their ancient charters or from " nature " (see p. 195), which the British Parliament could not legally deprive them of. The real question

ENGLISH INN OF THE EARLY NINETEENTH CENTURY
From an old English print. In front of the inn of the *Galloping Horse* is a
watering trough, which a maid is pumping full.

at issue was a question of self-government. The colonies felt that
they were quite capable of governing themselves, and that they
ought to be allowed to decide what was wise or necessary for
them to do. The British government felt that the colonies were
British possessions, and that as long as Great Britain protected the
colonies from foreign aggression they were in duty bound to submit
to such laws as Parliament thought wise or necessary.

The quarrel lasted ten years (1765–1775). The more the colonists discussed their rights, the more rights they discovered. The
final and most extreme formulation of colonial rights is to be found
in the famous Declaration of Independence (1776). The Declaration of Independence was based on a new theory of the British
Empire. According to this theory, the empire was composed of
several nations or "peoples" — the English people, the Irish
people, the people in the various colonies. Each of these groups
was free and had a natural right to govern itself. They were all
nevertheless united by a common allegiance to the king. In

short, the theory of the Declaration of Independence was that the British Empire was a voluntary association of free peoples.

With the aid of France the colonies won their independence (1783) and later established the United States of America under our present constitution (1787). Thus by trying to govern the colonies against their will, England lost a valuable part of her empire. What effect did this experience have in changing England's method of governing her empire? Not much, if any. For half a century, at least, the old method prevailed. But towards the middle of the nineteenth century the British government began to adopt a more liberal method of colonial government. This change was associated with two new ideas which were spreading through Europe at that time, one political, the other economic.

How the two ideas of popular government and free trade helped to change the English method of governing her empire. One of these two new ideas we are already familiar with. We have already seen how, after 1830 especially, most of the European countries, including England, adopted popular government. But if self-government was good for the people in Europe, why was it not good for the people outside Europe? At least it might be asked why Englishmen in Canada, Australia, and South Africa were not as well able to govern themselves as Englishmen in England. Many people said: " We lost the American colonies by stupidly trying to govern them against their will. There's no use repeating this blunder. If the colonies are fitted for self-government and want to govern themselves, the wise thing is to give them what they want."

The other new idea goes under the name of " free trade." Many years before, in 1776, Adam Smith had published one of the most famous and influential books on economic theory ever written — *The Wealth of Nations*. He said that the prosperity of a nation did not necessarily depend on a " favorable balance of trade," and that therefore protective tariffs were often — usually, indeed — harmful. This idea was taken over by English economists in the early nineteenth century — Ricardo, Cairnes, John Stuart Mill. All nations, they said, would be more prosperous if they would adopt the principle of free trade. Each country would then produce the things it could most cheaply produce, and buy of foreign countries other things which could be more cheaply produced in those countries. The result would be maximum production at minimum cost. After 1830 the question of free trade became a practical political question. Many restrictions on trade were abandoned and finally, in 1846, the famous " corn laws " (tariffs on the importation of wheat) were abolished. This may be taken as the measure, and 1846 as the date, which marked England's adoption of the principle of free trade.

The theory and practice of free trade were closely connected with the theory and practice of governing the colonies. Formerly colonies were thought to be valuable chiefly because their trade could be largely confined to the mother country. But if this was a mistake, what then was the value of the colonies? Some people said that they had no value and might as well be given up altogether. In any case, if the colonies were to be free to trade as they liked, there was less need for supervising their government. They might as well be left to govern themselves and make their own trade regulations, if any.

Thus in the middle of the nineteenth century the two new ideas of popular government and free trade prepared the way for a more liberal treatment of colonies. In these years the British government accordingly conceded the right of self-government to its English-speaking colonies.

The self-governing dominions: How England strengthened her empire by loosening its bonds. The English rarely change a custom or an institution until some practical difficulty forces them to do so. Therefore, in spite of the spread of liberal theories of colonial government, they made no change in the government of the colonies until one of them revolted. This revolt occurred in Canada.

Canada, originally settled by the French, was acquired by England in the Seven Years' War (1763), and during the American Revolution it remained loyal to the mother country. In 1791 it was divided into two provinces — Upper Canada (Ontario), and Lower Canada (Quebec). These provinces were governed much as the American colonies were governed before they won their independence. In each province there was an assembly elected

ENGLISH POSTCHAISE, ABOUT 1816
From an engraving by Vernet.

by the people and a royal governor appointed by the British government. In each province the assembly and the governor were almost always quarreling. The assembly, supported by the people, wanted to govern without interference by the governor. The governor, representing the British government, frequently vetoed laws passed by the assembly, or issued ordinances on his own authority. In Lower Canada this quarrel was more bitter than elsewhere because the people were mainly French. Finally, in 1837, the French people of Lower Canada, infuriated by certain arbitrary acts of the governor, began an armed rebellion in which they were promptly joined by some of the English people in Upper Canada.

The Canadian Rebellion of 1837 was easily crushed by British troops, but afterwards the British government sent Lord Durham to Canada to inquire into the grievances of the people and to suggest methods of redressing them. Lord Durham made an elaborate report which is important because it marks the beginning of a new policy of colonial government. In his report Lord Durham said that the Canadians could very well govern themselves through their assemblies, and that they would be more loyal to England if they were allowed to do so. He also said that it would be better if all the provinces in North American were united in some kind of federation. These two suggestions — *responsible self-government* and *colonial federation* — were afterwards applied, not only to the government of Canada but to other English-speaking colonies.

The Dominion of Canada. In 1840 Upper and Lower Canada were united into one province of Canada. In 1848 Lord Elgin, the royal governor, adopted the practice of appointing his cabinet of ministers from the leaders of the party that had a majority in the assembly. The ministers governed as long as their measures were supported by the assembly. If their measures were defeated in the assembly, they either resigned or called a new election. If the people, in the elections, supported the ministers, they remained in office; if not, a new ministry was formed. Thus the same system of government was established in Canada that existed in England. The royal governor played the same part in the government of Canada that the king played in the government of England. He was only a nominal ruler. The real ruler was the prime minister, supported by the dominant party in the assembly.

In course of time the various British provinces in North America were united in one federation. In 1867 New Brunswick and Nova Scotia united with the former province of Canada (Ontario and Quebec), in a federation known as the Dominion of Canada. Prince Edward's Island joined the federation in 1873. Meantime, as the western country was settled, new provinces were created — Manitoba and British Columbia. In 1878 all of the provinces (except Newfoundland, which remained an independent colony) were included in the federation. Each province had its own government for purely local affairs but no longer had a royal governor. There was now only one royal governor for the federation; and the federation was governed by the federal parliament through a cabinet of ministers appointed by the royal governor from the dominant party in parliament.

Thus Canada was given self-government. The British government has nothing to do with the government of Canada except

LAYING THE FIRST CABLE BETWEEN ENGLAND AND HOLLAND

From the *Illustrated London News*, June, 1853. "The King of Holland's speech at the opening of the States General at the Hague, was transmitted . . . to London . . . being the first public intelligence dispatched by the new route."

to manage its relations with foreign countries and to defend it from foreign aggression. Otherwise Canada is virtually as independent of Great Britain as the United States is, and if it demanded complete separation from the British Empire it would undoubtedly get it. Newfoundland has essentially the same kind of independent government as the Dominion of Canada.

New Zealand and the Commonwealth of Australia. The first English colony established in Australia was New South Wales (1788), which in the nineteenth century developed into a prosperous sheep-raising country and in 1855 was given a form of self-government similar to that established in the province of Canada. In 1851 the southern part of New South Wales was erected into the separate province of Victoria, and in 1859 the northern part was erected into the separate province of Queensland. Meantime four other colonies were founded — Western Australia, Southern Australia, and the island colonies of Tasmania and New Zealand. To these provinces self-government was also conceded.

The federation of the Australian provinces was early discussed, but long delayed on account of economic differences. New South Wales followed England in adopting the policy of free trade, while the other provinces favored protective tariffs. But in the latter part of the century they were led to unite by a common desire to exclude Chinese immigrants and by a common opposition to German colonies recently established in the region. After long discussion a federal constitution was drafted and enacted into law by the British Parliament. The federation thus created is known as the Commonwealth of Australia and includes all of the provinces except New Zealand (an island 1200 miles from the continent of Australia). The government of the commonwealth is much like that of the United States. Each province has a government much like the governments of our states. The federal government is composed of a Senate and a House of Representatives, very much as our federal government is. There is a High Court very similar in its functions to our Supreme Court. But the chief executive is not a president elected for a period of years. The chief executive is a prime minister who holds office, as the prime minister in England does, only so long as his measures are supported by a majority in the legislature.

Thus Australia is a federation enjoying responsible government, just as Canada is. New Zealand, like Newfoundland, enjoys responsible government but remains outside the federation.

The Union of South Africa. The southern point of Africa, the Cape of Good Hope, was first possessed by the Portuguese but was taken from them by the Dutch, and from the Dutch by the English (1806). This region, known as Cape Colony, was settled by a mixed population of English and Boers (a race descended from Dutch and French settlers). As the English moved in, the Boers moved north and east and settled Natal, the Orange Free State, and the Transvaal. Cape Colony was given self-government in 1872, Natal in 1893. Towards the middle of the century the Orange Free State and the Transvaal were recognized as virtually independent states. But friendly relations between the Boers and the English were always difficult to maintain, and after the discovery of diamonds and gold in South Africa (1867 ; 1886), bitter hostilities developed which finally led to the Boer War. The result was that the Orange Free State and the Transvaal were annexed to the British Empire (see p. 619), with a promise that self-government would be conceded as soon as practicable. This was done in 1906 and 1907. Two years later (1909) the four provinces of Cape Colony, Natal,

Orange Free State, and the Transvaal were united in a federation known as the Union of South Africa. As in Canada and Australia, each province has its own government for local affairs; but the federation is ruled by the Union parliament, under a prime minister who represents the majority party in the parliament. As it happened, the first prime minister of the new federal government was General Botha, who but a few years before had led the Boer armies in their gallant but losing fight against the British army.

Thus during the years 1837 to 1909 (the period during which democratic government was being established in European countries) a degree of self-government amounting virtually to independence was conceded to those parts of the empire inhabited in whole or in part by English-speaking people — Canada, Newfoundland, Australia, New Zealand, and South Africa. Since the war these countries, together with Great Britain, have been given a new name — the British Commonwealth of Nations. This is a new sort of empire — an empire which is a voluntary association of free peoples (the Boers of South Africa would perhaps not admit this). Will this principle of imperial government be extended to the rest of Britain's possessions — to India for example, with its hundreds of millions of non-English people? Only the future can answer that question.

Meantime another people, nearer home, objected strenuously to British rule. These were the Irish. How did they fare in the struggle for self-government?

Ireland and her grievances: How Gladstone gave the Irish some things they wanted, but not the chief thing, which was " home rule." The story of Ireland is an unhappy one. Conquered by Henry VIII in the sixteenth century, it remained until the twentieth subject to the alien rule of England. The English have been unusually successful in governing subject peoples, but the government of Ireland must be counted one of their failures. In the nineteenth century Irish grievances were therefore many, of long standing, and very real. Yet not until the first ministry of Gladstone (1868–1874) was any serious attempt made to redress them. What were these grievances, and what did Gladstone do to redress them?

The grievances of Ireland may be treated under three heads: (1) religion; (2) land; and (3) home rule.

1. *Religion.* The religious difficulties arose from the fact that the majority of the inhabitants of Ireland were Irish and Catholic, while a minority (chiefly in the northern province of Ulster) were Protestants of English or Scotch ancestry. The laws imposed on Ireland were unjust to the Irish Catholics in two respects. First, Catholics were excluded from Parliament, so that the majority of the people in Ireland could be represented in Parliament only by men of an alien and hostile religion. Second, the Protestant (Anglican) Church was established by law in Ireland. This meant that the Irish Catholics had to pay taxes to maintain churches which they did not attend and to support the Protestant clergy, many of whom, having no parishioners in Ireland, lived in England. Meantime, the Catholic services were held in dilapidated buildings, or in the open, and the priests were as poor as the people they served.

The first of these grievances was redressed in 1829 by the Catholic Emancipation Act. Henceforth Catholics were free to hold office and could be elected to Parliament. The second was redressed by the first Gladstone ministry in 1868. Gladstone said that there were three branches of the " Irish upas tree " which needed to be cut off. One of these was the " Irish Church " — that is, the Anglican Church established in Ireland. By a law of 1868 the Irish Church was " disestablished." This meant that the Protestant Church in Ireland was no longer supported by taxes imposed on the people. The church was also partly " disendowed." This meant that some of the property of the Irish Church was taken over by Parliament and applied to other purposes. Henceforth the Irish Catholics were not required to pay taxes for the support of any church. The disestablishment of the Irish Church was the only one of Gladstone's many Irish reform measures which was entirely effective.

2. *Land.* The great majority of the Irish were farmers. But the land was not owned by the farmers who tilled it. It was owned for the most part by wealthy landlords, many of whom were Englishmen who lived in England and rarely visited their Irish estates. On these estates the mass of the Irish lived and worked as " ten-

DERBY DAY, 1856
National Gallery, London

From a painting by Frith. The Derby (pronounced *Darby*) was then, as it is now, the great horse-racing event of the year.

ants." Since there were always more men seeking farms than there were farms, the landlords had a good thing of it. They could charge a high rent, and if the tenant failed to pay the rent promptly — or even if he did pay it promptly — the landlord could evict him at will, or at very short notice. To make matters worse, any improvements made by the tenant (such as the building of a barn or a cowshed) became the property of the landlord, and the tenant, if evicted, could claim no compensation for such improvements. The result was that the Irish tenant farmers lived in wretched hovels, were frequently evicted for non-payment of rent, and had little to eat except potatoes. When the potato crop failed there was a famine. In famine years, such as 1839 and 1846, thousands of people died of starvation; and every year other thousands, in desperation, migrated to the United States. As a result of starvation and migration, the population of Ireland fell from 8,300,000 in 1845 to 5,100,000 in 1881.

To improve the condition of the Irish farmers, Gladstone introduced the Land Act of 1870. This law provided that the landlord could not evict a tenant so long as he paid his rent, and that the tenant, if evicted for other reasons than non-payment of rent, should be paid for all improvements he had made on the land. The law also provided a method by which the tenants could buy their farms from the landlord. The only result of this law was that the landlords raised their rents, and evictions were more frequent than before. In his second ministry, Gladstone therefore had Parliament pass the Land Act of 1881, which was designed to establish fair and fixed rents, and deprived the landlords of the right to raise them arbitrarily. This act did almost as little to improve matters as the first one.

A PILGRIM'S PROGRESS

From a cartoon by Swain in *Punch*, April 15, 1893. Gladstone is represented as Christian passing through the valley of Home Rule, between the Irish Nationalist bog on the one side, and the Ulster Last Ditch on the other. Do you know from what part of Bunyan's *Pilgrim's Progress* this idea was taken?

The failure of these measures convinced the Irish that partial reforms were useless. They therefore demanded complete home rule.

3. *Home rule.* In the eighteenth century the Irish had had a parliament of their own, at Dublin; but in 1801 they were induced to give up their own parliament and instead to choose representatives to the English Parliament. At first the Irish members in the English Parliament had supported Gladstone's early reforms; but the failure of the first Land Act convinced them that nothing would end their troubles except the restoration of the Irish parliament. After 1879, under the leadership of a brilliant and aggressive man, Charles Stuart Parnell, the Irish party in Parliament and the people in Ireland concentrated all their efforts on the attempt to obtain home rule. The Irish members of Parliament resorted to obstructive tactics, talking endlessly on every question that came up, in order to delay the business of the House. In Ireland the people resorted to violence. They tried to intimidate their landlords by mutilating their cattle and burning their houses. Some landlords

were killed, and in 1882 two English officials were assassinated while crossing Phoenix Park in Dublin.

Under pressure of such tactics Gladstone decided that the wise thing to do was to give the Irish what they wanted. April 8, 1886, two months after the formation of his third ministry, he therefore introduced the first Home Rule bill into Parliament. The bill proposed to give Ireland a parliament of its own, with powers similar to, although not so extensive as, those enjoyed by the Dominion parliament of Canada. At the same time Gladstone introduced a new " land bill " providing an elaborate method for the purchase of farms by the Irish tenants with the aid of the British government.

The Home Rule bill encountered bitter opposition. Lord Salisbury, the Conservative leader, said that the Irish were incapable of self-government and that they were so hostile to England and the British Empire that it would be unsafe to give them home rule in any case. John Bright, a Liberal humanitarian who had warmly supported Irish reform, objected to the measure because under home rule the Irish Catholic majority would dominate and oppress the Protestant minority. Even among Liberals the opposition was so strong that ninety-three members of the party refused to support their leader and voted with the Conservatives. The bill was therefore defeated, and Gladstone resigned after having been in office less than six months.

Gladstone was nevertheless more than ever convinced that home rule was the only solution of the Irish problem. Six years later, when the Liberals were once more returned to power, the " Grand Old Man " formed his fourth ministry. In 1893 he introduced the second Home Rule bill. It was the old story over again. The debates were more notable for epithets than for arguments, and on one occasion certain members of Parliament engaged in fisticuffs on the floor of the House. The bill was finally carried in the Commons, but only by a small majority of thirty-four votes; and it was immediately rejected by the Lords. Divided and weakened, the Liberals retired from power in 1895, and for ten years England was governed by the Conservative party. Not until after the Great War did Ireland finally obtain home rule (see p. 765).

Why Part III ends with this chapter. In 1831, immediately following the July Revolution in France, Alexis de Tocqueville, a young Frenchman, visited the United States. In 1835 he published a book that made him famous — *Democracy in America*. His purpose in visiting the United States, he tells us, was to observe democracy at first hand in the country where it was most firmly established, in order to learn what " Europe has to fear or to hope for from its progress." His observations in the United States only confirmed him in the belief that the great French Revolution of 1789 had started a movement towards democratic government which could not be repressed; and he predicted that in no great time democracy, whether upper-class people liked it or not, would be the prevailing form of government in the Western world.

Within less than a hundred years after the French Revolution, De Tocqueville's prediction had virtually come true. With the adoption of a democratic suffrage in England, nearly every country in Europe had a form of government which in theory admitted the right of popular self-government and in practice gave to the mass of the people at least some share in electing their rulers. In Part III we have traced the history of the political revolution by which absolute monarchy disappeared in Europe and was replaced by some form or other of popular government. By 1871, or at latest by 1885, that revolution was, if not completed, at least assured of success. That is why, with this chapter, we shall close Part III, which we have called the Age of Political Revolution.

Meantime, another revolution, beginning long before 1871 but having its most important effects after that date, was occurring. This is called the Industrial Revolution. It will be the subject of Part IV.

QUESTIONS

1. What great events between 1860 and 1871 contributed to the progress of human freedom and popular government? What resemblance is there between the American Civil War and the wars in Italy and Germany about the same time?

2. How was Russia governed at the time of the accession of Alexander II? Describe the rise of the reform movement in Russia. How did the Western or Liberal party differ from the Slavophile or Nationalist party?

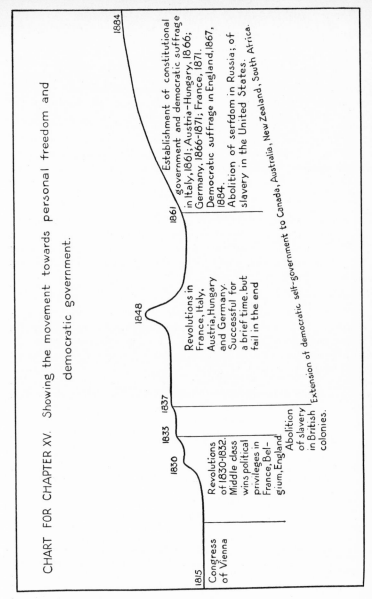

CHART FOR CHAPTER XV. Showing the movement towards personal freedom and democratic government.

1815
Congress of Vienna

1830
1833 1837
Revolutions of 1830-1832. Middle class wins political privileges in France, Belgium, England.

Abolition of slavery in British colonies.

Extension of democratic self-government to Canada, Australia, New Zealand, South Africa.

1848
Revolutions in France, Italy, Austria, Hungary and Germany. Successful for a brief time, but fail in the end.

1861
Establishment of constitutional government and democratic suffrage in Italy, 1861; Austria-Hungary, 1866; Germany, 1866-1871; France, 1871. Democratic suffrage in England, 1867, 1884.
Abolition of serfdom in Russia; of slavery in the United States.

1884

493

How were the serfs emancipated in Russia? What other reforms were adopted in Russia between 1861 and 1881?

3. What was the People's Charter? the Chartist movement? Why did the question of Parliamentary reform revive in England after 1860? Contrast Gladstone and Disraeli as to personal appearance, characteristics, etc. Describe the circumstances leading to the passing of the Reform Bill of 1867. What was accomplished by this law? What were the provisions of the reform bills of 1884–1885?

4. What were the chief countries within the British Empire in 1775? What disputes led to the American Revolution? What theory of the British Empire was put forth by the revolting colonies? What was the cause of the Canadian Rebellion of 1837? Why were the English more favorable to free government for the colonies in 1837 than they were in 1775? What was the importance of Lord Durham's report on Canada? Tell all you can about the formation (1) of the federation known as the Dominion of Canada; (2) of the Commonwealth of Australia; (3) of the Union of South Africa. What powers has the British government over the self-governing dominions? Were they obliged to support Great Britain in the Great War, or was their support voluntary? How does the government of Australia resemble that of the United States? How does it resemble that of Great Britain?

5. What were the chief grievances of Ireland in the nineteenth century? What was the "Irish Church" and why did the Irish object to it? When was it disestablished? Describe the situation of the Irish tenant farmers in the middle of the nineteenth century. What effect did the Irish famines have on the United States? What did Gladstone do to improve the condition of the Irish tenant farmers? What was the Home Rule movement? What were the Gladstone Home Rule bills? Why did they fail to pass?

SELECTED READINGS

Brief accounts. Robinson and Beard, *Modern Europe*, II, 190–198, 201–232. Robinson and Beard, *Outlines*, II, chs. xxi–xxii. Hazen, *Modern Europe*, chs. xxvii–xxviii, xxxii. Hayes, *Modern Europe*, II, chs. xxii, xxix. Ashley, *Modern Civilization*, chs. xv, xvii–xviii. Schevill, *History of Europe*, chs. xxviii, xxxi. Schapiro, *European History* (revised ed.), chs. xi, xvi. Hazen, *Europe since 1815*, ch. xx. G. M. Trevelyan, *British History*, xxi–xxii, xxiv. On Ireland and the British colonies: Robinson and Beard, *Modern Europe* (revised ed.), II, ch. vi. E. Barker, *Ireland in the Last Fifty Years*. E. Scott, *Short History of Australia*. A. Jenner, *Stories from South African History*. E. St. Aubyn, *Life on a South African Farm*. Sir Harry Johnson, *Pioneers of South Africa*. On the development of democracy in the smaller countries: Hazen, *Europe since 1815*, chs. xv–xvii. Schapiro, *European History* (revised ed.), chs. xix, xxii.

Biography. A. Maurois, *Disraeli.* G. M. Trevelyan, *John Bright.* L. Strachey, *Queen Victoria.* F. Ponsonby, *Sidelights on Queen Victoria.* G. Brandes, *Lord Beaconsfield* (Disraeli). G. W. E. Russell, *Life of Gladstone.* J. Bryce, *Gladstone.* J. A. Froude, *Disraeli.* P. Kropotkin, *Memoirs of a Revolutionist.* M. Degoboril, *When I was a Boy in Russia.* R. Cohen, *Out of the Shadow,* Part I. C. Breshkovsky, *Little Grandmother of the Russian Revolution.*

Sources. Robinson and Beard, *Readings in Modern History,* II, 245 (the People's Charter); 255 (Gladstone's defense of popular suffrage); 258 (working of cabinet government in England); 345 (Kropotkin's description of serfdom in Russia); 348 (Russian edict of emancipation). A. B. Keith, *Selected Speeches and Documents on British Colonial History,* 2 vols. B. Deutsch and A. Yarmolinsky, *Modern Russian Poetry.* Scott and Baltzly, *Readings in European History,* ch. viii.

LARGE FACTS TO REMEMBER ABOUT PART III

1. *New ideas in the eighteenth century.* The "philosophers" prepare the way for the French Revolution.

2. *The French Revolution, 1789–1795.* Destroys government by king and nobles. Establishes equality before the law, and government by the people.

3. *Napoleon, 1799–1815.* Organizes and maintains the revolutionary changes in French institutions. Establishes European empire.

4. *Temporary reaction, 1815–1825.* Settlement of Europe at the Congress of Vienna. Concert of Europe tries to repress liberal ideas.

5. *Revival of revolutions in behalf of "Liberty, Equality, Fraternity," 1830–1848.* Middle-class liberal governments established in France, Belgium, and England, 1830–1832. Grand upheaval of 1848. Temporary success, ending in complete failure.

6. *National and democratic reorganization, 1859–1885.* Italian unification under Cavour. German unity under Bismarck. Reorganization of Austrian Empire. Third French Republic. Liberal reforms in Russia. Democratic suffrage in England. Self-government extended to some of the British colonies.

MICHAEL FARADAY IN HIS LABORATORY

From a sketch by Maclise in *Fraser's Magazine*. Faraday (1791–1867) was one of the great scientists of the nineteenth century. He was noted for his discoveries in chemistry, but more so for the discovery of the induction of electric currents and the effect of magnetism on polarized light.

PART IV

THE AGE OF INDUSTRIAL REVOLUTION

In which a pertinent question is asked and briefly answered.
The great prophets of democratic government, such as Mazzini,
believed that when the people were allowed to govern themselves
everything would be well — poverty would disappear, justice would
reign, and nations would dwell together in peace and harmony.
The establishment of democratic government in Europe did not
bring about this happy state. On the contrary, during the fifty
years following the establishment of democratic government in
Europe, the conflict between rich and poor was even more intense
than before. The nations, instead of dwelling together in harmony,
hastened to enlarge their armies and navies, engaged in a competition for the control of " backward countries," became every year
more jealous and suspicious of each other, and at last plunged the
European world into the most desperate, the most widespread, and
the most disastrous war ever known.

Why? Why was it that the establishment of democratic government in Europe, belying the hopes of its prophets, failed to bring
about peace and goodwill, either within or between the nations?
This is the pertinent question which we have to ask.

Many attempts have been made to answer this question. Some
have said : " The so-called democratic governments were not really
democratic." Others have said : " It was a mistake to suppose
that democratic government would bring about peace and good
will." Still others have said : " Government has nothing to do with
it ; it is the nature of men to fight, and they will do so under any
form of government." These answers are all interesting, but if we
ask History to tell us which is the true one, she only looks Sphinx-
like and says nothing. History tells us *what*, but if we ask her
why, she can answer only by giving us more of the *what*. Historians
can therefore answer the question *why* only by saying that some-

thing happened which the prophets of democratic government could not foresee — something which democratic government was not well suited to deal with successfully.

What was this something that happened? The answer is to be found in Part IV. Briefly, this is what happened: A great economic and industrial revolution, the beginnings of which may be traced back to the eighteenth century and beyond, was rapidly accomplished in the latter half of the nineteenth century. As a result of this revolution the old ways of life — ways of living and making a living; ways of learning and of gaining experience of life; habits of thought and of conduct — were rapidly and profoundly changed. In every country in which the Industrial Revolution occurred, economic and social problems arose in such a bewildering variety of new forms that neither the people nor the law-makers whom the people chose to represent them were competent to deal with them successfully. That is to say, during the fifty years following the establishment of democratic government in Europe the conditions of life changed so rapidly that people could not adjust themselves to the new conditions without stress and conflict.

In Part IV we shall learn something about this Industrial Revolution and about the conflicts that it engendered — social conflicts within the nations and economic conflicts between the nations. Now if we inquire as to the primary cause of the Industrial Revolution which we are about to study, the answer is: science and invention, and the rapid multiplication of power-driven machines. First of all, therefore, we must learn something about the coming of machines, and how they changed the conditions of life.

CHAPTER XVI. THE INDUSTRIAL REVOLUTION: HOW SCIENCE GAVE MEN MACHINES TO WORK FOR THEM, AND HOW THE MACHINES CHANGED THE CONDITIONS UNDER WHICH MEN HAD TO LIVE AND LABOR

Things are in the saddle and ride mankind. EMERSON

Men have been using machines for a long time. Aristotle said that " man is a political animal." That is a good definition — one of the best. But man might also be defined as the animal that uses machines — or tools, since machines are only complicated tools. Of course other animals (the dog, for example) use tools too, but only such as come " f.o.b." The dog is not fully equipped with the extras. He has only the tools that he is born with — claws and teeth. If he wishes to store food he can only dig a hole in the ground. Man can store food far better because, by attaching to his hand artificial tools — saws, hammers, planes, chisels — he can build a storehouse. If the dog has a grudge, the most he can do is to attack his enemy with teeth and claws. But the intelligent man, in dealing with an enemy, is at once more polite and more deadly: he uses an automatic — or a fountain pen. This suggests another definition of man : *Man is the animal that uses artificial tools.*

Such tools man has been using for a very long time ; and our marvelous machines are only the latest stage in the slow and painful effort of man to master his world by means of tools. The jack in your automobile kit is only a perfected lever, and the lever has been in use since primitive man discovered how to pry up a stone with a stick. The pullman car is only a palatial wagon, the wagon is a super-cart, and the cart goes back to the time when some ingenious fellow invented a wheel, perhaps by cutting a four-inch slab from the end of a log. Long before the age of written records man had invented the fundamental tools: (1) fire, which made possible the art of cooking, the smelting and hardening of metals, and the making of bricks, glass, and pottery; (2) implements and weapons, such as the ax, the knife, the plow, the bow and arrow; (3) means of conveyance, such as the wheeled cart, the rowboat, and the sailboat; (4) domesticated animals (a kind of invention and a kind of tool), such as dogs, goats, cattle. These achievements were all accomplished eight or ten thousand years ago. Without them primitive civilization, or any subsequent civilization, including our own, would have been quite impossible.

Why men have infinitely more and better machines now than formerly. Although all civilization is based on the use of tools, the important thing to note about modern civilization is this: Within a hundred and fifty years infinitely more and better tools have been invented than were invented in all the preceding centuries. In the year 1800 no European country had a postal system more rapid than that of the ancient Roman Empire. Few ships sailed the Atlantic which could not have been overhauled by a Phoenician trireme. The royal highways in France were no better — were indeed hardly as good — as the Roman roads built seventeen centuries before. The farmer still used the wooden plow and the ox team. The artisan still made shoes and built furniture with tools invented by primitive men. If Julius Caesar had come back in 1800 to make a new conquest of Gaul, the only thing that need really have discouraged him were the muskets and cannon — and even these totally new weapons he might have mastered more easily than Napoleon could have mastered the weapons used in the Great War. Within a short hundred years the external conditions of life have been revolutionized by machines and devices which multiply a thousandfold the power of men to *make* things, to *move* things, and to *communicate* information.

Why this extremely rapid speeding-up of inventions within the last two centuries? The answer is: science, which is only another name for *systematic knowledge of the physical universe*. Before the eighteenth century there was relatively little knowledge of that kind, and little desire for it. For the most part, men regarded the natural physical world as a mystery, and as peopled by spirits which might be propitiated but could not be mastered. If someone stumbled by accident on a natural force, such as magnetism, he was likely to regard it as an enemy to be avoided rather than a friend to be cultivated. Previous to the eighteenth century we may say that man had an " inferiority complex " towards nature. But in the seventeenth and eighteenth centuries an intellectual revolution occurred (see Chapter VII), the result of which was that men gradually lost this inferiority complex. They discovered that nature might be the friend of man. Nature came then to be regarded as something filled with secret forces which might be mastered by reason and harnessed in the service of man. The result of this changed attitude has been the development, within the last hundred and fifty years, of modern science — of systematic knowledge of the physical, chemical, and biological structure of the natural world, such as never before existed.

It is thus scientific knowledge, and especially the deliberate intention of increasing it, that has made possible the rapid multiplication of machines during the last century. For the first time in history thousands of learned men, working in thousands of laboratories, in universities and elsewhere, are giving all their time to studying the structure of the physical universe. Modern science is a deliberately organized conspiracy to rob Nature of her secrets and to pilfer her concealed stores of power. Hence invention and discovery no longer come by accident. They do not take us by surprise. On the contrary, they are anticipated. We predict them. In large measure science has replaced necessity as the " mother of invention "; and a far more prolific mother she has proved to be.

How the multiplication of machines has changed the conditions of life. Perhaps in most respects modern civilization can hardly be said to surpass the ancient Greeks. Our athletes may slightly surpass in strength and swiftness the performers in the Olympic games. But has Tolstoy, or any other modern, excelled Socrates in wisdom? What modern philosopher has thought more profoundly than Plato or Aristotle? Who has written a more stirring tragedy than Euripides, a better comedy than Aristophanes, a more admirable history than Thucydides? What modern statue is more beautiful than the Venus de Milo, what building more perfect than the Parthenon? Who shall say that Bismarck was a wiser statesman than Pericles, or Napoleon a greater military genius than Caesar or Alexander?

But whether superior or not, modern civilization *differs* from all previous civilizations, and that chiefly in two respects: (1) man has more power over things; (2) things have more power over man. This new relation between man and things has done more than revolutionize industry; it has modified and is modifying our habits and institutions, and by modifying our habits and institutions it has changed and is changing our thinking. Briefly we may say that the new relation between men and things is changing our habits and thinking by (1) enabling more people to live; (2) providing them with more food, clothing, and luxuries than formerly; (3) making them live crowded together in cities; (4) making them more dependent upon each other, throughout the world, for the things they need; and (5) making them live and work in a more uniform way. We must now consider each of these points in more detail.

How science has enabled more people to live. One of the most striking changes during the nineteenth century in Europe was the great increase in population. In 1685 the population of England was about 5,000,000. For centuries the increase had been so slight that Gregory King, an economist living in the early eighteenth century, estimated that there would not be 11,000,000 people in England until the year 2300. But in fact there were 11,000,000 in England in 1815. In 1910 there were 36,900,000. Between 1801 and 1910 the population of France increased from about 25,000,000 to 39,000,000; during the same period the population in the territories included in the German Empire of 1871 increased from 24,000,000 to 65,000,000. Nothing like this rapid increase had ever been known before.

The explanation is not that many more people were born each year, but that far fewer died. In England before 1750 there were years in which 75 per cent of all children died before they were five years old, and thousands of those who escaped the perils of infancy were carried off in youth or middle age by the frequent epidemics of plague, typhus, smallpox, diphtheria, and like scourges. The high death-rate before the nineteenth century was owing chiefly to the lack of medical knowledge. People, including physicians, knew little or nothing about sanitation, the proper methods of caring for young children, or the prevention or cure of disease. We still know little enough about the human body and the diseases that it is heir to; but nearly everything we do know has been discovered during the last century and a half. The progress which has been made in that time may be illustrated by four crucial discoveries.

In 1798 Dr. Jenner, an English physician, demonstrated the possibility (which had already been suggested by a Frenchman, Rabaut-Pommier) of preventing smallpox by vaccination. Vaccination is based upon the fact that the body can be made immune to certain poisons. For instance, if you are not accustomed to taking strychnine, a large dose will kill you. But if you take a slight dose today, and a slightly larger one tomorrow, and go on increasing the dose gradually, the body builds up a defense against strychnine. When the doctor vaccinates you for smallpox, he really gives you a small dose of smallpox; and by fighting this mild case the body builds up a defensive process which prevents it from catching the severe form which may be going the rounds in the community. Dr. Jenner's discovery opened up a wide field of experiment and discovery — namely, the possibility of making the human body immune to certain diseases by injecting into the body a small dose of the very poison that causes the disease.

Such diseases, it is now believed, are likely to be caused by "germs." The existence of these miserable little creatures was made known about the middle of the nineteenth century by Louis Pasteur, a French professor of chemistry. Pasteur proved by experiment that the fermentation in wine and beer is due, not to "spontaneous generation," but to the presence of minute living organisms — bacteria. Pasteur's discovery was the foundation of modern bacteriology, and of modern medical science in so far as it is based upon the theory that disease is caused by minute living organisms. Knowing the cause of a disease often enables us to avoid it, even if it still remains difficult to cure.

© *William Thompson*

PASTEUR (1822–1895)

By discovering that fermentation is caused by bacteria, Pasteur laid the foundation of modern medicine.

For example, typhoid fever is still a difficult disease to cure if you get it; but if you drink no water nor milk containing typhoid germs, you are pretty certain not to get typhoid fever.

Pasteur's discovery enabled Dr. Joseph Lister to lay the foundations of modern antiseptic surgery. In the seventeenth century surgery was still a crude and painful kind of hack-work. Afterwards, when an anaesthetic was given the patient to deaden the pain, operations were less difficult; but even then it was a lucky chance if the patient did not die of infection in the wound. Lister thought that such infection might be caused by bacteria such as Pasteur had discovered in wine and beer. Was there something that might be put into the wound to kill the bacteria? There was — carbolic acid, a crude antiseptic but an effective one. Lister afterwards demonstrated that it was unnecessary to put an antiseptic in the wound itself; that it was quite as effective to sterilize everything that touched the open wound — knife, hands, absorbent cotton, bandages. Without Lister's discovery the amazing advances of modern surgery would have been impossible.

It was one thing to know that disease and infection were caused by germs; another to learn something definite about the nature of a particular germ that caused a particular disease. In 1876 Robert Koch, a German physician, managed to obtain a " pure culture " of the germ which caused the disease of anthrax — that is, he was able to produce the germ in the laboratory in such a way that he could study and experiment with it. As a result, he soon discovered

© *William Thompson*

PASTEUR'S EXPERIMENTAL FARM AT RAMBOUILLET, FRANCE
The pasteurization of milk to kill bacteria in it is a process developed by
Pasteur.

an antitoxin which, injected into the body of the patient, would
cure the disease by killing the germ. Koch's discoveries led to a
new method of attacking disease — the attempt to discover specific
antitoxins for specific diseases. Such antitoxins have been discovered for certain diseases, notably for diphtheria. At one time
Koch thought he had discovered an antitoxin for tuberculosis, but
that was not the case. Some day — soon, we all hope — scientists
may discover effective antitoxins for tuberculosis, meningitis,
infantile paralysis, and influenza.

These are only the most striking examples of the progress of
medical science in the last century. One result of this new knowledge has been to free the Western world from the terror of great
scourges — plague, typhus, smallpox, diphtheria, yellow fever, and
the like. Another result has been to lower the death-rate and
greatly increase the number of people in the world. To be free of
terror is certainly a good thing. Whether it is a good thing to
have many more people in the world depends — it depends on
whether they can find the means of living in decency and comfort.

HOSPITAL, MIDDLESEX, EARLY NINETEENTH CENTURY

From an aquatint by Pugin and Rowlandson.   The woman at the left is standing before the fireplace by which the room was warmed.

**How science and invention made possible an increase in the
production of wealth.**   Medical science keeps people from dying,
but it does not provide them with the means of living.   If 150
million people were to live in England, France, and Germany, where
formerly only 60 million had lived none too well, there had to be
a great speeding up of the production of wealth.   There was; and
just as the increase in population was due to the application of
science to the prevention and cure of disease, so the increase in
wealth was due to the application of science and invention to
agriculture and industry.

In the eighteenth century, farming was still carried on much as it
had been in Roman times.   Since then agriculture has been revolutionized mainly by three things: (1) better adaptation of crops to
soils; (2) the use of artificial fertilizers; (3) the use of improved
machinery.

If one crop is raised on a given field year after year, the soil soon becomes impoverished.   Formerly, to prevent this, each field was allowed to " lie fallow " for perhaps one year out of three.   But in the nineteenth century it was found that by raising a greater variety of crops and changing the crop raised on any given field from year to year, the fertility of the soil could be preserved without allowing the field to lie fallow.   More important still was the discovery of artificial fertilizers.   What soil needs especially is nitrogen.   In 1840 and 1855 Von Liebig, a German scientist, published two books on agricultural chemistry which showed that nitrogen products spread over the soil would serve as well as natural manures.   Since then artificial fertilizers have been increasingly used, with the result of (1) increasing the fertility of farm lands, and (2) bringing under cultivation much land that without fertilizers would produce little or nothing.   Finally, the invention of machinery — steel plows, drills, harrows, steam plows, tractors, threshing machines, self-binders, hay-loaders, and the like — enabled one laborer to do the work of many.

The result of these improvements was already notable by the middle of the nineteenth century.   For example, in 1849, enough wheat was raised in England to feed five million more people than were fed by English wheat in 1811.   In general the result of science and invention applied to agriculture was (1) to increase the amount of land cultivated; (2) to increase the yield per acre; (3) to decrease, relatively, the number of laborers needed on the farms.

The revolution in industry was even more important than the revolution in agriculture.   In the eighteenth century two vital changes were introduced into the manufacture of cotton cloth in England: (1) the use of improved machines for spinning and weaving; (2) the use of water power and steam power for running the machines.   In the nineteenth century these new methods were adopted in other industries, first in England, and then in other countries.   The transformation of industry was slow at first but was accelerated after the middle of the century.   Innumerable machines were invented for every sort of manufacturing process. The steam engine was supplemented by the electric dynamo and the gas engine.   The use of steam power created an enormous demand for iron and coal and gave an unprecedented impetus to the mining

COFFEE PERCOLATOR
Exhibited at the Universal Exposition, Paris, 1855.

of iron and coal. Besides, the increased use of machines created a demand for machines to make machines. For example, a modern automobile is a machine which people use. But before this machine can be assembled, the parts have to be made, and many machines are necessary to make the parts. Every new machine creates a need for other machines to make it, other tools to keep it in order. Thus machines breed machines and industries breed industries, so that much of modern industry is devoted, not to making things people consume directly, but to making the machines that make machines that make the things they consume. The story of modern industry is like the story of the " House that Jack Built."

Now anyone can see how machines produce wealth (that is, make things people want) more rapidly than hand labor can. For evidence of this fact you have only to observe an ordinary cement mixer in the street, or step into a print shop and watch the printing machine set type, or stand before a city skyscraper and wonder how long it would take to build it by hand labor.   Machines are stronger than men.   Since they do not tire, they can work night and day; and as they are perfected they become more automatic, so that one man can supervise many machines.   In 1913 the machines of Great Britain made seven billion yards of cotton cloth for export alone. The total population of Great Britain, working by the methods of 1750, could have made only a fraction of that amount.

That machines increase the numbers of things produced is obvious — so obvious that we are likely to exaggerate their capacity to increase real wealth.   There are no very reliable statistics as to the increase in wealth during the last hundred years.   It is estimated that in 1800 the wealth of Great Britain, if equally divided among all the inhabitants, would have given to each person $700; in 1885 the total wealth so divided would have given each person $2075.   But in 1885 a dollar would buy much less than in 1800, so that the real increase was not so great as the apparent increase. The total wealth of the United States in 1912 was placed at 186 billion dollars; in 1922 at 320 billion.   This was an increase of 72 per cent in dollars.   But the population had meantime grown, so that the increase for each person was only 50 per cent.   Besides, the value of the dollar in 1922 was little more than half what it was in 1912.   Thus the increase in real wealth between 1912 and 1922 was just about nothing.

Nevertheless, with all these allowances made, it is still true that the use of power-driven machinery in industry has resulted in a great increase in the production of wealth — a more than sufficient increase, at all events, to support the increased population.   Not only are more people enabled to live; on the whole they are enabled to live more comfortably — to have better food, clothes, and houses, to work fewer hours, and to enjoy more amusement and relaxation. And if the increased wealth were distributed more evenly among the people, this would be even truer than it is.

How science and invention have crowded people together in cities.   Although many people have been enabled to live in Europe, they have found it necessary, in order to do so, to crowd together in

MESSRS. SCHEUTZ'S "NEW CALCULATING MACHINE"
Exhibited at the Exposition of 1855.

cities.   This also is one of the results of science and invention and of
the revolution in industry which science and invention have brought
about.

In the eighteenth century any farmer's wife could spin cotton
thread, or set up a hand loom for weaving in her spare moments.
But the new power-driven machines were cumbersome and expensive.   The result was that in the nineteenth century industries came
more and more to be carried on in great factories, under one management employing great armies of laborers; and the factories were
located in cities, or else cities grew up where the industries were
located.   We have already seen how the cloth and iron industries of
England, located near the supplies of coal, built up the cities of
Manchester and Birmingham (p. 328).   An example nearer home is
the city of Akron, Ohio.   In 1890 the population of Akron was
27,000; in 1910 it was nearly 70,000; in 1925 it was nearly 208,000.
The explanation of this rapid growth is the fact that most of the
automobile tires in the United States are manufactured in Akron.
Industries enlarge cities, of course, because they employ hundreds
and thousands of laborers.   The presence of laborers creates a
demand for more grocers, butchers, lawyers, doctors, druggists,
actors, street-car conductors, school teachers, ministers, bankers,
and the like.

STEAM SEWING-MACHINES, IN HOLLOWAY AND COMPANY'S FACTORY

From a sketch in the *Illustrated London News*, 1854. Twenty young women
were employed in this factory. At the back is the engine room.

Thus the revolution in industry has led to one of the striking facts
of the last hundred years — the enormous growth of cities. In the
eighteenth century the largest city in Europe was Paris, with a
population of 600,000. London had a population of only about
500,000. Today London has a population of over 7,000,000;
Paris nearly 3,000,000; Berlin about 4,000,000. In the eighteenth
century there were scarcely half-a-dozen cities in Europe with a
population of more than 200,000. Today there are between seventy
and eighty such cities. In the eighteenth century there was no
country in which a majority of the people lived in cities. Today
there is scarcely a country in which the majority of the people do
not live in cities. In England three-fourths of the people live in
cities. Even in a great agricultural country like the United States
less than half the people live in the country.

In the eighteenth century, if seven million people had been
gathered in London they could not have lived there. The products
of their labor could not have been marketed; they would have
perished for want of food. Today seven millions do actually live in
London — none too well, it is true. Why is it possible for so many
more people to live in cities today than could have done so in
the eighteenth century? Once more the answer is: science and
invention.

How science and invention are making people throughout the world more dependent on each other. The millions of people crowded together in cities are of course supported by the industries established in the cities.   A stranger driving into Akron for the first time might naturally remark, " Well, this is quite a city.   What are the industries that support it? "   The answer would be: " Rubber." But the workers of Akron cannot eat rubber tires, nor can the mechanics of Detroit clothe themselves in Ford cars.   Things made in cities have to be sold outside, while food, raw materials, and other necessities have to be brought in from outside.   Now the larger the industry, the farther afield the manufacturer has to go to obtain raw materials and to find markets for his finished product ; the larger the city, the farther afield it is necessary to go to obtain food and other necessities for the people.

How far afield can the manufacturer go for markets and raw material?   How far can a city go for food and necessities?   This depends on the means of transportation and communication. You do not need to be told that the means of transportation and communication have been revolutionized within the last fifty years by the use of steam and electricity.   In 1830 it was thought marvelous to be able, any day in the week, to take a stagecoach from London and arrive at Edinburgh, four hundred miles distant, in forty hours.   Already (1825) George Stephenson had built a steam engine capable of carrying passengers and freight ; but unfortunately its smokestack got red before it reached its maximum speed of eight miles per hour.   Improvements made his engine a " going concern " by 1830 ; yet as late as 1870 there were no more than 15,000 miles of railroads in Great Britain.   In 1807 Robert Fulton managed to run a steamboat on the Hudson River ; in 1838 four steamships crossed the Atlantic ; but not until after 1860 did sailing ships cease to be the chief carriers.   At the beginning of the twentieth century automobiles were still novelties.   They were called " horseless carriages " — and looked the part.   In 1836 S. F. B. Morse succeeded in sending an intelligible message by electric telegraph ; in 1851 the first cable was laid between England and France ; in 1866 the first permanent cable was laid between England and the United States.   The first telephone message was heard in

© *William Thompson*

First Engine Used on a German Railway

1876; the first Marconi wireless message in 1896. We should not pay too much attention to the early dates of some of these inventions; the principal fact is that modern methods of communication and transportation, in anything like their present efficiency, have been in use no more than fifty years. It is also during the last fifty years that modern industries and modern cities, in anything like their present size, have been built up.

Now there are two important points to be noted. The first is this. Our giant industries are possible because the railroad, the steamship, and the telegraph enable the manufacturer to go as far afield as he likes — throughout the world in fact — for markets and raw materials. Our enormous cities are possible for a similar reason — because adequate supplies of food and necessities can be rapidly and systematically brought in from every part of the world. In other words, one important result of great industrial cities and rapid means of transportation is that the *area of exchanges tends to become world wide.* The second point is that this widening of the area of exchanges tends to *draw the world together by making the*

Deutsches Museum, Munich

DAIMLER'S FIRST MOTORCYCLE, 1885

people in different communities more dependent on each other. These
two points may be illustrated by two examples.

In 1903 Henry Ford formed a company to make a cheap automobile. To do this it was essential to use machine labor in place of
hand labor wherever possible. Mr. Ford had therefore to invest
millions of dollars in elaborate and expensive machines to make his
cheap Ford cars. In order to sell his car cheaply and at the same
time make a profit on his investment, it was necessary to make and
sell an enormous number of cars. In 1926 he made and sold
approximately a million and a quarter cars. So many cars could
not be sold in Detroit, or even in the state of Michigan. To
market his cars Mr. Ford had to go farther afield than that; he had
to go into every community in the United States and even into
foreign countries. To attract people's attention to his cars it was
necessary to advertise them. To distribute them, the services of
the railroads and steamships were essential. To sell them, agents
had to be established in every town in the country, and rapid
communication maintained between the agents and Mr. Ford. It
is easy to see that without the railroads and the telegraph Mr.
Ford could not have distributed and sold so many cars in one year.

It is also easy to see how the actual process of distributing and selling so many cars made a great many people in all parts of the world more dependent on each other. Who were these people? We can enumerate some of them: Mr. Ford and the laborers who worked for him; newspapers seeking news; advertising agencies seeking customers; railroad companies and their stockholders seeking profits from freight; local dealers making a living selling Ford cars; mechanics and farmers and clerks and professors needing cheap cars; producers of oil and rubber throughout the world; manufacturers of rubber tires in Akron; men and women in obscure villages and along the highways adding a few dollars to their income by setting up gas pumps and hot-dog stands; all these and many others were drawn together, were made in some measure more dependent on each other, because they gained or lost with the rise or fall in prestige of the most famous, the most used, and the most derided vehicle that ever bumped over country roads — the little old " Tin Lizzy."

The example of the Ford cars shows how large-scale manufacturing and rapid transportation make people *within the same country* more dependent on each other. Another example will show how large-scale manufacturing and rapid transportation make the people of *different countries* dependent on each other.

In the eighteenth century the people of England could have lived very well on what was raised and made in England. It is true that there was a considerable commerce with the outside world. Sailing ships in their leisurely fashion brought sugar, cotton, and tobacco from America in exchange for British cloth, ironware, and furniture. British cloth was carried to Holland; wines were imported from France and Portugal, and spices and silks from the East Indies. But in 1750 the entire export shipping from all the British ports was only 600,000 tons. A few of the largest modern ships could have carried it all in a dozen trips. If England had suddenly been cut off entirely from the outside world, many people would have suffered temporary distress; but the mass of the people would have managed well enough.

How different is the situation today, when three-fourths of the people are crowded together in cities and live by industry and

© *Deutsches Museum, Munich*

First Steam Automobile of Serpollet, 1891

commerce! In the year 1924 the total export shipping from all British ports was 88,780,000 tons; the imports 87,057,000 tons. If the British Isles were effectively blockaded today, millions of people would have no choice but to migrate or starve — and that within a very short time. The reason is, of course, that the people of England raise less food than they need and make more things than they can use. The excess of coal, cloth, ironware, and other products must therefore be sold abroad in exchange for food and other necessities — particularly for the raw materials (such as cotton and rubber) needed in industry. In 1926 there was imported into England food valued at more than $2,500,000,000 and raw materials valued at nearly $2,000,000,000. In the same year commodities were exported to the value of about $3,750,000,000. Where does England sell her manufactured commodities? Where does she buy her food and raw materials? The answer is: Everywhere. In the *Statesman's Year Book* you may see a list of the countries trading with Great Britain. Practically every country in Europe, Asia, and America exchanges its own products for British products.

Thus England is no longer a self-sufficing country. Through industry and commerce she is linked to every country in the world ; and to that extent her people are dependent on the people of every country in the world.   Even a slight disturbance in this intricate network of relations results in suffering.   The Great War raised price levels and diminished the buying power of most European countries — a state of affairs which had much the same effect on international exchange as throwing sand in the transmission would have on the running of an automobile.   The result is that since the war some two or three millions of English workers have been without jobs, because foreign countries cannot afford to buy — at prices for which they can be produced — enough English commodities to keep the people of Great Britain fully employed.

England is an extreme example.   But what is true of England is true in lesser degree of other countries.   The application of power-driven machinery to manufactures and to transportation is drawing the whole world together in a complicated network of exchanges which makes the people of each country more and more dependent on the people of every other country.

These are some of the ways in which science and invention have given men control over things.   But by giving men control over things, they have also given things control over men.   Let us see how this comes about.

How the machines we have mastered make us work for them in their own way.   Fifty years ago Emerson said : " Things are in the saddle and ride mankind."   The things which are in the saddle are chiefly machines.   Every year it becomes more true that the machines we have mastered enslave us.   The reason for this is the very simple one that we care for machines, whereas machines care nothing for us.   They will work for us only in their own way, and even in that way only if we pay strict attention to them.   The result is that we have to adjust our habits of work to theirs.

One striking example of this we have already noted : Machines are forcing the majority of people to live crowded together in cities. Machines don't care where they live ; but they often work best in unlovely places, or else they make the places where they work unlovely ; and so men have to live in those unattractive places. Professor J. M. Clark has put this fact very well :

Ride through the industrial district stretching from South Chicago to Gary, and as you view the expanse of ugly flats and barrens, ask yourself why these people are here. Is this a place men would choose to live in? Certainly not, if they were free to move out to those blue, wooded hills beckoning in the distance. These people never wanted to live here. But the machines did, and that settled it.[1]

The total population of the region, Mr. Clark goes on to say, consists of 100,000 people and six blast furnaces. The only beings who wanted to live in the region are the blast furnaces. The 100,000 people are there because the blast furnaces are there, and for no other reason.

Not only are the blast furnaces willing to live anywhere — they don't care how long they work. They never demanded the eight-hour day, with time-and-a-half for overtime. On the contrary, they say in effect: "The harder you work us the better we will pay you. Work us one hour or twenty-four hours a day, just as you please; but we shall rust out when we are idle just as quickly as we shall wear out when we are busy. Consequently, if you want the maximum of service from us you must be here attending to us twenty-four hours a day."

Therefore the owner of the machines says to the laborer seeking a job: "I can give you a job if you will work nights and sleep daytimes."

The laborer would much prefer to work daytimes. The owner of the machines would just as soon have him work daytimes. But the blast furnace says: "Someone has to work nights if I am to serve you best." So the owner and the laborer, the one seeking profits and the other seeking wages, both submit to the inexorable decree of the machine.

The machine determines not only where and when the laborer shall work but how he shall work. A hundred years ago the village shoemaker was a familiar figure. With a few tools he made shoes to order, taking the measure, cutting the leather, punching the holes, waxing the thread, and stitching the seams. He was something of an artist, proud of his skill in design and execution; an

[1] John M. Clark, "The Empire of Machines," *Yale Review*, Oct. 1922. Copyright by the Yale University Press.

independent man, working when and how he pleased; and something of a philosopher, discussing the state of the nation with customers or cronies. But with the coming of the machine the village shoemaker disappeared. He could not compete with the machines, and he was too poor to own them. So he went, hat in hand, to the machine. To the machine he said: " I am a skilled shoemaker. I want a job making shoes."

But the machine replied somewhat as follows: " I have no use for shoemakers. I make the shoes myself much faster than you can. I want someone to run *me*. To do that effectively you must cease to be an artist and a philosopher and become a kind of machine yourself. You can never be as precise and effective as a machine, but you must become as nearly so as your poor abilities permit. Just stand here and work me and be careful I don't catch your finger." So the poor fellow stands or sits in front of the machine, performing with monotonous regularity, for eight hours a day, a single simple operation which consists of pulling a lever, slipping a piece of leather into the machine, pushing a lever, and taking the leather out of the machine. The shoemaker has ceased to be an artist in shoes; he has become a laborer — that is to say, an animated cog in the machine process.

How the machines we have mastered make us do more things in a more uniform way. Machines enslave, not the laborer merely, but all of us. We are so delighted with all these new toys that we scarcely realize how they insensibly shape all our activities. It is probably a mistake to think that the machines, being indifferent, haven't a sense of humor. That is only because they order us about without words. If machines could speak, they might very well say something like this: " We save you much time and effort and so provide you with immense leisure to do as you like; in return for this boon we require only that you shall do more things, do them more quickly, and do them as far as possible in the same way." This is the great practical joke machines have played on us.

One aspect of this mechanical pleasantry is this: Whereas we have infinitely more time-saving machines than people had fifty years ago, we seem always more rushed for time than people

were fifty years ago. How can this be? Take a simple example.
If a business man living in Buffalo needs to go to New York, the
automobile or the railroad obviously enable him to go there in less
time than he could have gone by earlier means of travel. But a
hundred years ago, before the age of steam or electricity, a business
man in Buffalo would neither have needed nor have expected to go
to New York very often. Today his business interests are likely to
extend throughout the United States, and even into foreign countries. He may therefore need to go to New York once a month, or
once a week. The point is that machines, in saving us time in going
to distant places, create the need or the desire to go to distant
places more frequently.

Besides requiring us to do more things and to do them more
rapidly, machines rather insist on our doing them more or less in the
same way. Machines urge us to practice the goose-step. The
machine itself has no use for eccentric parts. A temperamental
brake-band which takes a notion to expand when the other three
brake-bands contract is a nuisance to be discarded. The machine
feels the same way about eccentric individuals. The old-fashioned
shoemaker could go his own gait — begin work when he pleased,
work slowly or rapidly, and lay off when he felt like it. But in a
modern shoe factory, where gangs of men work in eight-hour shifts,
the individual is an essential part of the machine process. Like the
brake-band, he must do as his fellow-workers do — begin on time,
work with a certain speed, and quit at a given moment. The
eccentric laborer is as much a nuisance as the temperamental brake-
band.

Not in factories only, but in the ordinary relations of life, the
machine urges us to acquire more uniform habits. The more we are
crowded together into cities, the faster we move about ; the more we
use machines for business or pleasure, the more need there is for
uniformity of action. The simplest example of this is to be seen on
any city street. Fifty years ago there was but one rule of the road :
" Keep to the right." Today the regulation of traffic is a serious
problem. Stand on any crowded avenue of a great city. Solid
masses of people and vehicles are moving up the avenue. All
watch the lights. The red light comes on, and everyone stops.

© *William Thompson*

MADAME CURIE IN HER LABORATORY

Madame Curie and her husband Pierre, who died in 1906, are famous for their
discovery of radium and for their experiments in connection with it.

The green comes on, and everyone moves forward. The jay-walker
is a nuisance, to be arrested — or taken to the hospital.

Machines can't speak, but they have an official spokesman who
announces every hour of the day what it is the machines desire of us.
This spokesman is like the traffic cop. And what does he say?
" Watch the lights! Step lively! "

**How the coming of the machines brought about new conflicts
both within and between the nations.** In this chapter we have
described some of the ways in which cience and invention have
changed the conditions of life. Scientific knowledge has enabled

more people to live on the earth and has made them more secure against death and disease. The machines which science has made possible have greatly increased the wealth in the world, enabling the majority of people to have conveniences and comforts which their grandfathers knew nothing of. Most people are freer today than formerly to move about, to see new places, and to relieve the monotony of life by amusements and relaxations. Every week, by means of the screen and the printed page and the radio, there is laid before them a transcript and a picture of the wide world and its doings; so that they may, even if they do not, emancipate themselves in some measure from ignorance and provincialism, and in some measure become acquainted with the common experience of mankind.

This is much. But one might reasonably have expected that science and invention would do more for the world than this. Since we have unprecedented power to make things, to find out where and when they are needed, and to transport them to the people who want them, one might suppose that everyone would have enough and be content. Since people throughout the world know each other so much better than formerly and are so much more dependent on each other for the things they need, one might suppose that suspicion and conflict would largely have disappeared. But unfortunately we all seem to be quite as discontented as ever and quite as much given to suspicion and conflict.

Perhaps the reason is that our knowledge and power have not been properly applied. Neither knowledge nor power is equally distributed. Some individuals, classes, and nations have control of the things that other individuals, classes, and nations need or desire. This, of course, has always been the case. But the power that arises from the possession of things is greater now than formerly. It is greater because, in the making and transportation of things, the individual counts for less and the machines for more. The machines are enormously expensive. Therefore the individuals, classes, and nations that own and control the machines have an unprecedented power over the lives and fortunes of the masses of people throughout the world who need the things which the machines make and distribute.

Thus it happened that the coming of the machines, and the Industrial Revolution which they brought with them, gave rise to new conflicts. From 1815 until the close of the Franco-Prussian War (1871) the great conflict within each country had been mainly *political* — concerned chiefly with the form of government. But during the last quarter of the nineteenth century the great conflict within each of the industrialized countries became mainly *economic and social* — concerned with the rival interests of capital and labor, with labor unions and strikes, and with the advantages or dangers of socialism and of socialistic legislation in behalf of the poor. In short, after 1871 the dispute over political democracy was largely replaced by the dispute over social and economic democracy.

Likewise, the conflict between the nations changed its character. From 1815 until after the Franco-Prussian War international disputes had been concerned largely with *political* questions — the repression of liberal or democratic revolutionary movements and the establishment of national independence or unity. After the Franco-Prussian War international disputes were concerned more with *economic* questions — with the exploitation of " backward countries," the control of raw materials, and the opening up of new markets throughout the world.

These new conflicts we shall have to study in the following chapters. First of all we must see how the coming of the machines, by separating the men who owned the machines from those who worked them, led to the conflict between capital and labor, and how this in turn gave rise to modern socialism and to the question of social reform.

QUESTIONS

1. Suppose a few ordinary American families were shipwrecked on a tropical or semi-tropical island without anything except what they would be likely to have with them. Describe in some detail the "civilization" they might create there.

2. How long has man been a tool-using animal? What were some of the earliest tools? Why are these the most important of all tools? How far could civilization have developed without fire? without domesticated animals?

3. What new idea of nature became current in the seventeenth and eighteenth centuries? How did this new idea lead to the development

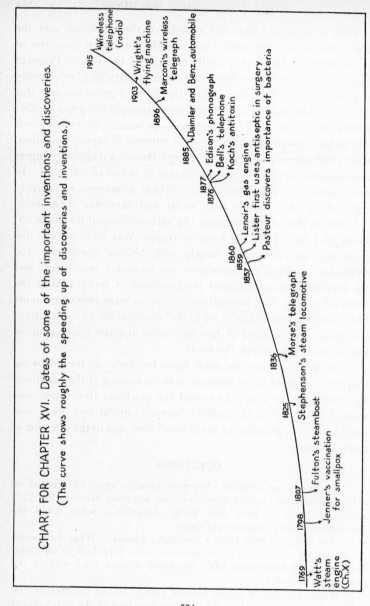

CHART FOR CHAPTER XVI. Dates of some of the important inventions and discoveries.
(The curve shows roughly the speeding up of discoveries and inventions.)

1769 — Watt's steam engine (Ch.X)

1798 — Jenner's vaccination for smallpox

1807 — Fulton's steamboat

1825 — Stephenson's steam locomotive

1836 — Morse's telegraph

1857 — Pasteur discovers importance of bacteria

1859 — Lister first uses antiseptic in surgery
      Lenoir's gas engine

1860

1876 — Koch's antitoxin
      Bell's telephone

1877 — Edison's phonograph

1885 — Daimler and Benz, automobile

1896 — Marconi's wireless telegraph

1903 — Wright's flying machine

1915 — Wireless telephone (radio)

of modern science? How does modern science make possible the rapid increase of inventions? How does every invention lead to further inventions? How do machines breed machines? What do you consider the most important inventions or discoveries of the last two centuries? What, if any, inventions or discoveries of great importance have been made within your memory?

4. How much has the population of Europe increased in the last century and a half? What has made this great increase possible? How has modern science contributed to the increase of the food supply?

5. How do you explain the great growth of cities in the last century? Why would such large cities have been impossible in the eighteenth century? What would happen to Henry Ford's plant at Detroit if all the railroads were out of commission for two years?

6. How do machines determine the conditions under which men have to work and live? Since we have so many machines to work for us, why do we not have more time and leisure? How do machines make it necessary for people to act more alike? to think more alike?

7. Make a list (1) of the ways in which machines have made life harder and less satisfactory for the average person than it used to be; (2) of the ways in which machines have made life better and more satisfactory.

8. Write a brief statement (from 300 to 500 words) of the ways in which machines have helped to make the people of the United States a united and democratic nation.

SELECTED READINGS

Brief accounts. Hayes and Moon, *Modern History*, ch. xiv. Hayes, *Modern Europe*, II, ch. xviii. Robinson and Beard, *Development of Modern Europe*, II, ch. xviii. Robinson and Beard, *Outlines*, II, ch. xiv. Schapiro, *European History* (revised ed.), chs. iii, xxvi, xxvii. F. A. Ogg, *Economic Development of Modern Europe*, chs. vii, xi, xvi. H. W. Van Loon, *Ancient Man: the Beginning of Civilization* and *Man the Miracle Maker*.

Books on science and invention. G. Iles, *Leading American Inventions* and *Flame, Electricity and the Camera: Man's Progress from the First Kindling of Fire to the Wireless Telegraph*. H. Thompson, *The Age of Invention*. E. W. Bryan, *The Progress of Invention in the Nineteenth Century* (illustrated). C. H. Cochrane, *The Wonders of Modern Invention* (illustrated). T. C. Martin and S. L. Coles, *The Story of Electricity*. C. C. Turner, *The Romance of Aeronautics*. H. N. Casson, *The History of the Telephone*. G. Bright, *The Story of the Atlantic Cable*. Robert Hoe, *A Short History of Printing*. J. Cleland, *Historical Account of the Steam Engine*. W. K. Towers, *Masters of Space: Morse, Thompson, Bell, Marconi*. S. I. Prime, *Life of S. F. B. Morse*. J. W. Grant, *Watt and the Steam Age*. R. H. Thurston, *Robert Fulton*. F. L. Dyer and J. C. Martin, *Edison, His Life and Inventions*. M. Curie, *Pierre Curie*.

EARLY IRON-WORKING FACTORY NEAR BRISTOL, 1854

CHAPTER XVII. HOW THE INDUSTRIAL REVOLUTION GAVE RISE TO MODERN SOCIALISM AND THE CONFLICT OVER SOCIAL REFORM, 1871–1914

One fact is common to all past ages, namely, the exploitation of one part of society by another. KARL MARX

Why new disputes arose after 1871 to replace the old. In this chapter and the next three we shall have to study the momentous period from 1871 to 1914. At the beginning of this period it was clear that the coming form of government was bound to be democratic. It was no longer possible to maintain the old autocracy of kings. In most of the states of Europe the people had won, to a greater or less extent, the right of choosing their rulers. According to the great prophets of democratic government the years that followed should therefore have been years of increasing peace and harmony.

On the contrary, the period from 1871 to 1914 was a time of great stress and conflict — a time of ruthless competition in business. These years witnessed the rapid development of railroads, of steamship lines, of steel plants; the rise of "big business," of "giant trusts" and "soulless corporations," of multimillionaires living in palaces; and the rise of great industrial cities inhabited by thousands — sometimes hundreds of thousands — of industrial workers

526

living in dingy houses or foul, musty-smelling tenements. It was a time of labor unions, strikes, lockouts, and picketing; a time when strikers threw bombs, and armed men employed by corporations shot down strikers. In these years the menace of revolutionary socialism appeared, and the doctrines of anarchy and terrorism made their devious ways through Europe. In these years a president of the French Republic, two presidents of the United States, and a Russian tsar were assassinated. In these years legislators engaged in heated debates over socialism, social legislation, military budgets, clericalism, and corruption in high places. In these years Africa was partitioned and Asia exploited by the European powers, many colonial wars were fought, and writers proved that wars were no longer possible. In these years armies and navies were enlarged and perfected, peace societies flourished, the Hague Tribunal was established to abate the evils of war, and writers proved that war was a necessary and beneficent instrument in the progress of the human race.

In this welter of issues and disputes one conflict stands out above all others. In every country in which an industrial revolution occurred there arose a persistent conflict between labor and capital — between the employers and the industrial workers, the men who owned the industrial machines and the men who worked them. In this chapter we shall see why there was a conflict of interest between labor and capital, what methods the laborers used to defend their interests, and how the " labor problem " gave rise to modern socialism and the movement for social reform.

How the machines elbowed their way in between employers and laborers and gave them conflicting interests to quarrel about. Before the coming of the machines, under the guild system of industry (see p. 29), there was little difference between employer and laborer. Ordinarily the master workman of a guild had a little shop on the ground floor of his house, with living rooms above. In his shop he worked at his trade of making — let us say, hats. He provided the tools and the raw material and sold the finished product over the counter. He was therefore capitalist, laborer, and merchant, all in one. To help him he might employ a journeyman or two, and several apprentices, paying the journeyman wages and

PIANO FACTORY OF PLEYEL, WOLFF, & CO., NEAR PARIS, 1870
From a sketch in *L'Illustration*.

giving the apprentice board and lodging. These men were laborers only, the master being their employer. There was no sharp distinction between employer and laborer. All worked side by side, ate very likely at the same table, and lived in the same house.

With the introduction of power-driven machinery the guild system of industry disappeared and the " factory system " took its place. To build the factory and install the expensive machines much money was required. The capitalist who furnished the money therefore owned the factory and the machines, provided the raw material, and sold the finished product. To run the machines many laborers were required. These the capitalist or " manager " employed, paying them wages. The capitalist did not work with his laborers; still less did he live with them. Both capitalist and laborer were connected with the industry, but their interests in it were different and seemingly conflicting. The capitalist was directly interested in the factory and the machines, in buying the raw material as cheaply as possible, in making the finished product as well as possible, in selling it at as high a price as possible, and in paying as low wages as possible. The laborers, on the other hand, were directly interested in only one thing — wages. They desired to get the highest wages possible for the least work.

In this conflict the capitalist-employer usually had a great advantage, because there were usually more workers than jobs. One laborer, working one of the new machines for weaving cloth, for example, could make as much cloth as a dozen men using the old hand looms. Besides, the machines could be worked by women and children. Hence in the early stages of the Industrial Revolution in England the conditions in the factory towns were appalling. A parliamentary committee appointed in 1838 to make an investigation reported that the streets of every large town swarmed with children, eight or ten years of age, going to and from the factories, where they worked ten or twelve hours a day with a half-hour off for dinner and an equal time for tea. In some industries fifty cents a week was an average wage. In 1840 the parliamentary commissioner said that it was unwise to tell the whole truth since, if the truth were told, people would either not believe it or else they would think the evils beyond remedy.

In the latter part of the nineteenth century such conditions did not usually prevail. But however high wages might be, the lion's share of the enormous increase in the production of wealth went to the employer class. The reason is that the machines, which were responsible for the great increase of wealth, were owned by the capitalist. The profits created by the machines therefore went to the capitalist-employer and were used by him to install more or better machines, which in turn created more profits for the capitalist-employer. Thus it happened that the machines elbowed their way in between the employer and the laborer, separated them into two distinct classes, and turned the major part of the wealth they created over to the employer, leaving the laborer to get on with such wages as the employer could be forced to give him.

How the laborers obtained two weapons with which to defend their interests — the right to vote and the right to strike. In the early and middle years of the nineteenth century the workers were relatively helpless. They were neither numerous nor well organized. Besides, most of their " betters " told them that there had always been rich and poor, and that it was the will of God that it should be so. But even in these years there were some, such as Mazzini, who told the workers that when kings and aristocrats were overthrown, all would be well. Therefore Mazzini counseled the workers to work for the establishment of a democratic republic.

The workers followed Mazzini's advice. We have already seen how in the revolutions of 1830 and 1848 the workers in every country followed the radical leaders who were in favor of giving all men, rich and poor alike, the right to vote. We have seen how the workers in England prepared the People's Charter, with its famous six points, one of which demanded universal manhood suffrage. In none of these revolutions did the mass of the workers obtain the right to vote. But at last, during the years 1859 to 1884, some form of democratic government was established in most of the countries of western Europe. Thus we may say that in the last quarter of the nineteenth century the workers obtained one weapon with which to defend their interests — the political weapon, the right to vote.

Meantime the workers — many of them at least — did not share Mazzini's idea that the right to vote would alone enable them to defend their rights against the employers. Besides the political weapon they wanted another — the economic weapon. They felt that if all the workers of a certain industry could form associations, agreeing to work only for certain wages and certain hours, they would be able to force the employers to accept their terms. This of course involved the right to " strike " — that is, to refuse to work at all unless their demands were met. This right to form labor unions and to strike for better wages or fewer hours is known as the right of " collective bargaining." Many workers felt that this right was more important than the right to vote; and indeed one reason why they wanted the right to vote was so that they might, by their votes, force governments to give them the right to engage in collective bargaining. They felt that as long as governments were controlled by the rich — by the employers and those who sympathized with the employers — there was slight hope that laws would be passed giving the workers the right to form labor unions and to strike for higher wages. Generally speaking, it was in the last quarter of the nineteenth century that the workers obtained, or were in the way of

HAND-TO-HAND FIGHTING DURING THE STRIKE AT CREUZOT, 1870
From a sketch in *L'Illustration*.

obtaining, this second weapon with which to defend their interests
— the economic weapon, the right to engage in collective bargaining.

Meantime the workers were provided with two social philosophies
which justified them in their conflict with their employers: socialism
and anarchism.

**Scientific socialism: How Karl Marx attempted to prove that the
workers were slaves of the capitalists, but promised them a better
time coming.** Many books have been written to point out the
evils of existing society and to describe one that would be better.
Plato's *Republic* was one of the first and the most famous of these.
Another was Sir Thomas More's *Utopia*, written in the sixteenth
century. Ever since that time the word *utopia* has been used to
describe (and usually to condemn) any ideal society or form of
government in which, if it could be established, everyone would
have enough and be happy and content. All these ideal societies
are based on a great *if*. The argument is: " If people would only
change their ways of thinking and behaving, injustice and suffering
might easily be abolished."

In the early nineteenth century many men, distressed by the poverty of the mass of the people — especially the industrial workers — suggested ways of transforming society, to the end that poverty might be abolished.? Among these were Saint-Simon and Fourier (see p. 337). Since their suggested reforms were primarily concerned with transforming society as a whole rather than government

German Tourist Information Office
KARL MARX (1818–1883)

in particular, they were called *Socialists*, and the movement in thought which they represented is known as *socialism*. Since their schemes were somewhat like those of Plato and Sir Thomas More, this early type of socialism is known as *utopian socialism*.

Between 1848 and 1875, however, this early type of socialism was replaced by a new type, known as *scientific socialism*. The founder and prophet of modern scientific socialism was Karl Marx, whose writings have had a profound influence on the social and political thought of the last fifty years. More than any other man, it was Karl Marx who provided the workingmen's political parties of Europe with a social philosophy and a program for social reform.

Karl Marx was born in Treves, Germany, in 1818, of well-to-do parents. He was educated at the universities of Bonn and of Berlin, where he studied history and philosophy. He married Jenny von Westphalen, the daughter of a high government official. With his powerful intelligence, his excellent education, and his advantageous family connections, Marx might have been a university professor or a high government official, rich and respected and respectable. But although possessed of a powerful and ruthless intelligence, he had a tender heart which inspired in him a passionate sympathy for the poor. Like Mazzini, therefore, Marx abandoned all his fine chances in life to become the unwearied champion of the oppressed. In 1842 he became the editor of a democratic newspaper called the *Rhenish Gazette*. It was suppressed the next year, whereupon Marx went to Paris, which was then the center of the Socialist movement. Expelled from France in 1845, he went to Brussels, only to return to Paris, where he took an active part in the Revolution of 1848. Fleeing from France after the collapse of the revolution, Marx settled in London, where for many years he lived in dire poverty in order to devote himself to expounding the socialistic doctrine and organizing the workers throughout Europe. He died in 1883.

Marx had no patience with the utopian schemes of Saint-Simon, Fourier, and their followers. During the Paris Revolution of 1848 he and his friend Friedrich Engels issued *The Communist Manifesto*, calling, in stirring words, to the workers of Europe to unite and throw off their chains. They used the word *Communist* instead of *Socialist*, to make it clear that they were not Socialists of the utopian sort. But the greatest book written by Marx was a long and learned work which cost him many years of close study and hard writing. Ever since, it has cost many people many days of hard reading. This work is entitled *Das Kapital* (" Capital "), and the first volume of it appeared in 1867. These two works, particularly *Das Kapital*, contain the gospel of modern scientific socialism.

What is this gospel? It consists of two parts: (1) an economic theory which aims to show the injustice of the present capitalistic system of industry; and (2) a philosophy of history which aims to prove that the capitalistic system of industry will in the course of time destroy itself.

1. The *economic theory* of Marx may be briefly stated as follows. (1) All wealth is produced by human labor. Capital in the form of machines, buildings, etc., is the result of labor in the past and is therefore " stored up " labor. (2) Although labor creates all wealth, the laborers, under the capitalistic system, do not receive the total product. They receive in fact only a very small part of it — just enough of it for themselves and their families to live on, a mere " living wage." (3) The difference between what the laborers produce and what they receive is " surplus " wealth. This entire surplus is taken by the capitalists, who are the owners of machines

and all " stored-up " capital. Thus the capitalist class reaps where it has not sown, taking the greater part of the wealth produced by the laborers.

2. Marx's *philosophy of history* aims to prove that this unjust system must disappear. What will bring it to an end? It is no use, Marx says, to write nice books describing an ideal society; no use trying to persuade people to be wise and just, or to expect those who have the good things of life to give them up voluntarily. All that is a utopian dream. All historical changes, he said, are brought about by those silent economic forces that are stronger than men's wills and desires. A proper study of history shows that this has been so in the past. Why should we not expect it to be so in the future? Instead of talking about the ideal society we should like to have, let us study history and see what kind of changes the future has in store for us whether we like them or not.

History shows us, according to Marx, that in every age government and society are controlled by the class which possesses the chief source of wealth. In the Middle Ages the chief source of wealth was land; hence the feudal nobles, who possessed the land, had everything their own way and controlled society through a government by kings and nobles. But in the eighteenth and nineteenth centuries, with the coming of power-driven machines, the chief source of wealth came to be " capital," in the form of money, machines, and industries. Hence the possessors of capital (middle-class business men, bankers, and manufacturers) elbowed the nobles out of the seats of power, and in place of the old governments by kings and nobles established governments suitable to their purposes — governments by representative assemblies. Thus through the silent operation of economic forces the feudal land-owning system gave way to the bourgeois-capitalistic system under which we live. But just as the feudal nobles were shoved aside by the middle-class capitalists, so the middle-class capitalists will in the course of time be shoved aside by the mass of the people — the " proletariat."

Why will this happen? It will happen, Marx said, because it is the nature of the capitalist system to destroy itself. The capitalist system is a competitive system — every man for himself and the

German Tourist Information Office

MODERN STEEL PLANT. INTERIOR OF THE ROLLING MILL OF THE UNITED STEEL WORKS AT HOERDE

Compare this with the early nineteenth century cutlery establishment shown in Chapter XIII.

devil take the hindmost. Each owner of industry seeks to make his industry bigger and bigger, and himself richer and richer. In this struggle for survival, the weaker will be destroyed by the stronger; industry and capital will be more and more concentrated; and presently all land and capital will be in the hands of a very few capitalists. Meantime this process will have reduced the mass of the people to the level of wage-slaves. When this process has worked itself out, the owners of capital will be so few, and the system so obviously unjust, that the mass of the people will quietly dispossess the capitalists and themselves take over the wealth and the means of producing wealth which is theirs by right.

The essence of Marx's scientific socialism is this: The workers are at present enslaved to the capitalists; but the stars in their courses, rather than the feeble wills of men, are bringing about their liberation. What Marx gave the workers was a new philosophy-religion — a religion to console them in their present distress, a philosophy pointing out the good time coming. This good time coming was the " social revolution," a kind of promised land to which the workers could look forward with faith and hope.

Anarchism: How Proudhon and Bakunin proclaimed that all government is an evil and ought to be abolished. Socialism and anarchism agreed in this: that under the present system of society the workers were enslaved. They differed radically in this: that whereas socialism would free the workers by placing the great industries under the control of democratic governments, anarchism would free the workers by abolishing all government.

The theory of anarchism is an old one; but in its modern form it was first formulated clearly by Pierre Joseph Proudhon (1809–1865), who also coined the word *anarchism* by which the modern theory is known. In 1840 Proudhon published a book entitled *What is Property?* According to Proudhon the answer is, " Property is theft." But the possession of property is guaranteed by government — that is, by the exercise of organized force. He says it matters little whether property is owned by individuals or by the government, since in either case some people will be forcibly deprived of the use of it. The real evil which robs people of their liberty is thus organized force in the form of governments. Men will not be free, therefore, until all governments, all force, all compulsion are done away with. " No more parties, no more authority; absolute liberty for man and citizen." Such was Proudhon's theory of anarchism — a highly idealistic doctrine, since it assumed that men are naturally good, and that if they were never restrained by force they would all live happily together.

Proudhon's anarchism would probably have had little influence if it had not been adopted and propagated by Mikhail Bakunin (1814–1876). Bakunin, a Russian noble, was educated in Germany and later went to France, where he met Proudhon and was engaged in the Revolution of 1848. He was ordered to return to Russia, and when he refused to return, the Russian government confiscated his property. In 1849 he was engaged in revolutionary activities in Dresden, but was arrested, returned to Russia, and exiled to Siberia. Escaping in 1861, he returned to Europe and joined an organization founded by Karl Marx five years before — the

International Workingmen's Association, commonly known as the first " International." The International had adopted the scientific socialism of Marx; but Bakunin tried to get it to adopt his anarchist philosophy. In opposition to Marx, Bakunin urged the workers not to vote at elections, not to form political parties, and not to work for laws designed to protect the interests of the working classes. He said: " We object to all legislation, all authority, and all influence . . . official and legal, even when it is based on universal suffrage." After three years of violent disputes between Marx and Bakunin, the latter was expelled from the International at the Hague Congress in 1872.

Although expelled from the International, Bakunin had his followers, and his doctrines lived on. They had a curious history. Bakunin himself was a mild-mannered man, chiefly interested in propagating the theory that government is an evil and ought to be abolished. Many peaceful men have embraced the doctrine. The famous Russian novelist, Count Leo Tolstoy, was an Anarchist of this sort. He taught that it was wrong to exert physical force of any kind against anyone. But he accepted the teaching of Jesus literally — that it was as wrong to resist the use of force as it was to exert it. He was a " passive-resistance " Anarchist, and there have been many such.

Few of the followers of Proudhon and Bakunin were willing to carry their doctrine to this logical conclusion. Believing that government was an evil, they felt that something more than talk was necessary to get rid of it. The use of force might be wrong, but as long as governments used force to persecute Anarchists it was right for Anarchists to use force to terrorize governments. Thus the Russian revolutionists known as " Terrorists " organized themselves secretly, engineered plots for the assassination of officials in high places, and ended by killing the Tsar Alexander II in 1881. In western Europe also there were little scattered secret groups of Anarchists, associating themselves with the labor unions, advocating the " general strike," and laying plans for the coming social revolution. Some of them were extremists, eager for the adoption of the methods of the Russian Terrorists. In 1892 a bomb was exploded in the French Chamber of Deputies by the Anarchist, Vaillant.

His defense was: "There can be no innocent bourgeois." In 1894 President Carnot was assassinated at Lyon. A few years later the Empress Elizabeth of Austria and President McKinley of the United States suffered the same fate.

Such is the inconsistency of the human mind! A doctrine designed to free mankind from the use of physical force came to be professed by stern fanatics, who dedicated their lives to the sacred cause of bringing peace on earth and goodwill to men by means of bombs and daggers. The result was that in the popular mind anarchism came to be associated with extreme violence; an Anarchist was thought of as a bearded and sinister-looking person with a bomb in his pocket, waiting for the appointed time to blow up a building or murder a president or a king.

A HAND AGAINST EVERY MAN

From a cartoon by Parkinson in *Judy*, 1892. It reflects the fear of anarchist and socialist ideas common in the late nineteenth century. Anarchy is setting off dynamite to blow up society, which rests on law, property, and religion.

How the industrial workers were supported by many people who became socialistic without being Socialists. Outside of Russia, anarchism had but little influence. The great majority of the industrial workers of western Europe accepted Marxian socialism. To defend their interests they formed labor unions, and in order to obtain higher wages and shorter hours of labor the labor unions organized strikes, which sometimes succeeded and sometimes failed, and were in any case expensive. Sooner or later, therefore, in nearly every country, the workers made use of the political weapon. They organized political parties of their own. The first of these was the German Social-Democratic Labor Party (1875). Similar parties were organized in other countries: in Belgium, the Socialist party, 1885; in Austria, the Social Democratic party, 1888; in France, the United Socialist party, 1905; in Great Britain, the Labor party,

1906. All of these parties accepted the Marxian doctrine of socialism, or some modification of it, and all adopted a program of social reform designed to protect the interests of the workingmen against capitalists, the poor against the rich.

At first these Socialist workingmen's parties polled but few votes, but after about 1900 they had a rapid and an astonishing success. By 1914 the Socialist parties in Germany and France, for example, were among the strongest parties in those countries. But it would be a great mistake to suppose that the industrial workers achieved this success by themselves, or that all of the people who voted for Socialist candidates were Socialists. In this movement for social reform the industrial workers were supported by many people who were not themselves industrial workers, many people who were socialistic without being Socialists. We must now see who these people were, and why they supported the Socialist parties.

One marked characteristic of the last fifty years has been the growth, among all classes of people, of a *sense of social responsibility*. What does this mean? It means something more than sympathy with the poor and oppressed. Humane sympathy is nothing new in the world; but formerly the relief of poverty was commonly left to the churches and to kind-hearted individuals. It is easy for you or me to give a dime to a beggar; easy for the churches or the government to provide homes for the aged and the infirm. "How grateful they must be," we are apt to think; and perhaps we are mildly surprised or indignant if the beggar scowls at us while taking our dime, or if the aged seem not entirely happy in their scrubbed homes that smell of soap or formaldehyde. But the beggar may very well ask, "Why am I, and not you, the beggar?" And those old people in the poorhouse may be thinking, "Why is it that after working hard all our lives we have not enough to live on when we are old and helpless?"

During the last fifty years intelligent and well-to-do people have taken these questions more seriously. Much more than formerly, such people are apt to say: "Perhaps it is the beggar's misfortune, rather than his fault, that he is a beggar. Perhaps it is the fault of society — of all of us — if the common man cannot earn enough to keep himself when he is old. Perhaps it is our business to *prevent* poverty rather than simply to *relieve* it. Perhaps it is the duty of governments, with all of modern scientific knowledge at their disposal, to devise laws which will abolish poverty by distributing the accumulated wealth of society more justly." Thus it happened that many educated and well-to-do people sympathized with the industrial workers. Some of them even accepted the Marxian doctrine of socialism; but most of them preferred a less revolutionary doctrine. They therefore called themselves either " Christian Socialists " or " State Socialists."

Christian socialism spread chiefly within the churches. Many ministers and priests felt that the capitalist system was unchristian, since it imposed poverty on the mass of the workers while the rich employers and capitalists lived in palaces. In Catholic countries Christian socialism was made respectable by Pope Leo XIII, who issued in 1891 an official letter in which he deplored the greed of employers and declared that the conditions of labor ought to be improved. Following this lead, Catholic political parties, such as the Center party in Germany and the Catholic party in Belgium, although strongly opposed to Marxian socialism, were quite ready to support the Socialist parties in their effort to obtain social reform — legislation favorable to the working classes.

Towards the end of the nineteenth century State socialism was made respectable by professors of economics in the universities. In the early nineteenth century the British school of " classical economists," followers of Adam Smith, taught the *laissez-faire* theory of government — the " let alone " theory. They said: " Governments should confine their activities to the protection of life and property and the defense of the country against its enemies; they should not try to regulate trade or industry, or to bring about a more equitable distribution of wealth between rich and poor." In the middle of the century John Stuart Mill criticized this doctrine, and towards the end of the century certain German economists (Professors Schmoller, Roscher, and Wagner) abandoned it altogether. They said: " It is the duty of the government to advance the welfare of all the people, not only by protecting life and property but by passing laws which will distribute property more equitably and make life more worth living for the mass of the people." These

TELEGRAPH OFFICE, 1870
From a contemporary drawing.

economists did not agree with Marx that labor is the sole source of wealth ; they did not accept his doctrine of the " social revolution." Their ideas spread to other countries, and thousands of people in every country, including the so-called " intellectuals " — professors, publicists, and writers of books — came to look with favor on social reform, and even to advocate the state ownership of certain industries, such as railroads and telegraph lines, which affected the lives of all the people. Thus a great many people who were not themselves industrial workers came to look with favor on the effort of the industrial workers to better their condition. Thousands of moderately well-to-do people — shopkeepers, clerks, doctors, lawyers, professors, school teachers, and small farmers — voted for the candidates of the Socialist parties because these parties favored a more equitable distribution of wealth among the people as a whole.

Meantime, just as the workers found many socialistic friends to support them in their conflict with capital, so the capitalists found many anti-socialistic friends to support them in their conflict with labor.

How many people, for religious or patriotic reasons, supported the capitalists against the workers. Of course it is easy to understand why the capitalists — the owners of big and little industries — were not in favor of the socialistic programs of reform. They naturally wished to conduct their businesses as they judged best. To them strikes were an evil, because they wasted time and demoralized the workers. They felt that it was necessary to resist the labor unions even when their demands might be justified. It would never do to yield to a threatened strike since, if the workers got what they wanted the first time, they would try it again, and there would be no end to their demands for higher wages and shorter hours. Besides, the capitalists often maintained that the unhampered development of business was a good thing for everyone, including the laborers. They said in substance: "If you interfere with our business by strikes or by hostile legislation, our profits will be reduced. With reduced profits we cannot afford to expand our business and perhaps we shall be forced to close it down altogether. In either case there will be hard times, and many laborers will be out of jobs. Interfere with industry and you hamper the very thing which makes the entire community prosperous."

The argument of the great capitalists seemed very reasonable to many people besides the owners of the great industries. It seemed reasonable to the owners of small businesses, to rich landowners, to bankers and promoters, to speculators on the stock exchange, to lawyers who looked after the interests of business corporations, to the people who lived on money invested in stocks and bonds, and to the thousands of people who were connected in a business or social way with the rich and powerful classes.

But people are not influenced solely by their economic interests or their social connections; and in every country thousands, even millions, of people, rich and poor alike, united in opposition to socialism on religious or patriotic grounds.

1. *Religious opposition to socialism.* Marxian socialism was strongly "anti-clerical." Marx believed that Christianity was a religion cleverly designed to keep the poor enslaved by teaching them that they would be rewarded in a future life if they patiently endured the trials and tribulations of this one. Following Marx,

the Socialist working classes of Europe were commonly indifferent or actively hostile to the churches, Catholic and Protestant alike. Religious people naturally resented the contempt with which Socialists spoke of their most cherished beliefs; and many people who were not themselves religious felt that if Christianity were discredited the very foundations of morality would be destroyed. Socialism was therefore feared and hated by conservative-minded people because socialistic ideas were " anti-religious," " atheistical," and " immoral " in their tendency.

2. *Patriotic opposition to socialism.* Marxian socialism was " international " in its outlook.   Marx taught that the real opposition of interests in modern society was not between one nation and another but between the workers of all nations and the capitalists of all nations.   The opposition between one nation and another — such, for example, as the rivalry between France and Germany which led to the Franco-Prussian War — was a sham opposition, a kind of game played by the ruling classes in both countries in order to arouse the patriotic emotions of the people and so keep them enslaved by keeping them divided.   The Socialist working classes in Europe generally accepted this doctrine.   No war, they said, could ever benefit the workers of either country concerned in it; whichever country won the war, the people in both would suffer from it and pay for it.   The Socialist parties were therefore generally anti-military and anti-nationalist.   They opposed big armies and navies, denounced secret diplomacy and secret treaties, and maintained that the colonial expansion of European powers in Africa and Asia was a game beneficial to the rich but likely to involve the people in expensive and disastrous wars.   Socialism was therefore feared and hated by many people, not only because it was anti-religious but also because it seemed unpatriotic, if not actually treasonable.

Thus it happened that just as the workers found many friends who were not themselves industrial workers, so the capitalists found many friends who were not themselves capitalists.   And just as the workers and their friends were inclined to support the workingmen's Socialist parties, so the capitalists and their friends were inclined to support the old conservative parties.   Between

1900 and 1914 this separation of the people into conservative and radical groups became more or less pronounced in nearly every European country. Moreover, the conflict between them came to be something more than a mere quarrel over wages and hours of labor. Generally speaking, they divided on three main issues: (1) *social reform* — the question of the extent to which the government should make laws designed to benefit the poor as against the rich; (2) *national defense* — the question as to whether it was necessary or wise to build up great armies and navies in order to preserve the peace by a vigorous defense of national interests; (3) *imperialism* — the question as to whether it was necessary or wise for European powers to acquire colonies and " spheres of influence " in Africa and Asia. The workingmen's Socialist parties were strongly in favor of the first — social reform; and they were inclined to be anti-nationalist, anti-militarist, and anti-imperialistic. The conservative parties, on the other hand, were strongly nationalist and imperialistic, but they were inclined to be indifferent, if not actively hostile, to social reform.

A look backward and a look forward.   In this chapter we have learned how the Industrial Revolution separated the employers from the laborers and gave them conflicting interests to quarrel about. We have seen how this conflict gave rise to a new social and political philosophy, known as socialism. We have seen how the working classes formed political parties, based on the philosophy of socialism and presenting certain specific programs of social reform. We have seen how the people divided, some supporting the working classes and some the capitalist classes. We have also seen how the two groups of people were opposed to each other, not only on the question of social reform but on the two other important questions — the question of nationalism and the question of imperialism. We have dealt with these new conflicts in a general way, as they arose in Europe as a whole. In the next chapter we shall deal with them more concretely, as they arose and worked themselves out in certain countries. The countries chosen to illustrate concretely the rise of the social conflict are Germany, France, and England.

CHART FOR CHAPTER XVII. Showing how the rise of the social conflict transformed old parties and led to the formation of new ones.

1815	1875	1900	1914

Landowning Conservative parties. Oppose movement for popular government.
→ Abandon opposition to popular government. Become merged in → capitalist Conservative parties. (Pro-nationalist, pro-imperialist, anti-socialist.)

Middle-class Liberal parties. Favor middle-class control of government, but oppose democratic suffrage.

Conservative Liberals join →

Continue with declining influence as → middle-class Liberal parties. (Mildly pro-nationalist, pro-social reform, anti-imperialist, anti-socialist)

Progressive Liberals join →

Lower-class Radical or Republican parties. Favor democratic government.

Continue with increasing influence as → Socialist or Labor parties. (Strongly pro-socialist, pro-social reform, anti-militarist, anti-imperialist.)

Radical Left Wing forms new →

Anarchist, Communist, and (Ch XVIII) Syndicalist parties. (Irreconcilably opposed to existing social system.)

QUESTIONS

1. How did the Industrial Revolution change the relation of laborers and employers? Why were wages low in the early stages of the Industrial Revolution? When did the laborers obtain the right to vote and to strike? How did they use these weapons to defend their interests?

2. Who was Karl Marx? What were his chief writings? State briefly his theory of scientific socialism. Do you see any similarity between Marx's theory of historical progress and Darwin's theory of biological evolution? (For Darwin's theory, see p. 648.)

3. What was Proudhon's theory of anarchism? How did the anarchism of Tolstoy differ from the anarchism of the man who threw a bomb into the French Chamber of Deputies? Why did most people come to associate anarchism with extreme violence?

4. Name some of the Socialist parties formed between 1875 and 1906. What is meant by " Christian socialism "? by " state socialism "? What is the difference between state socialism and Marxian socialism? What classes of people were inclined to sympathize with the laborers? Why did most of them prefer to be called "Christian Socialists," or "State Socialists," rather than "Marxian Socialists"?

5. Why were the capitalists opposed to socialism and to social reform? Why did many people who were not capitalists oppose socialism and the Socialist parties? What is meant by nationalism? by militarism? by imperialism? How did the capitalistic Conservative parties and the workingmen's Socialist parties differ in respect to these issues?

SELECTED READINGS

Brief accounts. Robinson and Beard, *Outlines*, II, ch. xiv. Hayes, *Modern Europe*, II, chs. xviii, xxi. Schevill, *History of Europe*, ch. xxiv. Hazen, *Modern Europe*, ch. xv, and *Europe since 1815* (revised ed.), I, chs. iv, xv. Ashley, *Modern Civilization*, ch. xxiv. Schapiro, *European History* (revised ed.) chs. iii, xviii. Seignobos, *Contemporary Civilization*, ch. xix. F. A. Ogg, *Economic Development of Modern Europe*, chs. xxi-xxiii. Brief histories of socialism: S. P. Orth, *Socialism and Democracy in Europe;* J. R. MacDonald, *The Socialist Movement;* J. Spargo, *Socialism.*

Biographies. J. Spargo, *Karl Marx.* A. Bebel, *My Life.* The following works throw light on the conditions that gave rise to the social conflict. M. R. Parkman, *Heroines of Service.* H. Begbie, *Life of General William Booth*, and *Twice-Born Men.* A. Patri, *A Schoolmaster in a Great City.*

Sources. Robinson and Beard, *Readings in Modern History*, II, 489 (Communist manifesto); 493 (Gotha Program); 495 (program of the Fabian Society). R. C. K. Ensor, *Modern Socialism as Set Forth by Socialists.* Henry George, *Progress and Poverty.* (Many times printed. The most convenient edition is *Significant Passages from Henry George's Progress and Poverty*, N. Y., 1898). Scott and Baltzly, *Readings in European History*, ch. xi.

SILHOUETTES DRAWN IN 1887

The artist has pictured a few of the various types of vehicles to be seen prome-
nading in the streets of Paris, London, or Berlin.

CHAPTER XVIII. HOW THE SOCIAL CONFLICT DEVEL-OPED IN THREE COUNTRIES — GERMANY, FRANCE, AND ENGLAND

The association of progress with poverty is the great enigma of our times.
HENRY GEORGE

An apology for neglecting the history of many countries. In the
last chapter we learned something about the general character of the
social conflict. What was said of it would be true of any country
in which the Industrial Revolution occurred. But the special
problems which it raised, the particular conflicts which these problems gave rise to, and the measures taken to solve the problems
were somewhat different in different countries. In this chapter we
shall study the social conflict more concretely, as it developed in
particular countries; and the countries chosen for this purpose
are Germany, France, and England.

Why do we choose these countries, rejecting so many others?
Partly, no doubt, because these were the countries whose activities
were likely to have a greater influence in Europe than the activities
of any others; but chiefly because these countries differed widely in
historical traditions, in political customs, and in national temperament. Germany is chosen because it represents the Germanic
countries and the countries with a strong monarchical tradition.
France is chosen because it represents the Latin countries, and
because its political traditions were revolutionary and democratic.

547

England is chosen because — well, because it is England, an island country separated from the Continent, a country whose traditions were neither revolutionary nor monarchical but a little of both, a country whose political customs were different from those of any Continental country.   These three countries will therefore provide us with all the variety we need for illustrative purposes.   By studying their history we shall meet with various brands of socialism, with various kinds of political parties and political conflicts, and with various types of practical programs for social reform.

I. Germany, 1871–1914

We meet Bismarck again and learn briefly what he was up to after 1871.   When last we heard of Bismarck he had just completed the formation of the new German Empire after the Franco-Prussian War (see p. 454).   For nearly twenty years (1871–1890) he held the office of chancellor (prime minister) in the imperial government; and during that time he was, far more than the emperor himself, the real ruler of Germany.   Bismarck had no faith in the capacity of the people to govern themselves successfully.   He therefore tried to organize the government of the new empire in such a way that the emperor and his ministers would never be dependent on the will of the people, never have to submit to the dictation of the popular assembly (*Reichstag*), never have to make serious concessions to the radical parties, whether Liberal or Socialist.   Bismarck's methods were nevertheless often very devious; and as it happened, in order to accomplish this last object, he found it convenient, during the first seven years of his chancellorship, to join hands with the Liberals and to adopt, or seem to adopt, a Liberal policy.

How Bismarck became a Liberal in order to make the new empire a " going concern," 1871–1878.   The problem which confronted Bismarck in 1871 was similar to that which confronted Washington and Hamilton in 1787 when the present Constitution of the United States was adopted.   In 1787 few people in the United States were very enthusiastic about the new federal union.   Much the same condition existed in Germany in 1871.   Many people were indifferent to the new empire; many were hostile. Bismarck's problem was to get the new imperial institutions to work smoothly, to win the support of the people who were indifferent, to reconcile those who were hostile. In short, his first task was to make the new empire a " going concern."

The attitude of the people towards Bismarck and the new empire was reflected by the political parties in the Reichstag. The Conservative party was chiefly a Prussian party, composed of the land-owning nobles and of high officers in the government and the army. Like Bismarck, the Conservatives were opposed to popular government; unlike him many of them were at first not very enthusiastic about the new empire. The Progressive Liberal party was composed mostly of workingmen and lower middle-class people. The Progressive Liberals were less interested in the government of the empire than in the government of Prussia; and they disliked Bismarck because he was opposed to any reform of the Prussian government. The Center party was a new party, formed by the Catholics, who were a minority in the empire, and who feared that the imperial government might interfere with their religious liberty. These were the parties that at first were hostile to Bismarck and not much interested in the new empire.

One party only was enthusiastic about the new empire and ready to help Bismarck make it a success. This was the National Liberal party. It was composed of upper middle-class people, educated and fairly wealthy or well-to-do people — business men, officials, lawyers, professors, and men of letters. The National Liberals admired Bismarck and believed that the unification of Germany under the German Empire was a great step forward for Germany. They wished to make the new empire a successful and a powerful state. In all this they agreed with Bismarck. But unlike Bismarck, they accepted the ordinary liberal doctrines. They believed in free trade, free speech, free press, and popular government. They were anti-clerical — opposed to the political doctrines of the Catholic Church. Above all, they believed that the Reichstag should, like the English House of Commons, exercise a controlling influence over the emperor and his ministers. The National Liberals were ready to help Bismarck make the new empire a strong and successful government, if he would fall in with their ideas and make it a truly liberal government.

At first, therefore, Bismarck had to work with the National Liberal party, not only because it was one of the strongest parties in the Reichstag but because it was the only party that was ready to support him. To get their support he had to adopt, temporarily, a liberal policy. To please the Liberals he adopted and partly carried out a policy of free trade. To please them he had to allow the Reichstag a greater control over the army than he would have preferred. But the chief of Bismarck's liberal activities was his fight with the Catholic Church. This struggle is known as the *Kulturkampf* ("fight for civilization"). In 1872–1874 many anti-clerical laws were passed. The Jesuits were expelled from Germany, and diplomatic relations with the Pope suspended. In Prussia, Catholic schools were subject to government supervision, and no one was permitted to become a Catholic priest unless he was a German who had studied three years in a German university. These anti-clerical laws pleased the Liberals, but they were not so popular in Germany as Bismarck doubtless hoped they would be. It was found impossible to enforce most of them, and they strengthened rather than weakened the church in Germany.

Bismarck always regarded his alliance with the National Liberals as temporary — a necessary move in the political game. In his *Reminiscences* he says that the granting of universal suffrage in the constitution of the empire was " a species of political blackmail." In order to get the support of the German Liberals for the unification of Germany and the establishment of the empire it was necessary to bribe them with the promise of popular government. When the empire was once firmly established it would be easy, Bismarck said, to " set the clock back."

In 1878 it seemed to Bismarck that the time had come to set the clock back. With the help of the Liberals, the difficult task of adjusting the relations of the states to the federal government had been fairly well accomplished. The new empire was recognized as the strongest state in Europe, and Bismarck was at the height of his fame and influence. Bismarck felt, therefore, that the Liberals had served their purpose, and he determined to break with them at the first favorable opportunity, and to base his government on the support of the Conservative parties. In doing this he was greatly helped by the rise of socialism and the popular fear of the new doctrines.

How the rise of socialism helped Bismarck to break with the National Liberal party. For some years the doctrines of socialism had been spreading among the German workingmen. Until 1875 the workingmen were divided into two associations — the followers of Lassalle and the followers of Marx. But in 1875 a congress was held at Gotha in order to compromise their differences; and under the leadership of William Liebknecht and August Bebel, two devoted followers of Marx, the two associations were united into one — the German Social-Democratic Labor party, whose members were commonly called the " Social Democrats."

The new party adopted what is known as the Gotha Program, consisting of (1) a statement of principles and (2) a practical political program. In its *statement of principles* the Gotha Program accepted the scientific socialism of Marx. It declared that " labor is the sole source of wealth," and that therefore the " means of wealth " (land, factories, and machines by which labor produces wealth) should be transferred from private ownership to state ownership. In its *platform of political action* the Gotha Program declared that the new party would work for social legislation beneficial to the mass of the people, and especially to the industrial workers. In short, immediate social reform, and the ultimate transfer of the great industries from private to public ownership — such was the Gotha Program of the new Social-Democratic Labor party.

Two years later (1877) the new party polled nearly half a million votes, and elected twelve deputies to the Reichstag. Many people began to take an interest in the new party and its activities, to fear it, and to wonder if something should not be done to suppress it. Among those who felt that socialism was a dangerous menace to society was Bismarck. In the Reichstag he had often thundered against the Socialists and their ideas — " utopian nonsense, the ideas of those who believe that roast pigeons will fly into their mouths." Bismarck seems often to have been greatly favored by luck; and as it happened, in 1878, just when he was preparing to break with the National Liberal party, two lucky chances enabled him to make use of the Socialist menace to accomplish that object.

One day in May, 1878, Bismarck was informed that a man by the name of Hödel had fired a shot at the aged Emperor William. Bismarck exclaimed, " Now we've got them." His informant asked, " The Socialists, Your Excellency? " Bismarck replied, " No, the Liberals." Bismarck knew well that the National Liberals were strongly opposed to socialism. But he knew that the attempt on the emperor's life would be charged to the Socialists; and he hoped that the fear of socialism would make even Liberal ideas unpopular. He at once introduced into the Reichstag a hastily prepared measure designed to suppress the Socialist party. The Liberal parties opposed it and it was rejected. Then a second lucky chance favored Bismarck's plans. The emperor was fired upon a second time, by a man named Nobiling, and seriously wounded. Hearing of this, Bismarck said, " In that case we will dissolve the Reichstag." He hoped that in the new elections the people would desert the Liberal parties.

Bismarck's hopes were justified. The people were infuriated by these attempts to assassinate their beloved emperor. It mattered not that the first assassin, Hödel, was a worthless fellow who had been expelled from the Socialist party, and that the second, Nobiling, had never been a member of it. The people easily believed that such acts were the natural result of Socialist ideas, and Bismarck used every means to confirm them in that belief. People wanted socialism suppressed. They were indignant with the Liberal deputies in the last Reichstag who had voted against Bismarck's repressive measures. The result of the new elections was therefore what Bismarck had desired — the liberal parties lost control of the Reichstag.

Bismarck now abandoned his Liberal policies and made his peace with the Conservatives. To win over the Catholic Center he abandoned the *Kulturkampf*. The laws against the Catholic priests (except those against the Jesuits) were suspended. As it happened, in 1878 a new Pope was elected — Leo XIII. Leo proved to be more friendly to modern ideas than Pius IX had been.

ATTEMPTED ASSASSINATION OF WILLIAM I
From a sketch by H. Lüders in the *Illustrirte Zeitung*, May 25, 1878.

He gave Catholics to understand that it was quite possible for them to be good Catholics and at the same time loyal to the governments under which they lived.   This smoothed the way for re-establishing friendly relations between the German government and the papacy. These measures pleased the Center party and made it more disposed to support Bismarck's measures.

The Conservative party was won over, partly by Bismarck's hostility to the Socialists, and partly by the fact that he was now ready to abandon the policy of free trade.   The great landowners of Prussia wanted duties levied on farm products, especially on the importation of Russian grain, so that they could get higher prices for their own products.   At the same time the people interested in developing German industries, especially the iron and cloth industries, wanted tariffs on manufactured commodities in order to protect them against English competition.   To please the landowners and the manufacturers Bismarck therefore introduced a tariff bill into the Reichstag in 1879.   Supported by the Conservatives, by those National Liberals who represented the great industrial interests, and by the Center, the tariff bill was passed by a large majority.   This was a great victory for Bismarck, not only because the Liberals were defeated but because it was the beginning of the disruption of the powerful National Liberal Party. From this time on something less than half of the old National Liberals continued to support Bismarck; the rest of them ultimately formed a union with the Progressive Liberals.

Bismarck's break with the Liberals was now complete. From 1879 to 1890 his government was supported by a " Conservative block " composed of the Conservatives, the Center, and what remained of the old National Liberals. With this strong Conservative support Bismarck set himself the congenial task of destroying the Social-Democratic party and utterly rooting out Socialist ideas. Thus the clock would be effectively " set back." Let us see whether he succeeded.

How Bismarck tried in vain to destroy socialism in Germany, 1878–1890. In his effort to destroy socialism Bismarck employed two methods. The first was to make it dangerous to be a Socialist or to belong to a Socialist organization. As soon as the new Reichstag assembled in 1878, measures were passed outlawing the Socialist party, suppressing its newspapers, and prohibiting its meetings. Socialist meetings had to be held on the sly. Newspapers had to be printed abroad and smuggled into Germany. Leaders were arrested and imprisoned or else expelled from the country. These laws were in force until 1890. During this time the life of the German Socialist was that of a criminal seeking to escape the police.

The second method employed by Bismarck was to wean the working classes away from Socialist ideas by conferring benefits upon them. In 1883, 1884, and 1887 he with difficulty got the Reichstag to pass what were called the Social Insurance Acts. These laws provided that in case of illness, accident, or old-age incapacity, the workers should be paid a sum of money on which to live.

The world was much astonished, and somewhat amused, to see Bismarck, the tough old Conservative, favor what was then regarded as a species of state socialism. But Bismarck's " socialism " was designed only in part to benefit the workers. It was chiefly designed to place them under obligations to the government, in the hope that they would then hesitate to join a Socialist organiza-

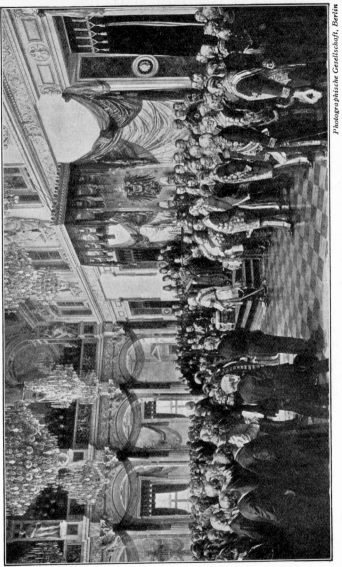

THE OPENING OF THE FIRST REICHSTAG UNDER WILLIAM II, JUNE 25, 1888

From a painting by Anton von Werner. Emperor William I was succeeded by Frederick III, who reigned three months. William II then became emperor. He is shown reading an address. Bismarck stands at the foot of the steps.

tion for fear of losing their insurance.   In advocating the law of 1884, Bismarck said:

Give the workingman the right to work as long as he is healthy; assure him care when he is sick; assure him maintenance when he is old.   If you do that and do not fear the sacrifice, or cry out "state socialism" — if the state will show a little more Christian solicitude for the workingmen, then I believe the gentlemen of the Social-Democratic program will sound their bird-calls in vain.

Bismarck's attempt to destroy socialism was a complete failure. For twelve years, in spite of repressive laws and a vigilant police, the Socialists managed to hold together somehow.   Somehow secret meetings were held and newspapers — printed abroad and smuggled in — were somehow circulated.   At each election candidates were agreed upon by the party that had no legal existence, and more people voted for the Socialist candidates during the years of repressive legislation than ever before.   In 1887 the Socialist candidates polled 673,000 votes; in 1890, nearly a million and a half.   For twelve years Bismarck had used all the resources of a powerful government to destroy the Social-Democratic party; at the end of that time the party was three times as strong as it had been in the beginning.

August Bebel, in his book entitled *My Life*, gives us an interesting account of his experiences, in prison and out, as a leader of the Socialists.   Anyone who wishes to understand modern socialism should read his book.   Bebel was no wild-eyed Anarchist carrying a bomb under his coat-tail.   He was a self-educated workingman, mild and humane, saddened by the misery of life and inspired by a deep sympathy for the poor.   For Bebel and his companions, socialism was a religion.   They regarded themselves as martyrs enduring persecution for an ideal of human happiness.   They never doubted that ideas were stronger than policemen's clubs and prison bars; and Bebel was not so much angry with Bismarck as sorry for him, regretting that so great a man could be so blind to the truth. Speaking of Bismarck, he says:

Bismarck was always a man of wrath, eager to crush and abolish any tendency of the times, which he found inconvenient or disagreeable, by the application of coercive measures.   He applied such measures to the Roman Catholic Church, the Polish National movement, and to Social Democracy. And he was never converted from this standpoint, although at the end of his life it was plain as day that it had been a mistake. He was the vanquished, not the victor.[1]

There is much truth in this. The mighty Bismarck, who easily outwitted diplomatists and defeated kings and emperors, was beaten by a handful of obscure men like Bebel and Liebknecht. In 1890, the very year that Bismarck retired, the repressive laws were repealed. The Social-Democratic party at once resumed its public activities, and after 1890 it rapidly increased in numbers and influence.

New York Public Library

BISMARCK AND HIS DOGS

An engraving made about the time of Bismarck's retirement from office, 1890.

What is the explanation of this rapid growth of the Social-Democratic party? Does it mean that the German people were turning Socialists and preparing for the social revolution predicted by Karl Marx? Not at all. It means that during the period from 1890 to 1914 the Socialists adopted less revolutionary doctrines. As their doctrines became less revolutionary they became less feared, and many people who were not Socialists voted for the candidates of the Socialist party.

How the Socialists revised their doctrines and thereby won many votes. In 1890, when Bismarck's repressive measures were repealed, Karl Marx had been dead seven years, and his great influence was declining. Many Socialists felt that he had been mistaken in predicting the speedy collapse of the capitalist system. The capitalist system seemed, indeed, to be thriving mightily. Germany was rapidly becoming one of the leading industrial coun-

[1] August Bebel, *My Life*. Reprinted by permission of the University of Chicago Press.

tries of the world.   Statistics seemed to prove that land and capital were not being concentrated in the hands of very rich capitalists and that the mass of the people were not being reduced to wage slaves.   On the contrary, Germany was prospering, and the working classes were better off than formerly.   The social revolution seemed a long time coming.   Many Socialists felt, therefore, that the doctrines of Marx needed to be revised.   The leader of the " Revisionists " was Edward Bernstein.   Bernstein maintained that the social revolution would come, not by any sudden revolutionary upheaval, but by a slow and peaceful evolution.   The thing for the Socialists to do, he said, was to gain political power and to get what they wanted by forcing the government to pass laws favorable to the mass of the people.

The Socialists revised their program at a conference at Erfurt in 1891.   The Erfurt Program reaffirmed the theories of Karl Marx, but it did not emphasize the idea of the coming social revolution so much as the Gotha Program had done.   In the Erfurt Program the chief emphasis was placed on the practical legislative reforms which the party would work for.   The list of reforms demanded was a long one.   It may be summarized under two main heads :

1. *General measures designed to benefit the people as a whole:* (1) universal, equal, and direct suffrage, with vote by ballot, for all men and women twenty years of age or over, and abolition of all laws restricting the rights of women as compared with men ; (2) direct control of legislation by the people through the initiative and referendum ; (3) military training for all citizens and the abolition of standing armies; (4) complete freedom of the press, of religion, and of assembly; (5) income taxes in proportion to wealth ; (6) compulsory universal education in free public schools; (7) free legal advice and free administration of justice; (8) free medical service and free burial for the poor.

2. *Special measures designed to benefit the industrial workers:* (1) eight-hour working day; (2) one day of continuous rest every week for all workers; (3) non-employment of children under fourteen; (4) prohibition of night work, with certain exceptions; (5) complete right of forming labor unions and of collective bar-

gaining; (6) extension of the system of workmen's insurance; (7) official inspection of factories to secure the rights of laborers.

It is easy to see that such a program would appeal to many people. The first part would appeal to many people who were neither industrial workers nor Socialists. People who wanted equal rights for women, democratic suffrage, or the initiative and referendum; people who wanted free education, free medical and legal service, heavy taxes on the rich; people who were opposed to huge armies and compulsory military service — to all such the Socialist program was attractive. And in fact the success of the Social-Democratic party in winning the votes of these people was striking. In 1898 the party polled more than two million votes; in 1907 more than three million; in 1912 more than four million. At the opening of the Great War in 1914 the Social-Democratic party was the strongest party in the Reichstag, with a representation of 110 deputies. Three-fourths of the people who voted for these deputies were not themselves members of the Socialistic organization. They were small shopkeepers, clerks, school teachers, doctors, lawyers, professors, men of letters, or small farmers. Thus it happened that during the years 1891–1914 the Social-Democratic party replaced the old Liberal parties as the party which represented the interests of the mass of the people in opposition to the upper and ruling classes.

What part of the Socialist program was enacted into law? Not all of it by any means. During the years 1891–1914 something was done to realize the second part of the Erfurt Program. Bismarck's labor insurance measures were extended and improved; and in 1911 the so-called Code of Social Insurance was adopted — the most elaborate system of labor insurance in the world. It provided for compulsory insurance for virtually all workers (including teachers and actors) receiving less than $500 a year. The necessary fund was raised by contributions from the workers, from the employers, and in some cases from the state or the local government. From this fund ill or injured workers so insured received enough to live on while disabled; and all persons so insured received a pension when they became too old to work. There was also a Commercial Code, a set of regulations enacted by the various states or by the imperial government and designed to protect the interests of the industrial workers by limiting the hours of labor, restricting the employment of women and children, and requiring employers to establish in their industries safe and sanitary conditions for their employees. Although such measures were often supported by the Conservatives and the Center, the Social Democrats exerted a great influence in creating the public opinion that made it possible to enact them.

Much less was done to realize the first part of the Erfurt Program, since the Conservative parties, upon which the government relied for support, rarely favored any part of it. The Prussian system of voting, in which the poor man's vote counted for much less than that of the rich man, remained in force. In the German Empire women were not given the right to vote until after the war. Needless to say, the standing army was not abolished. On the contrary, it was during these years (1891–1914) that Germany became more aggressively militaristic than ever. Her army was steadily strengthened; her navy became, next to that of Great Britain, the best in Europe. The government adopted an aggressive policy of colonial expansion; and the emperor, William II, by often " shaking the mailed fist " did much to increase international fear and to bring about the great war. The Social Democrats were never strong enough to control the government, never strong enough to make much headway against the powerful current of patriotic national sentiment which favored a militaristic and an imperialistic policy. Yet they were too strong to be ignored. In the years before the Great War they represented the mass of the poor and the moderately well-to-do people who wished to transform the Germany which Bismarck had created into a less militaristic, less imperialistic, and a far more socialistic state.

II. FRANCE, 1875–1914

How the third French Republic proved more stable than many people thought it would. After the fall of Napoleon's empire in 1870–1871, it was at first uncertain whether the National Assembly would retain a republican form of government or restore the Bourbon monarchy; but finally it adopted the constitution known as the

" Constitution of the Third French Republic " (1875).   The constitution was the result of a compromise between the moderate Royalists and the conservative Republicans in the Assembly; and like most compromises it was thoroughly disliked by many people, and was not entirely satisfactory even to the people who fashioned it (see page 458).

Thus in 1875 it seemed touch-and-go with the new form of government. Would the republic endure? Would the monarchy be restored? This uncertainty was bad for the nerves, and slight events were likely to be magnified into serious crises which seemed to threaten the existence of the government. The earliest of these crises occurred in 1877, and is known as the " Sixteenth of May."

At that time the president of the republic was Marshal MacMahon, a former Royalist but a very loyal Frenchman who had in good faith accepted the Constitution of 1875. But he was a very conservative man, and he worked with the Royalists and Clericals in the Chamber of Deputies in spite of the fact that the majority of the Chamber was Republican. The ablest leader of the Republicans was Léon Gambetta, a shrewd politician and a powerful orator. Gambetta believed that the Royalists and the Clericals were secretly conspiring to overthrow the republic at the first opportunity, and that the president was either their accomplice or their tool. He therefore used his influence to unite all Republicans against the president and his policies.

The strongest card Gambetta could play was " clericalism." Public opinion in France had been strongly anti-clerical ever since 1789, because most of the clergy had been opposed to the Revolution and to the movement for popular government. Even those who were Catholics in religion were often anti-clerical in politics. The priest, they said, should "stay in his church" and not meddle with politics. Gambetta used this dislike of priests in politics to unite the people against President MacMahon. In one of his most famous speeches in the chamber he exclaimed: " Clericalism — there is the enemy! " — a phrase which became a Republican slogan throughout the country. Irritated by Gambetta's opposition, President MacMahon decided to test his position by a popular vote. On May 16, 1877, he appointed a Clerical ministry under the Duke of Broglie, and shortly after dissolved the Chamber of Deputies, hoping that the new elections would give him a Conservative majority.

The president's action created great excitement. To Gambetta and the Radical Republicans the " Sixteenth of May " seemed but the first step in a *coup d'état* designed to restore the monarchy. During the elections Gambetta toured the country, denouncing clericalism and calling on all patriots to rally to the defense of the republic. His enemies called him a " commercial traveler for the republic," but he proudly accepted the designation, and used it to strengthen his crusade. The elections proved a victory for the Republicans. In January, 1879, MacMahon therefore resigned his office, and the Senate and Chamber of Deputies elected Jules Grévy, a Republican, as president. The Republicans celebrated their triumph by moving the seat of government from Versailles to Paris and by proclaiming July 14 (the anniversary of the taking of the Bastille) as a national holiday. The crisis of the Sixteenth of May was over. The new régime seemed to be firmly established.

Yet less than ten years later (1889) another crisis, the famous Boulanger Affair, threatened the existence of the republic. Although France was economically prosperous, the political life of the country was hectic and uninspiring. To counterbalance the loss of Alsace-Lorraine, the government adopted a policy of colonial expansion in far-off China which was more criticized than applauded. In reprisal for the Sixteenth of May it passed laws designed to abolish the influence of the priests in the schools, and thereby incurred the enmity of the great body of French Catholics, even those who favored the republic. The Chamber of Deputies was filled with inferior men, who were charged, and too often with reason, with being less interested in good government than in lining their own pockets. After the death of Gambetta in 1882 no first-rate leader appeared, capable of arousing popular enthusiasm for the republic or of uniting the Republican parties. Scandal smirched even the highest office when it transpired that President Grévy's son-in-law, a prominent deputy, was using his position to obtain the coveted badge of the Legion of Honor for people who would pay well for it. Although not himself involved, President Grévy was forced to resign (1887).   The very next year the Panama Company, organized to build a Panama Canal, went bankrupt, and many Frenchmen lost the hard-earned savings invested in it, while many politicians, so it was charged, carried off the spoils.

Such evidences of incompetence and corruption discredited the republic, and raised the hopes of the Royalists and Clericals.   And as it happened, there appeared on the scene a man who suddenly became a popular idol.   This man was Georges Boulanger, an officer in the army.   In 1886 he was made minister of war.   Already popular in the army, he suddenly enlisted the enthusiasm of the people.   He made a handsome figure, in uniform, riding a fine black horse. He talked much of a " war of revenge " against Germany.   He talked vaguely about necessary political reforms.   The Royalists took him up, hoping to make use of him.   So popular was he that in 1889 he was elected to the Chamber by five departments, including the Department of Paris. He became the man of the hour.   He was the " man on horseback " whom the people seemed eager to follow.   For months nothing was talked of but " Boulangism."   What would the great man do?   No one knew.   He did not know himself; but people believed that he was preparing a *coup d'état* — preparing to use his military power and his political popularity to set aside the republic and establish a dictatorship, or restore the Bourbon monarchy.

A DEMONSTRATION FOR BOULANGER AT EYZIES

From *L'Illustration* of May, 1888.

Had Boulanger been another Napoleon, the third republic would perhaps have come to an inglorious end in 1889.   But in fact Boulanger possessed neither intelligence nor character; and when the government decreed his arrest he fled the country, leaving his Royalist and Clerical friends in the lurch.   It was a ridiculous conclusion to so many brave words, and in France nothing is so fatal as to be ridiculous.   The people only laughed at the poor general who ran away.   What is more, they laughed at the Royalists and

Clericals who had supported him. This universal laughter cleared the air, and gave the republic a new lease of life.

The rise of socialism: How new parties were formed and old parties transformed, 1890–1905. The existence of the republic was not again seriously threatened, but the ten years following the Boulanger Affair was a period of great political excitement and of great political confusion. The excitement was provided by the Dreyfus Affair, of which we shall learn something presently. The confusion was the result, in part at least, of the rise of new political parties and the changing policies and alignments of the old ones. Of the new parties that were formed the chief were the Socialist party and the Radical Socialist party. First of all, therefore, we must learn something about the rise of socialism in France.

Before 1871 France was the chief center of socialism in Europe. We have already learned about the early type of utopian socialism as advocated by Saint-Simon and Fourier and Proudhon (see pp. 337, 536). After the collapse of the Revolution of 1848 the Socialist leaders were exiled and their organization broken up. The workers were discouraged. Utopian socialism seemed a mere dream; and for twenty-five years (apart from the short uprising of the Commune of Paris in 1871), socialism was practically a dead thing in France. But about 1875 the workers began once more to agitate and to organize. In 1876 the first French labor congress was held in Paris. In 1879 the third labor congress met at Marseille and took the name of the "Federation of Socialist Workingmen of France." This may be taken as the beginning of the modern French Socialist party.

One of the chief leaders of the Marseille Congress was Jules Guesde. He had taken part in the Paris Commune of 1871. Afterwards exiled, he went to Switzerland, where he met German and other Socialist leaders and was converted to the scientific socialism of Marx. Returning to France, he established in Paris a newspaper called *Equality*, and in the first number of this paper (1877) he announced the Marxian doctrine: "We believe that the natural and scientific evolution of mankind leads inevitably to the collective appropriation of the soil and the instruments of production (machines)." It was largely under the leadership of Guesde

FIRST LOCOMOTIVE THROUGH THE MONT CENIS TUNNEL
This event occurred in 1871.   The piercing of the Alps was an engineering feat
of considerable difficulty.

that the Marseille congress repudiated utopian socialism and accepted the scientific socialism of Karl Marx.

No sooner had the workers accepted the scientific socialism of Marx than they began to quarrel about the meaning of it.   The chief question which divided them was this: Should the socialists become a political party and try to bring about the social revolution by gaining control of the government?   The followers of Jules Guesde were inclined to say: " No, it is impossible to bring about the social revolution by political action."   But the followers of Paul Brousse, a rival Socialist leader, were inclined to say: " Yes, it is possible to help the social revolution along by passing laws favorable to the working classes."   The former were therefore called " Guesdists " or " Impossibilists "; the latter were called " Broussists " or " Possibilists " or " Revisionists."   (See p. 558.)

For many years the French Socialists remained weak and divided.   But during the years 1889 to 1905 the ideas of the Broussists or Possibilists gained ground, the various groups were more inclined to take part in elections, and the number of Socialist deputies in the chamber increased. They were led by three able men — Alexandre Millerand, Aristide Briand, and Jean Jaurès. In 1899 the Socialists were strong enough to gain representation in the Republican ministry of Waldeck-Rousseau; and finally, in 1905, most of the Socialist groups united to form the United Socialist party. In 1906 the new party polled 1,120,000 votes. From that time until the Great War it was one of the strongest parties in the Chamber.

In France, as in Germany, many people who were neither workingmen nor Socialists favored the social legislation advocated by the United Socialist party. But they did not like to be called Socialists. They preferred the term *radical*. Ever since 1871, to go no farther back, many good Republicans had been radicals — Radical Republicans. But when good Radical Republicans began to advocate measures of social reform — such as limitation of hours of labor, income taxes on the rich, and the like — it seemed proper, in order to distinguish them from ordinary Radical Republicans, to dub them " Radical Socialists." The name stuck, and about 1901 the deputies who were something more than Republicans but something less than Socialists organized as a separate group or party — the Radical Socialists. The name is misleading. It seems to mean that a Radical Socialist is more radical than an ordinary Socialist, whereas in fact he is less so. Strictly speaking, the Radical Socialists were not Socialists at all; they were Republicans with socialistic sympathies.

In France, as in all Continental countries, radical parties sit on the left side of the chamber; conservative parties on the right; and moderate parties in the center. Until about 1900 the chief party of the Left was the Radical Republican party. After 1900 two new parties took their seats on the Left — the Radical Socialists and the United Socialists. Henceforth these three parties constituted the Left. They had much in common. They were all democratic, anti-royalist, anti-clerical, and more or less anti-militaristic. They all, more or less, represented the poor or the moderately well-to-do. They could therefore often work together against the parties of the Right.

Meantime the parties of the Right — Royalists and Clericals — were modifying their policies and changing their names. Royalism seemed a bit ridiculous after the flight of Boulanger; and three years later (1892) Pope Leo XIII, in an official letter, advised French Catholics to give up their struggle against the republic. Most French Catholics were glad to accept this advice, and many Clericals in the Chamber broke away from the Royalists. For some years they were known as " Ralliés " — those who *rallied* to the support of the republic; but in 1901, under the lead of Count de Mun, a well-organized Catholic group was formed which called itself the party of Liberal Action.

The Liberal Action was Liberal in two respects only: (1) it supported the republic, and (2) it favored a program of social reform. Ten years earlier (1891) Pope Leo had officially expressed his sympathy for the working classes. Although denouncing Marxian socialism as an evil to be combated, he declared that every man has a right to live, and therefore to a living wage. He advised the workers to form labor unions, and urged governments to pass laws to protect the interest of the working classes. The solution of the modern conflict between capital and labor was to be found, not in Marxian socialism, but in Christian socialism — such in effect was the Pope's doctrine. The Liberal Action, like the Catholic Center in Germany, accepted the papal program of social reform, and in such matters often voted with the parties of the Left. But it sat on the Right, and in most respects was a conservative party: (1) it opposed Marxian socialism; (2) it opposed anti-clerical laws; and (3) although it accepted the republic it believed rather in government *for* the people than in government *by* the people.

Many former Royalists and Clericals refused to join the party of Liberal Action — for one reason because they could not accept its program of social reform. They were opposed to socialism in all its forms. They might have said, paraphrasing the famous words of Gambetta: " Socialism — there is the enemy! " They felt that the parties of the Left (United Socialists, Radical Socialists, and Radical Republicans) were all tarred with the same black stick. They were all socialistic. Besides, they were all *pacifist* — opposed to a strong army and to a vigorous foreign policy. Unless checked, they would end by destroying private property and by leaving France an easy prey to its enemies — to Germany above all. Thus many former Royalists and Clericals united with many conservative Republicans to form a new party in the Chamber of Deputies. The new party represented the old landed aristocracy and the new business aristocracy created by the Industrial Revolution. It was republican, but extremely conservative, anti-socialist, and strongly patriotic and nationalist. The party called itself the Republican Democratic Union, but its members were popularly known as " Nationalists."

Thus there appeared, about the beginning of the twentieth century, two strong parties on the Left and two on the Right. Between these Right and Left parties sat the various Republican parties of the Center, and without the aid of some of the Center groups neither the Right nor the Left could long control the Chamber. During the early years of the twentieth century the Chamber was controlled by a strong combination of the Republican parties of the Center and the Socialist parties of the Left. The event which brought about this combination was the famous Dreyfus Affair. We must now see how the Dreyfus Affair united the Republicans and the Socialists, and what use the Republican-Socialist combination made of its power.

The Dreyfus Affair and the social and anti-clerical legislation which followed it, 1894–1910. Alfred Dreyfus was a Jew, a captain in the army, and a Republican in politics. In 1894 he was accused of selling military secrets to the German government, tried by court-martial, and sentenced to servitude for life on Devil's Island. About the same time further revelation seemed to prove that certain Jewish bankers had united with certain Republican officials to make money corruptly out of the building of the Panama Canal. Nationalists and Clericals made the most of these events. France was being betrayed, they said — betrayed by Jews and corrupt Republican politicians. It was better to have a monarchy, they declared, than a corrupt republic. They felt that it was the duty of all true Frenchmen to unite in support of the church and the army against unpatriotic Jews, radicals, Socialists, and pacifists. At first the Socialist workingmen hardly knew what side to take

THE TRIUMPH OF JUSTICE

A Dutch cartoon referring to the reversal of Dreyfus' sentence. Dreyfus is
shown in the chariot of Justice. The horses are led by two men active on his
behalf. The one with glasses is Zola, the famous novelist. Behind are military
officers who were responsible for the false charges.

in this exciting crisis. They had no love for the Nationalists or
the Liberal Action; but neither had they much love for Jews, since
Jews were often bankers, and bankers represented the " money
power " and the capitalist system to which they had always been
so much opposed.

Thus for some years the trend of opinion was strongly anti-
Dreyfus, pro-army, and nationalist. But between 1897 and 1899
further revelations placed the affair in an entirely new light. It
was discovered that Dreyfus had been falsely accused. The
evidence against him had been forged to shield the real culprit,
Major Esterházy, who was not a Republican but a Royalist. In
the light of these revelations the affair seemed to prove, not that
Jews and Republicans were corrupt, but that Nationalists, Royalists, and Clericals were using the army for the unpatriotic purpose
of destroying the republic. The result was one of those quick re-
versals of public opinion which often occur in France. Dreyfus
became something of a national hero, and the great majority of
Frenchmen rallied to the defense of the republic against the triple
danger of royalism, clericalism, and militarism. In 1899 a Republi-

can-Socialist ministry was formed under the leadership of Waldeck-Rousseau, a Republican.   It was known as the " Cabinet of Republican Defense," and its declared object was " the energetic defense of Republican institutions."   For the first time a Socialist, Alexandre Millerand, became a cabinet minister; and for some years thereafter the government of France was largely controlled by a combination of the Republican and Socialist parties of the Left.

The first use which the Republican-Socialist combination made of its power was to pass a series of anti-military and anti-clerical laws.   Army officers of Royalist sympathies were replaced by Republicans.   The term of military service, hitherto three years, was reduced to two.   Having republicanized the army, the government took up the more difficult task of disestablishing the Catholic Church.   For a hundred years the relations of the French government and the Catholic Church had been regulated by Napoleon's famous Concordat with the Pope in 1801 (see p. 272).   According to this agreement the government appointed the bishops and paid the salaries of all the clergy.   Yet the clergy had been for the most part anti-republican and monarchist.   To good Republicans it seemed absurd for the government of a republic to support a church which used its influence to destroy the republic.   The result was that, under the ministry of Émile Combes, the Separation Law was passed (1905).   By this law the Catholic Church was disestablished in France.   The government ceased to appoint the bishops, and no longer paid the clergy salaries.   The church buildings, regarded as public property, were no longer to be reserved for the exclusive use of the Catholic religion.   Henceforth the Catholic Church was to have only such privileges (with certain minor exceptions) as all other religious organizations had.

These anti-military and anti-clerical laws could not have been passed without the support of the Radical Socialists and the Socialists.   In return for their support the Republican ministries made concessions in the matter of social legislation.   In 1899 the Republican ministry of Waldeck-Rousseau pledged the government " not to confine itself to mere political reform, but to embark upon the new path of social reform."   Therefore, during the period from 1900 to 1910 the growing strength of the Socialist party enabled its leaders, Millerand and Jaurès, to obtain some protection for the industrial workers. The hours of labor in factories were reduced from twelve to ten. The employment of women and children in mines was forbidden. The Sunday Rest Law of 1906 entitled employees to one day's rest in seven. But the most notable achievement of the Socialists in the matter of social legislation was the Old-Age Insurance Act of 1910. This law, following the German system, established compulsory insurance for all wage-earners (with certain exceptions) earning less than $580 a year. The necessary funds were to be contributed chiefly by the government but partly by the persons insured; and out of this fund each insured person was to receive, after the age of sixty, $85 a year for the rest of his life.

Thus the Socialist party obtained something in the way of social legislation. It might have obtained more, perhaps, had it been supported by the labor unions. But in France the labor unions (*syndicats*) had little faith in either the doctrines or the methods of the Socialist party. The labor unions adopted another doctrine, which is known as *syndicalism*.

Syndicalism: How it differed from socialism in theory and practice. Many French workingmen were dissatisfied with the United Socialist party for various reasons. In the first place the Socialist party had virtually abandoned the idea of Marx that the social revolution would come by a violent upheaval. To many French workers this seemed like a back-sliding in the faith. Why talk of a social revolution at all, they said, if it meant no more than a few laws limiting the hours of labor and requiring manufacturers to provide sanitary wash basins in factories? How could there be a social revolution without a revolution?

In the second place, the tradition of revolution was very strong in France. Since the great Revolution of 1789, the French workers, especially in Paris, had often enough taken part in real revolutions. They had raised barricades, fought the police, and assisted in overturning governments. The memory of the " glorious days " of 1830, of 1848, and of 1871 still remained vivid in spite of failure; and even if he had no present intention of resorting to violence, the French worker liked to talk of the revolution, and to

A STRIKE OF RAILWAY WORKERS

The railway which was being constructed in 1888 from Limoges to Brives, in
France, was delayed by a strike for higher wages.

anticipate the good time coming when the revolution would be
accomplished.

There was a third reason for the dissatisfaction of the French
workers, and this is the most important of all.   The Frenchman —
especially the working-class Frenchman — is by tradition and by
temperament suspicious of men in high office.   He easily suspects
the honesty of politicians and ministers.   The French workers
were therefore afraid that their own leaders, once elected to political
office, would become corrupted.   They were more convinced than
ever when Millerand, the first Socialist to become a cabinet minister, advocated the use of troops to suppress a labor union strike
(1902).   This is what happens, they said, when Socialists meddle in
politics.   As soon as our leaders are given office they betray us.
Seduced by power, they turn bourgeois, and instead of defending
socialism they defend the capitalist system.

For these reasons the French labor unions remained aloof from
the Socialist party.   In 1895 the various *syndicats* united to form
a General Confederation of Labor (*Confédération générale du Tra-*

vail) popularly known as the C. G. T. ; and in 1906, at the Amiens conference, the C. G. T. definitely refused to join with the United Socialist party which had been formed the year before. " We Syndicalists," the conference declared in effect, " are not opposed to the aims of the Socialists. But the aims of the Socialists are too limited. The social revolution can be brought about only by taking the property of the capitalist classes, and as a means to that end we recommend the general strike. Let the workers vote for Socialist deputies if they please ; let the Socialist deputies vote for laws limiting the hours of labor, increasing wages, and the like. But meantime let the workers prepare, through the *syndicats*, for the great general strike which will give them control of society and enable them to bring about the social revolution."

Between 1906 and 1910 the *syndicats* accordingly made much use of the strike for obtaining their ends. In 1906 a general strike was called for May 1 to compel the government to pass a law establishing an eight-hour day. In March, 1907, a strike of the gas and electric workers plunged Paris in darkness, and in 1909 there was a serious strike of the postal and telegraph operatives. But the most serious test of Syndicalist methods was the great railway strike of 1910. For a time all the railways of France were at a standstill. Food was lacking in the cities. Riots occurred and property was destroyed. The prime minister at that time was Aristide Briand, formerly a Socialist ; and the strikers expected that Briand would sympathize with them. They were greatly mistaken. Briand broke the strike by a novel method. He regarded the strike as a form of sedition, arrested the leaders, and " mobilized " the strikers. That is, he called the strikers to perform military service. If the strikers refused to obey the mobilization order, they were liable to be court-martialed for desertion. Thus the strikers were offered the choice between suppressing their own strike or being tried for treason. The strike collapsed.

The failure of the great strike of 1910 weakened syndicalism, but it did not destroy the faith of the Syndicalists. It seemed only to show that the time for a successful general strike was not yet. Meantime — patience, more effective organization, and propaganda ! The great day would come sometime.

III. England, 1895–1910

Some remarks on the English, designed to explain why the working classes are socialistic without being Socialists. In studying the history of Germany in the latter nineteenth and early twentieth centuries we found that one outstanding fact was the spread of socialism among the industrial workers. Another was the formation by the workers of a new political party to defend their interests — the Social-Democratic Labor party. In France, also, socialism spread among the workers; and in France, also, a new party was formed — the United Socialist party. How about England? Did socialism spread among the British workers, and did they also form a Socialist workingman's political party?

Most writers will answer, " No." They will tell you that the great majority of British workers never became Socialists, and that when the British workers formed a new political party they did not call it a Socialist party — they called it the Labor party. All this is true. Yet there are two very curious and interesting facts about this British Labor party. The first is that the chief leaders of the party have always been Socialists. The second is that the practical program of the party is essentially the same as that of the Socialist parties in Germany and France. Why is it that the British workers follow Socialist leaders, support a socialistic program, and yet refuse to call themselves Socialists?

One reason is that socialism, as formulated by Karl Marx, set forth a theory of what would happen in the future. The English dislike to commit themselves to any line of action in the future. They like to be free to act as seems best and see how it works out; then they can form subtle theories to explain what they have done. Socialism may be established in England some day; but the English will not call it socialism until long afterwards, when someone will write a brilliant book proving that after all England has been a socialistic state for a long time. Then everyone will be surprised, agree that it is so, and go about his business. Another reason is that the English dislike new names. They change their ways readily enough, but they stick to the old names. This enables them to tell themselves and others that they have not changed at all. " We had a king in the thirteenth century; we still have a king. We were not Socialists in 1850; why should we be Socialists now? " This is what the English seem to want us to believe.

The dislike of new theories and new names is very strong among the working classes. Long before they had heard of Marxian socialism they had elected to the House of Commons a few " Labor members." When they were convinced that it was necessary to form a political party and to adopt a socialistic program of reform, they did so; but they stuck to the old names. They continued to talk, as they had always done, of the " principles of trade union-ism." They called the men whom they elected to Parliament what they had always called them — Labor members. And so when they formed a new party they naturally gave it a good old British-sounding name — Labor party.

© *Underwood and Underwood*

VICTORIA, QUEEN OF ENGLAND

With her daughter, Victoria, wife of Frederick III of Germany. Queen Victoria reigned from 1837 to 1901.

Why and how the British Labor party was formed, 1899–1906. For many years the British laboring classes took no steps to form a political party of their own. They felt that they could get what they wanted through the trade unions. After the repeal of the old laws against the trade unions in 1875 the number of unions in-creased — slowly at first, rapidly after about 1884. By 1905 there were 1136 unions in Great Britain. They were well organized and well managed. Each union governed itself and looked after the interests of its own members; but there were two organizations which represented the interests and reflected the ideas of the unions as a whole. These were the annual Trade Union Congress and the General Federation of Trade Unions.

During these early years the unions relied upon strikes and collective bargaining to defend the interests of the workers. Between 1881 and 1905 there were in Great Britain some thirty thousand strikes, involving 181,407 industrial establishments, and nearly nine million workers. About half of these strikes were successful in forcing employers to raise wages or shorten hours. The unions themselves took no part in politics. Most of the industrial workers supported the old Liberal party of Gladstone, hoping that the " Grand Old Man " would take care of their interests. But from the first, some of the working class thought they ought to elect candidates of their own; and after 1874 there were always a few Labor members in the House of Commons. The Labor members usually supported the Liberal party, and were therefore known as " Liberal-Labor," shortened in popular speech to " Lib-Labs."

Thus until about 1899 the British working classes tried to defend their interests by strikes and collective bargaining, and by voting for Liberal or Liberal-Labor members in the House of Commons. But by the end of the century they were convinced that these methods were not in themselves sufficient. They felt that they must go into the political game in earnest. The result of this change of mind was the formation of the British Labor party. What was it that convinced the industrial workers that they needed a political party of their own? Three things chiefly: (1) the spread of socialism among the workers; (2) the Taff-Vale decision, which threatened to make strikes impossible; (3) the indifference of the old parties to the interests of the laboring classes.

1. *Socialism.* Socialism had little or no influence among the English workers until about 1880. In that year many workers were reading *Progress and Poverty* (published in 1879) — a powerful attack on private property in land, by an American writer, Henry George. In 1881 Henry Hyndman and the poet William Morris founded the Social Democratic Federation for propagating the scientific socialism of Karl Marx. In 1883 the Fabian Society was founded. This society proved to be, and still is, the most famous and influential of Socialist organizations in Great Britain. It was never strong in numbers, but it included among its members many famous scholars and writers, such as the economists Sidney and Beatrice Webb, the novelist H. G. Wells, and the satirist and play-

wright George Bernard Shaw.   The object of the Fabians was not
to bring about a political or social revolution, but to change the
ideas of people by talking and writing.   They were disciples of
Marx without his passionate hatreds.   They did not preach class
war.   They ridiculed existing ideas and customs, in the spirit of
Bernard Shaw, or calmly collected information about the conditions
of the laboring classes, after the manner of Sidney and Beatrice
Webb.   It is owing chiefly to the Fabians that Englishmen no
longer shudder when the word *socialism* is heard.

The Socialist organizations never had many members.   With
true British conservatism, the workers refused to label themselves
Socialists.   But Socialist discussion and propaganda influenced
them more than they knew.   It helped to convince them that there
was a sharp conflict between the interests of the upper classes and
the working classes, and that since the interests of the upper classes
were represented by the two old parties (Liberal and Conservative),
the interests of the working classes would never be properly attended
to until there was a workingman's party to do it.

2. *The Taff-Vale Decision, 1901.*   This decision grew out of a
strike of union workers on the Taff-Vale Railroad in Wales.   When
the company tried to bring in non-union workers (" black-legs" or
" scabs ") to break the strike, the union strikers resorted to picketing — that is, they tried by persuasion or intimidation to prevent
the new men from taking their jobs.   The company then sued the
trade union for damages, and the House of Lords — the highest
court in the land — decided that the union was liable and must pay.
This decision was a vital blow to the trade unions.   Strikes were
in any case expensive and wasteful, and too often not successful.
They could never succeed unless the small funds of the union could
be used to support the strikers while they were out of work.   If,
in addition, the unions were to be made liable for damages in every
strike, it would be practically impossible to carry on strikes at all.
Thus the principal weapon of trade unionism — collective bargaining — was rendered useless.

3. *Indifference of the Conservative and Liberal parties.*   For years
the workers had relied on the old parties — the Liberal party especially — to defend their interests in Parliament.   But even the great

Liberal leader, Gladstone, the "Grand Old Man," never really understood why the workers were dissatisfied. The Grand Old Man died in 1898. Meantime, the Conservative party, which was in power from 1895 to 1905, was even less interested than the Liberals in the demands of the laboring classes. The truth is that the extension of the suffrage to the workers in 1867 and 1884 had changed the government of England very little. England was still governed, as it had been for centuries, by the upper classes. The workers were becoming convinced of this. What would the Conservative party ever do for the laboring man? What had even the Liberal party ever done? Nothing, really, since they had no interest in doing anything. And what could a dozen "Lib-Labs" in the House of Commons do for them? Nothing, really, since they had no power to do anything.

For all of these reasons the industrial workers were convinced that they must form a party of their own. The first step was taken in 1899 by a special conference composed chiefly of representatives from the Trade Union Congress, the Social Democratic Federation, and the Fabian Society. This conference voted to establish

a distinct Labor group in Parliament . . . to co-operate with any party which, for the time being, may be engaged in promoting legislation in the direct interest of Labor, and be equally ready to associate themselves with any party in opposing measures having an opposite tendency.

This was the real beginning of the British Labor party. But for some years there were disputes between the Socialist and non-Socialist members. The former wished the new party to call itself "Socialist" and to adopt a more socialistic program; the latter, or some of them, wished to exclude the Socialists altogether. In 1904 it was voted not to exclude the Socialists; in 1906 it was voted to call the party simply the "Labor party." The Labor party was supported mainly by non-Socialist trade unionists; nevertheless its principal leaders (Ramsay MacDonald, Arthur Henderson, Philip Snowden, and Keir Hardie) were Socialists, and its program of social reform was similar to that of the Socialist parties in Germany and France. For the first time the laboring classes were represented in Parliament by a party strong enough to make itself felt. In 1906 the new party elected twenty-nine members to the House of Commons. By 1910 its representation had increased to forty members.

How the Liberal party became more liberal and united with the Labor party to carry through a program of social reform, 1906–1914. After ten years of power the Conservatives were thoroughly unpopular, chiefly because they had involved the country in the Boer War (see p. 616), which was won only with great difficulty and added nothing to the glory of Great Britain either at home or abroad. Criticized for their successes as well as their failures, the Conservatives were hopelessly defeated in the elections of 1906. Under Sir Henry Campbell-Bannerman, a Liberal ministry was formed, which was supported by the Labor party and the Irish Nationalists — in all, a combination of 514 members against 156 Conservatives. For ten years England was governed by this Liberal-Labor-Irish combination which, under able leaders, carried through an extensive program of social reform. Who were the leaders? What was the program?

The chief Liberal leaders were Herbert H. Asquith (prime minister, 1908–1916) and David Lloyd George (chancellor of the exchequer, 1908–1916). Mr. Asquith, like most of the Liberal leaders up to this time, was well born, and possessed of all the advantages of upper-class education and social connections. He was a Liberal of the school of Gladstone — that is to say, a pretty conservative Liberal; but he recognized that the Liberal party could retain power only by embarking on a program of social reform in the interests of the common people. Honest and just, he had a clear, cold mind, capable of seeing all sides of a difficult situation, and admirably suited to reconciling the divergent and often conflicting ideas of the men who served under him. He would never himself have initiated a program of social reform; but his guiding hand was indispensable to getting such a program through Parliament.

The man who initiated the program of social reform (based very largely on the economic researches of the Fabian Society, and especially those of Sidney and Beatrice Webb) was one of the most striking figures of recent times — David Lloyd George. He was the son of a poor Welsh schoolmaster, a man of the common people,

© *Ewing Galloway*

THE HOUSES OF PARLIAMENT IN LONDON

This fine building, in which the Commons and the House of Lords assemble, was built in 1840–1860, from plans by Sir Charles Barry. The clock in the tower is called "Big Ben." Its tones have been heard in the United States by radio.

knowing their lives and understanding their hopes and fears. Without much learning, he was gifted with the qualities of political genius. He possessed tireless energy. He was none too scrupulous, but his mind was far too quick and flexible ever to be disconcerted by either friend or enemy. He had to an unusual degree that quality of great leaders — a magnetic personality, capable without effort of attracting the constant attention of the multitude and of winning a new friend with every handshake and every twinkle of his merry eyes. Above all, he possessed the gift of speech suited to every occasion. He was lucid and persuasive in exposition; capable of beclouding an issue with a fog of words or of evading it with clever and humorous badinage; capable also of rising in crucial moments to real eloquence, passionate, denunciatory, appealing.

These two great leaders were supported by many able men in their own party, such as John Morley, the historian; Edward Grey; and the brilliant Winston Churchill, an aristocrat of Liberal views. Of equal importance were the leaders of the Labor party and of the Socialists: John Burns, Ramsay MacDonald, Arthur Henderson, Philip Snowden, and Keir Hardie.

Such were the leaders. What was the program? The program consisted of measures designed: (1) to benefit the workers directly; (2) to distribute the burdens of government more equally between the rich and the poor; (3) to weaken the political power of the aristocracy and the Conservative party.

1. *Measures designed to help the workers directly.* Laws regulating the conditions of labor in factories had often been passed before, and in 1902, under the Conservative government, all previous laws of that sort were systematized in a single " Factory Code." In 1906 Parliament adopted a similar code for mines. The employment of women and children in mines was forbidden, and the conditions of labor strictly regulated. In 1908 the hours of labor in mines were limited to eight hours per day. In 1906 a workingman's Compensation Law was passed which compelled employers to pay laborers for injuries sustained while working.

The most important measures of this sort were the pension and insurance laws. The Old-Age Pension Act (1908) provided that laborers reaching the age of seventy should receive a dollar a week from the government. The Labor Exchange Act (1909) established a series of bureaus designed to help the unemployed find jobs. In 1911 the National Insurance Act was adopted. This act was modeled upon the German Social Insurance laws. It provided for a fund made up from contributions by the government, the employers, and the laborers. From this fund laborers unable to work on account of illness or injury were to receive a certain small sum each week for a limited time. Laborers in certain industries who lost their jobs and were unable to obtain new ones were likewise to be assisted for a limited time.

The sums received by the laborers were very small, but these measures had a greater significance than can be measured by the sums of money paid to the laborers. They were based upon the idea that the wage-earner does not receive his just share of the wealth created by labor and capital and that consequently the government and the employers are bound to make it up to him when he needs it. This is as much as to admit, what the Socialists claimed, that the capitalist system is unjust and needs to be changed.

2. *Measures designed to equalize the burdens of government: The Budget of 1909.* The famous Lloyd George Budget of 1909 was the outcome of financial difficulties. Military and naval expenses were, as they always had been, very great. In addition, the Old-Age Pension Act of 1908 greatly increased the expenses of government. Where was the money to come from? The Conservatives were in favor of laying duties on imports. But the Liberals said that tariffs would burden the poor as much as the rich. Lloyd George said that the time had come to " lay the heaviest burdens on the broadest backs." The broadest backs, according to him, were those of the owners of the great landed estates. A great part of the small island of England was owned by a few people — the nobles and the gentry. Much of this land was unproductive, kept for parks and game preserves. Very beautiful these were, but producing nothing and serving the ease and comfort only of the privileged few. In a country crowded with people, many of whom were living on the edge of starvation, the exclusive possession of the land by a few

seemed doubly unjust. " Who ordained that a few should have the land of Great Britain as a perquisite ! " Lloyd George exclaimed. " Who made ten thousand people owners of the soil, and the rest of us trespassers in the land of our birth ! "

Lloyd George's Budget was therefore designed to lay extra burdens upon the privileged possessors of the land. Its main provisions were : (1) a tax of 20 per cent upon the increase in land values, when the increase was due, not to improvements made by the owner but to growth of population or to industrial development ; (2) a tax of 2 per cent on " idle land " — land not under cultivation, especially parks and game preserves ; (3) a tax of 5 per cent on " mining royalties." The fortunate possessors of the land where iron and coal deposits were found received a certain sum for every ton taken from the mines, thus growing rich from luck rather than by any labor or merit of their own. These royalties were now to be taxed.

The object of Lloyd George's Budget was thus twofold : (1) to lay extra tax burdens on the owners of the land ; (2) to induce landowners to put idle land to some use. The budget was more than a revenue measure ; it was also a measure of social reform intended to equalize the possessions of the rich and the poor.

3. *Measures designed to lessen the political power of the Conservative party.* Lloyd George was at once denounced by the Conservative landowners. They said he was dishonest — a demagogue, an intriguing politician. Lord Lansdowne likened him to a " robbergull," who lives by stealing fishes from other gulls. The budget was described as a barefaced confiscation of private property, the effect of which would be to undermine the social and political system of Great Britain. The Conservatives determined to defeat the budget at all hazards. This they could not do in the House of Commons, where the Liberal majority was overwhelming. But the House of Lords was strongly Conservative. When the budget was laid before the House of Lords, it was therefore rejected.

The rejection of the budget by the Lords created a more serious situation than the budget itself. No bill could become a law without the consent of the Lords ; but it had long been a parliamentary custom that the Lords could not amend or reject a " money bill." Was the budget a money bill? The Conservatives said it was not really a money bill, but a measure designed to effect a radical change in the social system. The Liberals maintained that it was a true money bill since its primary object was to raise revenue. The prime minister, Mr. Asquith, stated that the action of the Lords in rejecting the budget was "a breach of the constitution and a usurpation of the rights of the Commons." He therefore dissolved Parliament and referred the question to the people. The results of the elections were: Conservatives, 272; Liberals, 274; Labor party, 41; Irish Nationalists, 81. The Conservatives gained many seats, but the Liberals, with the support of the Labor party and the Nationalists, still controlled the House of Commons. The new House of Commons passed the budget once more (1910), and the Lords reluctantly assented to it also.

Having passed the budget, the Liberal ministry determined to curb the power of the Lords. For this purpose the Parliament Act was passed in 1911. It provided that money bills passed by the House of Commons should become effective within one month, with or without the Lord's consent, and that all other bills which were rejected by the Lords should become effective when passed by three successive sessions of the Commons. Henceforth the Lords could not permanently block any measure which the Commons was determined to carry through.

In the last three chapters we have been studying the period from 1871 to 1914 from the point of view of the *social conflict*. We have seen how science and invention and the use of machines changed the conditions of life, resulted in a rapid industrial revolution, and gave rise to conflicts within each country between capital and labor, the rich and the poor. We have studied this social conflict as it developed in western Europe generally, and more in detail as it developed in three representative countries — Germany, France, and England. In the following chapters we shall study the period from 1871 to 1914 from the point of view of *international conflict*. We shall see how the Industrial Revolution led to the expansion of the great powers in Africa and Asia; how their conflicts for the control of these so-called "backward" countries led to the formation of powerful international alliances; and how the rivalry of these alliances finally led to the Great War. First of all, let us see how the Industrial Revolution led to a scramble for colonies in Africa and Asia.

QUESTIONS

1. Why may Germany, France, and England be taken as representing the social conflict in western Europe?

2. What were the chief parties in the German Reichstag in 1871? Why did Bismarck rely chiefly on the National Liberals until 1878? What was the *Kulturkampf?* Why did Bismarck abandon the Liberals and turn to the Conservatives and the Center in 1878?

3. When was the Social-Democratic Labor Party formed? What was the Gotha Program? How did Bismarck try to destroy the Social-Democratic Labor Party? How did he try to counteract the spread of socialism among the working classes? How do you explain the rapid increase in the votes polled by the Social Democrats after 1891? What was the Revisionist movement? How did the Erfurt Program differ from the Gotha Program? What part of the latter program was enacted into law?

4. What were the chief political parties in France in 1875? What were their respective attitudes towards the republic? What was the crisis of the "Sixteenth of May"? the Boulanger crisis? Tell all you can about the spread of Marxian socialism in France. What was the difference between the Possibilists and the Impossibilists? When was the United Socialist Party founded? What was its program? Who were the Radical Socialists? Why is this name somewhat inappropriate? What was the party of Liberal Action? Who were the Nationalists? How did this party come to be formed?

5. What was the Dreyfus Affair? How and why did public opinion change in respect to the affair? Why did the Republican and the Socialist parties unite in 1899 to form the ministry of Waldeck-Rousseau? Why was this ministry called the "Cabinet of Republican Defense"? What parties for the most part controlled the government of France from 1899 to 1910? What anti-military and anti-clerical laws were passed? What laws beneficial to the working classes were passed? Who were the Syndicalists? How did their ideas differ from those of the Socialists?

6. Tell all you can about the rise of socialism in England. How does Fabian socialism differ from Marxian socialism? Explain how the British Labor party came to be formed. Why did the working classes think it necessary to form a political party about 1899? What was the program of the new Labor party? Who were its leaders? Is the Labor

CHART FOR CHAPTER XVIII. Showing the rise of socialism and of the social conflict in Germany, France, and England, 1875-1914.

GERMANY

1875	1878		1890	1891		1914

Social-Democratic Labor party. Gotha Program.

Bismarck's repressive laws against the Socialists. Social Insurance Acts.

Revisionist Movement. Erfurt Program.

Rapid growth of Socialist party. Extension of social legislation. Code of Social Insurance, 1911. Commercial Code.

FRANCE

1879		1894		1899		1905		1914

Federation of Socialist Workingmen

Division of Socialists. Possibilists and Impossibilists.

Dreyfus Affair.

Radical Socialist party. Anti-military, anti-clerical, and social legislation.

United Socialist party organized.

ENGLAND

1875	1881	1883		1899		1906		1914

Beginning of rapid organization of trade unions.

Social Democratic Federation.

Fabian Society

Working class votes with old parties; relies on strikes.

Organization of the British Labor party.

Union of Labor party and Liberals. Lloyd George program of social reform. Old-Age Pension Act. Insurance Act. Land taxes.

party a Socialist party? If not, why does it have Socialists for its leaders?

7. Why were the Conservatives defeated in the elections of 1906? Who were the leaders of the Liberal party from 1906 to 1914? How did the liberalism of Lloyd George differ from the liberalism of Gladstone? Why did the Labor party support the Liberal government from 1906 to 1914? What program of social reform was enacted into law between 1906 and 1910?

8. Comparing the history of Germany, France, and England, from 1871 to 1914, what similarities do you see in respect to the formation of new parties? In respect to the chief questions at issue? In respect to the kinds of laws passed?

SELECTED READINGS

Brief accounts. Hazen, *Modern Europe*, pp. 458–508, 551–561, and *Europe since 1815* (revised ed.), I, chs. xvii–xviii, xxiv. Robinson and Beard, *Outlines*, II, chs. xvii–xviii. Robinson and Beard, *Development of Modern Europe* (revised ed.), II, ch. iv. Schapiro, *European History* (revised ed.), chs. xvi (last part), xviii, xx. Flick, *Modern World History*, chs. xxi–xxii. Hayes, *Modern Europe*, II, 297–319, 331–367, 397–426. Schevill, *History of Europe*, ch. xxix. F. A. Ogg, *Economic Development of Modern Europe*, chs. xxii–xxv. G. P. Gooch, *History of Our Times*.

Biographies. For lives of Bismarck, see the references for Chapter XIII. A. Bebel, *My Life*. F. Dilnot, *Lloyd George, the Man and His Story*. M. G. Hamilton, *Ramsay MacDonald*. H. H. Tiltman, *Life of Ramsay MacDonald*. H. Stannard, *Gambetta*. A. Dreyfus, *Five Years of My Life*.

Historical novels. A. France, *M. Bergerac in Paris*.

Sources. Robinson and Beard, *Readings in Modern History*, II, 493 (the Gotha Program); 495 (program of the Fabian Society). C. J. H. Hayes, *British Social Legislation*, p. 167 (the Pension Act); p. 408 (the land taxes); p. 502 (the Parliament Act). Scott and Baltzly, *Readings in European History*, ch. ix.

PRINCIPAL STREET IN A VILLAGE OF FRENCH CAMEROON, AFRICA

CHAPTER XIX. HOW THE INDUSTRIAL REVOLUTION LED TO A SCRAMBLE FOR THE CONTROL OF "BACKWARD COUNTRIES," 1875–1905

Take up the white man's burden. RUDYARD KIPLING

Philanthropy is all very well, but philanthropy plus five per cent is a good deal better. CECIL RHODES

The extent and the importance of the new colonial movement. The acquisition of colonies beyond the sea is an old story in European history. In the sixteenth century Spain and Portugal were the great colonial powers. In the seventeenth century Holland, France, and Great Britain acquired colonial possessions in the East and the West Indies, and in North America. For a century and a half, from 1660 to 1815, the rivalry of these countries for colonies and commercial advantages made part of every European war. The result of this long struggle was in the main a victory for Great Britain. By 1815 France had lost her colonial empire in North America and in India. The Dutch and the Portuguese retained but a part of their former possessions in the East. The Spanish colonies in South America were in revolt, and by 1825 most of them had won their independence. Meantime the British Empire, except for the loss of the American colonies, had steadily increased in extent. In 1815 it comprised Canada, Australia, New Zealand, the continent of India, Cape Colony in southern Africa, the islands of Malta and Minorca and the rock of Gibraltar in the Mediterranean, besides many naval and coaling stations in the three oceans.

In the history of colonial conflict the year 1815 marks the end of an era. For more than half a century after that date few colonies were acquired by any European country, and none of the wars of that period grew out of colonial or commercial rivalry. From 1815 to 1875 the people of Europe were chiefly occupied with the struggle for political liberty and national independence; and in this period of political liberalism the trend of thought was anti-colonial. The social philosopher, Jeremy Bentham, wrote a famous work entitled *Emancipate Your Colonies*. He said that colonies were a burden rather than an advantage to any country. In the middle of the nineteenth century this view was widely held, and even in England many people looked forward to the time when colonial empires, including the British Empire, would disappear. This idea was known as the " Little England " theory. It was satirized by Lord John Russell, who said: " When I was young it was thought the mark of a wise statesman that he had turned a small kingdom into a great empire. In my old age it appears to be thought the object of a statesman to turn a great empire into a small kingdom."

But the " Little Englanders " were sadly mistaken in their predictions. In the last quarter of the nineteenth century there was a remarkable revival of interest in colonies, not only in England but in most European countries. Colonial societies were organized, and innumerable books and pamphlets were written to prove that colonies were a necessity instead of a burden. This revived interest was accompanied by a rapid expansion of European political and economic power in Africa and Asia. Within a period of twenty-five years (1875–1900) Africa, hitherto the " Dark Continent " and largely an unexplored wilderness, was almost entirely partitioned by Great Britain, France, Germany, Belgium, and Portugal. Russia built a railroad across Siberia, and extended her influence east into Manchuria and south into central Asia. France occupied Indo-China (Cochin China, Cambodia, Anam, and Tonkin). Great

American Museum of Natural History
STREET SCENE IN ALGIERS
Some people wear Arab, some European, costume.   Many signs are in French.

Britain pushed north from India into Afghanistan, west into Persia, and east into Tibet.   The chief European powers acquired naval ports and economic concessions in China.   The United States acquired the Hawaiian Islands and conquered Porto Rico and the Philippine Islands from Spain.   (See map, pp. 624–625.)

No such rapid expansion of European political and economic power throughout the world had ever been known before.   Great Britain increased her empire by one-third, and added 57,000,000 people to her subject population.   In 1880 France had virtually no colonies save Algeria; in 1904 she had an empire of 3,500,000 square miles, and a subject population of 37,000,000.   Between 1884 and 1900 Germany acquired colonies totaling 1,000,000 square miles, with a native population of 14,000,000.   What is the explanation of this startling revival of the colonial movement, of this sudden scramble for the control of " backward countries "?

How the Industrial Revolution led to the scramble for possessions in Asia and Africa.   Many explanations have been given for the new colonial movement.   Some writers have said overpopulation was the cause; every country needed colonies to which its people could migrate and still live under the old flag.   Others have said that colonies were desirable because they furnished markets for the products of the mother country; that colonies made a country richer by enlarging its commerce. Still others have said that regardless of whether colonies were necessary or desirable, it was a right — even a duty — of Europeans to colonize backward countries in order to bring to the benighted natives the blessings of Christian civilization.

But these are not so much the *causes* as the convenient *justifications* of the colonial movement. The real explanation of the new colonial movement after 1875 is to be found in the economic changes brought about in Europe by the Industrial Revolution. These changes we may best understand by considering three things: (1) the increased demand for raw materials; (2) the activities of European business men in promoting new enterprises; (3) the existence of surplus capital in banks, seeking investment.

1. *Increased demand for raw materials.* The demand for raw materials was of course nothing new. In the eighteenth century the makers of cotton cloth in England needed raw cotton, which they got from America. But one result of the Industrial Revolution was that Europe needed more raw materials, and more kinds of raw materials, than ever before. At the Peace Conference in 1919 the French economic experts made a list of the raw materials that were essential to modern industry. The list included, among other things, raw silk, cork, cotton, iron, tin, copper, zinc, nickel, gold, platinum, silver, mercury, arsenic, coal, rubber, and oil.

Now the point is that many of these things cannot be obtained in Europe. Take the familiar examples of oil and rubber. Before 1875 neither was of special importance. But the gasoline engine and the automobile made oil and rubber of vital importance in every country where the Industrial Revolution occurred. There is very little oil in Europe, but much in the United States, Central America, and Asia. The result is that European governments and business men, not wishing to be dependent on the United States for oil, seek to control those backward countries where it may be found. In modern days the search for oil has replaced the medieval search for the Holy Grail. The same is true in the case of rubber, which is to be had chiefly in Africa, the Malay Peninsula, and the tropical regions of America.   Every industrial country needs rubber; and every time you blow out a tire you are contributing to the influences that have driven business men and governments to seek control of backward countries.

2. *New business enterprises.*   In the early nineteenth century England was the chief industrial country.   At that time English business men found plenty of opportunities for new enterprises at home or in France, Germany, or the United States.   But towards the end of the nineteenth century, as these countries became highly industrialized, opportunities for new enterprise in Europe and in the United States declined, or at least the competition became keener and the profits relatively less.   Thus it happened that from about 1875 on, business men in Europe and the United States became more interested in opportunities for new enterprise in the undeveloped countries of Africa and Asia.   Africa is rich in coal and copper, gold and rubber.   Asia is rich in mineral resources and oil fields.   To develop these resources railroads would have to be built, telegraph lines strung, and factories constructed.   What unlimited opportunities for profit these backward countries offered to the far-sighted and adventurous business men of Europe and the United States!

Opportunities for profit — but on two conditions: first, that plenty of cheap labor could be obtained; second, that the property rights acquired could be protected.   In Africa the labor problem was difficult, unless the blacks could be made to work.   In the more thickly peopled countries, such as Egypt, Syria, China, or India, the labor problems presented fewer difficulties.   The natives, accustomed to labor and to cheap living, would work for trifling sums compared with the high wages demanded by the labor unions in Europe.   But if the prospective profits from enterprises in Asia and Africa were great, the risk was also great.   Europeans who invested heavily in oil wells, coal mines, or railroads in these countries might find their properties wrecked by natives or confiscated by native governments.   Thus European business men who invested money in these countries needed to be backed and protected by their own governments; and so wherever their money was invested they were eager to have some European government, prefer-

STREET SCENE IN CAIRO, EGYPT

Count the different types of transportation that can be seen in this view.

ably their own, establish a "sphere of influence," a protectorate, or a colony.

3. *Surplus capital in banks.* The Industrial Revolution, by increasing the wealth in the world, gave to bankers a power which they had never had before. The great development of modern banking occurred after 1850, and especially after 1875. As wealth was accumulated it was deposited in banks. People with great incomes and people with small incomes put their money in banks. Insurance companies with enormous accumulations, big business men with big surpluses, little business men with little surpluses, put their money in banks. Little banks put their accumulated deposits in bigger banks. Bigger banks consolidated and devoted their energies to investment on a grand scale. Thus there came into existence a new type of bankers — the "investment bankers." Examples are the J. P. Morgan Company of New York, the Rothschilds of London, Vienna, and Paris. These investment banks had control of millions and even billions of dollars of surplus capital

which they sought to invest in government loans or great industrial enterprises, of course at as high rates of interest as possible.

Before 1875 the only country with much surplus capital was Great Britain. In those years British surplus capital was invested in British industry, or in industrial enterprises in France, Germany, and above all in the United States. But in the last quarter of the nineteenth century France, Germany, Italy, Belgium, and the United States became industrial countries also. They also accumulated surplus capital of their own — even more than they needed; and so they no longer borrowed so much from Great Britain. Thus after 1875 there was accumulated in banks in Europe and the United States more surplus capital than could profitably be invested in these countries. The investment bankers, like the enterprising business men, therefore looked out over the wide world for new opportunities. For them, too, Africa and Asia offered an inviting field. They were willing enough to finance bankrupt native governments such as Egypt and Persia, to underwrite the loans for building railways and steamship lines, and to provide credit for the development of oil wells and rubber plantations.

Who then were chiefly benefited by the colonial expansion in Africa and Asia after 1875? Chiefly European manufacturers seeking cheap raw materials; business men and corporations interested in colonial mines, railways, or plantations; and bankers with money to lend at high rates of interest. Besides these there were the manufacturers of steel and iron goods and other equipment needed in the colonies; the manufacturers of arms and armaments; officers in the army and navy; administrative officials; and young men hoping to make careers or fortunes for themselves in new countries. Generally speaking, the classes that benefited by the colonial movement, and who therefore favored it, were the upper classes, who had wealth and influence — the capitalists, the people who owned and controlled the machines created by the industrial revolution. The mass of the people, the workers of the machines, benefited little or not at all by the colonial movement, and were either indifferent or opposed to it. In every country the political party in favor of colonial expansion was the conservative, upper-class party; the party opposed to it was the poor man's party — the Socialist parties in Germany and France, the Labor party in Great Britain.

It is a mistake to think that governments were primarily responsible for the colonial movement after 1875. Governments did not always, or usually, take the initiative. In those days there was a famous slogan: " Trade follows the flag! " It would be truer to say, " The flag follows trade "; truer still to say, " The flag follows capital." The colonial movement after 1875 was no doubt the result of many influences, but the chief of these was the expansion of capital and business enterprise. Governments established spheres of influence, protectorates, and colonies in order to safeguard European capital and business enterprise.

We have now learned something, in a general way, of the influences that brought about the extension of European power in Africa and Asia after 1875. But these influences will be better understood if they are illustrated by some concrete examples. To show why Europeans were interested in Africa, and how European powers acquired possessions there, we shall relate three stories — a story of rubber, a story of gold and diamonds, and a story of high finance.

A story of rubber. In 1876 the King of Belgium was Leopold II. Leopold was an accomplished man of the world, and a shrewd business man who loved money and the good things that money can buy. As a king he was active and ambitious, interested as a king should be in increasing the prestige of his country. As an educated and traveled man, quick to see the trend of events, Leopold was much interested in Africa, the great Dark Continent, which was just then much in the public eye because of Dr. Livingstone's missionary efforts and explorations and the expedition of Henry M. Stanley in search of the lost explorer. Accordingly, in 1876, Leopold summoned to meet at Brussels an international " Geographic Conference " of scientists, explorers, and public men. Speaking before this conference he said: " To open to civilization the only part of our globe where it has not penetrated, to pierce the darkness which envelops whole populations, is a crusade, if I may say so — a crusade worthy of this century of progress."

The outcome of the conference was the formation of the " International Association for the Exploration and Civilization of Africa."

Leopold's next step was to circulate a prospectus setting forth the opportunities for railroad-building in Africa. With the aid of some Belgian business men a capital of a million francs was raised and placed at the disposal of a " Committee for the Study of the African Congo." In 1879 the committee sent Henry M. Stanley to Africa. Stanley's party sailed up the Congo River, constructed portages, built roads and bridges, established stations, and above all made treaties with the native chieftains which guaranteed them " protection " in the possession of their lands. Unfortunately for Leopold, the French were already established in the Congo; but in 1885 an international conference of the European Powers, which met at Berlin to adjust the African claims of various states, recognized Leopold's claim to the upper Congo.

In 1885 the territory which Leopold thus acquired was given the name of the " Congo Free State." Leopold was the " sovereign " of the Congo Free State, a dominion of some 900,000 square miles. In his capacity as sovereign, Leopold declared all " vacant lands " the property of the state, conferred on the state a monopoly of all rubber and ivory produced in the vacant lands, and forbade the natives to sell rubber or ivory to anyone except the state. The state was Leopold. The vacant lands (all of the lands except the small possessions of the scattered tribes) contained vast herds of ivory-bearing elephants, and were suited to producing enormous quantities of rubber. But how get the rubber and ivory? European labor was not to be thought of. The climate was unsuited to Europeans, and in any case European labor was much too expensive. Leopold's vast enterprise had already left him nearly bankrupt. Would the natives willingly labor to enrich the Belgian king? They would not. Therefore Leopold, in his capacity as sovereign, levied taxes on the natives — that is, required each village to deliver regularly a certain amount of ivory and rubber. Native troops (natives found it easier to serve in the army than to work) were organized and armed to enforce the collection of the ivory and rubber from the villages. Native women were sometimes held as hostages until the rubber and ivory were delivered. Native insurrections were ruthlessly put down.

Leopold was a humanitarian, true; but he had ventured so deep that unless he got rubber and ivory he was ruined. Therefore, like many another humane man, he "countenanced" the atrocities. That is, he countenanced them from Brussels or the Riviera; he was not present in Africa watching the business. At all events the natives were subjected to torture and involuntary servitude in order to enrich the King of Belgium. Meantime, they took on European civilization to the extent of learning a few French words and acquiring a taste for gin.

Whether civilizing or not, the enterprise was a gamble for great stakes, which in the end succeeded. During the ten years from 1890 to 1900 the demand for rubber increased, and Leopold's profits from rubber alone were some $15,000,000. These did not include the profits to corporations, such as the American Congo Company, to which Leopold had granted concessions and whose methods of collecting rubber were similar to those of Leopold. Leopold's great fortune was spent partly in building splendid palaces, partly in land speculations on the Riviera, partly in making Ostende the most famous bathing resort in the world.

Meantime rumors of "Belgian atrocities" spread through Europe. Criticism led to investigation. Investigation led to the intervention of the Belgian government. In 1908 Leopold renounced his sovereignty, and the Congo Free State became the Belgian Congo. Since then the production of rubber and ivory has continued, under somewhat more humane conditions, to the benefit of buyers and sellers of rubber — including you and me, if we own automobiles.

A story of gold and diamonds. The expansion of British power in Africa started from two opposite points on the continent — Egypt, and the Cape of Good Hope. The Cape of Good Hope was taken from the Dutch by the English in 1806. In 1870 British possessions in South Africa, known as Cape Colony and Natal, extended north to the Orange River. Meantime the Boers (the people of Dutch and French origin) had moved to the north and east and had established there two independent republics — the Orange Free State and the Transvaal Republic.

In 1867 and 1870 there occurred two events of great importance for South Africa. The first was the discovery of diamonds near Kimberley. The second was the arrival in Cape Colony of a young Englishman named Cecil Rhodes.

One day in 1867 a Dutch farmer saw some children playing marbles with round stones which they had picked up in the gravel. One of the stones struck the farmer on account of its brilliant luster. He took it off to town where, upon examination, it turned out to be a diamond worth $2500. Similar stones were easily found in the region round about, one of which (the famous " Star of South Africa ") eventually sold for $125,000. The upshot of these discoveries was that Griqualand West, a sort of " no man's land " between The Orange Free State and British Cape Colony, proved to be the seat of the richest diamond deposits in the world. Needless to say, men came running from the four quarters of the globe. Within a few years the place was a country of tents and shacks, housing one of the most picturesque gangs of adventurers ever huddled together.

In 1870, at the beginning of this scramble for diamonds, Cecil Rhodes, a boy of seventeen, arrived in Cape Colony. He did not come for the diamonds. His ambition was to go to Oxford and be a lawyer or a minister of the gospel. But his health was poor, and he was sent out to work for his brother, Herbert. Years after, when he was rich and famous, Cecil Rhodes said: " They will tell you that I came out on account of my health, or from love of adventure, and to some extent that may be true; but the real reason is that I could no longer stand the eternal cold mutton." No man profited so much from the wealth of South Africa as Cecil Rhodes; no man did more to bring that country under the British flag. Perhaps one of the most effective causes of British expansion in Africa was Cecil Rhodes's aversion to cold mutton.

For a year the boy worked with his brother, Herbert, trying to raise cotton in Cape Colony. But in 1871 the two men moved on to the diamond fields, where they obtained a claim; and there we may picture Cecil " wearing flannels of the school playing-field, somewhat shrunken from strenuous rather than effective washing that still left the color of red dust, . . . his tall figure crumpled up on an inverted bucket, as he sat scraping his gravel surrounded by

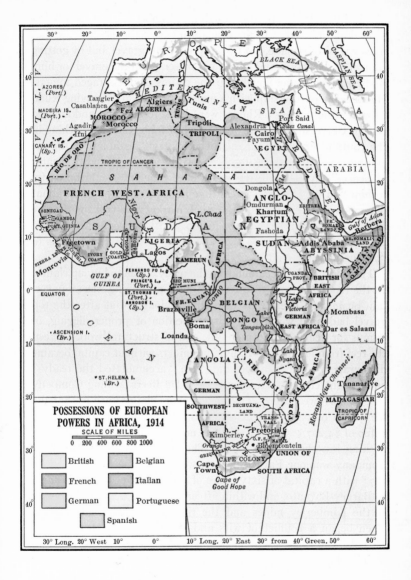

POSSESSIONS OF EUROPEAN
POWERS IN AFRICA, 1914

SCALE OF MILES

0   200 400 600 800 1000

British   Belgian

French   Italian

German   Portuguese

Spanish

his dusky Zulus." In this rough-and-tumble life his health improved and his latent business acumen emerged. He foresaw that money was to be made, not by scraping in the gravel, but by getting control of the claims and letting others scrape in the gravel for him. As he got money he bought up the claims of discouraged miners. He formed a partnership with a man named Rudd. Leaving Rudd to watch the business, Rhodes went back to England and entered Oxford University. There he listened to John Ruskin preaching to the youth of England to make their country " again a royal throne of kings; a sceptered isle, for all the world a source of light, a center of peace." An Oxford degree, Rhodes thought, would be useful to him " in his career." Meantime he learned all he could about diamonds and business and the stock market; and all the time he kept in touch with the situation in South Africa through his partner, Rudd, to whom he wrote that the main thing at present was to " accumulate the ready."

The purpose of " accumulating the ready " was to buy up claims. In the ten years from 1870 to 1880 diamond-mining was an uncertain business. There were diamonds a-plenty; but after the top gravel had been worked, it was a question of proper digging, of pumps for keeping the water out, and of structural work to keep the reef from falling in. Individual miners without capital became discouraged. Rhodes never did. He " accumulated the ready " and bought claims. He founded the De Beers Mining Company (1880), borrowed money, and bought more claims until in 1885 the De Beers Company, of which Rhodes was chief owner, had a capital value of $4,207,505. But this was not enough. Rhodes aimed at nothing less than a monopoly. The chief rival of the De Beers Company was one Barnett Isaacs, who had come to the mines in 1873 with a capital of sixty boxes of cigars, had changed his name to Barney Barnato, and within fifteen years had become the owner of the Kimberley mines and the richest man in South Africa. Then began a conflict of wits and wealth between Rhodes and Barnato, the Englishman and the Jew, for the mastery of the diamond fields. Rhodes won. It was a war of money and of clever juggling with stocks. Rhodes won because, with his English connections, he obtained the support of the great Rothschild bankers of London, and because he was more clever at the stock-market game than his rival.

The result was that in 1888 the two mining properties of Rhodes and Barnato were consolidated into the De Beers Consolidated Mines. This new company, controlled by Rhodes, Barnato, and two other men, presently had a monopoly of the diamond fields of South Africa, which produced 90 per cent of the world's supply. But even this was not enough. Rhodes had meantime become interested in the gold fields discovered in the Transvaal, and there he founded the Consolidated Gold Fields of South Africa — a company which ultimately gained a monopoly of the gold production. During the ten years from 1890 to 1900 Rhodes was virtually master of these two monopolies, and his personal income from properties of all sorts must have been close to $5,000,000 annually.

Strange as it may seem, Cecil Rhodes cared little for money in itself. What he enjoyed was the game; what he wanted was power; and like many men of genius he convinced himself that the power he acquired could be used for the benefit of mankind. As it happens, we know what dreams he dreamed and what faith inspired him. The faith was childlike and the dreams magnificent. Let us take a look at them.

Early in life Rhodes decided that God's purpose, as revealed in the history of mankind, was to produce a race of men fitted to establish peace, liberty, and justice in the world. The race obviously most fitted to do this was the Anglo-Saxon race; hence it followed that the surest way to promote the fulfillment of God's purpose in the world was to labor for the extension of the British Empire. Rhodes therefore dreamed of a British Empire which would some day include the United States, a great part of Asia, and all of Africa. Since it was not for one man, even a Cecil Rhodes, to attain the whole of this great object, he limited his activities to Africa alone.

Rhodes therefore used his great wealth for the philanthropic purpose of extending the British Empire in South Africa, and at the same time he used the extension of the empire in South Africa to increase his wealth. " Philanthropy is all very well in its way," he said, " but philanthropy plus 5 per cent is a good deal better."

STATUE OF CECIL RHODES AT CAPETOWN

Cecil Rhodes (1853–1902) left a large sum of money, derived from his gold and
diamond mines, to provide scholarships at the University of Oxford for two hundred young men from outlying parts of the British Empire, and also from
Germany and the United States.

He took part in the political game, acquired control of newspapers,
subscribed to party funds, and was elected to office. His first
object was to extend the British flag over Bechuanaland, which
lay between the Transvaal and German West Africa — the " Suez
Canal of South Africa," as he called it. His first efforts failed;
but in 1885, partly through Rhodes's influence, but chiefly through
the pressure of imperialist influences in England, the British
government took possession of Bechuanaland.

North of Bechuanaland and the Transvaal was an immense up-
land country, fertile and well watered, rich in gold and other minerals. By the right of possession, said to be " nine points of the
law," this country belonged to a warlike native tribe known as the
Matabeles. But by the law of Rhodes's philosophy it should belong
to the British Empire. With the consent of the British commissioner of South Africa, Rhodes sent three agents to talk with the
king of the Matabeles — King Lobengula. The result of this talk
was that Lobengula, without very well knowing what he was
doing, signed a document (1888) by which he granted to the agents

of Rhodes all the mineral rights of his country, in return for which he received 1000 rifles, 100,000 cartridges, a yearly income of $500, and a second-hand steamboat. The next year Rhodes organized the British South Africa Company. The charter of this company, granted by the British government, conferred upon the company for twenty-five years the right to develop mines, grant land, establish a police force, and make treaties with the natives. The country was known as Rhodesia; and for more than thirty years it was virtually owned and governed by the British South Africa Company — that is to say, by Cecil Rhodes.

King Lobengula was not pleased with these proceedings. He wrote a letter of protest to Queen Victoria, in which he said:

Some time ago a party of men came into my country, the principal one appearing to be a man called Rudd. They asked me for a place to dig gold and said they would give me certain things for the right to do so. I told them to bring what they would and I would show them what I would give. A document was written and presented to me for signature. I asked what it contained, and was told that in it were my words and the words of those men. I put my hand to it. About three months afterwards I heard from other sources that I had given by that document the right to all the minerals in my country.

Thus Lobengula lost his country but learned something of European "civilization."

A story of high finance. The story of high finance I have selected to tell has to do with the British occupation of Egypt. Other stories might have been selected; but this one shows very well how surplus capital stored up in Europe found its way into backward countries and created difficult situations which in turn led to political intervention — something which no one had originally intended or desired.

Ismail Pasha, the semi-independent ruler of Egypt (1863–1879) under the Sultan of Turkey, was one of the most observed and talked-of figures of his time. An ungainly looking person he was, short and fat, with drooping eyelids, tangled red eyebrows, and ears that did not match. Yet he was a clever and gifted man. Well educated and speaking French fluently, he was shrewd and good-natured and witty; he knew how to be all things to all men, knew how to fascinate them and to win their approval of whatever fantastic schemes he might wish to promote.

Ismail, like Cecil Rhodes, cherished a dream of power, and like Rhodes he needed millions for the realization of his dream. By expensive gifts to the sultan he had himself raised to the dignity of khedive. He started ambitious projects for the improvement of harbors, the construction of docks, the building of railroads and telegraph lines, and the establishment of schools. The great object of Ismail was to Europeanize Egypt, and to transform Alexandria and Cairo into splendid capitals rivaling Paris and Vienna. Such public expenditures called for private economies. But unhappily Ismail was the most reckless spendthrift of his age. Whether at home or abroad he lived lavishly and every month invented a hundred useless ways of depleting his fortunes.

When he became viceroy, in 1863, the public debt was already some $20,000,000. Within three years Ismail had increased the debt to $500,000,000. Where did he get all this money to spend? Where could he get more to spend in the same careless way?

Ismail got his money through the European bankers, who arranged loans for the Egyptian government. The year before Ismail's accession his predecessor had arranged, through the banking firm of Froeling and Göschen of London, for a loan of $16,500,-000. What happened was something like this. The bankers offered Egyptian bonds for sale. The face value of the bonds was, let us say, $100 each, bearing 7 per cent interest. Now, since the rate of interest was pretty high, many people were willing to invest their money in these bonds; but since they could not be sure the Egyptian government would be able to pay the interest and principal, they were not willing to pay $100 for a bond. They were willing to pay perhaps $75 a bond. This meant that the bondholders got about 10 per cent interest on the money invested. The bankers got a tidy sum for selling the bonds. The Egyptian government got the rest — that is, not the $16,500,000, but only about $12,375,000. Of course the Egyptian government had to pay 7 per cent on the $16,500,000. During Ismail's reign many loans of this sort were arranged for him by the European bankers. It

A VIEW OF CAIRO, CAPITAL OF MODERN EGYPT

The building in the foreground is the Mosque of Sultan Hasan, which dates from A.D. 1357.

was expensive borrowing for Ismail; safe and profitable business for the bankers; and profitable investment for the people who bought the bonds. But was it safe for the people who bought the bonds? That was the rub of the whole matter.

Ismail did not worry so long as he had money in his pocket. The bankers did not worry so long as they made a good profit loaning other people's money to Ismail. So the game continued. Between 1864 and 1874 new loans were arranged, chiefly through English and French bankers, amounting to about $385,000,000. But as Ismail's debt increased, people were more chary about buying the bonds — were unwilling to pay even so much as $75 for a hundred-dollar bond. The result was that out of the $385,000,000 of bonds sold, Ismail really got no more than $250,000,000. Some of this money he squandered. Some he spent on useful building. For example, $15,000,000 was paid to an English company for harbor construction in Alexandria. The work was well done; but Mr. Rivers Wilson, an Englishman who knew, said that $7,500,000 would have been a fair price for the work. Thus Ismail paid going and coming. A good part of the money he borrowed remained in Europe, in the form of fees to the bankers and high interest to the bondholders; a good part of the money he actually got came back to Europe in the form of over-payment for construction work done in Egypt — work sometimes well done, sometimes badly done.

This dizzy game could not go on forever. The bankers found it more and more difficult to sell Egyptian bonds. Ismail found it difficult to borrow enough to pay the interest on what he had already borrowed. Then the bondholders said: " Pay us our interest! " What could poor Ismail say, except: " I can't unless the bankers will arrange a new loan for me." What could the bankers say, except: " People won't buy more bonds, since you can't pay the interest on those they now hold." There was one other thing the bondholders and bankers could say. They could say: " The British and French governments ought to intervene in Egypt and straighten out its affairs, so that the European bondholders can get their money back — with interest at 10 per cent."

Ismail himself, not knowing where to turn for more money, asked for the appointment of British and French experts to advise him what to do. At first the British government refused to interfere in Egypt in any way; but in 1876 it authorized Mr. Stephen Cave to make an examination into the state of Egyptian finances. Mr. Cave's report showed that the Egyptian debt could be paid only by increasing the taxes and by cutting down the expenses. Ismail was incapable of cutting down expenses, and the upshot was that the British and French governments persuaded the Turkish sultan to depose Ismail and appoint as khedive his son Tewfik (1879).

Under the new khedive the British and French governments took charge of Egyptian finances — an arrangement known as the Dual Control (1879-1883). The severe economies and heavy taxes enforced by the Dual Control were unpopular. People in Egypt began to cry, " Down with the foreigners! " Meantime a disgruntled army officer, Ahmed Pasha Arabi, quarreled with the khedive, and, partly to save his own skin, threatened to lead a military revolt against both the khedive and the Dual Control. There were in Alexandria many Europeans — diplomatic officers, business men, tourists. They became alarmed for their safety and appealed to the British and French governments for military protection. Whether they were in much danger is uncertain. At all events the British and French governments, in order to " strengthen the authority of the khedive," made a naval demonstration by sending some warships to Alexandria (1882). One result of this demonstration was a riot in Alexandria in which some Europeans were killed. Another result was that Arabi began to fortify Alexandria.

The British government then decided to land an army in Egypt and invited the French government to join in this enterprise. The French government refused; and on July 10, 1882, the French warships withdrew, leaving the British fleet alone in the harbor. July 11, Admiral Seymour bombarded Alexandria, the city surrendered, British troops were landed, and Egypt soon passed under the control of Great Britain. At that time, and many times subsequently, the British government announced that it would withdraw its troops as soon as order was established. For some years disorder was greater than ever. But even when order was established, and in spite of many promises, Great Britain retained her control of Egypt. This seemed necessary, partly to protect English investments in Egypt and partly to strengthen her control of the Suez Canal. Several years before, the British government had purchased the khedive's shares in the canal, and its financial control of the canal was now made secure by the military occupation of Egypt.

Under British rule the Egyptians were as well governed as Orientals were likely to be by Europeans. Life and property were safeguarded. Roads were improved. The death-rate was lowered. Schools were established. Yet the natives, most of them, were never reconciled to British rule, although they preferred British rule to that of any other European country. Were they better governed by Great Britain than they would have been by themselves? Probably. Were they better off — happier? Perhaps not, if they thought not, since " nothing good or evil is but thinking makes it so."

While the European powers were engaged, by these methods, in partitioning Africa, they were also engaged, by somewhat similar methods, in "opening up" the rich Oriental empire of China. Let us now see how that was done.

How China was " opened up " and forced to grant valuable concessions to foreign powers. If you should say to an educated Chinese that the civilization of China is inferior to that of Europe, he would probably produce an inscrutable smile, as much as to say: " These Europeans! How young they are! They have wonderful machines, and they know how to fight. Like children, they are pleased with toys. Otherwise they know little. They have not wisdom." Perhaps he would be right. The civilization of China is much older than that of Europe, her traditions in many ways more humane, the wisdom her philosophers have accumulated more profound. In one sense only was China, at the close of the nineteenth century, a backward country — the inventions and the power-driven machines of Europe had never been applied to the development of her immense resources. Rich, populous, and unwarlike, China therefore offered to Europe the most attractive opportunity in the world as a field for economic exploitation — for the acquisition of territory, the opening up of mines, the building of railroads, the investment of capital.

Until 1842 China was almost entirely closed to foreigners. The chief exception was that British merchants enjoyed certain strictly limited rights of trading in Canton. Long-standing difficulties between English and Chinese merchants ended in the so-called

Opium War (1839-1842), the result of which was that the island of Hong Kong was ceded to Great Britain, and six of the principal Chinese ports (known as "treaty ports") were opened to British and other foreign subjects for residence and trade.

This may be taken as the beginning of the opening up of China. During the next fifty years European trade with China developed rapidly. The number of Europeans residing in the treaty ports increased; consular and other agents of the European governments were appointed to look after the interests of their subjects residing in China; and in the wake of the merchants and government agents came the missionaries, seeking to convert the Chinese from their "heathen ways" to the true religion (Methodist, Baptist, Anglican, or Catholic, as the case might be). Yet the Chinese never welcomed the foreigners, the "barbarians" as they called them.

© *Wide World Photos*

ONE OF THE OLDEST BUDDHAS

This stone image, found recently in China, weighs about two tons and is believed to have been carved about 400 A.D.

The government resented political interference, while the people were irritated by the arrogance and strange customs of the barbarians and were often infuriated by the missionaries who told them that their religion was false and their customs immoral and degrading. Conflict was therefore incessant. Conflict led to diplomatic protest, and even war; and as a result of constant pressure the Chi-

nese government was forced to make a great many " concessions "
to the European powers and to the United States — concessions,
many of them, which one independent European power would not
think of making to another.

These concessions (known as " extra-territorial " rights) were of
various sorts. First, certain Chinese territory was ceded outright :
to Great Britain, the island of Hong Kong and part of the mainland
opposite ; to France, the provinces of Cochin China, Cambodia,
Anam, and Tonkin in the southeast (French Indo-China) ; to Russia,
territory north of the Amur River, including the port of Vladivostok. Second, warships of European powers were privileged to
visit any Chinese port, and even to sail up the Yangtze River.
Third, in all the treaty ports (about sixteen in all) foreign residents
were subject, not to Chinese law or Chinese courts but to the law
and courts of their own country. Fourth, import duties on certain
commodities, fixed at the low rate of 5 per cent, could not be raised
except by the consent of the foreign governments concerned.
Finally, the Chinese government was under obligation to protect
Europeans in teaching and practicing the principles of Christianity.

**How Japan took a hand in the opening up of China, and what
came of it, 1894–1900.** In 1894 Japan took a hand in the opening
up of China. The Japanese, unlike the Chinese, had welcomed
the introduction of European customs. They established a strong
government along European lines ; they organized an army and
navy equipped in the European manner and led by officers trained
in European schools ; they mastered the mechanical and technical
secrets of European industry ; they adopted the European calendar,
and to some extent the European dress and customs. One other
aspect of European civilization the Japanese adopted — the determination to use their new power to defend and extend the
interests of Japan throughout the Eastern world. The place where
Japanese interests needed most to be defended in 1894 was Korea
(Chosen).

Korea is the peninsula which extends from the Chinese mainland
out into the Pacific, towards Japan. For more than two centuries
it had been a semi-independent kingdom which paid tribute to the
Chinese ruler and recognized his " suzerainty." But there were

A NATIONAL TREASURE OF JAPAN

An ancient bronze lantern (foreground) and the entrance gate (background) to the temple at Nara which houses the Daibutsu — a gigantic statue of Buddha dating from 750 A.D. The woodwork of the entrance gate is a dull but luminous red, the plaster white, and the roof of green-gray tiles. The photograph was taken from the steps of the temple itself.

in Korea almost as many Japanese as Chinese, and the constant quarrels between them embittered the relations between China and Japan. The result of this quarrel was the Chino-Japanese War (1894–1895), in which China, employing antiquated methods of fighting, was quickly and hopelessly defeated by Japan. By the Treaty of Shimonoseki (April 17, 1895), China acknowledged the independence of Korea. In addition, she was required to cede to Japan the admirable naval port of Port Arthur; to pay an indemnity of $57,000,000; and to open up to Japan four new treaty ports. Japan was now in an excellent position to compete with Russia, Great Britain, and France in the further exploitation of China.

The ease with which Japan had defeated China alarmed the European powers. Since the time of Marco Polo it had been understood that Oriental people were rich and industrious, but " no warriors at all." Now the Japanese had proved themselves very good warriors indeed. This was something new in the world. Russia was more alarmed than the others, for the simple reason that she wanted for herself the very thing which Japan had taken from China — Port Arthur. Japan was thus a menace to Russia because she had taken Port Arthur from China before Russia had a chance to do it. Russia therefore induced France and Germany to join her in " advising " Japan to restore Port Arthur to China. They said that the occupation of Port Arthur by Japan would menace the capital of China and " render illusory " the independence of Korea. Unable to resist the three European powers, Japan very reluctantly restored Port Arthur to China. As a compensation, the three European powers " advised " China to pay to Japan an additional indemnity of $24,000,000.

Having " protected " China from the encroachments of Japan, the European powers hastened to claim their reward. Russia, France, Germany, and Great Britain insisted on lending China money enough (more than enough in fact) to pay her indemnity to Japan, and it was agreed that in case of failure to pay the interest the management of the Chinese customs were to be taken over by the European powers concerned. But the privilege of loaning money was not enough. By a secret treaty China granted to a Russian corporation the right to build the Siberian railroad through Manchuria. France demanded and obtained additional territory in southern China, together with the right of opening mines and building railroads. Meantime Germany was determined not to be left out in the cold. In 1896 the emperor instructed his ambassador to " keep his eyes open for an event suitable as a cause for advance." The suitable event occurred in 1897, when some German Catholic missionaries in China were murdered, and about ten days later German warships steamed into Kiaochow Bay. The Chinese government, finding no European friends to protect her against Germany, yielded to the German demands. These were: (1) the lease to Germany for ninety-nine years of Kiaochow Bay; and (2) special privileges in respect to the opening of mines and building railroads in the rich province of Shantung (March 6, 1898).

The other powers were not to be outdone by Germany. No sooner had the German fleet entered Kiaochow Bay than a Russian fleet entered Port Arthur. As soon as Germany obtained the lease of Port Kiaochow, Russia demanded and obtained, on similar terms, the lease of Port Arthur (March, 1898). Shortly after Port Arthur was leased to Russia, Great Britain obtained a similar lease of Weihaiwei for " as long a period as Port Arthur shall remain in the possession of Russia " (July, 1898). Fortunately, China had many ports, and so there was one left for France. France demanded and obtained for ninety-nine years, on the same terms that Russia received Port Arthur, a lease of Kwangchow Bay (April 10, 1898). But with France in Kwangchow, Weihaiwei was not enough for Great Britain. She therefore demanded and obtained a lease of Kowloon (June 9, 1898). (See map, pp. 624–625.)

How the scramble for colonies resulted in a number of colonial wars, 1898–1905. For twenty-five years the European powers had been engaged in establishing their political and economic power in Africa and Asia. Difficulties with the natives had sometimes occurred, and the powers had sometimes come into conflict over their respective claims. But until the end of the century these difficulties had not been very serious. Then, in quick succession, there occurred four serious colonial wars, and one serious diplomatic dispute that nearly precipitated a European war. We must now learn something about these wars.

THE GREAT BUDDHA AT KAMAKURA

This bronze statue, fifty-two feet high, dates from the thirteenth century. The temple by which it was originally protected has been destroyed by fire and earthquake. Secluded in a quiet valley, this Buddha impresses one with the contemplative calm so characteristic of the Japanese. As Kipling says, one "may hear the soul of all the East about him at Kamakura."

1. *The Spanish-American War, 1898.* In 1895 a rebellion broke out in the Spanish colony of Cuba, and for three years a destructive and indecisive struggle was carried on between the insurgents and the Spanish authorities. At that time Americans had about $50,000,000 invested in Cuban sugar and tobacco plantations, iron mines, railroads, and shipping companies. American inves-

tors were hard hit by the rebellion, and naturally wished that it would end. Besides, many people in the United States sympathized with the Cubans in their struggle for liberty. Then on February 15, 1898, the American battleship *Maine* was blown up in Habana (Havana) Harbor. What caused the explosion is not known, but most Americans believed that the Spanish authorities were responsible. "Remember the *Maine!*" became a popular cry, and in April the American Congress, declaring that the Cubans "ought to be independent," declared war on Spain.

The war lasted ten months. The Spanish fleet in Cuban waters was destroyed and the American army occupied Cuba and Porto Rico. Meantime, Commodore Dewey sailed for the Philippines, which were at that time also colonies of Spain, destroyed the Spanish war-vessels in Manila Harbor and occupied the city of Manila. In negotiating the terms of peace, the United States naturally insisted that Spain should recognize the independence of Cuba. But it was more difficult to decide what should be done with the Philippines. The islands were said to be "rich in mineral resources." Manila was a valuable naval base, coveted by Japan. Yet since the United States claimed to be fighting for the unselfish purpose of freeing Cuba it seemed a bit hypocritical to grab the Philippines because they were rich in mineral resources.

This question troubled President McKinley greatly. He tells us that night after night, unable to decide this momentous question, he walked the floor until midnight. Often he asked for divine guidance. And then, suddenly, he knew not how, it was clear to him that the United States must keep the Philippines. To restore them to Spain would be "dishonorable"; to allow them to fall into the hands of Germany or Japan would be "bad business"; to recognize their independence would mean misrule and anarchy. For these reasons President McKinley decided that the United States must take the Philippines, "educate the Filipinos, and uplift and civilize and Christianize them as our fellow-men." So in the end the United States took the Philippines — and also Porto Rico.

2. *The Fashoda Affair, 1898.* While the Spanish-American War was being fought, France and England were on the verge of war over

American Museum of Natural History
RUINS OF A TEMPLE IN KARNAK
Karnak, on the east bank of the Nile, is on the site of ancient Thebes.

the Fashoda Affair. After occupying Egypt in 1882 the British
had extended their occupation up the Nile into the Egyptian
Sudan. In 1898 General Kitchener occupied Khartum and raised
the British flag. Meantime France had built up a great empire on
the Niger River and north of the Belgian Congo; and in 1896 the
French authorities had ordered Captain Marchand to lead an expedition from the Congo to the upper Nile. With a score of French
officers and some two hundred natives, Marchand pushed into the
uncharted wilderness and after two years of heroic effort finally
arrived at Fashoda, July 10, 1898. Thus in 1898 the British flag
was flying at Khartum and the French flag was flying at Fashoda,
five hundred miles farther south. One day Marchand (now a
major) learned that Kitchener was approaching with troops,
artillery, and gunboats. When the gunboats arrived, Captain
Marchand was invited on board. Kitchener complimented the
major on his splendid expedition but informed him that he must
protest against the presence of the French in the Nile Valley as a
direct violation of Anglo-Egyptian rights in the Sudan. Major
Marchand begged the English general to observe that the French
flag, which now in fact floated over Fashoda, had been placed there

by order of the French government.   General Kitchener replied that he nevertheless intended to raise the English and Egyptian flags, and expressed the hope that no resistance would be offered. He said that he would be glad to place a gunboat at the disposal of the major and his party to facilitate their withdrawal.   To this the gallant major replied that he must of course yield to superior force, but that he and his troops would die at their posts rather than withdraw without orders from Paris.

Having thus tested each other's diplomatic courage, the two eminent commanders agreed to refer the dispute to London and Paris.   They then separated, after a further exchange of compliments and gifts of fresh vegetables and wine.   Kitchener raised the British and Egyptian flags, and returned to Khartum.   Marchand remained at Fashoda, guarding the tricolor.

This dramatic encounter in the heart of Africa brought France and Great Britain to the verge of war.   At first it seemed as though neither government would back down.   The British prime minister, Lord Salisbury, declared that the entire Sudan was subject to Anglo-Egyptian sovereignty by right of conquest, and that no part of it could be conceded to France.   The French minister of foreign affairs, M. Delcassé, at first refused to withdraw from Fashoda, hoping no doubt by a brave front to induce the British government to concede some part of the Sudan to France.   To strengthen his position he appealed for aid to Russia, at that time an ally of France. But the tsar's government warned him not to count on Russian aid in case the dispute ended in war.   Unable to obtain aid from Russia or concessions from Great Britain, the French government at last yielded, quite aware that the British had every military advantage.   In ordering Marchand to withdraw from Fashoda (1899), Delcassé explained that the major was only an "emissary of civilization."   We must suppose that had Marchand represented France instead of civilization, the French government would have been in honor bound to support him.

3. *The Boer War, 1899–1902.*   The Fashoda scare had scarcely blown over before Great Britain was at war with the two Boer republics in South Africa — the Orange Free State and the Transvaal Republic.   After the discovery of gold in the Transvaal (1886)

the country was filled with gold-seekers, chiefly from British Cape Colony. The Boers disliked the foreigners (whom they called *Uitlanders*) and thought it unjust that they should reap the profits of the gold discovered in the country of the Boers. Under the leadership of the president of the republic, Oom Paul Kruger, the Boers passed laws restricting the political rights of the Uitlanders. According to a law of 1894 no Uitlander could vote until he was forty years of age, or become a citizen until he had resided in the country for fourteen years.

The Uitlanders resented these restrictions. They said that since they were a majority of the population, owned two-thirds of the land, and paid nine-tenths of the taxes, it was unjust to deny them equal political privileges. Undoubtedly it was. But President Kruger saw clearly that if the Uitlanders were given equal political privileges they would control the government, and the Boers would be a subject minority in their own country. Undoubtedly that would be unjust also.

Such was the situation when Cecil Rhodes took a hand in the affair. In 1895 Rhodes was at the height of his power. He was a multimillionaire. He was the premier of Cape Colony and the virtual ruler of Rhodesia. He was the most respected and well-beloved man in South Africa. His chief object was to bring all of South Africa under the rule of Great Britain. In November, 1895, Rhodes therefore entered into a secret conspiracy with the Transvaal Uitlanders to overthrow by armed force the government of the Transvaal Republic. The Uitlanders were to prepare for an armed uprising. With Rhodes's connivance arms and ammunition were to be smuggled in to them. Meantime a band of filibusters, armed at Rhodes's expense, were to be stationed in Rhodesia on the Transvaal frontier under the leadership of Dr. Jameson, a trusted friend of Rhodes. When the Uitlanders gave the signal, Jameson was to cross the frontier and help them carry through the revolution. The scheme might have succeeded but for one thing. Jameson was too impatient to wait. In spite of instructions to lie low until further orders, he made his famous raid into the Transvaal before the others were ready (December 29, 1895). The Uitlanders of course did nothing, the raiders were arrested, and the conspiracy failed.

When Rhodes heard that Jameson was on the march, he exclaimed in dismay, " Jameson has upset my applecart ! " He had indeed. It soon transpired that Cecil Rhodes, known throughout South Africa as a " square-dealer," was responsible for the conspiracy; Jameson responsible only for its failure. Rhodes's popularity collapsed like a pricked balloon. He resigned as premier of Cape Colony, and was censured by the British Government. Friends of a lifetime turned away in contempt. Yet Rhodes had acted from the highest motives — the profound conviction that by extending the British Empire he would be doing the will of God. Perhaps the ways of God are mysterious, and past finding out.

New York Public Library

THE RHODES COLOSSUS

Cartoon by Sambourne in *Punch*, 1892. Rhodes aimed to acquire for Great Britain territory from Cape Colony to Egypt, so that a railroad and telegraph line (note the line in his hands) could be run from Cape-town to Cairo. This cartoon represents the popular slogan of the time : "From the Cape to Cairo."

The Rhodes conspiracy led directly to the Boer War. It infuriated the Boers and united them against the English. It inspired the German emperor to send his congratulations to President Kruger in a telegram that was published throughout the world. It aroused sympathy for the Boers everywhere, even in England. Above all, it left the Uitlanders in the Transvaal worse off than before and finally, in 1899, they appealed to the British government to intervene on their behalf. October 9, when the veldt was nicely covered with fresh grass for his cavalry horses, President Kruger abruptly terminated negotiations by sending an ultimatum to the British government. October 11, the British government declared war on the Transvaal.

In England it was thought the war would soon be over. As a matter of fact, it lasted three years. Lord Roberts, with 250,000 soldiers, did indeed easily defeat the Boer army of 40,000 men. The Boer capital at Pretoria was occupied, and President Kruger fled to Germany. But the remnants of the Boer army, supported by the people, kept up a stubborn guerilla warfare. Such resistance, in so extensive a country, required drastic measures. Lord Kitchener, appointed to replace Lord Roberts, conducted systematic campaigns in one district after another; and in order to maintain his conquests he constructed chains of blockhouses or corrals in which the population, including women and children, were imprisoned. Superior forces and ruthless methods at last brought the Boers to submit. May 31, 1902, a treaty of peace was signed by which the Boers recognized the sovereignty of the King of England, on condition that the Boer language be used in schools and in the courts, and the conquered republics (the Orange Free State had joined the Transvaal in the war) should be given self-government as soon as possible. In compensation for destroyed farms the British government agreed to pay $15,000,000.

4. *The Boxer Rebellion in China, 1900.* While the Boer War was still on, the European powers, the United States, and Japan were engaged in suppressing the Boxer Rebellion in China. As a result of the ruthless aggressions of foreign powers in China, the mass of the Chinese people became every year more incensed against the " barbarians." The barbarians brought strange machines that made deep cuts in the country-side, or plowed through cemeteries where honored ancestors had lain undisturbed through the ages. They even took the people's farms for their railroads, promising to pay for them. Promising to pay, oh yes! But where was the money? (Very likely in the pockets of corrupt Chinese officials!) And then there was a failure of the harvest, and famine in some of the provinces (1899). Doubtless the hated missionaries, preaching a false religion, were the cause of all their troubles. So the people reasoned.

Popular hatred of the barbarians was encouraged and directed by certain secret societies, such as the " Plum-Blossom Fists," the " Great Sword Society," the " Fists of Public Harmony." The latter was a kind of Chinese Y. M. C. A. — highly religious and patriotic, and given to gymnastic exercises such as boxing. Hence the name " Boxers," which the Europeans gave to the members of all of these societies; and as they were all active in the popular uprisings, the movement came to be known as the Boxer Rebellion.

From December, 1899, to June, 1900, disturbances spread through the northern provinces. Railroads were destroyed, missions burned, some foreign missionaries and many Chinese Christian converts killed. Encouraged by some of the Chinese officials and joined by Chinese troops, the insurgents gained control of the capital, Peking; and from June 9 until August 15 the ambassadors of eleven foreign powers, together with other foreigners to the number of 1500, were besieged in the British Legation. The German ambassador, Von Keller, was killed on his way to a conference with a Chinese official. The foreign buildings, missions, and churches in Peking were looted; the wealthiest part of the city was laid waste; the business section caught fire and was burned to the ground.

All this time the European governments were organizing a relief expedition. Finally an army of about 2000 troops — Russian, French, German, British, and American — reached Peking and on August 15 rescued the besieged foreigners. The empress and her court fled from the city, and the insurrection was ruthlessly put down. The foreign troops, with or without the consent of their officers, massacred some thousands of Chinese, systematically pillaged the shops, and looted public buildings. With equal ruthlessness the insurrection was suppressed in the provinces, notably in Manchuria, which was overrun and occupied by the Russian army.

Having suppressed the rebellion, the allied powers presented to the Chinese government a long list of demands, the chief of which were the following: (1) punishment of certain Chinese officials; (2) prohibition of the importation into China of arms and ammunition for two years; (3) military defense of the foreign legations in Peking, and military occupation of the chief points between Peking and the seacoast; (4) an indemnity of about $386,000,000, to be paid off in thirty-nine years out of the Chinese customs and the salt tax. The indemnity was intended to cover only the value of property destroyed and the cost of suppressing the insurrection. The United States, whose share was regarded as moderate, received

DAIREN, MANCHURIA   © *Ewing Galloway*

This is the central plaza. Dairen has the reputation of being one of the best-planned cities of the Far East.

$24,440,000 — twice as much as her actual claims were afterwards found to be. In 1908 the United States renounced $10,785,296 of her indemnity, and the Chinese government has since used this sum to educate Chinese students in the United States.

One important result of the Boxer Rebellion was that it brought to an end for the time being the break-up of China. European governments were convinced that breaking up China was more difficult than they had supposed. The Chinese governing classes were convinced at last that China must be reformed or cease to exist. " China for the Chinese " became the cry; and under the lead of the empress dowager a serious attempt was made to reform the political, military, and educational institutions of China along the lines already followed by Japan (1901–1911). Another result of the Boxer Rebellion was that it had a great influence in bringing on the Russo-Japanese War.

5. *The Russo-Japanese War, 1904–1905.* In 1895, after her successful war against China, Japan had been forced by Russia, France, and Germany to restore Port Arthur to China. The Japanese had accepted, but had never forgotten, this humiliation.

Russia they regarded as chiefly responsible for it; and since 1895 they had watched Russia take over Manchuria and that very Port Arthur which Russia had advised Japan to restore to China! Meantime the astute Japanese had bided their time and prepared for the day of reckoning. Every year the Japanese army and navy were strengthened, and in 1902 Great Britain was induced to sign with Japan a treaty of alliance in which the two powers agreed to work together in defense of their interests in the Far East against Russia and France.

Courtesy of Art and Archaeology

DAIKOKU, JAPANESE GOD OF PLENTY

The god is represented as seated upon a bale of rice. The hammer in his hand symbolizes mining.

Strengthened by this alliance, Japan was ready to resist the further extension of Russian power. Two points of dispute arose. One concerned Manchuria, the other Korea. In July, 1903, Japan agreed to give Russia a free hand in extending her economic and political control over Manchuria, on condition that Russia should give Japan a free hand in Korea. Russia refused this offer. Japan then suddenly broke off diplomatic relations with Russia (February 5, 1904).

The war between Japan and Russia was fought neither on Japanese nor on Russian territory, but in Manchuria — that is to say, on territory belonging to China, a neutral state. The Japanese campaign aimed to accomplish four things: (1) to drive the Russians out of Korea; (2) to take Port Arthur; (3) to destroy the Russian fleet; (4) to defeat the Russian army in Manchuria. All of these objects were attained. The Russians had not expected Japan to make war and were not prepared for it. The Japanese were — thoroughly prepared. Korea was soon occupied by the Japanese. In Manchuria the Japanese general, Oyama, defeated

By Burton Holmes, from Ewing Galloway

STREET IN MUKDEN, MANCHURIA

Near here one of the decisive battles of the Russo-Japanese war was fought. The commercial importance of Mukden is declining. It is losing its trade to Dairen, which has the advantage of being a seaport.

General Kuropatkin in the ten-day battle of Liaoyang (August 23–September 2, 1904), and again in the fifteen days of desperate fighting known as the Battle of Mukden (February 25–March 10, 1905). Port Arthur had meantime been taken in January; and to complete the tale of disaster the Russian fleet, sent out from the Baltic, was located and destroyed by the Japanese (May 27–28, 1905) before it reached Vladivostok.

Both governments were now ready to make peace. The Russians might indeed have continued the war, but all the chances were against them, and the people at home, having no interest in the war, were clamoring for peace and even threatening to overturn the tsar's government by revolution. On the suggestion of Japan, and with the tsar's consent, President Roosevelt therefore invited the two governments to meet and discuss the terms of peace. The conference was held at Portsmouth, New Hampshire. In the

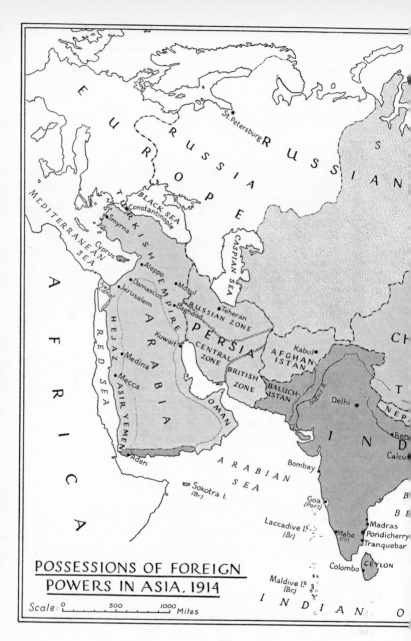

POSSESSIONS OF FOREIGN
POWERS IN ASIA, 1914

Scale: 0 ___ 500 ___ 1000 Miles

Legend

- British possessions
- Russian possessions
- British sphere of influence in Persia
- Russian sphere of influence in Persia
- Dutch possessions
- French possessions

ERIA

MPIRE

MONGOLIA

E REPUBLIC

L.Baikal

Irkutsk

Urga

Peking

CHINA

Yangtze R.

asa

A

BURMA

SIAM

Bangkok

Andaman (Br.) Is

Nicobar Is (Br.)

FEDERATED MALAY STATES

Singapore

SUMATRA

DUTCH

BORNEO

SARAWAK

EAST

INDIES

CELEBES

MANCHURIA

Mukden

Liaoyang

LIAO TUNG

Port Arthur (Jap.)

SHANTUNG Wei-hai-wei(Br.)

Kiaochow (Ger.)

Shanghai

KOREA (Jap.)

Formosa (Jap.)

Canton

Kwangchow (Fr.)

Kowloon(Br.)

Hong Kong (Br.)

Hainan

SEA OF OKHOTSK

Amur R.

Vladivostok

SEA OF JAPAN

Tokyo

Yokohama

JAPAN

PACIFIC OCEAN

Bonin Is (Jap.)

Ladrone Is (Ger.)

Caroline Is (Ger.)

Pelew Is (Ger.)

Manila

PHILIPPINE IS (U.S.)

SOUTH CHINA SEA

CELEBES SEA

CELEBES

N. GUINEA (Br.)

ARAFURA SEA

FRENCH INDO-CHINA

Peace of Portsmouth (September 5, 1905), Russia agreed: (1) to recognize Japan's special interests in Korea; (2) to transfer to Japan her lease of Port Arthur; (3) to evacuate Manchuria. Thus Japan gained more than she had demanded before the war began. Her revenge for the humiliation of 1895 at the hands of Russia was more than complete.

How the colonial wars raised the specter of a European war, and what people thought about it. The colonial wars were important, not only in themselves, but because they made people think more seriously about colonial expansion and its possible consequences. For twenty-five years people had for the most part watched the merry scramble for colonies and concessions without thinking too much about the rights and the wrongs of it, or about the dangers that might arise out of it. Then, quite suddenly, one war after another came out of it, like rabbits emerging from a conjurer's hat. Wars in China and Africa were bad enough. But what if this tangled skein of interests and rivalries should lead to a European war? The colonial wars raised on the horizon the fearful specter of a European war. The result was that people began to ask two questions. One was: " Is all this ruthless aggression in backward countries right or decent? " The other was: " Is it safe? "

In answer to the first question many people said, " No, it is neither right nor decent." In most countries, during the early years of the twentieth century, there accordingly developed a certain anti-colonial and pacifist sentiment. In France and Great Britain the liberal and radical parties which represented this sentiment came into power (see pp. 569, 579). In Russia popular opposition to the Russo-Japanese War resulted in the Revolution of 1905, which forced the tsar to grant a constitution and checked, for the time being at least, Russian schemes for expansion in the Far East. Many books were published by able and prominent men denouncing the ruthless exploitation of backward countries as a modern form of imperialism. The " new imperialism," they said, was not only unjust to the subject peoples, but contrary to the principles of European democracy. At the same time peace societies multiplied and increased their membership. They denounced war as morally wrong and economically unprofitable.

Statistics were relied upon, by practical men and dreamers, to prove that a European war would be a disaster to all concerned. The cost of modern war was so great, and the European countries were so dependent on each other in respect to trade and finance, that a general war would ruin all the participants, victors as well as vanquished. It was a " great illusion " to suppose that any modern nation could profit by even a victorious war.

Governments themselves were alarmed at the prospect of a European war. In 1899, at the request of the Tsar of Russia, an international conference was assembled at the Hague in Holland. The first Hague Conference declared that a reduction of armaments was " extremely desirable." It declared that the offer of any state to " mediate " a dispute between two other states could never be regarded as " an unfriendly act." It agreed upon a proper method for submitting disputes to impartial arbitration. A second Hague Conference assembled in 1907 established a permanent court of arbitration known as the Hague Tribunal. It was composed of salaried judges, appointed for twelve years, and its purpose was the settlement of disputes which any governments might be willing to submit to it. For housing this court a splendid building was provided by the generosity of Andrew Carnegie, multimillionaire and author of a book entitled *Democracy Triumphant*. To the lovers of peace the establishment of the Hague Tribunal seemed a decisive event — a turning point in the history of Europe. " After centuries of effort," a contemporary writer said, " mankind has at last been placed on the road which leads to the remote goal of international peace."

But the statesmen and diplomats of Europe had rather less faith in the Hague Tribunal than the writer just quoted. Confronted by the possibility of a European war, the statesmen in each country were disposed to ask, " Are we prepared for it? Would we stand alone, or would we have powerful allies? " One important result of the colonial wars was that the governments of Europe, in defense of their colonial interests and as a safeguard in case of a European war, hastened to strengthen old alliances and to form new ones. The outcome was that by 1907 Europe was divided into two hostile groups of powers — the Triple Alliance and the Triple

Entente.   In the next chapter we shall see how these alliances were formed to preserve the peace, and how their rivalries in fact led to the Great War.

QUESTIONS

1. What were the chief colonizing countries in the sixteenth century? What wars grew out of colonial rivalry in the eighteenth century?   What colonial possessions did Great Britain have in 1815?

2. Why was there little colonial expansion between 1815 and 1875? What was the "Little England" movement?   Why did the interest in colonization revive after 1875?   Why were business men and bankers especially interested in colonization?   Generally speaking, what classes of people favored colonial expansion?   What classes were indifferent or hostile to it?   What political parties were anti-colonial?

3. Explain how Belgium acquired the Congo.   Who was Cecil Rhodes, and why did he go to Africa?   How did he acquire wealth and power in South Africa?   Why did he think it was the duty of Great Britain to acquire control of Africa?

4. Who was Ismail Pasha, and what were his ambitions?   How did European bankers supply him with money?   Why did he have to pay high rates of interest?   Who profited by his borrowings?   How did the British government gradually become involved in Egyptian affairs? Why, after having promised to withdraw from Egypt, did Great Britain retain control of it?

5. How was China gradually opened up to Europeans?   What were the early concessions made to European Powers?   What were "treaty ports"?   What was the cause of the Chino-Japanese War of 1894?   Why was Japan able to defeat China easily?   What did Japan gain by this war?   Why did Russia, France, and Germany force Japan to give Port Arthur back to China?   What further concession did the European powers demand of China after the Chino-Japanese War?

6. What were the four colonial wars between 1898 and 1905?   Explain what is meant by the "Fashoda Affair."   What was the cause of the Spanish-American War?   Why did the United States take the Philippines?   What was the cause of the Boer War?   Why did it last longer than was expected?   What was the Boxer Rebellion, and how was it suppressed?   What was the cause of the Russo-Japanese War?   What did Japan gain by it?

7. What effect did the colonial wars have on the trend of thought in Europe?   What influence did the colonial wars have on political history in France, 1899–1910? upon political history in England, 1906–1910? upon political history in Russia in 1905?   What were the Hague conferences, and what provision did they make for preventing war?

CHART FOR CHAPTER XIX. Showing how the scramble for colonies led to many colonial wars.

Russo-Japanese War, 1904-1905

Boer War 1899-1902

Boxer Rebellion 1900

Spanish American War, 1898

Fashoda Affair, 1898

1842 .... 1898 Colonial Wars and Disputes 1905

Scramble for Colonies and Concessions

Opening-up of China { European powers, United States, and Japan force China to grant treaty port concessions, cessions of territory, and lease of naval ports. } leads to: Boxer Rebellion, 1900. Russo-Japanese War, 1904-1905.

Partition of Africa { Great Britain acquires South Africa, Egypt, Sudan. France acquires Tunis (Ch.XX), French Congo. Belgium acquires Belgian Congo. Germany acquires Southwest Africa, East Africa (Ch.XXIII) } leads to: Fashoda Affair, 1898. Boer War, 1899-1902.

United States acquires financial interests in Spanish West Indies. } leads to: Spanish-American War, 1898.

629

SELECTED READINGS

Brief accounts. Robinson and Beard, *Outlines*, II, 425–432, 466–501, and *Development of Modern Europe* (revised ed.), II, chs. v, viii. Hayes and Moon, *Modern History*, ch. xxii–xxiii. Hayes, *Modern Europe*, II, 547–596. Schapiro, *European History* (revised ed.), chs. xxx–xxxii. Hazen, *Modern Europe*, chs. xxix, xxxiii, and *Europe since 1815* (revised ed.), I, chs. xxvi, xxxii. Flick, *Modern World History*, chs. xxiv, xxvii, xxxi. P. Slosson, *Twentieth Century Europe*, chs. vi–vii. G. P. Gooch, *Modern Europe*, ch. iii.

Longer accounts. P. T. Moon, *Modern Imperialism*. H. A. Gibbons, *New Map of Africa* and *New Map of Asia*. H. H. Johnston, *The Opening up of Africa*. D. Reitz, *Commando*. (An interesting account of the Boer War by an eyewitness.) K. S. Latourette, *The Development of China* and *The Development of Japan*. P. J. Treat, *The Far East*. R. K. Douglas, *Europe in the Far East*. R. Van Bergen, *Story of Japan*. E. D. Morel, *The Black Man's Burden*. (A hostile but well-informed discussion of European exploitation of backward countries.) D. Crawford, *Thinking Black*. (A vivid account of native life in Africa by a man who lived there twenty-two years.) The following books throw light on Chinese and Japanese civilization: M. E. Burton, *Notable Women of Modern China*. E. Sugimoto, *A Daughter of the Samurai*. S. L. Gulick, *Working Women of Japan*. E. Cooper, *My Lady of the Chinese Courtyard*. (Familiar letters of an upperclass Chinese family.) Y. Lee, *When I Was a Boy in China*. G. L. Dickinson, *Letters from a Chinese Official*. (Fictitious letters presenting an Englishman's idea of the Chinese view of Western civilization.) For interesting illustrative material see Scott and Baltzly, *Readings in European History*, ch. xii.

Biographies. David Livingstone, *Missionary Travels in Africa*. H. M. Stanley, *In Darkest Africa* and *How I Found Livingstone*. B. Williams, *Cecil Rhodes*. G. Le Sueur, *Cecil Rhodes*. P. Jourdan, *Cecil Rhodes*. (Le Sueur and Jourdan each served Rhodes as private secretary. They present different views of the man.)

A STATION ON THE FRONTIER BETWEEN FRANCE AND GERMANY
At the left are the offices of the German customs inspectors and at the right those of the French.

CHAPTER XX. ALLIANCES AND ARMAMENTS: HOW THE GREAT POWERS PREPARED FOR WAR IN TIME OF PEACE, AND HOW THE WAR CAME BECAUSE THE GREAT POWERS WERE SO WELL PREPARED FOR IT

It will be better to depend upon the great armaments for maintaining peace.
CAPTAIN MAHAN

The moral is obvious: it is that great armaments lead inevitably to war.
SIR EDWARD GREY

The purpose of this chapter. One of the two great alliances existed long before the colonial wars described in the last chapter. This was the *Triple Alliance* of Germany, Austria, and Italy (1879–1882). It grew out of the fears and rivalries engendered by the Franco-Prussian War, and was largely the work of Bismarck, who wished to make the new German Empire too strong to be successfully attacked by any or all of its enemies. For nearly twenty-five years this was the only great alliance in Europe. Then, within a few years (1904–1907), a second and rival alliance was formed. This was the *Triple Entente* of France, Russia, and Great Britain. It was the result partly of the rivalries engendered by the colonial wars, and partly of the growing fear of Germany. From 1907 to

1914 these two combinations of great powers, each commanding military and naval resources never before dreamed of, confronted each other in an attitude of watchful waiting.

None of the great powers desired a European war. On the contrary, every one of them desired to prevent such a war. The great armaments and the great alliances existed not to make war, but to preserve the peace. Nevertheless the mere existence of great armaments and powerful alliances really endangered the peace they were designed to preserve. Armaments and alliances increased the mutual fears of the great powers, and their mutual fears led to aggressive talk and action which only increased their fears, until at last their fears and aggressions together plunged Europe into the Great War. For forty years the motto of the great powers was: " In time of peace prepare for war "; and the war came in the end because the great powers were so well prepared for it.

How could such good intentions lead to such deplorable results? That is what we must try to make clear in the present chapter. Let us first consider the influences that led to the formation of the great alliances, and then the series of diplomatic crises to which their rivalries gave rise.

I. The Formation of the Great Alliances, 1894–1907

The Triple Alliance: How Bismarck tried to form an alliance with Austria and Russia and why he failed. Before 1871 Bismarck had done what he could to bring about three wars. But after 1871 he suddenly turned into a man of peace. The reason is simple. Before 1871 he desired war in order to bring about the territorial unity of Germany; after 1871, in order to perfect and strengthen the institutions of the new empire, he desired to keep the peace in Europe. This he thought would not be easy, since in creating the German Empire he had made many enemies. Any one power Bismarck did not fear; what he feared was a coalition. One day one of his friends said to him: " Count, fear of a coalition seems to be your nightmare." Bismarck replied: " Yes, necessarily so." The aim of all Bismarck's diplomacy after 1871 was to safeguard Germany against a coalition of hostile powers.

The country most feared by Bismarck was France. For France,

the defeat of 1871 had been a great humiliation, and Bismarck took it for granted that France was, and must remain, the chief enemy. Therefore he did what he could to keep France weak and to embroil her with her neighbors. He used his influence to sustain the new republic in France, thinking that a republican form of government would necessarily be a weak one. Besides, he encouraged the French government to embark on a policy of colonial expansion. He supported the French occupation of Tunis in 1881. He placed no obstacles in the way of French expansion in Morocco, in the African Congo, or in Indo-China. He felt that these triumphs would console the French for the loss of Alsace-Lorraine. More important still, he felt that France could not build up an empire in Africa and Asia without sooner or later coming into conflict with Great Britain, as in fact happened in 1898 (*Fashoda Affair*).

But Bismarck felt that the most effective way of preventing France from forming a coalition was to form one of his own — to make Germany the center of an alliance too strong to be successfully attacked by any coalition that France could possibly form. His first idea was to make an alliance with Russia and Austria. The Russian tsar was grateful to Germany for her goodwill during one of the numerous Polish insurrections (1863). The Austrian government did not feel too badly about the defeat in 1866 because Bismarck had been easy in the terms imposed on Austria at the peace. Accordingly, in 1872, the three emperors — Alexander, Francis Joseph, and William — met in Berlin, and the year following signed an agreement known as the League of the Three Emperors.

This friendly understanding was short-lived. The reason is that Austria and Russia could not reconcile their differences in the Balkans. Most of the Balkan peoples were, like the Russians, Slavs; and most of them were, like the Russians, Christians. Yet they were subject to the Mohammedan Turks. Russia hoped to increase her power in the Balkans by freeing these people from Turkish rule. Austria was necessarily opposed to Russia in all this. There were many Slav people in the Austro-Hungarian Monarchy and they disliked being ruled by the Germans of Austria and the Magyars of Hungary as much as the Slavs of

Serbia and Montenegro disliked being ruled by the Turks. Consequently, if Russia succeeded in freeing the Balkan Slavs from Turkish rule, would she not then take up the cause of the Austrian Slavs and help them break up the Austrian empire? For this reason it was impossible for Austria and Russia to be very good friends.

The quarrel between Russia and Austria came to a head in 1875–1877. In 1875 the Serbians, Montenegrins, and Bulgarians revolted against Turkey. The revolt was on the point of failing when Russia intervened by making war on Turkey (*Russian-Turkish War*). The Turks were hopelessly defeated and were forced by the Russians to agree to the Treaty of San Stefano (1878). By this treaty Serbia, Montenegro, and Rumania were to become independent states; Bulgaria was to be greatly enlarged and permitted to govern itself, although still nominally part of the Turkish Empire; and Turkey was to cede Kars and Batum to Russia and to pay her a heavy indemnity. This was a great victory for Russia.

Austria was alarmed by the great extension of Russian influence in the Balkans. Fortunately for her, she was supported by Disraeli, the prime minister of Great Britain, who felt that British interests in the Near East required him to defend Turkey against Russia. Therefore both Great Britain and Austria demanded that the Treaty of San Stefano should be laid before a European congress for revision. Opposed by Austria and Great Britain, and unable to obtain the support of Germany, Russia consented to the revision of her hard-won Treaty of San Stefano.

The revision was made by a congress of European powers — the famous Congress of Berlin (1878). It was the most brilliant assembly of statesmen since the Congress of Paris in 1856. Next to Bismarck, whose reputation was now at its height, the most observed of all the representatives was Disraeli — the most observed and the most influential. "That old Jew, he is the man," Bismarck said. But it was Bismarck himself, the "Iron Chancellor," who was the star performer of the play. Many of the decisions had already been agreed upon before the congress assembled. The chief decisions thus arrived at, and sanctioned by the congress, were the following: (1) Bulgaria was reduced to its former boundaries, the territory added by the Treaty of San Stefano being restored to Turkey.

THE CONGRESS OF BERLIN, 1878

From a painting by Anton von Werner. Bismarck is shaking hands with Count Schuvalov. Disraeli, leaning on a cane, is talking to Prince Gortchakov. Behind Disraeli is the French representative, Waddington. To the right are Turkish representatives, wearing the fez.

(2) Austria was permitted to take over, for administrative purposes, the Turkish province of Bosnia-Herzegovina. (3) In return for British aid, Turkey ceded to Great Britain the island of Cyprus. (4) The independence of Serbia, Montenegro, and Rumania was recognized. (See map, pp. 644–645.)

Thus the result of the revision of the Treaty of San Stefano was that Turkey, Great Britain, and Austria profited at the expense of Russia. Bismarck had professed to be neutral. " My only desire is, like a good broker, to put the business through," he said. But by merely remaining neutral, the influence of Germany was really exerted in favor of Austria and against Russia. The tsar and his government knew this well. They were furious with Bismarck for the part he played; and Bismarck had to abandon, at least for the time being, his scheme of a triple alliance of Germany, Austria, and Russia.

How Germany and Austria formed an alliance (1879), and how Italy was admitted, thus creating the Triple Alliance (1882). The hostility of Russia after the Congress of Berlin was such that Germany and Austria hastened to sign a treaty known as the Dual Alliance (1879). The terms of this treaty, which were kept secret for many years, were: (1) that if either party to the alliance were attacked by Russia, the other would come to the aid of the one so attacked; (2) that if any third power (France was understood) should attack either party to the alliance, the other would remain neutral, unless Russia joined the attacking party (France), in which case the two (Germany and Austria) would join their forces. This alliance was directed primarily against Russia, secondarily against France. It safeguarded Austria against attack by Russia; it safeguarded Germany against attack by France assisted by Russia.

Three years later Italy was admitted to the German-Austrian alliance, thus creating the famous Triple Alliance (1882). This may seem strange, since Italy and Austria were enemies of long standing. The circumstances which drove Italy into the camp of her enemy, Austria, were complicated; but they may be stated simply as follows.

Italy was profoundly irritated by the results of the Congress of Berlin, because Austria obtained Bosnia-Herzegovina while she herself obtained nothing. Count Corti, the Italian ambassador, returning from the congress, explained that he returned at least " with clean hands." The Italians would have preferred something more substantial. They were still more irritated when it presently appeared that France as well as Austria had obtained something at the Congress of Berlin. When M. Waddington, the French ambassador, learned that Great Britain had obtained Cyprus, he threatened to pack up his trunks and leave the congress. Bismarck and Lord Salisbury pacified him by promising that neither Germany nor Great Britain would object if France saw fit to take possession of the Turkish province of Tunis. Acting upon this promise, France took possession of Tunis in 1881.

This act infuriated the Italians. Tunis was just across the sea from Italy, and it was the site of Carthage, which the ancient Romans had conquered. Hence for both geographical and sentimental reasons, the Italians thought that if any European country ever obtained Tunis, Italy was the proper country to do it. Now France had stepped in before them. Outwitted by both France and Austria, the Italians felt that they were being left behind in the scramble for territory. When France occupied Tunis, the Italian government therefore sought an alliance with Germany. But Bismarck said that " the key to the door which leads to us must be sought in Vienna." He meant that if Italy wanted to form an alliance with Germany she would first have to make her peace with Austria. This was difficult, but it was finally done. The result was that in 1882 the three powers signed the famous Triple Alliance treaty.

The chief provisions of this alliance were: (1) If Italy were attacked by France, Germany and Austria were to come to her assistance; if Germany were attacked by France, Italy was to come to her assistance. (2) If any one or two parties to the alliance were attacked by any two of the great powers, the other one or two parties to the alliance must join in the war against the attacking power or powers. The treaty was to be kept secret and to run for five years. It was renewed in 1887, with some modifications, and periodically thereafter until the Great War of 1914, when it broke down because of Italy's refusal to join Germany and Austria.

Thus Bismarck made Germany the center of a powerful alliance. It was not precisely the alliance he desired, but it served the purpose, especially since, in the period 1881–1890, he managed to restore friendly relations between Germany and Russia. His purpose was purely defensive — to keep the peace in Europe by securing Germany against attack by one or more great powers.

The Triple Entente: How Russia and France formed an alliance as soon as Bismarck ceased to govern Germany. Even after the Triple Alliance was formed, Bismarck did not abandon hope of restoring friendly relations with Russia. He once said that there were two dangers Germany must avoid at all hazards. One was the enmity of Great Britain. The other was an alliance between Russia and France. His conduct at the Congress of Berlin had won the goodwill of Great Britain, but it had lost the goodwill of Russia. Would Russia now turn to France? This was what Bismarck feared and what he tried to prevent. In order to prevent it he was willing to make many concessions. These concessions were formulated in a treaty between Russia and Germany, which Bismarck called his " Reinsurance Treaty " (1887). By this treaty Russia promised not to join France if France made war on Germany; and in return Germany promised to support Russian interests in the Balkans even, to some extent, against Austria.

The Reinsurance Treaty was to run for three years, and in 1890, when it lapsed, Russia was willing to renew it. Bismarck was willing to renew it too; but before a new treaty could be signed Bismarck had ceased to be chancellor, and the direction of German affairs was taken over by the young Emperor William II. Unlike Bismarck, the new emperor thought, or was persuaded by others to think, that Germany as well as Austria had interests in the Balkans, and that Germany and Austria ought to join to defend their common interests there against Russia. Therefore, when the Russian government asked for a renewal of the Reinsurance Treaty of 1887, the German emperor refused to renew it.

This change of policy on the part of Germany was soon followed by the formation of an alliance between Russia and France. For some years the relations of the two countries had been friendly. Since 1888 the Russian government had floated loans in Paris, and much of the money used to build the Siberian railway had been subscribed by the French people. This relation of debtor and creditor helped to draw the two countries together; but above all,

it was a common fear of Germany that united them. The result was that in 1894 the two governments made binding a military convention drafted two years earlier. The terms of this defensive alliance (which were not precisely known, even to the French parliament, until 1918) were as follows: (1) If France were attacked by Germany, or by Italy supported by Germany, Russia would employ all of her forces to attack Germany; (2) if Russia were attacked by Germany, or by Austria supported by Germany, France would employ all her forces to attack Germany; (3) the forces available for these purposes should be: for France, 1,300,000 men; for Russia, from 700,000 to 800,000 men.

Thus four years after the retirement of Bismarck the very thing occurred which he most feared and had labored for twenty years to prevent — a Franco-Russian mili-

DROPPING THE PILOT

This is one of the most famous of the cartoons of Tenniel. It appeared in London *Punch*, March, 1890, on the occasion of the retirement of Bismarck. The captain, young Emperor William II, is watching his old pilot, Bismarck, leave the ship.

tary alliance. This alliance was the first stage in building up the Triple Entente. The second was the formation of a " cordial understanding " between England and France in 1904.

The Triple Entente: How England and France, having been enemies for two hundred years, suddenly became friends, 1904. For two hundred years England and France had been on opposite sides in all the great European wars. In the time of Louis XIV, again in the eighteenth century, and once more in the time of Napoleon they had fought over colonies and trade privileges. So persistent was this opposition that diplomats regarded the hostility of England and France as the basic fact of international politics. Even as late as 1898 the two countries were on the verge of war over the Fashoda Affair. Yet within six years after Fashoda they compromised their rivalries and became friends. The change was so startling that it was called a "diplomatic revolution." What is the explanation of this sudden friendship between ancient enemies?

One explanation is their fear of each other. Although they had been rivals for two hundred years, there had been no war between them since 1815, and most people had come to think that war was improbable, if not impossible, between two such highly civilized countries. But this feeling of confidence was destroyed by the colonial wars at the close of the nineteenth century. The expansion of both countries in Africa and Asia had once more, as in the eighteenth century, created serious conflicts between them. The Fashoda Affair of 1898 had made this clear. It had flared up like a fire in the night, revealing the fact that England and France might easily find themselves at war before they were aware. After 1898, therefore, statesmen in both countries began to seek the terms of an agreement that might remove the danger of a war between them.

But the chief reason for the sudden friendship of England and France was their common fear of Germany. French fear of Germany needs little explaining. The French had not forgotten the loss of Alsace-Lorraine in 1871. The diplomatic ascendancy of Germany in the time of Bismarck was irritating to French pride, and the boastful speeches of the young Emperor William II were even more so. France was therefore only too willing to form alliances against Germany — not because she wished to provoke a war against that country, but because she wished to be too strong to be safely bullied.

English fear of Germany does need a little explaining. As long as France was her chief colonial rival, England naturally sought the friendship of the German country — Austria or Prussia — which was opposed to the extension of French power in Europe. This is why England welcomed the unification of Germany and was

MILITARY PREPARATIONS IN AUSTRIA

This engraving from *L'Illustration* of 1888 shows that the French kept a watchful eye on military preparations in neighboring countries.

always on good terms with Bismarck. Bismarck said that Germany's sphere of influence was in Europe. He said that Germany had " hay enough on her fork " already without burdening herself with colonies. This was exactly what England wanted — a strong Germany that would check the power of France in Europe without interfering with England's colonial and naval supremacy.

But what if the powerful Germany should try to become a great colonial and naval power? Then Germany might replace France as England's chief rival, in which case England would as naturally seek the aid of France against Germany as she had formerly sought the aid of Germany against France.

This is exactly what happened after the retirement of Bismarck in 1890. The young Emperor William II abandoned the anti-colonial policy of Bismarck. He said that Germany, as well as England, must become a world power, and he talked of " smashing " anyone or anything that stood in the way. At first his speeches seemed only amusing. But it turned out that they meant something. They meant something because there were in Germany the same powerful influences in favor of colonial expansion that existed in France and England. Since 1871 Germany had rapidly been industrialized. The population had increased from 41,000,000 to 65,000,000; the number of people living in cities had increased 25 to 50 per cent; the capital in the *Deutsche Bank* had increased from 60,000,000 to 7,000,000,000 marks; the steel production from 500,000 to 12,000,000 tons. In merchant and passenger ships Germany had come to rank next to Great Britain. In short, within twenty-five years Germany had become the second industrial country of Europe.

Now the result of this industrial revolution was the same in Germany as elsewhere. It created the same demand for raw materials. Moreover, business men and bankers in Germany, as well as in France and Great Britain, were seeking opportunities in backward countries. These powerful influences Bismarck had held in check for a time. The new Emperor William encouraged them. His flamboyant speeches were eagerly welcomed by the influential classes — diplomats and administrators, manufacturers, bankers, professors, and colonial societies. It was not, however, the emperor's speeches but the Industrial Revolution that was forcing Germany to become a world power.

The English are not easily alarmed, but after 1900 there were two aspects of German policy that seemed to the English a little ominous. These were (1) the German activities in Turkey and (2) the German plans for a big navy.

1. *German activities in Turkey.* Unlike Bismarck, the Emperor William took a great interest in Turkey. He established friendly relations with the Turkish government and permitted German officers to help the sultan organize and equip his army. In 1898 he visited the sultan at Constantinople and Damascus. At Damascus he made one of his famous speeches in which he assured the sultan and the 300,000,000 Mohammedans who venerated him as a caliph, that at all times the German Emperor would be their friend. Meantime German and Austrian financiers were organizing the famous " Baghdad Railway " project. The scheme was to construct a great trunk line running from Constantinople through Asia Minor and Syria to Baghdad, and ultimately to the Persian

Gulf. In 1902 the first concessions for such a railway were obtained from the Turkish government; and German and Austrian business men and bankers were already talking of Turkey as a German sphere of influence. The English did not like this very much. Hitherto England had been the " friend " of the sultan, protecting him against the aggressions of Russia. Now it seemed that Russian aggressions in Turkey were less to be feared, perhaps, than the growing influence of Germany.

2. *German plans for a big navy.* But the thing that alarmed England most of all was the emperor's naval policy. Bismarck, not being in favor of colonial expansion, had never favored a big navy. Besides, he felt that if Germany built up a big navy, she would lose the goodwill of England — one of the two things he most wished to avoid. But there was a strong sentiment in Germany in favor of a big navy. " We need a big navy," the Germans said, " to protect our commerce and to defend our colonial interests. Look what happened to Spain in the Spanish-American War! In case of war with England, Germany would be as helpless on the sea as Spain was. That must never happen. Germany has colonies — in Africa; she has concessions — in China and Turkey; she has an immense commerce over seas. These interests must not be left at the mercy of England. Germany must be, if not the first, at least the second, naval power." Therefore the German government adopted a " big navy " program. This navy program, worked out between 1898 and 1906, was intended to make Germany the second naval power in Europe.

The result of these two fears — the fear of France and England for each other, and their common fear of Germany — was the famous *Entente Cordiale* of 1904. The place where the two countries were most likely to come into serious conflict was Egypt and Morocco. Both Egypt and Morocco were nominally parts of the Turkish Empire. Egypt had nevertheless been controlled by England since the military occupation in 1882, and in Morocco French investments and business ventures were so great that the French government already looked upon it as a kind of French sphere of influence. Yet neither government had ever recognized the superior rights of the other in either province. The substance

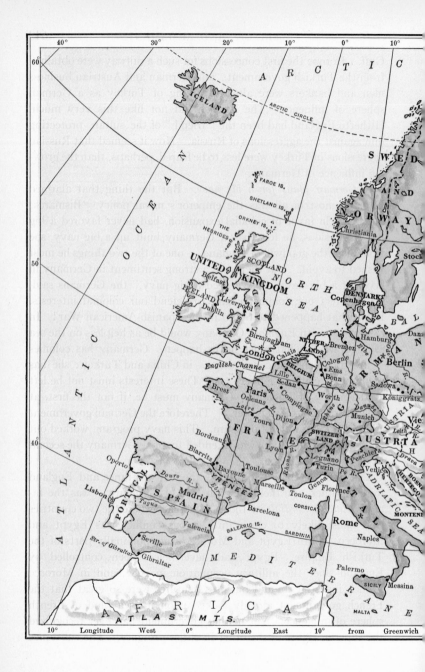

ICELAND

ARCTIC CIRCLE

FAROE IS.

SHETLAND IS.

ORKNEY IS.

THE HEBRIDES

SWEDEN

NORWAY

Christiania

Stock

ARCTIC

ATLANTIC OCEAN

NORTH SEA

UNITED KINGDOM

SCOTLAND

Belfast

IRELAND

Dublin

Liverpool

WALES

Birmingham

London

English Channel

Calais

NETHER-LANDS

BELGIUM

Cologne

Bonn

Ems

Lille

Sedan

Compiègne

DENMARK

Copenhagen

BALTIC

Hamburg

Danz

Elbe

Bremen

Berlin

Sadowa

Königgrätz

Brest

Paris

Orleans

Loire

Tours

R.

Worth

Danube

R.

Munich

AUSTRIA

Vie

Dijon

R.

FRANCE

Bordeaux

Lyon

Rhone R.

SWITZER-LAND

Legnano

Turin

Po R.

Peschiera

Leith

R.

Drava R.

BOSNIA

HERZEGO.

Biarritz

Bayonne

PYRENEES

Toulouse

Marseille

Toulon

Genoa

Florence

Venice

ADRIATIC SEA

MONTE

Oporto

PORTUGAL

Douro R.

SPAIN

Madrid

Ebro R.

Tagus

Barcelona

Valencia

CORSICA

ITALY

Rome

Naples

Lisbon

Str. of Gibraltar

Seville

Gibraltar

BALEARIC IS.

SARDINIA

MEDITERRANEAN

Palermo

SICILY

Messina

MALTA

AFRICA

ATLAS MTS.

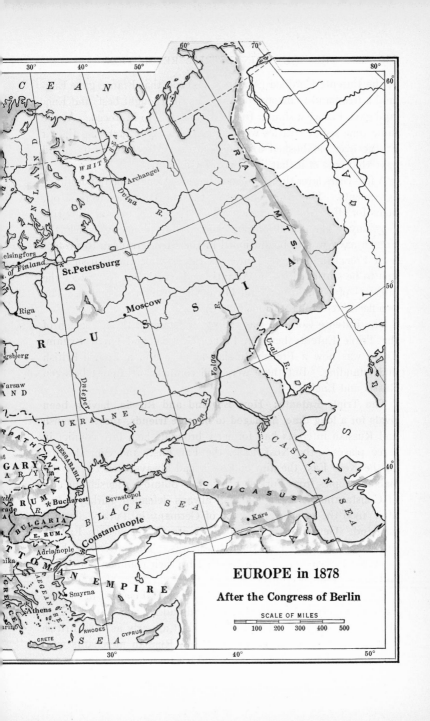

EUROPE in 1878

After the Congress of Berlin

SCALE OF MILES

0   100   200   300   400   500

of the Entente Cordiale (April 8, 1904) was that France gave England a free hand to dispose of Egypt as she thought best, and England gave France a similar freedom in respect to Morocco. At the same time secret treaties were signed with Spain, agreeing that if France ever established a protectorate in Morocco, Spain should have that part of it that lies opposite Gibraltar.

A few years later these agreements were strengthened by military agreements. The army officers of the two countries worked out plans for effective co-operation in case they were ever at war with Germany. The naval officers worked out plans by which the French navy was to be stationed in the Mediterranean to protect both French and English interests there, while the British navy was to be stationed in the Atlantic and North Sea to protect the interests of both France and Great Britain in that region. The two fleets were thus stationed in 1912.

The Entente Cordiale was the second stage in the formation of the Triple Entente between France, Russia, and Great Britain. There was now a French-Russian alliance and a French-British understanding. But there were still conflicts of interest between Russia and England.

The Triple Entente: How England and Russia, having been rivals for a long time, managed to become friends, 1907. English and Russian interests had formerly brought them into conflict in three places — the Near East, the Far East, and central Asia. In the Near East the aim of Russia had always been to free the Balkan peoples from Turkish rule and to obtain for herself the city of Constantinople. England had always defended Turkey. But after 1900 the growing influence of Germany in Turkey alarmed England. Germany seemed to be a greater menace to English interests in the Near East than Russia was. Thus after 1900 England and Russia were drawn together by their common opposition to German influence in the Near East.

For a time English and Russian interests had clashed in the Far East, especially in China. For many decades England had reaped the chief profits of the China trade. But as early as 1888 British consuls in Hong Kong complained that Russian merchants were becoming serious rivals in the silk and tea trade; and at the time of the Boxer Rebellion, Great Britain was much alarmed by the Russian occupation of Manchuria. This was one of the reasons why she made the alliance with Japan in 1902. Then came the Russo-Japanese War; Russia was forced out of Manchuria, the activities of Russia in China declined, and the British-Russian rivalry in the Far East ceased to be a serious one.

There was a third place where British and Russian interests clashed. This was in central Asia Great Britain, extending her conquests north from India, had gained a foothold in Afghanistan, whereas Russia had pushed south from Siberia to the frontiers of Afghanistan. Besides, both Russian and British citizens had invested much money in profitable enterprises in Persia, and the Russian and British governments were equally interested in establishing a sphere of influence there. In 1907, since the rivalry of the two countries in the Near East and the Far East was no longer serious, it seemed possible to come to some agreement in respect to Afghanistan and Persia; and this was the more desirable since both countries had established friendly relations with France.

The outcome of this situation was the Anglo-Russian Convention of 1907. By this convention Russia agreed that Afghanistan lay " outside the sphere of Russian influence "; Great Britain agreed not to annex Afghanistan (for the present at least), and to accord to Russia favorable trade privileges in that country. The agreement in regard to Persia began by saying that Russia and Great Britain would " respect the integrity and independence of Persia." It then proceeded to divide Persia into three zones — North Persia, Central Persia, and South Persia. The two countries agreed (1) that in the northern zone Great Britain would not obtain concessions for her citizens nor object to those demanded by Russia for her citizens; (2) that in the southern zone Russia would not obtain concessions for her citizens or object to those demanded by Great Britain for her citizens; (3) that in the central zone both countries might obtain concessions for their citizens. After this convention was signed the London *Punch* published a cartoon showing the Persian cat being torn into three pieces by the Russian Bear and the British Lion; and in fact the essence of the Anglo-Russian Convention was that the two countries agreed to share and share alike in the exploitation of Persia, to the exclusion of all other countries. (See map pp. 624–625.)

This convention completed the formation of the Triple Entente. The six great powers were now grouped in two rival alliances: (1) the Triple Alliance of Germany, Austria, and Italy; (2) the Triple Entente of France, Russia, and Great Britain. The result was that every international question became more serious than it would otherwise have been, because any question that concerned any one of the great powers, however trivial it might be, was likely to involve them all, since they were all bound together by diplomatic and military alliances. The existence of the great alliances, formed to preserve the peace, really endangered it by raising every dispute to the dignity of a " European crisis."

We shall presently study these crises and see how they led to the Great War. But before doing that there is another thing which must be understood. This is a state of mind, a widely accepted idea that war between races and nations is inevitable, and in the long run even beneficial. One way to make war inevitable is to think that it is. The Great War was the result, partly of the conflicts of the European powers, but partly, also, of the idea that such conflicts, with war as the final arbiter, are grounded in the nature of things and therefore not to be avoided. This idea we may call the " philosophy of imperialism."

The philosophy of imperialism: What it was, and how it helped to bring about the Great War. Many people accepted the philosophy of imperialism because it seemed to be confirmed by natural science. In 1859 Charles Darwin, an English biologist, published a book entitled *The Origin of Species*. It was one of the most important books ever published, because the central idea of the work has had a profound influence upon all modern thought from that time to this. Darwin maintained that the various species of plants and animals as we know them were not originally created in their present form. He said they had been gradually " evolved " from very simple forms of life. Every plant and animal, according to this theory, endeavors to live and reproduce its kind; but more individuals are born than can find proper nourishment. The result is a " struggle for existence " in which the strongest shove aside or

CHARLES DARWIN (1809–1882)

His book, *The Origin of Species* (1859), exerted a greater influence on the trend of thought than any other book of the nineteenth century.

destroy the weak.   Thus, according to this theory of evolution, the law of life is not peace but conflict.

Darwin did not apply this theory to the relations of men to each other.   But other writers did.   They pointed out that from the earliest times tribes and nations had fought for food and wealth and desirable territories.   Those that were the most numerous, or the most intelligent, or possessed the best weapons, shoved aside or enslaved or destroyed the others.   The victors established their customs and laws, their language, their religion — in short, their civilization.   According to these writers the progress of civilization was brought about in the past, and could be continued in the future, only through the incessant conflict of peoples and races.   According to these writers war is one form of this conflict and therefore a natural, and even a necessary, means of human progress.

Meantime, this theory seemed to be confirmed by the great nationalist wars of the period from 1859 to 1871.   The very year that Darwin's book was published, Cavour began the war of Italian independence against Austria; and the next ten years witnessed the Austro-Prussian War, the Franco-Prussian War, and the American Civil War.   For the most part, people thought of these wars as victories in the cause of human freedom.   The Italians had at last won independence from Austrian domination.   The Germans had achieved what they had so long struggled for in vain: national unity and constitutional government.   The French won once more what they had previously won and lost: republican liberty.   The Americans, after thirty years of heated discussion over slavery, had abolished it.   National independence, political liberty, the abolition of slavery — who could doubt that these were worthy objects?   Who could doubt that the achievement of these worthy objects was a victory for human progress?   And yet these worthy objects had been achieved by war.   They had been achieved, as Bismarck said, not by peaceful discussion but by " blood and iron."

But if liberty could be achieved only by blood and iron, must it not be maintained by the same means?   It was easy to think so. " In time of peace," said President Grant, repeating an old Roman proverb, " prepare for war."   For fifty years following the wars of national independence, every country, according to its fears and its abilities, enlarged and perfected its army until Europe became, as someone said, an " armed camp." Not for aggression were the national armies perfected, but for defense. Since war was always possible and sometimes necessary, it was thought to be the sacred duty of every free people to defend its hard-won independence.

In strengthening the spirit of nationalism and of militarism no one did more during these years than Bismarck. From 1871 to 1890 he was the virtual ruler of Germany and the central figure of Europe. For twenty years his caustic epigrams and cynical observations were everywhere known and everywhere repeated. Everywhere people were familiar with his striking portrait — the massive face whose rugged, deep-lined features seemed hammered out of bronze; the inscrutable eyes looking darkly and ominously out from under the spiked iron helmet of the German army officer. Lesser rulers and statesmen imitated his practices without his skill, and accepted his philosophy without tempering it with his common sense. His philosophy was simple and easily learned. He took it for granted that any nation which wished to play a great part in the modern world must rely upon shrewd diplomacy backed by an adequate army. Bismarck, like Napoleon, believed that " God is on the side of the big battalions."

The philosophy of imperialism provided a justification not only for the national conflicts in Europe, but also for the ruthless exploitation of backward countries. " By what right," many people asked, " do European countries deprive the Africans of their country and exact concessions from the Chinese against their will? " " By the right of conquest, the right of the stronger," some people replied. But most people were too tender-minded to be satisfied with so bald and brutal an answer as that. They wanted to think that in taking control of Africa and Asia the European governments were doing something that it was necessary for them to do, something that was beneficial to everyone concerned.

There were plenty of politicians and writers who were able to give them the answer they wanted. The Frenchman, or the Englishman, or the American, or the German reasoned in this way: " My country is a great country; its laws and customs are excellent — the very best in fact. It would be well if all people were as moral and intelligent and wisely governed as we are. It is a pity that the Africans, the Filipinos, and the Hindus live in ignorance, worship false gods, and adhere to degrading customs; a pity that they cannot or will not develop the natural resources of their rich countries for the benefit of mankind. Is it therefore not the right, is it not the duty, of the more civilized peoples to do for the backward peoples what they cannot or will not do for themselves? The British take control of Egypt, the French of Tunis, the Americans of the Philippines, because they have the power. It is right for them to use this power because by so doing they are spreading throughout the world a superior civilization."

It is a mistake to suppose that this philosophy flourished only in Germany. It was preached by prominent writers in every country. An influential American writer before the war was Captain A. T. Mahan, the author of popular books on the influence of sea power in history. In 1912 he published a book entitled *Armaments and Arbitration,* in which he maintained that if arbitration were substituted for armies and navies, European civilization " might not survive, having lost its fighting energy." A far more influential American was Theodore Roosevelt, the beloved " Teddy." He was always preaching the " strenuous life." Diplomacy, he said, should be supported by the " big stick." It was his idea that America should " play a great part in the world, and especially . . . perform those deeds of blood, of valor, which above everything else bring national renown."

Similar ideas were expressed by British writers. In 1890 the famous scientist, Karl Pearson, delivered a lecture on *National Life from the Standpoint of Science.* His idea is expressed in the following sentence: " History shows me one way, and one way only, in which a high state of civilization has been produced — namely, the struggle of race with race, and the survival of the physically and mentally fitter race." About 1898 Wilfred Scawin Blunt noted in his diary that the imperialist philosophy was becoming popular in England, especially among the younger men. Gerald Balfour, Mr. Blunt says, maintained that " patriotism was the imperial instinct of Englishmen, who should support their country's quarrels even when in the wrong"; and this idea he "based on the application to . . . politics of Darwin's law of the selection of the fittest, or rather of what is an exaggerated interpretation of that law." George Wyndam and the "young imperialists," according to Mr. Blunt, "are going in for England's overlordship and they won't stand half measures." These ideas Mr. Blunt called a species of "scientific inhumanity."

German writers were not the only, but only the most systematic and thoroughgoing, expounders of the philosophy of imperialism. In 1883 Gumplowicz published a scholarly book of great influence entitled *The Race Conflict*, in which he aimed to prove that " the perpetual struggle of races is the law of history, while perpetual peace is the dream of idealists." Heinrich von Treitschke had even greater influence on popular thought in Germany. From 1874 until his death in 1896 he lectured at the University of Berlin to crowds of students and others, preaching with passionate conviction the doctrine of patriotic nationalism, and of militarism and war as a means of human progress. His ideas are expressed in a book translated under the title *Politics*. " War," he said, " is both justifiable and moral, and the hope of perpetual peace is not only impossible, but immoral as well." " Our age is the age of iron; and if the strong vanquish the weak, it is the law of life."

During the ten years before the war a widely read German writer was Friedrich von Bernhardi, whose most important books were *Germany and the Next War*, and *Our Future*. The latter was translated under the misleading title *Britain as Germany's Vassal*, in 1912. He said:

If it were not for war, we should probably find that inferior races would overcome healthy, youthful ones by their wealth and numbers. (p. 111)

We must strenuously combat the peace propaganda. . . . We must become convinced that war is a political necessity, and that it is fought in the interest of biological, social, and moral progress. (p.105)

These are only a few of the many examples of the philosophy of imperialism that might be given. It is clear that some writers formulated this philosophy in a *realistic* way : they emphasized the fact that the strong will naturally shove aside the weak. Other writers formulated it in a more *idealistic* way : they emphasized the notion that it is the duty of the superior races to civilize the inferior. The latter method was the more effective because it appealed to a greater number of people.

Of this latter group of writers one of the most influential was Rudyard Kipling, the author of many stories and poems. (*Plain Tales from the Hills, The Seven Seas*, etc.) Kipling was an artist, a heaven-born teller of interesting tales in prose and verse. He describes vividly, and often with brutal frankness, the relations of the English and the natives subject to British rule; and yet he contrives to invest the whole business with a kind of romantic glamour. He makes it appear that after all the English, in spreading their empire throughout the world, are sacrificing their ease and comfort for the benefit of mankind. In one famous poem, " The White Man's Burden," Kipling expressed the essence of this sentimental and romantic faith:

> Take up the White Man's burden,
> Send forth the best ye breed,
> Go bind your sons to exile,
> To serve your captive's need,
> To wait in heavy harness
> On fluttered folk and wild —
> Your new-caught sullen people,
> Half devil and half child.

We have now described the formation of the great alliances — the Triple Alliance, and the Triple Entente; and we have set forth the philosophy which justified them. It remains to be seen how the conflict between these alliances, and the acts of men who were influenced by this philosophy, led to the Great War.

Between 1905 and 1914 five serious diplomatic conflicts or " crises " occurred. Two of them (the first and second Morocco crises, 1905, 1911) greatly intensified the hostility between France and Germany. Two of them (the Bosnian crisis, 1908, and the Balkan War crisis, 1912–1913) greatly intensified the hostility between Austria and Russia. The last one (the Sarajevo crisis, 1914) brought on the war. All of these disputes were concerned with the same fundamental rivalries. Each one seemed more serious than the last. As we review them now, they all convey an ominous warning, like the bumping of a derailed train on the ties before it takes the fatal plunge into the ditch.

II. THE CONFLICT OF THE GREAT ALLIANCES

First and second Morocco crises, 1905, 1911: How they intensified the hostility between France and Germany. After the "cordial understanding" between England and France the French government at once took steps to strengthen its control of Morocco. The finances of that country needed attention. The sultan had spent money recklessly; and, unable to increase his revenue by taxes, he had borrowed through French bankers the sum of 62,500,000 francs, pledging 60 per cent of his customs duties as security for the loan. For these reasons the French government felt that the time had come to set the affairs of Morocco in order. Late in 1904 the sultan was accordingly asked to agree to certain reforms. These included: (1) the establishment in Morocco of a military force commanded by French officers; (2) the establishment in Morocco, under French direction, of a state bank to manage the sultan's finances. These reforms, if agreed to, would have given France the same kind of control in Morocco that Great Britain had in Egypt.

At first the German government did nothing; but a few months later it intervened in a most dramatic fashion. The Emperor William made an official visit to the sultan of Morocco. Landing from the royal yacht at Tangier, March, 1905, the kaiser mounted a horse, rode through the streets of the city, and made one of his famous speeches. Addressing the representative of the sultan, he said:

> Today I pay my visit to the sultan in his character of independent sovereign. I hope that, under the sultan's sovereignty, a free Morocco will remain open to the pacific competition of all nations, without monopoly and without annexations. I am resolved to do all in my power properly to safeguard the interests of Germany, since I regard the sultan as being an absolutely free sovereign.

The result of the emperor's visit was that the sultan refused to accept the reforms proposed by France unless they were approved by the European powers. The German government also demanded that the French proposals be submitted to a conference of the powers. From the point of view of international law, Germany had every right to protest. From the point of view of international etiquette, her method of doing so had the appearance of a defiance of France — almost of an insult, like a slap in the face, publicly administered. What then would France do? The French foreign minister, Delcassé, was ready to refuse the German demands, even if it meant war. But the French premier, M. Rouvier, was unwilling to run the risk. He therefore agreed to refer the question of reforms in Morocco to a conference of the European powers. His concession on behalf of peace was generally regarded as a blow to French pride and a victory for German diplomacy.

The conference assembled at Algeciras, in Spain, January 16, 1906. After three months of negotiation it adopted the Act of Algeciras, April 7. In form, the Act of Algeciras recognized the " sovereignty " of the Sultan of Morocco, guaranteed the " integrity " of his territory, and declared that the country should be freely open to the trade of all nations. In reality, the act deprived the sultan of his sovereignty and placed the country largely under the control of France and Spain. This was accomplished chiefly through two provisions: (1) the establishment of a police force commanded by French and Spanish officers; (2) the establishment, to manage the finances of the country, of a state bank at Tangier, in which France, Spain, and Great Britain had the controlling interest. The Act of Algeciras was a great diplomatic victory for France.

The state bank established at Tangier did not succeed in straightening out the sultan's finances. Every year the public debt increased. This was partly due to the extravagance of the sultan, partly to the conflict between the natives and the French. By 1910 the sultan's debt to foreign (chiefly French, Spanish, and English) bondholders was nearly three times what it had been in 1904. Meantime the native police force, commanded by French and Spanish officers, was unable to maintain order. The presence of the foreigners was offensive to the natives. As the debt increased, it was necessary to increase the taxes, and these still further incensed the natives and multiplied the uprisings. M. Tardieu

MARKET OUTSIDE THE WALLS OF TANGIER, MOROCCO

William II visited the sultan in this city in 1905, at the time when he made his famous protest against French intervention in Morocco, thus precipitating the first "Morocco crisis."

put the situation in a nutshell: "Without money, no soldiers; for in the absence of pay they desert. Without soldiers, no money; for taxes do not come in unless they are collected. It was a vicious circle." It was indeed! The more the French did to restore order, the more disorder there was; the more they did to help the sultan pay his debts, the greater his debt became. The French government therefore resolved to help the sultan still further by relieving him of all responsibility. In 1911, on the ground that the lives of foreigners were in danger, a French army marched to the interior and occupied the capital city, Fez.

The occupation of Fez startled Europe. It was taken for granted that the French intended to transform the "independent"

Morocco into a French "protectorate." Once more Germany protested, in the same dramatic way as before. In July, 1911, a German gunboat, manned by 125 men, entered the port of Agadir on the west coast of Morocco. Another crisis was at hand. Throughout the summer of 1911 everyone was asking, "Will there be war?" Unless either Germany or France backed down, war was indeed almost certain.

France had no intention of yielding this time, as she had in 1905. One reason was that her army was larger and better equipped. Another was that she could count with much greater certainty on the support of Great Britain. The British government requested Germany to withdraw its gunboats; and in order to make it clear that England would support France in this quarrel, Lloyd George, the chancellor of the exchequer, made a famous speech in which he said:

I would make great sacrifices for peace. . . . But if . . . peace could only be preserved by . . . allowing Britain to be treated as if she were of no account in the council of nations, then I say emphatically that peace at that price would be a humiliation intolerable for a great country like ours to endure.

Unwilling to fight both France and Great Britain, Germany yielded. She agreed that France might establish a protectorate in Morocco. As a compensation, France agreed to cede to Germany a part of the French Congo.

The crisis was over, and everyone was relieved. But the crisis had important results. It intensified the hostility of the Germans towards the French, and of the French towards the Germans. It intensified the rivalry of the great alliances — the Triple Alliance and the Triple Entente. Above all, it left many people in every country with a feeling that a European war, happily averted in this instance, was only postponed. More than ever before people felt, and said, "After all, a war is inevitable; it is only a question of time."

The Bosnian crisis, 1908, and the Balkan War crisis, 1913: How they intensified the hostility between Austria and Russia. These crises were but the prelude to the Sarajevo crisis of 1914 which brought on the Great War. They all had to do with the rivalries of

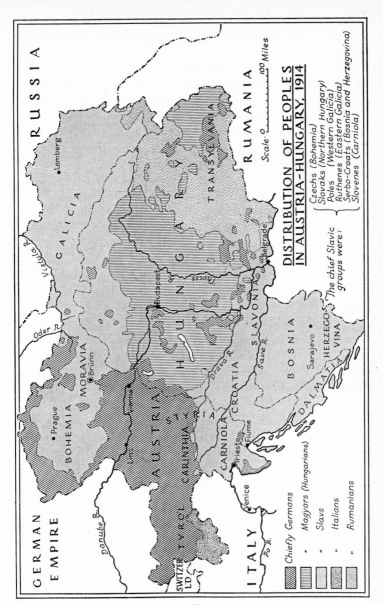

DISTRIBUTION OF PEOPLES
IN AUSTRIA-HUNGARY, 1914

Scale 0 _____ 100 Miles

The chief Slavic groups were:

{ Czechs (Bohemia)
Slovaks (Northern Hungary)
Poles (Western Galicia)
Ruthenes (Eastern Galicia)
Serbo-Croats (Bosnia and Herzegovina)
Slovenes (Carniola) }

▨ Chiefly Germans
▤ " Magyars (Hungarians)
░ " Slavs
▥ " Italians
▦ " Rumanians

Austria, Russia, the Balkan states, and Turkey. These rivalries need a little explaining.

The first thing to get clear is the nature of the Austro-Hungarian Monarchy. The main point is that a great number of different and hostile nationalities were bound together, much against the will of some of them. There were in the monarchy nearly 50,000,000 people. Of these, something more than one-fourth were Germans, something less than one-fourth were Magyars (Hungarians), and about one-half were Slavs. But the Slavs, although more numerous than either the Germans or the Magyars, were less influential in governing the monarchy. There were two reasons for that. First, they were themselves divided into many groups — Poles, Czechs, Slovaks, Ruthenians, Croats, Serbs, and Slovenes. Second, the Slavs were located around the fringes of the monarchy, while the Germans and Magyars occupied the center. For these reasons the Germans and the Magyars were the dominant groups. They really governed the monarchy, while the Slavs were subject nations.

The Slavs were therefore discontented. They felt that they were governed by alien peoples who disliked them, disregarded their interests, and discriminated against their language, their customs, and their religion. The result was that many of the Slav groups within the monarchy wanted to get out of it. The Poles wanted to join with the German and Russian Poles to form an independent Poland. The Czechs and Slovaks wished to govern themselves as they had formerly done when Bohemia was a kingdom. The Serbo-Croats and the Slovenes wished to be united with the independent Kingdom of Serbia to form a " greater Serbia."

This desire for political independence and union with their Slav brothers outside the monarchy is known as the Pan-Slav movement. The most active center of the movement was the Kingdom of Serbia. Little Serbia wished to become a greater Serbia, and the first step was the annexation of the province of Bosnia-Herzegovina, which was nominally part of the Turkish Empire but by the Congress of Berlin in 1878 had been turned over to Austria for purposes of administration (see p. 636). By annexing this province, Serbia would double her population and at the same time obtain an

© *National Feature Photos*
An Old Street in Biskra, Algeria, Which Once Belonged to Turkey

outlet on the sea. But what chance had Serbia of annexing this province? Alone, little Serbia had no chance at all, since both Turkey and Austria would object. But Serbia was supported by Russia. The Russians sympathized with their Slav brothers and the Russian government would be sure to support them in their effort to be free from both Turkish and Austrian rule. Thus back of the scheme for a greater Serbia was Russia, and Russia was allied with France and Great Britain. From the point of view of the Austro-Hungarian government Serbia was merely a pawn in the hands of the Triple Entente. This is why the Austro-Hungarian government felt that the movement for a greater Serbia must be suppressed at all hazards.

In 1907 the Austro-Hungarian government therefore determined that, upon the first favorable opportunity, it would block the Serbian scheme by annexing Bosnia-Herzegovina. The opportunity came with the so-called Young Turk Revolution of 1908. The Young Turk Revolution had been brewing for some time.

Many patriotic Turks, especially those of good families who had traveled in Europe and studied in French and German universities, were much concerned with the weakness of Turkey. Let us put ourselves in the place of a patriotic young Turk in the year 1907. As he looks back over the history of the nineteenth century, these are the events that strike him as significant. In 1829 Greece, with the aid of Russia, France, and England, won its independence. In 1830 France seized the Turkish province of Algeria. In 1878 the European powers at the Congress of Berlin deprived Turkey of Serbia, Montenegro, Rumania, Cyprus, and virtually of Bulgaria and Bosnia-Herzegovina. In 1881 France seized Tunis. In 1882 Great Britain occupied Egypt. In 1906 Morocco was virtually turned over to France and Spain. It seemed that Turkey was no more than a tasty artichoke which the European powers were eating, one leaf at a time.

In order to prevent the further dissolution of the empire, patriotic Turks formed the Young Turk Association. Its motto was " Union and Progress." By *progress* the Young Turks meant that Turkey must adopt the European form of government, introduce European machines and industrial methods, develop the natural resources of the country, and so become strong, like the European countries. By *union* the Young Turks meant that Turkey must use this new power to defend herself against aggression, and even to reunite with the empire those provinces which the European powers had taken from her. With these aims in view, the Young Turks staged a revolution in July, 1908. The old sultan, Abdul Hamid, easily gave way. A liberal constitution was then proclaimed. Once in control of the government, the Young Turks introduced some reforms and assembled a Turkish national parliament. To this parliament the people of Bosnia-Herzegovina were invited to send representatives. This act furnished the Austro-Hungarian government with the opportunity it was looking for. In order to prevent Bosnia-Herzegovina from being either reannexed to Turkey or annexed to Serbia, it announced, on October 7, 1908, that it was formally annexed to Austria-Hungary.

The annexation of Bosnia to Austria created the diplomatic crisis of 1908. In Serbia there was tremendous excitement. The

THE 13TH ARMY CORPS CROSSING THE SAVE RIVER

From a sketch by Franz Schlegel in the *Illustrirte Zeitung*, 1878. This was an incident in the first occupation of Bosnia by the Austrians, determined upon by the Congress of Berlin.

hope of making a greater Serbia, with an outlet on the sea, had received a serious setback. Crowds gathered in the streets of Sofia crying, " Down with Austria ! " The Austrian flag was burned. The windows of the Austrian embassy were smashed. A Serbian newspaper demanded " immediate mobilization and war to life and death against the [Austrian] monarchy." Russia supported Serbia, saying that the annexation was a violation of the Treaty of Berlin and not to be permitted. Thus the issue was clearly drawn, and war was likely to result unless either Austria or Russia yielded. Which power would back down? It depended on their respective allies.

The German emperor was furious with Austria. He said that the annexation was a species of " brigandage " and in any case a mistake, since it would weaken German and Austrian influence with the Turkish government and so endanger the Baghdad Railway project. But the German chancellor, Von Bülow, said that Germany must support Austria without reserve. When it comes to a " question of bending or breaking," he said, " Russia will climb down from her high horse and will also call her vassal Serbia to order."

His prophecy proved correct. Russia could not count on the support either of France or of Great Britain. Both governments protested against the annexation, but neither was willing to go to war in support of Serbian interests. They made this clear to Russia, and so Russia yielded and warned Serbia that she must yield also. " Do not begin a war now," the Russian minister Guchkov said to the Serbian minister, " for that would be suicide. Conceal your intentions and prepare yourselves. Your days of joy will come."

Thus the Bosnian crisis passed, but Serbia and Russia began at once to prepare for the " days of joy " to come. After 1908 Russia tried to unite the Balkan states in a league which she could use either against Turkey or Austria. This was difficult because Bulgaria and Serbia were enemies of long standing. But they had one thing in common — hatred of Turkey. Therefore, in 1912, Russia finally induced Bulgaria to sign a secret treaty with Serbia which provided that in case of a successful war with Turkey Bulgaria should annex the greater part of Turkish Macedonia, while Serbia should annex the rest of Macedonia and the province of Albania on the Adriatic coast. Shortly afterwards the two states entered into military conventions with Greece. These arrangements were known as the Balkan League of 1912.

The Balkan states were now eager for a war with Turkey — especially so since Turkey had become involved in a war with Italy over the possession of Tripoli. They therefore complained that Turkey was oppressing her Christian subjects in Macedonia. They had, however, agreed not to begin a war with Turkey without Russia's consent; and Russia, not yet ready for the war, refused to give her consent. But the Balkan states were not to be restrained. Little Montenegro suddenly declared war on her own account, and invited the Balkan League to join in a " holy war against the infidel Turk." In spite of the protest of Russia and the other great powers, Bulgaria, Serbia, and Greece entered the war (October, 1912). The four states, with well-equipped armies totaling 750,000 soldiers, quickly and hopelessly defeated the Turkish army of 400,000 and occupied the greater part of European Turkey.

The first Balkan War created another European crisis. Again

RUSSIA

HUNGARY

MOLDAVIA

BESSARABIA

WALACHIA

R U MANIA

Belgrade

BOSNIA

Bucharest

Danube R.

②

BLACK

SEA

Nish

SERBIA

BULGARIA

Slivnitza

Sofia

MONTE-
NEGRO

Cetinje

Scutari

Dulcigno

ALBANIA

Durazzo

Kirk Kilise

Adrianople

Luleburgaz

Constantinople

①

MACEDONIA

Monastir

THRACE TURKEY

A D R I A T I C   S E A

Salonika

MARMORA
SEA

THESSALY

Janina

AEGEAN

TURKEY

IN

SEA

I O N I A N   I S L A N D S

G R E E C E

SEA

ASIA

Smyrna

I O N I A N

SEA

MOREA

Athens

Rhodes

M E D I T E R R A N E A N   S E A

Scale: 0 ———— 100 Miles

CRETE
to Greece 1913

TERRITORIAL ADJUSTMENTS FOLLOWING THE BALKAN WARS, 1913

665

the danger point was the hostility of Serbia and Austria. Serbia's chief object in the war was to obtain Albania. This would give her that outlet on the sea which Austria had prevented her from getting by annexing Bosnia in 1908. But Austria was now just as determined to prevent Serbia from getting Albania as she had formerly been to prevent her from getting Bosnia. This once more raised the old question: Would Russia now support Serbia? A European war once more seemed possible. In order to avert it the great powers met in conference at London. Austria insisted that Serbia must not get Albania. Once more Russia yielded. She warned Serbia that " we are not going to war with the Triple Alliance on account of a Serbian seaport in Albania." The powers agreed, therefore, that the province of Albania should be erected into an independent kingdom. Thus, to preserve the peace, the interests of Serbia were once more sacrificed.

Serbia, prevented by Austria from obtaining Albania, asked for a larger share of Macedonia than had been agreed to in the treaty with Bulgaria. Bulgaria refused. Serbia therefore declared war on Bulgaria and was shortly joined by Greece, Montenegro, Rumania, and Turkey. This was the second Balkan War (1913). Bulgaria was hopelessly defeated and forced to accept the Treaty of Bucharest (August 10, 1913). By this treaty Bulgaria's share of Macedonia was greatly diminished. Serbia obtained the greater part of Macedonia, including Monastir. Greece obtained Salonika and the coast of Thessaly. Rumania obtained a slice of Bulgaria. Turkey recovered part of Thrace.

Thus another crisis had passed. Again Russia and Serbia had yielded to the demands of Austria and Germany. But more than ever Serbia and Russia were determined to gain their ends. At the Bucharest peace conference the Serbian minister, Pashitch, said to the Russian minister: " The first game [against Turkey] is won; we must now prepare for the second, against Austria." Within less than a year the final and fatal crisis occurred.

The Sarajevo crisis, June 28–July 28, 1914: How the death of an archduke was of vital interest to five great powers. During the Great War not much was known about the events that led up to it. The government of each country wished to show that it was not responsible; the people in each country wished to believe this. Therefore the people in Germany and Austria were told, and believed, that France, Russia, and Great Britain were responsible for the war. The people in France, Great Britain, and Russia were told, and believed, that Germany had deliberately plotted to bring on the war in order to establish her ascendancy in Europe. Since the war a great deal of new information has come to light; and today few historians who have studied the question carefully believe that any one government or group of allied governments was alone responsible. The truth seems to be that each government was determined to defend what it regarded as its " vital interests " and to remain faithful to its treaty obligations. Each government desired to do this without bringing on a general European war; but each government was willing to *risk* a general war rather than to abandon its vital interests or prove unfaithful to its treaty obligations. The war was the result of what *all* the great powers did rather than of what any one of them did. Let us see what each one did and how the sum of their acts was the Great War.

After the Balkan Wars Serbian propaganda against the Austro-Hungarian Monarchy became more unrestrained than ever. The members of a certain secret political society, together with a certain Dimitrievich (an officer in the Serbian army), were much alarmed because the Austrian emperor, old Francis Joseph, would soon be succeeded by the Archduke Francis Ferdinand. Francis Ferdinand, they felt, would introduce reforms tending to satisfy the Austrian Slavs and thus make them less desirous of becoming part of the greater Serbia. They therefore decided to assassinate the archduke, and they enlisted some young Bosnians in the plot. When it was learned that the archduke intended to visit Sarajevo, in Bosnia, to attend a military review, the conspirators decided to assassinate him there. Members of the Serbian government knew of the plot long before the archduke visited Sarajevo. The Serbian government, however, did nothing, or next to nothing, to suppress the plot, and on June 28, 1914, the Archduke Francis Ferdinand was killed in the streets of Sarajevo. This crime was the immediate exciting cause of the Great War.

The Austrian government, convinced that the Serbian propaganda threatened the existence of the Austro-Hungarian monarchy, had already determined to take the first opportunity to eliminate Serbia " as a political power in the Balkans." The assassination of Francis Ferdinand provided a most favorable opportunity. The Austrian government therefore determined to make war on Serbia, if it could count on German support in case Russia came to the aid of Serbia. On July 5, 1914, the German government said in effect to Austria: " Serbia needs to be taught a lesson. The assassination of the archduke is a most excellent opportunity for doing it. Go ahead with your war. Russia is not yet ready for war, and she will probably back down as she did in 1908 and 1913. But if Russia makes war on you in behalf of Serbia, Germany will stand by you, as she is bound by treaty to do."

With this assurance of German support, Austria presented an ultimatum to Serbia on July 23. The ultimatum required the Serbian government to agree, within forty-eight hours, to certain demands, the chief of which were the following: (1) the suppression of all anti-Austrian publications; (2) the suppression of anti-Austrian secret societies; (3) the elimination of anti-Austrian propaganda from the schools; (4) the removal of Serbian officials guilty of anti-Austrian propaganda; (5) that Austrian officials should be permitted to take part in suppressing the anti-Austrian propaganda in Serbia; (6) that Austrian officials should be permitted to take part in the Serbian proceedings against the authors of the Sarajevo crime.

The most important of these demands for Austria, the most humiliating for Serbia, were the fifth and sixth. On July 25 the Serbian government replied to the ultimatum, accepting all of the demands except the fifth and sixth. These it did not reject outright; but further information was requested as to the exact meaning of the two demands. The reply of the Serbian government was judged unsatisfactory, and on July 28 the Austrian government declared war on Serbia.

What, then, would Russia do? The most influential man in the Russian government was the minister of foreign affairs — Sazonov. Sazonov was bitterly hostile to Austria, and he believed that a war with Austria was necessary sooner or later in order to maintain the prestige of Russia and to free the Austrian and Balkan Slavs from Austrian domination. He would have preferred to postpone the war, but now that Serbia was seriously threatened he determined to support her at all hazards. On July 25 he told the British ambassador that Russia was prepared to " face all the risks of war." This time, if Sazonov had his way, there would be no backing down as there had been in 1908 and 1913.

Why was Russia prepared to face all the risks of war? Because, as Sazonov said, " France has placed herself unreservedly on Russia's side." The most influential man in the French government was the president — Raymond Poincaré. He was a man of boundless energy, clear convictions, and great ability in imposing his views on his colleagues. The great French war premier, Clemenceau, said of him : " He knows everything and understands nothing." Poincaré believed sincerely that France was in great danger from German hostility and that French vital interests required a close alliance with Russia and Great Britain. He and his colleagues in the French government therefore assured Russia, several times during the crucial days from July 25 to July 31, that if Russia became involved in a war with Germany, France would " fulfill her treaty obligations." This was understood by the Russian government to mean that France would make war on Germany.

Thus up to July 28 the situation seemed to be shaping as follows. Austria was determined to make war on Serbia. If Austria made war on Serbia, Russia was determined to make war on Austria. If Russia made war on Austria, Germany was determined to make war on Russia. If Germany made war on Russia, France was determined to make war on Germany. In this event what was the British government determined to do?

No one knew what the British government would do. The foreign minister, Sir Edward Grey, would not promise France that Great Britain would support France and Russia, nor would he promise Germany that Great Britain would remain neutral. He was desperately anxious to prevent a general war, and between July 20 and 26 he made three proposals for settling the quarrel peaceably. The first two proposals fell through largely on account of the objections of France and Russia; the last one fell through largely because Germany rejected it. Thus until July 28, the day on which Austria declared war on Serbia, the British government was

Wide World Photos

VISCOUNT GREY OF FALLODON, 1862–

In 1916, owing to failing eyesight, Sir Edward Grey resigned his office as secretary of foreign affairs and accepted a peerage.

trying to find a peaceful method of settling the quarrel, while the other four powers were either indifferent or opposed to its proposals.

The truth is that until July 28 the governments of the great powers felt that the situation, while very serious, would probably not bring on a general war. Each side hoped, and because it hoped was inclined to believe, that the other side would back down at the last moment. But the Austrian declaration of war on Serbia on July 28 was a turning-point in the crisis. From that day the great powers were faced with the startling fact that unless something was done quickly the "inevitable" war was upon them.

The Sarajevo crisis, July 28–August 4, 1914: How the vital interests and treaty obligations of the great powers involved them in the Austro-Serbian War. Until July 28 none of the great powers except Great Britain had done much, if anything, to preserve the peace. But on July 28 Germany changed her attitude. By that time it was clear that Russia would not back down. Besides, the Serbian government had accepted the Austrian demands, with some reservations. Emperor William said that the Serbian reply to Austria's demands was a great victory for Austria, and that as a result of it " every cause of war [on Serbia] has vanished." Supported by England, Germany therefore proposed (July 28) the following plan: (1) that Austria should occupy Belgrade as a pledge that Serbia would carry out her promises; (2) that Austria should assure Russia that she had no intention of annexing any

Serbian territory; (3) that military operations, both by Austria and by Russia, should be suspended in order to give the powers time to find a settlement satisfactory to Serbia, Austria, and Russia.

This was the so-called " pledge plan." It reached Vienna on July 29, and was accompanied by a note in which the German government urged Austria in strong terms to accept it. On July 30 the German government sent a second note to Austria which stated in part:

We stand, in case Austria refuses all mediation, before a conflagration in which England will be against us; Italy and Rumania, to all appearances, will not go with us, and we shall be opposed by four great powers. On Germany, thanks to England's opposition, the principal burden of the fight would fall. Austria's political prestige, . . . as well as her just claims against Serbia, could all be satisfied by the occupation of Belgrade or other places. . . . Under these circumstances, we must urgently and impressively suggest . . . the acceptance of mediation on the above-mentioned honorable conditions. The responsibility for the consequences that would otherwise follow would be an uncommonly heavy one, both for Austria and for us.

Until war actually broke out, Germany continued to urge Austria, in the strongest terms, to be satisfied with some plan of mediation.

While Germany was trying to restrain Austria, what were Great Britain and France doing to restrain Russia? Sir Edward Grey accepted the pledge plan as an excellent one. He advised Russia to suspend military operations and to agree to the plan proposed by Germany, but he took the view that unless Austria could be induced to accept it first there was no reason to put much pressure on Russia to do so. His chief effort to maintain peace after July 28 consisted in urging Germany to put pressure on Austria.

France did even less than Great Britain to restrain Russia. The vital question on July 29–30 was whether Russia would mobilize her army against both Austria and Germany. Every government in Europe understood that such action, being equivalent to a declaration of war, would precipitate a general European war without fail. July 29 the Russian government telegraphed to Paris asking whether France would approve of Russian mobilization. The French government replied that France was " fully prepared to fulfill all the obligations of the alliance," but it advised Russia to carry out her mobilization as secretly as possible so that Germany would have no excuse for mobilization.

Meanwhile, what of Austria and Russia? Could they have been restrained in any case? Austria refused to listen to German advice. The Austrian government refused the pledge plan, stating that military operations against Serbia could not be suspended. The attitude of Austria was this: We are bound to go on with the war against Serbia; if Russia intervenes, the responsibility for a European war will be hers. The Russian government was equally stubborn. July 29 it was decided to mobilize the entire Russian army against both Austria and Germany. A few hours later the tsar, as a result of a personal appeal from the German emperor, ordered the mobilization against Germany suspended. But on July 30 Sazonov and the military leaders induced the tsar to change his mind, and the mobilization against Germany continued. Russia's attitude was this: We are determined to make war on Austria unless Austria abandons her war on Serbia; if a European war is precipitated it will be Austria's fault, not ours.

The mobilization of the Russian army was equivalent to a declaration of war against Austria and Germany. Every government in Europe took it for granted that Germany would mobilize immediately, since in modern war any country with twenty-four hours' start has a great advantage. Yet Emperor William still hoped to preserve the peace. Instead of mobilizing his army at once he proclaimed the " state of imminent danger of war." He then notified the Russian government that unless Russia suspended her mobilization within twelve hours, Germany would declare war on Russia. The German ultimatum was sent at 3 : 30 P.M. on July 31. The emperor waited — not twelve hours only, but twenty-four hours — for the Russian reply, which never came. Finally, at six o'clock in the afternoon of August 1, Germany declared war on Russia.

On July 31 Germany sent an ultimatum to France as well as to Russia. The French government was asked to say, within forty-eight hours, whether it would remain neutral in case of a war between Germany and Russia. The French government delayed its answer until the next day. On the evening of July 31 the ministers held a conference at President Poincaré's house, after which, at one o'clock in the morning of August 1, the Russian ambassador telegraphed to the Russian government: " The French minister of war declared to me with hearty high spirits that the French government has firmly decided on war." Thus it seems that even before Germany declared war on Russia, the French government had decided to support Russia. On the afternoon of August 1 the French government replied to the German ultimatum by saying that it would " consult its interests." The French army began to mobilize the same day, and two days later Germany declared war on France.

Thus on August 1 Russia and France were virtually at war with Austria and Germany. Both sides were desperately anxious to know what Great Britain would do. But the British government was still unable to promise either to come in or stay out. Sir Edward Grey told the German ambassador that he could not formulate any terms on which Great Britain would remain neutral. He told the French ambassador that he could not promise that Great Britain would make war on Germany. Why was it that as late as August 1, when the European war had already begun, Sir Edward could make no promises to either side?

The reason is that in 1911 Sir Edward had, without the knowledge of Parliament, secretly arranged with the French government that the French fleet should safeguard both French and British interests in the Mediterranean, while the British fleet should safeguard both French and British interests in the English Channel. The result was that in 1914 France was open to German naval attack unless the British fleet defended her coasts. Sir Edward could not promise Germany to remain neutral, because he firmly believed that Great Britain was bound by these arrangements to join France in the war. But he could not promise France to join her in the war because he did not know whether Parliament, which alone could declare war, would be willing to do so. He had in fact got himself into a bad hole. He hoped to make good his promises to France, but in order to do so he had to wait until something happened to convince the British Parliament and people that it was necessary to declare war on Germany.

This something which he was waiting for was the German invasion of Belgium. It was well known that the easiest way for Germany to attack France was through Belgium, and all the German military plans had been made on that basis. But the English people had always objected strongly to having any Continental great power gain control of either Belgium or Holland. They had often fought to prevent France from doing so — in the time of Louis XIV, in the time of Napoleon. Sir Edward Grey knew that if Germany invaded Belgium it would be much easier to get Parliament to declare war on her. The German government knew this too. Wishing to offend Great Britain as little as possible, the German government tried to get through Belgium without violating her neutrality. On August 2 it asked the Belgian government to permit the German army to march through Belgium, promising (1) to guarantee its independence, (2) not to annex any of its territory, and (3) to pay an indemnity for the privilege. The Belgian government refused this request, and on August 4 the German army invaded Belgium.

The British government was now ready to act. August 3, foreseeing that Germany would invade Belgium, the ministers recommended that Parliament declare war on Germany. On that day Sir Edward Grey revealed for the first time the precise nature of Great Britain's obligations to France. He said that in his opinion Great Britain was bound to support France in the war. He said further that in his opinion both the interests and the honor of Great Britain required her to defend Belgium against German aggression (see p. 326). Three members of the cabinet resigned rather than take this step. But Parliament was convinced; and on August 4 Great Britain declared war on Germany.

We ask but do not answer the important question, *Who was responsible for the Great War?* Ever since 1914 historians and others have been trying to answer this question. Some say that Germany and Austria were responsible. Some say that Russia and France were responsible. Some say that all the great powers were jointly responsible. Some say that the system of alliances was responsible. Some say that human nature was responsible. What shall we say?

In trying to answer this question, much useless confusion is created by failing to distinguish two things: (1) what each country did; and (2) whether it should have done what it did. What each government did can be determined with reasonable accuracy. That each government was *responsible* for what it did can hardly be disputed. But was it *justified* in doing what it did? That is another question altogether. It is in answering that question that people differ and probably always will differ.

Let us state as simply as possible the essential action of each government which helped to bring on the Great War. Then each reader can answer for himself the question of whether it was justified in doing what it did.

1. The war might have been avoided if the Serbian government had prevented the assassination of the Archduke Francis Ferdinand, or if it had accepted without reservation the Austrian ultimatum. The Serbian government was *responsible* for doing what it did in both instances. Was it *justified* in doing what it did?

2. The war might have been avoided if the Austrian government had been satisfied with the Serbian reply, or if it had been willing to mediate the quarrel as the German government advised it to do. The Austrian government was *responsible* for refusing to accept the Serbian reply and for refusing to be guided by the advice of Germany. Was it *justified* in refusing?

3. The war might have been avoided if the Russian government had not insisted on making war on Austria in defense of Serbia. The Russian government was *responsible* for making war on Austria. Was it *justified* in doing so?

4. The war might have been avoided if the German government had not, in the first place, given Austria a free hand in dealing with Serbia; or if it had refused to make war on Russia, in support of Austria. The German government was *responsible* for what it did in both respects. Was it *justified* in so doing?

5. The war might have been avoided if the French government had refused, as it refused in 1908 and in 1913, to become involved in a war in defense of Russian and Serbian interests. The French government was *responsible* for repeatedly assuring Russia that it

would support Russia if Russia became involved in a war with Germany. Was it *justified* in making these promises?

6. The war might have been avoided (but this is perhaps less certain) if the British government had from the first made it clear either that it would or that it would not support France if France became involved in a war with Germany. The British government was *responsible* for refusing to make this clear until the war had begun. Was it *justified* in doing so?

In one sense it is easy to answer all these questions with an emphatic " No!" Knowing now what the war was like, we can easily say that none of the governments concerned was justified in doing what it did — that anything else would have been better. In fact, if the statesmen and diplomats of Europe had known in 1914 what a general European war would mean, as well as they knew in 1918, there wouldn't have been any general European war. They would all have hastened to settle the trifling Serbo-Austrian quarrel by peaceful means. We cannot condemn the statesmen of Europe for not knowing in 1914 what they knew in 1918. But this we can say: In 1914 every statesman in Europe knew that a general European war would be an unparalleled disaster. With their eyes open, they *risked* that disaster in behalf of " vital interests," treaty obligations, and " national honor." They were *responsible* for taking that risk. Were they *justified* in doing so?

QUESTIONS

1. Why did Bismarck take it for granted that France would always be hostile to Germany? What did he do to prevent France from forming alliances? Why did he fear a coalition against Germany? Why did he wish to make an alliance with Russia and Austria? What was the "League of the Three Emperors"?

2. Why did the interests of Russia and Austria clash? How did the Russian-Turkish War interfere with Bismarck's plans for an alliance with Russia? What were the terms of the Treaty of San Stefano? Why was the Congress of Berlin assembled, and what did it do?

3. Why did Germany and Austria form an alliance in 1879? What were the terms of this alliance? Why did Italy join this alliance in 1882? Why was Bismarck anxious to keep the goodwill of Russia? What were the terms of the "Reinsurance Treaty" of 1887?

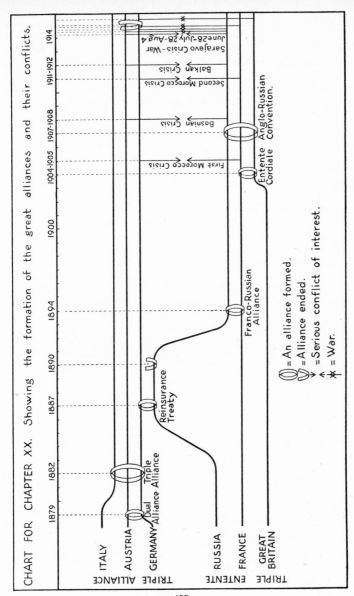

CHART FOR CHAPTER XX. Showing the formation of the great alliances and their conflicts.

1879 1882 1887 1890 1894 1900 1904-1905 1907-1908 1911-1912 1914

ITALY
AUSTRIA
GERMANY — Dual Alliance
Triple Alliance

RUSSIA
FRANCE
GREAT BRITAIN

TRIPLE ALLIANCE
TRIPLE ENTENTE

Reinsurance Treaty

Franco-Russian Alliance

Entente Cordiale
Anglo-Russian Convention.

First Morocco Crisis
Bosnian Crisis
Second Morocco Crisis
Balkan Crisis
Sarajevo Crisis — War
June 28 - July 28 - Aug. 4

= An alliance formed.
= Alliance ended.
= Serious conflict of interest.
= War.

4. What changes were made in German policy after the retirement of Bismarck in 1890? Why did France and Russia form an alliance in 1894? What were the terms of this alliance? Why did France and England suddenly become friends between 1898 and 1904? What were the terms of the "cordial understanding" of 1904? What were the terms of the Anglo-Russian Convention of 1907? Why were the agreements between Germany, Austria, and Italy called an "alliance," while the agreements between France, Russia, and Great Britain were called an *entente* ("understanding")?

5. What is meant by the "philosophy of imperialism"? What influences made it popular in the latter nineteenth and early twentieth centuries? Why is Rudyard Kipling sometimes called the "poet of imperialism"? State the argument justifying the control of backward countries by Europeans. State the argument justifying war as essential to the progress of civilization. How would you refute these arguments?

6. What were the great diplomatic crises between 1905 and 1914? Give a brief account of the first and second Morocco crises. How did these crises affect the relations of France and Germany? What was the Pan-Slav movement? How did it embitter the relations of Austria and Serbia? of Austria and Russia? Why did the annexation of Bosnia to Austria in 1908 create a European crisis? Why was Russia interested in forming a Balkan league? How did the first Balkan War create a European crisis? How was it settled? Why was there a second Balkan War?

7. Who was responsible for the assassination of the Archduke Francis Ferdinand? To what extent was the Serbian government implicated in this crime? What were the terms of the Austrian ultimatum to Serbia? Did Serbia accept the ultimatum or not? Why was Austria determined to make war on Serbia? Why was Russia determined to support Serbia? Did Austria have a better justification for her action than Russia had for hers? Why did Germany give Austria a free hand in dealing with Serbia? What did Germany do to restrain Austria after July 28? What did England and France do to restrain Russia after July 28? Why did the proposals of Sir Edward Grey for a peaceful settlement of the quarrel fall through? What was the pledge plan? Who proposed it? What countries supported it? What countries rejected it?

8. What action on the part of the Austrian government was most important in bringing on the war? on the part of the Russian government? on the part of the French government? on the part of the German government? on the part of the British government? Were they all justified in what they did? Were some more justified than others? Do you think there would have been a general European war if the great powers had not been bound by treaties of alliance?

SELECTED READINGS

Brief accounts. Robinson and Beard, *Development of Modern Europe* (revised ed.), II, ch. ix. Hayes, *Modern Europe* (revised ed.), II, ch. xxx. Schevill, *History of Europe*, ch. xxxii. Webster, *World History*, ch. xix. Hayes and Moon, *Modern History*, ch. xxiv. Schapiro, *European History* (revised ed.), chs. xxxiii–xxxiv. F. L. Benns, *Europe since 1914*, ch. i.

Longer accounts. G. P. Gooch, *Modern Europe*, chs. ii, v, x, xi, xii, xiv–xvi. C. Seymour, *Diplomatic Background of the War*, chs. ii, iii, vii–xii. P. Slosson, *Twentieth Century Europe*, chs. viii–x. The Sarajevo crisis and the immediate origins of the war have been fully treated in many books, and very different conclusions have been reached. Among the best of these books may be mentioned: S. B. Fay, *Origins of the World War*, Vol. II. P. Renouvin, *The Immediate Origins of the War*. A. Fabre-Luce, *The Limitations of Victory*. H. Lutz, *Sir Edward Grey and the World War*. A writer who maintains that France and Russia were chiefly responsible for the war is H. E. Barnes, author of *Genesis of the World War*. Two who maintain that Germany was chiefly responsible: H. W. Wilson, *The War Guilt*. B. Schmitt, *The Coming of the War, 1914*.

Books on imperialism and the philosophy of imperialism. F. Von Bernhardi, *Germany and the Next War*. A. T. Mahan, *Arms and Armaments*. K. Pearson, *National Life from the Point of View of Science*. N. Angel, *The Great Illusion*. G. Nasmyth, *Social Progress and the Darwinian Theory*. G. H. Perris, *A Short History of War and Peace*. H. N. Brailsford, *The War of Steel and Gold*.

Sources. Selections are in Scott and Baltzly, *Readings in European History*, ch. xii.

FRENCH PEASANTS FLEEING FROM THEIR HOMES BEFORE THE GERMAN
DRIVE IN MAY, 1918

CHAPTER XXI.   THE GREAT WAR, 1914–1918: HOW EU-
ROPE WAS TURNED UPSIDE DOWN IN ORDER TO MAKE
THE WORLD SAFE FOR DEMOCRACY

Patriotism is not enough.   EDITH CAVELL

Death is not an adventure to those who stand face to face with it.
ERICH M. REMARQUE

**Why the people in every country supported the war with enthu-
siasm.**   In no country did the mass of the people desire war
or know much about the events that led up to it.   During the
critical days from July 28 to August 1 they knew that war was
a possibility.   They hoped it would be averted, and because they
hoped it would be averted they believed up to the last moment that
it would be.

Yet when it came, the mass of the people in every country, after
the first moment of hesitation, supported the war with enthusiasm.
It was easy for them to believe that this war was different from any
other, and in this view they were confirmed by official propaganda.
The war was scarcely begun before each government published
a number of carefully selected diplomatic documents — the French
Yellow Book, the English Blue Book, the German White Book, etc.

680

Each of these books seemed to prove that the government concerned had done all in its power to preserve the peace, and that it
was the enemy governments that had desired war.   Thus the great
majority of people in every country supported the war with enthusiasm, partly because they felt it was their patriotic duty to do so,
partly because they believed with passionate conviction that it was
for them a war of self-defense against sinister and aggressive enemies.

The enthusiasm with which people supported the war in the
beginning was all the greater because they believed that it would
soon end in the defeat of their enemies.   The Germans said that
their armies would eat Christmas dinner in Paris.   The French and
English looked forward to a war of six months, or at most of a year.
A few were wiser.   Lord Kitchener said the war would last three
years.   The English Labor leader, John Burns, made the following
prediction to a friend: " A war with the Central Powers will last
three years.   It will cost us $35,000,000,000.   We shall lose a
million men.   It will end in world revolution."   But such ideas
were thought to be wild.   It was commonly thought that under
modern conditions twelve months of war would bankrupt every
country involved.

These optimistic hopes were soon dispelled.   The war lasted
four years, and no four years in the world's history were ever so
filled with striking events and desperate activities.   To relate these
events with any degree of completeness would require many
volumes.   We must somehow compress the narrative into a single
chapter.   Our aim must therefore be to get a general idea of the
war; to understand how the outstanding events were related to
each other, and how they contributed to the final result — the
defeat of the Central Powers.   We can do this more easily if we
think of the war as divided into three periods, as follows:

1. *First Period*, 1914–1916.   After the first optimistic hopes
were dispelled the war settled down to an indecisive struggle.   At
the end of two years the Central Powers had the upper hand on
land, the Allies had the upper hand on the sea.   No victory was in
sight for either side.

2. *Second Period*, 1917.   While each side still hoped for victory,
neither side was very confident.   On both sides there was talk of

a compromise peace.   Meanwhile, two important events changed the situation.   These events were: (1) the entrance of the United States, on the side of the Allies; (2) the Russian Revolution and the withdrawal of Russia from the war.   The first encouraged the Allies, the second encouraged the Central Powers.

3. *Third Period*, 1918.   The Central Powers staked everything on a new offensive.   By strengthening the western front with troops no longer needed against Russia, they hoped to break the French and British lines before the United States could come to their assistance.   The failure of the great drive was followed by revolution in Austria and Germany, and these in turn by the armistice which ended the war.

The story of the war will be more easily followed and remembered if these three periods, and their chief characteristics, are kept in mind.

I. FIRST PERIOD, 1914–1916: NO VICTORY IN SIGHT FOR EITHER SIDE

Military and naval strength of the Central and Allied Powers, and how time fought on the side of the latter.   At the beginning of the war the Central Powers were Germany and Austria.   Italy refused to join them, on the ground that the Central Powers were not attacked but were themselves the aggressors.   The Allied Powers were France, Russia, Great Britain, and Serbia.   What was the relative military and naval strength of the two sides at the opening of the war?   In this comparison we may omit Serbia.

The principal naval power was, of course, Great Britain, which had by far the largest and most efficient navy in the world.   Adding to this the French, Russian, and Japanese navies (Japan entered the war August 23, 1914), the Allies had from the first an incomparable naval superiority over the Central Powers.

In respect to armies the two sides were more evenly balanced. The armies of all the contending countries, save that of Great Britain, were " citizen armies."   In every Continental country all able-bodied young men, with few exceptions, were required, from about the age of twenty, to spend two or three years in continuous military training.   These made up the active army.

Having served their two or three years " with the colors," they returned to civil life. But until about the age of forty-five every man was still enrolled in some branch of the reserve army, had his uniform and equipment, belonged to a certain regiment, and always knew exactly what to do and where to go when the dreaded " mobilization " was declared. This is why all the Continental countries could immediately put into the field such enormous armies of trained soldiers. The British army was not a citizen army but a professional army. Nevertheless, although differently recruited, the British army, like the Continental armies, was composed of regulars and reserves.

In 1914 the active armies of the Central Powers (Austria and Germany) totaled about 1,000,000; their reserves totaled about 8,000,000. The active armies of the Allied Powers (France, Russia, and Great Britain) totaled a little less than 2,000,000; their reserves a little more than 10,000,000. The military strength of the Allied Powers was not, however, so great as these figures imply. First, their superiority in number of soldiers was largely due to the huge Russian army (active army, 1,000,000; reserves, 6,000,000); but the Russian army was far inferior in every other respect — in equipment, organization, training, and morale. Second, the Allied Powers were separated geographically, and could not co-operate effectively by transferring their troops easily from one front to another. The Central Powers had the great advantage of fighting on what the military men call " inside lines." Their plan of campaign had long since been worked out in a unified way. They knew just what they intended to do, and could easily and quickly move troops from one front to another where they happened to be most needed. We may say, therefore, that while the Allied Powers possessed a great naval superiority, in military effectiveness the two sides were about evenly balanced.

But there was another factor in the situation which was of great importance. This was *time*. In population from which new armies could in time be recruited and in economic resources for supporting a long war, the Allied Powers were far superior to the Central Powers. All they needed was time to make effective use of these resources. Time fought on the side of the Allied Powers.

The Germans understood this well.   Their best chance of winning
the war lay in winning it quickly, by inflicting a decisive defeat on
one enemy or the other at the very start.

**How the Germans expected to win the war quickly, and how they
nearly succeeded: First Battle of the Marne, September 6–12,
1914.**   The Germans had long since worked out to the last detail
a plan of campaign in case of a war on two fronts — against Russia
in the east and France in the west.   Thinking that the Russians
would mobilize slowly, the plan was to inflict a sudden and crushing
defeat on France, forcing her to make peace; and then, with
Austrian aid, to defeat Russia at leisure.

With amazing speed and precision the German armies were
mobilized on the western front.   The Germans did not intend to
invade France directly, through Alsace-Lorraine, since on that
frontier the French had two strongly fortified regions — one
around Toul and Verdun, the other around Épinal and Belfort.
The plan was to invade France where her frontier was unfortified.
To do this the German armies had to pass through Luxembourg
and Belgium.   When the advance guard of Germans entered
Luxembourg the Grand Duchess motored out and wheeled her
car across the road, but she was swept aside, and the German
armies passed on into Belgium.   The Belgians resisted more
effectively.   Although their army was not large, the Belgians
relied upon the excellent forts at Liége and Namur to delay the
Germans until the French and British came to their assistance.
Much to the surprise of the Allies, and perhaps to the Germans
themselves, these strong forts were battered to pieces in a few
hours by the German 42-centimeter howitzers.   The Germans
entered Belgium on August 3.   August 18, Brussels was taken,
and on August 22–23 the forts of Namur were demolished.   Belgian resistance had delayed the Germans eighteen days.

This delay of eighteen days was of priceless importance to the
French and British.   Like the Germans, the British had long ago
prepared for war.   With a speed and precision equal to that of the
Germans they transported an army of 160,000 to Belgium.   At the
same time the French commander, General Joffre, moved three
armies into Belgium to stay the invasion of the Germans.   August

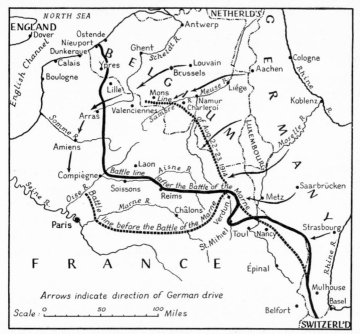

FIRST BATTLE OF THE MARNE, SEPTEMBER, 1914

22–23 the French and British first met the Germans, at Charleroi
and Mons; but the Germans were victorious, and on August 23
General Joffre was forced to order a " strategic retreat " into
France.

For nearly two weeks (August 24 – September 5) this famous
retreat from Mons continued.   The German armies of Von Kluck
and Von Bülow poured into France.   Day after day they marched
steadily on, past Lille, Valenciennes, Laon, pushing the French and
British back towards the Marne River.   By September 3 Von
Kluck's army was within twenty-five miles of Paris.   The French
government bundled up its effects and moved to Bordeaux.   It
was thought that Paris was the objective of Von Kluck's army.
But this was not so.   The object of the Germans was to inflict
a decisive defeat on the British and French armies retreating
before them, and then turn east and come in behind the French

armies on the fortified frontier at Toul and Verdun, Épinal, and Belfort.

General Joffre knew that at the proper time he must halt the retreat and make a stand. On September 5 the Allied armies stretched behind the Marne River from Paris to Verdun. Here General Joffre made his stand. Both sides realized that a decisive moment had arrived. " The time has come," General Joffre said, " to advance at all costs, and to die where you stand rather than give way." A German army order of September 6 states: " The great decision is undoubtedly at hand. Tomorrow the whole strength of the army is to be engaged along the whole line from Paris to Verdun. Everything depends on the result of tomorrow."

The famous first " Battle of the Marne " was not decided on the morrow. It lasted nearly a week (September 6–12, 1914). In the end the Germans were defeated. The victory of the Allies was due chiefly to three things: (1) As the French retreated from Belgium they were all the time in closer touch with their base of supplies, whereas the Germans, as they advanced into France, were every day farther from their base of supplies. This gave the French a great advantage in a battle lasting several days. (2) When the French-British line made its stand on the Marne a new French army was sent up to the left of the British. General von Kluck, on the German right wing, did not know this at first. Thinking that the British were still the extreme left of the French line, he moved too far east, only to find the new French army on his extreme right. To avoid being outflanked he had to execute a hasty retreat. (3) The French center was commanded by General Foch (later commander-in-chief of the Allied forces), whose brilliant tactics forced General von Hausen to fall back in confusion. This necessitated the retreat of the entire German army.

On September 10 the battle was virtually won. The French hoped to push the Germans out of France. But the Germans retired only to the north of the Aisne (September 12). There they remained. In December the French government returned to Paris. The western front now became " stabilized." It ran roughly from Nieuport, in Belgium, south to a point north of Compiègne and Soissons, east round Verdun, south to St. Mihiel,

© *William Thompson*

BARBED WIRE IN THE STREETS OF REIMS

Barbed wire was extensively used as a barricade to protect the trenches and fortifications. Reims, with its beautiful Gothic cathedral, suffered great damages during the many bombardments near it.

and southeast to the Swiss frontier — a distance of nearly 600 miles. Along this line the two armies " dug themselves in." With slight modifications on either side, this remained the line of the western front during the war, except for the last desperate drive of the Germans in 1918.

The Battle of the Marne was the decisive event of the early years. It meant that the attempt of the Germans to win the war quickly by a crushing victory had failed. It gave the Allied Powers time to bring into play their superior resources in man-power and wealth. It meant that the war was to be a long and desperate struggle.

War on the eastern front, 1914–1916: How the Russian " steam roller " did some damage at first but later proved ineffective. In 1914 the Germans employed their major force against France. The Allies hoped, therefore, that the huge Russian armies (the Russian " steam roller " according to the popular phrase) would by sheer numbers overwhelm the Germans and Austrians. At the very first the Russians seemed about to justify these hopes.

Although Von Hindenburg won a brilliant victory at Tannenberg (August 26–30, 1914) and drove the Russians out of East Prussia, the Austrian armies proved less effective. They were unable to make much headway against Serbia, and in September they were badly defeated by the Russians, who made a virtual conquest of the Austrian province of Galicia, including the city of Lemberg.

These early successes encouraged the Allies to hope for victory in the near future. They even discussed the question of dividing the spoils of victory. Secret treaties were signed by France, Russia, and Great Britain in which it was agreed that Russia should get Constantinople; France, Alsace-Lorraine; and Great Britain, the German colonies. In order to make victory more certain they invited Italy to join them. In 1914, Italy had refused to join Germany and Austria, on the ground that they had not been attacked but were themselves the aggressors. The Allies now promised that in case of victory Italy should get part of the Austrian Tyrol, the city of Trieste, and certain parts of the Turkish Empire. With this bargain struck, Italy declared war on Austria (May 23, 1915).

But the hopes of the Allies were premature. Italy was at first of little aid. An Allied naval expedition designed to take Constantinople (the so-called " Gallipoli Expedition," February–March, 1915) was a dismal failure. Worst of all, in the summer and fall of 1915 the Central Powers carried everything before them on the eastern front. In May and June General Mackensen recaptured Lemberg and drove the Russians out of the greater part of Galicia. In August and September General Hindenburg took Warsaw and conquered nearly all of Russian Poland. In this terrible campaign a million Russian soldiers were captured and two million killed or wounded. Having so far crippled Russia that she was little to be feared for the time being, the German and Austrian armies, aided by Bulgaria (which declared war, October, 1915), conquered Serbia, Montenegro, and Albania.

Thus at the beginning of 1916 the Central Powers had reason to be confident of success. In the west they held Belgium and a considerable part of northern France. In the east they had crippled Russia, occupied Russian Poland, and virtually conquered the

Balkans.   In one respect only were they at a serious disadvantage
— the Allies controlled the sea.

**The naval war, 1914–1916: How the Allies profited by controlling
the sea.**   The one decisive advantage which enabled the Allies to
win the war was control of the sea.   The first and essential task
was to destroy the German fleet or hold it in German ports.   This
was on the whole effectively done from the first, except for the
submarines.   German cruisers sometimes escaped and bombarded
English coast towns or inflicted serious losses on British merchant
vessels.   The German Far-Eastern fleet defeated a British squadron
off the coast of South America (November, 1914), but was itself
destroyed a little later.   In May, 1916, the German fleet at last
ventured out into the North Sea and attacked the British fleet near
Jutland, off the coast of Denmark.   The Battle of Jutland was the
one considerable naval battle of the war; but although the British
suffered serious losses, the German fleet returned to port, where it
remained until the close of the war.

Control of the sea was of the greatest value to the Allies in many
ways.   It enabled British merchant ships to transport troops to
France — from Canada, Australia, and above all from England and
(later) from the United States.   It enabled the Allies to conquer
the German colonies and to sweep German commerce from the sea.
But the great objective of the naval war was to blockade the
Central Powers and force them to submit in the end from lack of
food and supplies, even if they could not be defeated by force
of arms.   This could not be done without violating the rules of
international law.   According to international law it was permis-
sible for a neutral country, such as the United States, to export food
or supplies not defined as " contraband of war " into Germany
through the neutral countries, Holland and Denmark.   But in a
life-and-death struggle belligerent countries have rarely paid much
attention to the rules of international law.   It was so in this war.
Great Britain gradually extended the list of contraband articles
until it included nearly everything the Germans needed for any
purpose.   In this way the British navy pretty effectively prevented the importation of commodities into Germany through the
North Sea.

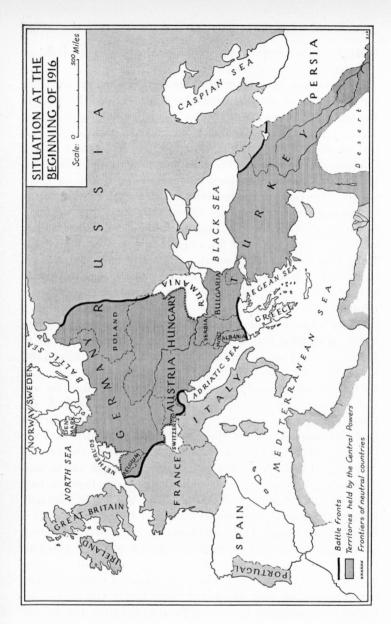

SITUATION AT THE
BEGINNING OF 1916

Scale: 0 ___ 500 Miles

NORWAY/SWEDEN

RUSSIA

CASPIAN SEA

BALTIC SEA

DEN-
MARK

NETHERL'DS

NORTH SEA

GREAT BRITAIN

IRELAND

BELGIUM

GERMANY

POLAND

BLACK SEA

ROMANIA

SERBIA

BULGARIA

TURKEY

PERSIA

Desert

AEGEAN SEA

GREECE

ALBANIA

ADRIATIC SEA

AUSTRIA HUNGARY

SWITZERL'D

FRANCE

ITALY

MEDITERRANEAN SEA

SPAIN

PORTUGAL

Battle Fronts

Territories held by the Central Powers

xxxxx   Frontiers of neutral countries

690

For Germany this was a serious matter, and likely to become more so as the war went on.   How could Germany break this blockade? Her one chance was by means of the submarines, with which she was far better provided than all other countries combined.   Submarines could easily slip out into the North Sea and, without warning, torpedo British naval vessels, or destroy British or neutral merchant ships carrying supplies to Great Britain or France.   But this use of the submarine raised a question of international law also. The submarine could not easily destroy merchant ships, and at the same time save the crew and passengers.   In a life-and-death struggle, however, the Germans were no more willing than the British to observe the rules of international law.   The German government therefore announced that after February 18, 1915, the waters around the British Isles would be regarded as a " war area," that all enemy warships found there would be sunk, and that " neutral vessels may be exposed to danger."

With this warning Germany began her first effort to break the blockade.   Many warships and merchant vessels were destroyed; and during the year it became clear that the Allied control of the sea would not prove to be so easy as had been thought.   The most dramatic episode in the first submarine war was the sinking of the *Lusitania*.   The *Lusitania* was a British merchant liner; but during the war it was registered as an " auxiliary cruiser " in the British navy.   This made it a war vessel, likely to be carrying arms and ammunition, and sure to be armed to defend itself.   On May 1, 1915, the *Lusitania* left New York City carrying a cargo of high explosives in the hold, and about 1900 passengers.   Six days later it was torpedoed by a German submarine off the coast of Ireland, and sank immediately, with the loss of more than half the passengers, of whom 114 were Americans.

This event proved at once the effectiveness of the submarine and the ruthless inhumanity involved in the use of it.   Nevertheless, the sinking of the *Lusitania* was a German blunder.   As a military measure it gained the Germans little or nothing; as a frightful act of inhumanity it did much to lose them whatever sympathy they may have had in the United States.   Thousands of Americans clamored for an immediate declaration of war.   President Wilson protested vigorously, and for nearly a year there followed an exchange of diplomatic notes which seemed at times to be but the preliminary to such a declaration. But at last (May 5, 1916) the German government promised to abandon the "unrestricted" submarine war until further notice — that is, it promised not to sink merchant vessels without warning, or without due provision for the safety of the passengers.

Two great but futile efforts to break the western front: Battle of Verdun, February–July, 1916 ; Battle of the Somme, July–November, 1916. The Germans abandoned unrestricted submarine warfare chiefly in order to conciliate the United States. But they were no doubt the more willing to do this because of their sweeping victories in the east (see p. 688). Russia was badly crippled and the Balkans conquered. Elated by these victories, the Germans thought the time had come to end the war by breaking the western line and forcing the French to make peace.

They chose Verdun as the point of attack. For months they assembled supplies of big guns and shells and concentrated troops behind the Verdun "salient" (bulge). They began the attack February 21 with a bombardment which in scope and intensity had never before been experienced. This was no "battle" in the old sense. It lasted five months — from February to July. Week after week, under cover of the terrific bombardment, the Germans pushed in their troops, steeling themselves to the inevitable slaughter in the hope that in the end a crushing defeat would justify whatever sacrifice of life was found necessary. The French rallied to the defense of Verdun with a resolution that won the admiration of the world, even of the Germans themselves. It was a resolution born of despair. "They shall not pass!" became a national cry. The heroic resistance of the French soldiers at Verdun must be counted the most splendid example of sheer nerve and valor exhibited during the war. At last the German emperor, appalled by the frightful loss of life and the growing uncertainty of victory in the end, gave "the momentous order for the cessation of the offensive at Verdun." The Germans had sacrificed 300,000 lives in the hope of a decisive victory. They had gained nothing but 130 square miles of French territory.

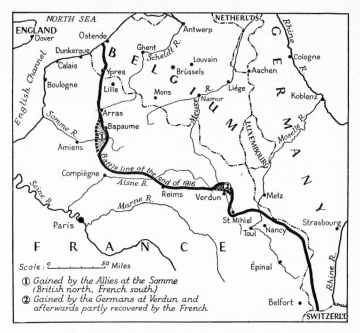

BATTLES OF VERDUN AND THE SOMME, 1916

The gains of the Germans at Verdun and of the Allies on the Somme, made after months of fighting and at such frightful cost in lives, left the western front virtually as it was before.

Like the first Battle of the Marne, the Battle of Verdun was a decisive event. A second time the Germans had determined to put France out of the war by a crushing defeat; a second time they had failed. This terrible failure, in a battle of their own choosing, with every advantage of preparation, depressed the Central Powers and encouraged the Allies. During the course of the Battle of Verdun, the Allies therefore prepared a counter-offensive. The point chosen was the Somme River, near Bapaume. Here the French and British made a concentrated drive on the German lines which lasted, with short lulls in the fighting, from July to November, 1916. After four months of desperate fighting, at the cost of more than half a million of men, the Allies had pushed the Germans back over an area of perhaps 120 square miles. But the German lines were never broken, nor in danger of being broken, and in some respects they were stronger at the end than at the beginning of the battle.

The final result of these two long and desperate battles was a deadlock. More than a million lives had been sacrificed without substantial result. At the end of 1916 the Central Powers seemed impregnable on land; the Allies controlled the sea. Neither side was any longer very confident of winning the war.

How the war became more ruthless and expensive, and why the people on both sides began to talk of peace. The nature of the Great War was unforeseen. Even the military men who had been studying the art of war for twenty-five years found that the conditions of modern warfare defeated their expectations and disarranged their plans. The art of war had, as it were, to be learned over again, and from week to week, from month to month, new methods of fighting had to be adopted and tried out.

One of these changes concerned forts. The Belgians had constructed forts at Liége and Namur. For forty years the French had spent vast sums in the elaborate fortification of the Alsace-Lorraine frontier. Forts had always been effective in past wars — the best ones rarely being taken except after long sieges. It was supposed they would be equally effective now. As a matter of fact they proved useless. With their 42-centimeter howitzers, the Germans battered the excellent Liége and Namur forts to pieces in a few hours. Forts were not only useless, they were worse than useless, since under bombardment they became death-traps. Two weeks of fighting proved that forty years of fort construction and maintenance was wasted effort.

Another change concerned "battles." In former days campaigns, and even wars, were won by pitched battles lasting a day, three days — at most, two weeks. Armies fought in the open, marched and countermarched, maneuvering for position. At the Battle of Austerlitz, Napoleon stood on a height of ground and through glasses surveyed the entire field. He could see, or easily learn, whether the right wing was advancing according to plan, whether the center was holding; and at the crucial moment he could send in the Old Guard of cavalry to make the decisive drive.

This was no longer possible. At the Battle of the Marne the line of battle extended from Paris to Verdun — a distance of 125 miles. The Allies had not " an army," but six armies — five French and one British. General Joffre could not stand on a height of ground and see this battle. He had to sit in a room and listen to reports over a telephone. He had to trust, far more than Napoleon ever did, to the wisdom and discretion of his several subordinate commanders. Even subordinate commanders could not see their own or the enemy army. General von Kluck endangered German success because he did not know that a new French army was advancing on his right. The German plan of campaign in August, 1914, had been carefully devised on the model of the campaign in 1870. The Germans had foreseen everything — with one exception. What they had not foreseen was that the scale of modern war was too large to be safely planned on the model of any previous war.

Another novelty was " trench war." After the Battle of the Marne the line of battle extended from Nieuport in Belgium to the Swiss frontier — a distance of 600 miles. Useless to try to " turn the flank " of this battle line. Useless, as the operations at Verdun and the Somme indicated, to try to break through the center. With little change, the line remained stabilized for four years. On both sides elaborate trenches were constructed, running zigzag in parallel lines, with stairs going up and down and underground rooms in which supplies were kept or soldiers rested when off duty. Between the lines of the opposing armies was " no man's land," obstructed with mounds of earth and barbed wire entanglements, often electrically charged. The characteristic operation was " going over the top." In this operation the soldiers made a concerted rush out of the trenches, worming their way through the entanglements, skulking along behind hillocks, through shell holes, or through the shell-stripped timber. " Going over the top " was a helter-skelter attack, at this point or that, wherever it was thought possible to take a few prisoners or destroy a small section of enemy trenches.

For this sort of war, cavalry was useless. But artillery was absolutely indispensable, both for destroying trenches and for

© Bong and Company, Berlin

FIRST AID IN THE TRENCHES

From a painting by P. Halke. A section of the German trenches is shown here, with Red Cross officials applying first aid to the wounded.

creating a smoke screen or " barrage," under cover of which infantry could cross " no man's land " unseen.   Advancing under a barrage, it was often difficult to tell whether the dropping shells came from friendly or hostile batteries.   The famous Austrian violinist, Fritz Kreisler, in his little book, *Four Weeks in the Trenches*, tells how his trained ear enabled him to be of peculiar service in the first days of the war.   He noticed that shells as they went over had a rising whine until they reached their highest point, and then a falling whine as they descended.   He informed a superior officer that he

could actually determine by the sound the exact place where a shell was reaching its acme [highest point] . . .   A few days later I was sent on a reconnoitering tour, . . . and it was later on reported to me that I had succeeded in giving to our batteries almost the exact range of the Russian guns. . . .   It is the only instance where my musical ear was of value during my service.[1]

Few men had the ear of a Fritz Kreisler, and ordinarily other means had to be found for locating enemy positions.   The airplane

[1] Fritz Kreisler, *Four Weeks in the Trenches*, pp. 28, 29.   Houghton Mifflin Company.

provided one of the new methods of doing this, besides being useful for dropping bombs on trenches and on accumulations of ammunition and stores behind the lines. Heavy artillery, 75's, and machine guns, supplemented with airplanes, poison gas, and armored-tanks lumbering through underbrush, over ditches, hillocks, and trenches with the easy flexibility and the resistless power of some dull-eyed prehistoric mammal — these were the indispensable instruments preparing the way for the common soldier with the old-fashioned but still effective bayonet.

To provide the millions of soldiers in the trenches with equipment, arms, big guns, shells, airplanes, tanks, food, and hospital service was a task more complicated and more expensive than anyone had dreamed of. A tenth of the population had to be mobilized as soldiers; more than another tenth was engaged in providing the soldiers with needed supplies. Never before did war so greatly transform the occupations of the people and the industrial activities of the nations concerned. Factories turned to the manufacture of munitions, airplanes, poison gas, big guns, lorries, uniforms, and hospital supplies. Boys and old men, girls and women of all ages, found employment in munition factories; as secretaries and typists; with the Red Cross " over there "; as nurses, at home or abroad; or as drivers of Ford cars and trucks back of the lines. In the end success depended quite as much upon the man-power and economic resources of the nation concerned as upon the size of armies; upon the quantity production of supplies and the effective organization of transport service as upon the genius of military commanders.

Above all, men and money were needed. The daily cost of the war mounted steadily, reaching fabulous sums. It is estimated that the total cost of the war in money spent was $186,000,000,000, and in property destroyed approximately $30,000,000,000, making a grand total of $216,000,000,000. Such amounts are beyond the imagination to grasp. The cost is more easily realized if we remember that the British Empire alone spent on an average $24,000,000 a day, or $1,000,000 an hour. Worse than the cost in money was the frightful cost in life. It is estimated that during the war nearly 65,000,000 men were mobilized; that of these about 8,360,000 were killed or died of illness, and about 21,000,000 were wounded.   There was scarcely a family in the chief European countries concerned that did not count its dead or maimed or missing members.

Four years of unprecedented activity, of suspense and suffering, of fear and anger and hope deferred created a strain that was terrific, exalting some, depressing others, and stringing the nerves of all. Little wonder that the people in each country gladly believed all the evil reports of their enemies.   Stories of " atrocities " were circulated and credited in every country.   In Allied countries it was believed that the Germans had devastated Belgium, massacred children, outraged women, crucified men; in Germany and Austria it was believed that the Russians had been guilty of similar atrocities in Galicia and East Prussia, and that the Belgian civilians behind curtained windows had shot down German soldiers, or poisoned the food and water provided for them.   Atrocity stories were not made up out of whole cloth.   They were for the most part based on incidents that were magnified as they were repeated from mouth to mouth, or rumors which, in this heated air of fear and hatred, were inflated beyond recognition and accepted without question as indisputable fact.   In every war people are amazed at the atrocities committed by the enemy, forgetting that war is itself the chief of atrocities.

Curiously enough the soldiers were less given to hating the enemy, and less disposed to credit the atrocity stories, than the civilians at home.   Civilians noted that soldiers were oddly changed after the first twelve months of war.   Something had happened to them. Returning home on short leaves they often seemed almost strangers to their parents and friends.   After the first glad greetings, they were curiously silent.   They seemed little disposed to talk of the war, and they exhibited an unaccountable dislike of being regarded as gallant heroes fighting for " freedom " and " national independence."

The explanation is perhaps that fighting the war in the trenches was an experience that could not be understood by those who remained at home fighting the war in office chairs.   The soldiers felt that the people " back home " were talking about something of which they really knew nothing.   They knew nothing of the dreary

© *William Thompson*

CLEMENCEAU AND FOCH COMING FROM HEADQUARTERS ON THE SOMME,
OCTOBER, 1918

Clemenceau (1841–1929), minister of war and prime minister during the latter
years of the war, is in civilian garb. Foch (1851–1929) commanded the French
armies of the north, then became chief of the general staff, and in 1918 was
made commander-in-chief of all the Allied armies.

and desperate business of trench warfare — of war shorn of all the
romance of dress parade, and flags flying in the breeze to the strains
of martial music. Trench war meant wallowing in the mud and
slime, fighting vermin, fighting utter exhaustion of body and
spirit, and fighting the still more dreadful " shell shock " induced by
the perpetual racket of machine guns and the terrible detonation of
the heavy artillery. In this inferno time stood still; the past
seemed unreal and the future non-existent. To the soldiers who
survived, the cheerful conversation of the people " back there,"
still talking of " national honor " and of the war for " freedom and
democracy," seemed too often but the shrill prattle of children
whose toys had been upset.

After two years the fearful price of this war was still far from
being paid; but the strain was beginning to tell, and people on both
sides were wondering whether the objects of the war were worth
the cost. What indeed were those objects? Could they in any
case be attained? The war seemed to have reached a deadlock.
The Central Powers were on the whole triumphant on land, but

their desperate effort at Verdun to end the war had failed. The Allies were masters of the sea, but they had barely been able to hold the western front. Moreover their efforts in the east had failed, and their ally, Russia, was a crippled and uncertain support. In this time of exhaustion and low spirits, when no one could foresee the end, people on both sides began to talk of peace.

II. SECOND PERIOD, 1917: PEACE PROPOSALS; THE UNITED
    STATES ENTERS THE WAR; RUSSIA WITHDRAWS

Peace proposals: How President Wilson asked the belligerents to say what they were fighting for, and why they told him less than they might have done. The first official move towards peace was made by the Central Powers. December 12, 1916, the German government sent to the United States a note to be forwarded to the Allied governments. The note stated that the Central Powers " propose . . . to enter into peace negotiations. They feel sure that the proposals which they would bring forward . . . would serve as a basis for the re-establishment of lasting peace." The Allied governments rejected this proposal. Believing that the offer was designed to " create dissentions . . . in Allied countries," they declared that " no peace is possible so long as they [the Allies] have not secured reparation for violated liberties, recognition of the principle of nationalities, and the free existence of small states."

Meantime, President Wilson felt that the time had come when the United States might venture to make a move towards peace. On December 18, 1916, he accordingly sent a note (prepared before he learned of the German proposal) to all the belligerent governments. He said that he was " merely proposing that *soundings be taken* . . . to learn how near the haven of peace may be." He pointed out that the " objects which the statesmen . . . on both sides have in mind in this war are virtually the same, *as stated in general terms* to their own people and to the world." If this was indeed so, the President said, would it not be well to state these objects in more detailed and specific terms? The belligerent governments might then find that the differences between them were not so great as they supposed, and perhaps by a little concession on both sides this frightful war might be ended.

Both sides replied to President Wilson's note. The German government, speaking for the Central Powers, declined to state its peace terms, but proposed " an immediate meeting of delegates of the belligerent states at some neutral place," for the discussion of peace. The Allied governments, in a joint note, deplored President Wilson's statement that the objects for which both sides were fighting seemed to be the same. The Allies had often stated the objects for which they were fighting, in general terms to be sure; but the civilized world knew what these terms implied. They implied:

first of all, the restoration of Belgium, Serbia, and Montenegro; . . . the evacuation of invaded territories in France, in Russia, in Rumania, with just reparation; . . . the restoration of [Alsace-Lorraine to France]; the liberation of the Italians, as also of the Slavs, Rumanes, and Czechoslovaks from foreign domination; the setting-free of the populations subject to the bloody tyranny of the Turks; and the turning out of Europe of the Ottoman Empire as decidedly foreign to Western civilization.

In pursuance of these aims the Allies declared that they would " make all sacrifices to carry to a victorious end the conflict upon which . . . depend not only their own welfare and prosperity but the future of civilization itself."

Thus it seems that the Central Powers were willing to enter a peace conference but not to publish their peace terms, while the Allies were willing to publish their peace terms — or some of them — but not to enter a peace conference. What is the explanation of this difference of attitude?

First, as to the Central Powers. Their attitude was apparently determined by a sharp difference of opinion between the civil and the military authorities. The German chancellor, Bethmann-Hollweg, doubted whether a complete victory was possible, especially if the United States should join the Allies. The blockade was beginning to tell, and the people, especially in Austria, were weary of the war. The Austrian minister, Count Czernin, told the emperor in confidence that for Austria " another winter's campaign is out of the question." For these reasons it seemed that the Central Powers could probably make a better peace now than later.

But the military authorities were still confident of winning a complete victory. This was the opinion especially of Ludendorff, the virtual chief of the German general staff. Ludendorff has been called the " evil genius of Germany." He was arrogant and overbearing, and he used his great influence to discredit anyone who talked of a compromise peace. This is perhaps why the civil authorities were unwilling to publish any terms of peace. To publish the terms demanded by Ludendorff would discredit them before the world. To publish any reasonable terms would enable the military authorities to discredit them in the eyes of their own people.

Second, as to the Allied Powers. The attitude of the Allies was determined by many things. They had no faith in the sincerity of the Central Powers in proposing a peace conference. They knew that the military victories of the Central Powers would give them a certain advantage in any negotiation that might take place. But above all, the Allied governments were fighting for certain objects which they were unwilling to reveal, either to the Central Powers or to President Wilson. These objects were defined in the famous " secret treaties " between the Allied governments, some of which they had negotiated in 1915 and 1916 and some of which they were at this very time preparing.

In the secret treaties the Allied governments agreed that at the close of the war, if they were successful, they would demand: (1) for Russia, Constantinople and Poland; (2) for Great Britain, the German colonies and the " neutral zone " in Persia; (3) for France, Alsace-Lorraine and the domination of the left bank of the Rhine; (4) for Italy, the city of Trieste and the major part of Albania and the Austrian Tyrol; (5) for all four powers, appropriate parts of the Turkish Empire. The Allies felt that the secret treaties must at all hazards be kept secret, since these treaties disproved their repeated assertion that they were fighting for defense only and not for conquest. Above all, to reveal the terms of the treaties would lose them the sympathy of President Wilson and perhaps make it impossible to induce the United States to enter the war.

Thus the attempt of President Wilson to bring about peace at the beginning of 1917 came to nothing. Meantime, the failure of the peace proposals was followed by two events of the greatest importance. These were: (1) the Russian Revolution in March, 1917, and the practical withdrawal of Russia from the war; (2) the entrance of the United States into the war on the side of the Allies in April, 1917. We must now learn something of these events.

How President Wilson declared for " a peace without victory," and then decided to make war on Germany, April 6, 1917. In 1914 most people in the United States thought that the European war was no affair of theirs. This war grew out of a quarrel between Austria and Serbia — something about which the people of the United States knew nothing and cared less; and in any case the traditional policy of the United States was not to meddle in European quarrels. President Wilson therefore issued a proclamation of neutrality, and advised everyone to be neutral " in thought and deed." This was a council of perfection, for people had their sympathies — some for the Germans, some for the Allies; but very few indeed thought it possible that the United States would ever take part in the war.

Yet as the war dragged on, a great many people came to the conclusion that the United States must sooner or later join the Allies. The development of this pro-war sentiment in the United States was the result chiefly of two things: (1) Allied propaganda; (2) the German submarine warfare.

1. *Allied propaganda.* What the people of the United States read in the newspapers and elsewhere about the origin of the war, and about the war itself, came almost exclusively from British and French sources. The United States heard the Allied side of the story but not the German side. They were told, and believed, that Germany had deliberately plotted to bring on the war in order to make herself master of Europe and the world. They were told, and believed, that the Germans were guilty of unheard-of atrocities in Belgium and France. The Belgian atrocities were vouched for by an official British investigation, signed by James Bryce, which was widely read in the United States; and the name of Bryce carried immense weight because he was well known and liked in the United States, and was in fact a man of judicious intelligence and of unquestioned honesty.

2. *The German submarine warfare.* Meantime the submarine warfare seemed to confirm all that had been reported about German brutality. The sinking of the *Lusitania*, especially, aroused intense indignation in the United States. It seemed a brutal and senseless act, a violation of all humane feeling as well as of the laws of civilized warfare. Some people pointed out that Great Britain violated the rules of war also. But Great Britain had done no more than confiscate property; Germany had destroyed the lives of innocent women and children. Most people believed the Allies were fighting in defense of the sacred cause of freedom and humanity against the ascendancy of brutality and barbarism; and that they were defending the United States as well as themselves, for if Germany won the war she might then turn against the United States as the sole power that blocked her path to world domination.

By the end of 1916 pro-war sentiment was strong in the eastern states, but far less so in the western states. President Wilson had just been re-elected (in November, 1916), mainly by the votes of people who supported him on the ground that " he has kept us out of war." But he was barely re-elected; and after the failure of the peace proposals he realized that he could not keep the United States out of the war much longer. On January 22, 1917, the President therefore took a very important step towards intervention. This was his famous Address to the Senate, in which he stated the conditions of a peace to which the United States would be willing to give its " formal and solemn adherence."

The necessary conditions of such a peace, according to the President, were the following: (1) " It must be a peace without victory . . . Only a peace between equals can last. (2) Peace must be based on " the principle that governments derive all their just authority from the consent of the governed." (3) There must be " freedom of the seas . . . the free, constant, and unthreatened intercourse of nations." (4) There must be a limitation of armies and of all programs of military preparation." (5) All nations must " henceforth avoid entangling alliances which would draw them into competitions of power, catch them in a net of intrigue and selfish rivalry. . ."

These were the conditions. If peace could be made on the basis of these principles, then it would be possible to organize a " league for peace," which would give to all nations security and guarantee the world against future wars such as the present. For such ideal objects the United States would work, but for no others.

If this famous address was intended as a warning that the United States might soon enter the war it was well timed. Nine days after it was delivered the German government, thinking that the United States could not in any case give much assistance to the Allies, announced the renewal of unrestricted submarine warfare — that all sea traffic within certain " war zones " around Great Britain, France, and Italy would " without further notice be prevented by all weapons." At first the submarines proved very effective. Within the war zones neither warships nor merchant nor passenger vessels were safe. The Allied governments told President Wilson that unless the United States joined them, their hope of winning the war was slight. Public opinion in the United States had become more and more hostile to Germany, and after the renewal of unrestricted submarine warfare the President felt that it was no longer possible to remain neutral. Acting on his recommendation, Congress therefore declared war on Germany, April 6, 1917.

The entrance of the United States encouraged the Allies, but at first they did not know whether the President could do more than give the Allies naval support in fighting the submarines. Perhaps he did not desire to do more. One phrase in the President's address of January 22 had greatly alarmed the Allies: " It must be a peace without victory." Few famous phrases ever astonished or angered so many people as this one. What could the extraordinary man mean? The Allies wanted no peace without victory. They wanted victory; and for victory they needed an American army — a big one — and they needed it at once. " In heaven's name," they said, " don't talk of a peace without victory ! The situation is desperate. Time is precious. Send us an army, and do it quickly." But the United States had no army. Could one be raised, organized, and equipped within a year, or two years? Could it be safely transported, escaping the submarines? These were the vital questions — terrible questions — which, in the spring of 1917 no one could answer.

© *Bong and Company, Berlin*

STORMING OF LA VACQUERIE NEAR CAMBRAI BY TROOPS FROM BADEN, DEC. 3, 1917

From a painting by Karl Albrecht. The village was practically demolished by the bombardment preceding the attack.

Meantime, the need for quick action on the part of the United States was all the greater because of another event of vital importance. This was the Russian Revolution (March 12, 1917), which virtually put Russia out of the war, and enabled Germany to throw all of her forces against the western front.

The Russian Revolution of March 12, 1917: How the Russians dethroned the tsar, and by so doing pleased the Allies. The Russian Revolution of 1917 was the result, partly of the war, partly of the reform movement that had been gathering force for a hundred years. Before 1914 the reformers had twice forced concessions from the tsars, and on both occasions it was an unsuccessful war that had enabled them to do so. During the years 1860–1881, following the Crimean War, serfdom was abolished, local assemblies (*zemstvos*) created, and a certain freedom of the press granted (see p. 467). But the assassination of Alexander II discredited the reformers, and until 1905 the old oppressive methods of government were revived. Then the failure of the Russo-Japanese War led to the Revolution of 1905 which forced the tsar to establish a national legislature, of which the lower chamber (*Duma*) was elected by the people — or some of them. But the Duma, although it managed to exist, never had much real power; and during the years 1908–1914 the tsar and his ministers continued to govern much as they always had done.

In spite of failure, the reform movement went on, and in 1914 there were three distinct parties, each having its own idea of what the reforms should be. (1) The Constitutional Democratic party (popularly known as the " Cadets ") was supported by the upper middle classes, who wanted a constitutional government such as the countries of western Europe had. (2) The Social Revolutionary party was supported by the peasants and led by middle-class radicals. It was chiefly interested in having the land of the nobles divided among the peasants. (3) The Socialist party of the industrial workers in the cities accepted the doctrines of Karl Marx, advocated the abolition of private property, and demanded that the workers should share in the management of industrial enterprises. But the Socialists differed as to the best method of gaining these ends. The *Menscheviki* (" Minority ") believed that social and economic reforms might be brought about slowly and peacefully. The *Bolsheviki* (" Majority ") believed the workers could get what they wanted only by a sudden and violent revolution which would establish the " dictatorship of the proletariat " and deprive the upper classes at a single stroke of both their wealth and their power.

Besides these reform parties there were certain subject nationalities in Russia demanding the privilege of governing themselves. The Finns, the Letts, the Lithuanians, the Poles, the Ukrainians, and the Georgians regarded themselves as different from the " Russians." Each group wished to have its own parliament, and to preserve its language and customs. Their idea was that Russia should be a federation of self-governing peoples, united under the tsar and a federal parliament. Then there were the Jews, who wanted to preserve their religion and their customs unmolested.

When the war broke out in 1914 all the parties except the Bolsheviks supported it with enthusiasm. True " Russians " regarded it as a noble crusade for the liberation of their brother Christians and Slavs from Austrian or Turkish tyranny. The Constitutional Democrats thought that the tsar would now give Russia a real constitution. The peasants thought they would now get the land of the nobles. Poles, Finns, and Jews thought that if they supported the war the Russians, in all decency, would cease to oppress them by trying to deprive them of their language and customs.

But this enthusiasm for the war did not last. Early victories were followed by disastrous defeats. The loss of life was frightful. People asked why Russia, with the largest armies of all, should always be defeated. Their answer was — and it was the true one — that the civil and military officials were inefficient and corrupt. Yet the tsar and his ministers refused to listen to advice and ruthlessly suppressed all criticism. Thus after two years of failure the people were disillusioned. They asked, " What are we fighting for ? Are we fighting for a blind tsar who listens only to a stupid and corrupt aristocracy ? "

All this discontent came to a head in the winter of 1916-1917. Army officers and members of the Duma openly charged the government with corruption and incompetence. Peasants began to attack the country houses of the nobles. Workmen in the towns refused to work. To meet disaffection the tsar used the only methods he knew. Instead of trying to remove the cause of the discontent he tried to suppress it. On March 11, 1917, he ordered the Duma to adjourn its sessions, and the workmen of Petrograd (St. Petersburg) to cease striking and go back to work.

These decrees precipitated the revolution. The Duma remained in session. Some troops in Petrograd, who were ordered to fire on the striking workmen, mutinied and joined the workers. The workers and soldiers formed a Soldiers' and Workingmen's *Soviet* (" Council "). March 12, after some street-fighting, the soldiers and the police of Petrograd joined the revolutionists. Several armies throughout the country declared their support of the revolution. The tsar and his ministers ordered a special train to take them to Petrograd, in the hope of restoring order there; but the workmen sidetracked the train and uncoupled the engine. When Nicholas II, Tsar of all the Russias, was left sitting in a train shunted off on a sidetrack, the game was played out. It was played out because the power of the tsar depended on obedience backed by military force. The workmen refused to obey; the soldiers refused to compel them. The end of tsardom was as easy as that. Three days later, March 15, Nicholas abdicated the throne.

The revolution of March, 1917, was the calmest and most joyous revolution ever seen. There was almost no bloodshed, because there was almost no resistance. Tsardom simply collapsed without a sound. Everywhere people heard the news with joy. They felt that at last they were free. A new day had dawned in which everything would be right and everyone happy. People went about smiling. Soldiers fraternized with workmen. Distinctions of rank and of wealth were momentarily forgotten. Strangers in the streets and shops greeted each other as brothers. Work was suspended so that all could be merry and drink toasts to the regeneration of Russia.

A provisional government was at once organized under the presidency of Prince Lvov, a landowner. The new government was controlled by the Constitutional Democrats, but it included one Social Revolutionary — Alexander Kerensky. It proclaimed freedom of the press and of religion, liberated political prisoners, and invited political exiles to return to Russia. It provided for the election of a national assembly to form a constitution for Russia. It assured the Allies that Russia, now emancipated from the corrupt tsardom, would prosecute the war with renewed enthusiasm and efficiency.

After the first shock of surprise, the Russian Revolution was regarded in Allied countries as a godsend. For two years the Allied governments had assured the world that they were fighting for freedom and justice. But skeptics said, " How can you say that when you are allied with tsardom, the most unjust and oppressive government in Europe? " Now all this was changed. The revolution made it easier for the Allies to convince President Wilson that they were fighting for freedom. It made it easier for President Wilson to bring the United States into the war on the side of the Allies. It made it possible for him to say, and for the people to believe, that the Allies were fighting to " make the world safe for democracy." Therefore in March, 1917, there was rejoicing in Paris, London, Rome, and Washington over the Russian Revolution. It was expected that a free Russia would bring to the Allies a more effective support, both moral and military, than she had ever yet been able to do.

The Russian Revolution of November 7, 1917: How the Russians refused to fight, and by so doing pleased the Central Powers. The rejoicing of the Allies was short-lived. The provisional government could not redeem its promise to prosecute the war vigorously, because it did not represent the ideas of the people as a whole. Russia fell into a kind of anarchy. To the workmen the revolution meant that they were to share in the management of industry. They therefore refused to work, and began to break up the machinery. To the peasants the revolution meant that they were to have the land of the nobles. They therefore refused to pay rents and taxes and began to pillage the country houses. To the soldiers the revolution meant freedom from discipline. They therefore deposed or killed their officers and elected others from the ranks. Above all, to the mass of the people — workers, peasants, and soldiers — the revolution meant, not a more vigorous prosecution of the war, but the end of war. Therefore, throughout the country, workmen and soldiers formed local councils called *soviets*, which ignored the provisional government and clamored for peace at any price.

To meet this situation, the provisional government was reorganized (May, 1917), with Alexander Kerensky at its head. Since Kerensky was a Social Revolutionary, it was thought that he would be listened to by the workers and the peasants. He tried in vain to restore discipline in the army, and even led a campaign against the Germans, only to be hopelessly defeated. Aware that Russia would not fight, he tried to persuade the Allied governments to renounce their secret treaties and to make peace with the Central Powers on the basis of " no annexations and no indemnities." The Allied governments refused to do either.

Thus the authority of the provisional government declined. The real authority was in the hands of the local soviets, and the soviets were more and more directed by Bolshevik leaders. The

© *Press Cliché*

LENIN ADDRESSING THE PEOPLE FROM A TRUCK

Lenin will always be remembered as the founder of the Soviet Republic.

result was a second revolution, directed by Nicolai Lenin, one of the most remarkable men of his time.   November 7, 1917, the provisional government was overthrown and replaced by the " Soviet Republic."   It was the " dictatorship of the proletariat " dreamed of by the radical Socialists — the Bolsheviks.   The object of the Soviet Republic was to carry through the social revolution.   As a preliminary to that object, the new government declared a truce with the Central Powers in December, 1917; and in March, 1918, made peace with them (*Peace of Brest-Litovsk*, see p. 713).

Thus the Russian Revolution, which at first encouraged the Allies, proved to be a disaster to them.   Never, therefore, were the Allies more discouraged than in the summer and fall of 1917.   The United States had declared war, but was as yet of little aid.   Russia, instead of renewing the war with vigor, was spreading the dangerous doctrine of " peace with no annexations and no indemnities." Worst of all, the doctrine found adherents in France and England. Lord Lansdowne published a letter in which he suggested that it might be better to make a compromise peace than to continue a hopeless struggle.   Joseph Caillaux and other prominent French-men spread the "pacifist" doctrine in France.   Entire companies of French soldiers, influenced by the peace talk, refused to fight and went home.   In August the Pope made an appeal to both sides to end the war on reasonable terms by mutual concessions.

Meantime, what of the Central Powers?   It appears that the Austrian government was ready to discuss peace on the Russian basis of " no annexations and no indemnities."   Perhaps the German civil officials would have been willing also.   But the military leaders were more than ever convinced that they could win the war. The submarine war was not so effective as they had hoped, it is true. But Russia was out of the war.   The United States was not yet of real assistance.   "Defeatist" sentiment seemed to be strong in the Allied countries.   In this situation the Germans staked all their hope on one last desperate drive against the western front before the United States could land an effective army in France.

III. THIRD PERIOD, 1918: PEACE OF BREST-LITOVSK; LAST GERMAN DRIVE; ARMISTICE

How the Germans made peace with soviet Russia at Brest-Litovsk, March 3, 1918.   Although Russia was really out of the war after the first revolution (March, 1917) the Germans could not safely remove their troops to the western front until peace was formally made.   It was well understood that the soviet government, under the leadership of Lenin, was quite willing to make peace. The Bolshevists were opposed to war on principle, and they had been opposed to this war from the start.   On December 15, 1917, the soviet government accordingly agreed to an armistice with the Central Powers, and on December 22 began negotiations with them at Brest-Litovsk.

At the Brest-Litovsk conference the soviet government proposed to make peace on the basis of no annexations and no indemnities. The Central Powers agreed to this in principle, but said they could not evacuate Poland, Lithuania, Estonia, Finland, or Ukrainia since the people of these regions did not regard themselves as Russians. This was a way of saying that the Central Powers were determined to deprive the soviet government of a great part of the former

Russian Empire. The soviet government refused to make peace on these terms, and the conference at Brest-Litovsk was broken off on January 14, 1918.

Then the soviet government made a curious announcement. It notified all the powers that Russia, although she had not been able to make peace with the Central Powers, was nevertheless not at war with them. " There is neither peace nor war between Russia and the Central Powers " — such was the astonishing declaration of the soviet government. Unfortunately, since one power can make war, one power cannot alone get out of it. In February, 1918, the German armies rapidly overran and occupied all of Russian Poland, Lithuania, Courland, Estonia, Livonia, and the greater part of Ukrainia. The soviet government discovered that it could not be " out of the war " without making peace. It therefore submitted, under protest, to the German terms, and on March 3, 1918, the Peace of Brest-Litovsk was signed.

By this treaty the soviet government abandoned all claims to Poland, Lithuania, Estonia, Livonia, and Finland, and ceded Kars and Batum to Turkey. In addition it signed an agreement which made enormously valuable economic and commercial concessions to Germany and Austria. By the Peace of Brest-Litovsk the soviet government lost a fourth of Russia's former territory and population and more than half of its former coal and iron resources. In much of this last territory new states were in the process of formation — in Poland, Finland, Lithuania, and Ukrainia ; but for the time being the political and economic independence of these new states was at the mercy of the Central Powers.

Thus by March, 1918, the Central Powers had won the war in the east. The question was, could they win it in the west also ?

The great German drive of 1918: Second Battle of the Marne, July 15–August 2, 1918. The Peace of Brest-Litovsk was of great service to the military leaders of Germany because it encouraged the war-weary people to make one more great sacrifice. The people were told that, with Russia out of it, Germany could now, by a last desperate effort, win the war. They were told that the French were too exhausted to withstand another attack. They were told that the United States was sending troops to France, but that the army

© *William Thompson*

THE BLOCKED HARBOR AT ZEEBRUGGE, BELGIUM

On the night of April 22, 1918, between 11 : 20 P.M. and 1 : 30 A.M., the harbor of Zeebrugge, which German submarines had been using as a base of operations, was blocked by the British, by sinking two of their own ships in the entrance. This was one of the most daring naval operations of the war.

of the United States could not be of any real use until 1919 at the earliest. So the German people were encouraged to make a last effort.

The German hope of breaking the western front in the spring and summer of 1918 was not altogether a vain one. The Germans had certain military advantages. Whereas the French and the British were finding it difficult to keep their ranks filled, the Germans were able to move nearly their entire eastern army to the western front. Besides, the Germans could concentrate great numbers at those points where they intended to make their drive, whereas the Allies, not knowing where the attack was to be made, had to be ready to defend their line at every point.

With these advantages, the Germans began their last great drive in March, 1918. They first struck the British line near St. Quentin and forced it back nearly to Amiens. Then in May they struck the French line further south and pushed it back to Château-Thierry. Within three months the apparently resistless Germans had made a great bend in the western front between Arras and Reims. Once more, as in 1914, they were on the Marne River, this time within fifty miles of Paris. Powerful guns, at a distance of seventy miles, had dropped shells in the capital of France. To the war-weary

Allied peoples it seemed that four years of desperate resistance would go for nothing, and that the Germans would win in spite of everything.

But the situation was really less desperate than the Allies feared, less promising than the Germans hoped. The great drive had cost the Germans heavily in men and munitions, and the difficulty of replacing them increased week by week. The submarine warfare failed to break the blockade, and the undernourished people of Austria and Germany were being slowly starved into submission. Austria was already a spent force; the Germans were fighting on their nerve.

While the Germans were becoming weaker every month, the Allies were becoming stronger. Resorting to military conscription, the United States had raised and equipped a great army; and in the early summer of 1918 American troops were being landed in France with a speed and efficiency which few people had supposed possible. During the month of April, 118,642 men were safely transported. By the end of July nearly 1,000,000 American soldiers were in France. It is true that they were incompletely trained. But their mere presence in France encouraged the Allies to hold out — gave them that last measure of desperate courage necessary to win the war. Completely trained or not, there they were, ready and eager to be called upon in an emergency.

The emergency was at hand on July 15, 1918, when the Germans began a desperate attempt to break the western front at Château-Thierry. This was the beginning of the second Battle of the Marne (July 15–August 2). If the Germans could break through, the French could no longer hold Reims, and the entire line would have to fall back. Realizing this, "every division of American troops with any sort of training was made available for use in a counter-offensive." During the first three days the Germans made slight gains, but the Allied lines held, and the American troops proved not only that they could be relied upon but that they could fight with an aggressiveness impossible for troops that had been exhausted by years of service. On July 18 General Foch (recently made commander-in-chief of the Allied forces) decided that the time had come for a counter-offensive. The plan was to " pinch " the

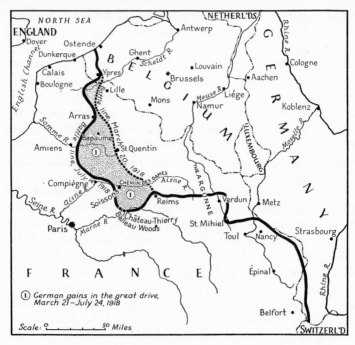

SECOND BATTLE OF THE MARNE, JULY, 1918

The southern "salient" (bulge) at Château-Thierry and Belleau is where the
French and American armies began the counter-attack which forced the Germans to retreat.

German salient at Château-Thierry, the Americans pushing in from
the west side, the French from the east side.   Unable to resist the
pressure from both sides, the Germans were forced to retreat.

By July 29 the Château-Thierry salient was " reduced," and on
August 2 the French occupied Soissons.   It was the beginning of
the end.   The German chancellor, Hertling, said:

I was convinced that before the first of September our adver-
saries would send us peace proposals. . . .   We expected grave
events in Paris by the end of July.   That was on the fifteenth.
On the eighteenth even the most optimistic among us understood
that all was lost.   The history of the world was played out in three
days.

© *William Thompson*

GENERAL PERSHING RECEIVING MARSHAL FOCH AT AMERICAN HEAD-
QUARTERS, CHAUMONT

Compare Marshal Foch's " traveling carriage " with that of Napoleon, p. 288.

**How the Austrian and German people, relying on the promises
of President Wilson, refused to fight any longer: Armistice, November 11, 1918.** It was quite true that " all was lost " when the
German armies began to retreat. All was lost, not so much because
the German armies were defeated as because the soldiers in the
ranks and the people at home were unwilling to fight any longer.
They were unwilling to fight longer, partly because the retreat of
the armies made it clear that the complete victory which had been
promised was out of the question, partly because they were too
exhausted to make another effort. But there was another and very
important reason for the refusal of the Austrian and German people
to fight any longer. This was their belief that President Wilson
would obtain for them a just and honorable peace.

In his Address to the Senate, January 22, 1917, before the United
States entered the war, President Wilson had said that the peace
must be " a peace without victory." Such a peace the Germans
and Austrians were now eager to accept. But in later addresses,
after the United States entered the war, President Wilson said that

German Tourist Information Office

LOCOMOTIVE ASSEMBLING PLANT, KRUPP WORKS, ESSEN

The Krupp Works furnished most of the artillery used by the Germans during the war. At one of the Krupp plants, the "Big Bertha" was built. Since the war, locomotives and agricultural implements have been the chief output.

the Allies "must win the war" (*Address to Congress, December 4, 1917*). To win the war, he said, the Allies must use "force, force to the uttermost, force without stint or limit" (*Baltimore Speech, April 6, 1918*). There seemed to be an inconsistency here. How could President Wilson convince the Allies that the war must be pushed to a victorious end, and at the same time convince the Germans that the war would result in a peace without victory?

That was a difficult task indeed; but President Wilson accomplished it with amazing success. In all of his addresses after the United States entered the war he explained, or explained away, the seeming inconsistency. He did it by making a distinction between the German people and the "masters of the German people." The "masters of the German people" were the emperor, his ministers, and his military leaders. These masters, the President said, had enslaved the German people. They had plotted to bring about the war in order to enslave the world; they alone were "guilty" of the war; the German people had no part in that guilt. For this reason the Allies were not making war on the German people, but only on the "military masters of the German people" (*Address of*

August 27, 1917). With the masters of the German people the Allies must therefore wage the war to a complete and final victory. But with the German people the Allies would make a just and honorable peace.

What were the terms of the just peace which President Wilson promised the Austrian and German people? These terms were clearly stated in the most famous of all his addresses — the Address to Congress, January 8, 1918, in which he formulated " the world's peace program " under fourteen heads, as follows :

1. Open covenants of peace openly arrived at, after which there shall be no private international understandings of any kind. . . .
2. Absolute freedom of navigation upon the seas outside the territorial waters alike in peace and in war. . . .
3. The removal, so far as possible, of all economic barriers [tariffs, etc.]. . . .
4. Adequate guarantees given and taken that national armaments will be reduced to the lowest point consistent with domestic safety. . . .
5. An . . . impartial adjustment of colonial claims. . . .
6. The evacuation of Russian territory . . . and an unhampered opportunity for the determination of her own political development . . . under institutions of her own choosing.
7. Belgium must be evacuated and restored. . . .
8. All French territory should be freed [and Alsace-Lorraine restored to France]. . . .
9. Readjustment of the frontiers of Italy . . . along lines of nationality. . . .
10. The peoples of Austria-Hungary should be accorded . . . autonomous development. . . .
11. Rumania, Serbia, Montenegro should be evacuated . . . Serbia accorded free access to the sea. . . .
12. Nationalities now under Turkish rule should be assured . . . autonomous development. . . .
13. An independent Polish state should be erected . . . inhabited by Polish populations [with] free and secure access to the sea. . . .
14. A general association of nations must be formed under specific covenants for the purpose of affording mutual guarantees of political independence and territorial integrity to great and small states alike.

These were the famous " Fourteen Points." Translated into all languages, they were everywhere read. And the essence of the

Fourteen Points was embodied in five phrases or slogans which in those days were everywhere familiar and everywhere repeated: (1) "Open Diplomacy"; (2) "Freedom of the Seas"; (3) "No Annexations"; (4) "National Self-Determination"; (5) "A League of Nations." In that last desperate year of 1918, war-weary and peace-loving people throughout the world eagerly welcomed these phrases as a new gospel for the nations, revealing the way of salvation. No people welcomed them more eagerly than the Austrians and the Germans. In the promises of France and Great Britain, of Clemenceau and Lloyd George, they had no confidence. But they believed that President Wilson meant what he said, and that he could do what he promised.

Thus it was that the German and Austrian people, utterly exhausted, faced with defeat, and relying on the promises of President Wilson, turned against their "military masters" as soon as the German armies began to retreat in 1918. In October and November the subject nations of Austria-Hungary revolted. Emperor Charles fled the country, and the old monarchy broke up into three independent republics — Czechoslovakia, Hungary, and German Austria. In November the revolution spread rapidly throughout Germany. In every German state rulers were deposed and republics established. On November 8 the revolutionists gained control of Berlin. Emperor William took refuge with the army; but the military leaders told him that they could not answer for his safety, since the soldiers sympathized with the revolutionists and were on the verge of mutiny. On November 10 the emperor therefore slipped across the frontier into Holland; and on November 28 the self-exiled monarch signed a formal abdication of the crown of Prussia and the German Empire.

With thrones crashing at home and the army on the verge of mutiny, it was useless for the military leaders to resist longer. A German delegation, headed by Matthias Erzberger, was received on November 8 by Marshal Foch and notified of the terms of the armistice. On November 11 the armistice was proclaimed. It was signed at five o'clock in the morning. At eleven o'clock the order was given to cease firing. All along the western front, for the first time in four years, the big guns were silent. The war was over.

CHART FOR CHAPTER XXI   Showing the ups and downs of the Allied Powers on land and sea.

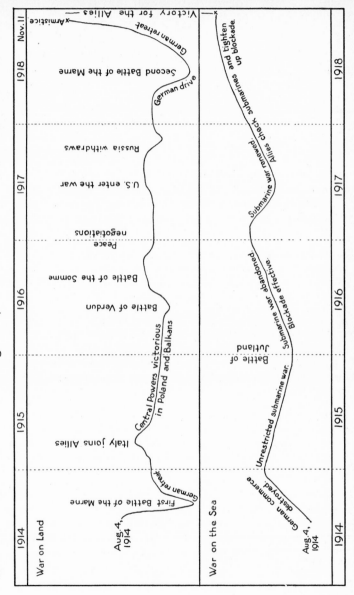

QUESTIONS

1. Give the dates of the three periods into which the Great War may be divided. What were the chief events of each period?

2. Compare the two sides in military and naval strength. What were the chief advantages of the Central Powers? of the Allies? Why did the Germans invade France by way of Belgium? Why did they lose the first Battle of the Marne? Why was this battle a decisive one?

3. What victories did the Central Powers win in 1915? What was the object of the Allied naval campaign? What was the importance of the Battle of Jutland? What did the Germans aim to accomplish by the submarine war? Why did they abandon unrestricted submarine warfare? What measures did the Allies take to "blockade" Germany? What was the object of the Battle of Verdun? of the Battle of the Somme? Why were these battles discouraging to both sides?

4. How did this war differ from earlier wars in the number of troops involved? in the character of its battles and the methods of fighting? in its effect upon the industries of the countries involved? Why were civilians more directly involved than in previous wars?

5. Why did the belligerents begin to talk of peace at the close of 1916? What were the German peace proposals of December 1916? Why did the Allies reject them? Why did President Wilson take part in the discussion of peace? What were the "peace terms" proposed by him in January, 1917?

6. What two major events of 1917 greatly influenced the course of the war? How did the first Russian Revolution come about? By what parties was it supported? How did these parties differ in their ideas of the revolution, and in their attitude towards the war? What was the second Russian Revolution? How did the Bolshevik government try to bring about a general peace? How were they forced to make the Peace of Brest-Litovsk? Why was the Russian Revolution of great advantage to the Central Powers?

7. Why did the United States enter the war in 1917? What were the "war aims" of the United States as stated by President Wilson? Why did the Allies not expect much aid from the United States at first? How did the German military leaders underestimate the importance of the entrance of the United States into the war? What was the object of the great German drive of 1918? Why did it fail? What part did the United States troops take in the second Battle of the Marne?

8. What were the famous "Fourteen Points"? Why were the Fourteen Points welcomed in Germany and Austria? What influence did President Wilson's "peace program" have in breaking the resistance of the Central Powers and in winning the war?

SELECTED READINGS

Brief accounts. Hayes and Moon, *Modern History*, ch. xxv. Hayes, *Modern Europe* (revised ed.), II, ch. xxxi. Schevill, *History of Europe*, ch. xxxiii. Gooch, *Modern Europe*, chs. xvii–xviii. Robinson and Beard, *Outlines* (revised ed.), II, chs. x–xi. A. C. Flick, *Modern World History*, chs. xxxv–xxxvi. Webster, *World History*, ch. xx. D. M. Kettelby, *Modern Times*, ch. ix.

Longer accounts. F. L. Benns, *Europe since 1914*, chs. ii–vi. Slosson, *Twentieth Century Europe*, chs. xi–xiv. G. Ashton, *History of the Great War* (Home University Library). C. E. Fayle, *History of the Great War*. J. E. Edmonds, *History of the Great War*. C. J. H. Hayes, *History of the Great War*. A. F. Pollard, *History of the Great War*. F. H. Simonds, *History of the World War*, 5 vols. (illustrated). D. W. Johnson, *Topography and Strategy of the War* (illustrated). Winston L. S. Churchill, *The World Crisis*.

Fictitious or real accounts (by people who took part in the war or observed it at close quarters). Fritz Kreisler, *Four Weeks in the Trenches*. M. Aldrich, *Hilltop on the Marne*. H. Barbusse, *Under Fire*. J. W. Gerard, *My Four Years in Germany*. A. Seeger, *Letters and Diary*. D. W. A. Hankey, *A Student in Arms*. R. Bending, *A Fatalist at War*. L. Renn, *War*. E. M. Remarque, *All Quiet on the Western Front*. M. Anderson, *What Price Glory*. H. M. Tomlinson, *All Our Yesterdays*. R. Graves, *Good-Bye To All That*. A. Zweig, *The Case of Sergeant Grischa*.

War poetry. *A Book of Verse of the Great War*. R. Brooke, *1914 and Other Poems*. G. H. Clark, *Treasury of War Poetry*.

Sources. Scott and Baltzly, *Readings in European History*, chs. xiv–xv.

THE CATHEDRAL OF NOTRE DAME, THE PONT SULLY, AND THE SEINE
From an etching by Béjot.

CHAPTER XXII. THE PEACE CONFERENCE OF 1919, IN WHICH MANY TREATIES WERE SOMEHOW MADE

It must be a peace without victory. . . . Only a peace between equals can last.
WOODROW WILSON

The Armistice of 1918: In which it appears that President Wilson was able to keep his promises only in part. In November, 1918, President Wilson was at the height of his fame, and few men ever stood so high in the world's estimation. From the time the United States entered the war he had served as the spokesman of the Allies, voicing with emotional fervor those ideals of human brotherhood which in all ages have stirred the heart of mankind. The ideal of peace and goodwill to men had often been voiced before by the saints and sages of the world; but it was a new thing for the ruler of a great state to make it the guiding principle of practical politics. Common men throughout the world, weary of war and destruction, gave to the President's addresses an approval never before accorded to the words of any statesman. With the powerful support of public opinion in every country, President Wilson hoped to keep his promises and to carry through his program; and when the resistance of the Central Powers was broken, he proposed to the Allies that an armistice should be declared and peace negotiated on the basis of the Fourteen Points.

724

It turned out to be easier to make promises than to keep them. In all the Allied countries there were many people who wanted to continue the war until the Germans were entirely crushed. " Why stop fighting now," they asked, " when we have the Germans on the run? Why negotiate with the Germans at all? Let us push on into Germany, occupy Berlin, and crush the German army. We want ' unconditional surrender ' first; then a ' dictated peace.' " The Allied governments did not insist on these extreme measures. They agreed to an armistice, and they even agreed to negotiate the peace on the basis of the Fourteen Points. But in return President Wilson had to agree to certain things which were not in harmony with the spirit of his program.

First, although the Allied governments accepted the Fourteen Points as the basis of peace, they refused to be bound by Point Two on the freedom of the seas, and they insisted that Germany should pay for " all damage done to the civilian population of the Allies and their property by the aggressions of Germany by land, by sea, and from the air." Second, although they agreed to make peace on the basis of the Fourteen Points with these exceptions, they refused to negotiate with Germany. They insisted that the terms of peace should be determined by the Allied governments in a conference at which the Central Powers were not to be represented. Third, although the Allies were willing to stop fighting before Germany was entirely crushed, the terms of the armistice were such as amounted virtually to unconditional surrender.

The terms of the armistice, November 11, 1918, were as follows: (1) German troops were to be withdrawn from Russia, Rumania, Austria-Hungary, Turkey; Belgium, Alsace-Lorraine, and all other territory west of the Rhine River. (2) The Allied troops were to occupy German territory up to the Rhine River, together with the three principal " bridgeheads " at Mainz, Cologne, and Koblenz, to a depth of thirty kilometers on the east side of the Rhine. (3) The economic blockade of Germany was to continue during the peace negotiations. In short, the terms of the armistice, once carried out, would place Germany at the mercy of the Allies and enable the Allied governments to dictate the terms of peace.

With these agreements made, the Peace Conference was assembled in Paris (1919). The results of the conference, and of certain agreements made after it adjourned, were embodied in five treaties: (1) the Treaty of Versailles with Germany, June 28, 1919; (2) the Treaty of Saint-Germain with Austria, September 10, 1919; (3) the Treaty of Neuilly with Bulgaria, November 27, 1919; (4) the Treaty of Trianon with Hungary, June 4, 1920; (5) the Treaty of Sèvres with Turkey, August 10, 1920 (modified in important respects by the Treaty of Lausanne, July 24, 1923). It would be quite impossible to give even a summary of these treaties. The Treaty of Versailles alone fills a book of more than two hundred pages of close print. It will be more useful to see in a general way how the map of Europe was changed by these treaties, and what new institutions were established to preserve the peace between nations.

The natural starting-point is President Wilson's Fourteen Points. They provided a set of general principles for making peace with all the enemy countries. The Allied Powers had agreed, with certain reservations, to make peace on the basis of these principles. Would they live up to this promise? Could they live up to it? The central feature of the Peace Conference was the effort of President Wilson and his supporters to make the peace conform to the Fourteen Points. How far did he succeed, and in what respects did he fail?

The Paris Peace Conference: How it worked and what powers really made the peace. January 18, 1919, the Peace Conference held its first session. Thirty-two states were represented by seventy delegates — a brilliant assembly of the most distinguished political leaders of the world. There was President Wilson, whose presence in Europe was the occasion for popular demonstrations such as perhaps had never before been elicited by any man. There was Clemenceau, the hard-headed French premier — the old " Tiger," who in the darkest hour of the war had assumed direction of the French government and had inspired the French people and the French armies with a desperate determination to win. There was Lloyd George, the brilliant and versatile little Welshman who had replaced Asquith as prime minister in 1916, when the war

THE " BIG FOUR "
Left to right: Lloyd George, Orlando, Clemenceau, and Wilson.

seemed lost, and by his great energy, his infectious enthusiasm, and his genius for leadership had injected a new spirit into the British conduct of the war.   There was Orlando, premier of Italy; Marquis Saionji, premier of Japan; Émile Vandervelde, Belgian patriot and Socialist statesman; Venizelos of Greece — one of the most engaging personalities and one of the shrewdest diplomats of Europe; and many others, famous in their own countries but little more than names to the rest of the world.   Besides the seventy delegates, each delegation was accompanied by a staff of assistants, secretaries, interpreters, and " experts " — economists, geographers, and historians — whose business it was to prepare exact information on the history, geography, and economic conditions of the countries whose claims had now to be adjusted.

As the first of the famous Fourteen Points, President Wilson demanded " open covenants [treaties] openly arrived at."   Many people therefore expected that the peace would be made in an open assembly of all the delegates.   But such a procedure would have been quite impossible. Never before had such a mass, and such a mess, of complicated business come before any body of men. The questions were far too complicated to be settled in so large an assembly. Before they could be even intelligently discussed, voluminous reports had to be prepared by the experts and mastered as well as time permitted by the responsible delegates. Besides, it was inevitable that the great powers that had done most to win victory should have more weight in making peace than the small states that had done little or nothing.

So it happened that the treaties were not " openly arrived at " in public sessions of the conference. At first the conference was managed by a supreme council of ten — two delegates each from France, Great Britain, the United States, Italy, and Japan. The council of ten was soon reduced to five. Later Japan was dropped from the inner council, and there remained the " Big Four " — Wilson, Clemenceau, Lloyd George, and Orlando. Finally Orlando, offended at the proposed settlement of Italy's claims in the Adriatic, withdrew, and the chief decisions for a time fell to the " Big Three " — Wilson, Clemenceau, and Lloyd George. Thus the decisions of the Peace Conference were the result in large part of the conflict of ideas and interests of the five principal Allied Powers; and of these the predominant influence was exercised by the United States, France, and Great Britain.

Why it was impossible for President Wilson to make the peace square with the Fourteen Points. In practical life no one is always able to do what he thinks ideally best. It was so with President Wilson at Paris. In applying the Fourteen Points to the settlement of Europe he had to make concessions: (1) to facts; (2) to people.

William James, the philosopher, once said that he was always up against the " irreducible brute fact." With the best will in the world, it was impossible to make the Fourteen Points square with the " irreducible brute facts " of European life. For example, one of President Wilson's most cherished principles was the " self-determination of nations." The idea was that each nation should govern itself. It is a very good idea. But the frontiers between the European nations are not clear-cut. Between Germany and

Poland, for example, are large areas inhabited by both Germans and Poles. Where, then, draw the frontier of the new Polish state? It was impossible to draw it so that all Poles would live in Poland and all Germans in Germany. The same difficulty existed in drawing the frontier of most of the new states. Thus no solution of the question of frontiers was possible without violating to some extent the principle of the self-determination of nations.

President Wilson found it necessary to make concessions, not only to the brute facts of European geography, but to the opinions, the fears and animosities, of the people with whom the treaty had to be made. He discovered that the Allied governments were bound by secret territorial bargains of which he said he had never heard. He found popular opinion in the Allied countries less favorable to the Fourteen Points than he had expected. After the signing of the armistice his influence began to decline. This astonished him, but it need not astonish us. While the principal object was still to win the war, it was easy and consoling for people to think with President Wilson, " We are fighting for freedom and justice, not for selfish advantage." But once the victory was won, the high emotional strain under which people had lived for four years relaxed, and old habits of thought revived. Then people began to think less about the high ideals they had fought for and more about making Germany repay them for their sacrifices. They can scarcely be blamed for that. Having been thoroughly taught to hate the Germans, they could not all at once cease to hate them. In all the Allied countries, including the United States, the majority of the people expected their delegates at the Peace Conference to punish Germany for beginning the war, to weaken her so that she could not begin another, and to obtain for the Allied countries some compensation for their losses.

It was therefore quite impossible for President Wilson to make the peace conform to the Fourteen Points in every respect. In order to get some things he wanted, he had to give up others. What he wanted most of all was the League of Nations (Point Fourteen). To get this he made many concessions. What were they? Point Two (freedom of the seas) was conceded in the armistice. Points One and Three (open diplomacy and free trade) were virtually ignored. But besides these concessions, President Wilson made five great compromises. These compromises had to do with (1) disarmament; (2) the left bank and the Saar Valley; (3) the Italian frontier; (4) colonies and spheres of influence; (5) reparations.

The great compromises: (1) Disarmament for the Central Powers alone. Point Four reads: " adequate guarantees given and taken that national armaments will be reduced to the lowest point consistent with domestic safety." President Wilson thought of this point as bound up with the League of Nations; with a League of Nations to settle disputes, there would be no need for great armies and navies. But there never was at any time the slightest chance of getting the great powers, or the small ones either, to abolish their armies and navies. The League of Nations was not yet established, and no one knew whether it would work or not. Besides, people in the Allied countries were convinced that Germany alone was responsible for the war. " What would have happened in 1914," they asked, " if France had not had a powerful army? " Although defeated, Germany was still so much feared that her ports were blockaded and her territory occupied by Allied troops. To the people in the Allied countries disarmament for themselves seemed the height of folly. The sensible thing, they thought, was to disarm Germany but keep the Allied armies as a guarantee that Germany would never again be able to endanger the peace of the world.

The only " adequate guarantees " on disarmament were given by Germany and the other Central Powers. The Treaty of Versailles required that the German army should be limited to 100,000 men. Compulsory military training was forbidden; enlistments were to be voluntary and for a period of not less than twelve years. The size of the navy was limited, the use of submarines and military airplanes forbidden. Similar restrictions were imposed on Austria, Hungary, and Bulgaria in the treaties with those countries. Thus the Central Powers alone were disarmed. As for the Allied countries, the question of disarmament was referred for consideration to the future League of Nations.

The great compromises: (2) The " left bank " and the Saar Valley. This compromise had to do with the French-German frontier. Point Eight of President Wilson's Fourteen Points called for the restoration of Alsace-Lorraine, taken from France in 1871. But the French people were not satisfied with the mere restoration of Alsace-Lorraine. France had suffered terrible devastation during the war, and would have lost more by defeat than any other country. Thoroughly convinced that Germany had deliberately brought on the war, the French people wanted above everything else to weaken Germany and strengthen France. To accomplish this most Frenchmen desired, not only to disarm Germany but to deprive her of the control of the entire left bank of the Rhine and to annex to France that part of it known as the Saar Valley or the Saar Basin.

The " left bank " is the name given to that part of the German Empire lying west of the Rhine, between Lorraine and the Dutch frontier — a very rich industrial region inhabited by more than 5,000,000 Germans. Marshal Foch favored the outright annexation of the left bank; but the proposal of the French delegates at the Peace Conference was that this region should be separated from Germany and erected into a separate state subject to the military and economic control of France for an indefinite period. The Saar Valley, which is only a small part of the left bank, is on the Lorraine frontier. Its special value is in its coal mines, which before the war yielded 17,000,000 tons a year, or 8 per cent of the coal produced in the German Empire. Unlike the rest of the left bank, the Saar had, by the Treaty of Paris in 1814, been left to France; but in 1815 it had been given to Prussia. The French now proposed to " reannex " the Saar to France, to " restore the historic boundary of 1814."

These proposals, which would have turned over to French rule more than 5,000,000 Germans, produced the most serious crisis of the Peace Conference. President Wilson absolutely refused to assent to so flagrant a violation of the principle of self-determination. Lloyd George was opposed to the French proposals also. But he had less faith than President Wilson had in the League of Nations as a means of giving France security. Besides, he wished

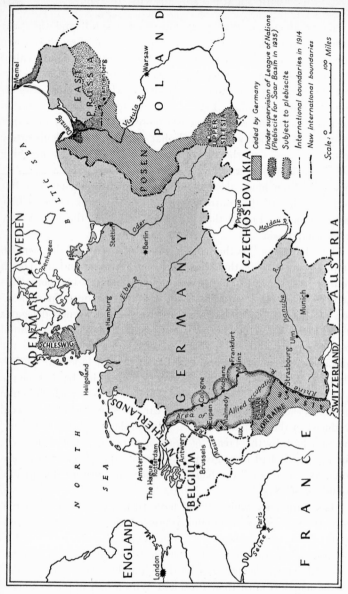

Ceded by Germany

Under supervision of League of Nations
(Plebiscite for Saar Basin in 1935)

Subject to plebiscite

International boundaries in 1914

New international boundaries

Scale: 0 ——————— 100 Miles

BOUNDARIES OF GERMANY AS DETERMINED BY THE TREATY OF VERSAILLES, 1919

at all hazards to prevent a breach between the three powers — France, Great Britain, and the United States. He therefore skillfully contrived to place obstacles in the way of the French plan, without clearly siding with President Wilson. For six weeks the conflict continued without result. President Wilson fell ill under the strain; and on April 7 he ordered the *George Washington* to sail immediately from New York for France. This act seemed to the world to signify that the President was preparing to withdraw from the Peace Conference. Whatever the President's intention may have been, the crisis was safely passed, and in the following weeks, by virtue of concessions on both sides, a compromise was finally arranged in respect to the left bank and the Saar Valley.

The essential features of this compromise were as follows. Clemenceau agreed not to insist on the annexation of any German territory except Alsace-Lorraine. President Wilson agreed (1) to sign a military treaty with France and Great Britain to guarantee France against future attack by Germany; (2) to deprive Germany of the control of the left bank for a period of fifteen years according to the following conditions: (*a*) during the fifteen-year period the left bank was to be occupied by Allied troops at German expense; (*b*) the Saar Valley was to be placed under the sovereignty of the League of Nations and its mines to be placed at the disposal of France; (*c*) at the close of the fifteen-year period all the Allied troops were to be withdrawn from the left bank, and the people of the Saar Valley were to decide by popular vote whether they wished to be united with Germany or with France, or to continue as a separate state under the protection of the League of Nations.

The settlement of the left bank and the Saar Valley gave the French less than they desired but more than could be easily reconciled with the ideal principles of the Fourteen Points.

The great compromises: (3) The Italian frontier. Even after the completion of Italian unification in 1870 there were some territories on the northern and eastern frontiers which were inhabited mostly by Italians but were still parts of the Austro-Hungarian Monarchy. The chief of these regions were: (1) the city of

Trent and the territory in the southern part of what is known as the Tyrol or the Trentino; (2) the city of Trieste and the surrounding territory at the head of the Adriatic. Italian patriots had long clamored for the " redemption " of their Italian brothers living under foreign rule, and one of Italy's objects in joining the Allies in 1915 had been to obtain the Austrian territories inhabited by Italians. So it was that " Trent and Trieste " became the popular Italian slogan during the war.

If the Italian delegates at the Peace Conference had asked only for the territory inhabited by Italians, no objections would have been raised. But they asked for much more than that. They asked not only for the southern Trentino, which is inhabited by Italians, but for the northern part, which is almost entirely German in population. They asked not only for Trieste but for the Istrian Peninsula and the city of Fiume, which were largely Slavic in population. In justification of these demands, they argued as follows: " (1) The Trentino is the natural gateway into Italy through the mountains. It will be of no use to us for military defense against Germany and Austria unless we possess the northern approaches to the passes; (2) when we entered the war the Allies promised us, by the secret Treaty of London (1915), not only Trieste and most of the Trentino, but also the Istrian Peninsula and part of Dalmatia. Italy has carried out her part of the bargain and the Allies must carry out their part, even if it does violate the principle of self-determination."

France and Great Britain could not well object to ceding to Italy what they had promised in the secret Treaty of London. But the United States had not signed the secret Treaty of London. President Wilson said that he had never heard of this treaty; and anyway he claimed that when the Allies agreed to make peace on the basis of the Fourteen Points the secret treaties were thereby canceled. He therefore refused to agree to the extreme demands of the Italians. Nevertheless, he was willing to make many concessions. On the advice of the American experts, he agreed that Italy should have the entire Trentino, Trieste, and a considerable part of Istria, thus turning over to Italian rule some hundreds of thousands of Germans and Slavs; but on the question of Fiume

President Wilson stood firm. Fiume was not only inhabited chiefly by Slavs; it was the principal available outlet to the sea for the new state of Yugoslavia. To give it to Italy would be to give her a dangerous control over the economic life of the newly created Slavic state.

The question of Fiume created another crisis in the Peace Conference. President Wilson hoped to win his point by appealing in a public statement to the Italian people over the heads of her representatives. The only effect of this act was that Orlando and Sonnino withdrew temporarily from the conference, while the Italian people, who a few months earlier had welcomed the President as a deliverer, now denounced him as a pro-German and demolished the statues formerly erected in his honor. Meantime, Gabriele d'Annunzio, the Italian poet and novelist, gathered a band of free-booters, seized Fiume, and announced that he would hold it for Italy whatever the Peace Conference might decide. Thereupon, the conference abandoned the attempt to settle the question, leaving Italy and the new state of Yugoslavia to settle it as they could. In the end (*Treaty of Rapallo, 1920, modified in 1924*) Italy obtained both Istria and Fiume, but agreed that Yugoslavia should have free commercial use of the city.

The great compromises: (4) Colonies and spheres of influence. Everyone knew that the war was partly caused by the rivalries of the great states over colonies, trade privileges, and spheres of influence in the so-called backward countries. If these rivalries could be abolished, at least one cause of war would disappear. This was doubtless why President Wilson included in his Fourteen Points the following: Point Three, " Removal, so far as possible, of all economic barriers [tariffs]; " and Point Five, " An absolutely impartial adjustment of colonial claims, the interest of the populations concerned having equal weight with the claims of the governments whose title is to be determined." To what extent did the Peace Conference abide by these principles?

The chief " economic barriers " were the tariffs levied by the several countries on the imports from other countries. President Wilson said that by Point Three he did not mean that tariffs should be abolished, but only that in levying tariffs there should be " no

discrimination against some nations that does not apply to others."
But even so it was certain that none of the Allied countries — least
of all the United States — would consent to a treaty that restricted
its right to levy such tariffs as it pleased.   At all events, no attempt
was made to restrict the right of the Allied states to erect " economic barriers."   Germany alone was forbidden, for a brief period
of about five years, to discriminate against the trade of any of the
Allied states.

Point Five, calling for " impartial adjustment of colonial claims,"
was likewise ignored, or nearly so.   The Treaty of Versailles deprived Germany of all her colonial possessions and distributed them
among Great Britain, France, Japan.   To Great Britain was
given German East Africa and a small part of the German Kamerun; to the British self-governing colonies — South Africa, Australia, and New Zealand — were given German Southwest Africa,
German New Guinea, and German Samoa.   France received the
greater part of German Togoland and the Kamerun.   Japan received the German Pacific islands north of the equator and the
rich province of Shantung, which Germany had obtained from
China in 1898.

In like manner the Allied states divided among themselves a
great part of the former Ottoman Empire.   The eventual partition of the Ottoman Empire had been agreed upon during the war
in the secret treaties signed by the Allied governments (see p. 702).
Russia, having withdrawn from the war after the Bolshevik revolution, was not represented at the Peace Conference.   But France,
Great Britain, and Italy insisted that the terms of the secret
treaties, with some modifications, should be carried out; and this
was done by the Treaty of Sèvres with Turkey (1920).   Nevertheless, a vigorous Turkish nationalist uprising, under the lead
of Kemal Pasha, made it impossible, short of a new war with
Turkey, to enforce this treaty; and in the end the Allied states
agreed to a new treaty, known as the Treaty of Lausanne (1923).

By the Treaty of Lausanne, Turkey retained Asia Minor, the
city of Constantinople, and the territory in Thrace as far west
as the city of Adrianople.   The remainder of the former Ottoman
Empire was disposed of as follows: Syria, including Damascus,

was given to France; Mesopotamia, Transjordan, and Palestine (including Jerusalem), were given to Great Britain; the islands in the Aegean known as the Dodecanese Islands were given, with two exceptions, to Italy; the Arabian territory along the Red Sea, known as the Hejaz, was made independent; Armenia, which by the Treaty of Sèvres had been made a free republic, was restored to Turkey. In all of these arrangements the interests and desires of the native populations were largely ignored.

President Wilson consented to the distribution of German colonies and to the partition of the Ottoman Empire with much reluctance. He was especially opposed to the transfer of Shantung to Japan, believing that by every principle of justice it should be restored to China; but he had to be content with the promise of Japan that she would herself restore Shantung to China sometime in the future. (This was later done, at the Washington Conference, 1921–1922.) Although he consented to the distribution of the German colonies among the Allied states, President Wilson insisted that a new method should be adopted for administering them. This is known as the system of " mandates." For example, the former German colony of East Africa was turned over to Great Britain. But it is not, strictly speaking, a British colony in the old sehse; it is a territory administered by Great Britain under a " mandate " from the League of Nations. This means that Great Britain is bound to give to the League a periodical accounting of her administration of East Africa. The theory is that the governments which administer " mandated " territories do so as trustees on behalf of all the states that are members of the League. Most of the former German colonies are held as mandates; and this is true also of Syria and Mesopotamia.

The great compromises: (5) Reparations. The Fourteen Points did not mention reparations; but in his other addresses President Wilson had said that there must not be any " punitive indemnities " — that is, money exacted from the vanquished as a *punishment*. Nevertheless, the terms of the armistice required Germany to pay for " damage done to the civilian population of the Allies and their property by the aggressions of Germany by land, by sea, and from the air." The theory was that payment for damage done was not " punitive indemnity " but merely just reparation. The conference had therefore to determine: (1) what was to be included in damage done; and (2) the amount of such damage done.

First, what was to be included in damage done? During the war Germany had destroyed many farms and houses in France and Belgium. This was clearly damage done by Germany to civilians. In addition, the people of France had had to pay taxes to equip their soldiers. This was also damage to civilians; but was it done by Germany? Again, thousands of English soldiers had been killed, leaving their families without means of livelihood, and the English were taxed to pay pensions to these people. This, too, was damage done to civilians; but was it done by Germany? There were extremists at the conference who wished to include in damage done by Germany the entire cost of the war. But President Wilson and others would not assent to this, so that in the end the bill for damages was expected to include only the value of property actually destroyed and pensions paid by the Allied states to wounded veterans or the families of soldiers killed in the war.

Second, what sum would cover these two items? The economic experts soon discovered that the sum would be enormous — far more, in their opinion, than Germany could pay. The question then became, not how much damage Germany had done, but : What was the maximum sum that Germany could possibly pay? The American experts estimated that Germany might possibly pay $25,000,000,000, with interest, if the payments were spread over a period of years. But Clemenceau and Lloyd George both said that it would never do to fix the amount at so low a figure. " The French and British people," they said in substance, " have been led to expect that the Germans will pay for the war. In fact we have virtually told them as much; and if we now announce that Germany can pay no more than this small sum of $25,000,000,000, they will turn us out of office and appoint others in our places. Then the work of the conference will have to begin all over again."

Thus the question changed once more and became : How require Germany to pay the largest sum possible without saying precisely what that sum might turn out to be? In the end it was determined that Germany should pay, before 1921, the sum of $5,000,000,000, without interest, and thereafter such sums annually as might be fixed by an international Reparations Commission. In 1921 the Commission determined the conditions under which Germany should pay, over a long period of time, capital and interest amounting to $33,000,000,000 — with the possibility that more might be required later if it should later appear that Germany was able to pay more. Germany objected to this settlement on the ground that the total amount required of her was not fixed and was in any case beyond her capacity. After ten years of bitterness and strife over reparations, the sum to be demanded of Germany was reduced to about $27,000,000,000 (see p. 807).

These were the five great compromises — the five important respects in which the peace did not conform to the spirit of the Fourteen Points. In what respects *did* the peace conform to the Fourteen Points? In two very important respects. (1) The Peace Conference remade the political map of Europe so that it conformed to the principle of the self-determination of nations far more strictly than before the war. (2) The Peace Conference established the League of Nations. We must now see how this was done.

The self-determination of Nations: (1) The restoration of Poland. The desire for national independence was one of the chief political aspirations of the nineteenth century. National independence was won by the Italians and the Germans in the time of Cavour and Bismarck (1860–1871); but in 1914 many nations of eastern Europe were still subject to governments which they regarded as foreign. These subject nations were nearly all included within the territory ruled by four great powers — Germany, Russia, Austria-Hungary, and Turkey. One of the chief results of the Great War was the liberation of the subject nations and the creation of a large number of new " national " states.

One of the most important of the new national states was Poland — an old state restored. For centuries Poland had been an independent kingdom; but in the latter eighteenth century it had been partitioned between Russia, Prussia, and Austria (see p. 138). The Poles had never been reconciled to the loss of their independence,

RUSSIAN WOOD CARVERS   © *William Thompson*

The home was the workshop for such workmen, and all members of the family assisted.

and throughout the nineteenth century the partition of Poland was remembered as a high-handed crime against human liberty. It was doubtless for this reason that President Wilson, in his Fourteen Points, made a special case of Poland. Point Thirteen reads: " An independent Polish state should be erected . . . inhabited by Polish populations [with] free and secure access to the sea. . . ." At the close of the war, when revolution swept over Germany and Austria, the Poles formerly subject to Russia, Germany, and Austria, reunited to establish the Polish Republic. Therefore when the Peace Conference met, an independent Polish state had already been erected. The work of the Peace Conference was limited to defining the boundaries of the new republic.

This was no easy task, since both the eastern and western frontiers of Poland were inhabited by mixed populations. In the first place, the Poles claimed all of the old Austrian provinces of Galicia, although the population of eastern Galicia was mainly Ruthenian. However, the chief city of eastern Galicia — Lemberg,

© *Press Cliché*

TUNGUS WOMEN, IN SIBERIA
Probably these women were not much interested in the Peace Conference.

now called Lwów — was Polish, and the people of wealth and influence were Poles. The Polish Republic was therefore prepared
to fight rather than abandon any part of Galicia; and so the Peace
Conference decided that all of Galicia should be united with Poland,
with the proviso that eastern Galicia should enjoy " home rule "
under its own parliament for a period of twenty-five years.

The eastern and northern frontiers were also difficult to define,
since there was a wide region inhabited by a mixed population of
Poles, Russians, Lithuanians, and Ukrainians. Both Poland and
Russia claimed this region; and the Peace Conference, although it
established a provisional boundary, left the final settlement to
Poland and Russia. In 1920 they settled it by a short war in
which Poland was successful.

More difficult still was the task of drawing the boundary between
Poland and Germany. The two regions in dispute were Upper
Silesia and the so-called " Polish Corridor." Upper Silesia had the
same kind of importance as the Saar Valley. It was a rich industrial region which, before the war, yielded 23 per cent of Germany's
coal. The majority of the people were Poles, but it was uncertain

whether or not a majority would prefer to be united with Poland. The matter was therefore left to the people of Upper Silesia to decide; and the result of the plebiscite or referendum was that a large majority voted in favor of having Upper Silesia united with Germany. In this, as in most other plebiscites of a similar nature, the defeated party claimed that the voting was unfairly, or even corruptly, managed.

The other region in dispute concerned chiefly the city of Danzig on the Baltic near the mouth of the Vistula River. The Poles desired, and President Wilson urged, that they be given " free and secure access to the sea." This was done by giving Poland a strip of territory (the so-called " Corridor ") running up to the Baltic at Danzig. The Germans objected to this arrangement for two reasons: (1) because it separated East Prussia from the rest of Prussia; (2) because the city of Danzig and the surrounding terri- tory was inhabited almost entirely by Germans. The Peace Con- ference nevertheless decided to give Poland the " Corridor," on the ground that it was less of an injustice to include a great many Germans in Poland than it was to leave the mouth of Poland's chief river and her chief available seaport in the control of a hostile Germany. As a concession to Germany, Danzig was made a " free city " under the protection of the League of Nations, although as a seaport, for the purpose of administering the customs, it was placed under the control of Poland. (See map, p. 732.)

In the old Russian Empire there were subject nations besides the Poles. Since Russia was not represented at the Peace Confer- ence, the conference had nothing directly to do with these nations; but as a result of the Bolshevik revolution and of the war, four new states were established. They were Lithuania, Latvia, Estonia, and Finland. The Republic of Ukrainia, established in 1918, lost its independence and was reunited with Russia; but in 1920 the Ukrainian Socialist Soviet Republic was established and recognized by the Russian government.

The self-determination of nations: (2) How the Austro- Hungarian Monarchy was divided among five nations. The Austro-Hungarian Monarchy was a curious conglomeration of national groups — Germans, Magyars, Czechs, Slovaks, Ruma-

© *William Thompson*
AIRPLANE VIEW OF THE HARBOR OF REVAL, ESTONIA
Reval (Tallinn), the capital of the Estonian Republic, has always been an important port because of its excellent harbor. It was in medieval times one of the cities of the Hanseatic League.

nians, Serbo-Croats, Slovenes, and Italians. The groups that largely dominated the government were the Germans and the Magyars. The Slavs regarded themselves as oppressed subject nations. They had therefore supported the war with no great enthusiasm, and when the Central Powers were defeated in 1918 they revolted. Within a month the authority of the Austro-Hungarian government collapsed; and when the Peace Conference met there was no longer any Austria-Hungary to deal with, but only the fragments into which it had been broken by defeat and revolution. The major part of the former monarchy was claimed by five states, one of them an old state, the others new ones. The five states were Czechoslovakia, Yugoslavia, Austria, Hungary, and Rumania. The task of the Peace Conference was largely confined to determining the boundaries of these states.

The task was a difficult one. In a country of such mixed population it was difficult enough in any case to draw satisfactory national boundaries. But the task was made still more difficult because the various national groups were bitterly jealous of each

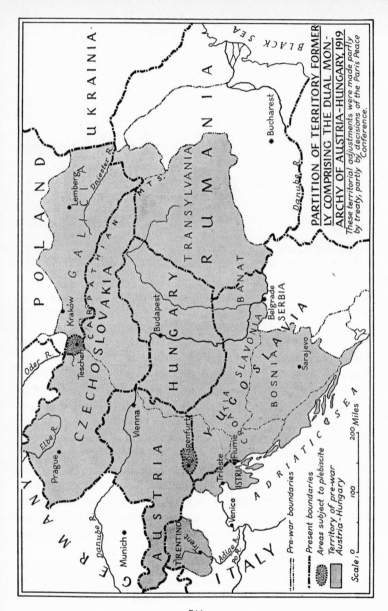

PARTITION OF TERRITORY FORMER-
LY COMPRISING THE DUAL MON-
ARCHY OF AUSTRIA-HUNGARY, 1919

These territorial adjustments were made partly
by treaty, partly by decisions of the Paris Peace
Conference.

BLACK SEA

UKRAINIA

POLAND

GERMANY

ITALY

RUMANIA

HUNGARY

AUSTRIA

CZECHOSLOVAKIA

GALICIA

TRANSYLVANIA

BANAT

SERBIA

BOSNIA

SLAVONIA

CROATIA

ISTRIA

CARPATHIAN MT S.

TRENTINO

• Bucharest

Lemberg •

Kraków •

Budapest •

Vienna •

Prague •

Munich •

Belgrade

Sarajevo •

Trieste

Fiume

Venice

Teschen

Klagenfurt

Trent •

Dniester R.

Danube R.

Oder R.

Elbe R.

Adige R.

Po R.

ADRIATIC SEA

Pre-war boundaries
Present boundaries
Areas subject to plebiscite
Territory of pre-war
Austria-Hungary

Scale: 0   100   200 Miles

744

other, and each claimed far more territory than could be justified on any ground. The result was that the recommendations of the experts — especially the American experts — had more weight in the decisions than the claims of the various peoples concerned. No satisfactory or strictly just division of territory was possible; but the division actually made was rather more than fair to the Slavic nations, and rather less than fair to the Magyars and the Germans. This was due to the fact that the Magyars and the Germans were regarded as largely responsible for Austria-Hungary's part in the war. They were still thought of as the " enemy," while the subject Slavic nations, who had for the most part supported the war only under compulsion, were regarded as friends of the Allies. We must now see how the Peace Conference applied the principle of self-determination in dividing the old Austro-Hungarian Monarchy among five nations.

1. *The Republic of Czechoslovakia.* The country of the Czechs is Bohemia, which before the seventeenth century had been a semi-independent kingdom. The ancient frontier of Bohemia on the north and west was the circular range of the Carpathian Mountains, and the Czechs now asked that this " historic frontier " be made the boundary of the new state. The objection to doing this was that within the western rim of the Carpathians there were about 3,000,000 Germans who might properly be united with either Germany or Austria. But the Czechs demanded the old mountain frontier partly because of the military defense against Germany and partly because it contained resources necessary for the economic development of the country.

Although demanding the historic frontier on the west and north, the Czechs objected to it on the south and east. They advanced three reasons for including within the new state of Czechoslovakia a considerable part of ancient Hungary. (1) They wished to unite with Bohemia that part of Hungary which was inhabited by the Slovaks — a Slavic people closely related to the Czechs. (2) They wished the new state to extend far enough east so that its frontier would join that of Rumania, thus enabling these two states to defend themselves more easily against Hungary. (3) They wished the southern frontier to touch on the Danube, so that the new state,

Czechoslovak Consulate, New York

WORK OF PEASANTS OF RUTHENIA, IN EASTERN CZECHOSLOVAKIA

The pottery and the woven material made in Czechoslovakia are strikingly colored.

which had no seacoast, would at least have access to the waterway leading to the Black Sea.   To concede the last two demands would make it necessary to include within Czechoslovakia more than a million Magyars and Ruthenians.

In spite of the opposition of the Germans and the Magyars, the Peace Conference gave the Czechs practically the frontiers which they wanted.   The result is that Czechoslovakia can hardly be called a " national " state.   The Czechs and the Slovaks are really two nations rather than one.   Besides, nearly one-third of the total population of 14,000,000 is neither Czech nor Slovak, but German, Magyar, and Ruthenian.   In arranging the boundaries of Czechoslovakia the conference departed rather far from the principle of self-determination in order to gratify the patriotic sentiments of the Czechs, or to safeguard their military and economic interests.

2. *The Kingdom of Rumania.*   Before the war Rumania was an independent kingdom lying between the Black Sea and the Austro-Hungarian Monarchy.   It had long coveted the Hungarian prov-

Czechoslovak Consulate, New York

DWELLING HOUSE IN CZECHOSLOVAKIA

Many houses of this type may be seen in Czechoslovakia.   Notice the mud wall
at the right.

ince of Transylvania (meaning the province across the Carpathian
Mountains), which was largely inhabited by Rumanians.   Rumania now asked not only for that part of Transylvania inhabited
by Rumanians, but also for a generous slice of territory to the west
inhabited largely by Magyars.   This they said was necessary in
order that Rumania might control the railroads connecting northern and southern Transylvania.   In addition, the Rumanians
claimed a district in southern Hungary, known as the Banat of
Temesvar, inhabited partly by Rumanians and partly by Serbs.
The Peace Conference gave the Rumanians most of the territory
they asked for, except the western third of the Banat of Temesvar,
which went to Yugoslavia.

Rumania was thus greatly enlarged — chiefly at the expense of
Hungary.   Like Czechoslovakia, it now contains many people,
chiefly Magyars, who are of alien speech and customs, who profess
different religions (the Magyars are Roman Catholic while the
Rumanians are mainly Orthodox Catholic), and who therefore
regard themselves as subject to foreign rule.

3. *The Kingdom of Yugoslavia.*   The new state of Yugoslavia
was made up of the old Kingdoms of Serbia and Montenegro, some

small parts of Bulgaria, and those parts of the Austro-Hungarian Monarchy which were inhabited by Slavs more or less related to the Serbs — the provinces of Croatia, Bosnia-Herzegovina, and part of the Banat of Temesvar. It was the realization of the dream of a greater Serbia which created the bitter rivalry between Serbia and Austria-Hungary before the war (see p. 660). Although inhabited mainly by Slavs, Yugoslavia contains half a million Germans, an equal number of Magyars, 150,000 Rumanians, and 175,000 Italians. Besides, the Slavic groups that make up the majority of the population (Serbs, Croats, Slovenes) differ a good deal in language and customs. It was easy for them to unite against the alien rule of Austria-Hungary; it has been less easy for them to unite for the purpose of ruling themselves.

Thus the territory inhabited by the subject nations of the old Austro-Hungarian Monarchy was distributed among three states — Czechoslovakia, Rumania, and Yugoslavia. There remained the territory inhabited by the two dominating nations — the Magyars of Hungary, and the Germans of Austria proper. How much was left for them? Very little.

4. *The Republic of Austria.* After the defeat of the Central Powers, the Germans of Austria, like the other nations, freed themselves from their Habsburg rulers. When the boundaries of Czechoslovakia, Rumania, Yugoslavia, and Italy were once determined, there were only about 6,500,000 Austrian Germans left unaccounted for. According to the principle of nationality, it would have been proper to unite them with the German Republic. The Austrian Germans in fact requested that this be done, and the American delegation to the Peace Conference approved of it. But France was strongly opposed to any enlargement of her old enemy, Germany, and so the conference decided that the Austrian Germans must form a little inland state of their own. It is one of the smallest states of Europe. Nearly a third of its population lives in the capital city of Vienna. It has few resources and is dependent for food on the outside world. It was still further weakened by being required to assume, jointly with Hungary, responsibility for reparations to the Allied countries for damage done to civilian property during the war.

Czechoslovak Consulate, New York
WELL SWEEP IN MORAVIA, CZECHOSLOVAKIA

5. *The Kingdom of Hungary.* The Magyars, like the Austrian Germans, were regarded by the Peace Conference as the "enemy," and as such were shown no favors. Much of ancient Hungary — even of that part of Hungary inhabited by Magyars — was turned over to Czechoslovakia, Rumania, and Yugoslavia. The Hungary that remained under Magyar control was a small state of about 35,000 square miles, with a population of no more than 8,000,000. Together with the Republic of Austria, the government of Hungary was made responsible for reparations. During the Peace Conference a Bolshevist régime was temporarily established in Hungary, only to be followed by a strongly reactionist movement which aimed to restore the Habsburg dynasty. The Peace Conference intervened to prevent this, declaring that " such a restoration would be at variance with the whole basis of the peace settlement, and would neither be recognized nor tolerated." So for a time Hungary was a monarchy without a king.

The self-determination of nations: (3) To what extent did the peace treaties really conform to the principle of self-determination ?

The Peace Conference has often been severely criticized for flagrant violation of the principle of self-determination. What can be said in its defense? Consider, first, the treatment accorded to Asiatic peoples in Asia. The result of the war and the peace was to destroy the ancient Ottoman Empire. But the millions of people in Syria, Mesopotamia, and Palestine formerly subject to the Turks were not made independent. They were only transferred from Turkish rule to French and English rule. In defense of the Peace Conference some writers say that these people were incapable of self-government; others say that they are far better off under French and British rule than under Turkish rule; still others say that in any case their rights are sufficiently safeguarded by the adoption of the mandate system (see p. 737). In spite of all this it must be admitted that in dealing with Asiatic peoples the Peace Conference paid very little attention to the principle of self-determination.

Consider, second, the treatment accorded European peoples. It is true, as we have seen, that in arranging the boundaries of central and eastern Europe there were many violations of the principle of self-determination. Many Germans were left subject to Czechoslovakia, Poland, Rumania, Yugoslavia, and Italy — altogether perhaps five or six million. Many Magyars were left subject to Czechoslovakia, Rumania, and Yugoslavia — altogether perhaps two million. And in all the countries of central and western Europe there were still, as before the war, millions of Jews subject to alien rule.

These are notable exceptions to the principle of national independence. But if we compare the political map of Europe in 1914 with that of 1920, it is clear that the war and the peace resulted in a great triumph for President Wilson's principle of self-determination. In 1914 the number of Slavs and Italians subject to the alien rule of Germany, Austria-Hungary, and Russia was about 50,000,000. The war and the peace liberated these peoples and permitted them to establish governments of their own choosing. For the first time in history the political boundaries of central and eastern Europe corresponded in some fashion, even if only roughly, to national boundaries. So far as Europe is concerned, it may therefore be said that the peace treaties conformed to the principle of self-determination of nations to a far greater extent than they violated it.

Whether the creation of so many new states in central and eastern Europe was a wise measure is another question, which only the future can answer. Certainly not all is peace and harmony among the liberated nations. National hatreds still exist — between the Poles and the Germans, the Magyars and the Rumanians, the Yugoslavs and the Italians. The " minority groups " within the new states although guaranteed by the treaties equal rights in respect to citizenship, language, education, and religion, are still often oppressed, and in any case discontented. The little land-locked states of Hungary and Austria are indeed independent national states; but, surrounded by hostile and more powerful neighbors, they do not count national independence a great blessing.

Before the war the Balkan Peninsula, divided among small warring states, was recognized as a " danger zone " always threatening the peace of Europe. The chief service of the Austro-Hungarian Monarchy was that it kept this region in at least some kind of order; and perhaps the worst that can be said of the peace settlement is that by destroying the Austro-Hungarian Monarchy it " Balkanized " the whole of eastern Europe, and thereby greatly increased the danger of perpetual war. This danger was clearly recognized by the Greek statesman, Venizelos. " Without the League of Nations," he said, " southeastern Europe would face the future with despair in its heart."

This brings us to the second of President Wilson's two leading ideas. He regarded the League of Nations as the foundation of his entire peace program; and he might have said: " Without the League of Nations the Peace Conference is a failure, and the future of the world is without hope."

The League of Nations: How the Covenant was drafted, modified, and adopted. The idea of a league of states to prevent war is an old one. We have already learned something about the projects for such a league that were published in the seventeenth and eighteenth centuries (see pp. 204–207). We have seen that over and over again the peace societies of the nineteenth century urged the formation of such a league (see p. 341). The formation of the

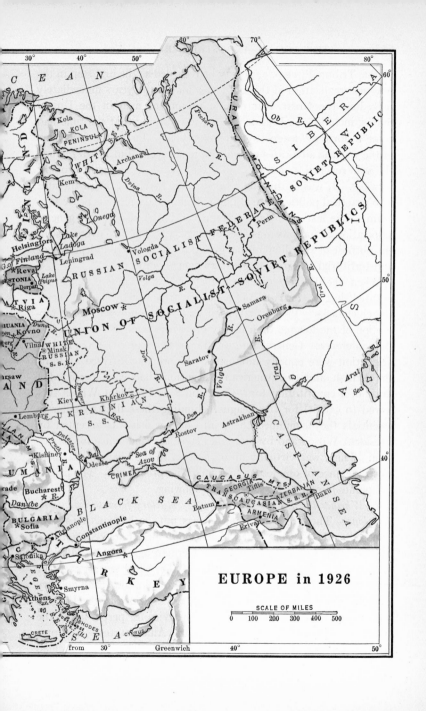

EUROPE in 1926

SCALE OF MILES

0   100   200   300   400   500

Hague Tribunal (see p. 627) may be regarded as the first step in the practical realization of this old idea; and in the years immediately preceding the Great War certain prominent men in the United States, including ex-President Taft, were urging that the time had come to form a " league to enforce peace." During the first years of the war the advocates of peace were silenced; but in 1917, when the war reached a deadlock, peace proposals were again brought forward. It was at this time that President Wilson thrust the idea into practical politics by making it the foundation of his peace program. The last of his famous Fourteen Points reads: " A general association of nations must be formed under specific covenants for the purpose of affording mutual guarantees of political independence and territorial integrity to great and small states alike."

When the Peace Conference met, it was therefore taken for granted that the formation of a League of Nations would be one of the chief tasks. President Wilson was more interested in the formation of the League than in any other question that came before the conference. General Smuts and Lord Robert Cecil of the British delegation were equally interested. Before they arrived at Paris the British and the American delegations had each prepared a draft of a constitution (or " Covenant," as President Wilson preferred to call it) for the League. Finding these drafts similar in essentials they combined them into one, which was accepted by President Wilson and by him laid before the conference for discussion. There was virtually no opposition to the League, but there was difference of opinion as to some of its provisions. The principal points in controversy were the following.

1. *Whether the League should employ military force to execute its decisions.* The French delegation was not, as is sometimes said, opposed to the League; but Clemenceau hoped to make it a means of protecting France against future German aggression. His idea was that the League should consist of the Allied states, together with such neutral states as might wish to join, and that military force should be employed to back up the decisions of the League. This would have been no more than a device for perpetuating the political and military ascendancy of the Allied states. The proposal received little support and was rejected. Thus it was decided

that the League was not to be a " super-state," with an army and navy to enforce its decisions.

2. *Whether the League should declare in favor of religious and racial equality.* President Wilson wished to introduce a clause declaring that all religions should be treated alike. But if all religions were to be treated alike, why not all races? The Japanese were quick to see the importance of this. They were displeased with the laws which prohibited the immigration of Japanese into the United States and into Australia. Therefore they proposed that the Covenant should include a clause declaring that all races should be treated equally by the states that were members of the League. President Wilson and Lloyd George, because of strong national opposition in the United States and Australia, could not support this proposal. It was therefore rejected, and President Wilson dropped his scheme for proclaiming religious equality. Thus it was decided that the League of Nations would not declare that all nations and all religions had a right to equal treatment.

3. *Whether the League should recognize the Monroe Doctrine.* The chief object of the League was to prevent war. If a war threatened between two South American states, the League would presumably take a hand in the dispute in order to prevent the war. But President Wilson knew that the people of the United States would seriously object to that. In 1823 President Monroe had declared that the United States would object to any intervention by the European powers in the political affairs of the Western Hemisphere; and ever since 1823 the United States had jealously maintained this so-called Monroe Doctrine. President Wilson therefore insisted that the League should recognize the Monroe Doctrine. France objected to this, but in the end President Wilson had his way. Thus it was decided that the League would not act in the Western Hemisphere contrary to the Monroe Doctrine.

With some slight modifications, therefore, the Covenant of the League as presented by President Wilson was adopted. It was incorporated in the treaty with Germany — the Treaty of Versailles.

The League of Nations: How the League was organized, and what it can do to prevent war. The first members of the League were: (1) all of the states that entered into the treaty with Germany (President Wilson signed the treaty, but the Senate refused to ratify it, so the United States is not a member of the League); (2) most of the neutral states that wished to join. Altogether this made forty-two states. Besides, separate representation was given to five countries within the British Empire — Canada, Australia, New Zealand, South Africa, and India. The former " enemy " states (Germany, Austria, Hungary, Bulgaria, and Turkey), and Russia and Mexico, whose governments the Allied states refused to recognize, were excluded. Any state may be admitted if approved by two-thirds of the member states. Any member may withdraw after two years' notice. Since the founding of the League, Brazil and Costa Rica have withdrawn; Germany, Austria, Hungary, and several other states have been admitted.

The League is established at Geneva, Switzerland, and is supported by a budget to which the members contribute roughly in proportion to their capacity. It acts through the following four bodies:

1. *The Secretariat* — a permanent body of officials who conduct the necessary correspondence.

2. *The Council*, which is composed of: (1) one member each from France, Great Britain, Italy, Japan, and (since her admission to the League) Germany; and (2) one member each from nine of the smaller states (not always the same nine). The Council meets once a year and is the directing or executive body of the League.

3. *The Assembly*, composed of not more than three representatives from each member of the League. As each state has but one vote, the smallest state has as much weight in voting as the largest. The Assembly admits new members, and designates the nine small states that shall be represented on the Council. Otherwise it does little except discuss " international conditions whose continuance might endanger the peace of the world."

4. *The International Court of Justice*, provided for by the Covenant, but operating under a separate agreement, was not established until 1921. It is a judicial body for settling disputes between states in which *legal rights*, as distinguished from *political interests*, are involved.

The primary object of the League is to prevent war. What can the League do to realize that object? Strictly speaking, the League cannot itself prevent war. It is not a super-state with armies and navies to execute its decisions. It is rather an *international agency* of the member states. In joining the League the member states have authorized the League to do certain things, and they have pledged themselves to follow certain recommendations which it makes. What are the things which the League is authorized to do, and what are the recommendations which the member states are pledged to follow? They have to do chiefly with (1) reduction of armaments, (2) mediation, (3) arbitration, and (4) international boycott.

1. *Reduction of armaments.* One of President Wilson's Fourteen Points called for a reduction of armies and navies. The Peace Conference referred this matter to the League; and Article VIII of the Covenant authorizes the Council of the League to formulate plans for a general reduction of armaments. This is all the League can do. It has no power whatever to compel the member states to reduce their armies or navies, nor are they in any way pledged to follow its recommendation in respect to such reduction.

2. *Mediation.* It had long been recognized by international law that when war threatened between two states, any other state might offer its " good offices," and if this offer was accepted it would try to " mediate " the dispute. No state was likely to offer its good offices until it was quite sure that the two quarreling states desired it to do so. The trouble in the past has been that what is everybody's business is nobody's business. The advantage of the League is that it makes it somebody's business to step in. Article XI provides: (1) that any member state may call the attention of either the Council or the Assembly to " any circumstance whatever which threatens to disturb international peace "; and (2) that whenever there is danger of war the Council " shall take any action that may be deemed wise " to prevent it.

3. *Arbitration.* In the past, states have often settled their disputes by referring them to a board of arbitration; but even when this was done, neither state was required to accept the decision of the arbiters. The advantage of the League is that all of the

member states are pledged, by Article XII, to submit disputes which they cannot themselves settle, either to arbitration or to the Council of the League. In the latter case, if the Council makes a unanimous decision which is accepted by one of the states, the other state is pledged to accept it also. And in no case may a state, without violating its pledge, begin war until three months after the board of arbitration or the Council has rendered its decision.

4. *International boycott.* The League cannot itself employ force; but it may recommend it. If any member state goes to war in violation of any of the provisions of the League Covenant, the other member states are expected to boycott that state — that is, to discontinue all commercial and financial relations with it. In extreme cases the Council may recommend the member states to employ their armies and navies to compel the offending state to keep the peace.

Thus the League of Nations does not abolish war. It does not even outlaw war. But it *creates a presumption* against it. It is a solemn international agreement by most of the nations of the world that henceforth they will settle their disputes peaceably; and it establishes regular methods of procedure for doing so.

Such in brief was the work of the Peace Conference. Many people objected to the settlement because it was too lenient with the defeated powers; many denounced it because it was too severe; many defended it on the ground that, considering all the circumstances, it was the best settlement that could be made at the time. Perhaps we cannot do better than to recall a famous saying of Benjamin Franklin: " There never was a good war or a bad peace."

Of all the treaties drafted by the Peace Conference, the most important was the Treaty of Versailles with Germany. Germany was commonly regarded by the Allies as having been guilty of plotting the war. It was the military strength of Germany that made victory for the Allies doubtful for four years. It was Germany that the Allies still feared. The completion of the German treaty was therefore regarded as bringing the war to a final conclusion.

The Germans had no part in framing the treaty. When it was completed a German delegation, headed by Count Brockdorff-

Rantzau, was admitted to the conference and informed of its terms. The Germans prepared a long protest and pleaded for a revision of the settlement. They denied (what the treaty virtually asserted) that Germany was solely responsible for the war. They objected to the provisions of the treaty on the ground that they were a flagrant violation of the Fourteen Points which the Allies had accepted as the basis of peace. The Peace Conference refused to modify the treaty; but, although Brockdorff-Rantzau, speaking for the German delegation, refused to sign it, the German government was helpless. The Allies still maintained the blockade, and their troops guarded the Rhine. Accordingly, on June 23 the German national assembly voted to accept under protest the drastic terms laid down.

The signing of the treaty, carefully staged, was the most dramatic occasion of the Peace Conference. The treaty was not signed at Paris, where the conference held its sessions. To point the moral of the tale and to heighten the effect of victory, the place appointed for signing the treaty was the famous Hall of Mirrors in the château at Versailles, where the victorious Germans, after the Franco-Prussian War in 1871, had proclaimed the German Empire. In this historic room, on June 28, 1919 — exactly five years after the assassination of the Archduke Francis Ferdinand — the Germans affixed their signatures to the treaty that had been imposed upon them by superior force.

QUESTIONS

1. What were the terms of the Armistice of 1918? What part of the Fourteen Points did the armistice accept as the basis of peace? Why did the popularity and influence of President Wilson decline after the armistice?

2. Who were some of the principal leaders at the Peace Conference? How was the conference organized? What powers were chiefly responsible for the peace settlement? Why was it not possible to make peace strictly in accordance with the Fourteen Points? What part of the peace program was President Wilson most interested in? Which of the Fourteen Points were ignored at the Peace Conference? What concessions did President Wilson make in respect to open diplomacy? in respect to disarmament? in respect to the self-determination of nations?

CHART FOR CHAPTER XXII. How the peace squared with the Fourteen Points: which of the points were kept upright, and which were kept nearly upright but not quite.

1) Open covenants openly arrived at.	2) Freedom of the seas.	3) Removal of economic barriers.	4) Disarmament.	5) Impartial adjustment of colonial claims.	6) Evacuation of Russian territory, and non-interference in Russian affairs.	7) Belgium evacuated and restored.
Largely ignored.	Abandoned before the Peace Conference.	Ignored.	Germany and Austria alone required to disarm.	German colonies given to Allied powers.	Territory evacuated by Central Powers. Allies try to overthrow soviet government.	Carried out.

8) Alsace-Lorraine restored to France.	9) Readjustment of Italian frontier along lines of nationality.	10) Self-determination for the peoples of Austria-Hungary.	11) Self-determination for Rumania, Montenegro, Serbia.	12) Self-determination for nations subject to Turkish rule.	13) Self-determination for Poland, and free access to the sea.	14) League of Nations.
Carried out.	Carried out. But some Germans and Slavs subject to Italy.	Carried out in the main. Some Germans and Magyars subject to Slavic states.	Carried out in the main.	Largely ignored.	Carried out.	Carried out

3. Why did the question of the "left bank" create a crisis in the Peace Conference? What arrangements were made with respect to the left bank? Why was Italy given the Trentino and Trieste? What was the dispute over Fiume, and how was it finally settled? What were the chief difficulties in arranging the boundaries of Poland? What new states were created out of the old Austro-Hungarian Monarchy? What old states obtained some of former Austro-Hungarian territory? Why were many Germans included in Czechoslovakia? Why were many Magyars included in Rumania? Why were the Austrian Germans not permitted to unite with the new German Republic? What new states were created out of the former Russian Empire?

4. What disposition was made of the territory of the former Ottoman Empire? What became of the German colonies? What were the "mandates"? How old is the idea of a league of European states? Name a project for such a league published in the seventeenth century; in the eighteenth century. How was the draft of the League prepared? What differences over the League arose in the Peace Conference? How is the League organized? Is it a "super-state"? Can it prevent war? How does it proceed? What can it do to lessen the likelihood of war?

5. In what respects did President Wilson fail to get the kind of peace he wanted? In what respects did he succeed? What did President Wilson mean by saying, "It must be a peace without victory"? Was the peace of 1919 a peace without victory? Was it a peace between equals? If you were asked to justify the peace settlement, what could you say in its favor? If you were asked to condemn it, what could you say against it?

SELECTED READINGS

Brief accounts. Hayes and Moon, *Modern Europe*, ch. xxxvii.   Robinson and Beard, *Development of Modern Europe* (revised ed.), II, ch. xii. Hayes, *Modern Europe*, II, xxxiii.   Schapiro, *Modern History* (revised ed.), ch. xxxvi.   Flick, *Modern World History*, ch. xxxvii.   P. Slosson, *Twentieth Century History*, chs. xv–xvi.   F. L. Benns, *Europe since 1914*, chs. vii–viii. G. P. Gooch, *Modern Europe*, ch. xix.   R. Muir, *Political Consequences of the Great War* (Home University Library).   A. L. Bowley, *Some Economic Consequences of the Great War* (Home University Library).

Longer accounts. R. S. Baker, *Woodrow Wilson and World Settlement*, 3 vols. (A defense of President Wilson by one of his great admirers.) J. M. Keynes, *Economic Consequences of the Peace*. (An able criticism of the peace settlement.)   A. Tardieu, *The Truth About the Peace*. (An account by a Frenchman from a French point of view.)   C. H. Haskins and R. M. Lord, *Some Problems of the Peace Conference*.   E. M. House and C. Seymour, *What Really Happened at Paris*.   C. T. Thompson, *The Peace Conference Day by Day*.   The text of the League and many other sources are in Baker's *Woodrow Wilson*, Vol. III, and Scott and Baltzly, *Readings in European History*, ch. xiv, sec. 5.

ONE OF THE LARGE SOVIET FARMS

One hundred and fifty tractors are used by the peasants on this farm.

CHAPTER XXIII. THE NEW WORLD OF TODAY, WHICH IS ONLY THE OLD WORLD OF YESTERDAY TRYING TO GET ITS BEARINGS

Hope, often disappointed but always renewed, must be the anchor by which . . . democracy and its fortunes will have to ride out this latest storm. LORD BRYCE

Some remarks about the age in which we live. After the French Revolution Talleyrand said: " No one who has not lived before 1789 knows how pleasant life can be." After the Great War many people looked back to the good old days before 1914 when, as they liked to think, life was much pleasanter. Perhaps they were right — or it may be only that they were growing old. But certainly the world after the war, whether better or worse, was in many ways different from the world before the war.

Yet in what essential way different? It is difficult to say. The prevailing form of government was still democratic and indeed in some countries, such as Germany, democratic government was more firmly established than ever. On the other hand, there were some countries, such as Italy, in which democratic government was replaced by a dictatorship. Some people said that dictatorship was only a temporary phase. Others said it was a sign that democratic government was about played out and destined to be replaced by some form better suited to the complex economic conditions of modern life. International conflict was still rife, but there was the League of Nations and the World Court. Some people said these new institutions would enable the world to avoid another catastrophe like the Great War. Others said not.

762

Perhaps the chief characteristic of the decade after the war was that the world had been suddenly turned upside down, and no one could see how it was to be set right side up. Of course some people said, as some in all ages have said, that the world never was right side up and never will be. How, they asked, could anything reasonable be expected of a creature like man — a creature intelligent enough to bring forth the marvels of modern civilization, and yet stupid enough to employ his intelligence in a desperate and concerted effort to destroy the very civilization he had created? Surely, they said, nothing can be expected of such a creature except that he will do something new, something at once brilliant and insane, something at all events unexpected.

The world after the war may be compared to a vigorous, conceited, and aggressive man who has been knocked out by a sudden blow between the eyes. He recovers consciousness, but is still dazed. "What has happened?" he asks. "Where am I? What's the idea?" He has lost a little of his old confidence and conceit. Slowly and painfully he picks himself up, trying to get his bearings. The world after the war was like that. It had been knocked out by the war. It was asking, "What has happened? What's to be done?" It was looking about, taking stock, trying to get its bearings. The most we can do is to see what the demoralized world has done since 1919 to right itself, to get its bearings.

This brief survey of the period since the war may conveniently be made under three heads: (1) the extension of democratic government; (2) new experiments in government; (3) international relations and the League of Nations.

I. THE EXTENSION OF DEMOCRATIC GOVERNMENT

How women in many countries obtained the right to vote. During the war President Wilson said that the world must be made safe for democracy. Some wit replied that it would be more to the point to make democracy safe for the world. However that may be, one thing is certain — since 1914 there has been a marked extension of democratic government in many countries. One aspect of this was the rapid extension of the suffrage to women.

In the nineteenth century, governments were thought to be democratic which granted the suffrage to all men of a certain age. " Universal manhood suffrage " was the test of democracy. Nevertheless, there were always some people who demanded the same rights for women as for men. Among the early advocates of women's suffrage was the Frenchman, Condorcet, one of the Girondist leaders in the Revolution. Another was the Englishwoman, Mary Wollstonecraft, who published an eloquent plea entitled *Vindication of the Rights of Woman* (1792). Not until the late nineteenth century, however, was the woman suffrage movement of such importance. In 1869 John Stuart Mill, famous philosopher and political economist, published a powerful defense of equal rights for women entitled, *Subjection of Women*. From about that time the woman suffrage movement gathered force. Societies were formed, especially in England and the United States; and even before the war, full or limited rights of voting were extended to women in certain American states (Wyoming was the first, 1869), and in Finland (1906) and Norway (1907).

In the years before the war the woman suffrage movement acquired a spectacular interest through the activities of the English " suffragettes." In 1903 Emmeline Pankhurst and her two daughters organized the Woman's Social and Political Union, which adopted more militant methods of promoting the same cause. Instead of arguing, the suffragettes created disturbances. They broke up public meetings, smashed windows, mutilated works of art in public galleries, fought the police, and in the opinion of most people made nuisances of themselves generally. The idea was to force the issue. Such tactics gained them nothing except notoriety. Then came the war, which the women, including the suffragettes, supported loyally; and after the war the English government which had refused to make concessions under threats granted equal rights as a recognition of services performed. In 1918 limited rights of voting were granted to women; in 1919 many legal inequalities were abolished; and finally, in 1928, women received the same right of voting as men.

Since the beginning of the war most countries have made similar concessions. In the United States a constitutional amendment accorded women the same rights of voting as men (1920); and full or partial rights of voting are now enjoyed by women in Holland, Denmark, Sweden, Austria, Germany, Czechoslovakia, Estonia, Latvia, Lithuania, and Russia. Of the European countries that fought to make the world safe for democracy, France and Italy are the only ones that have refused to grant the suffrage to women.

Progress of democracy in the British Empire. During the war British statesmen claimed to be fighting in " defense of small nations " and for the " self-determination of nations." Critics were inclined to say: " That is all very well, but how about Ireland? How about Egypt? How about India? Why should these nations not be ' self-determined ' "? Since the war Great Britain has made certain concessions to these nations.

As we have seen (p. 490), Gladstone twice tried in vain to give Ireland home rule. Nothing further was attempted until 1912, when the Liberal ministry of Asquith introduced a new Home Rule bill, which was finally passed in 1914. Because of strenuous opposition to the measure by the Protestants of Ulster (North Ireland) the operation of the act was suspended during the war. Meantime there arose in southern Ireland what was known as the Sinn Fein movement. The words *Sinn Fein* mean " we ourselves," and the object of the Sinn Feiners was to obtain complete independence for Ireland. In 1916 the Sinn Feiners started a rebellion at Dublin and proclaimed an independent " Irish Republic." The rebellion was ruthlessly repressed, and during the last years of the war Ireland was governed by martial law.

In the election of 1918 most of the Irish members chosen were Sinn Feiners, and instead of taking their seats in the House of Commons in London they organized a parliament of their own in Dublin, elected Eamon de Valera president, and defied the British government. For three years there was a futile struggle between the British and the North Irish on the one hand and the Sinn Feiners on the other. Finally, in 1921, a settlement was arranged. South Ireland (Catholic) was permitted to have a parliament of its own, with much the same privileges of self-government as those that Canada and the other self-governing dominions enjoy. North Ireland (Protestant) was either to join the "Irish Free State" or to

© *International News Photos*

FLESK CASTLE, NEAR KILLARNEY

Killarney, in southern Ireland, is famed for its three beautiful lakes. The lower lake, Lough Leane, is studded with islands, many of which contain historic ruins. The Flesk River flows into this lake.

retain the connection with Great Britain which had formerly existed. It voted not to join the Irish Free State. Thus the Irish question was settled by dividing Ireland into two parts. South Ireland constitutes the Irish Free State, which is a self-governing dominion within the British Empire. North Ireland remains, as formerly, a part of Great Britain, governed by the British Parliament to which it sends representatives.

The British government has also made certain concessions to the Egyptian demand for national independence and self-government. Before the war the status of Egypt was peculiar. Technically a part of the Ottoman Empire, it had in fact been governed by Great Britain since the military intervention of 1882 (see p. 607). The British government had often promised to withdraw from Egypt, but never did so; and during the war it formally declared the country to be a British "protectorate." The Egyptians protested, and at the Peace Conference tried in vain to obtain a hearing; but in 1922 the British government voluntarily abandoned its protectorate and permitted the Egyptians to form a government of their own.

A democratic government was at once organized under Sultan Fuad, who took the title of King of Egypt. Even so, Egypt was far from being an independent state. A British high commissioner was kept in the country to watch over affairs, and British troops remained there to protect British interests. Nationalist agitation continued, and conflicts sometimes resulted in violence. Finally, in 1929, the Labor goverment of Ramsay MacDonald made further concessions. The British high commissioner was withdrawn. British troops were withdrawn, except in the Suez Canal zone; and the British government promised to support the Egyptian application for membership in the League of Nations. Nevertheless, Egypt is by no means an independent state. The relations between the Egyptian and the British governments are far from harmonious, and what new difficulties may arise no one can say.

In India, as well as in Ireland and Egypt, the war greatly stimulated nationalist sentiment. India remained loyal to Great Britain during the war, incurring in support of it a debt of $700,000,000; and educated Indians felt that in return they were entitled to self-government. In 1919 the British government made certain concessions by passing the Government of India Act. This act established local governments in the provinces and also a national legislature composed of two chambers in which the people of India are represented. Although these measures gave the Indians a share in their own government, the ultimate control still remained in the hands of the British. Many of the people were not satisfied with these limited concessions, and the agitation for independence continued.

The chief leader of the Indian nationalist movement was M. K. Gandhi, one of the most striking personalities of the time. His followers call him *Mahatma* (" the saintly man "). Gandhi was educated in England, practiced law in Bombay, and then went to South Africa. In 1914 he returned to India to promote the cause of Indian independence. He preached a doctrine of " civil disobedience " and non-resistance. He said in effect: " You will

© *Ewing Galloway*

VIEW OF KHYBER PASS, THE GATEWAY BETWEEN NORTHWEST INDIA AND
SOVIET RUSSIA

never get rid of the British by argument or by forcible resistance.
They will always beat you at that game. But you can succeed by
non-resistance. Therefore refuse to associate with the British.
Refuse to co-operate with them in any way. Take no part in elections. Accept no offices. Make no use of British courts, and
recognize no decisions rendered by them. The British cannot long
govern a nation that totally ignores their presence."

The result of Gandhi's teaching was to strengthen the desire for
national independence. He urged his followers not to resort to
violence of any kind, but to follow strictly the method of peaceful
non-resistance. Some of them found this too difficult, and in 1922
there were numerous riots. Gandhi was arrested, the riots were
suppressed, and during the next two years the non-resistance movement declined. Some of Gandhi's followers accordingly abandoned
the idea of complete independence. They organized the *Swaraj*
(" Home Rule ") party. Thus there came to be two parties; the
followers of Gandhi, who demand complete independence; and the
Swaraj, which ask only that India be given the same freedom within

the empire that Canada and the other self-governing dominions have.

Which party is the stronger it is difficult to say. But at all events, in 1930 the legislative assembly declared itself in favor of complete national independence. Gandhi felt that the time was ripe to carry through his program of non-co-operation and non-resistance. In March, 1930, he therefore inaugurated a second civil disobedience campaign by a public and dramatic violation of the salt law. The British government in India has a monopoly of the sale of salt, and the people are forbidden to obtain it otherwise. In order to advertise his program and arouse the people, Gandhi and about seventy-five followers made a long march from the interior to the sea. Everywhere thousands of people gathered to see the great leader and hear him preach his doctrine. When he arrived at the coast the saintly man waded into the sea, filled some jars with water, and proceeded to manufacture a little salt. The act was to be the signal for a nation-wide boycott — a nation-wide refusal to recognize British law in India, or to have anything to do with the British.

Gandhi's attempt to bring about a nation-wide boycott was not successful. But the dissatisfaction with British rule was so widespread in India that late in 1930 an Anglo-Indian Conference was assembled in London to discuss the whole question of British-Indian relations, and in 1931 it formulated a program which, if carried out, would give to India much the same rights of self-government as those enjoyed by the self-governing dominions (see p. 487).

The granting of liberal concessions to subject states was accompanied and partly caused by the growth of liberal and socialistic sentiment in England itself. After 1919 the most notable fact in British politics was the increasing strength of the Labor party. England was hard hit by the war. A few people had made fortunes, but the mass of the people found it hard to make both ends meet. The war debt was enormous, and to pay it the income tax was raised, so that even moderately well-to-do people paid one-fourth of their income to the government. Prices were extremely high, industry languished for want of markets abroad, and great numbers of men, including soldiers returned from the trenches,

THE PALACE OF THE VICEROY AT NEW DELHI

New Delhi, the capital of all India, has been designed and built since 1911. The palace of the viceroy and the two secretariat buildings stand upon a huge rock, overlooking the plain below.

were without jobs. In 1926 there was a most serious general strike, involving 2,000,000 workers, which temporarily paralyzed the entire economic life of the country and seemed at the time to bring England to the verge of social revolution.

In this era of distress the Labor party appealed to the mass of the people, who found life hard. It proposed to serve the interests of those who " live by working " against those who " live by owning." In general it aimed " to secure for the producers by hand or brain the full fruits of their industry and the most equitable distribution [of wealth] that may be possible." In particular it declared in favor of national ownership of mines, land, railways, and electric power; and it accepted the principle that every man has " the right to work or to maintenance." Such a program was popular, and the Labor party replaced the Liberals as the second strongest party in the Parliament. In the elections of 1923 the return was: Conservatives, 258; Labor, 192; Liberals, 159. For the first time a Labor ministry was formed, under Ramsay Mac-Donald. Before the year was out, it was overthrown by a combination of Liberals and Conservatives, and the Conservative ministry of Mr. Baldwin was formed. The Conservatives, in concession to public opinion, extended the system of old-age pensions and of unemployment insurance. But the conditions of industry improved very little, the great problem of unemployment remained unsolved, and the foreign policy of the government was unpopular. The result was that in the elections of 1929 the Labor party was returned to power, and the second ministry of Ramsay MacDonald was formed.

Democratic government in the new states of eastern Europe. Before the war, central and eastern Europe and the Near East were largely controlled by four great powers — the German Empire, the Austro-Hungarian Monarchy, the Russian Empire, and the Ottoman Empire. One of the

Turkish Embassy, Washington

STREET IN ANGORA, THE NEW CAPITAL OF TURKEY

Only a few years ago this street was unpaved and lined with ramshackle buildings.

chief results of the war was that the German Hohenzollern dynasty and the Russian tsars lost their power, and the Austro-Hungarian Monarchy and the Ottoman Empire disappeared. In place of these four imperial powers many new states, mostly republics, were established.

During the hundred years before the war the European powers had taken over one province after another of the extensive Ottoman Empire. The war completed this process. Having lost their former subject provinces, the Turks established in Asia Minor the Turkish Republic. The capital of the new republic was transferred from Constantinople (Istanbul) to Angora. The new government consists of a national assembly elected by all adult men of Turkish nationality, and a president elected by the assembly. Equality of political and religious rights was established, although Greeks and Armenians were expelled on the ground of alien nationality. Besides adopting a democratic government, the Turks determined to become " modern " by introducing western European customs. Men were ordered to wear the European hat instead of the Turkish fez, and women were encouraged to appear unveiled. Efforts were made to substitute the Roman alphabet for the Arabic. Polygamy was virtually abolished. As a small republic Turkey is more independent than formerly, since the special privileges of European powers, called " capitulations," have been abolished. On the whole the Turks feel that they are better off without imperial possessions. These changes were largely brought about under the leadership of Kemal Pasha, who is at present (1931) exercising the powers of a dictator under the form of a republic.

In the territory formerly controlled by Russia, Germany, and Austria-Hungary many new states were established after the war — Yugoslavia, Austria, Hungary, the enlarged Rumania, Czechoslovakia, Poland, Lithuania, Latvia, Estonia, and Finland. Yugoslavia and Rumania are kingdoms. Hungary would have re-established the Habsburg dynasty if the powers at the Peace Conference had not intervened. All the other states are republics, with an executive elected either by the people or by the legislative asemblies. In all of the new states inequality of rights was done away with. In all of them a democratic suffrage was established. In all of them the ministers who exercise executive power are responsible to the legislatures, after the English and French system.

The chief difficulty in most, if not all, of the new states arises out of racial and religious differences. In Czechoslovakia there are difficulties between the Germans, the Czechs, and the Slovaks. In Yugoslavia there are even sharper difficulties between Serbs, Croats, and Slovenes. In all of the new states there is the Jewish problem. In Poland and Yugoslavia these difficulties led to the establishment of virtual dictatorships. Yet on the whole we may say that the attempt to apply to eastern Europe the principle of

KEMAL PASHA AND ATTENDANTS

Nominally president, virtually dictator, Kemal Pasha has taken the leading part in organizing the new Turkish Republic.

the self-determination of nations has not so far proved a failure. Most of the people are better satisfied under the new governments than they were under the old.

Of all the new governments established as a result of the war, the most important are the Russian Soviet Republic and the German Republic. The Russian Soviet Republic is one of the new experiments in government which we shall consider later (see p. 790). We must now learn something about the new Germany.

The German Republic: How a new constitution was made for the old *Reich*, 1919. It has sometimes been said that the German people exhibited a mean spirit by supporting their government while it won victories, only to desert it when it lost the war. There may be some truth in this charge, but it is not the whole truth. The defeat of the German armies was no doubt the immediate cause of the revolution of 1918, but it was not the sole cause. It merely brought to a head a widespread discontent with the imperial government which existed before the war began. Although proud of German prestige and power, the common people everywhere disliked the excessive burden of military service, were irritated by the insolence and arrogance of the military officers, and were dissatisfied because the Reichstag, supposed to represent the people, had but little control of the emperor and his ministers. Besides, in the smaller states, such as Bavaria, there was a strong " anti-Prussian " sentiment — the feeling that the imperial government was only a device by which Prussia dominated Germany for the benefit of the Prussian landowning and military aristocracy.

When the war came, criticism was mostly silenced for the time being. The great majority of the people believed that they were fighting in defense of their country, against sinister and aggressive enemies. For three years the people made the necessary sacrifices willingly. They were proud of their army, and confident of victory. But after three years the old discontent began to revive. In 1917 the Socialists and the Center party urged the government to make peace on reasonable terms. They criticized the emperor for being too much guided by the military officials and demanded that the Reichstag should be given a greater share in determining the policies of the war. Then came the disastrous retreat of the armies in 1918. Realizing that Germany had lost the war, and that four years of terrible sacrifices had been in vain, the German people within a few days swept away the imperial system which Bismarck had labored for twenty years to consolidate.

The revolution created a widespread fear in Europe that Germany might follow the lead of Russia and " go Bolshevik." The German Communists, led by Karl Liebknecht and Rosa Luxemburg, had taken a very active part in the revolution, hoping to gain control of the government and inaugurate in Germany the Russian soviet system. But their hopes were disappointed. The first ministry formed after the revolution was controlled by the Socialists, with Friedrich Ebert as chancellor; and the first important act of the Ebert government was to call for the election, by all adult men and women, of a national assembly to draft a new constitution. Foreseeing that the national assembly would not adopt a soviet régime, the Communists tried (January 5, 1919) to overthrow the Ebert government by force as the first step in a German Bolshevik revolution. The revolt was ruthlessly suppressed by the Socialist government. Liebknecht and Rosa Luxemburg were arrested. The latter was killed on the way to prison, by a mob; the former was shot while attempting to escape. This quieted the fear that Germany would go Bolshevik.

Elections for the national assembly were held in January, 1919. The Communists took no part in the elections, but all the old parties put up candidates and set forth their views on the constitution to be adopted. The old parties now appeared with new names, which we must learn, since they are still used. The old Conservative party became the Nationalist party. The National Liberal party called itself the People's party. The Catholic Center preferred the name Christian People's party. The Progressive Liberal party changed to the Democratic party. During the war the Social Democrats had divided into two groups — the Majority Socialists, who supported the war, and the Independent Socialists, who refused to support it. These names they retained until 1922, when the two groups united (United Socialist Democratic party). In the elections more than ten million

© *Wide World Photos*

EBERT (1870–1925)

Friedrich Ebert, a leader of the Socialist party in Germany, became chancellor, then provisional president of the German Republic. He served a second term at the request of the Reichstag.

votes were cast, and among the 421 members elected, 39 were women. Ten of the members belonged to no party, the rest were divided among the various parties as follows: Nationalists 42; People's party 21; Christian People's party 88; Democratic party 75; Majority Socialists 163; Independent Socialists 22.

The national assembly met at Weimar, February 6, 1919. What form of government did the various parties favor? The forty-two Nationalists, representing the old landowning aristocracy and the big business interests, desired to establish a monarchical form of government. All the others felt that the time had come to establish a republic. The vital question was, what kind of republic — conservative middle-class republic, democratic republic, or socialistic republic? The three parties of the Left (Democrats, Majority Socialists, and Independent Socialists) preferred the latter type — that is, they wanted a constitution which would make a special point of safeguarding the interests of the mass of the poor against the rich. The three parties of the Right were on the whole opposed to socialistic experiments — they wanted a constitution that would safeguard property against the danger of communism and bolshevism. Since the parties of the Right had only 151 votes, while the parties of the Left had 270, we might suppose that the latter would have everything their own way and establish a radical socialistic republic.

But in fact the Socialists did not get all that they wanted. The action of the Weimar assembly depended less upon the differences which divided the various parties than on the mutual fears which bound them together. The parties of the Left feared above everything the restoration of the Hohenzollern monarchy, and in order to prevent that they made concessions to the parties of the Right. The parties of the Right feared above everything communism and bolshevism, and in order to avoid those evils they made concessions to the parties of the Left. The result was a compromise. The new German constitution, while more democratic than the parties of the Right desired, was less socialistic than the parties of the Left would have preferred. This may be why it has, on the whole, proved so satisfactory to the mass of the German people.

The new constitution is based on the principle that all citizens have equal rights. It states that " all Germans are equal before the law. Men and women have fundamentally the same civil rights and duties. Privileges and discriminations due to birth or rank . . . are abolished. Titles of nobility . . . may not hereafter be granted." The constitution also recognizes the principle that " political authority is derived from the people." The federal government, and the governments of the several states that compose the commonwealth (*Reich*), must be republican in form. " The German commonwealth is a republic. . . . Every

German Tourist Information Office

PRESIDENT VON HINDENBURG AND CABINET LEAVING BERLIN CATHEDRAL

They have been attending services on the opening of the Reichstag.

state must have a republican constitution. The representatives of the people must be elected by the universal, equal, direct, and secret suffrage of all German citizens, both men and women, according to the principle of proportional representation."

The federal government consists of a president and two legislative chambers — the national assembly (*Reichstag*) and the national council (*Reichsrat*). The assembly is elected by all men and women over twenty years of age. It therefore represents the people. The council is composed of members appointed by the state governments. It represents the states. The president is elected directly by the people, for seven years. His position is like that of the President of France or the King of England. He represents the dignity and majesty of the nation, but has little real power. The real control of affairs is in the assembly. It makes the laws. The council may object to any measure, but by two-thirds vote the assembly may override the objection. The executive power is exercised by the chancellor and his cabinet of ministers, but the chancellor, although appointed by the president, is responsible to the assembly.

Under the new constitution Germany, like the United States, is a democratic federal republic. To what extent is it a " socialistic " republic? The most novel features of the German constitution are those which deal with economic life. It states that " the regulation of economic life must conform to the principles of justice, with the object of assuring humane conditions of life for all. . . . The right of private property is guaranteed by the constitution. Its nature and limits are defined by law." For certain purposes, " landed property may be confiscated " by the government, and:

The commonwealth may by law . . . transfer to public ownership private business enterprises adapted for socialization. . . . Labor is under the special protection of the commonwealth. . . . Every German shall have opportunity to earn his living. So long as suitable employment cannot be procured for him, his maintenance will be provided for. . . . Wage-earners are qualified to co-operate on equal terms with employers in the regulation of wages and working conditions.

Thus the constitution authorized the government to nationalize land and industry when the common interest seemed to demand it, and it imposed on the government the duty of providing either work or maintenance for all citizens. The constitution did not establish a socialistic régime, but it made it easy for the people to establish such a régime if they so desired.

The German Republic, 1919–1930: How it managed to live in spite of enemies and hard times. The new German Republic was confronted with difficulties that seemed insuperable and might have been so to a less competent and resolute people. The country had been exhausted by the war, and when the blockade was lifted the people were undernourished or starving. Industries were disorganized, the merchant marine had been destroyed and international commerce swept from the seas. Demobilized soldiers were looking for jobs that did not exist. While the old Hohenzollern government was held responsible for the disastrous defeat, the new republican government was held responsible for the almost equally disastrous peace. The German people expected to be paid back the money they had loaned the government in support of the war, and the Allies expected to be paid the huge indemnities imposed on Germany by the Treaty of Versailles. What could the untried government do to revive industry and commerce, restore prosperity to an impoverished people, and find the enormous sums necessary to pay its domestic and foreign debts?

It could in fact do but little, and for some years the situation became worse rather than better. One of the most difficult problems was presented by the decline in value of the mark. Before the war the German mark was worth twenty-five cents in American money. During the war the government issued great amounts of paper money, and after the war it continued to do so. The result was that the value of the mark declined. In January, 1923, an American dollar would buy, not merely four German marks, but 50,000 marks.

German Tourist Information Office

MUNICIPAL GAS WORKS OF BERLIN

These modern smokestacks resemble medieval towers. Since the war, German architects have introduced many innovations in building.

It was in this very month of January that the French armies occupied the Ruhr district, on the ground that the German government had failed to make the required indemnity payments (see p. 806). This event, having all the appearance of a renewal of the war, created a situation of which no one could foresee the end. The immediate result was that the mark began its so-called "toboggan slide." In November, 1923, the mark was quoted in Berlin at 2,520,000,000,000 to the dollar. At this rate a postage stamp was worth 50,000,000 marks. The mark had reached the bottom, it was worthless.

When the mark began to decline rapidly, people ceased to save money. Everyone spent his money on the day he got it, since it would almost certainly buy less the next day, and still less the next week. People who had contracted debts long since, when the mark was at a high value, hastened to pay them off now that the mark was of little or no value. The result was that thousands of people whose property was invested in securities or whose income depended on fixed rents, dividends, or salaries were utterly impoverished. Innumerable " well high born " counts, and former officials and professors and lawyers and doctors, taking any job they could get, were to be seen carrying away garbage, running street cars, or, with napkin over arm, serving as waiters in cheap restaurants. The collapse of the mark had " economically guillotined " an entire class and introduced intolerable confusion into the economic life of the country.

The new republic, unable either to avoid economic chaos or to defend the country against the aggressions of France, became somewhat unpopular. Many people looked back to the " good old days " before the war, when Germany was prosperous and powerful under the monarchy — the good old days when everything was ordered and secure, when no French troops occupied the Rhineland, and when everyone, although " forbidden to walk on the grass," could count the marks in his pocket, well knowing that they would buy as much tomorrow as they would today. In these years of depression the enemies of the republic took courage, and several futile attempts were made to restore the old monarchy or to bring about a Communist revolution.

In March, 1920, General Lüttwitz, with 8000 undemobilized soldiers, occupied Berlin and proclaimed as chancellor a former Prussian official by the name of Von Kapp. President Ebert and his cabinet, hastily decamping to Stuttgart, called upon the workers to " throttle this military dictatorship " by ceasing to work. The workers called a general strike, water and electricity were cut off in Berlin, the trains and street cars ceased to run, and the Lüttwitz-Kapp monarchist *Putsch* quickly collapsed. Encouraged by the weakness of the government and the success of the general strike, the Communists staged little revolutions in various parts of Germany, especially in the Ruhr district, where a " Red army " of 70,000 was collected. But the Red army was dispersed, and the Communist uprisings were ruthlessly suppressed.

During the next two years (1921–1922) the monarchists continued their intrigues, and in 1923 a second *Putsch* was hatched in Bavaria. General Ludendorff, supported by Adolf Hitler and other Bavarian monarchists, planned to march on Berlin and establish a Ludendorff dictatorship. But the leaders quarreled, and the so-called Ludendorff-Hitler *Putsch*, which the people ridiculed by calling it the "beer-cellar rebellion," came to nothing. In the same year certain Germans in the Ruhr district, with the connivance of the French authorities there, attempted to establish an independent "Rhineland Republic." The Rhineland Republic was proclaimed at Aachen and Koblenz in October, 1923, and formally recognized by the French government. But the mass of the people in the Rhineland remained loyal to the German Republic, and the separatist movement came to nothing.

Photo Julius Söhn

MODERN APARTMENT HOUSES IN DÜSSELDORF

This type of construction provides more window space and consequently more sunlight in an apartment house.

It is said to be darkest just before dawn. The lowest ebb in the fortunes of the German Republic was reached in 1923, with the collapse of the mark and the French occupation of the Ruhr. The beginning of better times dates from 1924 and is associated with two important events of that year — the adoption of the Dawes Plan and the stabilization of the mark. The Dawes Plan was a scheme, worked out by an international commission, designed to make it easier for Germany to make the reparation payments and providing for the evacuation of the Ruhr by the French at an early date (see p. 807). An essential part of the Dawes Plan was the arrangement of a foreign loan of $200,000,000 to the German government for the stabilization of the German mark. In desperation the German government had already, in 1923, made a limited issue of *Rentenmarks*, which it endeavored to maintain at the value of four to the dollar. Finally, in 1924, the old currency was retired, and new *Reichsmarks*, secured by the 200,000-000 gold dollars, were issued and maintained at the same value which the mark had had before the war.

Possessed of international credit and a stable currency, the economic recovery of Germany proceeded rapidly during the next six years. The impoverishment of the people and the abolition of military service made labor plentiful and cheap. To offset the loss of German coal fields, water power was scientifically developed for the production of electrical power. Industries were rebuilt on modern lines and more efficiently managed through the co-operation of employers and laborers. By 1929 German bank deposits totaled $2,125,000,000, and the tonnage of German merchant ships was second only to that of the ships of Great Britain. In this rapid return to economic prosperity Germany had one great advantage over the countries that won the war — thanks to the Treaty of Versailles she had neither army nor navy to support. This freed more than half a million men annually for productive labor and relieved the people of half a billion dollars in taxation. Ten years after the peace, Germany was rapidly becoming one of the leading industrial and commercial nations of the world.

With the return of economic prosperity, political life became more secure. The mass of the people were every year better satisfied with the republic, and attempts to overthrow it all but ceased. It is true that the economic depression of 1930 created widespread discontent. In the elections of September the National Socialist party (German Fascists), led by Adolph Hitler, startled the world by polling 6,000,000 votes and electing 107 deputies to the Reichstag. Since the party professes to favor a dictatorship on the Italian model, its success indicated a decline in the popularity of the republic; but at present (1931) it appears unlikely that Germany will abandon the republic for a Fascist state.

In making the republic popular during these years no one did more than President Paul von Hindenburg. In 1914, at the age of sixty-seven, he had come forth from a well-earned retirement to take command of the VIIIth German army. His decisive victory against the Russians at Tannenberg made him a national hero, and throughout the war it was on Von Hindenburg above all that the German people relied for success. After the war he once more retired. The loss of the war, which was the tragedy of his life, he accepted in silence. He did not, like Ludendorff, blame others for defeat. Although a loyal servant of the Hohen-

zollerns, he did not, like Ludendorff, engage in intrigues to overthrow the republic. In 1925, when President Ebert died, Von Hindenburg was elected to succeed him; and once more, at the great age of seventy-eight, the granite-faced old hero left retirement to serve his country.

Many people, in Germany and abroad, were alarmed, fearing that the new president would use his great influence to restore the monarchy which he had served all his life. But Hindenburg loved Germany more than he loved the Hohenzollerns. He took the oath of loyalty without reservation, refused to approve of ministers who were not "faithful to the Weimar constitution, and performed the duties of his office with dignity and ability. He

© *Ewing Galloway*

PRESIDENT VON HINDENBURG ON HIS
8OTH BIRTHDAY

A newspaper reporter once asked Von Hindenburg: "What do you do when you are nervous?" — "I whistle." — "But I've never heard you whistle." — "I never do."

became Germany's "grand old man," honored for his achievements, beloved for his honesty. It is one of history's happier ironies that this man, who represented all that the world had come to associate with German militarism and autocracy, should devote the last years of his life to instilling a love of the republic in the hearts of the German people.

II. New Experiments in Government: Italy and Russia

Fascist Italy: How the Italians found peace more burdensome than war. The great fact in Italian history after the war was the overthrow of the old form of parliamentary government and the establishment of Mussolini's dictatorship. Instead of being governed by elected representatives, the people were governed by Mussolini. But Mussolini could not have established or maintained his dictatorship if the mass of the people had not been willing to support him. Why were the people of Italy willing to give up the privilege of governing themselves? Why did they prefer to be governed by Mussolini? The answer is that after the war Italy fell into a kind of anarchy which the old government proved quite incompetent to remedy, and the mass of the people felt that it was better to be efficiently governed by Mussolini than to be so very badly governed by representatives of their own choosing. In order to understand the rise of Mussolini we must therefore learn something about the state of affairs in Italy immediately after the war.

During the years from 1919 to 1922 the majority of the people became increasingly dissatisfied with the government. In the first place, the government failed at the Peace Conference to obtain Fiume and other possessions which were thought necessary to compensate Italy for her services in the war. In the second place, the government proved incompetent to deal with the financial and economic difficulties that arose after the war was over. In 1920 the financial situation of the government was desperate; its expenses exceeded its income by more than three billion dollars. The value of the lira declined rapidly, prices soared, and the majority of the people were unable to meet the higher cost of living. Meantime, several millions of demobilized soldiers, having been promised a "regenerated Italy" for their services, returned to civil life only to find their old jobs filled and no new ones available.

Under the pressure of poverty and discontent many people — old soldiers, workmen, and farmers — turned to socialism and bolshevism. In 1919 the Socialist party elected 156 deputies to the parliament. It used its controlling influence to block the

measures of the government, sometimes interrupting the dignified proceedings of the chamber by singing " The Red Flag," cheering Lenin, and hissing the king. Extreme Socialists abandoned
the peaceful methods and moderate program of the party and endeavored by means of the general strike to establish the Russian
soviet system of government. In many parts of Italy the farmers
refused to pay rent, burned the houses, and seized the lands of the
large landowners. In the industrial cities the workers refused to
work, dispossessed the employers and owners of industries, and
tried to run the factories on their own account. Three years after
the Peace Conference the Italian government was bankrupt and
the country in a state of confusion bordering on anarchy. It was
this situation that enabled Mussolini to gain control of affairs.

**Fascist Italy: How Mussolini gained control of the government
by turning himself from a Socialist into a Fascist.** Benito Mussolini (born in 1883) was the son of a village blacksmith. He
acquired a little money by teaching, and then attended the universities of Lausanne and Geneva in Switzerland, working on the side
to pay his expenses. Returning to Italy he became an active Socialist, and in 1908 was arrested as a dangerous revolutionary. In
1914 he was editor of the official Socialist paper, *Avanti*. At first
he opposed the entrance of Italy into the war, but he soon changed
his views and himself served as a private soldier until 1917, when
he was wounded and discharged.

When Mussolini changed his views on the war, the Socialists
abandoned him and forced him to resign as editor of *Avanti*. He
then established a paper of his own, *The People of Italy;* and at
the close of the war he organized a society of ex-Socialists and
former soldiers which he called *Fascio di Combattimento* (" Union
of Combat "). The Fascist society advocated many social reforms, such as the heavy taxation of the rich. But its program
differed from that of the Socialists in two important respects.
First, the Fascists were strongly nationalist. They advocated
an aggressive foreign policy, especially the acquisition of Fiume
and Dalmatia, and they gave enthusiastic support to D'Annunzio
in his spectacular conquest of Fiume. Second, the Fascists were
bitterly opposed to communism and bolshevism. To resist these

unpatriotic movements, bands of young men, wearing black shirts and armed with guns and clubs, were sent out to break up Communist meetings and to destroy Communist printing presses, literature, and red flags.

These activities made the Fascist society popular throughout Italy. It was known, not for its socialistic ideas, but for its patriotic demonstrations. In 1921–1922 young men from all classes rushed to join the " Black Shirts "; and as the membership of the society increased, Mussolini emphasized more and more the ideas that would be approved by the people who joined. Employers wanted an end of strikes. Landowners wanted protection against peasant uprisings. Shopkeepers, lawyers, doctors, clerks, and teachers wanted a restoration of law and order and easier conditions of living. Patriots wanted something done to strengthen the government at home and to restore the prestige of Italy abroad. Fascism stood for all these desired things.

Meantime the government had done little if anything to remedy any of the evils of which people complained. One feeble ministry had followed another, until in 1922 the weakest of all the ministries was in power. The prime minister was a certain Mr. Facta, whom a colleague described as follows:

I saw him at least twice a week at the king's audiences and at the cabinet meetings, for a long series of months, but not the vaguest memory have I kept, either of a sentence, or a remark of any kind from this obliging little middle-class gentleman, always smiling and nodding and approving.

Tired of confusion and insecurity, the mass of the people turned to Fascism because they felt that something more heroic was needed than could be expected from a smiling little gentleman, always nodding and approving.

In the fall of 1922 Mussolini felt that he was strong enough to take the decisive step. At a great gathering of Fascists in Naples he declared: " Either the government will be given to us or we shall seize it by marching on Rome." The prime minister, Facta, hastily offered the Fascists certain offices in the cabinet. Instead of accepting this offer the Fascists began their famous " march on Rome." Facta proclaimed a state of siege, but the king, refusing to approve this measure, called upon Mussolini to form a ministry.   October 30, 1922, a cabinet was formed of which a majority were Fascists and Mussolini the dominating figure.   This was the beginning of his dictatorship.

Fascist Italy: How Mussolini transformed the old parliamentary government into the Fascist state. Mussolini first asked and obtained from parliament certain dictatorial powers for a period of fourteen months.   These powers he used to place the government of Italy in the hands of the Fascist society.   National and local offices were filled with his loyal Fascist supporters.   Then a law was passed which provided that in any election for parliament the party which polled a majority of the votes should be given two-thirds of the seats in the Chamber of Deputies.   This gave the Fascists control of parliament.   The government of the cities was changed so that municipal officers were no longer chosen by the people but appointed by Mussolini's government.   Mussolini was freed from responsibility to parliament and made accountable to the king alone.   His title was changed from " prime minister " to " Head of the Government," and all cabinet ministers were made dependent on his will.   Opposition to these measures was ruthlessly repressed, and it became dangerous, even for members of parliament, to write or to speak against the government or the Fascists.   In 1924 Matteotti, a Socialist deputy and the author of a book entitled *The Fascisti Exposed*, was carried off and murdered by some of Mussolini's Fascist supporters.

Once firmly established in power, Mussolini made certain important changes in economic organization.   This was effected in 1926 by the Legal Discipline of Collective Labor Relations Law. The law created six national confederations of employers and seven national confederations of workers.   These were in turn subdivided into local unions or syndicates of employers and workers.   No other associations of either employers or laborers were permitted. The syndicates had authority to make binding agreements respecting wages, hours of labor, and other matters of importance, and their decisions were binding on those employers and workers who did not belong to the syndicates as well as on those who did.   No employer or worker could belong to a syndicate unless he was acceptable to the government — that is, unless he was a member of the Fascist party. Thus it was very much to the interest of all employers and workers to join the Fascist party and support Mussolini's government.

Besides creating the national confederations and the local syndicates, the law of 1926 provided that the government should exercise a direct supervision over disputes between employers and laborers. When such disputes arise between employers and laborers in any business, the local syndicates try to reach an agreement. If they fail, the dispute is referred to a committee composed of employers and laborers not directly concerned in the dispute, acting under the supervision of the minister of corporations. If no settlement is made by the committee and the minister, the dispute comes before the established courts of justice, where it is finally disposed of. Strikes and lockouts are illegal.

This organization of industry prepared the way for Mussolini's organization of the Fascist state, which was accomplished by the electoral reform law of 1928. By this law the right to nominate candidates for parliament was given to the national confederations of employers and workers. The thirteen national confederations prepare a list of 800 candidates for the 400 seats in the Chamber of Deputies. These names are then sent to the Grand Council of the Fascist society, of which Mussolini is the head. The Grand Council then chooses (presumably but not necessarily from this list) 400 names which are then submitted to the people for approval or rejection. Each voter must vote for or against the entire list. In case the list is rejected by a majority of the voters, a second election is held in which all legal organizations with a membership of 5000 or more may prepare lists of candidates.

The first election under the new system was held in 1929. The list of 400 names, headed by Mussolini, was drawn up by the Grand Council and submitted to the people. Mussolini, and other prominent Fascists, made speeches urging the people to approve of it. No opposition speeches were permitted. The question on which the people voted was: " Do you approve of the list of deputies chosen by the Fascist Grand Council? " Of the 9,460,727 Italians who had a right to vote, 8,663,412 voted *yes;* 135,761 voted *no.*

GENERAL VIEW OF THE CITY OF ROME

Taken from the roof of St. Peter's. In the middle distance is the Tiber. In the foreground is Bernini's colonnade, which forms an approach to St. Peter's.

Even allowing for the fact that many may have voted *yes* because they were afraid to vote *no*, the result of the election indicated that a great majority of the people of Italy were quite satisfied with Mussolini and his Fascist state.

One of Mussolini's outstanding achievements was the settlement of the ancient quarrel between the Pope and the Italian government (see p. 452). Mussolini realized that his position would be much strengthened if he could win the approval of the Pope and the devout Catholics. In 1926 he therefore began negotiations with the papal court, and in February, 1929, three documents — a treaty, a concordat, and a financial agreement — were signed by the Pope and the Italian government.

The principle matters agreed upon were the following: (1) The Italian government recognized the complete independence of the " State of the Vatican City " under the sovereignty of the Pope. This smallest of states has an area of about 100 acres and a population of 500 people. As ruler, the Pope may send and receive ambassadors, coin money, issue postage stamps, and do all that any sovereign state may do, except make war. His realm is recognized as forever neutral and inviolable. (2) The Italian government recognized the Catholic religion as the only state religion; it agreed to enforce the canon law, and to established compulsory religious instruction in the schools. (3) The Pope for the first time recognized the Kingdom of Italy and renounced his claims to the States of the Church. In compensation for the lost territory the Italian government agreed to pay him 1,750,000,000 lira ($91,875,000).

The Fascist state seems to be firmly established, and the idea of Fascism has spread to other countries (see p. 782). But the Fascist state was created, and is sustained, by one man — Mussolini. What will happen after the death of Mussolini?

Soviet Russia: How Nicolai Lenin made good the prophecies of Karl Marx by establishing the " dictatorship of the proletariat." When the first Russian Revolution occurred in March, 1917 (see p. 706), there was living in exile in Switzerland a man whom few people had ever heard of. When he died seven years later his name was known throughout the world. Millions feared him as a devil; other millions worshiped him as a saint. The man's real name was Vladimir Ilyich Ulianov, but he had published books under the name of Nicolai Lenin. The world knew him and will always remember him as Lenin. Immediately after the first revolution he returned to Russia, became the leader of the majority (Bolshevik) Socialist party, and more than any other man was responsible for the second revolution of November, 1917 (see p. 710), and the establishment of the present Russian Soviet Republic.

When Lenin returned to Russia he was forty-seven years old. A contemporary described him as " a plump little man, with a high bulbous forehead, a snub nose, and a bald head." Another contemporary said of him: " Lenin seems to have two aspects, one gentle and smiling, the other hard and criminal." He was two men in one, Doctor Jekyll and Mr. Hyde, " who succeeded each other without ever meeting." Many great leaders in the crusade for human freedom have been like that. They have united a passionate sympathy for the poor and oppressed with a passionate hatred for those whom they held responsible for poverty and oppression.

Lenin was a disciple of Karl Marx. The central doctrine of Marx (see p. 533) was that under the present capitalist system the mass of the people (*proletariat*) produce all of the wealth by their labor; but the few idle rich (*bourgeois*) are able, by owning land and the industrial plants, to take most of the wealth for themselves. Marx prophesied that sooner or later there would be a social revolution in which the working classes would gain control of the government, dispossess the private owners of land and industry, and establish the common (*communist*) ownership of land and industry. Thus the wealth of society would be possessed by the people who created it by their labor.

This doctrine Lenin accepted. He never doubted that the social revolution would come, and after the revolution of 1917 he never doubted that the time was ripe for it in Russia. The " gentle and smiling " Lenin was the Lenin who felt a profound sympathy with the poverty and oppression under which the Russian people lived and had lived for centuries. The " hard and criminal " Lenin was the Lenin who never doubted

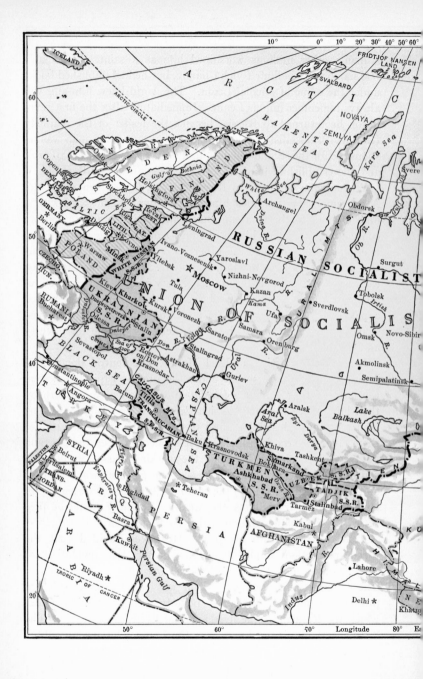

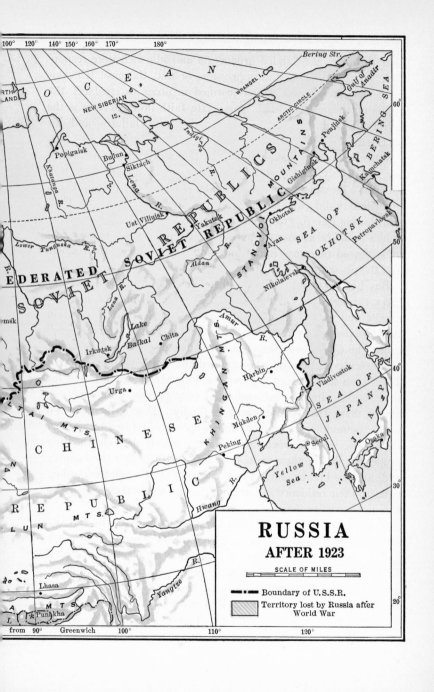

RUSSIA

AFTER 1923

SCALE OF MILES

Boundary of U.S.S.R.

Territory lost by Russia after
World War

that the tsars and landed aristocrats and idle rich were responsible for this poverty and oppression, or that the most ferocious methods were necessary and justified in order to establish the rights of the people.   This passionate faith in a doctrine is the secret of Lenin.   It explains his actions, his failures, and his successes.

When Lenin and his followers seized the government in November, 1917, only a small minority of the Russian people were Bolsheviks.   To win the sympathy of the mass of the people, Lenin immediately did two things.   He negotiated peace with the Central Powers (see p. 712), and he announced that the lands of the nobles would be at once turned over to the peasants.   These measures pleased two very important groups of people — the soldiers and the peasants.

But Lenin knew that he could neither maintain his power nor carry through the social revolution by peaceful means, since the middle and upper classes would fight to the last ditch to retain their property and influence.   An " extraordinary commission," called the *Cheka*, was therefore created and authorized to arrest and execute all persons who opposed the Bolshevik government. The Cheka inaugurated a government by terror which lasted for three years.   In the year 1918 some 6000 persons were executed, among them Tsar Nicholas and his family.   During the next two years the middle- and upper-class people who refused to support the Bolshevik government actively were mostly despoiled of their property.   Many thousands were shot.   Others fled the country and, like the French émigrés in the time of the French Revolution, took up their residence in foreign countries where they engaged in anti-Bolshevist propaganda.

Meantime certain former Russian generals, supported by " White armies," set up anti-Bolshevik governments — one in the north under Admiral Kolchak, one in the Baltic region under General Yudenich, and one in the south under General Denikin (later under General Wrangel).   To resist the White armies, the Bolshevik government organized a Red army of about 100,000 men, under the able leadership of Leon Trotsky.   General Yudenich came within sight of Petrograd (Leningrad as it was now called), but he was defeated and driven back. The army of Kolchak melted away. After the war the French and British governments, fearing the spread of bolshevism, landed troops in the Black Sea region in order to overthrow the Bolshevik government. But in November, 1920, General Wrangel and the French army which supported him were defeated.

Thus by 1920 the Bolshevik government had cleared European Russia of foreign and White armies, and it had dispossessed the middle and upper classes. The Bolsheviks were still a small minority of the people, but by means of the Cheka and the Red army they had terrorized the people into submission.

Meantime the Bolshevists assembled an All-Russian Congress which adopted a new constitution (1918) designed to establish and maintain their power. The name adopted for the new government was the Russian Socialist Federated Soviet Republic — popularly known as the R. S. F. S. R. (Later the Russian Socialist Federated Soviet Republic formed a union with similar republics established in Ukrainia, White Russia, the Caucasus, and three other neighboring countries. The official name of this larger union is Union of Socialist Soviet Republics — popularly known as the U. S. S. R.) The Russian Constitution of 1918 confers political privileges on all men and women of eighteen years of age or over who are productive workers, or the housekeepers of such workers, or soldiers, or sailors. The following classes of people may neither vote nor hold office: (1) those who employ hired labor for profit; (2) those engaged in buying and selling for profit; (3) those who have an income not derived from their labor; (4) priests or ministers of any church; (5) members of the former tsar's family, and agents or supporters of the former tsarist government. Thus the constitution is based on the radical socialist theory that political power should be confined to the proletariat — the workers. All others are regarded as capitalists — exploiters of the people and enemies of society.

The workers exercise political power through the local soviets. The village soviets are composed of the peasant farmers. The city soviets are composed of deputies chosen by the workers according to their occupation. The iron workers choose deputies to represent their interests, the miners choose deputies to represent their interests, and so do the soldiers and other groups. By an indirect and complicated system of election the village and city soviets choose deputies to the All-Russian Congress, which is composed of about 1500 members and meets once or twice a year. The All-Russian Congress may discuss and decide any question; but in fact it does very little except to elect the Central Executive Committee of 450 members. The Central Executive Committee, according to the constitution, is " the supreme legislative, executive, and controlling organ of the R. S. F. S. R." It meets four times a year, and when not in session delegates its power to two smaller bodies — the Council of Commissars (about 17 persons), and the Presidium (27 members).

Thus, according to the constitution, the peasants in the country and the workers in the cities govern themselves through the local soviets and the All-Russian Congress. But in fact the effective leadership and direction of the government is in the hands of the Bolshevik party. The Bolshevik party is not mentioned in the constitution. It has a membership of about one million, out of a total population of 140,000,000. It is strictly organized and rigidly governed. In each community there is a party " cell " — a little group of Bolsheviks who, like the American party bosses, take an active part in politics and have great influence in elections. The result is that while the soviets and even the All-Russian Congress are composed of many people who are not Bolsheviks, the Central Executive Committee and the Council of Commissars are composed only of Bolsheviks. Under constitutional forms Russia is pretty effectively governed by the Bolshevik party. Lenin himself said that without instructions from the Bolshevik party " not one institution in our republic can decide a single question of importance in matters of policy or organization."

Thus it happened that Lenin established in Russia what many radical Socialists had dreamed of since the time of Karl Marx — the " dictatorship of the proletariat." Perhaps it would be truer to say the " dictatorship *of* the Bolshevik party *for* the proletariat." What has the Bolshevik party done to make the mass of the people satisfied with their government?

Soviet Russia: How the soviet government moved toward the nationalization of land and industry by taking two steps forward and one step back. The great aim of Lenin and his followers was the "nationalization" of land and industry. Instead of being owned and managed by private individuals for their own profit, land and industry were to be owned and managed by the state for the common welfare. Therefore, as soon as he obtained power, Lenin proclaimed the nationalization of the land, and shortly after (1918), the nationalization of all industries except very small ones. At the same time the government created a Supreme Economic Council to manage the 37,000 industrial plants that were thus nationalized. The council was expected to supply the industries with raw material and machinery, to find workers, supply them with money and food, and manage the distribution of the product. To facilitate the work of the Council the peasants were ordered to turn over to the government all the grain they raised above what was necessary for their maintenance. In short, the Supreme Economic Council was expected to direct and supervise the production and distribution of wealth for the entire Russian nation.

To effect so great a revolution in the economic life of the country at one stroke proved quite impossible. During the war and the revolution Russian industry was badly disorganized, and production had fallen off. During the three years from 1918 to 1921, under government management, it fell into still worse confusion, and production continued to decline. The mining of metals practically ceased, and the production of coal, iron, oil, and cloth fell to less than half of the pre-war production. Since the ruble fell in value, prices and the cost of production and of living increased. The workers, assured that the government would provision them, idled on the job, or "deserted" — that is, refused to work at all.

But the government's chief difficulties came from the peasants. The peasants thought that the "nationalization" of the land meant that they could take over the lands of the nobles. This they proceeded to do; but they objected to turning over their grain to the government. When the government seized their grain by force, the peasants refused to raise more than was necessary for their own maintenance. In 1921 (a bad year on account of drought) the production of grain was less than half the amount raised before the war. The result was a severe famine, the government was unable to provision the workers in the cities, and the workers began to raise the cry, " Down with the soviet government ! "

Thus by 1921 the attempt of the soviet government to national-ize land and industry had resulted in alienating the peasants and many of the industrial workers — the two classes upon which the government chiefly relied for support. Either the resistance had to be crushed or the economic policy modified. Fortunately for the Bolsheviks, Lenin possessed what many ideal dreamers lack — a hard practical mind which understood that ideals cannot be realized by ignoring facts. The stubborn resistance of the peas-ants was a fact that could not be ignored. It was " easier to change their policy than to change the peasants." Having taken two steps forward toward the goal, Lenin decided that it was neces-sary to take one step backward. This he did by adopting (1921) a " New Economic Policy," popularly known as " the N. E. P." or Nep.

Under the Nep the soviet government gave up for the time being the attempt to nationalize all land and industry. The peasants were permitted to dispose of their grain as they liked, except that they were subject to a fixed tax, at first in grain, later in money. Although the government kept control of the larger industries, the smaller ones (those employing less than twenty workers) were restored to private ownership. In order to obtain needed capi-tal for industrial and commercial development, foreign capitalists were granted " concessions " for limited periods in various mining, transportation, and commercial enterprises. Thus after 1921 industry was only in part owned and controlled by the govern-ment, and the land was virtually restored to the peasants.

The new economic policy worked much better than the old one. Foreign capital flowed into Russia. The ruble was stabilized (1924), foreign commerce revived, and the government-owned industries were newly equipped and enlarged. Industrial recovery was so rapid that by 1928 the government adopted an elaborate plan which called for the expenditure, during the next five years, of $14,150,000,000 for electrification, improvement in industrial

© *Press Cliché*

THRESHING GRAIN IN RUSSIA UNDER THE SOVIET RÉGIME

equipment, and the extension of railroads and other means of transportation. By 1930 the output of Russian industries was on the whole as great as, and in some of the government-owned industries greater than, before the war.

With the return of economic prosperity the soviet government became every year more popular, and in 1928 it felt strong enough to take another step forward toward the nationalization of the land. It was alarmed by the fact that while the mass of the peasants remained wretchedly poor, a few prospered, enlarged their farms, and hired other peasants to work for them. These few "rich" peasants, called *kulaks*, made a little peasant aristocracy which might in time obtain most of the land and reduce the mass of the peasants to wage-earners. This would be to establish the very inequalities which the revolution had aimed to destroy. Another difficulty was the fact that the total amount of grain produced was much less than so rich a country might produce under large-scale scientific farming. The government therefore aimed to do two things: (1) to destroy the kulaks and (2) to increase the production of grain by introducing large-scale farming under scientific management and with the best modern equipment and machinery.

For several years the government had " made war on the kulaks " by excluding them from political privileges in the soviets and by taxing them more heavily than the poorer peasants. In 1928 it began in earnest the attempt to increase the production of grain by establishing large state farms (*sovkhozes*) — that is, farms owned and managed by the government. By 1930 there were some five thousand state farms. Here is a description of two of them by an eyewitness:

> Out in an endless plain . . . a town . . . with three-story concrete buildings, with a single central-heating station for the entire settlement, with post office, telegraph offices, flower beds, machine and tool plants, two-story theater and clubhouse, and with a perfect road on which we later drove at 100 kilometers [about 62 miles] an hour. Yet this is not a town. It is a single state farm. The manager of this sovkhoz . . . realized that if he told us his farm had an area of so many thousand hectares it would mean nothing concrete to us. So he took us in his Buick to the northern boundary of the farm. From there we traveled on one straight unending highway for eighty-six kilometers [about 55 miles]. It made an unforgettable impression. From farthest north to farthest south on this *Sovkhoz Number 2*, known as "Camel," would be an hour's non-stop dash by an express train.
>
> But the next day we visited an even bigger sovkhoz, "Gigant" or "Giant." Its director uses an airplane to get from one sector of his farm to the other. . . . Gigant covers a surface of 220,000 hectares — a hectare is about two and one-half acres — of which about 113,000 were cultivated this year. It employs 3,541 workers, 220 tractors, 230 combines, and 450 tractor seeding drills. Its machinery alone cost 7,000,000 rubles; its buildings, 16,000,000 rubles. It has a total population of 17,000. Both Gigant and Camel publish their own daily newspaper. Outside Russia the world's largest farm is that of Mr. John Campbell in Montana. But Gigant is seven times as big as Mr. Campbell's farm.[1]

Besides establishing state farms, the government encouraged the poor peasants in each community to unite their small farms in large co-operative enterprises organized and managed as the state farms were. To assist them in doing this the government

[1] *The Nation*, Oct. 8, 1930, p. 369.

provided a certain amount of capital for machinery and equipment. The union of small farms in " co-operatives " (*kolhozes*) proceeded rather slowly until 1930, but during that year the movement was very rapid. By March 1, 1930, the " co-operatives " included more than half of all the farms, and " in some regions, such as Northern Caucasus, Moscow, Ural, Crimea, Ukrainia, 70 per cent of all the farmers had joined the co-operatives." [1]

The Russian peasant is very conservative. He dislikes to surrender his small farm and the right to do as he likes, but the co-operative farming, conducted under a single management and by means of American tractors, harvesters, and thrashing machines, is more profitable. The situation was explained by a peasant as follows:

Of course the tractor makes the harvesting and planting easier in the commune [co-operative], and there's a nursery where you can put the children. But the worst thing about the commune is that you're not your own master. You have to work as the management directs and not as you want to do yourself. You have to eat where everyone else eats, whether you like it or not. . . . Still, I think I'll have to join : there's nothing else for a peasant to do in these days. [2]

Thus the soviet government moved forward towards one of its chief objects — the control of land and industry. But it had another and equally important object — the transformation of the ideas and culture of the people. We must now see what it did to achieve this object.

Soviet Russia : How the soviet government tried to change the ideas and culture of the people. Under the tsarist government the mass of the people were uneducated. In proportion to population the number of children in schools was only about one-eighth of the number in schools in the United States. To change this situation the soviet government established a system of free public schools, ranging from the kindergarten to the university, supported and controlled by the state. With few exceptions, no private schools were allowed. All children between the ages of three and

[1] *Current History*, Oct., 1930, p. 53.
[2] W. H. Chamberlin, *Soviet Russia*, p. 205. Little, Brown, and Company.

EDUCATION IN RUSSIA

© *Press Cliché*

An instructor teaching adults. So many of the peasants have had no formal education that the problem of providing adult education is acute. Classes are everywhere organized and taught by members of the former middle class.

sixteen are required to attend. The professional schools and the universities are open to those who desire and are capable of obtaining a higher education, except that where the facilities are inadequate the children of the poor are preferred to those of the rich and the well-to-do.

The educational program of the soviet government has two main objects. The first is to give to all children a practical education — to fit them for some useful occupation in the new social system which has been established in Russia. In the elementary and secondary schools geography, history, nature study, manual training, and elementary science are studied. So far as possible the child learns from observation and experiment rather than from books. He studies " topics " rather than " subjects." Perhaps the topic is " The City of Moscow." In connection with this topic the pupil studies history by learning something of past events in Moscow. He studies geography by visiting the Moscow River and looking at islands, shores, and peninsulas. He studies arithmetic by going out and measuring the nearest city block. In the universities natural science, history, economics, and the social sciences are studied more than Greek, Latin, philosophy, and the foreign languages.

The second aim of the soviet government is to give the people a new philosophy of life. Formerly society rested on the institution of private property. People were taught that it was well to become rich, and that if the mass of the people were poor it was either their fault or their misfortune. The soviet government wished to destroy this idea. In the schools the children are taught the extreme communist doctrine that private property is the cause of poverty and therefore an evil which must be abolished. They are taught, not to admire and envy those who are rich and have fine clothes and possessions, but to regard them with suspicion as anti-social and anti-patriotic. The result is that people do not exhibit their wealth even if they have it. The highest officials in the government receive no higher salaries than the skilled mechanics, and in the theaters and elsewhere it is impossible to tell who is an " important " person by his dress or his manner of living. The new philosophy aims to teach that " fine feathers do not make fine birds," and for the most part important and influential people take a conscious pride in living as simply as the mass of the people.

It was the theory of Karl Marx that the old religions, Catholic and Protestant, furnished the strongest support to the institution of private property and the enslavement of the poor by the rich. Lenin accepted the idea. " Religion is one of the forces of spiritual oppression," he said. " To him who works and is poor all his life religion teaches passivity and patience in earthly life, consoling him with the hope of a heavenly reward. . . . Religion is the opium of the people." The statement, " Religion is the opium of the people," which Lenin borrowed from Karl Marx, may be taken as a kind of official motto of the soviet government. It is inscribed on many of the public buildings. In the schools, and by official propaganda, the government teaches the doctrine that the old religious beliefs are not only untrue but hostile to the welfare of the people.

Holding these views, the soviet government confiscated the property of the old Russian established church, and refused to support the clergy. At first it declared that " the liberty of religious propaganda as well as anti-religious propaganda is guaranteed to all citizens." All churches were free to conduct public

© *Press Cliché*

A RUSSIAN MINER "LISTENING IN"

Radios are being widely distributed by the Soviet authorities and used as a
means of spreading education and Soviet ideas.

worship and to teach their doctrines. Under this régime of freedom the churches became active, and contrary to the expectation
of the government increased their membership. In 1929 the government therefore changed its policy. People were still free to
accept any religious belief, and the churches were free to hold
public worship. But the activities of the churches were greatly
restricted. They were forbidden to carry on organized charitable
or educational work, or to try and win converts to their faith.
Anyone in Russia may accept any religious belief he likes, and any
group of people may organize a church and hold religious services
publicly without interference. But they may not, as a church,
propagate their beliefs or engage in any activity not purely religious.

Thus the soviet government is frankly hostile to the old religions.
It frankly tries to convert all the people to its own professed philosophy of life — the extreme Socialist or Bolshevist doctrines.
Bolshevism is in fact regarded not merely as a theory of economic
reform, but as a philosophy of life, a religion. It has its dogmas,
its ceremonies, and its saints. Its dogmas are the theories of the

social revolution. The great days which it celebrates are the great days of the revolution. Its saints are Karl Marx and Lenin — especially Lenin. In the homes of thousands of Russians, Lenin's picture replaces the old sacred religious pictures, and thousands of Russians make reverent pilgrimages to his tomb as formerly they made pilgrimages to the holy places of the Christian religion.

The Russian Revolution aims to effect a complete transformation of society — the establishment of a Communist economic régime and the acceptance of a Communist philosophy of life. This is why it is, of all the events of our time, the most interesting and perhaps the most important.

III. INTERNATIONAL RELATIONS AND THE LEAGUE OF NATIONS

German reparations: How it took ten years to determine what amount Germany should pay. The Peace Conference left many questions undecided, some of which gave rise to disputes that threatened to disturb the peace of Europe. Most of these disputes had to do with boundary claims and will be considered in connection with the work of the League of Nations. But of all the questions left undecided by the Peace Conference, the most important, and the one which more than any other kept alive the hatreds engendered by the war, was the question of German reparations.

The Treaty of Versailles required Germany to pay, by 1921, the sum of $5,000,000,000, and thereafter such sums as the Inter-allied Reparations Commission might determine. In January, 1921, the Reparations Commission (composed of representatives of France, Belgium, Italy, and Great Britain) fixed the amount that Germany should pay, over a long period of years, at $56,500,-000,000. This amount the Germans regarded as far beyond their capacity to pay, and it was indeed about twice the amount which the American experts at the Peace Conference had recommended. In April, 1921, the Reparations Commission therefore reduced the amount. It now demanded that Germany should pay, over a long period of years, the sum of $33,000,000,000 — with the understanding that more might be required later if it should later appear that Germany was able to pay more. The Germans thought this amount still too great, and they especially objected to the demand because it left the Commission free to increase the amount if it saw fit. To accept this demand would be like signing a blank check which the Allied powers could fill in at their pleasure.

Under threat of military occupation the German government nevertheless formally yielded to the demand of the Commission. The first payments were made in 1921. The payments for 1922 were, at the request of the German government, partly postponed. In November, 1922, the German government asked that all the payments be postponed for three or four years, in order to give it time to stabilize the mark and bring about a revival of German industry and trade. This request was refused, and in 1923, upon the failure of Germany to make her payments, French and Belgium armies occupied the district of the Ruhr. The French government declared that it would not annex any German territory, but announced that its armies would remain in the Ruhr until Germany paid what she owed.

The immediate result of the French occupation of the Ruhr was that Germany was both less able and less willing to pay reparations than before. The Ruhr is a small district, but it is the " nerve center " of German industry. The French occupation of this district led to the collapse of the mark and the complete disorganization of German economic life and so made it impossible for Germany to pay the reparations demanded, even if she had desired to do so. But the Germans regarded the occupation as a virtual renewal of the war and a violation of the Treaty of Versailles. The government therefore adopted a policy of " passive resistance." It stopped all reparation payments and ordered the inhabitants of the Ruhr district to pay no taxes or customs levied by the French authorities. Thus in 1923 the dispute over reparations reached a complete deadlock. France refused to withdraw from the Ruhr until Germany paid; Germany refused to pay until France withdrew from the Ruhr.

To end this deadlock the British government proposed that the whole question of reparations should be examined by a committee of financial experts. The result was the formation of an international committee, headed by an American, Charles G. Dawes, and the adoption of the so-called Dawes Plan (1924). The Dawes Plan provided for the stabilization of the German mark by means of a foreign loan of $200,000,000. It recommended that Germany should pay, in reparations, $250,000,000 in 1924; increasing amounts annually up to $625,000,000 in 1928; and $625,000,000 annually for an indefinite period of years thereafter, with the provision that the amount might be raised or lowered according to the " index of prosperity " in Germany. If this plan was accepted by Germany, France was to withdraw from the Ruhr.

The Dawes Plan ended the deadlock over reparations. France evacuated the Ruhr (1925). The German mark was stabilized, German industry revived, and during the four years from 1924 to 1928 the German government made all of the required payments promptly. But one important point was left unsettled. The Dawes Plan did not fix the total amount to be required of Germany. The German government wanted this point settled. Besides, it was generally recognized by the best authorities that the annual payments fixed by the Dawes Plan were too high. The result was the appointment of a new committee and the adoption of a new plan, known as the Young Plan (1929). The Young Plan provided that Germany should pay a total sum of about $27,000,000,000. The payments were to be made over a period of fifty-nine years. During the first thirty-seven years the annual payments were to average $512,500,000; during the last twenty-two years they were to average $391,250,000. As a further concession to Germany, the allied troops were withdrawn from the Rhineland in 1929–1930 instead of in 1934 as provided by the Treaty of Versailles.

Thus after ten years of quarreling, the amount of German reparations was fixed at about the amount which the American experts had recommended at the Peace Conference in 1919. This amount Germany agreed to pay; and the Allied powers, confident of her ability and willingness to pay, withdrew their troops from German territory.

The League of Nations: What it did to preserve the peace and to promote international goodwill. When the League of Nations was first established, many people thought of it as a kind of court which would sit with folded hands until Europe was on the verge of war. Then, becoming suddenly active, it would do something to preserve the peace. It would be quite wrong to think of the League in that way. During the first ten years of its existence it was constantly occupied with a great variety of matters of international importance, only some of which had to do with quarrels likely to lead to war. These varied activities of the League may be conveniently considered under five heads: (1) settlement of quarrels between states; (2) assistance to bankrupt states; (3) administration of territories under its protection; (4) creation of a World Court; (5) disarmament.

1. *Settlement of quarrels between states.* Shortly after the war a quarrel arose between Sweden and Finland over the Aland Islands. These islands, lying between Finland and Sweden, were governed by Finland; but the inhabitants, being mostly of Swedish speech and nationality, desired to be united with Sweden. Foreseeing that the quarrel might become serious, the British government induced the two governments to refer their dispute to the League. After hearing the arguments on both sides, the Council of the League recommended the following solution: (1) that the islands should remain subject to Finland; (2) that the inhabitants of the islands should be guaranteed the privilege of self-government and the free use of the Swedish language; (3) that the islands should remain unfortified and be "neutralized" like Switzerland and Belgium. In this sensible way the quarrel was settled (1920–1922).

The League was concerned in many boundary disputes. Poland and Lithuania both claimed Vilna and Memel. Yugoslavia claimed territory which Albania insisted belonged to her, and Turkey claimed territory which, according to the British government, was part of her mandated colony of Mesopotamia. All of these disputes were referred to the League, and all of them, except the dispute over Vilna, were settled peaceably according to terms recommended by the League or by special commissions appointed by it. But far more important than these boundary disputes were two quarrels which, since they involved the question of "national honor," might easily have resulted in war had it not been for the intervention of the League.

The first of these was a quarrel between Italy and Greece. In 1923 a boundary commission appointed by the Conference of Ambassadors (an international body created in 1920, representing France, Italy, Great Britain, Japan, and the United States) was in Greece determining the boundary between Greece and Albania. In August of that year four Italian members of the commission were murdered on Greek soil. Mussolini at once presented to Greece an ultimatum demanding: (1) an indemnity of 50,000,000 lira; (2) an investigation of the murderers, to be conducted by the Greek government under the supervision of an Italian official. Greece rejected these demands on the ground that they outraged the " honor " and violated the " sovereignty " of the state. Mussolini promptly took possession of the Greek island of Corfu. Greece appealed to the League, but Mussolini announced that Italy would resent any outside interference.

Here, then, was a situation similar to that created by the murder of Archduke Francis Ferdinand in 1914. There was grave danger of war between Italy and Greece, and a war between Italy and Greece might very easily involve the other Balkan states, and possibly some of the great powers. It was just such a situation as this that the League had been created to deal with. It was the first real test of the power of the League to prevent war. Would it stand the test?

Unfortunately the test was not so clear-cut as it might have been, because the murdered men were members of a commission appointed by the Conference of Ambassadors, and the Conference of Ambassadors might resent any action by the League. Instead of acting on its own authority, the League therefore urged the Conference of Ambassadors to act. But at the same time it presented to the Conference of Ambassadors its own views as to what might be done. It recommended: (1) that the investigation of the murders be made by a Greek commission assisted by representatives of Italy and two other great powers, and under the supervision of a representative of the League of Nations; (2) that the 50,000,000 lira, instead of being paid at once to Italy, be deposited in a Swiss bank until the amount of indemnity could be impartially determined by the newly created World Court (see

p. 816). In the end the dispute was settled peaceably, through the Conference of Ambassadors but essentially according to the methods suggested by the League of Nations. The World Court awarded the indemnity of 50,000,000 lira to Italy, and Italy evacuated the island of Corfu.

A less important but more clear-cut test of the power of the League occurred two years later. In October, 1925, shots were exchanged between Greek and Bulgarian soldiers stationed on the frontier, the result of which was that a Greek was killed on Bulgarian soil. Greece demanded an indemnity and the prompt punishment of those guilty of the murder. Bulgaria appealed to the League, but Greece insisted that it was not a matter for the League, and very shortly hostilities began between the two countries.

The Council of the League acted with vigor and promptness. Through its president, Aristide Briand, it informed the two governments that the Council would take up the matter, and demanded that hostilities should cease immediately. To this demand the two governments yielded. The Council then appointed a commission to investigate the circumstances of the murder. On the basis of the commission's report it announced that Greece had no cause for war, since the murder was not premeditated, but that she had grounds for an indemnity which the Council recommended should be fixed at $220,000. Both governments accepted the decision. Thus by prompt action the League prevented a war after hostilities had actually begun.

2. *Assistance to bankrupt states.* No country came out of the war in a worse plight than Austria. It was burdened by a heavy war debt. It was incapable of raising enough food to support its people, and the high tariffs levied by hostile neighbors crippled its industry and its commerce. For three years after the war the people were partly supported by foreign charities and the government was kept going by foreign loans. But in 1922 the bankers advised against further loans. The government was bankrupt and the country on the verge of revolution. What could be done? It was at this point that the hapless and apparently hopeless question of Austrian finance was referred to the League of Nations.

The Council of the League appointed several committees to study the political, economic, and financial situation, and on the basis of their reports prepared three agreements, called " protocols," which were signed by the governments of Great Britain, France, Italy, Czechoslovakia, and Austria (October, 1922). The substance of these agreements was as follows: (1) The governments of Great Britain, Italy, France, and Czechoslovakia agreed to " respect the political independence " of Austria, and to grant her a further loan of $135,000,000. (2) Austria agreed to carry through financial reforms recommended by a commissioner-general and a financial committee representing the League of Nations.

The League appointed as commissioner-general Dr. Alfred Zimmerman, a Dutchman, who arrived in Vienna in December, 1922. Under his direction the financial committee worked out a series of drastic reforms. Expenses were reduced by dismissing about 80,000 useless government officials. Taxes were greatly increased. The issue of paper money was rigidly restricted, and a new monetary unit, called the *schilling*, was established and stabilized on a gold basis. For three years the government of a former great power took its orders from a group of economic experts directed by the citizen of a foreign country. Finally, in 1926, the finance committee announced that the government of the sovereign state of Austria could now be relied upon to manage its own affairs, and the League's control of Austrian finances came to an end.

Meantime, in 1923 the government of Hungary asked the League to prepare a plan for the reorganization of her finances. The situation in Hungary was not so desperate as that in Austria, but the plan adopted by the League was much the same. A finance committee was appointed, and Jeremiah Smith of Boston was named as commissioner-general. The commissioner-general began his task in May, 1924; and with the aid of the finance committee and a foreign loan guaranteed by the powers, the finances of Hungary were straightened out in a short time. In June, 1926, the League's supervision of Hungarian affairs came to an end.

3. *Supervision of territories under its protection.* The Peace Conference placed under the protection of the League of Nations the mandated colonies, the Saar Valley, and the free city of Danzig.

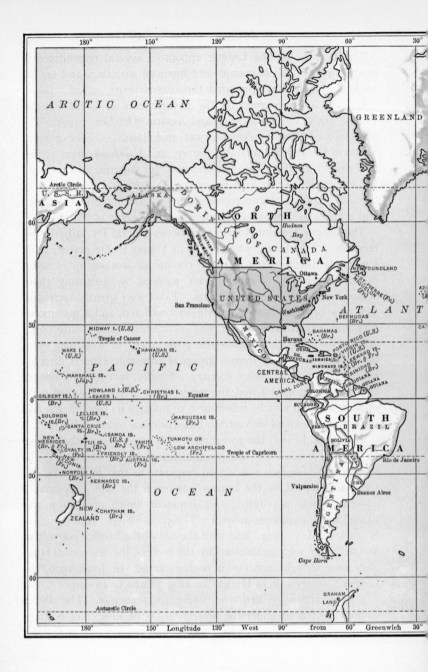

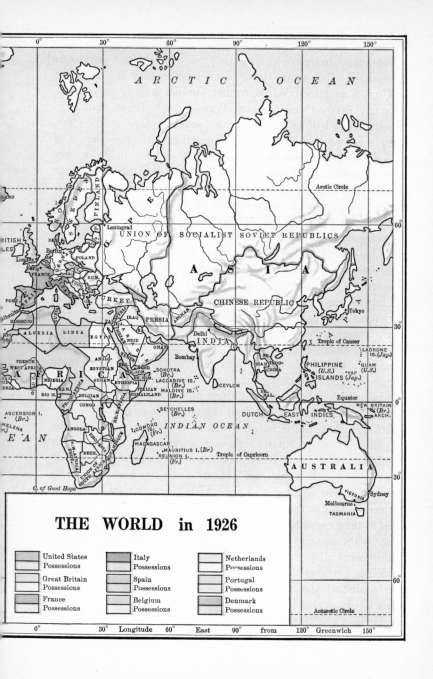

THE WORLD in 1926

Legend:

United States Possessions

Great Britain Possessions

France Possessions

Italy Possessions

Spain Possessions

Belgium Possessions

Netherlands Possessions

Portugal Possessions

Denmark Possessions

0°   30°   Longitude   60°   East   90°   from   120°   Greenwich   150°

The mandated colonies (see p. 737) were divided into three classes, according to the level of civilization they had attained. In Class A were included the former Turkish possessions — Mesopotamia, Syria, Palestine, and Transjordan. These were sufficiently civilized to be recognized as " provisionally " independent. They were supposed to govern themselves with a minimum of advice and supervision by the mandatory country to which they were assigned. In Class B were included the former German colonies in central Africa. Since they were less civilized, the mandatory countries were supposed to exercise a greater degree of control over them. In Class C were included the former German colony of Southwest Africa, and her possessions in the Pacific islands. These, being scarcely civilized at all, were to be administered by the mandatory country " as integral portions of its territory."

The business of the League was to see that these various classes of colonies were governed according to the provisions of the mandate system. Every year the mandatory countries — Great Britain, France, Belgium, and Japan — made reports on their administration of the colonies assigned to them. These reports were examined by the Permanent Mandate Commission of the League, which then either approved of the mandatory country's administration or suggested such changes as it might think wise. The League has interfered very little in the administration of the mandated colonies, but its influence is very considerable. It is in a position to know whether the colonies are being properly administered and, if they are not, to make the facts known to the world. The result is that the mandatory countries have been anxious to secure the approval of the League, and such suggestions as the League has seen fit to make have generally been acted upon by the mandatory countries concerned.

The Saar Valley was placed under the sovereignty of the League for fifteen years, at the end of which time the inhabitants were to decide whether the Saar should be united to France or to Germany (see p. 732). In 1920 the League created a Governing Commission for the Saar. It was composed of five members — a Frenchman, a Belgian, a Dane, a Canadian, and an inhabitant of

the Saar Valley. The Frenchman, M. Rault, was made president
of the commission. It was the intention of the League that the
government of the Saar should be strictly impartial, neither pro-
French nor pro-German. Unfortunately M. Rault and the Danish
and Belgian members of the commission were influenced by pro-
French sympathies, and as they controlled the commission, the
government of the Saar for the first three years was not at all satisfactory to the inhabitants. Discontent reached its height in 1923,
when the French occupied the Ruhr. The Saar miners went on
strike, the governing commission adopted a very repressive policy,
muzzled the press, and brought in French troops to maintain order.
Protests of the inhabitants led the British government to request
the League to make an investigation. The Council of the League
advised the commission to abandon its repressive measures and
to withdraw the French troops. In 1924 it appointed more impartial members on the commission, and in 1926 M. Rault resigned.
From that time on, the government of the Saar was more efficient
and more satisfactory to the inhabitants.

The Peace Conference made Danzig a free, self-governing city,
but gave to Poland the " free use and service of the port." To
guarantee this arrangement the city was placed under the protection of the League of Nations. The result is that there are in
Danzig three distinct authorities: the city government, composed
of an assembly and a senate; the customs commission, which
administers the customs; and the high commissioner, who represents the League of Nations. The chief duty of the high commissioner is to settle disputes arising out of the division of authority
between the city government and the customs commission. Since
1920 many such disputes have been settled by the parties themselves, under the mediation of the high commissioner. Others
have been referred to the Council of the League, and at least one
was of sufficient importance to be referred to the World Court.
Without the impartial mediation provided by the League of Nations, the peculiar arrangement made for Danzig would probably
have proved unworkable.

4. *The establishment of a World Court.* Article XIV of the
Covenant of the League required the Council to submit " plans

for the establishment of a Permanent Court of International Justice . . . competent to determine any dispute of an international character which the parties thereto submit to it." To draft such a plan the Council at once appointed a commission of jurists, headed by Elihu Root of the United States. With but few amendments, the plan drafted by the commission was adopted by the League, and became effective when it was ratified by twenty-eight states (1921). By 1930 it had been ratified by twenty-six additional states.

The Permanent Court of International Justice (commonly called the World Court) sits at the Hague in Holland. It is composed of fifteen judges, chosen for a term of nine years by the Council and the Assembly of the League of Nations. The World Court has authority to decide any dispute which any two or more states may submit to it. This is called its "voluntary jurisdiction." But certain states, in ratifying the World Court, have agreed to submit all legal disputes concerning treaties, questions of international law, and the breach of international obligation, and to accept the decision of the court in respect to such disputes. This is called the "compulsory" jurisdiction of the court. In 1930, twenty-five of the fifty-four states that had ratified the World Court had accepted this "compulsory" jurisdiction. Of these states only two — Great Britain and Germany — were great powers.

The World Court, although it sits at the Hague in Holland, is not to be confused with the Hague Tribunal established before the war (see p. 627). The Hague Tribunal is a court of arbitration. It does not determine whether states submitting disputes to it have violated international law or custom. It merely tries to arbitrate the dispute — that is, to find a settlement that the two states will agree to accept. The World Court is not a court of arbitration but a court of law. It decides which of two states in a dispute is in the wrong — that is, which has violated an international law, or wrongly interpreted a treaty, or failed to live up to an obligation. That is why the World Court is of far greater importance than the Hague Tribunal. For the first time many "sovereign and independent" states have recognized the validity of international law and have agreed to renounce their right to interpret that law as they please. The establishment of the World Court may easily prove to be the most important step which the League of Nations has as yet (1931) taken towards the abolition of war.

5. *Disarmament.* One of President Wilson's Fourteen Points called for the reduction of armaments to " the lowest point consistent with domestic safety." The Peace Conference required the Central Powers to disarm, but took no steps to disarm themselves, except to refer the question of general disarmament to the League of Nations. The League at once appointed a committee to prepare plans. The committee realized that no state would disarm until some other means of providing it with " security " against aggression was devised. The efforts of the League were therefore chiefly directed to finding some method of providing security as a preliminary step towards disarmament.

The first successful act to provide security was carried in 1925 at Locarno. The bitter hostility between France and Germany had by that time somewhat abated; and fortunately two men of great ability and influence (the Frenchman, Briand, and the German, Stresemann) desired to establish more friendly relations between the two countries. Under the leadership of these two men, representatives of France, Germany, Belgium, Great Britain, Italy, Poland, and Czechoslovakia met at Locarno in Switzerland and signed what are known as the Locarno Treaties. The essential points of the Locarno Treaties were: (1) Germany, France, Belgium, Great Britain, and Italy agreed to maintain the existing frontiers between Germany and Belgium, and between Germany and France; (2) Germany and Belgium, and Germany and France mutually agreed never to resort to war with each other except in case of a violation of the Locarno Treaties, or in cases provided for by the Covenant of the League of Nations.

Encouraged by the success of the Locarno Treaties, Briand initiated the famous movement to " outlaw war." On April 6, 1927, the tenth anniversary of the entrance of the United States into the Great War, he announced in the newspapers that France would be willing to sign with the United States an agreement to " outlaw war " between the two countries. In the official cor-

SIGNING THE TREATY OF LOCARNO IN LONDON

At the head of the table are Stanley Baldwin and Austin Chamberlain. On the right side is the French delegation, Briand second from end, leaning back in his chair. On the left side is the German delegation; the bald man in the center is Stresemann.

© *Wide World Photos*

respondence which followed, the American secretary of state, Kellogg, suggested that other countries be invited to join in this measure. The result was that in 1928 fifteen states signed at Paris what is known as the Paris Pact (in this country called the Kellogg Peace Pact) for outlawing war; and shortly afterwards thirty additional states subscribed to it. The Paris Pact is a solemn agreement by the principal states of the world to " renounce war as an instrument of national policy," and never to seek the solution of any disputes " of whatever nature . . . except by pacific means."

This famous declaration was regarded by many as a great step towards the abolition of war. Skeptics nevertheless pointed out that the declaration amounted to very little, since there were certain " reservations " which were understood, although not incorporated in the treaty. Each state reserved the right to make war: (1) in self-defense; (2) against any state which violated the declaration; (3) in cases provided for by the Locarno Treaties or the Covenant of the League of Nations. The first reservation is the important one. It is of course fairly easy for any state that desires to make war to claim that it is a war of self-defense. The Great War was regarded, by the people in each country concerned, as a war of self-defense. Nevertheless the declaration to outlaw war was an event of great importance. Any state which signed this solemn declaration will surely find it difficult to make war on the flimsy pretexts that have often been used in the past. The declaration to outlaw war does not abolish war; but it creates a strong moral presumption against it.

The Locarno Treaties and the Paris Pact were designed to provide that feeling of security which is necessary before any state will consent to reduce its armaments. In the way of actual disarmament very little has been accomplished. In 1922, on the invitation of President Harding, the first naval disarmament conference was held at Washington. The result of the Washington Conference was that Great Britain, Japan, France, Italy, and the United States agreed to limit — according to a certain ratio and for a period of years — the construction of big battleships. Since battleships proved to be of relatively little importance in the Great

British Government Official Photo

LEADING FIGURES AT THE NAVAL CONFERENCE IN LONDON, JANUARY, 1930
Left to right: Grandi, Stimson, Briand, MacDonald, Tardieu.

War, this agreement was of less importance than many people supposed. No limitation was placed on the construction of submarines, destroyers, and cruisers; and after 1922 the construction of these vessels rapidly increased. In 1930 a second conference was held, in London, at which the five powers tried to reach an agreement for the limitation of all naval construction. No agreement between the five powers was reached; but the United States, Great Britain, and Japan agreed to reduce — to a slight extent and according to a certain ratio — their programs for naval construction.

Besides the activities mentioned above, the League has been occupied with a great variety of other matters. It has taken an active part in organizing annual international labor conferences for the discussion and adjustment of international labor conditions. It has served as a kind of international research bureau for gathering information on a variety of subjects of interest to all nations — such as the customs, telegraph, railway, shipping, and cable services, the prevention of disease, the suppression of the opium traffic, and the so-called white slave trade.

On the other hand, the League has in many respects disappointed the hopes of its most enthusiastic supporters. It has not always succeeded in settling disputes among the small states, as for example in the case of Vilna. It has scarcely even attempted to settle the disputes between the great powers, as for example the dispute between France and Germany which led to the occupation of the Ruhr. It has not done much to protect the interests of native peoples in the mandated colonies. It has exhibited a less friendly attitude towards Russia than towards other European powers. In a word, the League has been largely controlled by the great powers — especially by France and Great Britain — and it has sometimes served their interests at the expense of the rights of small nations. In spite of all this it cannot be said that the League has as yet proved a failure. It may well be that of all the results of the war the establishment of the League of Nations will prove to be the most important.

No man can foretell the future, and prophecy is perhaps as futile as it is uncertain. Yet this much may safely be said. Science and technology have placed in the hands of men material forces the like of which have never before been known. But the Great War made it clear that these forces can be used for evil as well as for good, for death as well as for life. The most important question which confronts coming generations is this: Will the forces which men have mastered destroy the civilization which for centuries they have been creating? The Great War was a disaster to all concerned, victors as well as vanquished. The world cannot afford another such catastrophe. But in order to avoid it we must do something more than to rely upon the League of Nations. We must learn how to employ the material forces at our command for useful instead of for useless purposes. This will not be easy. But men have by sad experience learned much in the past. We may at least hope that they will learn something more in the future — for example, that national "interests" and national "honor" may be as well protected by friendly agreement as by hostile conflict. It is not entirely fantastic to suppose that within a hundred years the people of Europe and America may think of war as we think of dueling — as a romantic but senseless custom happily outmoded.

CHART FOR CHAPTER XXIII. Showing that many things have happened in different countries at the same time since 1918

	1918	1919	1920	1921	1922	1923	1924	1925	1926	1927	1928	1929	1930
GREAT BRITAIN	Limited suffrage for women	Limited self-government for India.		Irish Free State established, self-government.	Egypt given nominal self-government.	First Labor ministry.			General strike.		Full right of voting to women.	Second Labor ministry.	Anglo-Indian Conference.
GERMANY		Constitution of the republic.	Economic and political confusion. Collapse of the mark. Failure to pay reparations.			French occupy the Ruhr.	Stabilization of the mark.	Period of economic recovery and prosperity under presidency of Von Hindenburg. The republic becomes increasingly popular.					
ITALY	Period of economic and political weakness. Rise of Mussolini and the Fascist society.				Mussolini becomes minister.	Establishment of dictatorship of Mussolini.			New Fascist organization of economic life.		New law on right of voting.	New treaty with the Pope.	
RUSSIA	Bolshevik dictatorship established. Soviet constitution adopted.		Attempt to nationalize land and industry fails. N.E.P. adopted.				Ruble stabilized.	Period of rapid economic recovery and of growing popularity of soviet government.			Five-year economic plan.		Experiments in large-scale farming.
INTERNATIONAL RELATIONS	Reparations			Amount fixed by Commission.		Germany fails to pay. Ruhr occupied.	Dawes Plan.	Ruhr evacuated.				Young Plan.	Allies evacuate Rhineland. London Conference.
	Naval Disarmament				Washington Conference						Paris Pact to outlaw war.		
	League of Nations		World Court. Åland Islands dispute.		Manages finances of Austria.	Greek-Italian dispute. Manages finances of Hungary.	Geneva protocol.	Locarno Treaties.					

822

QUESTIONS

1. Tell all you can about the woman suffrage movement before the war. What effect did the war have on this movement? Give an account of the extension of self-government in the British Empire since the war.

2. What was the Weimar assembly? What parties were represented in it? How does the German constitution resemble that of the United States? Is it more democratic or less democratic? What provisions in it are "socialistic"? When and how was the German mark stabilized? Why did most of the currencies become unstabilized during the war? What attempts were made to overthrow the German Republic? Why did the republic become more popular after 1924?

3. Why did the Italian government become unpopular after the war? Tell all you can about the rise of Mussolini and the Fascist society? Why was the Fascist society popular? How did Mussolini gain control of the government? How was the dictatorship established? How did Mussolini organize the workers and the employers? Why is it to the interest of employers and workers to join the Fascist party? How is the legislature elected in Italy? Compare the government of Italy with that of the United States.

4. How did the Bolshevist party gain control in Russia? What was the Cheka? the Red army? What were the ideas of Karl Marx which Lenin adopted? Describe the working of the soviet constitution. How does this constitution differ from the Constitution of the United States? How does the soviet government resemble the Fascist government in Italy? How does it differ from the Fascist government? What is meant by the "nationalization of land and industry"? To what extent is land and industry in Russia nationalized? Explain what the Nep is, and tell why it was introduced. Tell all you can about the state farms and the co-operative farms. What is the character and the object of the public school system in Russia? What is the attitude of the soviet government towards religion? Does the government forbid the organization of churches or the holding of religious services? What restrictions are placed on the churches? Why do the workers and the peasants willingly submit to the dictatorship of the Bolshevist party in Russia?

5. What amount of reparations did the American experts at the Peace Conference think Germany could pay? What amount did the Reparations Commission demand at first? Why did Germany object to this demand? Why and when did the French occupy the Ruhr? What was the Dawes Plan? Why was it replaced by the Young Plan? What payments are required by the Young Plan?

6. What were the two most important disputes between states which the League of Nations helped to settle? Tell how each was settled.

What are the three kinds of "mandated colonies"? What does the League have to do with the administration of these colonies? What has the League to do with the government of the Saar Valley? What has the League to do with the government of Danzig? What measures did the Peace Conference take towards disarmament? What were the Locarno Treaties? Who started the movement to "outlaw war"? What was the Paris Pact, and how many states have signed it? What reservations were made in connection with this declaration to outlaw war? How was the World Court established? What is its "voluntary jurisdiction"? What is its "compulsory jurisdiction"? Which of the great powers have accepted its compulsory jurisdiction? How does the World Court differ from the Hague Tribunal?

7. Do you know what French statesman started the movement for organizing a "United States of Europe"? Would it be more difficult to establish a United States of Europe than it was to establish a United States of America? If so, why?

SELECTED READINGS

Brief accounts. Hayes, *Modern Europe* (revised ed.), II, chs. xxxiv–xxxv. Schapiro, *Modern History* (revised ed.), chs. xxxviii–xxxix. Flick, *Modern World History*, chs. xxxix-xlii. Robinson and Beard, *Development of Modern Europe* (revised ed.), II, chs. xiv–xv, xvii. R. L. Buell, *A History of Ten Years*, chs. iii (reparations), vi (Locarno Treaties), xiii (Soviet Russia), xvii (Fascist Italy). F. L. Benns, *Europe since 1914*, chs. ix (League of Nations), x (reparations), xii (German Republic), xvi (Fascist Italy), xvii (Soviet Russia).

Books dealing with special subjects. W. H. Chamberlin, *Soviet Russia*. B. Russell, *Bolshevism; Practice and Theory*. H. N. Brailsford, *How the Soviets Work*. A. Wicksteed, *Life under the Soviets*. S. Nearing, *Glimpses of the Soviet Republic*. M. Farbman, *After Lenin*. H. G. Daniels, *Rise of the German Republic*. G. H. Danton, *Germany after Ten Years*. E. Jaechk, *The New Germany*. W. Bolitho, *Italy under Mussolini* (hostile account). H. N. Gay, *Strenuous Italy* (friendly account). H. Schneider, *Making the Fascist State*. E. M. Sait, *Government and Politics in France*. R. L. Buell, *Contemporary French Politics* (1921). S. Huddleston, *France* (1927). F. A. Ogg, *English Government and Politics* (1929). R. H. Tawney, *British Labour Movement*. D. Gwynn, *The Irish Free State*. H. L. McBains and L. Rogers, *The New Constitutions of Europe*. M. W. Graham, *New Governments of Central Europe*. C. A. Beard, *Cross Currents in Europe Today* (1921). P. J. N. Baker, *The League of Nations at Work*. J. S. Bassett, *The League of Nations*. F. White, *Mandates*. M. O. Hudson, *The World Court*. W. Miller, *The Ottoman Empire and Its Successors, 1821–1927*. S. Nearing, *Whither China?* A. J. Brown, *Japan in the World Today*. N. D. Harris, *Europe and the East* (to 1926). H. A. Gibbons, *America's Place in the World*.

Biographies. S. Huddleston, *Those Europeans.* Count Sforza, *Makers of Modern Europe.* V. Marcu, *Lenin.* M. Sarfatti, *Life of Benito Mussolini.* B. Mussolini, *My Autobiography.* L. Trotzky, *My Life.* P. Scheidemann, *The Making of the New Germany.* R. Von Rheinbaben, *Stresemann: The Man and the Statesman.* M. Goldsmith and F. Voigt, *Hindenburg: The Man and the Legend.* H. H. Tiltman, *Life of Ramsay MacDonald.* M. G. Hamilton, *Ramsay MacDonald.* Marie of Russia, *Education of a Princess.* (A vivid and admirable account of the experiences of a Russian Grand Duchess, cousin of the late tsar, during and since the revolution.)

Sources. Scott and Baltzly, *Readings in European History,* ch. xv–xvi. For keeping abreast of the history of the world month by month, an excellent periodical is *Current History.* Systematically arranged information about all the countries of the world is published each year in the following manuals: *World Almanac; Statesman's Year Book; International Year Book; American Year Book.*

LARGE FACTS TO REMEMBER ABOUT PART IV

1. *Science and invention.* After 1875 the Age of Industrial Revolution succeeds the Age of Political Revolution. The Industrial Revolution the result of science and invention and the increasing use of machines.

2. *Social conflict and legislation.* The Industrial Revolution gives rise to conflict between employing and working classes, which leads to socialism and the social conflict in each industrial country. Social conflict and social legislation in three chief countries — Germany, France, England.

3. *Exploitation of backward countries.* The Industrial Revolution leads to demand for raw materials, markets, and opportunities to invest capital. The result is the rapid partition of Africa and the exploitation of Asia. This in turn leads to series of colonial wars, 1898–1905.

4. *Alliances, crises, and the Great War.* Colonial expansion and colonial wars result in formation of Triple Entente. Conflict of the two alliances, Triple Entente and Triple Alliance, results in diplomatic crises leading to the Great War, 1905–1914.

5. *Extension of democratic government.* The Great War results in the extension of democratic government, the destruction of four empires in eastern Europe, the creation of many new republics, the soviet régime in Russia, the Fascist régime in Italy, the League of Nations, the World Court, and the disarmament conferences.

INDEX

KEY TO MARKS OF PRONUNCIATION

ā as in āle, ȧ as in senȧte, â as in câre, ă as in ăm, ä as in ärm, à as in àsk; ē as in ēve, ė as in ėvent, ĕ as in ĕnd, ē̇ as in makēr; ī as in īce, ĭ as in ĭll; ō as in ōld, ô as in ôbey, ŏ as in ôrb, ŏ as in ŏdd; ū as in ūse, ů as in ůnite, û as in ûrn, ŭ as in ŭp, ü in the French word *menü* (purse the lips as if to pronounce ōō and then try to say ē); ōō as in fōōd, ŏŏ as in fŏŏt; **ou** as in out; **oi** as in oil; **ch** as in chair; **g** as in go; **ng** as in sing; **K** as the "ch" in the German word *ich;* **N** as in the French word *bon;* **zh** as the "z" in azure; **y** as in yet.